UNITED STATES ARMY IN WORLD WAR II

The Army Ground Forces

THE PROCUREMENT AND TRAINING OF GROUND COMBAT TROOPS

by Robert R. Palmer, Bell I. Wiley and William R. Keast, of the Historical Section Army Ground Forces

HISTORICAL DIVISION
DEPARTMENT OF THE ARMY
WASHINGTON, D.C. 1948

This volume is the second to be published in the series THE UNITED STATES ARMY IN WORLD WAR II, and the second in the subseries THE ARMY GROUND FORCES. All the volumes are closely related, and present a comprehensive account of the activities of the Military Establishment during World War II. A tentative list of subseries is appended at the end of this volume.

Library of Congress Catalog Card Number: 50–13989

Reprinted 1966

For sale by the Superintendent of Documents, U.S Government Printing Office
Washington, D.C. 20402 - Price $5.25

. . to Those Who Served

Foreword

The conflict with the Axis Powers confronted the United States Army with problems on a scale never faced before—problems as great in administration, training, supply, and logistics as in strategy and tactics. THE UNITED STATES ARMY IN WORLD WAR II sets forth in detail the nature of the problems faced, the methods used to solve them, and the mistakes made as well as the success achieved. The object is to provide a work of reference for military and civilian students as well as a record of achievements which deserve an honorable place in the pages of history. Its value to the thoughtful citizen as an aid to his comprehension of basic problems of national security has been a major consideration. Its preparation has also been prompted by the thought that in a faithful and comprehensive record all who participated in the Army's vast effort would find a recognition merited by their service and sacrifice.

The advantage to the Army and the scholar has been the decisive factor in proceeding with the least possible delay to the publication of such a series. No claim is made that it constitutes a final history. Many years will pass before the record of the war can be fully analyzed and appraised. In presenting an organized and documented narrative at this time, the Historical Division of the War Department has sought to furnish the War Department and the Army schools an early account of the experience acquired, and to stimulate further research by providing scholars with a guide to the mountainous accumulation of records produced by the war.

The decision to prepare a comprehensive account of military activities was made early in the war. Trained historians were assigned to the larger units of the Army and War Department to initiate the work of research, analysis, and writing. The results of their work, supplemented by additional research in records not readily available during the war, are presented in this series. The general plan provides for a division into subseries dealing with the War Department, the Army Air, Ground, and Service Forces, the technical services, and the theaters of operations. This division conforms to the organization of the Army during World War II and, though involving some overlapping in subject matter, has the advantage of presenting a systematic account of developments in each major field of responsibility as well as the points of view of the particular commands. The plan also includes volumes on such topics as statistics, order of battle, military training, the Women's Army Corps, and other subjects that transcend the limits of studies focused on an agency or command. The whole project is oriented toward an eventual summary and synthesis.

The studies in this volume were written during the war in the Historical Section of Headquarters, Army Ground Forces, where the authors had free access to the records and experience of the command. The Historical Division of the War Department has confined material changes to such additions of information, approved by the authors, as seemed necessary to round out the picture presented. The full and frank presentation of the wartime point of view of the Army Ground Forces, which has not been affected by the changes made, is regarded as one of the most valuable features of this particular series of studies.

Washington, D.C.
April 1947

HARRY J. MALONY
Brigadier General, U.S.A.
Chief, Historical Division
War Department Special Staff

Preface

In the series of historical studies of the Army Ground Forces, 1942–45, a volume previously published, *The Organization of Ground Combat Troops,* deals with policies governing the number, size, composition, and equipment of the ground combat units in World War II. This volume centers on training, the principal mission of the Army Ground Forces. Since the obtaining of qualified personnel proved to be basic to the fulfillment of this mission, the first three studies deal with the procurement of enlisted men and officers possessed of the qualities and aptitudes desired for service in ground combat. The three studies which follow discuss the policies and problems involved in the training of individuals, enlisted and commissioned, for their special functions in ground combat—a responsibility which the Commanding General of the Army Ground Forces received in March 1942 as successor to the chiefs of the statutory arms. The last four studies in the volume deal with the training of units, which the Army Ground Forces regarded as its principal and most urgent task.

The preparation for combat of a large force of combined arms, rather than school or replacement training, was the aspect of the mission of the Army Ground Forces to which initial priority was given by Lt. Gen. Lesley J. McNair, its commander until July 1944. The consequence was an emphasis on the field training of units, particularly of divisions. The building and training of infantry divisions and related activities are described in this volume. Other volumes will deal with such phases of training as the preparation for combat of special types of divisions, the maneuvers of corps and armies, and combined air-ground training.

In general, the principle governing the historical program of the Army Ground Forces was to concentrate on accomplishing what probably could not be done as well, if at all, after the war. Concretely, this meant exploiting the advantages of access to the records while these were being made, and of access to the officers of the command while the problems they faced and the solutions proposed were in the foreground of their thought and interest. The subjects chosen for intensive study reflect the major activities and problems of the Army Ground Forces. Inevitably this choice made the survey a study of high command and not of tactical units or of the establishments concerned with individual training.

The object has been to state not only what was done but also why the actions recorded were taken and what lessons were learned. The judgments expressed on military matters are those of the officers concerned. The function conceived as proper for the historians was to search out and state the facts which seemed to have a bearing on the major problems, proposals, and decisions of the Army Ground Forces, in the belief that in this context of facts the decisions of its commanders and the consequences of these decisions could best be understood. Research was carried beyond the records of AGF headquarters only so far as seemed necessary to explain the particular views and decisions of the commanders and staff of Army Ground Forces. The main effort was concentrated on exploring and setting forth the facts known to the headquarters at the time when action was recommended or taken. It is recognized that a knowledge of other facts will probably be needed to arrive at balanced judgments of its recommendations and decisions—a knowledge attainable only when the history of the part played by other agencies of the War Department and the Army has been written.

The first study in this volume was prepared by Dr. Robert R. Palmer, now Professor of History in Princeton University; the second, by Dr. Palmer and Maj. William R. Keast, now Assistant Professor of English in the University of Chicago; the third, by Dr. Palmer in collaboration with Major Keast; the fourth, fifth, and sixth, by Major Keast; and the seventh, eighth, ninth, and tenth, by Maj. Bell I. Wiley, now Professor of History in Louisiana State University. All were prepared in the AGF Historical Section, of which the undersigned was chief. The members of the Historical Section received invaluable advice and collaboration from the officers of Headquarters, Army Ground Forces. In particular, the studies in this volume owe much to the unfailing interest and helpfulness of Maj. Gen. James G. Christiansen, Chief of Staff of the Army Ground Forces.

Materials obtained from records and interviews in AGF headquarters were supplemented by observations and interviews in the field. Wherever testimony has been used the officers who gave it are named in the footnotes. No attempt is made here to include a complete list of those whose advice and comments, frequently sought, were freely given. For Major Wiley's studies such a list would include many officers and enlisted men of the 63d, 65th, 69th, 75th, 84th, 86th, 92d, 94th, and 95th Divisions. As the 65th was the last division activated, and as the period of its training paralleled the preparation of Major Wiley's study of divisional training, he visited it three times, at well-spaced intervals, and on each visit interviewed representative officers from the division commander down to platoon leaders.

The studies have been materially strengthened by editorial revision in the Historical Division of the War Department. This revision was carried out by Dr. Rudolph A. Winnacker, Chief of the Editorial Branch, Dr. Stetson Conn, Dr. Albert K. Weinberg, and other members of the editorial staff. Dr. Conn's assistance proved especially helpful in the revision and correction of statistical data to the extent permitted by figures now available. Dr. Weinberg rounded out some of the studies by incorporating material from related AGF monographs, in particular from the "History of the Replacement and School Command," prepared by Capt. William H. Willis. Maj. Ulysses G. Lee of the Historical Division contributed to the first study a section on Negro troops. Mr. W. Brooks Phillips performed the difficult task of providing a full index for the volume. To all those who have rendered assistance, the authors acknowledge their indebtedness.

At the end of the volume certain aids to the reader will be found: a glossary of the numerous abbreviations which appear in the text and tables; a footnote guide explaining the system of documentation; a bibliographical note to guide future students of the subjects treated through the archival materials used; and, at the end of the bibliographical note, a list of the studies prepared or initiated by the Historical Section of the Army Ground Forces during the war.

Washington, D.C.
April 1947

KENT ROBERTS GREENFIELD
Colonel, ORC

Contents

The Procurement of Enlisted Personnel: The Problem of Quality

by

Robert R. Palmer

Contents

Tables

I. The Classification of Enlisted Personnel

The armed forces of the United States at their peak strength during World War II numbered approximately 12,350,000. The Army's share of this total was roughly 8,300,000, of which about 7,300,000 were enlisted men. Another volume of this series has described the problems attending the allocation to ground combat units of an adequate proportion of the mobilized manpower.[1] Of equal concern to the Army Ground Forces was the quality of these men with respect to their basic aptitudes for service in the ground arms.

Even if these basic aptitudes had been firmly established by the system of classifying the Army's quota of the national manpower, not all of those found to possess them could have been assigned to the Army Ground Forces. The competing demands of the Air Forces for men with combat aptitudes and of both the Air and Service Forces for men with technical qualifications had to be met also. The supply necessary to meet all demands having quickly been found inadequate, priorities were established. In 1942 it was deemed necessary to give the Army Air Forces first call on the Army's quota of men in the highest brackets of general military aptitude. By the end of 1943 the operation of this priority and of other factors had reduced to a dangerously low level the number of men allotted to the Ground Forces who seemed likely to perform effectively in combat. In 1944 priority as between Air and Ground Forces was reversed, and the system of classification was revised to select more effectively for ground combat service the types of men who had an aptitude for such service.

The present study approaches the problem from the point of view of the Army Ground Forces, the major command responsible for the training of ground combat troops in World War II. It presents an analysis of the effects produced by the system of assignment used in 1942 and 1943, reviews the efforts and proposals which were made to obtain a larger share of men of the type needed to meet the requirements of ground combat in modern war, and describes the results of these efforts. An attempt has been made to indicate why certain efforts and proposals failed or were overruled, but in general only insofar as the reasons

[1] See "Mobilization of the Ground Army," in UNITED STATES ARMY IN WORLD WAR II: THE ARMY GROUND FORCES, *The Organization of Ground Combat Troops* (Washington, 1947).

230-171 O - 66 - 2

were known at Headquarters, Army Ground Forces. The views presented can be fully appraised only when the whole picture of the war effort has been more fully developed.

Although many in the armed forces seem at first to have shared the prevalent optimism regarding the abundance of the resources of the Nation both in materiel and personnel, the War Department had in practice recognized the necessity of using the existing aptitudes of its quota of manpower economically. It had built up, with the advice of experts in psychology and personnel management, a complex system of classification and assignment to make maximum use of civilian skills and personal aptitudes.[2] Its system made provision for specialists and administrative and clerical personnel. Its scheme of classification recognized differences in age, physical hardihood, mental endowment, education, occupational skill, and capacity for assuming responsibility, with the object of adapting these various personal aptitudes to military requirements. The purposes of the system, in ascending order of importance, were to maintain morale by giving men suitable assignments; to simplify, hasten, and economize the training effort; and to organize the available manpower in such a way as to deliver in the shortest time the maximum force against the enemy.

The Need for High-Grade Personnel in Ground Combat

Ground combat in World War II required complex skills, which were in large part technical. Even in the Infantry, the ground arm requiring the least technical training, the private had to understand the use of a dozen weapons. He had to acquire at least an elementary knowledge of many things besides: camouflage and concealment; mine removal and the detection of booby traps; patrolling, map reading, and combat intelligence; recognition of American, Allied, and enemy aircraft, armored vehicles, and other equipment; the use and disposal of captured equipment; the processing of prisoners of war; first aid, field sanitation, and maintenance of life and health out of doors over long periods and under conditions of extreme difficulty. Thus the trained ground soldier was, on the basis of military instead of civilian skills, almost as much a specialist as anyone in the Army. Moreover, the knowledge and skills which the infantryman might need in battle were such that they could not be reduced to an anticipated

[2] See the articles by Walter V. Bingham, Chief Psychologist, Personnel Procedure Section, the Adjutant General's Office, in *Annals of the American Academy of Political and Social Science,* March 1942, pp. 18–28, *Harper's,* September 1942, pp. 432–40, and *Science,* September 29, 1944, pp. 275–80.

routine. He had to know how to play his part under conditions of strain and confusion in the teamwork of squad and platoon, coordinating the various infantry weapons in a tactics of fire and movement. The mobile tactics and open formations of World War II demanded the greatest possible physical vigor and mental alertness in individual combat soldiers and required strong powers of leadership in commanders, even in units as small as the squad. The intelligence, skill, and stamina of semi-isolated riflemen and small-unit commanders were to determine not only individual survival on the battlefield but also in many cases the outcome of battle.

Although these facts were appreciated increasingly as the war proceeded, they were recognized from the beginning. In March 1942, when the Army Ground Forces was established, G-3 of the War Department General Staff endorsed the following public statement emphasizing the importance of having a high grade of personnel in ground combat units:[3]

> The increased tempo of war today, its rapid changes in local situations, and the great spaces it covers make it impossible for commanders to control the detailed action of subordinate units. Hence the accomplishment of the will of the commander depends, in final analysis, upon the ability of subordinates to make the proper decisions in unpredictable situations on the battlefield. These decisions require sound judgment and initiative—qualities which must be carefully developed and fostered in the training of every individual.

Yet the quality of manpower in the ground arms, when mobilization was nearly completed in the latter part of 1943, compared unfavorably with that of other elements of the Army. A sample consisting of 12,000 combat soldiers proved to be below the Army average in height, in weight, in intelligence, and in education. The infantrymen examined averaged over half an inch shorter and six pounds lighter than the average for the Army.[4]

The ground combat arms had failed to receive a proportionate share of the high-quality men assigned by reception centers to the major Army commands. During the representative year of 1943, about 2,600,000 men were processed by the Army at reception centers and assigned to the arms and services. About 40 percent of these men were sent to the ground combat arms. But only 34 percent of the men graded highest in intelligence and aptitude (AGCT Classes I and II) were so assigned, while 44 percent of those graded lowest (AGCT Classes IV

[3] Lt B. N. Harlow (Bureau of Public Relations, War Department), "Training for Military Service," *Annals of the American Academy of Political and Social Science*, March 1942, pp. 29–49. Stated by the editors to have been written in collaboration with G-3, WDGS.

[4] AGF memo for G-1 WD, 11 Nov 43, sub: Improvement of the Morale, Efficiency, and Effectiveness of Inf. 000.7/22 (Inf Prog).

and V) went to the ground combat arms.[5] Lt. Gen. Lesley J. McNair, Commanding General of the Army Ground Forces, felt very strongly on this matter. He came increasingly to believe that American soldiers were sustaining avoidable casualties and perhaps taking longer than necessary to win the war, because the men assigned to ground combat units did not represent a fair cross section of the nation's manpower.

The Army Classification System and the Army Ground Forces

There were various reasons for the relatively inferior quality of the human raw material made available to the ground combat arms during the first two years of the war. One was the absence of a central system of personnel classification and assignment for the Army and Navy as a whole. Another was, from the viewpoint of the Army Ground Forces, the shortcomings of the Army's own system of classification.

Underlying Selective Service was the idea that the military authorities could best determine where a man might most effectively serve, and that individuals should patriotically abstain from volunteering for this or that branch of the service. In fact, however, the Navy and the Marine Corps obtained their personnel entirely from volunteers until the end of 1942. They also procured a large proportion of their officers by granting commissions to civilians prior to training, largely on the basis of educational background. This practice contrasted with the Army system, in which most men went through basic training as enlisted men before they could become eligible as officer candidates. Direct commissioning of civilians by the Army, though practiced on a fairly large scale in the early period of mobilization, did not ordinarily affect men liable for Selective Service and was not used to obtain officers for combat assignments. But by voluntarily enlisting or by accepting a commission in the Navy or the Marines, many thousands of men of the finest physical types, and of a high degree of education and personal initiative, remained outside the operations of Selective Service and hence outside the Army. Not all of these men were used for combat duty by the Navy and the Marine Corps.

The Army classification system, designed to determine where men could serve most effectively, therefore applied to a group which, in its top strata, was

[5] These percentages were compiled from statistics of the AGO Classification and Replacement Branch, reports on Forms XOC–62, 63, 64. For a detailed breakdown of the 1943 statistics see Table No. 3.

less than representative of the national manpower. In addition, some of the best men received by the Army were not subject to normal classification. Until the end of 1942 the Army also accepted men of draft age as volunteers and permitted them to select their own branch of the service. In 1942 only about 5 percent of the volunteers chose the Infantry or Armored Force.[6] The overwhelming majority chose the Air Corps. They reached Army reception centers preclassified—earmarked for the Air Corps by their own wish. Only high-type men could qualify. By no means all were employed by the Army Air Forces on combat or flying duty.[7]

The Navy, the Marines, and the Army Air Forces therefore had the character of hand-picked organizations, a character preserved to a large extent by the Navy and the Marine Corps even after their resort to the draft (because of differences in induction standards), and by the Army Air Forces even though a large proportion of its personnel was obtained by nonvoluntary methods.

The Army classification system applied to the great bulk of men received by the Military Establishment during the war. Classification began on induction and followed the enlisted man through his military career, changing as he changed. Assignment and reassignment reflected the successive decisions of classifying officers. For most men the classification and corresponding assignment made at the time of induction determined their subsequent careers in the Army. Men were classified in three ways—by physical capacity, by intellectual capacity, and by occupational skill.

Classification and assignment within the Army by physical capacity was very broad. For induction, detailed and fairly high physical standards, including psychiatric standards, were prescribed.[8] Once in the Army, men were classified on simple lines. Whereas the British and German Armies recognized several grades of physical capacity, according to muscular strength, endurance, agility,

[6] "Armistice Day Address by Lt Gen L. J. McNair, 11 Nov 42," p. 5. AWC Library, Collection of McNair Speeches.

[7] The Air Corps is the permanent statutory organization of the air arm of the Military Establishment and is the principal component of the Army Air Forces. During World War II the strength of the Air Corps was 80 percent or more of the total strength of the Army Air Forces, the remainder being made up of various services and arms attached to the Air Forces. The preferential rules of 1942–43 discussed in the following pages applied to all men assigned to the Army Air Forces and shipped directly from reception centers to AAF basic training centers. Such men were actually members of the Air Corps; this study, however, follows the customary war and postwar practice of referring to them as personnel of the Army Air Forces.

[8] WD Mobilization Regulations (MR) 1–9, as amended.

coordination, and other criteria, and assigned men to positions making corresponding demands on physique, the United States Army recognized only one category of general service and one category of limited service. In July 1943 limited service was abolished as a category in classification. Physical grounds for assignment thereafter depended on individual cases rather than on types. The great majority of men qualified for general service. General-service men were assigned to units irrespective of finer physical gradations, largely on the basis of occupational skill. Consequently the question whether, in a given unit, a man would engage in hand-to-hand fighting, march long distances on foot, carry a heavy pack, or go without sleep and food counted very little in his original assignment. Modifications in this system were introduced in 1944, too late to affect the bulk of the Army.

Classification by intellectual capacity was more precise.[9] For this purpose inductees were given an Army General Classification Test (AGCT) designed to measure ability to learn. The confusion of AGCT scores with concepts of "I.Q." or "mental age" was forbidden by the War Department. The AGCT measured a compound of native endowments and of the effects of schooling and social experience, amounting to "intelligence" in the popular and practical sense in which it was useful to the Army. Scores were so arranged that 100 represented the expected median of all men tested. Numerical scores were grouped into five classes, of which Class I represented the men of highest intelligence and Class V the lowest. To qualify as an officer candidate a man had to fall in Class I or II. Class II was also the main source of good noncommissioned officers. Other things being equal (which they were not), all arms and services were to receive the same proportionate distribution of men in the five AGCT classes.

Of all provisions of the classification system those concerned with occupational skills were the most elaborate and the most refined.[10] The Army sought to meet its needs for specialists with men experienced in related occupations in civilian life. The purpose was the very important one of speeding up mobilization and training by utilizing the full capacities of the available manpower. Specialists, in this connection, included those pursuing relatively simple trades which could be learned in a few weeks or months. The need of the Army for specialists

[9] TM 12–260, WD, 31 Dec 42, Personnel Classification Tests.

[10] (1) AR 615–26, 15 Sep 42, sub: EM: Index and Specifications for Civ and Mil Occupational Specialists. (2) TM 12–426, WD, 1 Jul 44, sub: Civ Occupational Classification and Enl Pers. (3) WD Classification Memos, especially No. 9, 18 May 42, and No. 10, 1 Aug 42.

was made clear to the public, especially in the period before the declaration of war, when the distastefulness of compulsory military training could be relieved by pointing out its vocational value. The publicizing of technical requirements produced an expectation among many inductees that they could best contribute to the war effort by continuing with their usual occupations, somewhat modified, in the Army. The satisfaction or disappointment of these expectations became an important factor in morale.

To effect proper classification on all jobs performed by enlisted men, called "military occupational specialties" (MOS's), were given "specification serial numbers" (SSN's) on a scale from 001 to 999. Numbers below 500 designated military jobs having corresponding occupations in civilian life, such as Automobile Mechanic, 014, or Clerk-Typist, 405. Numbers above 500 designated jobs having no parallel in civilian life, such as Rifleman, 745, or Antitank Gunner, 610. An exception in the numbers above 500 was Laborer, 590. A special case was Basic, 521, since basic privates might be trained for any job as desired by commanders.

At the reception center the newly inducted man, after an interview, with or without vocational tests, was classified according to his occupational experience or aptitude. He received the specification serial number most closely corresponding to his main civilian skill. This number inevitably fell in the group of SSN's below 500. To fill the need for SSN's above 500 the classifying officer attempted to find related civilian trades. A man classified as Steward, 124, might be recommended for training as Mess Sergeant, 824. But for fighting jobs, such as Rifleman, 745, Tank Driver, 736, or Gunner, 603, there were, of course, no civilian equivalents.

The requirements of the Army, in terms of SSN's, were formulated primarily in unit Tables of Organization (T/O's), which showed what jobs existed in every unit and how many men were needed for each type of job. From the T/O's of all units the Adjutant General's Office computed "Requirement and Replacement Rates, Military Specialists."[11] These were for the guidance of reception centers in the assignment of newly inducted men. They converted the needs of every type of unit for each SSN into a rate per thousand enlisted men. For example, in the infantry regiment, the rate per thousand was 21.3 for cooks (SSN 060), 77.0 for light truck drivers (SSN 345), 177.5 for riflemen (SSN 745), and 50.7 for automatic riflemen (SSN 746). The Requirement and Replacement

[11] Reissued at fairly long intervals; figures in present paragraph are from issue of WD Memo W615-12-43, 28 Jan 43.

Rates also included figures for the over-all SSN needs of each arm and service. These figures served as a guide in the assignment of newly inducted men to replacement training centers.

The arms and services differed greatly in their needs for military occupational specialties. Some had a higher requirement rate than others for SSN's below 500, that is, for men to fill jobs for which there was a civilian counterpart. All the services except Military Police had more of such jobs than did any of the arms. (See Table No. 1.) At one extreme was the Transportation Corps, in which,

TABLE NO. 1

Distribution of Enlisted Men per Thousand in Various Arms and Services, 28 January 1943

Arm or Service	All SSN's below 500[a]	SSN 590 (Laborer)	SSN 521 (Basic)	All Other SSN's[b]	Total
Transportation	788	90	59	63	1,000
Engineers	725	1	120	154	1,000
Ordnance	641	45	171	143	1,000
Signal	579	......	107	314	1,000
Quartermaster	466	268	121	145	1,000
Medical	438	......	163	399	1,000
Chemical	409	182	116	293	1,000
Field Artillery	347	......	111	542	1,000
Tank Destroyer	338	......	109	553	1,000
Cavalry	322	1	91	586	1,000
Armored	253	3	89	655	1,000
Antiaircraft	224	......	106	670	1,000
Coast Artillery	197	......	99	704	1,000
Infantry	164	......	104	732	1,000
Military Police	108	......	112	780	1,000
Air Corps	198	......	117	685	1,000

Source: WD Memo W615-12-43, 28 Jan 43, sub: Reqmt & Repl Rates, Military Specialists (1943 Troop Basis).

[a] Men with jobs having counterparts in civilian life.

[b] Men with distinctly military jobs, having no civilian counterparts.

according to the Requirement and Replacement Rates, 788 out of every 1,000 enlisted men filled civilian-type jobs (SSN's below 500), while only 63 were engaged in work for which there was no civilian equivalent. In the Infantry, on the other hand, only 164 men out of 1,000 (mostly cooks, truck drivers, and radio operators) filled civilian-type jobs, and 732 were engaged in exclusively military occupations. In general, for the combat arms there was no specific vocational preparation in civilian life. In assigning newly inducted men to the combat arms, and especially to the Infantry, it was necessary to a large extent either to ignore civilian occupation or to assign men who had no established occupation, and who therefore, unless lack of established occupation was due to youth, were not likely to be the most desirable material.

Occupational classification, though not adapted primarily to the needs of the combat arms, was nevertheless the main basis of assignment. Reception centers, in filling requisitions of units or replacement training centers for personnel, supplied specialists in the proportions called for in the Requirement and Replacement Rates. For further guidance of the reception centers Army Regulations 615–26, dated 15 September 1942, offered suggestions for assignment. For boilermakers, bricklayers, riveters, and steelworkers, the suggested assignment was the Corps of Engineers. For longshoremen it was the Quartermaster Corps. Detectives were thought to be peculiarly suitable for the Provost Marshal General's Office, and "vice-squad patrolmen" for the Military Police. Miners might fit into either the Engineers or the Infantry. Suited for the Infantry primarily, according to these suggestions, were a few "specialists" of infrequent occurrence in the civilian population, such as parachute jumpers and mountaineers. Bookkeepers, file clerks, piano tuners, shipping clerks, and teachers were recommended "for any arm or service."[12] White-collar workers were not needed by the Army in proportion to their frequency in civilian society. They stood, therefore, a somewhat better chance of being assigned to the Infantry than did boilermakers or longshoremen.

The War Department was aware that civilian vocation was not in itself an adequate basis for military assignment. It realized that combat soldiers and combat leaders must learn their tasks after induction into the Army, regardless of previous occupation, and that to become a good soldier or a good leader required a considerable degree of intelligence. In March 1942 the Chief Psychologist, Personnel Procedures Bureau, Adjutant General's Office, in discussing the Army

[12] AR 615–26, 15 Sep 42, pp. 97ff.

classification system, emphasized that men suited for combat positions should not be kept blindly at their old trades while in the Army. A master plumber, he maintained, would be misused as a plumber if he could become the leader of a machine gun squad.[13] A certified public accountant, he added, would be wasted in the Finance Department if in fact he had the ability to become the commander of a tank destroyer battalion. To keep qualified men from combat or command positions was the worst form of "occupational casualty."[14]

The trouble was that no definite means had been developed to determine a man's potentialities as a fighter or a combat leader. The first principle of the system as a system was, after all, to provide men with suitable job experience to Army units according to a highly refined scheme of job analysis rooted in Army Tables of Organization. A sample study in 1943 indicated that, of enlisted men having civilian trades usable by the Army, only 17 percent "were used by the Army in some activity different from previous civilian experience."[15]

The net result was that men having established trades or skills in civilian life tended to be assigned to the noncombat elements of the Army. The problem of technical training in the Army was thereby simplified, but the problem of tactical and combat training was rendered more difficult. Skilled workmen in civilian life tended to be men of the higher intelligence levels, with a sense of responsibility and initiative, and possessed also of superior physiques. The loss of civilian skills to the ground arms was of slight importance, since most skills in the ground arms had in any case to be learned after induction; but the loss of the type of men who had acquired skills in civilian life left the ground arms with a subaverage portion of the available manpower.

There was one large exception to the placing of primary emphasis on occupational classification. In assignment to the Army Air Forces, classification by intellectual capacity was given precedence. During most of the period of rapid mobilization, from early in 1942 to the middle of 1943, the War Department ruled that a specified proportion of inductees sent to basic training centers of the Army Air Forces should be men scoring over 100 in the AGCT. The proportion varied but was always well above that found among inductees as a whole. The training program of the Air Forces, largely technical in nature, was simplified

[13] But in AR 615–26 plumbers were suggested for assignment to the Engineers or the Quartermaster Corps.

[14] W. V. Bingham, "The Army Personnel Classification System," *Annals of the American Academy of Political and Social Science*, March 1942, p. 21.

[15] *Report of the Army Service Forces, Fiscal Year 1943*, p. 136.

and accelerated by the receipt of a larger percentage of high-intelligence personnel. In view of the size of the Air Forces, the practice substantially reduced the number of high-intelligence men available to the remainder of the Army.

In principle, the War Department desired that all arms and services should receive an adequate proportion of the more intelligent men from whom officers might be developed. Instructions to reception centers read:[16]

> Mental ability will be distributed proportionately to all replacement training centers and units after occupational specialists required by installation or unit of assignment have been supplied, except when specifically directed to the contrary by the War Department. Particular attention will be given to the necessity of sending to the various arms and services all men who appear to have the proper qualifications for officer candidates in the respective arms and services.

But the "after" clause in the first sentence, by which men with established vocations went largely into the services, and the "except" clause, which during 1942 and 1943 covered the policy of assigning a larger proportion of men of high mental capacity to the Air Forces, meant that however evenly the reception centers distributed the remaining mental ability the combat ground arms would obtain less than their share of the high-intelligence men. The percentage of enlisted men "who appeared to have the proper qualifications for officer candidates" was in fact lower in the combat ground arms than in the rest of the Army.

For the purposes of the Army Ground Forces, the fundamental shortcoming of the classification system was that, while it indicated very definitely the occupational qualities of enlisted men for which the Army Service Forces could establish a claim, it indicated very indefinitely the qualities mainly required by the Army Ground Forces. A man's potentialities as a fighter or combat leader were intangible. To estimate them involved the prediction of how an individual would behave under future conditions of a kind to which he had never been subjected in the past. It was fairly safe to assume that a truck driver, if taught to drive an Army truck under tactical conditions in maneuvers, would be able to drive satisfactorily in a combat zone. It was more difficult to predict how a man would react in battle as a rifleman from anything known of him at the time of induction, or even during training, however much the training might simulate combat. It was not possible to predict with assurance, whatever signs of leadership a man might have shown as a civilian, that he would do well at officer candidate school or, if he did, how he would actually conduct himself as a lieutenant directing his platoon in battle.

[16] Par 23*b*, WD Classification Memo No. 9, 18 May 42.

In short, the qualities which it was most important for the Army Ground Forces to know were those on which psychological research was the least conclusive, and on which the records made by classifying officers were the most indefinite or silent. Attempts were made to put the desired information on the soldier's principal classification record, his "Form 20." It might be recorded that he had handled firearms as a civilian, or had gone on hunting trips—a fact which would perhaps be made the basis of assignment to the Infantry. It might be recorded that a man had supervised others in civilian life, as a foreman, office manager, or superintendent—a fact which would possibly be used as evidence of a capacity for military leadership. For the purpose to be served, however, such notations were desultory and inadequate. They lacked also the apparent definiteness of an SSN classification or an AGCT score; they did not constitute systematic classification. Putting a needle through the punched spaces in a stack of Form 20's did not make it possible to identify the men who would make the best riflemen or the best officer candidates.

In the absence of definite and reliable measures of the qualities needed in combat troops, the Army Ground Forces relied on more or less indirect indications of such qualities. The fact that the use of AGCT scores and vocational histories tended to put the men with most initiative and intelligence in technical positions, and that little use of physical classification was made at all, gave additional reason for the Army Ground Forces to stress intelligence, initiative, and physical strength as indirect indications of what was needed in combat troops. Physical ruggedness was emphasized as a sign of fighting capacity, not only because front-line soldiers needed to be strong but also because physical strength was to some extent correlated with aggressiveness and emotional stability. Achievement in a civilian vocation was held to be a sign of initiative, ambition, self-reliance, persistence, and learning ability, and hence an indirect measure of qualities needed in fighting men and battle commanders. High AGCT scores were stressed as a sign of potential leadership. It was well known, to be sure, that battle leaders required qualities not measured by the AGCT and that many men with exceptionally high AGCT scores often could not deal effectively with subordinates. The correlation between leadership qualities and AGCT scores was by no means perfect. But in the absence of definite leadership tests common to the whole Army no better index than the AGCT was available.

Officers of the Army Ground Forces came gradually, however, to question the whole system of classification and assignment. Their increasing doubts of its effectiveness in meeting the needs they represented were built up by experience.

At first, in 1942, in pointing out the consequences of basing preferential assignment to the Air Forces on mental classification, Army Ground Forces urged a more consistent adherence to the principle of assignment according to occupational skill. Protesting against an exception to the system, Army Ground Forces appealed to the system itself. Later, as the consequences of vocationalism became apparent, the value of the system as a whole came to be doubted. The War Department's decentralization of assignment procedures on 1 March 1943, and the consequent establishment of an active Classification and Replacement Division in the AGF headquarters staff, meant that more thought was given by AGF officers to the whole problem. After the middle of 1943 General McNair believed that assignment of inductees to branches of the Army should depend primarily on physical classification, with occupational assignment reserved for certain rare specialists only, and with no assignment on the basis of AGCT score alone. This was almost the reverse of the procedure under which the Army (almost completely mobilized by late 1943) had been formed.

II. Problems of Quality in the Period of Mobilization

The first "new" infantry divisions, neither Regular Army nor National Guard in origin, were activated in March 1942. In the same month the quality of manpower received by the ground arms began to decline below the national average. The role of the Army classification system in this decline was not at first appreciated and became fully evident only as experience accumulated. In 1942 the War Department sought a remedy in legislation which would permit the induction of younger, more vigorous men, and the Army Ground Forces was concerned with the effect of the preference accorded to the Army Air Forces in the assignment of men with high AGCT scores. In November 1942 legislation for the induction of men eighteen and nineteen years old was obtained, and the War Department directed the maximum practicable assignment of younger inductees to combat units.[1] But throughout 1943 preference to the Army Air Forces continued to affect adversely the quality of those men received by the Army Ground Forces. A further decline in the quality of ground combat troops was caused in 1942 and 1943 by the loss of men who applied for officer training in the Air and Service Forces, and in 1943 by the temporary withdrawal of thousands of highly intelligent men for the Army Specialized Training Program. By the middle of 1943 the basic causes for this qualitative deterioration in ground combat troops became apparent. Partial remedies could not provide a solution for the existing crisis. A radical change, involving a shift in emphasis from occupational and mental to physical qualifications in the Army classification system, was required to assure the effectiveness of ground troops in combat. In the preceding year and a half the quality of personnel in the Army Ground Forces had declined well below the national average in intelligence as well as in physical vigor.

[1] (1) Memo (C) of G-3 WD for TAG, 1 Dec 42, sub: Assignment of 18, 19, and 20 Year Old Enlisted Men. AGO Records, ACT 324.71 (11-12-42) (1) (Use of 18 and 19 Year Old Group) (R). (2) For discussion of policy and plans with Hq AGF see AGF file 327.3 (Selective Service Men) (S). By express direction of General Marshall not less than 25 percent of the men in combat units were to be 'teen-age men. Seventy-five percent were to be assigned to divisions activated after 1 January 1943.

Decline in the Quality of AGF Personnel

Before March 1942 the ground arms received a representative cross section of the manpower available to the Army. The best single precise index to quality of personnel (physical fitness of all general-service men being assumed equally adequate) was the score on the Army General Classification Test. In the six months preceding 1 March 1942, men processed and assigned by Army reception centers to replacement training centers were distributed by AGCT score as follows:

Class	*I*	*II*	*III*	*IV and V*	*Total*
Percent	6.9	26.8	31.1	35.2	100.0

Percentage distribution to the ground arms was as follows:

Class	*I*	*II*	*III*	*IV and V*	*Total*
Armored Force	7.4	28.0	32.7	31.9	100.0
Cavalry	7.1	27.2	30.8	34.9	100.0
Infantry	6.7	26.5	31.2	35.6	100.0
Coast Artillery	6.4	25.9	31.6	36.1	100.0
Field Artillery	6.3	25.9	31.2	36.6	100.0

This distribution by classes in the ground arms reflected the average for the Army as a whole before 1 March 1942.[2]

In February 1942 the War Department ordered that 75 percent of the white men sent to the Air Forces from reception centers were to have AGCT scores of 100 or over, that is, be in Classes I, II, or the upper half of III. This decision was based upon strategic requirements. The first offensive blows were to be delivered by the Army Air Forces. Preparing it for this role involved not only expanding it rapidly from a very small nucleus but also giving it first call on high-quality personnel. At the same time, in the spring and summer of 1942, the number of service units activated was greatly increased to build up a base in the British Isles for the large-scale air and ground operations then contemplated. As a consequence, the factors tending to lower the quality of manpower assigned to the ground combat arms began to operate with pronounced effect.

Percentage distribution, in terms of AGCT classes, for men processed and assigned by Army reception centers to replacement training centers in the six months following 1 March 1942 was as follows:

Class	*I*	*II*	*III*	*IV and V*	*Total*
Percent	6.5	25.7	31.0	36.8	100.0

[2] Percentages compiled by Historical Division, WDSS, from statistics of the AGO Classification and Replacement Branch, reports on Forms XOC–62, 63, 64.

Distribution to the ground arms by percentages was as follows:

Class	*I*	*II*	*III*	*IV and V*	*Total*
Armored Force	5.3	23.2	32.6	38.9	100.0
Infantry	5.3	22.1	29.0	43.6	100.0
Coast Artillery	4.6	21.5	31.7	42.2	100.0
Field Artillery	4.6	19.5	29.4	46.5	100.0
Cavalry	4.4	21.4	31.3	42.9	100.0

The percentage distribution during the same period of the men assigned to replacement training centers of the various arms and services is shown in Table No. 2. Only the Corps of Engineers ranked below the ground combat arms in the quality of personnel received, as reflected in AGCT scores.[3]

The same situation continued to prevail throughout 1943. Figures for all men assigned by reception centers to both units and replacement training centers during 1943 show that the ground combat arms stood considerably below the Air Forces and most of the services in quality of personnel received; divisions stood near the bottom of the list. Divisions, the major fighting units of the ground arms, received only 27.9 percent of their inductees in Classes I and II; the Air Forces, on the other hand, received 41.7 percent; service command service units (comprising permanent reception center personnel, etc.), 51.6 percent; and the Signal Corps, 58.0 percent. (See Table No. 3.) The ground combat arms were assigned about 40 percent of the men processed at reception centers during 1943, but only 28.5 percent of the top-quality Class I men.[4]

Not all the high-grade men assigned to the ground arms could be retained. Attrition was highest in this type of personnel. Some were lost as officer candidates when they elected to try for commissions outside the ground arms. In one infantry division in 1942, of 1,200 enlisted men accepted as officer candidates 800 elected officer training in quartermaster, medical administration, and finance.[5] Apart from the lesser danger, these branches were probably preferred in a belief that they offered opportunities for vocational self-improvement. Election of these branches by enlisted men in the combat ground arms was later prohibited by amendment to the Army Regulations. Through 1943 many intelligent enlisted men were also lost to the Army Specialized Training Program in the colleges. Through the whole period of mobilization soldiers in the ground arms were free

[3] *Ibid.*

[4] *Ibid.*

[5] AGF ltr to CGs, 4 Sep 42, sub: OCS. 352/301 (OCS).

TABLE NO. 2

Percentage Distribution by AGCT Classes of All Men Assigned by Reception Centers to Replacement Training Centers, by Branch, March–August 1942

Branch	Class		
	I and II	III	IV and V
Finance[a]	89.4	10.1	0.5
Chemical Warfare	51.2	27.6	21.2
Army Air Forces[a]	44.4	35.3	20.3
Ordnance	41.6	33.0	25.4
Signal Corps[a]	39.2	35.1	25.7
Military Police[a]	35.3	33.0	31.7
Medical	30.6	29.1	40.3
Quartermaster	28.5	29.4	42.1
Armored Force	28.5	32.6	38.9
Branch Immaterial[b]	28.5	28.2	43.3
Infantry	27.4	29.0	43.6
Coast Artillery	26.1	31.7	42.2
Cavalry	25.8	31.3	42.9
Field Artillery	24.1	29.4	46.5
Engineers	23.4	26.2	50.4

Source: Compiled by Historical Division, WDSS, from statistics of the AGO Classification and Replacement Branch reports on Forms XOC–62, 63, 64.

[a] These RTC's received white selectees only during this period. Negro men for these services and the Air Forces were assigned directly to units from reception centers or were trained at a BIRTC. Finance RTC, in addition to receiving no Negroes, received no Class V men.

[b] Most graduates of branch immaterial replacement training centers were assigned to the Infantry.

to volunteer as aviation cadets in the Air Corps. Transferred to the Air Forces, they might not succeed in becoming fliers. If not, they were retained by the Air Forces in ground positions. Many enlisted men, of sufficiently good physique and intelligence to qualify originally as aviation cadets, were shifted by this process from AGF units, in which they would probably have become at least squad or platoon leaders in combat, to the ground installations of the Air Forces, in which their functions were predominantly technical and mechanical. The Air Forces enjoyed this advantage in addition to obtaining large numbers of volunteer aviation cadets directly from the reception centers, and in addition also to the preferential assignment of high-quality men to AAF basic training centers under the rules in effect until June 1943.

230-171 O - 66 - 3

TABLE NO. 3

Distribution by AGCT Classes of All Men Inducted into the Army, Processed at Reception Centers, and Assigned to the Various Arms and Services during 1943

Branch	Classes I and II		Class III		Classes IV and V		Total
	Number	Percent	Number	Percent	Number	Percent	
ASTP	45,114	97.7	1,027	2.3	47	[a]	46,188
Signal Corps	43,202	58.0	18,849	25.0	12,775	17.0	74,826
Service Command Service Units	26,607	51.6	13,915	27.0	11,035	21.4	51,557
Miscellaneous (includes Finance and Military Intelligence)	29,141	43.6	17,827	26.6	19,926	29.8	66,894
Army Air Forces	247,141	41.7	185,489	31.3	159,282	27.0	591,912
Military Police	21,566	39.3	20,017	36.5	13,299	24.2	54,882
Ordnance	26,984	36.1	25,447	33.7	22,886	30.2	75,317
Chemical Warfare	8,454	33.9	7,165	28.8	9,303	37.3	24,922
Coast Artillery	9,496	33.0	9,851	34.3	9,406	32.7	28,753
Field Artillery	34,909	31.4	36,815	33.1	39,372	35.5	111,096
Armored	17,319	31.4	19,043	34.5	18,783	34.1	55,145
Medical	44,732	30.9	46,286	32.0	53,791	37.1	144,809
Infantry	102,223	30.2	110,561	32.6	125,942	37.2	338,726
Branch Immaterial[b]	23,674	29.7	25,538	32.0	30,536	38.3	79,748
Antiaircraft	60,491	29.1	69,815	33.6	77,513	37.3	207,819
Engineers	57,206	29.1	64,002	32.5	75,409	38.4	196,617
Tank Destroyer	13,731	28.2	16,516	33.9	18,447	37.9	48,694
Divisions	39,716	27.9	49,796	35.1	52,666	37.0	142,178
Cavalry	6,621	27.2	7,785	32.0	9,931	40.8	24,337
Quartermaster	35,099	21.3	42,373	25.7	87,464	53.0	164,936
Transportation	10,448	19.4	14,838	27.7	28,359	52.9	53,645
TOTAL	903,874	35.0	802,955	31.1	876,172	33.9	2,583,001
Ground Combat Arms	308,180	29.7	345,720	33.3	382,596	37.0	1,036,496
Services	348,553	36.5	271,746	28.5	334,294	35.0	954,593
Army Air Forces	247,141	41.7	185,489	31.3	159,282	27.0	591,912

Source: Compiled by Historical Division, WDSS, from statistics of the AGO Classification and Replacement Branch reports on Forms XOC–62, 63, 64.

[a] Less than 0.05 percent.

[b] Most men assigned to branch immaterial were subsequently assigned to the Infantry.

From an initially limited and constantly depleted stock of men in the higher AGCT grades the Army Ground Forces had to meet its own requirements for officer candidates, for men to be sent to enlisted specialist courses at the service schools, for parachute volunteers, and for cadremen for new units. Men remaining with their organizations were a very much picked-over lot. One commander observed in a moment of extreme discouragement that his hardest problem was to find competent enlisted men to act as instructors, because "everybody higher than a moron" had been pulled out for one reason or another.[6]

Lt. Gen. Ben Lear, Commanding General, Second Army, suggested in July 1942 that the ground arms should conduct a program of advertising of the kind used by the Navy, the Marine Corps, the Air Forces, and some branches of the Service Forces. In October he urged that[7]

> instead of offering "bait," we offer blood and sweat, and tell of the honor of the "hard way" by which, only, will this war be won. Once we have told them that, we can also tell them of opportunities for advancement. . . . We are scratching the bottom of the barrel now for officer candidates. We are decidedly short of the right material for noncommissioned officer leaders. We will pay for this dearly in battle.

Advertising was distasteful to General McNair. Yet the unpopularity of the Ground Forces was evident. Many speakers, including the Commanding General of the Army Service Forces, kept the public informed of the Army's technical needs.[8] General McNair undertook to stress combat needs in a radio talk on Armistice Day 1942, but addressed himself primarily to the men under his own command.[9] Warning against preferences for "the more genteel forms of warfare," he reminded his hearers that war was a matter of killing and that the American soldier had better put himself in a killing mood before reaching the battlefield. The "killer speech" caused unfavorable public comment, even after a year of declared war with enemies well known to be ruthless. Talking about the realities of war might win sympathy for the individual combat soldier, but it did not make the Army Ground Forces more popular with the average selectee.

Field commanders in 1942 protested repeatedly to Headquarters, Army Ground Forces, that they were receiving men of too low a mental quality to be trained. They said it was dangerous to entrust lethal weapons to men in AGCT

[6] Personal ltr of a commanding officer to Brig Gen J. M. Lentz, 22 Jun 43. Lentz Correspondence.

[7] Personal ltrs, Gen Lear to Gen McNair, 31 Jul and 22 Oct 42. Personal files of Gen Lear.

[8] Address by Gen Somervell, 28 Aug 42. 353.9/22.

[9] "Armistice Day Address by Lt Gen L. J. McNair, 11 Nov 42." AWC Library, Collection of McNair Speeches.

Class V, and wasteful to develop elaborate and expensive equipment and then place it in the hands of men incapable of using it properly. The antiaircraft, armored, tank destroyer, and airborne commanders stressed the special intricacy of their problems,[10] using an argument which the Air Forces had emphasized in seeking preferential assignment of personnel. The Antiaircraft Artillery Command declared that study of Tables of Organization showed that not more than 25 percent of the enlisted men in antiaircraft batteries could be of Classes IV and V, and requested permission to remove all Class V men in excess of 10 percent.[11] For airborne divisions it was proposed that all Class V men be removed.[12] The Replacement and School Command, pointing out that demonstration units had to function with great accuracy in the instruction of student officers, and declaring that they could not do so because of the high proportion of their Class IV and V men, requested a preferential status in assignment of high-grade men.[13] Commanders of tactical units very commonly asked for temporary preference until their units could be brought up to the Army average.[14] It was not at first realized in the field that the Army average was no longer the average for the ground arms.

These requests were rejected by General McNair.[15] He would grant no preference within the Ground Forces unless absolutely necessary. He insisted that the Army must deal with the manpower of the country as it found it, and that to favor one element in the Ground Forces would inevitably injure the others. An exception was made only for airborne divisions, which were authorized to clear out their Class IV and V men in excess of the Army average.[16] Since the Army average was better than the average for the ground arms, this policy constituted preferential treatment for the airborne divisions, but the airborne divisions constituted only about 2 percent of the strength of the Ground Forces.

[10] (1) AGF M/S, G-1 to CofS, 10 May 42. 327.3/212. (2) AGF 1st ind to Armd F, 3 Sep 42. 341/11 (Armd F). (3) AGF 2d ind to TDC, 20 Jul 42. 327.3/239. (4) See footnotes 11 and 12.

[11] AAC ltrs to CG AGF, 27 Apr and 15 Jul 42, sub: Class V Men Received at AA RTCs. 327.3/209.

[12] 101st A/B Div ltr to CG AGF, 7 Sep 42, sub: Qualification of Repls Received by 101st A/B Div. 327.3/287.

[13] (1) Papers in 327.3/300, Aug–Oct 42. (2) R&SC ltr (R) to G-1 AGF, 4 Dec 42, sub: Classification of Pers in Sch Trs. 201.6/6 (R).

[14] AGF 2d ind to II Corps, 26 May 42. 220.01/1 (4th Div).

[15] (1) AGF D/F, 13 May 42, sub: Allotments of EM. 327.3/7 (SS Men) (R). (2) AGF M/S, G-1 to G-3, 31 Jul 42, sub: Class and Grades of Men Received at AA Tng Cens. 327.3/209. (3) AGF M/S, AG Classification to G-3, 20 Jul 42. 327.3/301.

[16] AGF ltr to CGs, 18 Sep 42, sub: Improvement of Pers in A/B Divs. 201.31/106 (A/B).

Preferential Assignment to the Army Air Forces

As previously observed, the unfavorable effect of the classification system on the assignment to the Army Ground Forces of the type of personnel needed for its purposes was not at first appreciated and became fully evident only as experience accumulated. Army Ground Forces was preoccupied during 1942 and the first half of 1943 with the similar but more conspicuous effects of War Department rulings which accorded preference to the Army Air Forces in the assignment of inductees.

In January 1942 the Army Air Forces informed the War Department that almost half the men received by the Air Corps in 1941 had lacked the intelligence necessary for technical training, that comparative study of Tables of Organization showed a greater need in the Air Corps than in the other arms and services for highly trained technicians, and that "failure to properly accomplish the paramount mission of the Air Corps" might be expected unless corrective action was taken. It was recommended that 75 percent of all white inductees shipped from reception centers to the Army Air Forces have an AGCT score of 100 or over.[17] This recommendation was put into effect on 2 February 1942 by order of the War Department.[18]

To be understood this decision must be viewed in the light of broad strategic considerations with which the Army and the Nation were faced. At the beginning of 1942 it was already evident that rapid expansion of American air power was necessary if the Axis powers were to be held at bay for sufficient time to bring the full strength of the United States military might to the aid of the Allies. It also seemed clear, with Allied control of the high seas in doubt, that the first chance the United States would have to deal an offensive blow would be with its air arm. The problem of expansion imposed on the Air Forces was staggering. At the end of 1941 the Army Air Forces numbered only 350,000 out of a total army of 1,650,000 then mobilized. To meet the requirements of Allied strategy, the War Department in the Troop Basis of January 1942 called for expansion of the Air Forces within a year to a strength of 998,000 and, as soon as practicable, to 2,000,000. In August 1942 the goal was raised to 2,200,000. Expanding more

[17] AAF memo (R) for CofS USA, 24 Jan 42, sub: Intel Tests for Air Corps EM Prior to Entry in the Serv. AGO Records, 201.6 (1–24–42) ER (R).

[18] WD ltr (R) AG 201.6 (1–24–42) ER to CG First Corps Area, 2 Feb 42, sub: Intel Tests for Air Corps EM. AGO Records (R).

rapidly than called for by initial plans, the Army Air Forces numbered nearly 1,600,000 officers and men by the end of 1942.

To obtain the technical skills necessary for this swift and prodigious expansion the Army Air Forces, like the Ground Forces, was inadequately served by a system of classification based primarily on civilian skills. The development of the aviation industry was so far below the needs of war that the Air Forces, like the ground combat arms, was obliged to train men after induction in almost complete disregard of civilian vocation. There was no accepted criterion of the relative difficulty of comparable jobs in the various arms and services.[19] The *a priori* argument advanced by the Air Forces in the absence of such a criterion was a strong one.

General McNair freely expressed his appreciation of the difficulties which the Air Forces faced in expanding rapidly while preparing to meet its extraordinary responsibilities. In August 1942 he wrote regarding a failure of the Air Forces to cooperate in joint training: "They are extended beyond their capacity and we simply must be patient while they get straightened out and catch up with the procession."[20] On 30 December 1942 he wrote to Lt. Gen. Henry H. Arnold, Commanding General of the Army Air Forces: "As I have said many times to you and other air officers, the Ground Forces appreciate the tremendous load which the Army Air Forces are carrying, the difficulties they face in expanding so rapidly and so enormously, and the fact that they are fighting heavily in many theaters."[21] On the other hand, the policy of preferential assignment had been declared by the War Department to be a temporary expedient, and it was clearly General McNair's duty to point out the effect on the ground arms of the measures

[19] The following table, though based on samples too small to justify firm conclusions, suggests that a man of given intelligence would probably find it more difficult to become a tank mechanic at Fort Knox than an airplane mechanic at Chanute Field. The sampling indicated that, in certain comparable courses, the chances of men obtaining an average or better grade were as follows:

Course	*School*	*Chances per 100 AGCT*					*Number of Men in Sample*
		V	*IV*	*III*	*II*	*I*	
Airplane Mechanics	Chanute Field	6	21	44	69	90	99
Automotive Mechanics	Fort Knox	17	28	37	48	62	148
Tank Mechanics	Fort Knox	3	13	42	54	81	237

Source: WD TM 12–260, "Personnel Classification Tests," 31 Dec 42.

[20] Personal ltr of Gen McNair to Col Sterling Wood, 20 Aug 42, no sub. 353/128 (Air Gd).

[21] Memo (C) of Gen McNair for CG AAF, 30 Dec 42, sub: Aviation in Support of Ground Forces. 353/4 (Air Gd) (C).

deemed necessary to strengthen the Air Forces. In protesting the drain of intelligent men to the Air Forces, he rested the case of the Ground Forces on the need of such men as junior leaders in combat. In time he came to believe that the actual effect of the policies of Army assignment as applied in 1942 and 1943 was to give the Air Forces a degree of preference greater than the War Department had intended.

Officers in the War Department General Staff, particularly G–1, recognized the bad effects on the rest of the Army of preferential assignment to the Air Forces.[22] On 2 June 1942 General McNair, to support G–1, for the first time formally protested.[23] He noted, citing such figures as were then available, that continuation of the 75-percent rule for the Air Forces would jeopardize the officer candidate program of the ground arms, and that the using up of qualified Class I and Class II men as officer candidates would lower the quality of noncommissioned officers, "despite the fact that the nature of the current war indicates that a high premium must be placed upon the leadership of small units in order to attain success." He recommended rescission of the 75-percent rule and assignment at reception centers according to occupational experience or aptitude. The same view was taken by Lt. Gen. Brehon B. Somervell, Commanding General of the Services of Supply, who, in a personal memorandum for the Deputy Chief of Staff, pronounced the 75-percent rule "contrary to the best interests of the Army as a whole."[24] On 18 July 1942 the 75-percent rule was rescinded.[25]

General Arnold appealed to the Chief of Staff on 29 August for a reinstatement of preferential assignment.[26] The rapid commitment of air units to combat, he said, made necessary a great speeding up of training, which was feasible only with men of a high order of intelligence. He declared that since the rescission of the 75-percent rule the Army Air Forces was not receiving enough high-intelligence personnel to meet its requirements, and recommended that, of the 70,000 inductees then being received monthly by the Air Forces from reception centers,

[22] (1) AGF M/S, G–1 to CofS, 28 May 42, sub: Distrib of EM according to Intel Class. (2) WD memo WDGAP 220.31 for CofS USA, 6 Jun 42, sub: Asgmt of EM from Recp Cens. Both in 327.3/212.

[23] Memo of Gen McNair for G–1 WD, 2 Jun 42, sub: Distribution of EM according to Intel Classification. 327.3/212.

[24] SOS memo (S) SPEX of Gen Somervell for DCofS USA, 13 Jul 42. AGO Records, 220.31 (6–2–42)(S).

[25] (1) WD priority telg AG 324.71 (7–17–42) EC to CG First Corps Area, 18 Jul 42. 327.3/212. (2) WD Memo W615–13–42, 27 Aug 42, sub: Reqmt and Repl Rates for Occupational and Mil Specls.

[26] Memo (C) of Gen Arnold for CofS USA, 29 Aug 42, sub: Asgmt of EM for AAF from Recp Cens. AGO Records, 220.31 (6–2–42) (C).

52,000 (almost 75 percent) should have a score of at least 100 in both the Army General Classification Test and the Mechanical Aptitude Test.

General McNair advised against reinstatement of preference. He wrote to the War Department on 2 September 1942:[27]

I am opposed to the action recommended by the Commanding General, Army Air Forces. . . .

Practically all the comments . . . apply with equal force to the Army Ground Forces. It would be a fairly simple matter to compile data showing that not less than 66% of the men distributed to the Army Ground Forces from reception centers must have an AGCT score of 100 or better if the Army Ground Forces is to accomplish its mission. . . .

Since there was not this proportion of high-scoring men in the country, such preference to one branch must unavoidably injure another. The letter of General McNair continued:

The Army Air Forces have sources of manpower which are not available to the Army Ground Forces. They are permitted to drain the Army Ground Forces of all acceptable material for aviation cadets, air crew and glider pilot training. They secure a large number of highly intelligent personnel by recruiting.

The enormous problems of the Air Forces are appreciated. They should be assisted in every reasonable way. It is felt that the Ground Forces are contributing materially in developing the Air Forces and it is desired to increase this aid wherever practicable. While the Air Forces have heavy and important needs in enlisted technicians, they have a large proportion of commissioned officers (well over twice as large) which should permit the effective utilization of enlisted men of average intelligence. . . . The Ground Forces admittedly have fewer technical demands than the Air Forces, but need high-grade and intelligent enlisted men as combat leaders. . . . Thus it is reasonable to assert that the needs of the Ground Forces for high-grade leadership by non-commissioned officers counterbalance the needs of the Air Forces for enlisted technicians.

General Somervell, also, registered the protest of the Services of Supply. He declared that the 75-percent rule had handicapped both Army Ground Forces and Services of Supply, "particularly," he said (arguing the AGF case), "in the procurement and development of combat leaders."[28]

The problem was difficult. The decision had been made to employ air power in Europe on a large scale before the extensive employment of ground power. General Arnold rested the AAF case on over-all strategic plans which required development of aviation with the utmost speed. As a temporary solution the War

[27] Memo of Gen McNair for G–1 WD, 2 Sep 42, sub: Asgmt of EM for AAF from Recp Cens. 327.3/212.

[28] ASF memo (S) SPGAE 220.3 (9–5–42)–15 of Gen Somervell for G–1 WD, 5 Sep 42, sub as in n. 27. AGO Records, 220.31 (6–2–42) (S).

Department on 7 September 1942 ordered that the monthly quotas of the Air Forces for September and October include 50,000 men scoring 100 or better in both the AGCT and the Mechanical Aptitude Test. Approval was later extended through November.[29] This new preferential policy favored the Air Forces even more than the old 75-percent rule; although roughly half the men tested scored 100 on each test, only about 33 percent scored 100 on both.[30] Combining two kinds of ability, these men were exceptionally desirable. The Army Air Forces was now due to receive almost three-quarters of the new personnel assigned to it at reception centers from the top third of the available manpower.

G–1 of the War Department, supported by G–3, continued to oppose preferential assignment except as a temporary expedient. G–1 observed in September that the training problem of the Air Forces was common to the whole Army, and expressed a belief that the Army Air Forces was using men in positions not commensurate with their ability.[31] This belief was confirmed by a report of The Inspector General dated 13 November 1942. More than a third of the privates at various air bases, according to The Inspector General, were men in AGCT Classes I and II. Over half of these high-intelligence privates were acting in such jobs as "messengers, warehousemen, clerks, guards, orderlies, truck-drivers, firemen and assistant cooks." The Inspector General recommended that preferential assignment be suspended until the Army Air Forces effected a better distribution of its high-intelligence manpower.[32] It will be recalled that AGCT Classes I and II were the source of all officer candidates, and of the best noncommissioned officers, for the whole Army.

Also on 13 November, without having seen The Inspector General's report of that date, General McNair protested against the new preferential policy, which AGF officers regarded as an appalling diversion of the national intelligence from leadership into technical and mechanical jobs. General McNair cited a letter in which Lt Gen Dwight D. Eisenhower noted the weakness of junior leadership among American troops in Great Britain. He warned that it might become necessary to lower the qualifications for officer candidates in the ground arms from

[29] (1) WD memo (C) WDCSA 220.31 (9–2–42) for CG AAF, 7 Sep 42, sub as in n. 27. AGO Records, 220.3 (6–2–42). (2) TWX, TAG to Serv Comds, 2 Oct 42. 327.3/212.

[30] AGF M/S, AG Classification to G–1, 6 Nov 42, sub: Notes on Air Corps 75% Policy. 327.3/212.

[31] WD memo (C) WDGAP 220.31 for CofS USA, 18 Sep 42, sub: Asgmt of Recruits to Arms and Servs from Recp Cens. With concurrence of G–3, 24 Sep. AGO Records, 220.31 (6–2–42) (C).

[32] Extract from IG rpt attached as Tab 5 to WD memo (S) WDGAP 220.31 for CofS USA, 25 Nov 42, sub: Asgmt of Recruits to Arms and Servs from Recp Cens. AGO Records, 220.31 (6–2–42) (S).

110 to 90, or from the bottom of Class II to the bottom of Class III. "While I do not undertake to pass on the merits of the situation as a whole," he remarked in his memorandum to the War Department, "there is little doubt that the prevailing policy is having a detrimental effect on the leadership of the Ground Forces." [33]

Despite the views expressed by the Commanding Generals of the Army Ground Forces and of the Services of Supply, the recommendations of the two General Staff sections principally concerned, and the findings and recommendations of The Inspector General, it was nevertheless ruled on 28 November 1942, over the signature of the Deputy Chief of Staff, that "the Air Force contention must be recognized," and that preferential assignment to the Air Forces, kept for three months on a temporary basis, would remain in effect until 30 June 1943.[34] During this period 55 percent of the men assigned to the Air Forces by reception centers were to have scores of at least 100 on both the AGCT and the Mechanical Aptitude Test. Under the new 55-percent rule, as under the previous preferential policies, volunteer aviation cadets enlisted as such were not included in the quotas assigned to the Air Forces; this high-caliber group was obtained by the Air Forces independently of the normal assignments from reception centers.

The 55-percent rule was discontinued on 1 June 1943, a month before it was due to expire. Ground Forces officers again believed preferential assignment to be a thing of the past. But in effect preference was continued by a new procedure introduced at reception centers for the recruiting of aviation cadets. On 3 June 1943 the War Department directed that any inductee at a reception center who expressed a desire for flying training should be immediately assigned to the Air Forces as an aviation cadet if he met certain requirements. He was required to be a native-born citizen, between eighteen and twenty-six years of age, with a score of at least 100 on the AGCT, and "apparently" qualified physically for aviation-cadet training.[35]

In adopting this procedure the War Department sought to correct two conditions regarded as undesirable. One was the effect that lowering the draft age to

[33] (1) Memo of Gen McNair for G–1 WD, 13 Nov 42, sub: Preferential Treatment of AAF in Asgmt of Enl Pers. (2) AGF M/S, G–1 to CofS, 27 Oct 42, sub: Notes on Air Corps 75% Policy. Both in 327.3/212.

[34] (1) WD memo (S) WDCSA 220.31 (9–2–42) of Gen McNarney for G–3 WD, 28 Nov 42, sub: Asgmt of Recruits to Arms and Servs. AGO Records, 220.31 (6–2–42) (S). (2) WD memo WDGAP 220.31 for TAG, 29 Nov 42, sub: Recruits for the Air Corps. AGF Plans Sec file 155.

[35] WD ltr AG 221 Avn Cadets (5–15–43) OC–E–WDGAP to CGs, Serv Comds, 3 Jun 43, sub: Selection of Qualified Applicants for Flying Tng as Avn Cadets (Air Crew) at Recp Cens. 327.3/548.

eighteen had had in reducing the number of aviation cadets whom the Air Forces could attract as volunteers from civilian life through the Air Corps Enlisted Reserve. The other was the transfer to the Air Forces, as aviation cadets, of enlisted men already assigned and trained in Ground Forces organizations.

The latter drain and its disruptive effect on ground units had long been a subject of serious grievance to the Army Ground Forces. Under War Department policies in force any qualified enlisted man had been allowed to apply either for flying training or for officer candidate school.[36] Army Ground Forces conceded that fliers had to be of high caliber. It objected to the system of voluntary transfer only when it was used to obtain men for ground positions in the Air Forces. In short, it did not concede that Air Forces ground personnel had to be generally of higher mental and physical caliber than enlisted men in combat ground units. Yet such was the outcome of assigning to ground positions in the Air Forces men from ground units who, initially accepted as aviation cadets, had failed to be commissioned as pilots. As early as April 1942 the Chief of Staff of the Ground Forces, Maj. Gen. Mark W. Clark, recommended that aviation cadets recruited from AGF personnel be subjected to more careful examination so that those not ultimately used by the Air Forces as fliers might remain with the Ground Forces.[37] As late as December 1943 the AGF Chief of Staff, Brig. Gen. James G. Christiansen, observed to the War Department that of 1,800 aviation cadets obtained from the 44th Division in the preceding summer not one had returned to the Ground Forces, despite the certainty that not all had qualified for flying positions.[38] If it was necessary to select aviation cadets on liberal grounds, and then to reject large numbers as fliers, the Army Ground Forces desired that rejects originating with the ground arms be returned.[39]

Thus, one of the objects sought by the War Department through the new procedure for recruiting aviation cadets adopted on 3 June 1943 was to relieve this pressure on ground units by liberalizing the recruitment of air cadets at reception centers. Flight surgeons stationed at reception centers, after determin-

[36] (1) AR 615–160, 5 Nov 42. (2) WD Memo W615–55–43, 26 Jun 43, sub: Procedure on Applications from EM for Avn Cadet (Air Crew) Tng. 221/55 (Avn Cadets).

[37] AGF memo for G–1 WD, 30 Apr 42, sub: Procedure for Application and Enlmt of Avn Cadets. 221/22 (Flying Cadets).

[38] Tab B (S), sub: Summary of Conf on Medical Standards and Personnel, WD Gen Council Min (S), 13 Dec 43.

[39] (1) AGF memo for G–1 WD, 5 Aug 43, sub: Disposition of Non-Graduates of OCS and Avn Cadet Tng. 352/462 (OCS). (2) WD ltr AG 352 (5 Aug 43) OC–E–WDGAP to CG AGF, 16 Nov 43, sub as in (1). With atchd comment by G–1 AGF. 352/479 (OCS).

ing which inductees on a given day possessed qualifications for becoming aviation cadets, asked them if they desired to apply for flying training. To those who replied in the affirmative the flight surgeons gave a simple color-blindness test, adding nothing else to the physical examination as reported from the induction stations. Volunteers were also told that if they failed ultimately to be accepted as fliers they would remain in the Air Forces in ground positions.[40] Under this system, which became effective on 1 August 1943, the percentage of high-grade men received by the Air Forces from reception centers was greatly increased. In the last half of 1943 nearly 50 percent of the inductees shipped to the Air Forces fell in AGCT Classes I and II (with scores over 110), while only 30 percent of the inductees shipped to the ground arms fell in these categories.

The Ground Forces obtained certain concessions in the aviation cadet system. Recruiting at reception centers continued until March 1944, but in August 1943 the War Department made clear that, while enlisted men were free to apply, direct individual proselyting was forbidden.[41] In November 1943, facing a replacement crisis in infantry, the War Department ordered that aviation cadets should not be accepted from trainees in replacement training centers of either the Army Ground Forces or the Army Service Forces.[42] Finally, in March 1944, the need for aviation cadets having abated, the War Department ordered that no cadets should henceforth be taken from AGF or ASF units.[43] In the same month, also, as the infantry crisis grew more acute, the War Department reversed its priorities to the extent of transferring some 30,000 aviation cadets to the Army Ground Forces, mainly for use in the Infantry.

The Army Specialized Training Program and the Army Ground Forces

The critical shortage of infantrymen in the winter of 1943–44 was largely responsible for the virtual liquidation in February 1944 of the Army Specialized Training Program (ASTP), which had been initiated at the close of 1942 on broad grounds of public interest and policy. The ASTP had been approved by the Secretary of War in September 1942, in anticipation of the lowering of the draft age from twenty to eighteen. The program was established primarily to ensure a

[40] AGF M/S, C&RD to AG, 10 Nov 43, sub: Recp Cen Procedures in Asgmt of Pers to AAF. 327.3/548.

[41] (1) Papers in 221/57 (Flying Cadets). (2) AGF Wkly Dir, 10 Aug 43.

[42] WD memo WDGCT 320 RTC for CGs AGF, ASF, 15 Nov 43, sub: RTCs. 341/1173.

[43] Cir 93, WD, 3 Mar 44.

continuous flow of technically and professionally trained men for the prosecution of the war, men who could not be procured without deferments if the draft age should be lowered to eighteen. Continuous replenishment of the national stock of young men with such training was an urgent necessity, especially if the war should last more than four or five years.[44] There were strong arguments for training them in the colleges and universities. The training and educational facilities of the Army were believed to be insufficient in extent and character to give the type of education required. Moreover, the use of the colleges and universities would protect these institutions from impoverishment or collapse, and the provision of students by the Army might be expected to lower the resistance of civilian educators to the reduction of the draft age to eighteen. To avoid the shortcomings of the Student Army Training Corps of World War I, the plan for the ASTP was to be tied firmly to the military program of the Army. Selected enlisted men were to be assigned to various colleges and universities for academic instruction, but only after they had received basic military training, which was to be continued under a cadet organization while they were in college. Under the plan proposed, the Army would be assured of receiving from each oncoming age group a due proportion of men with advanced training, shaped with reference to ultimate military requirements. At first it was contemplated that most of these men would become officers after completing their college work.

On 30 September 1942 Army Ground Forces was requested to submit, within five days, its plan for application of the program to the Ground Forces. Given the effect of current policies on the quality of men being assigned to the Army Ground Forces in 1942, such a program was bound to present itself to that command as another means by which men of the higher intelligence levels would be withheld or withdrawn from combat positions. With four or five divisions being activated each month, and preferential assignment to the Air Forces in full effect, this was the period of worst personnel shortage in the history of the Ground Forces and of great strain in the procurement of officer candidates. "With 300,000 men short," exclaimed the AGF G–3, "we are asked to send men to college!" [45]

General McNair, taking a grave view of the Nation's requirements for effective strength in combat, based his opposition to the ASTP on strictly military

[44] (1) Joint Statement of Secretaries of War and Navy Depts, 17 Dec 42. (2) WD memo WDGAP 353 for CG SOS, 25 Sep 42, sub: The Army College Tng Programs Necessary to Provide Required College-Trained Men for Future Needs. 353/119 (S).

[45] AGF M/S (S), G–3 to G–1, 30 Sep 42, sub as in n. 44 (2). 353/119 (S).

considerations. Confronted with the ASTP proposal of 30 September 1942, he observed that a college program would further deplete units in training of high-grade men and would compete with the program of officer candidate schools, whose quotas the Ground Forces were already having difficulty in filling. He recommended that the college program not be launched until it was clear that the war would last beyond 1944.[46] For the time being the Army, in his opinion, had a sufficient backlog of college-trained men. Fourteen percent of the men who had entered the Army in 1942 had had some degree of college education, and General McNair believed that, in view of the general policy of providing liberal opportunities for promotion and of tapping all available manpower, not more than a quarter of the officer corps need be college graduates. Fearing that the military discipline and the few hours of military training received by ASTP men in colleges might be considered the equivalent of regular Army training, he advised against the introduction of this phase of the program. "If it is necessary to keep men in college to provide Army officers, then their whole effort might well be placed on academic studies, because, presumably, that is the reason for their going to college." [47]

The decision to institute the program had already been made when General McNair submitted these observations on 4 October 1942. With them he submitted a plan as requested. The plan took the form of estimates, necessarily hurried, of the number of graduates of the proposed program which Army Ground Forces could use. The organizers of the program construed these estimates as a statement that the Ground Forces "required" these graduates.[48] Army Ground Forces immediately disclaimed this interpretation. It was reiterated that, in the arms for which the Army Ground Forces was responsible, the supply of college men would last through 1944 and the facilities of the normal officer candidate schools were sufficient for officer training.[49]

The Army Specialized Training Program was formally established in December 1942. It differed from some of the preliminary proposals in placing attention not so much on the production of officers as on the production of specialists who might or might not ultimately be commissioned. The specialties were

[46] AGF memo (S) for CG SOS, 4 Oct 42, sub: The Army College Tng Prog. 353/119 (S)

[47] AGF M/S (S), DCofS to G-1, 6 Sep 42, sub as in n. 44 (2). 353/119 (S).

[48] Memo (S) of Col Herman Beukema for CG AGF, 4 Dec 42, sub: 1943 Reqmts of Offs Educated at College Level under ASTP. 353/119 (S).

[49] AGF memo (S) for CG SOS (attn Col Beukema), 11 Dec 42, sub as in n. 48. 353/119 (S).

chiefly scientific, engineering, medical, and linguistic. The maximum number of men to be in the program at any given time was set at 150,000. Enlisted men under twenty-two years of age, and having an AGCT score of 110 or more, were eligible. For advanced study men over twenty-two might be sent. "The mission of the Army Specialized Training Program," it was announced in February 1943, "is to prepare personnel for officer candidate schools and for other military tasks." [50]

On 25 January 1943 General McNair asked for reconsideration.[51] The Army Ground Forces feared that all Class I and most Class II men of the 18–22 age bracket would be taken from the ground combat arms, trained as specialists and technicians, and hence on leaving college be assigned to other forces for the duration of the war. The result would be to aggravate for Army Ground Forces the unfavorable consequences of the vocational emphasis in the classification system and of preference given the Air Forces in the distribution of intelligent personnel. General McNair asked that the Ground Forces be assured at least of receiving back from the ASTP the same number of Classes I and II men as might be transferred from the Ground Forces into the program—a request which, though urged upon the War Department, was not met. The answer given to the request for reconsideration was that the fears of Army Ground Forces arose from an erroneous and narrow conception of the program. The program, according to G–1 of the War Department, was designed to benefit the Army as a whole. It would not jeopardize the procurement of officer candidates; graduates would be assigned to the several arms and services in accordance with branch requirements for "specialized training."[52]

So critical did its own needs appear that Army Ground Forces thought it necessary to take measures by which it could receive back, or "require," ASTP graduates within the terms laid down by the War Department. Army Ground Forces was consistently disposed to value leadership above specialization. But with the ASTP in operation, many of the best potential leaders in the younger

[50] (1) WD Memo W350–144–42, 23 Dec 42, sub: Army and Navy Plans for the Use of College Facilities. 353/1 (ASTP). (2) WD Memo W350–36–43, 19 Feb 43, sub: ASTP: General Information and Procedures for Selection of Pers. 353/21 (ASTP). (3) WD Memo W350–47–43, 1 Mar 43, sub: ASTP Orgn and Opn. 353/20 (ASTP).

[51] Memo of Gen McNair for CofS USA, 25 Jan 43, sub: ASTP. 353/10 (ASTP).

[52] (1) WD memo WDGAP 353 for CG AGF, 2 Feb 43, sub: ASTP. 353/10 (ASTP). (2) Memo of Gen McNair for G–1 WD, 12 Feb 43, sub and location as in (1). (3) WD memo WDGAP 353 (2–15–43), 2 Mar 43, sub and location as in (1). (4) AGF memo for G–1 WD, 30 Jun 43, sub: Disposition of ASTP Trainees at End of Term. 353/60 (ASTP). (5) WD memo WDGAP 353 (1 Jul 43) for CG AGF, 16 Jul 43, sub and location as in (4).

age group would be obtainable only in the guise of specialists. To fill its need for intelligent personnel, Army Ground Forces had to express a need for men with specialized training.

One device was to make sure that the ASTP included courses of study useful to the ground arms.[53] If the colleges taught such subjects, Army Ground Forces could claim students on the basis of their specialized training. AGF staff officers, in conference with the Army Specialized Training Division and with civilian educators, arranged for courses to be given in basic engineering, surveying, internal combustion engines, communications, and acoustics and optics. Training in most of these subjects could be of value to any ground arm; the course in acoustics and optics was designed for artillerymen.

Numerical requirements of the Ground Forces for graduates of the ASTP were submitted on 27 March 1943.[54] Elaborate computations were made; though in the end they were not used, they illustrated the way in which the Army Ground Forces believed the program could be employed. The stated need for 1944 was 52,404 men, distributed among types of specialized training as follows:

ASTP Program	*Engineering*	*Scientific & Mathematical*	*Languages*	*Field Immaterial*	*Total AGF Requirements*	*Percent of Total AGF Requirements*
Advanced (4 yrs. college)	9,263		2,311	4,529	16,103	31
Basic (2 yrs. college)		26,181	5,419	4,701	36,301	69
TOTAL	9,263	26,181	7,730	9,230	52,404	100

These men were to be assigned, in proportions computed by the Army Ground Forces, to the various ground combat arms. Graduates of the Advanced ASTP (except engineers) were too specialized for exact assignment in the combat arms, and were less desired by the Army Ground Forces than were Basics (2-year college men). Later, in 1943, the Ground Forces called for 80 percent of Basics, hoping to obtain high-intelligence personnel for duty with troops as quickly as possible.[55]

[53] (1) AGF M/S, G–1 Enl Div to G–1, 13 Apr 43, sub: ASTP. 353/35 (ASTP). (2) AGF M/S, CofS to G–1, 20 Jul 43, sub: Disposition of ASTP Trainees at End of Term. 353/60 (ASTP). (3) ASTD memo SPASC/350 Engr (9 Sep 43) to CG AGF, 9 Sep 43, sub: Formal Concurrence on ASTP Curricula. 353/109 (ASTP).

[54] Memo (R) of Gen McNair for G–1 WD, 27 Mar 43, sub: Opn of ASTP. 353/1 (ASTP) (R).

[55] AGF M/S, G–1 to G–3, 12 Nov 43, sub: Revised Demand Schedule for ASTP. 220.3/5 (ASTP).

Of these 52,404 ASTP graduates the Army Ground Forces proposed, in March 1943, that all the 16,103 4-year college men and 13,421 of the 2-year college men be allowed to attend officer candidate schools. The figures were based on the concept that 25 percent of officers should be college graduates, 25 percent should have two years of college, and 50 percent should be commissioned on grounds of performance in the field irrespective of education. The reduction of the Troop Basis in June 1943, reducing the anticipated requirements for officers, made it impossible to consider commissioning so many ASTP graduates, long before the ASTP itself came to a virtual end.

The ASTP went into full operation on the campuses in the spring of 1943. The first college units were recruited, not from new inductees, but from men already in training. During 1943 about 100,000 students for the program were taken from the three major forces, and about 50,000 from new inductees.

Selection of the new inductees was by complex and constantly fluctuating procedures.[56] At first the required AGCT score was 110—the same as for officer candidates. It was soon raised to 115. At first it was intended to rely on voluntary applications of the kind used in recruiting officer candidates and aviation cadets. This not proving feasible, all eligible enlisted men were automatically passed through a testing and screening process (frequently altered), after which commanders designated those to be sent to college. Those eligible consisted of all enlisted men (with various exceptions, such as men in alerted units), who had completed basic training or part of it, who if under twenty-two had had a high-school education or its equivalent, and who if over twenty-two had had at least one year of college (with certain other conditions), and who in any case had an AGCT score of 115. Unit commanders, suffering constant drains to other activities, showed a want of alacrity in designating men for ASTP. Gen. George C. Marshall issued a memorandum explaining the ASTP and insisting on its support. Headquarters, Army Ground Forces, circulated this memorandum to the field for compliance.[57]

The Army Ground Forces supplied about 47 percent of the ASTP trainees drawn from the three major commands in May–July 1943. Even superficially

[56] (1) WD Memo W350–36–43, 19 Feb 43, sub: ASTP Gen Information and Procedures for Selection of Pers. 353/21 (ASTP). (2) AGF memo for G–1 WD, 16 Mar 43, sub: Opn of ASTP. 353/10 (ASTP). (3) WD Memo W350–198–43, 17 Jul 43, sub: Gen Qualifications for ASTP. 353/81 (ASTP). (4) WD Memo W350–197–43, 17 Jul 43, sub: Revised Procedures Governing the Selection and Asgmt of EM to ASTP. 353/88 (ASTP).

[57] (1) Memo of Gen Marshall for CG AGF, 1 Apr 43, sub: ASTP. (2) AGF ltr to CGs, 3 Apr 43, sub: ASTP. Both in 353/31 (ASTP).

230-171 O - 66 - 4

considered this was somewhat more than an even share, since the Ground Forces at their maximum comprised only 42 percent of the troops in the United States. In reality it was substantially more than an even share, since men with the required AGCT score of 115 were proportionately less numerous in the Ground Forces than in the Air or Service Forces.

Although the operation of preferential assignment policies had concentrated a large number of ASTP eligibles in the Army Air Forces, the latter supplied proportionately fewer men to the ASTP than did either the Ground or Service Forces during this initial period. (See Table No. 4.)

That men already trained and performing their jobs should be removed from troop units for a "specialized training" of rather distant military value was unavoidable under a principle that all enlisted men of a certain age and degree of

TABLE NO. 4

Provision of Students to the Army Specialized Training Program, First Three Training Cycles, May–July 1943

Item	Army Ground Forces		Army Air Forces		Army Service Forces		Total	
	Number	Percent	Number	Percent	Number	Percent	Number	Per-cent
Training Cycles:								
10 May 1943	3,096	57	218	4	2,151	39	5,465	100
14 June 1943	5,079	44	1,545	14	4,744	42	11,368	100
12 July 1943	12,626	47	6,341	23	8,183	30	27,150	100
In STARS[a]......	8,577	45	5,107	27	5,240	28	18,924	100
Total......	29,378	47	13,211	21	20,318	32	62,907	100
Total Enlisted Strength in United States, 31 July 1943...	1,925,773	42	1,506,746	33	1,179,788	25	4,612,307	100

Source: Memo for Director, ASTP, 21 Jul 43, sub: Number of Men in ASTP Institutions Supplied by Each of the Three Forces. Copy in AG Records, Hq AGF, 353/91 (ASTP).

[a] STARS (Specialized Training and Reassignment Units) were units intermediate between troop units and the ASTP units in the colleges, set up for the processing and storage of ASTP candidates.

intelligence had a right to be considered for college. But the result of these removals was deplored as wasteful by officers of the Ground Forces. Although the number of men removed from units was relatively not large, those removed tended to be men who occupied key positions; the loss was especially heavy in key units. Units with enlisted men of high intelligence, such as headquarters companies, engineer topographical companies, and radio intelligence signal companies, suffered most. One company of the latter type had 81 out of 250 men selected for the ASTP. On the other hand, units with few men of the required intelligence could least afford to lose even one. The Army Ground Forces finally obtained a limitation on the number of men who might be selected from a given unit.[58]

After July 1943, ASTP trainees came in increasing numbers from eligible men newly inducted into the Army. These were of three kinds: (1) inductees with an AGCT score of 115 or over; (2) enlisted reservists, or certain college students inducted into the Army but kept temporarily in a civilian status; and (3) A–12's, or certain high-school students who by preinduction tests had established their eligibility for the ASTP.[59]

Members of the first group were assigned on induction, as were inductees generally, to replacement training centers and to troop units, on the principle that they would later have the opportunity to go to college through the screening process to which the whole Army was subject. Their subsequent selection for ASTP meant that replacement centers trained men who did not become replacements and that units trained men whom they could not keep. Since every inductee with an AGCT of 115 might go to college sooner or later, it was wasteful to train them except in segregated groups. Army Ground Forces proposed on 20 August 1943 that all men eligible for ASTP should be screened at reception centers and given basic training in special battalions, and that all ASTP quotas in the future should be filled from such special battalions only. The Army Specialized Training Division agreed, with amendments to assure that eligible individuals still in troop units should not lose the right to receive specialized training. In the autumn of 1943 progress was made toward concentrating the selection of ASTP candidates in reception centers. The flow of such candidates into units was thereby checked and the integrity of tactical units and replace-

[58] AGF memo for G–1 WD, 6 Aug 43, sub: Restriction of AST Selection from AGF Units. 353/89 (ASTP).

[59] AGF M/S, G–1 to G–3 and CofS, 26 Jul 43, sub: Disposition of ASTP Eligibles upon Induction. 353/96 (ASTP).

ment training centers better preserved. The deliberate withholding of high-intelligence inductees from normal units was a price, however, which Army Ground Forces would have preferred not to pay.[60]

Members of the second and third groups, enlisted reservists and A–12's, were already earmarked for the ASTP when they entered upon active duty. They had to have basic training before proceeding to ASTP units in the colleges. The War Department ordered that their basic training be given by Army Ground Forces. Army Ground Forces drew up a modified Infantry Mobilization Training Program and arranged to segregate the candidates in special branch immaterial training battalions. In this way the waste of training them in regular units would be avoided. The War Department estimated that the enlisted reservists and A–12's earmarked for the ASTP would number 50,000, of whom 25,000 would begin basic training in June and 25,000 in July 1943. The Army Ground Forces provided facilities for 20,000 at Fort Benning and Camp Hood, available at this time because of the reduction in officer candidate quotas. Facilities for the remaining 30,000 were created at replacement training centers by stopping the production of 30,000 normal replacements.[61]

The 50,000 expected trainees were slow in appearing. Only 17,152 had been received by 15 August. Beds, equipment, training aids, enlisted cadres, and officer instructors for 32,848 men stood ready but idle. Of the total shortage of 32,848, the shortage of ASTP trainees expected in replacement training centers was 21,799. Twenty-three battalions of replacements could have been in training with the facilities reserved for the ASTP.[62]

With the invasion of Sicily in July 1943 a heavy demand for replacements set in. With Selective Service falling behind in the delivery of its quotas and with RTC quotas incorrectly adjusted to the actual rate of ground casualties, the replacement training centers could not meet the demand. Since the War Department now estimated that the remainder of the 50,000 ASTP trainees would become available in decreasing increments through January 1944, Army Ground Forces concentrated all ASTP basic training at Fort Benning and Camp Hood (later at Fort Benning only), in order to liberate the ASTP facilities at replacement training centers for ordinary replacement training.[63] But time had been

[60] See papers in 353/96 (ASTP).

[61] AGF ltr to R&SC, 19 May 43, sub: ASTP. 353/40 (ASTP).

[62] R&SC ltr to AGF, 17 Aug 43, sub: Non-Receipt of ASTP Candidates. 353/97 (ASTP).

[63] AGF ltr to R&SC, 27 Aug 43, sub: ASTP. 353/40 (ASTP).

lost in the face of a replacement crisis that rapidly grew acute. The Army Ground Forces was obliged to take replacements from divisions and other units in training to meet the heavy current demand. Shortages reappeared, training was interrupted, and readiness of units for combat was delayed. The number of infantrymen taken from divisions for replacement purposes, about 26,000 by January 1944, was comparable to the number of replacements who might have begun training in the summer of 1943 if replacement training facilities had not been reserved for ASTP trainees who failed to appear. The ASTP thus happened to contribute to the quantitative crisis which prevailed in the Infantry at the end of 1943. This crisis was soon to overwhelm the ASTP.

Men began to return from the ASTP to troop units, after a term on the campus, in the late summer of 1943. Frequently they could not be so assigned as to use their specialized training. Nor could they be allowed to qualify for commissions; with the reduction of the mobilization program in June the need for additional officers in the ground arms almost disappeared, and the scanty quotas of AGF officer candidate schools were filled with college men of another type, the ROTC students whom the Army was legally obliged to allow to try for commissions.

Thus, toward the end of 1943 the Army Specialized Training Division faced the critical problems of the morale of its trainees and of its usefulness to the Army. It proposed in October 1943 that new military occupational specialties be authorized by the War Department, that corresponding SSN's be listed in unit Tables of Organization, that the arms and services requisition men by these numbers, and that ASTP graduates be assigned to fill these requisitions with ratings as enlisted technicians in grades to be determined by the War Department.[64] This was an effort to create jobs worthy of the effort expended by men in college. It was an attempt to fit demand to production. The consuming agencies, such as Army Ground Forces, were to use men designated as specialists, not because they sensed a need, but because such men were becoming available.

Army Ground Forces nonconcurred in the proposal. Reasons given were that it would force commanders to ignore need, experience, and demonstrated leadership in making assignments; and that ASTP graduates, irrespective of their educational advantages, should demonstrate their ability in the unit to which they were assigned before receiving a promotion.[65] In January 1944 Headquarters,

[64] Draft memo of ASTD for G–1 WD, undated, sub: Asgmt of ASTP Graduates. 353/118 (ASTP).

[65] AGF memo for ASTD, 5 Oct 43, sub as in n. 64. 353/118 (ASTP).

Army Ground Forces, went as far as it thought possible to meet the proposal by issuing an assignment guide to the field, listing the SSN's in which men with "specialized training" might suitably serve, and urging special care in the assignment of graduates of the advanced phase of the program. But the guide was not made mandatory, commanders were left free to use their own judgment, and it was insisted that the development of leaders, not the placement of specialists, must be the chief aim in employing men sent to college by the Army.[66]

The Army Specialized Training Program, operating on a scale of 150,000 trainees, became especially vulnerable when personnel shortages threatened to impede military operations in late 1943. The ASTP served no need recognized as immediate by most elements in the Army. Once the need for more and better combat troops became critical it was one of the easiest items in the Troop Basis to sacrifice. On 5 November 1943 G-3 of the War Department proposed a reduction of the ASTP to 30,000 trainees, largely in medical and related subjects; four-fifths of the men in the ASTP would return to active service.[67] Army Ground Forces dispatched its concurrence to the War Department on the same day.[68] The Troop Basis published on 15 January 1944, reflecting a compromise between various points of view, called for a gradual reduction of the ASTP to 62,190 by the end of 1944.

A month later this figure was more than halved. Both the replacement crisis and the alarm regarding the condition to which the ground arms, particularly the Infantry, had declined influenced the outcome. The efficiency of divisions in training was being gravely impaired by the wholesale transfer of their infantry privates to the replacement stream. Many of these same divisions were scheduled for early movement to take part in the impending invasion of western Europe. Men who had already received basic training were needed to refill their ranks. Meanwhile the War Department had come to the conclusion that the quality of enlisted personnel in the Infantry must be raised. General Marshall on 10 February 1944 informed the Secretary of War that 134,000 men already basically trained were required for the coming operation in France and that "the outstanding deficiency currently noted in our divisions is the number of noncommissioned officers who are below satisfactory standards of intelligence and qualities of

[66] (1) Cir 255, WD, 16 Oct 43. (2) AGF ltr to CGs, 27 Jan 44, sub: Asgmt Guide for ASTP Graduates. 220.3/101 (ASTP).

[67] WD G-3 memo (C) for AGF, 5 Nov 43, sub: ASTP. 353/2 (ASTP) (C).

[68] AGF memo (C) for G-3 WD, 5 Nov 43, sub: ASTP. 353/2 (ASTP) (C).

leadership." He recommended withdrawing all but 30,000 trainees from the Army Specialized Training Program. The alternatives which he presented were to cut the ASTP or to disband 10 divisions, 3 tank battalions, and 26 antiaircraft battalions.[69]

The ASTP was immediately cut.[70] A large number of its trainees, almost overnight, became infantry privates. They could not be used immediately to meet the need for more intelligent noncommissioned officers because of their lack of military training and experience, and because most units, with their privates withdrawn as overseas replacements, had at least a full complement, and sometimes a surplus, of noncommissioned officers. It was desired and expected that ASTP trainees would soon show their superiority over the older noncommissioned officers, win ratings, and become leaders of small units.

For its trainees, the Army Specialized Training Program was a series of disillusionments. Some, had they not been sent to college, would undoubtedly have gone to officer candidate schools, to the advantage both of themselves and of the Army Ground Forces, though it is true that recruiting for ASTP came at a time when OCS quotas were declining. Among civilian educators participating in the ASTP the abrupt termination of their efforts, though accepted as a military necessity, was difficult to understand. It seemed arbitrary, after repeated declarations by the War Department of the importance of specialized training, suddenly to snatch away the young men undergoing such training, a select group numbering only 2 percent of the Army, for conversion into infantry privates.[71]

The fact was that a crisis had been developing for two years in the ground arms. Quantitatively, the provision for combat troops in the Troop Basis, especially for infantrymen, left no margin of safety. Qualitatively, the ground combat arms had been persistently denied a proportionate share of high-intelligence personnel. The extension of ground combat in the last part of 1943 made the consequences fully apparent. They could not be ignored on the eve of the invasion of France. Conversion of manpower from the Air and Service Forces to the Ground Forces, though contemplated at this time, was difficult to effect. The sacrifice of the ASTP was one means, among others, of meeting the critical need for a speedy rehabilitation of the ground arms.

[69] Memo (S) of Gen Marshall for the SW, 10 Feb 44, sub: Serv Pers Shortages. 353/100 (ASTP) (S).

[70] WD D/F ACofS G-1 to CG ASF, 16 Feb 44, sub: Reduction of ASTP. WDGAP 353 (ASTP). The reduction to 30,000 was to be completed by 1 April 1944.

[71] See for example the article entitled "014" by Andrew J. Green in the *American Association of University Professors Bulletin,* XXX (1944), pp. 217–21.

Limited-Service Men in the Army Ground Forces

Classification of enlisted men on physical grounds (including psychiatric) was so broad during the whole period of expansion of the Army that it might almost be said that there was no classification at all. A small minority, for a time, were classified as fit only for "limited service." Much thought was expended on the types of jobs to which limited-service men might be assigned. Another minority, including aviation cadets and parachute infantry, had to meet exceptional physical standards. But the overwhelming majority of soldiers, known as "general-service" men, were considered to be interchangeable so far as physique was concerned; assignment of these men depended on occupational specialty or intelligence rating.

It was not until August 1942 that the Army began to induct limited-service men in significant numbers.[72] As a category in classification, limited service was abolished a year later. Limited-service men, designated as such, were never a serious problem to the Army Ground Forces, though there was an apprehension that they might become so. The War Department ordered in August 1942 that permanent installations of the Air Forces and Ground Forces employ limited-service personnel to the maximum. The permanent installations of the Ground Forces (school troops and replacement training personnel were subject to rotation and hence not permanent) included the headquarters of Army Ground Forces and its subordinate nontactical commands and centers. These absorbed 13,000 limited-service men by the middle of 1943.

In September 1942, when the Army Ground Forces were 330,000 men short, the War Department directed that field units of the Ground Forces absorb a certain percentage of limited-service men. This policy was soon reversed. From October 1942 to July 1943, field-force commanders were authorized to arrange the transfer of limited-service men from tactical units to the service commands. General-service men were transferred into the Ground Forces from both service commands and defense commands. On the whole, so long as the distinction between general and limited service was in effect, Ground Forces tactical units, of both combat and service types, were composed of general-service men.[73]

[72] (1) WD ltr AG 220.31 (7–6–42) EC to CG AGF, 11 Jul 42, sub: Asgmt of Ltd Serv Pers. 327.3/35 (LS). (2) Par 20, WD Classification Memo 11, 1 Aug 42. (3) AGF ltr (S) to CGs, 30 Jul 42, sub: Ltd Serv Pers. 319.1/5 (RTC) (S). (4) AGF M/S(S), DCofS to G–1, 16 Aug 42. 327.3 (LS)(S).

[73] (1) Memo of Col Tate for DCofS AGF, 7 Sep 42, sub: Rpt on Meeting Held under Supervision of G–3 WD on Pers Matters. 327.3/42 (LS). (2) AGF memo for G–3 WD, 18 Sep 42, sub: Ltd Serv Pers for AGF Units. 327.3/42 (LS). (3) Cir 327, WD, 27 Sep 42. (4) WD Gen Council Min (S), 9 Oct 42. (5)

The main concern of Army Ground Forces was to assure the maintenance of this policy. As induction of limited-service men continued, plans were made to spread them as widely as possible. In February 1943 the War Department, on the basis of a study prepared by The Adjutant General, proposed to the Army Ground Forces that, in the distribution of limited-service men to be inducted in the future, 65 percent be assigned to the Service Forces, 20 percent to the Air Forces, and 15 percent to the Ground Forces.[74] The Adjutant General based the figures of 65 percent for the Service Forces and of 15 percent for the Ground Forces on detailed investigation of the physical requirements of individual enlisted men's jobs, using for AGF jobs a study made by the AGF headquarters staff.[75] No similar study of individual jobs in the Air Forces was made or used by The Adjutant General. The figure of 20 percent for the Air Forces was a flat percentage believed to be acceptable.

It was thought at AGF headquarters that 15 percent would be a fair proportion if it were really necessary to assign limited-service men to the Ground Forces. No such necessity was seen. All troops in the Army Ground Forces, including AGF service units, were intended (with insignificant exceptions) for employment in the combat zone. An unknown portion of the Army Air Forces (later established as about one-third) was intended to remain permanently in the United States. Most Air Forces personnel overseas would remain at some distance from the enemy. It therefore seemed unreasonable that the Air and Ground Forces should receive nearly the same proportion (20 and 15 percent respectively) of incoming limited-service men.

General McNair took the position that the physical hardihood of a soldier should be greater in direct ratio to his proximity to combat. Proximity to combat depended, not on type of job, but on type of unit. A cook or clerk, if in an infantry unit, was likely to have to fight and would certainly experience irregular conditions of living. On this point General McNair wrote to the War Department on 3 March 1943:[76]

To illustrate the foregoing. A cook in an infantry rifle company should not have poor eyes, flat feet or bad hearing, because he must be able to fire his weapons, be on his feet for

---

Papers in 327.3/67 and /73 (LS). (6) AGF ltr to CGs, 20 May 43, sub: Clearing Fld Force Units of Ltd Serv Pers. 327.3/188 (LS). (7) AGF M/S, G-3 to CofS, 31 Jul 43, sub: Disposition of Ltd Serv Pers in Grd Force Units. 327.3/193 (LS).

[74] WD memo (S) WDGAP 320.22 for CG AGF, 8 Feb 43, sub: Almt of Ltd Serv EM from Recp Cens. 327.3/8 (LS) (S).

[75] For the AGF study see 327.3/10 (LS) (C).

[76] AGF memo (S) for G-1 WD, 3 Mar 43, sub: Almt of Ltd Serv Men from Recp Cens. 327.3/8 (LS)(S).

long hours, and hear and understand whispered directions in the presence of the enemy. These requirements are not essential in a rear area installation. Perhaps a better illustration might be the comparison drawn between the *physical* demands made upon an automotive mechanic in an armored unit and one at an Air Corps field 100 or more miles in rear of the front lines.

It is desired to point out that Air Force combat units are peculiar in the respect that generally only a certain proportion of a combat unit can be considered as actually engaging in close combat. Dependent upon conditions, ground crews and administrative personnel of front line combat air units may be from 100 to 1,000 miles from the enemy. Such personnel can be more or less assured of regular meal hours, living conditions and medical attention.

It is further desired to point out that the Army Air Forces has, in effect, its own services of supply housekeeping installations of a permanent nature in the United States that can possibly absorb a large part, if not all, of the proposed 20% allotted to the Air Force. The Army Ground Forces cannot so place its 15% of limited service personnel.

General McNair recommended that the War Department make an impartial survey of the three major commands to determine, by study of the missions of units, the number of men in each command who would probably engage in close combat or be drawn into the area of close combat, and that distribution of general-service and limited-service men follow the findings of this survey.

No such survey was made. On the other hand, no limited-service men were, in principle, assigned to tactical units of the Ground Forces. Nor were they assigned except in restricted numbers to the permanent domestic establishments of the Air Forces. The solution adopted by the War Department was to cut down the intake of limited-service men in the spring of 1943.[77] The reduction of the Troop Basis on 1 July 1943, reducing the demands upon Selective Service, made it less necessary for the Army to accept physically inferior personnel. AGF officers had previously expressed the opinion that curtailment of the Troop Basis would be preferable to placing limited-service men, even those with noncombat jobs, in combat units.[78]

Effective 1 August 1943 the War Department introduced a new system of physical classification, outlined in Circular 161 and in successive circulars and directives. Limited service as a category in the classification of enlisted men was abolished. In practice each of the three major commands was to find a place for its physically inferior personnel. Reasons given for the change included the

[77] WD Manpower Bd, Information Bul 8, 24 Apr 43, sub: WD Manpower Policies. 320.2/6013.

[78] See memo (S) of Lt Col J. H. Featherston for G-1 AGF, 19 Nov 42, sub: WD Conf 18 Nov, Ref Use of Ltd Serv Pers by AGF Units, Tab E of the study in 327.3/10 (LS) (S); and item 3 in M/S, G-3 to G-1, 11 Nov 42, same file.

belief that to be labeled "limited service" lowered the morale of men so classified, that some men so classified should be dropped from the Army, and that others should be used for more arduous duties than were permissible as long as they were classified as limited service. Men who could not be utilized by the Army because of physical or mental defects were to be discharged. For the remainder it was desired that commanders, instead of using a simple distinction between general and limited service, make the physical condition of enlisted men a matter of more exact and continuing appraisal and utilize the maximum capabilities of their personnel according to "physical qualifications, prior training, skills, intelligence and aptitude." Among so many criteria, physical condition continued to be in practice a secondary consideration in assignment. In practice three kinds of physical condition were recognized. Men below physical standards of induction, who therefore might be subject to discharge on physical grounds, could be retained in the Army at the desire of their commanders if their skill and training made them useful to the service in jobs which they were physically capable of performing. Men above minimum standards for induction still fell into two classes resembling general and limited service. The War Department declared that it would "continue to accept, in controlled numbers, enlisted men who do not meet current physical standards for general military service." These were the old limited-service men under a new name, or rather under no name, a fact which made their administrative processing more difficult and probably less accurate. Such men were not to be assigned upon induction to divisions, combat support units, or replacement training centers of the Army Ground Forces. They might be assigned upon induction to service units in the Ground Forces, to the Service Forces, and to the Air Forces in numbers up to 20 percent of future quotas for the Air Forces and arms and services with the Air Forces. Transfer of limited-service men among the three major commands, without concurrence of the receiving command, was stopped. This meant that the Army Ground Forces could no longer automatically ship men of low physical quality to the service commands. What General McNair had long resisted now took place: the Army Ground Forces would have no limited-service men, because there was no limited service, but it would have to find jobs for men of low physical quality, unless their physical quality was low enough to justify discharge from the Army.[79]

[79] For preceding two paragraphs see Cir 161, WD, 14 Jul 43, and WD ltr AG 220.01 (5 Aug 43) OC-E-WDGAP-M for CGs, 13 Aug 43, sub: Elimination of term "Ltd Serv" with Reference to EM. 327.3/193 (LS).

Physically inferior men accumulated in the Ground Forces in various ways. Some men deteriorated physically while in training. Some of those who were received from overseas, defense commands, and other sources would formerly have been designated as "limited service." Although men "not meeting current physical standards for general military service" were not supposed to be assigned initially to combat units and replacement centers of the Ground Forces, a considerable number were in fact so assigned in the months following Circular 161.[80] The matter was complicated by divergence of professional judgment among medical officers in assessing a soldier's physical qualities, and by divergence of judgment among commanders in determining how a soldier, with a given physical condition as announced by the medical officers, should be assigned. Men regarded at reception centers as fit for general service might not be so regarded at replacement centers, in divisions, or at replacement depots. There were successive points along the line at which the medical decision or the command decision might change. In general, the nearer a soldier came to combat, as in replacement depots or when units were alerted, the more exacting the interpretation of physical standards became. Hence there was a constant tendency to reclassify as unfit for general duty men previously considered acceptable.

Unless of such poor quality as to warrant discharge, or unless they were over thirty, in which case they could still be transferred to the Army Service Forces, all these physically inferior enlisted men—those not meeting the standards of general service—after 1 August 1943 had to be retained in the Army Ground Forces. The Ground Forces obliged, in the words of the AGF G–1, "to swallow their own limited service men," entered reluctantly upon a program of reassignment and retraining of individuals. At first the attempt was made to adhere to the policy laid down by General McNair on 3 March, that is, the policy that assignment on physical grounds should depend on type of unit, not on type of job. Field commanders of the Ground Forces were instructed on 21 August 1943 to transfer enlisted men formerly classifiable as limited service from combat units to overhead installations, higher headquarters, and service-type units of the Ground Forces, reassigning equal numbers of general-service men from these organizations to combat units.[81]

[80] AGF 2d ind to ASF, 5 Nov 43, on ltr of CG IRTC, Cp Roberts, to CG AGF, 21 Oct 43, sub: Discharges in IRTC. 327.3/208 (LS).

[81] (1) AGF ltr to CGs, 21 Aug 43, sub: Disposition of Ltd Serv Pers in Ground Force Units. 327.3/193 (LS). (2) AGF ltr to CGs, 15 Oct 43, sub: Proper Asgmt of EM below Gen Serv Standards. 327.3/205 (LS). (3) AGF 2d ind to Second Army, 28 Sep 43, on ltr cited in (1). 327.3/193.

Virtually all troops in the Army Ground Forces, including service units, were intended not only for overseas duty but also for duty in the combat zones. Before the issuance of Circular 161, limited-service men in principle were not to be sent overseas. Now all men were eligible for overseas duty unless specifically disqualified. Defects disqualifying men for overseas duty, as announced by the War Department in Circular 189, 21 August 1943, were stated to include hernia, perforated eardrum, missing teeth, and "neuro-psychiatric condition of any kind." The last was in practice, of course, an extremely elastic and uncertain category when applied to men nervously keyed up by training for combat. Commanders of AGF units and replacement centers found themselves accumulating men who could not proceed overseas, and whom therefore it was a waste for the Army Ground Forces to train.

The net result was a wave of wholesale discharges from the Army. Circular 161 granted liberal powers to discharge men who could not be utilized "because of mental or physical defects." Many commanders found it easier to invoke this power than to carry out a complex program of reassignment and retraining, or to retain men of whose future qualifications for overseas service they were not certain. In the last months of 1943, AGF replacement training centers, although supposedly receiving only trainees qualified for general service, reported 10 percent of their trainees as "died or discharged." Another 8 percent failed to qualify for overseas duty.[82] Under Circular 161, tactical units of the Ground Forces discharged about 55,000 men in the period August–November 1943. An average of 500 men was discharged per division.[83] This was a time of critical demand for manpower. Men were discharged who were of better physical quality than other men inducted at the same time.[84]

In November 1943 the War Department rescinded Circular 161 and replaced it with Circular 293: Enlisted Men—Utilization of Manpower Based on Physical Capacity. It remained the basic expression of policy on the subject, to be restated in Circular 164, 26 April 1944.

Circular 293 prohibited the discharge from the Army of men able to do any

[82] Tab F (S) "Losses at RTC's," AGF memo (S) for G–1 WD, 21 Dec 43, sub: Utilization of Available Manpower Based on Physical Capacity. 327.3/8 (S).

[83] Tables in "Bulky Package" 327.3/209 (LS), compiled in compliance with AGF ltr, 12 Jan 44, sub: Utilization of Available Manpower. 320.2/7002.

[84] (1) AGF memo (C) for G–1 WD, 21 Sep 43, sub: Allocation of Recp Cen Pers to AGF. 327.3/13 (C). (2) Tab B (S) "Summary of Conferences on Med Standards and Pers Placement," WD Gen Council Min (S), 13 Dec 43.

useful work. It reaffirmed the policy that each of the three major commands must absorb its own "physically handicapped enlisted men," and that commanders of all echelons should be continuously responsible for proper classification, assignment, and reassignment. It tightened the list of specific disqualifications for overseas service. For example, men with "mild psycho-neuroses, transient in character" (what lay officers of Army Ground Forces considered normal nervous apprehension) could now proceed overseas in a combat capacity, as could also men who, despite missing teeth, had been able to earn a living in civil life. Men going overseas as trained members of organized units were not held to as high a physical standard as those going over as individual replacements. In general, any enlisted man retained in the Army, if not suffering from specified defects disqualifying him for overseas service, could be used for any duty of which his unit commander, acting with medical advice, believed him physically capable.

Discharges from the Army fell off sharply after publication of Circular 293. The number of physically inferior men requiring assignment correspondingly increased. It became necessary for General McNair to retreat from his preferred policy as stated on 3 March 1943, and to countenance the assignment of physically inferior personnel to combat units. In each individual case the lowest possible commander was to find an appropriate assignment. In a directive to the field dated 7 December 1943, implementing War Department Circular No. 293 and personally rewritten by General McNair, AGF commanders were ordered to assign men falling below general-service standards in the following priority: (1) to appropriate positions (such as cooks or clerks) within combat units; (2) to service-type units in divisions; (3) to service-type units under armies, corps, and special commands; and (4) to permanent overhead installations of Army Ground Forces.[85]

Circular 293, while tending to swell the number of physically inferior men in the Ground Forces, nevertheless affirmed, more explicitly than previous War Department instructions on the subject, the importance of physical condition as a basis of assignment. Circular 161, abolishing limited service, had recognized that a mere twofold classification, with all general-service men regarded as physically alike, was not enough. Circular 293 announced that enlisted men should "be assigned to the most active type of duty appropriate to their physical qualifications." The implication was that general-service men were not interchangeable; the strongest should be used as infantry riflemen, medical-aid men,

[85] AGF ltr to CGs, 7 Dec 43, sub: Utilization of Manpower Based on Physical Capacity. 327.3/209 (LS).

etc., and those of less exceptional physique as artillery gunners, airplane mechanics, ordnance technicians, etc. The implication was weakened by the addition, in Circular 293, of a modifying clause after the word "qualifications": "with due consideration to their civilian training and experience, education, intelligence, aptitude, leadership ability and acquired military occupational specialties."

With this experience freshly in mind General McNair came to the conclusion, stated in a memorandum of 21 December 1943, that, with "due consideration" to civilian training, the best solution for the problem of allocating suitable personnel to the Ground Forces would be to make physical qualities the primary basis of assignment. From this position, set forth in a comprehensive summary of the problem of quality in the Ground Forces, he was ready to proceed in 1944 with the development of the Physical Profile system.

III. Efforts to Improve the Quality of Ground Combat Troops

During the second half of 1943, as mobilization reached its final stages, the signs that all was not well with the personnel situation in the ground arms became unmistakable. One sign was provided in a survey made available in August 1943 by the Special Services Division, Army Service Forces. Asked what branch of the Army they would prefer to be in, if free to choose, only 11 percent of enlisted men in the Infantry, in contrast to 76 percent of enlisted men in the Air Corps, named their own branch. All ground combat arms fell below all the services in popularity, and all the services fell below the Air Corps. (See Table No. 5.) Unpopularity of the ground arms was perhaps due largely to relative danger. More than 80 percent of the enlisted men becoming casualties in the North African Theater of Operations at this time were in the ground arms, not counting medical aid men and combat engineers. More than 70 percent were in the Infantry alone. Unpopularity may be ascribed in part to the low pay and the generally lower intelligence rating of combat soldiers. High pay and high average intelligence in a branch gave members the sense, valuable for morale, of being a selected group.

In addition, surveys by the Special Services Division indicated that the better educated a man was the more willing he was to serve as a soldier. This may only reflect the fact that the more desirable positions were filled by educated rather than by uneducated men; it does not prove that the educated were more willing than the uneducated to serve as front-line fighters. Finally, the popularity of branches varied more or less directly with the satisfaction of enlisted men with their individual job assignments. Infantrymen disliked their jobs far more than did men of other branches. Enlisted men of the technical services and of the Air Corps were more satisfied. This was probably for a variety of reasons: that their jobs did not generally involve killing, hand-to-hand combat, or maximum personal discomfort; that their jobs were in many cases counterparts of customary civilian occupations; and that their jobs offered, or were believed to offer, vocational training of potential value after the war.

Under the new policies on physically limited men announced in Circular 161, in effect after 1 August 1943, physically inferior (formerly limited-service)

TABLE NO. 5

Relative Popularity of Arms and Services Among Enlisted Men in 1943

Arm or Service	Percentage Preferring Own Branch	Percentage Satisfied with Individual Assignment	Class I and II Men as Percent of Total Assigned in 1943	Average Annual Base Pay	Percentage Distribution of Casualties in NATO[a]
	(1)	(2)	(3)	(4)	(5)
Air Corps	76	53	42	[b]$1,152	5.0
Signal Corps	46	44	58	780	0.6
Ordnance	42	44	36	825	0.3
Quartermaster	38	40	21	750	0.4
Military Police	36	33	39	700	0.2
Medical	35	41	31	707	2.7
Engineers	32	33	29	720	4.7
Field Artillery	27	41	31	730	9.4
Armored	26	33	31	760	[c]
Antiaircraft	26	34	29	730	1.8
Infantry	11	17	30	700	70.8

Source: Columns 1 and 2: "What the Soldier Thinks," August 1943, Special Services Division, Army Service Forces. (C)
Column 3: Percentages compiled in Historical Division, WDSS, based on statistics of Classification and Replacement Branch, AGO, report on Forms XOC-62, 63, 64.
Column 4: AGF memo for G-1, WD, 25 October 1943, sub: Raising of Average Annual Pay of Infantry, Tab B. 000.7/1 (Inf Prog) (C).
Column 5: AGF staff study, "Memo for the Chief of Staff, AGF," 8 December 1943, Table VIII (C). 327.3/7 (S).

[a] To 30 September 1943. NATO was selected as the only theater in which extensive operations of all arms were conducted prior to the end of 1943. Percentages do not add to 100 because all arms and services are not included.

[b] Does not include flying pay.

[c] Included in Infantry, Field Artillery, etc. Not separable.

men began to accumulate in combat units. Twelve thousand combat soldiers at the AGF overseas replacement depot at Fort Meade were examined in November 1943. Since they were general-service men from units and replacement training centers in all parts of the country, they probably offered a cross section of personnel in the ground arms. They were inferior in height, weight, AGCT grade, and education to the average for the Army.[1] In AGCT grades, the average of all men inducted into the Army was considerably better in the second half of 1943

[1] (1) AGF memo, Repl Dep No. 1 for CG AGF, 9 Nov 43, sub: Characteristics of Enl Repl by Arm. 000.7/18 (Inf Prog). (2) Tab D, AGF memo (S) for G-1 WD, 21 Dec 43, sub: Utilization of Available Manpower Based on Physical Capacity. 327.3/8 (S).

230-171 O - 66 - 5

than in the first half. More than 38 percent of the men inducted were in Classes I and II, compared with an average for the year of 35 percent. Both the Service Forces and the Air Forces received a larger proportion of these high-quality men than during the first half of 1943 (41 percent and 49.5 percent respectively). Since the proportion of Classes I and II men received by the Ground Forces remained virtually unchanged (30 percent), the relative proportion of high-quality manpower assigned to the Ground Forces declined considerably in the second half of 1943.[2]

After the middle of 1943, United States forces overseas were increasingly committed to combat. An AGF observer with the Fifth Army in Italy reported: "Squad leaders and patrol leaders with initiative were scarce. . . . The assignment of Grade V intelligence men to infantry is murder." The surgeon of the XIV Corps, after the New Georgia campaign, made a study of war neurosis and found "tangible evidence that incompetent or questionable leadership in small units was an important causative factor." In units in New Georgia, where junior and noncommissioned officers had broken down, panic spread among the men and needless sacrifice of manpower resulted. When stronger leaders were transferred to infected units, cases of war neurosis declined. Breakdown of privates from unit to unit was in direct proportion to breakdown among junior commanders, enlisted and commissioned. It was found "that many unit leaders were not aware of their responsibilities as leaders." War neurosis was not frequent "in field artillery, engineer, quartermaster, signal and reconnaissance units of the divisions; Navy boat pool crews, air warning units, Marine defense battalions; and service units, as a whole." It occurred chiefly in the Infantry. Another medical officer reported: "I saw one whole platoon of an infantry company go out because the platoon sergeant went 'wacky.' It is very important to select strong leaders, men with strong minds, especially during training periods in the States. It cannot be over-emphasized that the non-commissioned officer is a key man of vital importance, because if he fails, the unit he is in charge of goes down with him."[3]

General McNair wished to show the shortage of combat leadership statistically. He adopted three premises: that the need for strong leadership was in direct relationship to exposure to danger; that danger was measurable by casualty

[2] Percentages compiled in Historical Division, WDSS, based on statistics of Classification and Replacement Branch, AGO, reports on Forms XOC–62, 63, 64.

[3] (1) Incl to unused draft of AGF memo for WD in 327.3/100 (S). (2) Sec II, OPD Information Bul (S) (OPDIB), 18 Mar 44.

rates; and that strong leaders would in almost all cases be men in the upper AGCT classes. He ordered an actual count by AGCT grade of men in all divisions and in nondivisional units in the Army Ground Forces as of 1 November 1943, totaling over 1,000,000 enlisted men.[4] Distribution of recent inductees, by AGCT score, among the three major forces, was likewise reviewed. AGF staff officers computed indices showing the comparative severity of battle casualties by branch, that is, the incidence of battle casualties by arm or service, in proportion to the strength of each arm or service in the theaters. Attention was focused on the North African Theater of Operations, in which sizable forces of all arms had been in combat for a considerable time. Findings were as follows:

	Battle Casualty Ratio[a] *(Air Corps=1.0)*	*Class I and II Men Among Assignees from Reception Centers*[b] *(Percent)*	
		Class I	*Class II*
AGF Combat Units	[c] 2.6	5.2	26.5
Air Corps	1.0	9.3	38.0
Service Personnel (Exc. AAF)	0.2	10.7	32.5

[a] Represents the relationship among the units shown of the incidence of battle casualties in proportion to strength of each arm in service in NATO up to 30 October 1943.

[b] Based on assignments during the period May–September 1943. The survey of 1,000,000 men in AGF on 1 November 1943 indicated that 3.1 percent of the total were AGCT Class I men and 23.5 percent were Class II.

[c] Ratio for infantry alone was 4.0.

It appeared that leaders were scarcest where the fighting was thickest. General McNair submitted these conclusions to the Chief of Staff, U.S. Army, on 17 December 1943. He wrote briefly:[5]

> From time to time in the past, this headquarters has pointed out that certain procedures in distributing manpower discriminate against the ground forces. The inclosed charts show the cumulative effect of such measures.
>
> While the situation is viewed as unfortunate, it is realized that it is now too late for effective remedial action. This study is submitted in order to make clear the composition of our war Army in its practically complete form.

Proposals for the Rehabilitation of the Ground Arms

In the summer of 1943, officers of both the G–1 and the G–3 sections of the AGF headquarters staff subjected the whole question of quality of personnel in the ground arms to a searching analysis. They were now impressed with the

[4] (1) AGF ltr to CGs, 13 Sep 43, sub: Age and Distribution in Divs and Nondiv Units. 201.6/483. (2) For results, see tables in incl to 327.3/7 (S).

[5] Memo (S) of Gen McNair for CofS USA, 17 Dec 43, sub: Distribution of Manpower. 327.3/7 (S).

adverse effect on the combat arms of the classification system itself, noting that the diversion of men with established civilian occupations from the combat arms drained away also the best minds, best physiques, and best leaders. It was observed that, from the peacetime necessity of attracting volunteers, the Army paid more money for the more skilled positions, not the more dangerous. "Such procedure," remarked G–1, Army Ground Forces, "should be unnecessary under a universal Selective Service System. In wartime, the money should go to the more dangerous positions." AGF headquarters itself, observed G–1 on 17 July, had in the past sanctioned these practices; and AGF field commanders had tended to assign their best men, and give the highest ratings, to administrative and technical positions at the expense of the combat elements within their own units. G–1 recommended a word of admonition to commanders, a restudy of grades and ratings, a program of publicity for the ground arms (such as General Lear had suggested a year before), and reassignment of high-caliber enlisted men within the Ground Forces from service to combat units.[6]

On the last point General McNair wished to proceed cautiously. He did not desire to upset by wholesale transfers units which at this late date were already organized and trained. A moderate directive was issued on 6 August, warning commanders against excessive emphasis on preinduction skills and ordering the transfer, within limits, of men physically and mentally capable of aggressive leadership from service to combat units.[7] For various reasons it proved impossible to avoid upsetting organized units in the following months. Units were being remodeled under new Tables of Organization, stripped for replacements, obliged to reshuffle their limited-service personnel, and tapped for ASTP candidates and aviation cadets. In such a turmoil of reassignment it was difficult to guide men into combat units on the basis of leadership qualities, especially since leadership qualities were not definitely indicated in classification records.

The problem of rehabilitating the ground arms could not be solved by the Army Ground Forces alone. It was desirable that front-line fighting soldiers be young, though not immature, with a minimum of dependents and family responsibilities, and physically and emotionally sturdy enough to have a maximum chance of survival. The attempt to concentrate such men in combat positions after the middle of 1943 was subject to severe limitations. The manpower controlled by the War Department was not a single internally fluid pool. It was to a

[6] AGF M/S (R), G–1 to CofS, 17 Jul 43, sub: Asgmt and Utilization of EM. 220.3/50 (R).

[7] AGF ltr (R) to CGs, 6 Aug 43, sub: Utilization of EM. 220.3/50 (R).

large extent frozen in each of the three major forces. To this administrative circumstance was added the fact that mobilization was already accomplished. Men were trained and functioning in their respective major forces—Ground, Air, or Service. As General McNair hesitated to upset his units by a general transfer into combat positions of suitable men irrespective of their current assignments, so also the War Department hesitated to upset the three major forces by transfer into Army Ground Forces of men who were potentially good combat soldiers but actually functioning in other jobs. This was the meaning of General McNair's statement, in December 1943, that it was too late for effective remedy of the unfortunate condition of the ground arms. It will presently be seen that in 1944 the War Department nevertheless did take measures to "unfreeze" the Army and to cause a flow of high-quality manpower into the Ground Forces.

Meanwhile the efforts of Army Ground Forces and the War Department to improve the quality of the ground arms branched into three lines: a reanalysis of the problem of Negro troops in relation to the general problem of quality; a definite program to raise the effectiveness of the Infantry; and a concerted drive to obtain modification of the Army system of classification and assignment.

The Quality of Negro Troops

From the beginning the problem of raising the quality of the Negro combat units had been of special concern to the Army Ground Forces. While the inclusion of Negro troops in the ground combat forces did not lower appreciably the over-all quality of the combat arms, their concentration into all-Negro units resulted in the production of a number of units generally characterized by a far greater proportion of low AGCT grades than in AGF units as a whole. This condition can be traced to deficiencies in the educational and environmental backgrounds of the bulk of Negro enlisted men. The contention of Army Ground Forces was not that Negro combat units could not be trained effectively but that units with disproportionately low AGCT grades could not be trained under normal methods in a normal period of time.

Under the provisions of the Selective Service Act and a presidential directive, the War Department required all arms and services to absorb Negro enlisted men on the general basis of the proportion of Negroes in the population of the country.[8] This figure, the "proper proportionate number" of Negro troops, was

[8] WD ltr AG 291.21 (10-9-40) M-A-M to CGs, 16 Oct 40, sub: WD Policy in Regard to Negroes. 314.7 (AGF Hist).

set at 10.6 percent, the percentage of Negroes registering in the draft. Since Negro personnel could not be shifted except to other Negro units,[9] large numbers of Class IV and Class V personnel, averaging from 75 to 90 percent, were concentrated in Negro units.

In the spring of 1942 the problem reached its initial crisis. Before this the Army, because of a shortage of training cadres, housing, and planned activations, had not taken its "proper proportionate number" of Negro troops. Those Negro combat units which were in the Army consisted of a few Regular and National Guard units and some new nondivisional units.[10] Selective Service had been urging the Army to increase its quota of Negro inductees to bring its percentage of Negroes up to 10.6. This would increase the number of Negroes inducted for the remainder of 1942 beyond the 10.6 percentage and would interfere with scheduled activations, both by the proportionate reduction of new white inductees planned for units already in the Troop Basis and by providing Negro inductees for whom no such units had been planned. If proportionate distribution were made to all arms and services, the War Department estimated that one-seventh, or a total of ten divisions, would have to be Negro.

The problem facing Ground Forces here was one of receiving larger numbers of poorer-quality enlisted personnel than it had expected, all of whom would have to be concentrated in specific units. In an attempt to avoid this heavy concentration which, it was predicted, would produce a number of units which would be all but ineffective, a member of the War Department G–3 proposed in November 1942 that, beginning in 1943, Negroes and whites be placed in the same units in a ratio of 1 to 10.6.[11] General McNair, fearing that such a move would further impair the general quality of combat units, proposed that large Negro combat units, with their heavy requirements of personnel experienced in administrative and technical skills, be discontinued. "If the size of Negro combat units were

[9] *Ibid.* The letter concluded with the statement that the policy of not placing Negroes and whites in the same regiments would be continued: "This policy has proven satisfactory over a long period of years and to make changes would produce situations destructive to morale and detrimental to the preparation for national defense."

[10] These included six infantry regiments (the 24th, 25th, 366th, 367th, 368th, and 372d), seven coast artillery regiments, one field artillery brigade, five field artillery regiments, two tank destroyer battalions, and one tank battalion. Four of the infantry regiments and several of the smaller units were tactically disposed under the defense commands. The other two infantry regiments were under Army Ground Forces, preparing for overseas movement.

[11] Draft memo (S) of Col (later Brig Gen) E. W. Chamberlain, WDGS, for Brig Gen I. H. Edwards, WD G–3, undated, sub: Negro Personnel TB 43. WD G–3 "Negro File" (S). See also Gen E. W. Chamberlain's manuscript "History of G–3, WD," Chap. V, "Negro Personnel."

limited to separate battalions," he wrote, "they would be fully suitable for battle employment, yet the organization would permit the maximum flexibility in such employment."[12] Neither proposal was accepted by the War Department and the problem remained unsolved, though not ignored.

To take care of additional Negro combat troops, new units were added to the Troop Basis. These units were primarily of combat-support types. Four Negro infantry divisions were provided in the 1942 Troop Basis, but only two of these were activated with Negro personnel. The decision to activate an armored division from the white elements of the 2d Cavalry Division left the Negro elements (the 4th Cavalry Brigade) intact to serve as a basis for expanding the Division into an all-Negro unit.[13] This expansion culminated in the reorganization of the 2d Cavalry Division in February 1943. By June 1943 the growth of AGF Negro units had reached its peak. The enlisted strength of AGF Negro units in that month totaled 167,957, or 10.46 percent of AGF enlisted strength. Of these, 99,045 were in the arms.

With the multiplication of Negro units came an intensification of problems growing out of the disproportionately low AGCT grades among the men available. The difficulties of training Negro combat troops at the accelerated pace required in wartime meant frequent failures in training tests, at times making necessary a deferment of overseas shipment dates. Adequate cadres for new units were becoming scarcer, and the personnel available for cadre and instructional purposes was being spread thinner and thinner. Loss rates for older units were higher than in comparable white units, and the prospect for improving their over-all quality was considerably lessened by the constant need of transfers. Newer units were no better off so far as AGCT distributions were concerned. The Commanding General of the Antiaircraft Artillery Command, in a letter to Army Ground Forces requesting permission to screen from sixteen Negro antiaircraft battalions enough high-scoring men to form three battalions with AGCT distributions relatively comparable to those of white antiaircraft battalions, expressed the problem thus:[14]

> My investigations have convinced me that if colored antiaircraft battalions can be made up of men who are in the proper ratio of Army General Classification Test grades they can

[12] AGF memo (S) for G–3 WD, 11 Nov 42, sub: Negro Personnel TB 43. 322.999/1 (Cld Trs) (S).

[13] WD memo WDGCT 320.2 (4–28–42) for CG AGF, 27 May 42, sub: Armored and Motorized Divs. 320.2/165 (S).

[14] Ltr (C) AAC 320/HN–GNSCS, CG AAC to CG AGF, 12 Mar 43, sub: Colored AA Units. 321/110 (CAC) (C).

be trained in a reasonable time into efficient combat units. It is to be expected that such colored units in action would reflect credit on the American Army and prove a source of pride to the colored race. No such results, however, can possibly be expected of colored antiaircraft units with their present composition of personnel. With this composition it is impossible to find or to develop qualified leaders in anything like sufficient numbers. Moreover, the great majority of the men are unable to grasp the barest fundamentals of the gunnery problems involved, and to care for and properly man the complicated equipment inherent in antiaircraft units. There are in the sixteen colored antiaircraft battalions approximately 10,000 men whose opportunities for mental development have been so restricted as to necessitate their classification in Army General Classification Test Grades IV and V. Of this number only about 3,000 could be employed to useful advantage within the sixteen battalions were all to be continued active.

Since similar requests had come from other arms and new proposals to limit the numbers of Class V men, white and Negro, were under consideration, no action was taken.[15]

Discussion of proposals to improve the quality of enlisted personnel in Negro combat units had been under way for some time. The transfer of low-scoring personnel to service units was proposed several times, but it was difficult to screen out high-scoring personnel for specific units without leaving large numbers of low-scoring personnel for whom no possible noncommissioned leadership would be available.[16] An example of the difficulties involved in shifting Class V men in excess of 10 percent from one division only is afforded by a proposal in one plan which would have entailed the relief of approximately 7,000 men. To obtain fillers in higher grades to replace them it would have been necessary to induct and screen 12,500 men.[17] This would still have left 12,500 men of Class V to be absorbed by other units. Among alternate and substitute proposals the following were included: shifting higher-level Negroes from service units into combat units and replacing them with white noncommissioned officers; splitting Negro divisions into combat teams or separate battalions which might be more easily trained and utilized than the full-sized divisions; restricting

[15] (1) M/S atchd to ltr cited in n. 14. (2) Subsequently, in an effort to lessen training difficulties, permission was granted to convert six Negro automatic weapons battalions to gun battalions on the ground that gun units required closer supervision and less individual action than automatic weapons units, and therefore had a higher absorption rate for Class IV and Class V men. See papers in 320.2/40 (TUB 43) (C).

[16] (1) Draft memo (S) of Brig Gen I. H. Edwards for CofS USA, 12 Mar 43, sub: Employment of Grade V Personnel in the Army. 327.2 (SS Men) (S). (2) Ltr (S) of CG AAC to CG AGF, 12 Mar 43, sub: Colored AA Units. 321/343 (CAC) (S). (3) WD memo WDGCT 291.21 (1-4-43) for CG AGF, 27 Apr 43, sub: Negro Personnel. 322.999/4 (Cld Trs) (S).

[17] WD memo WDGCT 291.21 (1-14-43) for CG AGF, 5 Mar 43, sub: Negro Personnel. 322.999.

the percentage of Negro Class V men inducted to the same percentage as that of white Class V's; discharging the majority of the men in Class V; and halting the commissioning of Negroes until noncommissioned grades had been filled with competent leaders.[18]

Most of these proposals were examined and discarded. One influential reason was that the War Department's plan to improve the quality of ground combat troops was scheduled to go into operation in the early future.

This plan involved establishing special training units (STU's), discharging men found unteachable, and ordering the transfer of excess high-intelligence personnel to the ground combat troops. Special training units, which received proportionately more Negro than white selectees, were established in June 1943 at reception centers to teach illiterates and Class V men the minimum reading ability and simple vocabulary needed for military training. Those found unteachable were to be discharged. At the same time the War Department directed that the waste of high-intelligence personnel be brought to an end. "Specifically," read the directive, "excess of men with high intelligence in units such as aviation squadrons, sanitary companies, and service units of the Quartermaster Corps and Engineer labor units will be reassigned to units where their skills and intelligence can be utilized more effectively."[19]

None of these efforts affected to any appreciable extent the distribution of AGCT scores in Ground Forces units. Of the men released from STU's for assignment to regular training in the first six months of operation, 98.7 percent were in Classes IV and V.[20] Of these, white divisions received 1,400 men, all but 24 of them in Classes IV and V; Negro divisions received 1 man (Class IV). Of men assigned to the Infantry 6,305 were white, all of them except 88 in Classes IV and V, while 907 were Negro, all but 10 of whom were in Classes IV and V. Relatively few STU men—10.3 percent in the first six months—were discharged from the

[18] (1) AGF memo (S) for CofS USA, 4 Jan 43, sub: Negro Personnel. 322.999/4 (Cld Trs) (S). (2) AGF memo (S) for CofS USA, 2 Feb 43, sub: Negro Personnel. 322.999/6 (S). (3) AGF memo (S), 9 Apr 43, sub: Negro Personnel. 291.2 (S). (4) Memo (C) of Gen J. A. Green, CG AAC, for Gen McNair, 19 Mar 43, sub: Colored AA Units. 321/110 (CAC) (C). (5) AGF ltr (S) to CG AAC, 1 Apr 43, sub: Negro AA Units. 321/343 (CAC)(S).

[19] WD ltr (R) AG 353 (10 Jun 43) OB–D–A, 17 Jun 43, sub: Sp Tng Units. 353/32 (R).

[20] Men were assigned to regular training from STU's, July 1943 to 31 December 1943, as follows:

	Class I	*Class II*	*Class III*	*Class IV*	*Class V*	*Total*
White	. . .	11 (.1%)	295 (1.9%)	11,837 (76.7%)	3,291 (21.3%)	15,434 (39%)
Negro	. . .	10 (.0%)	197 (.8%)	14,256 (59.2%)	9,624 (40.0%)	24,087 (61%)
TOTAL		21 (.1%)	492 (1.2%)	26,093 (66.0%)	12,915 (32.7%)	39,521 (100%)

Army as unteachable. While STU's increased the total manpower available to the Army, they did little to increase that portion from which leadership might be expected to come.

Moreover, the units specifically directed by the War Department to give up their excess "high-intelligence" personnel contained no marked excess of high AGCT men. In addition, the majority of these units were made up of Negro enlisted men.[21] In most cases there was not enough "high intelligence" in these units, as measured by AGCT scores, to raise the level of Negro ground combat units. In no case could this group of units furnish enough high-level personnel to affect the Ground Forces as a whole.

The Infantry Program

General Marshall was seriously disturbed by the 1943 surveys of the Special Services Division that indicated the low state of morale in the ground arms, especially in the Infantry. On 4 August he requested General McNair to suggest remedial action.[22] General McNair answered General Marshall's request by submitting the proposals which had been made by the AGF G-3 Section earlier in the month, which he had approved with minor reservations. "My only regret," he observed to General Marshall, "is that we did not start something along this line about two years ago."[23] These proposals aimed at an increase of pay and of public recognition for infantrymen and at assigning men to the Infantry on a more selective basis than in the past.[24]

[21] On 1 July 1943 the following numbers of types of units were within the continental limits of the United States:

218	Negro and 32 white aviation squadrons
13	Negro and 12 white engineer general service regiments
3	Negro and 1 white engineer separate battalions
87½	Negro and no white medical sanitary companies
40	Negro and 2 white quartermaster service battalions
18	Negro and 10 white quartermaster truck regiments
4	Negro and no white quartermaster fumigation and bath battalions
33	Negro and 13 white troop transport companies

Source: (1) Directory of the Army of the United States (Continental Limits of the United States), Army Air Forces Units, Attached Services, and Miscellaneous AAF Installations and Activities, July 1, 1943. AGO Records, 461 (1 Jul 43) OB-F-M. (2) Directory of the Army of the United States (Continental Limits of the United States), Exclusive of Army Air Forces and Attached Services, June 1, 1943. AGO Records, 461 (1 Jul 43) OB-I-M.

[22] Memo of Gen Marshall for Gen McNair, 4 Aug 43, sub not given. 000.7/35 (Inf Prog).

[23] AGF M/S (C), CG to CofS USA, 16 Aug 43, sub: Program for Improvement of the Morale, Efficiency, and Effectiveness of Inf. 000.7/1 (Inf Prog) (C).

[24] AGF memo (C) for CofS USA, 28 Aug 43, sub as in n. 23. 000.7/1 (Inf Prog) (C).

Army Ground Forces desired the adoption of "fighting pay" corresponding to "flying pay" in the Air Forces.[25] Holding that flying pay could be justified only on the ground of risk (not of skill, since medical officers, for example, were paid no more than aviators of the same rank), General McNair offered figures to show that service in the Infantry was more risky than service in the Air Forces. Even at this date, before major ground operations were well launched, the casualty rate for infantrymen in the combat zone was about the same as for Air Forces personnel on flying-pay status in the theaters. General McNair recommended that fighting pay be given for combat-zone service to members of arms in which the monthly casualty rate reached a periodically determined figure, initially 1.2 percent. This percentage had hitherto been reached only by the Infantry. Its adoption would therefore favor the Infantry without explicit discrimination. To stop the practice by which, through award of grades and ratings, the Army paid more for "clerical and trade skill" than for fighters and leaders, he recommended in addition that the average base pay of enlisted men in all the combatant arms be raised to the level prevailing in the Ordnance Department. (See Table No. 5.)

To obtain greater recognition for ground combat soldiers and hence to give them new incentives for efficiency, General McNair proposed the establishment of a Ground Medal to be awarded as liberally as the Air Medal. He proposed also that a title and grade of "Fighter" be established in the Infantry, that privates holding the title be addressed as such ("Fighter Jones" instead of "Private Jones"), and that all personnel earning the title, enlisted and commissioned, wear a fighter badge of appropriate design. Between fighting pay and the title of Fighter there was to be no connection.[26]

Finally, General McNair proposed that reception centers "assign, generally, to the infantry those selectees who are physically strong regardless of previous occupation, keeping the infantry intelligence level with the general average." He suggested that a physical test be given before assignment to the Infantry and that no selectees, unless of unusually good physique, be assigned to the Infantry if shorter than 5 feet 6 inches.[27]

[25] Tab B to AGF memo cited in n. 24.

[26] (1) Tab D to AGF memo cited in n. 24. (2) AGF memo for G-1 WD, 10 Aug 43, sub: Medal for Ground Trs. 200.6/80.

[27] Tab E to AGF memo cited in n. 24.

These proposals, submitted to the Chief of Staff, U.S. Army, on 28 August 1943, were unfavorably received by G–1 of the War Department General Staff.[28] G–1 thought that the American soldier would ridicule the term "Fighter," and on the matter of a Ground Medal he warned that "too liberal award of any decoration renders it valueless." Assignment to Infantry as suggested by General McNair, G–1 maintained, "violates all the principles of correct personnel classification and assignment." Treating together the proposal to raise base pay in all combat ground arms and the proposal for fighting pay especially designed by Army Ground Forces to favor the Infantry, G–1 declared that all arms would benefit, and that hence the Infantry would gain little. Nevertheless, G–1 considered the infantry problem to be critical—so critical as to require more fundamental correctives than those proposed by General McNair. It was suggested that the best correctives would be an intensive publicity campaign and "positive action by all commanding officers," chiefly to prevent individual misassignments. G–1 also favored an Infantry Badge in place of the fighter badge, and an increase of grades and ratings in infantry combat companies. During the succeeding months Army Ground Forces, adhering to its basic proposals, recommended various modifications of the program in order to win its acceptance.

Publicity, put forward as a major remedy by G–1 of the War Department, had also been recommended to General McNair by G–1 and G–3 of his own staff, but was one of the elements in their proposals on which he felt some reservation. He desired no high-pressure advertising.[29] He created a new section on his staff, called a "Special Information Section," to promote understanding and appreciation of the Infantry on the part of the public. About half a dozen officers and a similar number of enlisted men with newspaper or other writing experience were assigned to it. Civilian writers, magazine editors, cartoonists, song writers, and moving picture executives were asked to give prominence to the Infantry in their work, using the words "infantry" and "doughboy" wherever possible. General McNair wrote personally to a number of the leading newspaper and magazine publishers of the country.[30] The Special Information Section worked through the War Department Bureau of Public Relations. To guide the Bureau

[28] WD memo (C) WDGAP 330.11 for CofS USA, 14 Sep 43, sub: Reflection of Pride in Orgn and Satisfaction with Job Asgmt. 000.7/1 (Inf Prog)(C).

[29] AGF M/S (C), CG to CofS, 16 Aug 43, and G–3 to CofS, 21 Aug 43, sub: Prog for Improvement of Morale, Efficiency, and Effectiveness of Inf. 000.7/1 (Inf Prog)(C).

[30] See generally 000.7 (Inf Prog).

of Public Relations, General Marshall wrote to its head, observing that the Infantry had borne 60 percent of the casualties in Italy:[31]

> Men will stand almost anything if their work receives public acknowledgment. They are inclined to glory in its toughness and hazards if what they do is appreciated. There has been so little glamour in infantry work that the public is little aware of the requirements. On the contrary, if you will recall, I was opposed vigorously in the early formation of the Army for my attitude regarding the infantry soldier and his importance in our war army. It was to be all tanks and air, maybe a little artillery, with everybody motorized, etc. Now [in February 1944] the picture is being completed in accordance with the fundamental requirements of waging a successful war. The haphazard theorizing is found to be without solid foundation, and the influence of the more glamorous methods of making war is found not to be sufficient for the purposes of successful operation. . . .
>
> It might well be charged that we have made the mistake of having too much of air and tank and other special weapons and units and too little of the rifleman for whom all these other combat arms must concentrate to get him forward with the least punishment and loss. I don't want to discourage the rifleman and yet I want his role made clear and exalted. I don't want to unduly alarm the families of riflemen and yet it is important that some action be taken.

General McNair in March 1944 notified the Bureau of Public Relations that infantry units thus far stationed overseas, although constituting only 6 percent of the Army, had to date borne 53 percent of the casualties. He believed, however, that the figures should not be made public.[32]

Appreciation of the Infantry undoubtedly rose in 1944. How much this was due to efforts in public relations and how much to the facts of battle cannot be said. Infantry participated increasingly in overseas operations; the main offensive was no longer conducted by aviation. In the popular mind the well-publicized but somewhat fruitless bombing of Cassino seems to have brought a sudden realization of the infantryman's fundamental place. Yet it continued to be reported by qualified observers that the front line infantryman was in a bitter mood, believing himself an unappreciated and forgotten man, kept in combat until exhausted, wounded, or killed, and denied the comforts and advantages abundantly provided to rear-area troops. "The infantryman," wrote a medical officer in August 1944 after service in Italy, "is at present the least appropriately rewarded specialist in the Army."[33]

[31] Memo (S) of Gen Marshall for Gen Surles, 6 Feb 44, sub: Appreciation of Inf Soldier. 000.7/8 (Inf Prog) (S).

[32] AGF memo (S) for BPR WD, 18 Mar 44, sub: Inf Str and Casualty Figures. 000.7/8 (Inf Prog) (S).

[33] ASF Monthly Progress Rpt (S) 7, "Health," p. 11.

In place of the Ground Medal proposed by Army Ground Forces a Bronze Star Medal was established by executive order of the President in February 1944, to be awarded to members of any of the armed services "for heroic or meritorious achievement or service, not involving participation in aerial flight, in connection with military or naval operations against an enemy of the United States."[34] In place of the "Fighter" status originally proposed, Army Ground Forces (elaborating the recommendation of G–1, War Department) obtained authorization of the titles, with corresponding badges, of Expert Infantryman and Combat Infantryman.[35] The first could be won by meeting in training or combat certain standards with respect to infantry weapons and tactics and to physical endurance and good military behavior. The second could be won by "exemplary conduct in action against the enemy."[36]

Pursuing its idea of fighter-pay, Army Ground Forces desired that the award of the Expert Infantryman badge carry an increase of pay of $10 a month, that of Combat Infantryman $15.[37] After temporary objection by the Director of the Budget, sums of $5 and $10 respectively were obtained through legislation in June 1944.[38] Rearrangement of infantry Tables of Organization, prescribing higher grades for platoon, section, and squad leaders and increasing the number of privates first class, raised average infantry base pay from about $700 to about $743 a year.[39] Special compensation for the Infantry, which Army Ground Forces had wished to secure through fighter-pay, thus was obtained in part through Expert and Combat Infantryman badges, and in part by refusing increases of base pay to other arms than the Infantry. In contrast to the original AGF proposal, the plan adopted did not favor the front-line fighter as such but the Infantry as an arm.

[34] Executive Order No. 9419, 4 Feb 44, published in Bul 3, WD, Feb 44.

[35] AGF memo for CofS USA, 12 Oct 43, sub: Improvement of the Morale, Efficiency, and Effectiveness of Inf. 000.7/33 (Inf Prog).

[36] (1) AGF memo (C) for G–1 WD, 22 Oct 43, sub: WD Cir "Infantry Standards of Proficiency." 000.7/1 (C). (2) Cir 322, WD, 11 Dec 43, "Standards for Expert Infantryman Badge"; Cir 186, WD, 11 May 44, "Infantry Badge." (3) AGF ltr to CGs, 18 Jan 44, sub: Standards for Expert Infantryman Badge. 200.6/2 (Inf Badge).

[37] (1) AGF memo (C) for G–1 WD, 25 Oct 43, sub: Raising of Average Annual Pay for Inf. 000.7/1 (Inf Prog)(C). (2) AGF M/S, CofS to G–3, 27 Oct 43, sub: Inf Program. 000.7/22 (Inf Prog).

[38] (1) WD Gen Council Min (S), 25 Apr 44, 26 Jun 44. (2) Cir 271, WD, 3 Jul 44.

[39] (1) AGF M/S (C), G–3 to DCofS, 30 Oct 43. 000.7/101 (Inf Prog)(C). (2) Memo (C) of Gen McNarney for CGs AAF, AGF, ASF, 12 Dec 43, sub: Increased Pay for Inf NCOs. 000.7/1 (C). (3) Cir 323, WD, 13 Dec 43.

Selective assignment to the Infantry on physical grounds was regarded by General McNair as a principal feature of the infantry program. On 11 November 1943 he renewed his recommendation of 28 August, proposing that men "generally" be assigned to the Infantry according to physical strength, as shown by tests, irrespective of civilian occupation. A sample of 6,000 infantrymen examined in November 1943 disclosed that they averaged only 5 feet 7.74 inches in height, as compared with an Army average of 5 feet 8.41 inches. Height provided a rough measure of strength. Where in August he had suggested 5 feet 6 inches, he now suggested 5 feet 9 inches as the height below which future inductees should not normally be assigned to the Infantry.[40] Hope for such a program seemed to be given by the publication at this time of Circular 293, which directed, with reservations, the assignment of enlisted men "to the most active type of duty appropriate to their physical qualifications."

The Military Personnel Division, Army Service Forces, commenting on General McNair's proposal of 11 November, declared that the giving of physical tests at reception centers was impracticable. It added:[41]

> The Military Personnel Division, Army Service Forces, does not concur in a further screening of general service enlisted men at reception centers to assign the higher physically qualified men within general service standards to infantry replacement training centers and units. There is no argument against the need of physically qualified men in the infantry. The need is similar in the field artillery, armored force, mobile antiaircraft artillery, and other combat and service units such as combat and general service engineers.

The last sentence was precisely what the Army Ground Forces denied and believed to be implicitly denied also by the War Department in Circular 293.[42]

In divisions already in combat, the infantry rifle components were used up much faster than other components. The War Department, in January 1944, sought means of increasing the staying power of infantry.[43] The wear upon infantrymen was due in part to sickness and nonbattle casualties arising from the severe conditions in which infantrymen lived when in combat. General McNair suggested that with assignment of the strongest physical specimens to the Infan-

[40] (1) AGF M/Ss, CofS to G-3, 27 Oct 43; CG to CofS, 6 Nov 43, sub: Inf Program. (2) AGF memo for G-1 WD, 11 Nov 43, sub: Improvement of the Morale, Efficiency, and Effectiveness of Inf. Both in 000.7/22 (Inf Prog).

[41] MPD ASF memo (S) SPGAP/210.5 Gen (11 Nov 43)-89 for G-1 WD, 23 Nov 43, sub as in n. 40(2). 000.7/8 (Inf Prog) (S).

[42] See copy of Cir 293, WD, 11 Nov 43, annotated by CofS AGF. 327.3/209 (LS).

[43] WD memo (S) WDGCT 320.2 (20 Jan 44) for CG AGF, 20 Jan 44, sub: Inf Str in the Inf Div. 000.7/4 (Inf Prog) (S).

try this attrition might decline, and consequently that the various arms within a division would deteriorate at a more even rate. He renewed his proposals of 28 August and 11 November 1943.[44]

They were again disapproved, but not because of a failure to appreciate the gravity of the situation. Not only had General Marshall expressed his anxiety, but also the Chief of the G–1 Division of the General Staff had observed on 14 February that in consequence of emphasis on civilian skills "the combat arms got what was left after the Air Forces and Service Forces had selected the pick of the lot." [45] The latter stated, however, on 23 March 1944, that General McNair's proposals would destroy the "time tested policies" whereby civilian occupation and military training were considered in making assignments.[46] Meanwhile remedial action had been initiated. On 3 March 1944, reception centers were instructed to assign the physically strongest inductees to the Army Ground Forces. New procedures in classification, known as the "Physical Profile Plan" and designed to regularize this policy, were already being applied experimentally. These were believed by the War Department to be preferable to General McNair's clear-cut but somewhat arbitrary distinction by height.

Pending the decision of the War Department, Army Ground Forces renewed its effort to have the best physical specimens under its own jurisdiction assigned to the Infantry. On 20 February it dispatched a confidential letter to its subordinate commanders, pointing out that the Infantry had a scarcity value, that it comprised only 11 percent of the Troop Basis, that it was nevertheless the decisive arm, that it must therefore be scrupulously conserved, and that the strongest and healthiest men should be assigned to it. All commanders were enjoined to comply strictly with the provision in Circular 293 that enlisted men should be given the most active type of duty suited to their physical qualifications.[47]

The Physical Profile System

Proposals for selective assignment to the Infantry merged into a more comprehensive effort to obtain changes in the whole system of classification and

[44] (1) Memo (S) of Gen McNair for G–3 WD, 1 Feb 44, sub: Inf Str in Inf Div. (2) Memo of Gen McNair for G–1 WD, 17 Feb 44, sub: Improvement of the Effectiveness of Inf. Both in 000.7/8 (Inf Prog) (S).

[45] WD Gen Council Min (S), 14 Feb 44.

[46] (1) WD memo (S) WDGAP 330.11 (6 Mar 44), 23 Mar 44, sub: Improvement of the Morale, Efficiency, and Effectiveness of Inf. (2) MPD ASF memo (S) SPGAP/327.31 (17 Feb 44) for G–1 WD, 9 Mar 44, sub: Improvement of the Effectiveness of Inf. Both in 000.7/8 (Inf Prog) (S).

[47] AGF ltr (C) to CGs, 20 Feb 44, sub: Strengthening the Inf. 321/103 (Inf) (C).

assignment of enlisted personnel. General McNair had come to favor emphasis on physical classification as a means of procuring not only stronger but also more intelligent combat soldiers. If men were assigned primarily according to physique, then each major command would receive more nearly the same proportions of men of all intelligence levels and of various degrees of civilian accomplishment.

In December 1943, noting that discrimination against the ground arms in the distribution of men by AGCT grades had become accentuated in the preceding months, Army Ground Forces had again requested a more equal apportionment.[48] The Army Service Forces, through its Control Division, replied that the action recommended by the Army Ground Forces was not justified by the figures submitted; it held that the Ground Forces must unavoidably receive a less intelligent group of men, partly because of War Department priorities for aviation cadets and ASTP students, which militated against the Ground and Service Forces alike, and partly because "the primary factor" in assignment was to utilize civilian skills, which militated against the Ground Forces in particular. It was natural, Army Service Forces declared, for the Ground Forces to receive a lower percentage of men with high AGCT scores than the Service Forces, "because of greater requirements for such personnel in Army Service Forces." No change in AGCT distributions could be expected, it was added, as long as the main basis of assignment was the Requirement and Replacement Rates in which branch requirements for occupational specialists were set forth.[49]

It was clear, as it had been for some time, that the quality of personnel in the ground arms could be raised only through a radical change in the personnel policies of the Army. On 21 December 1943 General McNair proposed such a change to the War Department.[50] After summarizing the causes of the relatively low quality of personnel in the ground arms, he restated his belief that the subaverage percentage of ground soldiers in the upper intelligence levels had contributed to the high casualty rate of infantrymen. He ascribed the subaverage physical quality of the Infantry in part "to the fact that professional men or skilled workers come from the more privileged classes, which are better fed and housed, and, as a result, have better physiques, generally." He asserted that, with mobilization and training virtually complete, it was no longer necessary to

[48] AGF 3d ind (S) to ASF, 22 Dec 43. 327.3/100 (S).

[49] ASF 4th ind (S) to AGF, 12 Jan 44. 327.3/100 (S).

[50] AGF memo (S) for G–1 WD, 21 Dec 43, sub: Utilization of Available Manpower Based on Physical Capacity. 327.3/8 (S).

230-171 O - 66 - 6

utilize the civilian skills of soldiers and that "assignment by occupational specialty should be made secondary and be limited to that practicable within physical groupings, except for rare specialists." As additional proof of this point of view he summarized the methods of physical classification in the British, Canadian, and German Armies.

General McNair submitted a relatively simple plan. In effect the procedure he now proposed would be a simplified version of that followed under the Requirement and Replacement Rate Tables, except that the rates would measure physical rather than occupational needs in the Army, and would refer to the physical rather than occupational status of individual men. The recognition of three physical categories was involved: Category A, to include "men who must walk as riflemen, litter-bearers and linemen, and are capable of full combat service"; Category B, to include men able to function in service units, or in combat units in jobs carrying a place in the loading chart of a vehicle; and Category C, to include men permanently disqualified for shipment overseas. Various "units, establishments and components of the Army" should formulate their requirements for men in each category. "For example, an infantry unit might have 90% Category A and 10% Category B; a field artillery unit 70% Category A and 30% Category B; and a laundry unit 100% Category B." Reception centers and other assigning agencies should classify men in the three categories and send them to using organizations in the proportions determined for each organization. General McNair also recommended an equal distribution of AGCT classes to the three commands; the return to the Ground Forces of rejected aviation cadets originating in the ground arms who were being used by the Air Forces in ground assignments; and cessation of transfers from the Ground Forces for most forms of flying training.

By the end of January 1944 there was "unanimous agreement" in the War Department that better use must be made of soldiers according to physical capacity. It has not agreed that physical capacity should dominate assignment to the degree desired by General McNair. Nor were the details of implementation as suggested by General McNair accepted. The Surgeon General, G-1 of the War Department, and others submitted plans. They reached an agreement on what was called the "Physical Profile Plan," which reception centers began to employ experimentally in February 1944.[51]

The plan incorporated the main features of the AGF proposal, including

[51] (1) WD Gen Council Min (S), 31 Jan 44. (2) WD memo WDGAP 201.5 for CofS USA, 24 Feb 44, sub: Physical Profile. 220.01/1 (Phys Prof).

three categories known as A, B, and C.[52] Criteria determining classification in these categories were elaborately defined. Six elements in physical condition were distinguished: general stamina, upper extremities, lower extremities, hearing, vision, and emotional stability. In each element the soldier was graded from 1 down to 4. Grades 1 and 2 corresponded to qualification for general military service; Grade 3 to qualification for induction into the Army but not for general service (that is, the old limited service); and Grade 4 to a condition below minimum standards for induction. The six numbers obtained by grading, one for each element in physical condition, when read together in the proper order, as in "211211," constituted the soldier's "physical profile serial." A soldier profiled as 211211 would be of top quality in upper and lower extremities, vision, and emotional stability, and of good quality, though not superior, in general stamina and in hearing. Men with serials of 211211 or better were grouped in Profile A. Profile A qualified for strenuous combat duty. Serials below 211211 to and including 322231 were grouped in Profile B. A "B" man at the worst, that is, if profiled as 322231, would be a man emotionally stable, with adequate command of his arms, legs, and hearing, but with impaired vision and of limited stamina. Profile B qualified for less rigorous combat duty or for service duty in or near the battle areas. Serials below 322231 to and including 333231 were grouped in Profile C, which qualified for duty in base positions in the United States or overseas. Occurrence of a "4" anywhere in the serial signified a man below minimum standards for induction. Such a man who was already trained and functioning satisfactorily in an Army assignment, however, could be retained at the discretion of his commander; he was classified in a fourth category, Profile D.[53] It was of course not practicable to profile at once all of the more than seven million enlisted men in the Army. The War Department directed that reception centers should profile new inductees, that hospitals, reassignment centers, and redistribution stations should profile the men they processed, and that troop units should profile men as occasion arose—for example, in cases of reassignment. Inductees were to have their profiles reviewed after six weeks of basic training.

To determine requirements according to physical profile, staff officers at AGF headquarters studied every enlisted job in each of the ground arms, and also in each of the service branches to the extent that units of these branches

[52] (1) WD Memo W40–44, 18 May 44, sub: Physical Profile Plan. 220.01/1 (Phys Prof). (2) Supplement to MR 1–9, 22 May 44, sub: Physical Profile Serial. (3) AGF ltr to CGs, 20 Jun 44, sub: Physical Profile Plan. 220.01/7 (Phys Prof).

[53] The designation "BC" (below C) was sometimes used instead of "D."

belonged to the Ground Forces.[54] For each SSN the staff estimated the physical standards needed, translating these into the 6-digit physical profile serials. The same SSN might require different physical standards in different arms and services. For example, a bugler in either the Infantry or Field Artillery was designated as SSN 803; but buglers in the Infantry were considered to require a better physique than buglers in the Field Artillery. For each arm and service the SSN's were grouped into Profiles A, B, and C. The number of men required for each type of job was estimated according to current replacement rates. The proportion of men in each profile group needed by various arms and services was then announced to the War Department to be as follows:

Arm or Service	*Percentage Required in Each Profile Group*		
	A	*B*	*C*
Infantry	86	7	7
Field Artillery	80	5	15
Cavalry	71	13	16
Antiaircraft	65	23	12
Armored	61	18	21
Tank Destroyer	60	9	31
Signal	55	11	34
Chemical	40	25	35
Engineers	35	40	25
Medical	10	78	12
Quartermaster	10	50	40
Ordnance	5	30	65

Since the greatest proportion of the men received by the Ground Forces at this time (April 1944) were needed by the Infantry, General McNair recommended that 80 percent of new inductees made available to the Ground Forces be in Profile A.[55]

The War Department, accepting the AGF figures, ordered that new inductees should be shipped from reception centers to the three major commands as follows:

Command	*Percentage To Be Shipped in Each Profile Group*		
	A	*B*	*C*
Army Ground Forces	80	10	10
Army Air Forces	10	50	40
Army Service Forces	40	40	20

[54] Papers in 220.01/422 (sep file).

[55] AGF memo for G–1 WD, 17 Apr 44, sub: Physical Profile Plan. 220.01/1 (Phys Prof).

Representatives of the Army Ground Forces now appeared alongside those of the Air Forces at reception centers. They were authorized to determine which individual inductees, among those provided by each reception center to the Ground Forces as a whole on a given day, should go to infantry replacement centers, to field artillery replacement centers, to particular infantry or armored divisions, and so forth. In this way the headquarters of the Army Ground Forces could guide the flow of inductees to produce the percentages of A, B, and C men desired in each of the ground arms.

Reception centers might assign certain "critically needed specialists," as determined each month by the War Department, irrespective of physical profile, but in general they were to proceed as follows: They would first assure that at least 80 percent of the men assigned to Army Ground Forces were in Profile A, 10 percent in B, and so forth. They would then assign men to Army Air Forces and Army Service Forces by SSN's, in accordance with the Requirement and Replacement Rates, but taking care to keep within the prescribed distribution of physical capacities as far as possible. Classification officers were to "bear in mind that physical qualification is the first consideration and that occupational background is secondary in importance." The Army Ground Forces thus found its main contention accepted. Physique would be in principle the primary criterion in assignment.[56]

Though the Physical Profile system was fully in operation by June 1944, it came too late to affect the bulk of the Army. The invasion of western Europe was beginning. Half the divisions in the Army were overseas, the other half preparing for early shipment. Applying chiefly to newly inducted men, the profile system might most fully justify itself by raising the quality of replacements. This was a matter of great importance. Units in intensive combat sometimes received 100 percent of their strength in replacements within two or three months. Quality of replacements might therefore rapidly affect quality of the Army at the decisive spot—namely, in the front lines.

Limited Success of the Physical Profile System

During the last six months of 1944, well over the required 80 percent of men received from reception centers by the Army Ground Forces were in Profile A, and most of the remainder were in Profile B. But in practice the utilization of manpower according to physical capacity continued to fall short

[56] WD Memo W615–44, 6 Jun 44, sub: Asgmt of Enl Men from Recp Cens.

of what was desired by the Army Ground Forces. The high proportion of men in Profile A was in part deceptive. The Army at this time was not generally inducting men over twenty-six or of limited physical powers. The proportion of "A" men assigned to the Army Air Forces and Army Service Forces greatly exceeded the 10 percent and 40 percent respectively allotted.[57] This meant that for the quality of currently incoming manpower the profile system was not highly selective, that the idea of physical interchangeability persisted, and that of two men differing in physical capacity the stronger might still go to a service position while the weaker went into combat. For example, two men with serials of 111111 and 211211 both fell in Profile A; the latter might become an infantry rifleman while the former, excelling him in stamina and hearing, went to the Army Air Forces or the Army Service Forces, especially if he had a civilian specialty desired by one of these commands. In addition, profiling at reception centers was not very accurate. Medical officers at reception centers were too few for the purpose, and consequently they determined profiles by consulting the records of physical examinations transmitted from induction stations, supplementing them by an inspection so cursory that many inductees were not even required to strip.[58] The tendency, reinforced by the War Department directive that borderline cases should be graded upward, was to profile too high, to use the serial 111111 rather indiscriminately. Medical officers in the Ground Forces downgraded about one man in every nine after six weeks of basic training.[59]

The application of the Physical Profile system could not solve the problem posed by the excess of physically inferior men already in the Army Ground Forces in the summer of 1944.[60] Such men had accumulated since the directives of 1943 restricting transfer to service commands and curtailing discharges. Men newly received in Profile C, or downgraded into Profiles C or D, added to the number. With overhead positions in the Ground Forces being rapidly filled by men unqualified for overseas service, and with the shipment to theaters of units which might otherwise have found assignments for soldiers of low physical caliber, the disposition of handicapped personnel presented an insoluble problem.

[57] AGF memo for G–1 WD, 4 Oct 44, sub: Distribution of Pers According to Physical Profile. 220.01/34 (Phys Prof).

[58] (1) Memo of Lt Col T. A. McCrary, Enl Div G–1 AGF, for CofS AGF, 4 Jul 44, sub: Visit to Recp Cens. 220.01/35 (Phys Prof). (2) AGF M/S, C&RD to CofS, 8 Jul 44, sub: Inspection Trip. 220.01/31 (Phys Prof).

[59] AGF memo for TAG, 28 Oct 44, sub: Rpt of Losses and Gains by Physical Profile. 220.01/47 (Phys Prof).

[60] AGF M/S (C), G–1 to CofS, 22 Aug 44, sub: Excess Cl D Pers. 327.3/107 (LS)(C).

Every installation in the Ground Forces had its burden, wasteful to all concerned, of men who could be neither trained, utilized, nor transferred. In August 1944 the War Department indicated that, without publicity and under existing directives, discharges on physical grounds should be liberalized.[61] Tactical units of the Ground Forces were ordered to clear themselves of men unfit for overseas service, by discharge of those deemed absolutely unusable by the Army and by transfer of the remainder to the headquarters, special troops, of armies and corps for further screening and reassignment.[62]

For a time the Physical Profile system was virtually nullified by the fact that 18-year-olds and "pre-Pearl Harbor fathers" received special treatment, and, as a consequence, the Army Ground Forces had to assign inductees to the various arms almost irrespective of physical condition.

The teen-age question had first arisen at the end of 1942, when the draft age was lowered from twenty to eighteen. The War Department, wishing to use the younger age group in combat positions, had granted replacement training centers of the Army Ground Forces a high priority in assignment of inductees between the ages of eighteen and twenty, inclusive.[63] In May 1943 Army Ground Forces, anticipating unfavorable public comment if teen-age men went into combat after only thirteen weeks of training, the cycle then in effect at replacement centers, recommended that men of eighteen or nineteen be assigned to units which were not at that time moving rapidly overseas, and men of twenty or over to replacement centers.[64] The War Department had not believed this proposal to be feasible, because with the decline of activations incident to curtailment of the Troop Basis practically all inductees, whatever their age, had to be trained as replacements.[65] Then, with casualties mounting, the War Department

[61] (1) Extract (C) from Rpt of ASF conference at Ft Leonard Wood, 27–28 Jul 44. 327.3/107 (LS)(C). (2) Memo (C) of DCofS USA for CG AGF, 21 Aug 44, sub: Enl Men—Utilization of Manpower Based on Physical Capacity. 327.3/107 (LS)(C). (3) Cir 370, WD, 12 Sep 44.

[62] (1) AGF ltr (C) to CGs, 23 Aug 44, sub: Enl Men — Utilization of Manpower Based on Physical Capacity. 327.3/107 (LS)(C). (2) AGF ltr (R) to CGs, 13 Sep 44, sub: Transfer of Cl D Pers. 220.3/112 (LD)(R).

[63] (1) WD memo WDGCT 324.71 (11–12–43) for CofS USA, 12 Nov 43, sub: Use of 18–19 Age Gp. AGO Records, 324.71. (2) WD ltr (C) AG 324.71 (11–12–43) OC–E–WDGCT–M to CGs, 5 Dec 42, sub: Asgmt of 18, 19, and 20 Year Old Enl Men. 327.3/2 (C).

[64] (1) AGF M/S (C), G–1 to CofS, 11 May 43, sub: Advisability of Sending Loss Repls Overseas in 18–19 Year Age Gp with 13 Wks Tng. 341/174 (C). (2) AGF memo (C) for G–1 WD, 4 Jun 43, sub: Overseas Loss Repls within 18–19 Age Bracket. 327.3/2 (C).

[65] TAG 1st ind (C) to AGF, 29 Jun 43. 327.3/2 (C).

in February 1944 ordered that no 18-year-old should go overseas as a replacement until other sources of replacements, both units and replacement centers, had been exhausted.[66] The same ruling was applied to men with a child or children presumably conceived (not born) before the declaration of war, and with less than six months' service in the Army. In June 1944 it was ordered unconditionally that no man under nineteen should go overseas as a replacement for an infantry or armored unit.[67] It was therefore further ordered that no inductee younger than eighteen years and six months should be assigned to an infantry or armored replacement center.[68]

In June 1944 almost all inductees received by the Army Ground Forces were going to replacement centers, and of these more than 70 percent went to infantry and about 5 percent to armored. At the same time only half the inductees were over nineteen years of age, and only about three-quarters were over eighteen years and six months. To meet the need for infantry and armored replacements with men over eighteen years and six months took virtually all such men available, including those of Profiles B and C. Conversely, the field artillery, antiaircraft, cavalry, and tank destroyer replacement centers received hardly any trainees except youths under this age. These young men ranked high in Profile A's; yet the arms receiving them required fewer "A's" proportionately than did the Infantry. The AGF liaison officers at reception centers were therefore unable to perform a principal part of their mission—to steer into the Infantry the best physical specimens available to the Ground Forces. Age, not physique, for newly inducted men within the ground arms, became the main determinant of assignment.[69]

Policy was again reversed, therefore, at the end of August. Men under eighteen years and six months entered infantry and armored replacement centers. Effective 1 November 1944, by which time these men would have almost completed their training, the sending of men under nineteen as overseas infantry or armored replacements was again authorized. Older men were still to be sent

[66] WD memo (C) WDGCT 200 (26 Feb 44) for CG AGF, 26 Feb 44, sub: Repls. 320.2/107 (O'seas Repls)(C).

[67] WD memo (C) WDGCT 370.5 (24 Jun 44) for CG AGF, 24 Jun 44, sub: Repls. 320.2/107 (O'seas Repls)(C).

[68] WD D/F (C) WDGAP 220.3 to MPD ASF, 26 Jun 44. 320.2/107 (O'seas Repls)(C).

[69] (1) AGF memo (C) for G-3 WD, 28 Jul 44, sub: Repls. 320.2/107 (O'seas Repls)(C). (2) AGF M/S (C), C&RD to G-1, 3 Jul 44, sub: Physically Unfit Trainees. 220.3/3 (LD)(C). (3) Papers in 220.01/29, 33, and 35 (Phys Prof).

first, but the demand for infantry replacements was so heavy that in practice even the youngest men were needed.[70]

The effectiveness of the Physical Profile system was further limited by the continuance of systems of recruiting and volunteering. Volunteers at this time were 17-year-olds who, by high physical and mental qualifications, had gained admittance to one of the enlisted reserve programs. On 1 March 1944, 67 percent of these top-quality 17-year-olds were in the Navy reserve, 31 percent in the Air Corps reserve, and 2 percent in the Army Specialized Training Reserve Program (ASTRP).[71] Reservists, when called to active duty after reaching the age of eighteen, were not subjected to the Physical Profile system. As an Army procedure, the system naturally did not apply to Navy personnel. In practice it also did not apply to Army reservists. Each major force of the Army, which in effect meant the Air Forces, received its inducted reservists (who if profiled would have been mostly "A's") outside its prescribed quota of profile groupings.

At a time when about half the men processed by Selective Service were 18-year-olds, the most desirable element in this group, through preselection at the 17-year-old level, was outside the normal channels of classification and assignment.

Except insofar as the Navy or the Air Forces were not able to use all the reservists that they had recruited, the Ground and Service Forces could hope to receive from the reservist group only those who were enrolled in the ASTRP. The Army Service Forces, foreseeing dire consequences in 1945, when the current 17-year-olds would enter upon active duty, and desiring therefore to build up the ASTRP, requested General McNair to make a public statement on the attractiveness of service in the ground arms so that youngsters might be more inclined to elect the ASTRP.[72] General McNair was unwilling to make another "futile verbal gesture."[73] Instead, he protested to the War Department against the competition for manpower in preinduction reservist training. He recommended that 17-year-olds for the Army programs be procured by a single agency of the War Department acting centrally for the three major commands, and that reservists when inducted, except the relatively small number still going to the ASTP (much smaller than the number in the ASTRP), be classified and assigned at

[70] WD memo (S) WDGCT 370.5 (4 Aug 44) for AGF, ASF, 4 Aug 44, sub: Repls. 320.2/142 (O'seas Repls) (S).

[71] ASF memo, Div of Mil Tng for CG AGF, 17 Apr 44, sub: Development of ASTRP. 327.3/637.

[72] *Ibid.*

[73] AGF M/S, CG to G–1, 6 May 44, sub: ASTRP. 327.3/637.

reception centers according to the Physical Profile system.[74] No action was taken on this proposal.[75] "The War Department," reported an AGF staff officer, "will not eliminate the Air Corps Enlisted Reserve Program since it is the Army's only means of competing with the Navy, and the Navy has repeatedly indicated that they will not eliminate their recruiting program."[76]

The hope of the Army Ground Forces that the Physical Profile system would increase the percentage of high-intelligence men assigned to the ground combat arms met with disappointment. Young men with high intelligence and capacities for leadership continued to be drained off in large numbers, through the reserve programs, to the Navy, the Marine Corps, and the Army Air Forces. Furthermore, the tremendous mobilization of manpower in the preceding years had removed from the scope of Selective Service the best-qualified men, except the young men just attaining draft age. In all of 1944 the proportion of Class I and Class II men inducted into the Army was only 30.6 percent; this compares with a proportion of 35 percent among those inducted in 1943.[77]

Even if the quality of manpower available to the Army as a whole in 1944 and 1945 had remained as high as in the earlier years of the war, the application of the Physical Profile system could not have effected any major improvement in the quality of newly inducted men received by the Army Ground Forces, because the proportionate distribution of inductees among the major commands underwent a radical change during the last year of the war. Until the summer of 1944 the Army Ground Forces had been assigned only about 40 percent of the men processed at Army reception centers. After June 1944, because of the shortage of ground troops qualified for combat, the great majority of newly inducted men were assigned to the Ground Forces, the bulk of them to the Infantry. During the 6-month period November–April 1944–45, the Army Ground Forces received approximately 378,000 men from reception centers, or about 90 percent of the 420,000 men assigned to the three major commands of the Army.[78] With the

[74] (1) AGF memo (C) for G–3 WD, 17 Jun 44, sub: Asgmt of Enl Pers. 327.4/104 (C). (2) AGF memo for G–1 WD, 22 May 44, sub: Recruiting. 327.3/637.

[75] (1) WD D/F WDGAP (23 May 44) to CG AGF, 4 Jul 44. (2) AGF M/S, G–1 to CofS, 8 Jul 44, sub: Recruiting. Both in 327.3/637.

[76] Memo of Lt Col T. A. McCrary, Enl Div G–1 AGF, for CofS AGF, 4 Jul 44, sub: Visit to Recp Cens. 220.01/35 (Phys Prof).

[77] Percentages compiled in Historical Division, WDSS, based on statistics of Classification and Replacement Branch, AGO, reports on Forms XOC–62, 63, 64.

[78] (1) WD ltr (S) WDGCT (30 Oct 44) to CGs AGF, AAF, ASF, 30 Oct 44, sub: Allocation of Personnel. 327.3/104 (SS)(S). (2) Annual Report, 1945 (R), C&RD, AGF.

overwhelming majority of the men received by the Army through induction being assigned to the Army Ground Forces, no improvement in the classification system within the Army could have greatly increased the number of high-quality men assigned to the ground combat arms.

Since no major improvement in the quality of men available for assignment to ground combat training could be effected by the Army itself, the Commanding General of the Army Ground Forces proposed, on 15 June 1945, that the War Department initiate remedial measures "to effect total procurement of enlisted personnel for the armed forces through the medium of the Selective Service System and on a basis that will equalize age and intelligence distribution."[79] A corrective of unbalanced distribution as between the armed forces had been sought by an agreement with the Navy on 15 March 1945. In accordance with this pact the allocations to the Navy of 18-, 19-, and 20-year-old inductees was suspended for a 3-month period in order to compensate the Army for the large number of young men already in the Navy who were enlisted as 17-year-olds. The agreement, however, was conditioned by the authority given the Navy to screen substantial numbers of inductees, regardless of age, who successfully completed the "Eddy" radio aptitude test and who were preponderantly men of high intelligence.

The Eddy test provided the Navy with an efficient means of recruiting high-quality volunteers among 17-year-olds and other men about to be called up for induction. As a result of this device the Navy was found by Army Ground Forces to be still securing about half the eligible young men becoming eighteen years of age—the better half in terms of intelligence and physical stamina. In consequence, the young men inducted into the Army had to be obtained from a less desirable segment of the manpower being obtained by the armed forces. Increasingly, the Army had to draw upon men in the older age group to fill its induction quotas. Between August 1944 and April 1945 the percentage of Army selectees within the 18–25 year age group declined from 88 percent to 56 percent. During the same period the percentage of Profile A men received by Army Ground Forces from reception centers declined from 91 percent to 75 percent. In the spring of 1945 the Army Ground Forces desired that 95 percent of its infantry trainees should be Profile A men; actually only about 82 percent were in Profile A, and the other combat arms were all receiving less than 50 percent of men in

[79] AGF memo (S) for CofS USA, 15 Jun 45, sub: Procurement of Enl Pers for the Armed Forces. With atchd charts. 327.3/104 (SS)(S).

Profile A. With heavy replacement requirements in prospect for the war in the Pacific, the Army Ground Forces felt that this situation ought to be rectified.[80]

On 11 August, three days before V-J Day, the War Department responded to representations by the Army Ground Forces that efforts were being exerted to persuade the Navy Department to eliminate the use of the Eddy test in the Navy's personnel procurement program. The War Department agreed that the recommendation of the Commanding General, Army Ground Forces, presented a desirable objective, and stated that it was "continually exerting efforts to bring about total procurement of enlisted personnel for all of the armed forces through the medium of selective service."[81] No further action was taken, for with the end of the war the procurement of high-type personnel was no longer a problem. Induction schedules were substantially reduced after V-J Day, and the men inducted into the Army could be chosen from those best qualified for military service. In the last four months of 1945, 97 percent of the enlisted personnel received by Army Ground Forces from reception centers were Profile A men.[82]

The Physical Profile system did not receive a fair wartime test as a device for funneling a larger proportion of high-quality men into ground combat service. The system remained a hopeful experiment, the effectiveness of which cannot be properly judged on the basis of the Army's experience in 1944 and 1945.

The Transfer of High-Quality Personnel to the Ground Arms

Quantitative requirements in the Infantry in 1944, by forcing extensive transfers of manpower within the Army, made it possible to take positive measures for qualitative improvement. At the beginning of 1944 the nonalerted infantry divisions in the Army Ground Forces were understrength from furnishing overseas replacements. Each was further stripped for replacements until the latest feasible date before its embarkation. The depleted divisions were generally refilled with men of higher quality (in terms of AGCT scores) than those lost. The chief disadvantage was that the new men could be given only a limited amount of training before their divisions moved overseas.

As previously noted, the first element to be sacrificed to the growing need for combat soldiers was the Army Specialized Training Program. Following the

[80] *Ibid.*

[81] WD D/F (S) WDGAP 327 to CG AGF, 11 Aug 45, sub: Procurement of Enl Pers for the Armed Forces. 327.3/104 (SS)(S).

[82] Annual Report, 1945 (R), C&RD, AGF.

virtual dissolution of the ASTP in February 1944, the Ground Forces obtained 73,000 men, virtually all in the youngest and most vigorous age group and in AGCT Classes I and II. Almost 50,000 of these men had been members of the Ground Forces before their assignment to the ASTP.[83]

A few weeks later, on 29 March 1944, the War Department ordered the transfer to the Ground and Service Forces of 30,000 aviation cadets who were not needed by the Air Forces and who had originated in the other two commands.[84] Further recruiting of aviation cadets among AGF and ASF personnel was stopped.[85] Of the 30,000 transferred cadets the Ground Forces received 24,000, of whom 20,000 had formerly been members of the Army Ground Forces.[86] Most of the aviation cadets were in AGCT Classes I and II, and they were physically an even better lot than the ASTP students.

The War Department desired these men to be spread widely among receiving units, since the purpose was not merely to fill shortages but also to improve the quality of junior leadership in the ground arms. A War Department circular stressed the essential importance of "noncommissioned officers who *exercise command responsibilities,*" the italics serving to distinguish them from enlisted technicians who also wore chevrons.[87]

The Army Ground Forces assigned virtually all the aviation cadets and 55,500 of the ASTP students to divisions, the remainder of the ASTP students going to nondivisional units.[88] Units receiving ASTP students gave up, in partial exchange, a small number of Classes III, IV, and V men, of whom 15,000 were shipped by the Ground Forces to the Service Forces in the course of the ASTP transaction.[89] Thirty-five divisions, infantry, armored, and airborne, received on

[83] Papers in 353 (ASTP)(S) 1944, especially the following: (1) AGF M/S (S), G–1 to C&RD, 26 Feb 44, sub: Distribution of ASTP Pers. 353/101 (ASTP)(S). (2) AGF M/S (S), Sec to G–1, 14 Feb 44, sub: ASTP Graduates (Journal — CofS), 11 Feb 44. 353/101 (ASTP)(S). (3) WD D/F WDGAP 353 ASTP (S), G–1 to CG AGF, 16 Feb 44, sub: Reduction in ASTP. 353/100 (ASTP)(S). (4) AGF M/S (S), G–1 Control Div to G–1, 26 Feb 44, sub: Rpt concerning Distribution of ASTP Students. 353/100 (ASTP)(S).

[84] (1) WD Gen Council Min (S), 27 Mar 44. (2) WD memo WDGCT 220.3 (24 Mar 44) for CG AGF, 29 Mar 44, sub: Almt of Pers Released by AAF. 220.3/2119.

[85] Cir 93, WD, 3 Mar 44.

[86] AAF memo to G–3 WD, inclosed with WD memo cited in n. 84(2).

[87] Cir 70, WD, 16 Feb 44, sub: NCOs.

[88] (1) AGF ltr (R) to CGs, 26 Feb 44, sub: Distribution of ASTP Pers. 353/101 (ASTP)(R). (2) AGF ltr to CGs, 6 Apr 44, sub: Distribution of Avn Cadet Tng Pers. 220.3/2129½ (R). (3) AGF memo (R) to CG AAF, 6 Apr 44, sub: Almt of Pers Released by AAF. 220.3/115 (R).

[89] ASF memo SPX 220.3 (1 May 44) OC–T for CG AGF, 1 May 44, sub: Transfer of 15,000 AGF EM to ASF. 354.1/4 (Reassgmt Cens).

the average over 1,500 ASTP students each. Twenty-two divisions received on the average about 1,000 aviation cadets each. All divisions still in the United States, except those scheduled for earliest shipment overseas and the 10th Mountain Division, which contained an exceptional proportion of high-grade men, received infusions of the new manpower. Some infantry divisions, those which were most depleted or which had the lowest intelligence ratings, obtained over 3,000 men from the two sources combined. All divisions assigned the ASTP students and aviation cadets mainly to their infantry components.

The effect on the training of troops was immediate. Divisions whose officers and men were depressed by the loss of their old personnel, and discouraged by the thought that they might become purely replacement organizations doomed not to go overseas as units, were revived in spirit by the incoming trainloads of high-quality young men. The newcomers faced a difficult problem of personal readjustment, since their sudden transfer to the Infantry placed them in a type of service very different from all they had been led to expect. They nevertheless proved with a few exceptions to be excellent soldiers. With their superior intelligence they could absorb infantry training more rapidly than the type of men usually received by the ground arms. Divisions could therefore, despite personnel turnover, still meet the readiness dates required by strategic plans. After inspecting certain of these divisions General McNair reported that with a period of retraining they would be better divisions than those previously dispatched to the theaters.[90] The 26th Division, for example, benefited by the redistribution of men by AGCT classes as follows:[91]

	I	*II*	*III*	*IV – V*	*Total*
Percentage Distribution before Transfers of Aviation Cadets and ASTP Students (1 Nov 43)	4	30	36	30	100
Percentage Distribution after Transfers of Aviation Cadets and ASTP Students (after Mar 44)	8	36	30	26	100

The 26th Division was not entirely typical. Its earlier distribution was considerably better than that of most divisions, which in November 1943 had on the average about 28 percent of their enlisted personnel in AGCT Classes I and II, and 38 percent in Classes IV and V.[92] On the other hand, the 26th Division received fewer ASTP students and aviation cadets than most divisions.

[90] WD Gen Council Min (S), 10 Apr, 10 Jul 44.
[91] AGF memo (C) for G–3 WD, 17 Jun 44, sub: Asgmt of Enl Pers. 327.3/104 (C).
[92] See tables in 327.3/7 (sep file) (S).

With rising quantitative requirements, the War Department in April 1944 approved a program to encourage men in other arms and services to volunteer for the Infantry.[93] How much the quality of the Infantry improved through this process is not clear. Some Infantry volunteers were chronic malcontents dissatisfied in their old units. Others were culls made to volunteer for the Infantry by pressure from their commanders. But most seem to have been men desiring more active duty as the tempo of operations overseas speeded up. A study made at AGF headquarters in June 1944 indicated that Infantry volunteers were generally somewhat younger and of somewhat higher intelligence than the average infantryman in November 1943.[94] The total number of volunteers is difficult to ascertain since many were reassigned by commanders without reference to Washington. As of 30 September 1944, 22,822 voluntary transfers to the Infantry had been recorded by The Adjutant General, including about 13,000 from sources outside the Ground Forces, of which 7,051 were from the Service Forces and 4,548 from the Air Forces. In addition, in this period 25,000 volunteers were obtained for the parachute troops, most of whom were infantrymen; but 22,000 of the 25,000 came from within the Ground Forces—most, it may be supposed, from the Infantry itself.[95]

Inactivation of AGF units, notably antiaircraft, and conversion of their personnel to other arms, notably Infantry, was of the greatest importance in meeting quantitative requirements in 1944 but probably made no significant change in quality of personnel in the receiving units, except, to some degree, in age. A survey of 65,000 enlisted men in antiaircraft battalions in the Army Ground Forces in November 1943 disclosed that, though they were somewhat younger, they were distributed by AGCT classes in about the same proportion as men in divisions at that time.[96]

Average age in certain divisions was further reduced by the sudden absolute prohibition, imposed in June 1944, of the sending of 18-year-olds overseas as infantry or armored replacements. Over 22,000 men in training at this time in infantry and armored replacement centers were due to be graduated before their nineteenth birthdays. The Army Ground Forces assigned them to seventeen divisions, since it was permissible for 18-year-olds to go overseas as members of

[93] (1) Cir 132, WD, 6 Apr 44. (2) WD Gen Council Min (S), 8 May, 15 May, 5 Jun, 28 Aug 44.

[94] AGF M/S, C&RD to G–1, 9 Jun 44, sub: Transfer to Inf. 220.3/220 (Inf Prog).

[95] WD memo (R) AGPEA 220.3 (11 Oct 44), TAG for G–1, 11 Oct 44, sub: Voluntary Transfer and Asgmt of EM to Inf and Prcht Units. 220.3/106 (Inf)(R).

[96] See tables in 327.3/7 (sep file)(S).

organized units, and some would in any case be nineteen by the time their divisions were shipped. The seventeen divisions supplied 22,000 older men to overseas replacement depots to fill the gap created in the replacement stream.[97] Some of these "older men" were no doubt recently converted ASTP students, aviation cadets, or antiaircraft personnel with a minimum of infantry training. Infantry personnel of divisions shipped during most of 1944 had been almost completely renewed since the beginning of the year. In the last nine infantry divisions sent to the European Theater (those sent after October 1944) only a quarter of the enlisted men in the infantry regiments had been in the regiments since the preceding January.[98] Slightly less than a quarter had been ASTP students or aviation cadets. Slightly more than a quarter had been converted from other arms, mainly antiaircraft. Roughly the remaining quarter were recent graduates of the infantry replacement training centers, that is, men with only a little over four months' service in the Army. Experience of the latter three groups in their regiments ranged from five or six months down to a few days. Thus the divisions and their component infantry regiments were imperfectly trained according to the standards of the Army Ground Forces. But in the quality of individual infantrymen—in youth, intelligence, and physical vigor—they were better than most divisions shipped before the middle of 1944.

In addition to ASTP personnel and aviation cadets, the Army Ground Forces looked upon the enlisted men qualified for overseas duty who were serving in fixed installations in the Zone of Interior as a source to improve the quality of the combat arms. "Qualified for overseas duty" meant men who were qualified physically, were under thirty-five, had not served overseas since December 1941, and had been assigned to a fixed installation for over a year. At a time when the demand for combat troops was increasingly critical, with combat units being stripped for replacements and with the War Department concerned over the use of 18-year-olds and pre-Pearl Harbor fathers as infantry riflemen, some 600,000 able-bodied soldiers, enough for two or three field armies, were occupying jobs in overhead organizations which would never take them outside the United States. About 42,000 were in the Ground Forces, 158,000 in the Service Forces, and 400,000 in the Air Forces.[99]

On 14 January 1944, by an "Immediate Action" letter, the War Department directed that these men be reassigned, "as rapidly as practicable and in any event

[97] AGF ltr (R) to CGs, 20 Jul 44, sub: Asgmt of 18-year-old IRTC Graduates. 341/208 (R).

[98] AGF memo (S) for OPD, 19 Oct 44, sub: Pers Status of Certain Divs. 320.2/760 (S).

[99] Statistical Summary, Col 1, Rpt dated 18 Mar 44, as of 29 Feb 44, WD Gen Council Min (S), 14 Aug 44.

by 30 June 1944," to activities in which overseas duty was intended.[100] They were to be replaced in the Zone of Interior by civilians, WAC's, over-age enlisted men, physically inferior enlisted men, or enlisted men who had already served overseas. The deadline was later moved back to 31 October 1944, then abandoned altogether.[101] Men who could not be properly reassigned within their own major force were to be reported to The Adjutant General for disposition. On 20 January 1944, in discussing the 1944 Troop Basis, G–3 of the War Department announced that, "for both quantitative and qualificative reasons," extensive transfers of manpower among the major forces could be expected.[102]

The directive of 14 January was successfully carried out in the Ground Forces and the Service Forces. Trainer personnel at AGF schools and replacement centers, a form of overhead to which general-service men had formerly been assigned on the principle that they should be capable of rotation into tactical units, were now obtained from men not qualified for overseas service, including men who had seen overseas service already and whose presence as instructors was in any case thought to be desirable for that reason. Men not qualified for overseas service had been assigned to administrative overhead ever since August 1942. This process was speeded up and completed in 1944. By October 1944 virtually all the 42,000 qualified enlisted men in AGF Zone of Interior positions had been transferred to the field forces.[103]

The Army Air Forces found it more difficult to comply with the War Department directive. About a third of the strength of the Air Forces was in fixed installations in the Zone of Interior.[104] Since the beginning of mobilization no attempt had been made to assign physically limited men to the Air Forces in proportion to the requirements of the Air Forces for Zone of Interior personnel.

[100] (1) WD ltr (C) AG 220.3 (14 Jan 44) OB–C–A to CG AGF, 14 Jan 44, sub: EM — Utilization of Manpower Based on Physical Capacity. (2) WD ltr (C) AG 331.1 (21 Dec 43) OB–S–A, 5 Jan 44, sub as in (1). Both in 327.3/101 (LS)(C). (3) Cir 100, WD, 9 Mar 44.

[101] (1) WD ltr AG 220.3 (2 Oct 44) OC–E–WDGAP–MP–M to CGs AGF, ASF, and MDW, sub: EM—Utilization of Manpower Based on Physical Capacity. 220.3/305 (LD). (2) Papers in 320.2 (O'seas Repls 1944).

[102] WD memo (S) WDGCT 320 TB (30 Dec 43) for CofS USA, 20 Jan 44, sub: Implementation of 1944 TB. 310.2/8 (TUB 44)(S).

[103] (1) AGF 1st ind to CGs, 20 Jan 44, on WD ltr of 14 Jan cited in n. 100 (1). 220.3/305 (LD). (2) AGF ltr to CGs, 13 Apr 44, sub: Utilization and Conservation of Manpower. 220.3/357 (LD). (3) AGF ltr to CGs, 26 Aug 44, sub: EM — Utilization of Manpower Based on Physical Capacity. 220.3/552 (LD). (4) AGF 1st ind, 11 Oct 44, on WD ltr AGO B–C–A 220.3 (3 Oct 44) to CG AGF, 6 Oct 44, sub and location as in (3).

[104] "Army Strength Remaining in U. S. when Overseas Deployment is Complete," App "C" (Clear), WD Gen Council Min (S), 30 Oct 44.

230-171 O - 66 - 7

The number of physically limited men in the Air Forces in 1944, even when supplemented by men returned from overseas, was not sufficient to fill AAF Zone of Interior positions. The replacement of qualified men in such positions by an equal number of other men presented a staggering problem of reassignment and retraining. On 31 August 1944 there were still in AAF overhead positions 395,595 enlisted men qualified for overseas service—about 95 percent of all qualified men remaining in overhead positions in the United States.[105]

Noting the failure of the Air Forces to comply with the directive of 14 January, the War Department in September 1944 ordered that the Army Ground Forces, in each month from October to December inclusive, make available to the Army Air Forces 5,000 men not qualified for overseas service, receiving in return an equal number of men who were so qualified.[106] As far as was feasible the Army Ground Forces exchanged men who were equal in AGCT scores and attempted to supply men with SSN's usable by the Air Forces.[107] The advantage to be gained by the Army Ground Forces was in physical quality.

On 30 October the War Department took a more drastic step by ordering the Army Air Forces and the Army Service Forces each to transfer to the Army Ground Forces 25,000 enlisted men qualified for overseas duty.[108] This step, resulting from the increasingly critical shortage of men qualified for infantry duty, initiated an extensive process of transfer among the major commands that continued until the end of the war in Europe. Between October 1944 and May 1945 the Army Ground Forces received approximately 100,000 men from other Zone of Interior sources, almost all of whom were assigned to infantry advanced replacement training centers (IARTC's) for retraining as combat soldiers. The Air Forces supplied about 60,000 of these men, the Service Forces 28,000, and other Zone of Interior sources 12,500.[109]

Although all the men transferred to the Army Ground Forces were supposed to be qualified for infantry training—at least 90 percent were to be Profile A

[105] WD Gen Council Min (S), 9 Oct 44.

[106] (1) WD memo (R) WDGAP 220.33 for DCofS USA, 19 Sep 44, sub: Transfer of EM Physically Disqualified for O'seas. (2) WD D/F (R) WDGAP 220.03 to AGF, AAF, 12 Sep 44, sub: Transfer of EM. Both in 220.3/143 (R).

[107] See papers in 220.3/143 (R).

[108] (1) WD memo (S) WDGCT 220 (30 Oct 44) to CG AAF, 30 Oct 44, sub: Transfer of EM, as amended 23 Nov 44. (2) WD memo WDGCT 320 (RTC) (30 Oct 44) for CG AGF, 30 Oct 44, sub: Capacity of RTCs. Both in 220.01/5 (S).

[109] Statistics compiled from weekly report, "Analysis of Profiles and AGCT of EM received at AGF IARTC's from AAF, ASF and DC's," in 220.33 (Trans between Services), binders 1 and 2.

men—many of those shipped to IARTC's were not so qualified. Training centers actually received about 82 percent of Profile A men, and only about 90,000 of the total number received could be retrained as infantry. On the other hand, the men transferred into the Ground Forces were both physically and mentally superior to those being assigned to the Ground Forces by reception centers during this same period, as shown in the following tabulation:[110]

Accession of Enlisted Men by Army Ground Forces, January–April 1945

			Percentage Distribution by AGCT Classes		
	Number	*Percentage in Profile A*	*I–II*	*III*	*IV–V*
Transferred to AGF from Other ZI Sources (31 Dec 44–5 May 45)	65,010	85.0	32.5	34.5	33.0
Assigned to AGF by Reception Centers (1 Jan–30 Apr 45)	261,426	74.5	26.5	35.0	38.5

The transfer of men into the Army Ground Forces materially improved, therefore, the over-all quality of the manpower available to it in the winter and spring of 1944–45.

In exchange for the physically qualified men received from other Zone of Interior sources, the Army Ground Forces transferred to the Air and Service Forces a considerable number of men of low physical quality who could not be used for overseas duty. These transfers began in October 1944 and continued into the following summer. In the first four months of 1945 the Ground Forces transferred about 22,500 such men to the Air Forces and about 17,500 to the Service Forces.[111] These transfers likewise tended to raise the average quality of AGF troops by subtracting a sizable portion of the physically unqualified men from their number.

The large-scale transfers of physically qualified men into the Ground Forces in the winter and spring of 1944–45 helped to meet the shortage of infantry trainees as well as to improve the over-all quality of ground combat troops. By V-E Day the infantry crisis had abated, and the process of transfer among the major commands was reversed. The receipt of AAF and ASF men at IARTC's had practically ceased by April, and in early May the War Department ordered

[110] (1) *Ibid.* (2) Annual Report, 1945 (R), C&RD, AGF.

[111] Annual Report, 1945 (R), C&RD, AGF.

the Army Ground Forces to transfer to the Army Service Forces 12,500 partially trained infantrymen in order to meet shortages in ASF units that were to be sent overseas.[112]

The transfer of 100,000 men to the Ground Forces marked the climax of a process that had been going on since the beginning of 1944. To the end of 1943, the need for technical and flying personnel took priority in the assignment of manpower over the need for ground combat soldiers. Priorities were reversed in 1944. The need for combat soldiers, especially infantrymen, first assumed priority over the Army Specialized Training Program, the most easily dispensable large item in the Troop Basis. Then it took priority over the desirability of a large reserve of aviation cadets. In receiving ASTP students and aviation cadets the Ground Forces for the most part only received back men formerly lost—men withdrawn from training as ground combat soldiers in the days when college training and flying training were judged to be of higher priority. When the recruiting of aviation cadets in AGF organizations was discontinued, and the program of encouraging volunteering for the infantry was adopted, the benefits of voluntary interbranch transfer were withdrawn from the Air Corps and conferred on the Infantry. Nonvoluntary transfer to positions of higher combat value was first applied within the Army Ground Forces, notably in the conversion of antiaircraft personnel to infantry. In the fall of 1944 the process of transfer was extended to affect the other two major commands.

In all, the Army Ground Forces received about 200,000 enlisted men from other elements of the Army during 1944 and 1945, most of whom were of a comparatively high type both physically and mentally. These transfers were a recognition of the fact that the war had reached a phase in which, with the bulk of the Army overseas, the need for maintenance troops in the United States had diminished and the provision of qualified battle replacements had become a major concern of the War Department. The effect was to improve considerably the quality of the manpower available to the ground combat arms in the last year of World War II.

In retrospect, the experience of the Army Ground Forces with the quality of its personnel during the war pointed to basic shortcomings in the provisions for allocating the Nation's manpower, not only within the Army itself, but also among the Army, Navy, and Marine Corps. The fact that, within the Army, the men assigned to the ground combat arms after February 1942 were below

[112] (1) WD memo (R) SPGAG/220.3 Gen (9 May 45)–357 for CG AGF, 10 May 45, sub: Transfer of EM to ASF. (2) AGF ltr (R) to CG R&SC, 10 May 45, sub: Transfer of Inf EM to ASF. Both in 320.2 (ASF).

the average established by the Army General Classification Test is undeniable. Opinions will differ as to what facts had a decisive influence in producing this result. Some will argue that the absence of accurate tests indicative of combat aptitude and of the qualities of leadership was responsible. Others will emphasize the need for rapid mobilization, which put a premium on previous occupational experience in forming the Army, or will stress the decision, based on the strategic situation in the early years of the war, to assign preference to the Army Air Forces. Still others will find an explanation of the predicament of the Ground Forces in measures which permitted or forced the transfer of high-quality ground combat personnel to the Air and Service Forces and the Army Specialized Training Program and which did not provide for prompt return to the Ground Forces of men who failed to qualify for their new jobs.

The Army Ground Forces naturally protested against the diversion of high-quality personnel from ground combat assignments and pointed out the resulting effects on its efficiency in performing its mission. Its protests echoed, from the first, two of General McNair's deepest convictions regarding the conduct of war. One was that, in spite of peacetime impressions to the contrary, the United States did not have unlimited resources of high-caliber manpower with which to fight the enemy, and therefore that maximum economy and concentration on combat effectiveness would be necessary to win the war. The other was that, large as was the part which machines on the ground and in the air might be expected to play, the contact of fighting men with the enemy on the battlefield would be a decisive factor. Both of these views were verified by experience.

Remedies for the situation mentioned above were sought and applied. The one most effective in raising the quality of the Ground Forces was the wholesale restoration or transfer of large numbers of men from the ASTP and the Air and Service Forces in 1944 and 1945, made necessary by quantitative shortages in the Ground Forces which had reached critical proportions. But by February 1944, when large transfusions of high-quality men from other commands began, nearly half the divisions had been shipped overseas; the men who had been received by the Ground Forces during the period of mobilization had been built into the structure, and this had conditioned the training of all divisions activated since the outbreak of the war. The retraining of the divisions that did receive new men in 1944 had to be hasty and fell below the standards of the training program, so that the qualitative improvement did not result in a proportionate increase of combat efficiency. Another remedy tried was the Infantry Program, which gave infantrymen in combat somewhat better pay and a badge which became a coveted honor. Another was the Physical Profile system. Although it was adopted too late and administered too loosely to produce decisive results, it pointed out a direction in which a solution for the problem of pre-selecting men suitable to the needs of the Ground Forces might be found. A solution for the problem of assigning to the Ground Forces men with adequate combat qualifications will continue to be a matter for national concern until ground combat can safely be eliminated from calculations in regard to war.

The Procurement of Officers

by

Robert R. Palmer and William R. Keast

Contents

Tables

I. General Requirements and Policies

The proper training and effectiveness of enlisted men in combat depend on the competence and personal qualities of the officers commissioned to train and lead them. In all modern armies the majority of officers as well as of enlisted men have to be procured in time of war from the eligible civilian population and trained partially or completely for military duty after mobilization begins. In the United States this task is especially difficult because of the relatively small professional Army and the perennial minimization of the Military Establishment in times of peace. When the Army began to mobilize in 1940 it had only 14,000 professional officers. This number could not be increased materially during the war, though some officers who had resigned or retired from the Regular Army could be recalled to active duty, and graduations at the U.S. Military Academy were speeded up. The vast majority of the officers required in all branches for the multifarious tasks of planning, mobilization, training, administration, and combat of the Army, rapidly expanding to a mass of 8,300,000 men and women, had to be drawn from three sources: from those who had received some training in peacetime military agencies—the National Guard, the Officers' Reserve Corps, the Reserve Officers' Training Corps, and the Citizens' Military Training Camps; from the limited group of civilians whose technical or administrative skills could be used without military training; and from the officer candidate schools created in 1941 to convert eligible enlisted men into officers.

The situation in 1941 was better than in 1917. A backlog of ROTC officers had been trained in peacetime. Thanks to improved training in the National Guard and to the efficiency of the service schools of the Army between the two wars, many of the nonprofessional officers available had had a preparation which conformed more closely than in 1917 to professional military standards. But the demands of World War II were greater both in complexity and magnitude, and the task of procuring suitable officers in the numbers required was a huge one. By the end of 1943, when mobilization was nearly complete, about 19,000 officers of the National Guard were in the Federal service. Some 180,000 had been drawn from the Officers' Reserve Corps. Almost 100,000 civilians had been commissioned directly,[1] somewhat less than half as doctors, dentists, and chaplains, the remainder for technical and administrative positions. The largest number of new officers, approximately 300,000 by that time, had been commissioned after graduation from officer candidate schools or as aviation cadets. Altogether about 600,000 ex-civilians were serving as Army officers, according to plans laid and standards set by the small nucleus of the Regular Army. The 15,000 Regular Army officers were outnumbered in the ratio of about 40 to 1 by officers drawn from civilian sources since the beginning of the war.

In the period of mobilization preceding Pearl Harbor the non-Regular officers needed had been drawn chiefly from the "civilian components" of the Army, 18,000 from the National Guard and 80,000 from the Officers' Reserve Corps. Of the latter most were ROTC graduates who had continued their military studies and training since graduation from college. The officer candidate schools, established in July 1941, had by December 1941 produced only a few hundred lieutenants in each branch.[2] The further training of National Guard and Reserve officers, and the elimination of the more obviously unsuitable, were two of the advantages gained by prewar mobilization. With the outbreak of war and the rapid expansion of the Army the need for additional officers mounted sharply, and it was found that the readiness for combat of those already in service still left much to be desired. In February 1942, Lt. Gen. Lesley J. McNair, shortly before assuming command of the Army Ground Forces, stated his view of the situation in an address to a graduating class at the Command and General Staff School. He was reviewing the military training of the preceding year and a half, accomplished under his supervision as Chief of Staff of General Headquarters. He observed that this training had not yet produced first-class combat troops. Officers from the civilian components, instead of being immediately ready to assist in the task of converting a mass of civilians into soldiers, had themselves required a long period of further training. "The outstanding generalization of this experience, in my view," General McNair said, "is that we did not have in fact the great mass of trained officers that were carried on the books. . . . We have verified the inevitable—that inadequately trained officers cannot train troops effectively." [3]

[1] That is, without training; but about 12,000 were former officers, most of them with World War I experience.

[2] Status of Personnel, Army of the United States, Statistics Branch, WDGS, 15 Dec 43, gives officer strength by components at intervals from 30 Jun 40. 320.2/351 (C).

[3] Mimeographed copy of speech in "Addresses delivered by Lt. Gen. Lesley J. McNair." Army War College Library, VA25 M16.

In officer procurement the Army Ground Forces enjoyed certain advantages over the other major commands. Numerical requirements were proportionately lower in the Ground Forces, which according to the 1944 Troop Basis required only 54 officers for each 1,000 enlisted men, whereas the Service Forces required 97 and the Air Forces 156.[4] Since the expansion of the Ground Forces, great as it was, was not as great as that of the Air and Service Forces, the proportion of Regular Army officers remained somewhat higher in the ground arms than in the rest of the Army.[5] It was also of advantage to the Ground Forces that a high proportion of National Guard and Reserve officers had received their peacetime training in the traditional ground arms. These officers, when tested and sifted by experience, constituted a source from which competent leaders in the field grades could be developed.

On the other hand, the Army Ground Forces also faced peculiar difficulties in obtaining officers qualified to meet its requirements. The paramount requirement for officers in the ground arms was capacity to lead men in battle. Administrative positions had to be filled, but, because emergencies of battle might require one officer to step into the place of another, General McNair adhered strictly to the Army's policy of rotating officers between staff and command positions and between headquarters and the field. The specialization of ground officers beyond a certain point was regarded as undesirable, and the Army Ground Forces developed no class of administrative officers as such.[6] Specialties of civilian life, a common basis of commissions in the Army Service Forces, were of little value to a ground combat commander. Again, individual daring and personal skill, emphasized as necessary qualifications of flying officers of the Air Forces, did not suffice to meet the needs of ground combat. In officers of the ground arms these qualities had to be combined with ability to direct the performance of enlisted men and to cooperate with the plans of other officers amid the hazards and uncertainties of battle. The necessary qualities were summed up by the Army Ground Forces in the ideas of responsibility and leadership.

Emphasis on responsibility and troop leadership shaped the policies of the Army Ground Forces in procuring and training officers. In training, this meant

[4] The figures, according to the Troop Basis of 1 April 1944, were as follows: Ground Forces, 168,307; Air Forces, 313,448; Service Forces, 143,215.

[5] As of 31 December 1943, 3.5 percent of the AGF officers were Regular Army, as against 2.6 percent of the ASF and 1.4 percent of the AAF officers.

[6] See AGF memo for CofS USA, 3 Nov 43, sub: Inclusion of MOS Serial Numbers for Offs on T/Os. 210.01/286. AGF officers "are not specialists but are qualified to perform any duty within their arm commensurate with their grade."

keeping officers as much as possible with troops rather than on detached service or in Army schools. In procurement, it meant that very few appointments could be made directly from civilian life and that officers from the "civilian components" of the Army, the National Guard, and the Reserve Corps, and even those from the Regular Army, had to be carefully screened, especially for posts of higher command.

During the period of officer shortage in 1942 Army Ground Forces commissioned a few men directly from civilian life, but only for certain signal and ordnance units. This was accomplished by a process of affiliation in which a group of employees of an industrial concern were organized bodily as a military unit, the higher employees in the civilian group becoming officers in the military unit. The relation of officers and enlisted men under this system did not prove altogether satisfactory. Direct commissioning of civilians for other purposes was negligible in the Ground Forces.

By the summer of 1942, National Guard officers and many Reserve officers had been on active duty for over a year. A general weeding out had followed the GHQ maneuvers of 1941. Regimental commanders and officers for general staff work were needed in increasing numbers in 1942 to meet the activation program. On 16 July Army Ground Forces, observing that such key positions could now be filled by many officers of the Reserve components, directed subordinate commanders to submit lists of names of individuals believed to be qualified.[7] From these lists, appointments were made to new units and to headquarters staffs.

At the height of the officer shortage in the summer of 1942 many requests reached the War Department to expand the Reserve Officers' Training Corps. ROTC students constituted a deferred class under Selective Service and in 1942 they remained in the colleges. Army Ground Forces did not favor an increase in the number of students held in colleges, preferring that they be inducted into the Army and selected for officer candidate schools. The reason for this preference was in part the immediate need for a large supply of potential officer material. But the value as well as the timing of the product was considered. Graduates of the officer candidate schools had greater immediate value as platoon leaders than did recent graduates of the ROTC. After several months' service OCS graduates with similar education were found to be more valuable than recent products of the ROTC. "The three months of intensive training undergone in an officer candidate school under war conditions," Army Ground Forces notified the War

[7] AGF ltr (C) to CGs, 16 Jul 42, sub: Rpt on Qualification of Offs. 201.6/4 (C). Lists submitted from the field are in this file and in clear file 201.6/233ff.

Department, "is far superior to the full ROTC course." Army Ground Forces advised against expansion of the ROTC, and no expansion took place.[8] Instead, beginning in the summer of 1942, men who had not completed the full ROTC course before leaving college were, upon induction into the Army, assigned to officer candidate schools and given the regular OCS course.

Late in 1942 the War Department initiated plans for sending selected enlisted men to civilian colleges. At first this Army Specialized Training Program (ASTP) was thought of as a source of commissioned personnel. General McNair opposed it. It threatened, by diverting the ablest young men to the campuses, to keep them out of officer candidate schools at a time when officer candidates were urgently needed and difficult to procure. It was feared also that the most intelligent youth of the country, if educated at college in technical specialties, would be lost to the ground arms as combat leaders. General McNair believed that the Army possessed a sufficient backlog of college men to last through 1944.[9] Launched late in 1942 over the opposition of Army Ground Forces, the ASTP was virtually dissolved early in 1944. By that time the demand for new officers had almost ceased. Large numbers of ASTP trainees who might have become graduates of officer candidate schools remained enlisted men.

The officer candidate schools were established in July 1941 in accordance with plans written into Mobilization Regulations. They took the place of the officer training camps of World War I, but with the distinctive feature that candidates were restricted to warrant officers and enlisted men who had had a minimum of from four to six months of service at the date of admission.[10] The basic aim was to substitute a competitive and democratic system of procurement for the rather haphazard selection of young officers from a social and intellectual elite which had appeared necessary, for lack of a better means, in World War I. The Army Ground Forces profited immensely from the operation of these schools. It valued them highly as a means of procuring and training the type of junior officers it needed. They became by far the largest source of its commis-

[8] AGF memo for G–3 WD, 20 Jul 42, sub: Study on Expansion of ROTC. 326.6/64.

[9] AGF memo (S) for CG SOS, 4 Oct 42, sub: The Army College Tng Prog. 353/119 (S).

[10] (1) Four months for replacement trainees, six for other enlisted men. (2) Activation was initiated by WD memo G–3/25445 for the CofS, 19 Sep 40, sub: Officer Candidate Schs. AGO Records, AG 352 (9–19–40) (1) Sec 1, Part 1. (3) Basic plans are in MR 1–4 and 3–1. (4) The basic letter directing their activation is WD ltr 352 (4–10–41) MM–C, 26 Apr 41, sub: Officer Candidate Schools. (5) While the great majority of officer candidates in the ground arms were selected from the ranks, from 1942 onward they also trained ROTC men and Volunteer Officer Candidates who had been selected for officer training before induction into the Army.

sioned personnel. By the end of 1943, with mobilization almost complete, nearly 114,000 officers had been graduated from the officer candidate schools of the Army Ground Forces. They constituted about two-thirds of all officers serving in the ground arms. In the grades of captain and lieutenant the proportion of officer candidate school graduates was considerably higher than two-thirds. By the end of the war in the Pacific, more than 136,000 officers had been graduated from the AGF officer candidate schools. (See Table No. 2.) The officer problem in the Army Ground Forces was essentially a problem of procurement and training of officer candidates.

Every large AGF organization became a mosaic of officers from various sources. The higher echelons had the highest proportion from the Regular Army. At AGF headquarters, as of 31 December 1943, 48 percent of the commissioned personnel were Regular Army,[11] and until early 1944 no officer above lieutenant colonel belonged to the civilian components.[12] In divisions the proportion of Regulars averaged under 5 percent; the 31st Division, originally National Guard, contained less than 1 percent, with only five Regular Army officers assigned to it.[13] In regiments, OCS graduates outnumbered all others. One regimental commander, in a letter to a friend who had been designated to command a regiment in a new division, described the officer texture of a typical infantry regiment in 1943 as follows:[14]

> You will find your officer cadre something like this: Your executive officer probably a regular officer of the class of 1924 to '27, probably one regular battalion commander, one reserve officer and one National Guard. Probably two-thirds of your company commanders will be graduates of officer candidate schools, the remaining one-third will be principally National Guard and only a few reserve. My executive and I are at present the only two Regular Army officers in this regiment. I am the only graduate of West Point in this regiment .... [About 150 second lieutenants, the colonel explained, would be fresh out of officer candidate school.] Let me say a word about these OCS people in case you have not had any contact with them. They are far in the way the best that I have seen in the Army, and for the job they have to do I had just as soon have them as any graduate of the Military Academy joining his first regiment. They are well grounded, interested in their job, industrious, ambitious, and on the ball twenty-four hours a day. Since November 1,

[11] Hq AGF, Strength Report, Officers, 31 Dec 43. AGF AG Sec.

[12] Lieutenant Colonels V. A. St. Onge, J. H. Banville, and A. L. Harding, all ORC, were promoted to colonel on 22 January 1944. They were respectively, Chief of the Task Force Division, G-4; Chief of the Classification and Replacement Division, AG; and Chief of the Troop Movements Division, G-3.

[13] Status of Personnel, Army of the United States, Statistics Branch, WDGS, 15 Dec 43. 320.2/351 (C).

[14] Copy of personal ltr, 22 Mar 43, in confidential file, AGF G-1 Sec.

I have not had more than five cases which necessitated my taking disciplinary action, and of these five only one was a drinking case. They are much better behaved than any similar group of young men I have ever seen.

The selection and promotion of higher commanders in the Ground Forces involved special problems, policies, and relationships which did not attend the commissioning and assignment of junior officers and those in the lower field grades. All Army officers were officially commissioned and all officers in the higher grades were promoted by authority of The Adjutant General, acting as agent of the War Department. The commanders of newly activated regiments and groups in the Army Ground Forces were assigned on designation of the Commanding General of the Army Ground Forces. For a time General McNair delegated authority to assign officers up to and including the grade of colonel to his subordinate commanders. In August 1943 Army Ground Forces, to prevent the transfer of regimental and group commanders to staff work, as well as to avoid needless turnover and to extend the employment of officers returning from combat, assumed direct control over the assignment of colonels.[15] Army and corps commanders had shown an inclination to transfer the ablest colonels to their staffs, but General McNair believed strongly in the principle that the most vigorous and effective officers should occupy positions of command.

Gen. George C. Marshall, with the advice of his G–1, designated the general officers who were to command the largest ground force units—armies, corps, and divisions. The War Department also controlled promotions to general-officer grades. These were of special importance to the Army Ground Forces since until well into 1944 the number of general officers under its supervision was considerably larger than that in any other command of the Army. On 31 July 1943 the Army Ground Forces had 298 general officers, including 2 lieutenant generals (commanding the Second and Third Armies), almost 100 major generals, and over 200 brigadier generals, the total constituting nearly 30 percent of the general officers in the U.S. Army. The number subsequently declined as troops moved overseas.[16] In both the promotion of generals and their assignment to ground commands General McNair exercised a very considerable influence.

In the field of promotion to general-officer grades, General McNair was called upon, as commander of the Army Ground Forces, to advise regarding such

[15] (1) AGF ltr to CGs, 8 Oct 42, sub: Asgmt and Reasgmt of Individual Offs and Warrant Offs. (2) AGF M/S, CofS to G–1, 17 Aug 43, sub: Use of Regtl Comdrs on Corps or Army Staff. (3) AGF ltr to CGs, 29 Aug 43, sub: Asgmt of Offs. All in 210.31/3648.

[16] Monthly Strength of the Army, 31 Jul 43. AGO Machine Records Branch. 320.2 (C).

230-171 O - 66 - 8

promotions even in theaters of operations. It was important to maintain standards of promotion which were uniform as between ground commanders overseas and those at home who would presently go overseas in turn, both in order to maintain morale and to assure the placing of the best men available in important positions. Generals had to be interchangeable as between the Zone of Interior and theaters. Under the policy of using battle-experienced officers in training, many officers were brought back from theaters to the United States, where, if their experience had been in the ground arms, General McNair had to find posts for them commensurate with their rank. In the spring of 1943 General Marshall suggested to him that he dispatch a deputy to coordinate promotions overseas with those at home, thus extending an influence which General McNair evidently felt constrained to use sparingly. General Marshall wrote: "While your responsibility is technically confined to the continental United States outside the Coast Defense Commands, I want you to feel a responsibility to me regarding the entire field of Ground Force promotions. While G–1 keeps the check on this for me, your knowledge is more intimate in most cases."[17] General McNair preferred not to send a deputy into the theaters but to adhere to the existing procedure by which G–1 of the War Department General Staff sought the opinion of General McNair on the recommendations of theater commanders for promotions to general-officer grades.

By this system, common standards were maintained through G–1 of the War Department General Staff, which submitted to General McNair the recommendations of theater commanders for promotions to the general-officer grades. Sometimes, at least until the middle of 1943, when the need for additional generals rather suddenly declined (owing to previous promotions, Troop Basis reductions, and reorganization in the armored divisions), General McNair requested G–1 of the War Department to ask theater commanders for recommendations. Comparing the records of overseas officers with the records of officers under his own command, General McNair made recommendations as to whether the overseas officers, if they were in the Ground Forces, should be considered for promotion. His answer was frequently negative. "Age" (meaning older than about fifty for promotion to brigadier general) and "not sufficiently outstanding" were the most common reasons given for disapproval.[18]

In the field of assignments and promotions in the Ground Forces at home

[17] Memo (S) of Gen Marshall for Gen McNair, 29 Mar 43. 322.98/82 (S).

[18] Various cases appear in the AGF "commander files." 322.98 (S).

General McNair's recommendations normally prevailed. They were almost invariably decisive in the choice of division commanders. In all instances except two, suggestions for division command originated with General McNair; in only one instance did the War Department turn down a nominee of General McNair for division command, and this officer subsequently was given a division which he led with distinction in the European Theater.[19]

Because of these responsibilities, it was continuously necessary for General McNair to evaluate the performance of general officers, to keep in mind colonels best suited for promotion, to estimate the maximum future potentialities of officers known or described to him, and to watch and constantly reappraise the performance of men in positions which they already occupied. The responsibility was the greater since it was an accepted principle that a commander who carried a unit through its training should also lead it into battle. The effect of all training policies and directives depended on the force and intelligence of the commanders who carried them out. The quality of combat leadership down the whole chain of command depended, not on regulations and orders, but on the moral courage of commanders in eliminating ineffectual or unreliable subordinates, and on their discernment in finding the best men to replace them. It was an enormous waste and risk to appoint as a division commander a man who could not do the job, for not only was time lost in making the division ready to fight, but the limited opportunity for future battle commanders to gain experience in handling large units was misspent.

In choosing higher commanders General McNair relied mainly on a close study of their records. He attached great weight to General Efficiency Ratings, since they consolidated the judgments of all commanders under whom an officer had served during the preceding ten years. Only an officer with a high General Efficiency Rating—if possible above 6.5, rarely below 6.0—would be considered. Other things being equal, and age being within acceptable limits, he gave preference to seniority on the promotion list, regarding seniority as a measure of experience. Noting especially the succession of assignments in which an officer had spent his military career, he demanded definite evidence of successful duty with troops. It was a great advantage that he knew personally, from years past, most of the men coming within range of consideration.[20]

[19] (1) Statement of Gen A. R. Bolling to AGF Hist Off, 4 Jul 44. (2) Information obtained from McNair Personal Correspondence.

[20] Consultation of Hist Off with CofS AGF, and documents in file 322.98 (S).

Initial selection was only the beginning. Once appointed, high commanders remained under scrutiny of all higher echelons, including Army Ground Forces. If a commander failed to justify expectations, General McNair took the position that, once his shortcomings were verified, the sooner he was relieved the better, in order that his replacement might obtain a maximum of experience before facing the test of combat. At the same time caution had to be used against precipitate removals, not only to avoid injustice but also because the number of men qualified for high command was too small to permit waste.

A few concrete cases will illustrate ways in which General McNair handled his responsibility for the quality of his higher commanders.[21] They reflect his ideas of the qualifications necessary for military leadership.

The commander of a division was reported to have resorted to intimidation of enlisted men and to have upbraided and publicly humiliated his officers. Senior subordinates were seeking reassignment, and the whole division was reported to be restless and resentful. General McNair was in agreement with the corps commander that, while the general in question was rough in his methods, he was an able and valuable officer. He handled the matter unofficially, sending the division commander a short private homily on leadership:

> Methods of leadership, as we all know, vary widely. I hold to no one particular procedure; the only criterion is the results obtained. However, I refuse flatly to believe that our officers today, especially those of the Regular Army, are unwilling to follow a division commander in his efforts to build a new division. If you have experienced difficulty along this line, I believe that the fault is yours in part. Either you are too impatient, considering conditions, or your methods are faulty. There is something wrong, I incline to believe, even though your objectives are above reproach . . . . My whole experience fixes my belief that the first essential of an efficient command is a happy one—the happiness, or contentment, if you will, being based on confidence in the leadership and a realization that the leader's demands are just, reasonable, and necessary for victory in war.

The commander in question remained with his division, which presently quieted down, and he led it effectively in combat.

In another division an assistant commander made himself useless by excessive drinking. He was at times incoherent and unsteady, and was found by his subordinates to be unable to carry responsibility. The division commander long postponed action, but finally took steps resulting in his removal. The matter did not stop there. The division commander was himself removed. For allowing such

[21] The following paragraphs are based upon documents in the McNair Correspondence and in AGF file 322.98 (S).

a situation to develop so far, and for yielding to personal reluctance to hurt a brother officer, he was judged unsuited to command a division and was transferred to a nontactical post.

A third division was commanded by a major general on whom General McNair had passed a favorable though not final judgment. After the division had been under AGF control for some months, the corps commander recommended the division commander's reclassification; the army commander concurred. Army Ground Forces supported this recommendation, but General Marshall advised a period of waiting until, after longer service in the Army Ground Forces, the division commander's performance could be evaluated more fully. Five months later, after visiting the division, General McNair decided that the time had come to relieve the commander. He wrote to the War Department:

> This occasion, together with my previous observation of the officer, leads me to the conclusion that he is active, intelligent and intensely interested in his division. Doubtless he has the confidence of the mass of his troops, since he has served them devotedly. The fundamental difficulty, however, is that he has at best a restricted military horizon. He commands from his office. He seems incapable of training his division adequately, undoubtedly because he has no proper standard of training in his mind, due to his deficient military background .... I am convinced that the present condition of the division reflects essentially General ____________'s military ceiling, and it is too low, beyond all question. It would be utterly inexcusable to send 15,000 Americans into modern combat under such leadership.

Within a few days the commander in question was replaced.

The conviction of General McNair that every activity of a combat unit was a function of command, together with his adherence to strict accountability as the keystone of military organization, put a heavy strain on the energy and resourcefulness of his top commanders. He personally kept them aware of the weight of responsibility that goes with command. When informed that the commander of a unit that had been training for two years had asked for a G-2 to replace the one who had been given a new assignment, he wrote the commander a personal letter reading in part as follows:

> ... it is inconceivable to me that a division with the experience of yours must be furnished a ready-made G-2. Also, I cannot for one minute understand why a division which is nearing its second anniversary should find it necessary to go outside for an experienced [subordinate] commander. If a . . . division cannot build its own . . . commanders, in my view, there is something sadly lacking.
>
> There is no better way to build leaders than the sort of training which you have had during the last two years. Now you are asking for additional experienced officers out of the 14,000 with which we entered the war, in spite of the fact that the Army now has well over 600,000 officers. If you will ponder the broad situation you cannot but realize, I am

sure, that these fine big divisions must manufacture leaders, not only for their own use but for the higher echelons as well, since the latter do not have the troops with which to manufacture.

On the other hand, when a commander had, in his opinion, lived up to his heavy responsibilities, he bestowed praise in terms equally personal. To a National Guard officer who was about to take his division overseas he wrote:

> I was delighted, impressed, and touched by your letter of Monday. To you and to me it tells an inspiring story of sustained, untiring effort and outstanding achievement. In passing this remarkable paper to General Marshall, I have commented that if the . . . Division does not perform outstandingly in battle, I shall be forced to believe that there is no merit in training, or that the training of the Army Ground Forces has been all wrong . . . . It is all one more example of how a body of troops reflects the character and spirit of its commander. The . . . Division has a great commander, and I doubt not for a moment that no one realizes it better than the soldiers themselves.

The main difference between officers of the junior field and company grades and higher-ranking officers in the Ground Forces was that the latter, because of age and profession, had spent years in preparing themselves for the demands of war. Their specific training for the leadership of units in battle, like that of other officers, had taken place in the units themselves. By supervising the training of his unit, administering its affairs, and employing it in maneuvers, a commander trained himself for his role in combat. General McNair insisted that the principle of keeping officers with troops applied to generals as well as to others. On a few occasions, in connection with very recently developed procedures, high commanders were assembled for indoctrination. Such occasions were the demonstrations in 1942 of air-ground coordination at Fort Benning and of tank destroyer employment at Camp Hood. But as a rule General McNair frowned upon higher commanders taking trips which diverted them from their essential duties. The opening of operations in North Africa gave training commanders an inviting opportunity to make tours of observation. General McNair limited himself to one brief visit. When General Marshall asked whether it might be wise for division commanders, halfway through their divisional training periods, to see some combat operations in North Africa, General McNair replied that division commanders were needed with their divisions; he suggested that a few corps commanders go instead, especially since Gen. Dwight D. Eisenhower wished to limit the number of visitors in his theater.[22] Four AGF corps commanders conse-

[22] (1) Memo (S) of Gen McNair for CofS USA, 27 Feb 43, sub: Obsr Tours O'seas for High Comdrs. 322.98/77 (S). (2) On absence of general officers from units, see AGF ltr to CGs, 31 Jan 43, sub: Interferences with Tng. 353.02/78 (AGF).

quently made tours to North Africa in the spring of 1943. Later in the year Lt. Gen. Courtney H. Hodges, whose Third Army went overseas early in 1944, visited the battle zone in Italy. Maj. Gen. Harry F. Hazlett, commanding the Replacement and School Command, made a similar trip in February 1944.

The practice developed early in 1943 of appointing officers with battle experience to the command of troops who were in training in the United States. Officers with successful experience overseas were appointed to the general-officer positions of new divisions. The cessation of divisional activations in August 1943 terminated this practice. Officers were rotated between Army Ground Forces and the theaters. In the five months following 1 June 1943, Army Ground Forces released six major generals for overseas duty as individual replacements and received twelve major generals from overseas in return, of whom six were given command of divisions, one of a corps, and two of replacement training centers. In the same period Army Ground Forces released eight brigadier generals to theaters of operations and received ten in return.[23]

[23] Memo of Gen McNair for G–1 WD, 22 Oct 43, sub: Battle Experienced High Comdrs. 210.311/524.

II. Procurement During the Period of Mobilization, 1942-43

When the Army Ground Forces was established on 9 March 1942, it took over from the old chiefs of the ground combat arms the responsibility for the training of officer candidates. Since July 1941, when the officer candidate schools had begun to function, the number of candidates to be admitted had been determined by the War Department. No change in this arrangement was made with the establishment of Army Ground Forces; for another year, until March 1943, control over the size of OCS operations remained with the War Department. Although Army Ground Forces took over the personnel functions formerly performed in the offices of the Chiefs of Infantry, Field Artillery, Coast Artillery, and Cavalry, specific exception was made of functions relating to the procurement of officer candidates.[1] The War Department progressively stepped up OCS capacities to keep pace with expansion of the Troop Basis, in order to provide the necessary officers for new units well in advance of their activation. The OCS population, from slight beginnings in 1941, when only 1,389 officers were graduated, leaped upward in the spring of 1942; the number of enlisted candidates increased to a total of 31,025 by 15 January 1943. In all, 54,233 officers were graduated from AGF officer candidate schools during 1942. (See Tables Nos. 1 and 2.)

The Officer Shortage of 1942

While the officer candidate schools were expanding, the procurement of officer candidates in the prescribed numbers was difficult in the extreme. The rapid activations of 1942, outrunning the supply of inductees, left troop units with serious shortages of enlisted personnel.[2] It was necessary to resort to several expedients, including the recruitment of volunteer candidates from civilian life and the award of administrative commissions, to keep the officer candidate schools filled. An AGF directive to the field, dated 4 September 1942, pointed

[1] Par 5 *c* (8), Cir 59, WD, 2 Mar 42.

[2] Comparison of Enlisted Strengths of AGF — by Months (C), 24 May 43. 320.2/297½ (C).

TABLE NO. 1

*Number of Candidates in AGF Officer Candidate Schools, 1942–45**

School	1942			1943				1944							1945
	15 Apr	15 Jul	15 Oct	15 Jan	15 Apr	15 Jul	15 Oct	15 Jan	15 Apr	15 Jun	30 Jun	31 Jul	31 Oct	31 Jan
Antiaircraft Artillery	1,778	3,790	5,719	6,780	6,032	7,078	2,286	876	253	5	5	......	......	....
Armored	1,668	2,081	1,849	3,281	1,479	532	182	145	36	44	40	36	100	299
Cavalry	100	538	687	670	514	167	50	49	......	......	......	......	......	....
Coast Artillery	......	403	559	543	227	195	90	60	......	......	......	......	......	....
Field Artillery	1,318	5,045	4,959	5,340	4,294	1,496	254	255	133	147	132	104	48	456
Infantry	4,782	9,220	13,820	12,621	7,471	4,371	1,152	552	377	381	1,412	3,364	8,812	5,307
Tank Destroyer	......	....	1,657	1,790	1,301	779	354	66	......	......	......	......	......	....
TOTAL	9,646	21,077	29,250	31,025	21,318	14,618	4,368	2,003	799	577	1,589	3,504	8,960	6,062

Source: Statistics Branch, WDGS, Status of Personnel, AUS. 320.2 (C).

*Exclusive of ROTC candidates.

TABLE NO. 2

Graduation of Officer Candidates from AGF Service Schools, 1941–45

School	1941[a]	1942	1943	1944	1945[b]	1941–45[b]
Antiaircraft:						
Enlisted Men	341	9,637	13,370	303	......	23,651
ROTC	0	89	934	517	......	1,540
Total	341	9,726	14,304	820	......	25,191
Armored:						
Enlisted Men	177	4,998	4,590	164	733	10,662
ROTC	0	0	277	672	4	953
Total	177	4,998	4,867	836	737	11,615
Cavalry:						
Enlisted Men	181	1,536	1,464	60	......	3,241
ROTC	0	38	171	39	......	248
Total	181	1,574	1,635	99	......	3,489
Coast Artillery:						
Enlisted Men	......	913	899	55	......	1,867
ROTC	......	9	42	71	......	122
Total	......	922	941	126	......	1,989
Field Artillery:						
Enlisted Men	233	10,902	9,888	417	595	22,035
ROTC	0	70	1,840	1,640	13	3,563
Total	233	10,972	11,728	2,057	608	25,598
Infantry:						
Enlisted Men	457	24,169	19,424	4,135	8,304	56,489
ROTC	0	307	1,765	4,190	217	6,479
Total	457	24,476	21,189	8,325	8,521	62,968
Tank Destroyer:						
Enlisted Men	......	1,565	3,259	77	......	4,901
ROTC	......	0	186	194	......	380
Total	......	1,565	3,445	271	......	5,281
All Schools:						
Enlisted Men	1,389	53,720	52,894	5,211	9,632	122,846
ROTC	0	513	5,215	7,323	234	13,285
TOTAL	1,389	54,233	58,109	12,534	9,866	136,131

Source: Statistics compiled in Hist Div, WDSS, from records of AGO.
[a] First graduations, September 1941. No ROTC graduations until 1942.
[b] Includes graduations of enlisted candidates through 31 August 1945, and of ROTC candidates through 30 June 1945.

out the urgency of the OCS program, cited the case of a company commander relieved for not filling his OCS quota, and urged commanders to use "salesmanship" in recruiting candidates.[3]

In the procurement of officer candidates Army Ground Forces was handicapped by the fact that its enlisted ranks represented a subaverage cross section of the population of the United States.[4] A large proportion of the good men were kept from the Army by the recruiting methods used by the Navy and the Marine Corps. Within the Army the classification system, emphasizing achievement in civilian vocations, tended to concentrate high-grade personnel in technical and noncombat branches. In addition the Army Air Forces, under the "75-percent rule" and its successive equivalents, drew a large proportion of its inductees from the higher intelligence levels of men available to the Army, thereby reducing the number of men of officer caliber assigned to the Ground Forces. In some branches, such as Antiaircraft, Field Artillery, and Engineers, in which mathematical knowledge was needed, it was especially difficult in 1942 for AGF units to meet officer candidate quotas.[5] There was a marked tendency also for able-bodied officer candidates, after basic training in a combat arm, to elect officer candidate school in such branches as Quartermaster and Finance. This practice was stopped by an amendment to Army Regulations.[6] Until March 1944 enlisted men in the ground arms were free to volunteer for training as aviation cadets; thousands of high-quality men were lost by the Ground Forces to the Air Forces in this manner.

Since despite repeated screenings of its units the Army Ground Forces could not supply enough candidates to fill its own schools, AGF schools were thrown open to candidates secured from all branches of the Army.[7] Even this broadening of the base from which selections were to be made did not suffice. It became necessary in the interests of expediency to depart from the theory on which officer procurement had been based. The prevailing Army policy had been to secure new officers from the enlisted ranks of the Army, except for certain

[3] AGF ltr to CGs, 4 Sep 42, sub: Off Candidate Quotas. 352/301 (OCS).

[4] (1) See above, "Procurement of Enlisted Personnel: The Problem of Quality." (2) AGF M/S, G-1 to CofS, 7 Sep 42, sub: Offs for Engr, FA, AA. 352/315 (OCS). (3) AGF 3d wrapper ind to Mtn Tng Cen, 21 Sep 42, on AGF ltr, 8 Sep 42, sub: Apps for OCS. 352/317 (OCS).

[5] (1) WD ltr AG 352 (4-5-42) MT-A-M to CGs, 6 Apr 42, sub: Off Candidates, Technical Branches. 352/147 (OCS). (2) AGF ltr to CG Mtn Tng Cen, 8 Sep 42, sub: Applications for OCS. 352/317 (OCS).

[6] Sec III, Cir 358, WD, 28 Oct 42.

[7] (1) Par 6, Cir 48, WD, 19 Feb 42. (2) Cir 126, WD, 28 Apr 42.

specialists appointed directly from civilian life, and to award commissions within a branch for general duty, including combat leadership. Both these fundamentals had to be modified in 1942.

The volunteer officer candidate (VOC) plan, inaugurated in March 1942, was an attempt to tap a large pool of potential officer material—men deferred from military service.[8] Under the VOC scheme, a man deferred for dependency might apply for officer training with the understanding that if not selected at the replacement training center to which he was sent for basic training, or if not commissioned at an officer candidate school, he could return to civilian life and his former draft status. By December 1942, 38,134 VOC's had been accepted in the Army as a whole; 27,000 were attending officer candidate schools.[9] The program tapered off in 1943, when the need for officers declined, and disappeared late in that year when dependency ceased to confer draft exemption. The VOC program was a source of many officers who, but for the exigencies of procurement that forced its adoption, might have remained outside the military service altogether or accepted commissions in one of the services the officer procurement program of which was less restricted. In 1942 the VOC plan did much to solve, without lowering the quality of officer candidates, the problem of filling officer candidate schools.[10]

But going outside the Army for candidates did not entirely make up for the shortage of officer material. It became necessary in the summer of 1942 to make another breach in the established plan by redefining the qualifications for a commission. According to the original theory every officer was qualified to be a combat leader, and the OCS mission was defined accordingly: "To produce platoon commanders for units of the field forces." [11] Candidates judged to be lacking in leadership qualities were relieved from officer candidate schools. As the shortage of officers mounted, this practice seemed increasingly wasteful. Some 59,000 administrative positions in the Army at large had to be filled, none of which required combat leadership ability. To conserve some of the excellent material being squandered at officer candidate schools under the restrictive view

[8] (1) WD ltr AG 352 (3–19–42) TM–M to CGs, 24 Mar 42, sub: Attendance at OCS of Selective Service Registrants Deferred for Dependency Only. 352/138 (OCS).

[9] WD ltr AG 352 (12–28–42) OB–D–SPAGO to CGs, 30 Dec 42, sub: Volunteer Off Candidates (Quotas Allotted for January 1943). 352/408 (OCS).

[10] For relative performance of VOCs and regular candidates in OCS during 1942, see R&SC 1st ind to CG AGF, 5 Mar 43, on AGF ltr to CG R&SC, 30 Jan 43, sub: Reduction in Volunteer Off Candidate Prog. 352/409 (OCS).

[11] Par 6 *h*, Cir 126, WD, 28 Apr 42.

of fitness for commission, the War Department in June 1942 gave the schools a second mission: "To produce good administrators from those who lack combat leadership qualities." Only when a candidate was unfit for any type of commissioned duty was he to be relieved.[12]

This revision of procurement standards was not popular with the ground arms. The number of administrative positions in the arms was relatively not great. Double classification and complicated bookkeeping procedures reduced flexibility of assignment. In practice the restriction "commissioned for administrative duty only" was generally disregarded, officers being assigned to any duty for which they were needed.[13] No figures are available on the number of men so commissioned in the Ground Forces. By February 1943, the crisis in procurement having passed, the original standards for commission were reinstated and candidates once more had to qualify as potential combat leaders.[14]

With pressure of the strongest kind being exerted to find candidates for officer training, it was inevitable that the system would break down at some point. Actually, the breakdown occurred at several points.

To find enough candidates in units it was necessary to deplete the sources of good noncommissioned officers, a point emphasized by Lt. Gen. Ben Lear in a personal letter written in October 1942 to General McNair.[15] As the enlisted sources were repeatedly picked over, the quality of candidates declined. Despite the desire of officer candidate schools to graduate as many men as possible, the following table indicates that the proportion of enlisted candidates graduating fell steadily through 1942:

	Percentage Graduating		
School	*January 1942*	*July 1942*	*December 1942*
Antiaircraft	82.9 (Apr)	71.4	66.2
Armored	86.2	77.7	75.6
Cavalry	94.5 (Mar)	93.0	88.9
Coast Artillery		88.8	68.5
Field Artillery	80.3 (Feb)	78.3	62.9
Infantry	86.9	84.6	79.2
Tank Destroyer		91.4 (Oct)	88.1

[12] WD TAG ltr (C) to Comdts OCS's, 16 Jun 42, sub: Disposition of Off Candidates Who Lack Combat Leadership but Have Administrative Ability. 210.31/229 (C).

[13] Statement of Maj F. C. Ash, G–1 Sec Hq AGF, to AGF Hist Off.

[14] WD TAG ltr (C) to Comdts OCS's, 16 Feb 43, sub as in n. 12. 210.31/299 (C).

[15] Personal ltr of Gen Lear to Gen McNair, 22 Oct 42, quoted on p. 19 above. Personal files of Gen. Lear.

Academic failures, resulting chiefly from lack of proper educational background, rose at the Armored School from 3.2 percent in February to 14.8 percent in December; at the Coast Artillery School, from 1.1 percent in July to 21.9 percent in December; and at the Infantry School, from 1.9 percent in April to 17.3 percent in November.[16] In October 1942 Dr. James Grafton Rogers, visiting officer candidate schools at the request of General Marshall, found them "notably troubled by poor quality." [17] Maj. Gen. Harold R. Bull, commanding the Replacement and School Command, admitted that "emphasis on filling officer candidate quotas had influenced commanders in many instances to sacrifice quality for quantity." [18] General McNair defined the dilemma when he remarked to General Lear that "we must not set up arbitrary standards and ignore the fact that we must have officers." [19]

Numerous expedients were adopted at the officer candidate schools to combat or offset the poor quality of the available candidate material. Special tests were devised to screen out men who had been selected as officer candidates merely to fill quotas; preparatory schools were established to give basic training to candidates brought in from other arms; and the policy was adopted of turning back weak candidates to repeat all or part of the course in the hope of salvaging as many men as possible. The result was unavoidably an adulterated product. By the end of 1942 the quality of recent OCS graduates had declined so far that The Inspector General suggested sweeping reforms in the selection and training of officer candidates. Army Ground Forces opposed the recommendations, feeling that the trouble did not lie in the details of the selection system but rather in the reluctance of unit commanders to send key enlisted men to officer candidate school and in the shortage of high-intelligence personnel within the Army Ground Forces.[20]

The Officer Surplus of 1943 and the Control of OCS Production

The issue in 1942 had been numbers. With passage from shortage to surplus, difficulty in finding enough qualified men to fill quotas disappeared. Quality

[16] Percentages compiled by Ground Statistics Section, Hq AGF. These percentages do not include ROTC candidates, who, however, numbered less than 1 percent of the OCS graduates in 1942.

[17] James Grafton Rogers, "Some Over-all Comments on Army Training," 22 Oct 42. 095/41 (Rogers, J.G.).

[18] Gen H. R. Bull, "Comments on Rogers Report." 095/41 (Rogers, J. G.).

[19] Personal ltr of Gen McNair to Gen Lear, 6 Aug 42. McNair Correspondence.

[20] (1) AGF memo (S) for G–1 WD, 14 Mar 43, sub: OCSs. 352/60 (C). (2) Memo slips in 352/60 (C).

could again be insisted on and high standards reasserted. At the end of 1942 the War Department wrote a commentary on the problems of the year just past and a forecast of the year to come:[21]

While the reduction in officer candidate requirements will not operate to deny qualified applicants the opportunity to attend an officer candidate school, it will permit more careful selection, and will place officer candidate opportunities on a higher competitive basis. With a broad field from which to select a smaller number of candidates, commanders should give most careful attention to final selection to the end that the highest type of officer material available is selected.

But in 1943, as in 1942, the control of input continued to be central in officer procurement. The problem was no longer how to get enough suitable candidates, but how to avoid getting too many.

Although the Army Ground Forces was given control of the officer candidate schools of the ground arms in March 1942, it did not acquire control over the number of candidates to be trained. During 1942 it was responsible only for filling school quotas allotted to it by the War Department and for training the candidates. In March 1943, the procurement crisis of 1942 having passed, the War Department decided to delegate control over officer candidate enrollment to the three major commands. Since the officer candidate schools constituted by this time almost the only large source of new officers—direct Reserve appointments having ceased—this action in effect gave the three commands control over the whole officer procurement program. Effective with quotas for May 1943, the Commanding General, Army Ground Forces, was "to determine and maintain the proper number of candidates in schools under his jurisdiction." [22] Following by one month a similar delegation of authority over the planning of enlisted replacement production, this directive put Army Ground Forces into the personnel business on a large scale, considerably broadening the functions originally assigned to it.

The War Department continued to set the long-range goals for the officer procurement program and, because the Ground Forces lacked the necessary facilities, to supply estimates of anticipated replacement requirements. Operating within the framework of these broad guides, Army Ground Forces set monthly

[21] (1) WD ltr (R) AG 352 (12–20–42) OB–D–WDGAP to CGs, 24 Dec 42, sub: Candidates Selected to Attend OCS. 352/18 (R). (2) Cf. WD Memo W625–7–43, 1 Sep 43, sub: Acceptance and Selection of Applicants for OCSs. 352/471 (R).

[22] (1) WD ltr AG 352 (3–15–43) OB–D–WDGAP to CG AGF, 16 Mar 43, sub: Authorized Capacities of OCSs in the United States. 352/427 (OCS). (2) Change 5, AR 625–5, WD, 19 Mar 43.

OCS quotas until March 1944, when control over the procurement system passed again to the War Department.

When the Army Ground Forces assumed control over officer procurement on 16 March 1943, the number of candidates in AGF schools had already begun to decline. (See Table No. 1.) In 1943 the problem was to make an exact calculation of future requirements, in the hope that both underproduction and overproduction might be avoided.[23] Overproduction of officers was wasteful of manpower, added to difficulties of administration, necessitated the retraining of individuals, and shut the door to promotion to men newly inducted into the Army. Despite repeated reductions in numbers of officer candidates, Army Ground Forces failed to avoid overproduction in 1943. Future requirements, together with other variables, proved impossible to calculate exactly.

Army Ground Forces was slow to perceive the danger of overproduction. The War Department on 15 December 1942 made the first move to check the OCS output, reducing the capacity of the Infantry Officer Candidate School by almost 50 percent. Army Ground Forces protested strongly against the severity of this cut.[24] It wished a 25 percent overstrength in officers in troop units. This overstrength had been authorized by the War Department on 27 March 1942 but had been impossible to realize under conditions of general shortage. Officer overstrength had several uses. As an important element in the training program for 1943, Army Ground Forces planned to send officers in large numbers to advanced courses in the service schools. Units from which officers were detached for this purpose needed an overstrength in order to retain enough officers to conduct training. Overstrength also provided a means by which units in the United States might supply, without damage to themselves, officer replacements for battle and nonbattle losses overseas. Further, it constituted a reserve against normal attrition, assuring that a unit would have its tabular component of officers at the time of embarkation. Army Ground Forces feared that these requirements had been underestimated, but the War Department adhered to its decision of December. Moreover, in March 1943 when the War Department set the OCS quotas for May, it cut those of all the AGF branches except Antiaircraft.[25] (See Table No. 3.)

[23] AGF M/S, CofS to G–1 and G–3, 28 Mar 43, sub: Authorized Capacities of OCS in the U. S. 352/427 (OCS).

[24] (1) WD memo (S) WDGAP 352 OCS for CG AGF, 15 Dec 42, sub: Quarterly Capacities of OCS for AGF. (2) AGF M/S (S), G–3 to CofS, 28 Dec 42, sub as in (1). (3) AGF memo (S) for G–1 WD, 31 Dec 42, sub as in (1). All in 352/12 (OCS) (S).

[25] (1) AGF M/S, G–1 to ExO, 11 Mar 43, sub: OCS Quotas. AGF G–1 Control Div files. (2) AGF ltrs to R&SC AAC, Armd F, 31 Mar 43, sub: Authorized Capacities of OCSs in U. S. 352/427 (OCS).

When it received responsibility for determining OCS output, the first step taken by Army Ground Forces was to assemble the data necessary for calculation. Figures were obtained on the number of Ground Forces officers who were surplus in the defense commands and theaters, the number on loan to Army Service Forces, the number in AGF pools or held as overstrength in units, and the num-

TABLE NO. 3

*Authorized Monthly Quotas of AGF Officer Candidate Schools, 1943–45**

Month	AA	ARMD	CAV	CA	FA	INF	TD	Total
1943								
Jan–Apr	2,000	466	166	57	1,333	2,200	333	6,555
May–Jun	2,000	300	100	50	900	1,200	300	4,850
Jul	500	100	50	50	300	1,000	100	2,100
Aug–Sep	210	80	40	54	400	700	80	1,564
Oct–Nov	50	40	25	25	75	135	40	390
Dec	182	140	......	......	314	647	......	1,283
1944								
Jan	147	134	......	......	289	612	......	1,182
Feb	119	126	......	......	270	725	......	1,240
Mar	......	105	......	......	252	712	......	1,069
Apr	......	105	......	......	250	780	......	1,135
May	......	136	......	......	50	800	......	986
Jun	......	......	......	......	50	510	......	560
..	......	......	......	......	50	1,600	......	1,650
Jul–Oct	......	......	......	......	50	3,200	......	3,250
Nov	......	60	68	......	150	2,000	22	2,300
Dec	......	100	114	......	200	2,000	36	2,450
1945								
Jan–Sep	......	100	114	......	200	2,000	36	2,450
Oct	......	15	15	......	65	200	5	300

Sources: (1) WD ltrs to CG AGF: (S) WDGAP 352 OCS, 15 Dec 42, in 353/12 (OCS) (S); AGOT–S–WDGAP 352 (24 May 44), 27 May 44, in 352/408 (Inf OCS); (S) AGOT–S–A 352 (7 Jun 44), 10 Jun 44, in 352/105 (OCS) (S); AGOT–S–A 352 (20 Sep 44), 26 Sep 44, in 352/532 (OCS); (R) AGOT–S–A 352 (3 Oct 44), 11 Oct 44, in 352/7 (OCS) (R).

(2) AGF quota ltrs in 352 (OCS) diagonals 438, 451, 455, 465, 472, 477, 482, 500, 503, 504, 506, 508, 529, 532, 539, 564, 573, 575, 579, 584, 591, 599, and in 352 (Inf OCS) diagonals 408, 412, 415, and 429.

(3) AGF M/S (S), G–1 to ExO, 11 Mar 43, in AGF G–1 Control Div files.

*Quotas from July 1943 through May 1944 determined by AGF; quotas for other months determined by WD.

ber being currently produced in the candidate schools. The total represented progress already made toward meeting future requirements.[26] The method of computing requirements was that outlined by the War Department in its directive of 16 March. The main element in the calculation was the Troop Basis, which in the spring of 1943 called for 100 divisions, with supporting units, by the end of 1943. Officers under this program had to be available ninety days before activation of new units. Future overhead requirements and the number of ground officers needed for duty with the Air Forces also had to be estimated. In addition, provision had to be made against expected attrition in troop units and for a backlog of overseas officer replacements. For the latter, the War Department prescribed that 18,500 officers be held in readiness, mainly as overstrength in units.

The following formula was developed by G–1 of Army Ground Forces to calculate minimum quotas for officer candidate schools:[27]

1. Add:
   - Officer requirements to meet new activations (1943 Troop Basis).
   - 2 percent annual attrition loss on above.
   - 4 percent annual attrition loss on established units.
   - Estimate for overhead expansion and for arms and services with Army Air Forces.
   - War Department requirements for overseas loss replacements.
2. Deduct:
   - Surplus officers currently in units (in the United States and overseas).
   - Surplus officers in pools.
   - Candidates currently in schools.
3. Increase resultant figure by 20 percent to cover failures in officer candidate schools.
4. Divide by number of OCS cycles remaining in 1943.

This calculation was made for each of the seven arms and quasi arms in the Ground Forces.

Satisfactory calculation was difficult because of uncertainty of the main factor, the 1943 Troop Basis. On 14 April Army Ground Forces proposed to the War Department a general readjustment of mobilization which would decelerate activations and more fully synchronize the expansion of ground troops with the development of shipping facilities.[28] This program, if acted upon, would have

[26] AGF ltrs to AAC, Armd F, R&SC, 31 Mar 43, sub as in n. 25 (2). 352/427 (OCS).

[27] AGF M/S, Lt Col W. S. Renshaw to G–1, 31 Mar 43, sub: Rpt of Visit to School Establishments. AGF G–1 Sec files.

[28] Memo (S) of Gen McNair for G–3 WD, 14 Apr 43, sub: Modification of Mobilization Procedures. 381/177 (S).

reduced officer requirements for 1943, especially those of tank destroyer and antiaircraft units. No action was taken. On 4 May the Army Ground Forces learned from G-1 and G-3 of the War Department that activation of 10 divisions in 1944 could be expected, in addition to the 100 divisions planned for 1943.[29] In June the outlook reversed itself; the 100 divisions planned for 1943 were cut to 88, and there was no indication whether the remaining 12 (not to mention an additional 10) were only deferred to 1944 or permanently canceled. In July a new 1943 Troop Basis appeared. It not only dropped 12 divisions and their supporting units but also embodied reductions in Tables of Organization on which Army Ground Forces had long been working. The number of enlisted men to be mobilized by 31 December 1943 in ground combat units was diminished by about 400,000. Some 30,000 fewer officers would be required than were previously expected.

On 28 April, long before these reductions became official, G-1 of Army Ground Forces reported that officer requirements for 1943 would be met, with a small surplus to spare, at dates varying among the arms from July to October 1943. On those dates the officer candidate schools could be closed so far as 1943 requirements were concerned. It was undesirable to close the schools altogether; aside from the probable need for them in the more distant future, opportunity for officer training was important to the morale of enlisted men. To keep open this opportunity G-1 proposed a plan to admit twice as many men to officer candidate schools as it was practicable to commission, the half not qualifying for commissions to be diverted by process of elimination to advanced enlisted training. Nothing came of this proposal.[30]

On 8 May 1943 Army Ground Forces set OCS quotas for July, the first such quotas established under AGF authority.[31] Although the directive of 16 March had specified that AGF determination should begin with the quotas for May, the War Department had already announced May quotas. Commitments already made to enlisted men selected for officer training, and the length of time necessary to assemble data and compute new estimates, were such that Army Ground Forces retained the May quotas as announced. June quotas, which had to be announced by the middle of April, were made the same as those for May, again

[29] AGF M/S, G-1 to CofS, 4 May 43, sub: Off Requirements. AGF G-1 Sec files.

[30] AGF M/S, G-1 to CofS, 28 Apr 43, sub: Reduction of OCS Capacities and Reorganization. AGF G-1 Sec files.

[31] AGF ltrs to R&SC, AAC, Armd F, 12 May 43, sub: OCS Quota for July 1943. Confirming telephone instructions of 8 May. 352/438 (OCS).

because calculation of requirements had not been completed. July quotas, therefore, represented the first new departure.

The quotas for July applied drastic cuts except in Infantry and Coast Artillery. Field Artillery, Armored, and Tank Destroyer OCS quotas were reduced 67 percent; those of Antiaircraft, 75 percent; and those of Cavalry, 50 percent. Further reductions followed in August, and again in October. (See Table No. 3.) Announced respectively on 13 June and 10 August, these further reductions reflected the crystallization of the Troop Basis at the reduced level of 88 (later 90) divisions. Such uncertainty remained that capacities of the schools—their overhead and facilities as distinguished from actual monthly intake—were left relatively high until indications of the 1944 Troop Basis were forthcoming from the War Department in the later months of 1943.[32]

The quotas for July and the following months, small though they were, called for more officer candidates than were actually needed. This was because certain groups of personnel, irrespective of officer requirements, had to be allowed to qualify for commissions. The officer surplus caused by the sudden reduction of the Troop Basis was made larger by the necessity of putting these groups through the candidate schools.[33]

By far the largest group which, irrespective of requirements, had to be admitted to officer candidate schools consisted of men in the Advanced Reserve Officers' Training Corps program. These were college students who had contracted to pursue military training during their last two years of college with a view to qualifying for a commission, and toward whom it was felt that the Government had an obligation. Small numbers of these men had been admitted as officer candidates in 1942. They became eligible in large numbers between the summer of 1943 and the summer of 1944, the period of officer surplus in the ground arms. In 1944 the bulk of OCS graduates from the AGF schools were ROTC candidates. (See Table No. 2.) There were three types of ROTC candidates:[34]

1. *Second-Year Advanced ROTC's.* Members of the normal college class of 1943, having completed the entire ROTC course except for the summer camp, suspended since the outbreak of the war.

[32] (1) AGF M/S, G-1 to AG, 18 Jun 43, sub: OCS Capacities. (2) AGF ltrs to AAC, Armd F, 18 Jun, sub as in (1); to R&SC, 24 Jun. All in 352/448 (OCS).

[33] For this and the following five paragraphs see especially AGF memo (R) for G-1 WD, 24 May 43, sub: Procurement of Commissioned Offs. 210.1/315 (AUS).

[34] Papers in 210.1/85 and /86 (ORC), and in 352/403 (OCS).

2. *Second-Year Advanced ROTC's*. Members of the college class of 1944, qualifying by acceleration of studies for graduation before or about 30 September 1943, and having an almost complete 2-year advanced ROTC course.

3. *First-Year Advanced ROTC's*. Members of the normal college class of 1944, unable to graduate from college before induction into the Army, but with one year of advanced ROTC completed.

In general, ROTC students went to the officer candidate school of the arm in which their ROTC work had been done; but since ROTC units gave no tank destroyer or armored training, some redistribution among the arms was necessary in assignment to officer candidate school.

Another group to be sent to officer candidate schools consisted of enlisted men selected overseas for officer training. In 1943, there were no candidate schools overseas except in Great Britain and Australia. Selected candidates from other theaters returned to the United States. Room had to be made for them in AGF candidate schools.[35]

In May and June 1943 it was also necessary, for planning purposes, to include the Army Specialized Training Program. Army Ground Forces at this time considered allowing 25 percent of ASTP trainees, in general those who would eventually complete the "Advanced" or 4-year college program, to qualify for commissions. Only the longest-range planning was affected. As events turned out, with the reduction of the Troop Basis and the rising need for enlisted replacements it became impossible even to consider commissioning ASTP students. No quotas for them were ever allotted in the candidate schools.

Much the smallest group consisted of volunteer officer candidates. By 1943 the need for the VOC system had abated; the War Department greatly reduced the VOC program but was reluctant to stop it entirely. To keep it going, a nominal VOC quota was awarded by Army Ground Forces to each replacement training center. The system disappeared naturally, late in 1943, when dependency ceased to carry exemption from the draft.[36]

These special groups, coming into officer candidate schools, threatened to squeeze out ordinary enlisted men of the Army Ground Forces. It was highly

[35] AGF memo for G-1 WD, 11 Aug 43, sub: Return of Accepted Officer Candidates from Overseas Theaters and Bases. 352/464 (OCS).

[36] (1) WD ltr AG 352 (3-19-43) MT-M, 24 Mar 42, sub: Attendance at OCS of SS Registrants Deferred for Dependency Only. 352/138 (OCS). (2) AGF ltr to AAC, 28 Jul 43, sub: Volunteer Off Candidates. 352/456 (OCS).

desirable for morale purposes, irrespective of officer requirements, to allot nominal OCS quotas to tactical units and replacement training centers.

To lay plans for accommodating the various groups within the shrinking limits of officer candidate schools, and to clarify and stabilize the ultimate objectives in officer production, a committee of AGF staff officers prepared a detailed study on "Procurement of Commissioned Officers" which was submitted to the War Department on 24 May 1943.[37] The study presupposed the then existing 100-division program. It recommended that 50 percent of OCS capacity be reserved for the college sources—first for ROTC students until an undetermined date in 1944, then for ASTP graduates. The remaining 50 percent of capacity would be reserved for troop units and replacement training centers, in numbers divided between Army Ground Forces and overseas theaters in proportion to relative strengths. Reduction of OCS capacities, ensuing upon reduction of the Troop Basis, made these features of the plan unworkable. Not only did the long-run arrangements for ASTP never materialize but it proved impossible to maintain equality between the number of officer candidates from troop units and replacement centers and the number from the ROTC.

The ROTC problem, wrote G–1 of Army Ground Forces, "is, with the possible exception of ASTP, one of the most sensitive administrative problems we have at this time." [38] The difficulty was in putting through the limited capacities of the officer candidate schools a large number of ROTC students all of whom became available at about the same time. In this matter the plan set forth in the study of 24 May was followed.

Second-year advanced ROTC men, of the normal college class of 1943, having graduated from college in June, and lacking only the summer camp in the normal requirements for a Reserve commission, proceeded to officer candidate schools in June, July, August, and September. Pending the dates on which successive groups could be admitted, the War Department proposed that these men, who had four years of military training under college conditions, be used as instructors at replacement training centers. Army Ground Forces objected, noting that ROTC students had lacked opportunity to train with modern equipment and that replacement training was so important that it required the highest quality of instruction. Second-year advanced ROTC men were therefore kept

[37] AGF memo (R) for G–1, WD, 24 May 43, sub: Procurement of Commissioned Offs. 210.1/315 (AUS).

[38] AGF M/S, G–1 to CofS, 15 Jul 43, sub: ROTCs. 352/403 (OCS).

in pools, where they were redistributed among the arms, given some instruction, and then filtered gradually into the candidate schools.[39]

Second-year advanced ROTC men of the accelerated class of 1944 were allowed to remain in college until graduation, which occurred in most institutions before 30 September 1943. On graduation they went to officer candidate schools. The number of these men proved less than was anticipated. It was planned that they should reach officer candidate schools in October, November, and December. They began in fact to enter in September; in October and November they were so few that no OCS quotas were set especially for them, the few who appeared being admitted outside of quotas.[40] By December none of this ROTC group remained.

First-year advanced ROTC students were considerably short of having completed the ROTC course. They were sent upon induction to replacement training centers, where they received basic training in the various arms and were selected for officer candidate school, having to meet the usual requirements of intelligence and leadership. Those selected were then returned for further study to the colleges, under the administration of the Army Specialized Training Program. They were accepted as officer candidates as room became available in successive increments beginning in December 1943.

During the period beginning with the establishment of reduced OCS quotas by Army Ground Forces for July 1943 and lasting through May 1944, with the exception of October and November 1943, ROTC students formed a large majority of the candidates admitted to officer candidate schools. Several hundred candidates from overseas were also admitted. During the last six months of 1943 less than 2,000 officer candidates were selected from AGF units in the United States, including those of all seven ground arms. This was no more than had been admitted each month for Antiaircraft alone before July 1943. It was a minimum number judged necessary to maintain the morale of enlisted men and to avoid a situation in which college students would be given officer training while soldiers in the field were denied it.

To summarize, it was found impossible to prevent overproduction of officers in 1943 because, simultaneously with the sudden drop in requirements incident to the revision of the Troop Basis, roughly 15,000 ROTC students previously

[39] AGF memo for G-1 WD, 20 Jul 43, sub: Disposition of 2d Yr Advanced ROTC Students. 352/403 (OCS).

[40] The absence of ROTC quotas in October and November accounts for the low quotas of these months as shown in Table No. 3.

held on the campuses became available to the Ground Forces and for reasons of policy had to be allowed to qualify for commissions. Although only about half the available ROTC men were enrolled in officer candidate schools in 1943, they helped to increase the total number of OCS graduates from AGF schools during 1943 above that of 1942. In all, 58,109 OCS candidates were commissioned, of whom 5,215 were from the ROTC. (See Table No. 2.)

Liquidation of the Antiaircraft Surplus

Antiaircraft Artillery presented the extreme case of inability to make accurate prediction of officer requirements. By December 1943 a surplus of antiaircraft officers existed, variously estimated at from 5,000 to over 10,000.[41] Estimates differed because surplus could be variously defined, depending on provisions made for attrition, battle replacements, overhead, future activations, and so forth. A figure of 10,000 represented a strength of about 40 percent over Table of Organization requirements as of December 1943.

The main cause of surplus was the reduction at a late date of the planned strength of antiaircraft units. The reduction was more precipitous than the prior reductions to which other ground units had been subjected by the revision of the 1943 Troop Basis. Lack of complete understanding among the War Department, Army Ground Forces, and the Antiaircraft Command, and within the headquarters staff of Army Ground Forces, played its part in faulty planning of antiaircraft officer strength.

In 1942, when the main outlines of the war army were being drawn, enemy air power was of formidable proportions, and the War Department favored a maximum development of antiaircraft artillery. In the summer of 1942, in setting up the 1943 Troop Basis, the War Department prescribed an enlisted strength of over 600,000 in Antiaircraft, to be attained by 31 December 1943.[42] This strength was about half that contemplated for Infantry. General McNair on 29 October 1942 stated his belief that the strength proposed for Antiaircraft was too high (in proportion to other ground arms), considering the liberal provisions being made for expansion of the Army Air Forces, by which enemy air power would presumably be weakened.[43] The 1943 Troop Basis, announced officially in

[41] AGF M/S (S), 7 Dec 43, sub: Surplus CAC Officers. 321/407 (CAC) (S).

[42] (1) WD ltr (S) AG 320.2 (8–27–42) MS–C–M, 28 Aug 42, sub: TB for 1943. 320.2/4 (TUB 43) (S). (2) WD memo WDGCT 320.2 Gen (10–25–42), 25 Oct 42, sub as in (1). 320.2/5 (TUB 43)(S).

[43] AGF memo (S) for G–3 WD, 29 Oct 42, sub: TB for 1943. 320.2/5 (TUB 43)(S).

November 1942, left the figure for Antiaircraft still slightly over 600,000.[44] Recommendations made by General McNair on 14 April 1943 included the deferment of 88 antiaircraft battalions.[45] The recommendation was not accepted immediately, but in June 1943 the Committee on Revision of the Military Program, War Department General Staff, reduced by 58 the number of antiaircraft battalions.[46] General McNair urged a still larger cut on 22 June, recommending that an enlisted strength of 180,000 be transferred from Antiaircraft to other types of Ground Forces units.[47] As announced on 28 July, the reduced Troop Basis cut Antiaircraft about 62,000. Revised again as of 4 October, the Troop Basis finally embodied General McNair's views on the matter, cutting Antiaircraft by another 112,000 to a strength of 427,832 as of the end of 1943. Further planning reduced proposed strength as of the end of 1944 to 405,535. The decisive change was that of 4 October 1943, from which Antiaircraft Artillery emerged with only two-thirds of the strength originally expected. Until 4 October 1943, though not believing the current expansion of Antiaircraft to be wise, Army Ground Forces had to plan to have ready 24,350 antiaircraft officers, for tactical units only, by the end of the year. The number actually required after 4 October was only 18,845. Since officers had to be trained in advance this overproduction could hardly have been avoided.[48]

Overproduction might, nevertheless, have been smaller had different decisions been made in the first part of 1943. The Antiaircraft Command wished in March to curtail slightly the number of its officer candidates. The War Department, which at this time was fixing quotas for May, cut the OCS quotas for May in the other ground arms but not in Antiaircraft. On 11 March a conference was held at the headquarters of the Antiaircraft Command, at which Brig. Gen. John M. Lentz, G-3 of the Army Ground Forces, directed that the OCS quota remain at 2,000 a month.[49] This quota was maintained through June.

The studies completed by G-1 of Army Ground Forces late in April 1943 indicated an imminent overproduction of officers in all ground arms except Infantry. Too late to affect the June quotas, these studies led to the abrupt reduc-

[44] WD memo (S) WDGCT 320.2 Gen (11-24-42), 24 Nov 42, sub: TB for 1943. AGO Records, 322 (7-14-42) Sec 1 (S).

[45] Memo (S) of Gen McNair for G-3 WD, 14 Apr 43, sub: Modification of Mob Procedures. 381/177 (S).

[46] Memo (S) of Special Committee for DCofS USA, 13 Jun 43, sub: TUB 1943. 320.2/31 (TUB 43) (S).

[47] Memo (S) of Gen McNair for DCofS USA, 22 Jun 43, sub: TUB 1943. 320.2/31 (TUB 43) (S).

[48] Statistics from Tab B to memo of Gen McNair for CofS USA, 1 Feb 44. 321/408 (CAC)(S).

[49] AGF M/S, G-3 to CG, 11 Mar 43, sub: AA Schs. 352/12 (OCS) (S).

tions directed for July. A greater cut was then applied to Antiaircraft than to any other arm. In August the input into Antiaircraft Officer Candidate School was scarcely 10 percent of what it had been in June. No candidates entered in August except ROTC's, VOC's, and candidates from overseas. Except for these three groups, whose admission was prescribed by the War Department, only 145 candidates entered the Antiaircraft School from August to December, inclusive. These 145 represented a minimum believed necessary for the maintenance of morale.[50]

Since a slight officer surplus was accumulating even under the unreduced Troop Basis, the slashing of the program for Antiaircraft on 4 October 1943 produced an officer surplus of considerable size. At the same time it became clear that no increase in the strength of Antiaircraft would be called for in the Troop Basis of 1944 and that the surplus could therefore not be absorbed. In November Army Ground Forces took steps to encourage the shifting of officers in Antiaircraft to other arms by voluntary transfers, of which more than 5,000 were effected in the following four months.[51] It was decided to postpone transfer by nonvoluntary means until the settlement and publication of the 1944 Troop Basis, which, in defining the units scheduled for activation, would show into what arms surplus antiaircraft officers could most advantageously be moved.

On 4 December 1943 the Antiaircraft Command estimated its officer surplus at 5,836, and recommended suspension of its officer candidate school. G–1 of Army Ground Forces figured the surplus at approximately 10,500 and recommended block transfers to other arms by nonvoluntary means. G–3 of Army Ground Forces hesitated at block transfers, fearing the increase of school overhead which the retraining of Antiaircraft officers on a large scale would involve. G–3 believed the officer surplus in Antiaircraft to be exaggerated. G–1 assembled figures to show that antiaircraft tactical units were carrying, on the average, an officer strength of 141.5 percent. It was agreed to request the War Department for authority to suspend the Antiaircraft Officer Candidate School. This authority was granted on 12 January 1944. Meanwhile, on 4 January, Army Ground Forces canceled for February 1944 entrance into the Antiaircraft School of all candidates except those of the ROTC. A few weeks later the same policy was applied to ROTC men. Both ROTC and non-ROTC candidates, who together numbered only 144 for February, were shifted to the Infantry, Field Artillery, and Armored

[50] AGF M/S (S), G–1 to CofS, 29 Jan 44, sub: Surplus AA Offs. 321/408 (CAC) (S).

[51] (1) AGF ltr to CGs, 12 Nov 43, sub: Applications for Transfer or Detail. 210.31/601 (CAC). (2) AGF memo (S) for DCofS USA, 20 Mar 44, sub: Reduction in CAC Off Overstrength. 321/408 (CAC) (S).

Officer Candidate Schools, the only ones still open in the Ground Forces. The intake of the Antiaircraft School was thereby stopped.[52]

Late in January the officer surplus in Antiaircraft aroused the unfavorable attention of the War Department General Staff. The Inspector General submitted a highly critical report, and General Marshall made inquiry of General McNair. "This does not impress me as businesslike, certainly not efficient," he wrote, and added: "Is there any good explanation for this business to have continued the way it has without evident signs of correction?" In his reply General McNair outlined the main facts of the preceding year. Maj. Gen. Ray E. Porter, War Department G–3, expressed his opinion that Army Ground Forces was not responsible for the surplus in Antiaircraft.[53]

In retrospect, it would appear that the only time when Army Ground Forces might have acted to prevent the surplus was in March 1943, when the War Department left the OCS quotas untouched for Antiaircraft while reducing the others. Had Army Ground Forces at this time supported the desire of the Antiaircraft Command to curtail, the action of the War Department might have been different. But the Troop Basis for Antiaircraft was at that time so high, and such questions as attrition rates, replacement needs, and desirable overstrengths were so difficult to agree upon that there was room for legitimate difference of opinion.

By March 1944, 5,668 antiaircraft officers had been voluntarily transferred to other arms or services. The conversion of antiaircraft officers to other arms, chiefly to the Infantry, for which special retraining courses were established in certain of the AGF schools, was one feature of the officer program during 1944.

The Reclassification of Officers

From the beginning of 1943 the number of officers in the ground arms was in excess of Table of Organization requirements. The surplus increased following the reduction of the Troop Basis in July 1943, despite rigorous curtailment at that time in the output of the officer candidate schools. With the slowing down of promotions, the excess was concentrated in the grade of lieutenant. It amounted to about 30,000 in the last months of 1943.[54]

[52] For this paragraph see AGF memo slips in 321/407 and /408 (CAC) (S).

[53] Memos in 321/408 (CAC) (S).

[54] (1) AGF M/S, G–1 to CofS, 12 Oct 43, sub: OC Program. AGF G–1 Control Div files. (2) Statistical Tabulation: Authorized and Actual Strength of Offs in the AGF by Grade and Arm or Service. 320.2/352 (C).

In general, except in Antiaircraft Artillery, the excess over Table of Organization requirements in the Ground Forces did not represent a surplus in the sense of a superfluity. It did not mean that the total number of officers was substantially more than was needed for all purposes, immediate or eventual, or more than could profitably engage in some kind of activity. Of the excess, 18,500 officers were maintained by order of the War Department as a source of overseas replacements.[55] Since overseas replacements had to be furnished mainly in lieutenants, the degree to which lieutenants in the Ground Forces were actually surplus depended on the volume of overseas calls. Officers were needed for domestic purposes to meet varying and elastic needs. Overhead allotments had to be made, reserves against attrition built up, and so forth. The policy of improving the professional education of officers by sending them to service schools in large numbers required an excess over Tables of Organization strength, if insufficiency of officers on duty with units was not to handicap the training of the field forces.

While the existence of an officer surplus encouraged commanders in some instances to send officers to school or put them in overhead positions merely to keep them busy, it had the advantage of making possible a sustained policy of eliminating the least fit. In 1942 separation from the service for inefficiency had been unusual because of the shortage of officers. Vacancies were so numerous that an unsuitable officer would be reassigned to a position in which presumably he would be more effective. At the same time the wholesale operation of officer candidate schools and rapid promotions in all grades were producing officers whose competency was open to question. At the end of the year, as the pressure to produce numbers relaxed, attention turned to reclassification, the standard procedure by which officers were demoted or dropped because of inefficiency. In December 1942 General Lentz, in protesting against the severity with which the War Department then cut OCS capacities, argued that an overstrength of officers should be developed as an aid, among other things, to reclassification. He observed that, while more officers should be reclassified, they would not be unless a margin in numbers existed.[56]

The War Department continued for some time to study the matter. On 9 June 1943 it published the revised AR 605-230, designed to increase the use of

[55] WD ltr AG 352 (3-15-43) OB-D-WDGAP, 16 Mar 43, sub: Authorized Capacities of OCS in U. S. 352/427 (OCS). The figure of 3,000 prescribed in this letter for Field Artillery was later raised to 4,000, making the total 18,500.

[56] AGF M/S (S), G-3 to CofS, 28 Dec 42, sub: Quarterly Capacity of OCSs of AGF. 352/12 (OCS)(S).

reclassification. Army Ground Forces on 10 July enjoined subordinate commanders to employ fully the powers granted.[57] On 14 July, over the signature of General Marshall, a confidential radiogram was dispatched by the War Department directly to the field, including Ground Forces commanders down to the division:[58]

The officer problem demands closer attention. Out of 500,000 officers only four were eliminated from the Army for inefficiency during the month of May. . . . It is inconceivable that of 500,000 only four should fail to come up to the required standards of leadership. . . . Commanders of every echelon will be judged by their discernment and moral courage in the elimination of the unfit.

Inertia was great not only because of the personal embarrassments involved for individual commanders but also because the required administrative process remained formidable and indirect. Jurisdiction in reclassification cases rested with the commanding generals of the service commands. General McNair believed that Ground Forces commanders might use more initiative if cases could be settled nearer home. In August 1943 a plan was drawn up whereby reclassification jurisdiction would be granted to the Commanding General of the Army Ground Forces and delegated to commanders having general court-martial jurisdiction.[59] These included, by a recent action, commanders of armies, corps, divisions, special training commands, service schools, replacement training centers, and replacement depots. On 2 September Army Ground Forces requested permission to test the plan with the Second and Third Armies. The War Department disapproved. General McNair still favored the plan, for reasons indicated in the following note for his G–1 on 9 November:[60]

I favor requesting reconsideration. . . . Basic premise should be that the reclassification of officers is an important function of command, that the Chief of Staff, USA, has recently stressed the importance of this function and criticized the manner in which it was being performed by commanders. In spite of this fact, reclassification cases are heard, not by the responsible commander, but by service commanders who have no responsibility for the efficiency of ground force units.

Successful efforts were made to speed up the working of the existing system.[61]

[57] AGF ltr to CGs, 10 Jul 43, sub: Reclassification of Offs. 210.01/267.

[58] AGF Classified Radio File, CM–OUT–6035.

[59] AGF M/S, G–1 to CofS, 3 Nov 43, sub: Reclassification Jurisdiction. With supporting tabs. 210.01/274.

[60] AGF M/S, CG to G–1, 9 Nov 43, sub as in n. 59. 210.01/274.

[61] (1) Cir 280, WD, 5 Nov 43. (2) AGF M/S, G–1 to CG, 12 Nov 43, sub: Action on Reclassification Proceedings. 210.01/288.

The number of officers separated from the service by reclassification rose to over 200 a month. In December 1943, in the three major commands, the number was 286. Of these, 207 were in the Army Ground Forces.[62] A smaller number were separated under authority granted in AR 605–10, which provided that officers commissioned in the Army of the United States (that is, not in the Regular Army, the National Guard, and the Officers' Reserve Corps), and which applied, therefore, principally to graduates of officer candidate schools, might be eliminated without reclassification at any time within six months of receiving their commissions.[63] Because the AGF surplus was mainly in the younger age levels the Army Ground Forces derived little advantage from the policy of the War Department, adopted in January 1944, of relieving from active duty officers over thirty-eight for whom no suitable assignment existed.[64]

Notwithstanding the improvement in the use of reclassification under the existing system, of which Army Ground Forces had taken full advantage, the War Department on 4 January 1944 decentralized reclassification jurisdiction as General McNair desired.[65] Army Ground Forces delegated to immediate subordinate commanders, who were authorized to delegate in turn to commanders having general court-martial jurisdiction, the power to hear reclassification cases involving captains and lieutenants. To overcome the inertia of subordinate commanders, Army Ground Forces devised at General McNair's suggestion a special monthly report.[66] In this report, required in a directive of 8 March 1944, each commander was to give the number of cases in which he had instituted proceedings since last reporting, or else to state that no unsatisfactory officers were assigned or attached to his command.

One reason for the inertia of commanders in effecting the separation of unqualified officers from the service was that, until early in 1944, the overstrength system made it possible for a commander to rid his own unit of unwanted officers

[62] (1) Incl 6 to AGF M/S (S), 29 Jan 44. 210.31/1308 (S). (2) Memo (S) of Gen McNair for CofS USA, 1 Feb 44, sub: AA Off Pers. 321/408 (CAC) (S).

[63] (1) AGF ltr to CGs, 3 Dec 43, sub: Discharge of Offs under Provisions of Par 26, AR 605–10. 210.8/47. (2) Incl 6 to AGF memo (S) for G–1 WD, 29 Jan 44. 210.31/1308 (S).

[64] AGF M/S (R), G–1 to CofS, 22 Dec 43, sub: Relief from Active Duty of Offs for Whom no Suitable Asgmt Exists. 210.8/2 (R).

[65] (1) WD ltr (R) AG 201.6 (31 Dec 43) PO–M–A to CG AGF, 4 Jan 44, sub: Revision of AR 605–230. (2) AGF 1st ind to CGs, 8 Jan 44, on ltr cited in (1). Both in 210.01/304½ (R).

[66] (1) AGF M/S, CG to CofS, 28 Feb 44, sub: Elimination of Unfit Offs. (2) AGF ltr to CGs, 3 Mar 44, sub as in (1). (3) AGF memo for G–1 WD, 8 Mar 44, sub: Rpt on Progress in Elimination of Unfit Offs. All in 210.01/308.

by a less drastic method. The problem of eliminating unqualified officers was tied in with the general problem of surplus. When, on 16 March 1943, the War Department prescribed that 18,500 officers be maintained as a source of overseas replacements, it specified that except for small pools they should be carried as overstrength in tactical units.[67] A commissioned overstrength of 25 percent had been authorized by the War Department since 27 March 1942 for units in the United States.[68] The requirement for 18,500 officers in the seven arms and quasi arms constituted about 20 percent of the officers in those arms under Army Ground Forces, roughly, those in the continental United States, in 1943. In 1942 the shortage of officers made such overstrength impossible to realize. In 1943 many unit commanders showed a reluctance to requisition up to a full 125 percent of their tabular commissioned strength. Insofar as units failed to carry full overstrength, officers tended to accumulate in pools. To clear the pools and to distribute the accumulating surplus, of which the chief single component was the 18,500 officers produced as replacements, Army Ground Forces on 12 July 1943 made it mandatory for units to requisition up to the full 125 percent of tabular commissioned strength.[69] Although the directive was not universally acted on, unit overstrength increased in the latter half of 1943.

Pools also grew rapidly. After the reduction of the general Troop Basis in July 1943 and of the antiaircraft Troop Basis in October, units for which officers were produced in advance failed to come into being. Pools therefore expanded. Pools were kept at high levels by the increase in the number of officers returning from overseas, by the dissolution of air base security and barrage balloon battalions, by the dropping of officer overstrengths from units preparing for embarkation, and by OCS overproduction caused principally by the necessity of admitting ROTC candidates after the need for new officers had ceased. In the Infantry, the number of officer replacements maintained by order of the War Department—9,000 out of the 18,500—was larger than could be accommodated in infantry units even at a 25 percent overstrength. Infantry pools grew correspondingly, until the increase in battle casualties turned surplus into shortage.[70]

[67] (1) WD ltr AG 352 (3–15–43) OB–D–WDGAP to CG AGF, 16 Mar 43, sub: Authorized Capacities of OCSs in the United States. 352/427 (OCS). (2) AGF M/S, G–1 to CG, 5 Oct 43, sub: G–1 Matters as Result of Western Trip of Gen McNair. 353.02/245.

[68] WD ltr AG 320.3 (3–20–42) OP–A–M to CGs, 27 Mar 42, sub: Disposition of Pool of Offs. 320.2/1673.

[69] AGF ltr (R) to CGs, 12 Jul 43, sub: Off Overstrength. 320.2/234 (R).

[70] (1) AGF M/S, G–1 to CG, 5 Oct 43, sub: G–1 Matters as Result of Western Trip of Gen McNair. 353.02/245. (2) AGF memo for G–1 WD, 22 Oct 43, sub: Disposition of Surplus Offs. AGF G–1 Sec files.

Overstrength units, not pools, were the source from which officer replacements for overseas theaters were in principle to be taken. In the North African campaign, many second lieutenants had entered combat as replacements without adequate experience with troops in the United States. Army Ground Forces thereafter enforced stringently, with more success after the establishment of replacement depots under AGF command, the requirement that officer replacements serve at least three months with tactical units in the United States. It was ruled specifically that officers sent to replacement depots must have served with Table of Organization companies, batteries, or troops (not with units in replacement training centers); that in quality they should preferably be above the average of their units of origin; and that they must have gone through an infiltration course with overhead fire, fired a marksmanship course, and met other specified requirements.[71]

Divisions and other units required an overstrength in order to supply officer replacements without impairing their own organization. Unit overstrength, however, also entailed certain difficulties. If excessive, as it came to be in many antiaircraft units, overstrength could indeed be ruinous. Officers got in each other's way, confused command responsibilities, and spent their time either in idleness or in performing noncommissioned officers' work, to the disadvantage of all concerned. Usually, however, the trouble was not that overstrength was excessive but that it was known to be temporary.

Units dropped their overstrength on preparing to move overseas. In 1943 no distinction was made during the training period between officers who were overstrength and those who were not, all being assigned to a unit in the same fashion. A unit commander could knowingly go through his training period with officers whom he did not wish to take into combat, expecting to drop them as overstrength before embarkation. In these circumstances only the strongest commanders took action, by reclassification or otherwise, to separate unsuitable officers from the service. Ineffective officers, dropped as overstrength, might pass through a pool, be assigned to another unit, dropped again, and so forth. The pool-and-overstrength system was a kind of no man's land in which, if it was not carefully watched, unsuitable officers might be hidden indefinitely, and in which the best officers might deteriorate from lack of proper activity.

In pools it was especially difficult for all officers to be profitably occupied. General McNair raised this question in October 1943 on returning from an

[71] (1) AGF ltr to CGs, 19 Sep 43, sub: Requirements for Overseas Repl Offs. (2) AGF ltr to CGs, 1 Jan 44, sub as in (1). (3) AGF ltr to CGs, 5 Apr 44, sub as in (1). All in 210.31/27 (O'seas Repl Deps).

inspection trip. There were then 10,000 officers in AGF pools. G-1 of Army Ground Forces reported that they attended schools, served as supplementary instructors at replacement training centers, and were rotated into units as rapidly as possible to fill vacancies left when units furnished overseas replacements.[72] On 27 December 1943 The Inspector General reported very unfavorably on AGF pools, charging that they had become a means of avoiding reclassification of the unfit. It was believed at AGF headquarters, after consultation with the Replacement and School Command, that the charges were exaggerated.[73]

On 20 December, before The Inspector General's report, Army Ground Forces took steps to control the abuses of overstrength.[74] A directive of that date provided that unit commanders must fill their Table of Organization positions by organic assignment of officers in the prescribed grades. The new procedure forced a unit commander to determine during the training period those officers who should be permanently assigned and those who should be carried as overstrength. The unit commander, instead of carrying an undifferentiated group of officers from among whom he would be free to choose his permanent personnel before sailing, was committed to choosing them at once; he had to dispose of unsatisfactory individuals within his organic strength, either by initiating reclassification or by some other means of earmarking the unfit. The new policy was reinforced early in January 1944 by the delegation of reclassification jurisdiction to subordinate AGF commanders.

On 20 January 1944 the War Department abolished overstrength for most units in the United States, except in the grade of second lieutenant, in which an optional degree of overstrength was permitted.[75] Implementing this action, Army Ground Forces required the requisitioning of a 25 percent overstrength in second lieutenants by infantry and cavalry units, and of a 50 percent overstrength by field artillery, antiaircraft, armored, and tank destroyer units.[76] Since the surplus of officers, like the need for overseas replacements, was heavily

[72] AGF M/S, CG to G-1, 4 Oct 43, sub: G-1 Matters as Result of Western Trip of Gen McNair. 353.02/245.

[73] (1) AGF ltr (C) to R&SC, 31 Dec 43, sub: Off Repl Pools. (2) AGF M/S (C), 15 Jan 44. Both in 210.31/594 (C).

[74] (1) AGF ltr to CGs, 20 Dec 43, sub: Requisitions for Commissioned Pers. (2) AGF ltr to CGs, 20 Dec 43, sub: Asgmt of Offs (except General Offs). Both in 210.31/5054. Amended by ltrs, same subjects, 4 Mar 44. 210.31/5159.

[75] WD ltr (R) AG 320.2 (15 Jan 44) OB-S-C-M to CGs, 20 Jan 44, sub: Overstrength in Units in Continental U. S. 320.2/309 (R).

[76] AGF 1st ind (R) to CGs, 10 Feb 44, on ltr cited in n. 75. 320.2/309 (R).

230-171 O - 66 - 10

concentrated in second lieutenants, these measures helped materially to reduce the pools and to promote the training of officer replacements in tactical units.

For officers of the grades from first lieutenant through colonel, the distinction between organic assignment and attachment unassigned was further clarified.[77] Officers of these grades, whether in pools or serving in units in excess of Tables of Organization (no longer as "overstrength," since overstrength in these grades was abolished), were considered to be attached unassigned. They became subject to immediate organic assignment to Table of Organization positions in other units. All units were obliged to requisition officers, in the prescribed grades and numbers, to fill their tabular requirements. If they failed to submit proper requisitions, the Replacement and School Command, or, for antiaircraft officers, the Antiaircraft Command, assigned the necessary officers nevertheless. The effect was to force a distribution of officers, by organic assignment in grade, throughout the units and establishments of the Ground Forces. An inefficient officer so assigned could not be passed from one organization to another. By 1944 a commander could rid himself of the unqualified only by instituting appropriate proceedings.

[77] (1) AGF ltr to CGs, 25 Jan 44, sub: Asgmt and Attachment of Offs. 210.31/5111. (2) AGF memo for G-1 WD, 29 Jan 44, sub: Rpt on Offs Required by DCofS in WD Gen Council Min, 27 Dec 43. 210.31/1308 (S).

III. Problems of Redistribution and Replacement, 1944-45

The end of 1943 marked the termination of a major phase in the officer procurement program. Until that time the program had been geared to the requirements of mobilization. The chief determinant of the scope of the program had been the number of units to be activated; the chief guide to the pace of the program had been the rate of mobilization as indicated in successive revisions of the Troop Basis. The major problems had been, in 1942, to secure enough officers to supply the great numbers of units activated in that year, and, in 1943, to balance officer production against requirements as mobilization slowed down and the distribution of strength among combat arms was more firmly determined. As indicated above, one major result of the attempts to handle these problems was the production of a large surplus of officers in the Army Ground Forces by the end of 1943.

Increasingly thereafter the officer procurement program was directed toward providing replacements in such numbers and at such times as were required to maintain existing units at full strength. Officers had of course been shipped overseas as loss replacements throughout 1943, but the number so used had been small compared with the number assigned to units in training.

Passage from a mobilization to a replacement basis involved for officer procurement certain of the same shifts found necessary when the provision of enlisted replacements underwent a similar reorientation. The most critical of these was the change in branch requirement rates. During mobilization, distribution of officer requirements among the seven combat branches had been conditioned by the rate of expansion of each arm and by the backlog of officers available in the Regular and Reserve components. For the newer branches, especially Antiaircraft, in which many units were formed where none had existed before and in which there was almost no reserve of officers, procurement requirements had been very high—almost as high for Antiaircraft as for Infantry. Once mobilization had been completed, the distribution of requirements among the arms was governed almost entirely by the rate of attrition, in which combat loss was the critical factor. There was no correspondence between battle casualty rates in a particular branch and the earlier rate of expansion. In the Antiaircraft and Tank Destroyer branches, where the need for officers had been relatively high during 1942 and 1943, the requirement for replacements was very low. As with enlisted replacements, the demand for officer replacements was concentrated in the Infantry, which suffered the greatest proportionate loss. A major redistribution of officer production capacity—in effect, OCS capacity—was required as mobilization gave way to maintenance of units at effective strength. The severity of this redistribution was intensified by a number of factors not related to the general transition. Troop Basis cutbacks in certain branches, notably Antiaircraft and Tank Destroyer, by reducing the number of positions in these arms reduced further their lowered replacement requirements. At the same time officers made surplus by these Troop Basis changes were available for use as replacements in other arms, thus further lowering the OCS production requirement in the arms affected. In general it was in the branches which had been most inflated by rapid expansion during mobilization—Antiaircraft and Tank Destroyer—and those in which loss replacement rates were relatively low, that these Troop Basis cutbacks were made. The net effect was greatly to intensify the problems involved in shifting from a mobilization to a replacement basis.

This shift was fortunately not complicated for officer procurement, as it was for enlisted replacements, by sharp changes in the requirements rates for different types of specialists. Although a military occupational specialty classification was developed for officers, it was never a dominant influence in providing replacements.[1] Branch and rank were the real determinants; an infantry lieutenant was presumed to be qualified to lead any sort of infantry platoon. To be sure, demands for certain types of highly trained specialists had to be met, but these were never large enough to create a real problem in setting up the procurement program. A difficulty did arise from the concentration of requirements for officer replacements in the grade of lieutenant. Very few captains and almost no field officers were desired as replacements. Overseas commanders naturally preferred to receive replacements in the lowest grades and to promote within their organizations. Since the output of officer candidate schools, the chief source of replacements, was in the grade of lieutenant, overseas demands and continental sources were generally in line with one another. But there were large numbers of captains and field-grade officers on duty in Zone of Interior installations of the Ground Forces, required by War Department and AGF directives to serve overseas, for

[1] Statement of Col W. S. Renshaw, G–1 AGF, to AGF Hist Off, 11 Sep 45.

whom no need existed. Sent abroad, these men tended to accumulate in pools, where they often remained for months. Left in the United States they were a useless charge against authorized replacement pool capacity. Army Ground Forces took the position that overseas theaters should have been required to accept a quota of replacements in each rank.[2]

By the end of 1944 this situation had been reversed, at least in the Infantry. The shortage of field-grade officers was more critical than the shortage of lieutenants. Regimental and battalion commanders were needed in large numbers for combat duty; field officers were required for the expansion of the replacement system in the United States, and demand for rotational replacements and officers for special details was high. Drain on the Zone of Interior was severe. One division departing for overseas in late 1944 was 50 percent below strength in infantry lieutenant colonels. As late as April 1945, infantry replacement centers were operating with only 65 percent of the authorized strength in lieutenant colonels.[3]

Redistribution within the Ground Arms

Transition from the provision of officers for mobilization to provision of officer replacements was complicated also by the necessity of coping during much of 1944 with a problem left over from the mobilization period: the surplus of officers in certain of the ground arms, chiefly Antiaircraft, Coast Artillery (harbor defense), and Tank Destroyer. The mere existence of a surplus of officers, though serious in view of the impending general overstrength of the Army, would not have been alarming if the excess officers could have been put directly to use as replacements. But excesses were heaviest in the arms whose replacement requirements were lowest. On 31 March 1944 the overstrength in antiaircraft officers was sufficient to furnish 21 months' supply of replacements at rates then estimated; there were enough coast artillery (harbor defense) officers to provide replacements for 44.7 months. The surplus of officers in the Infantry, on the other hand, would supply replacements for only 1.5 months.[4] The elimination of the large surplus of officers was therefore essentially a problem of redistributing

[2] AGF study (S), 13 Jan 45, sub: Off O'seas Repl System. 327.3/114 (SS)(S). The study was presented to the War Department committee investigating the replacement system on 13 June 1945.

[3] AGF M/S (S), Maj Meyer, Inf Br, G–1, to Col Seaman, ExO, G–1, 3 Dec 45, sub: Study No. 6 in the History of the Army Ground Forces. 314.7 (AGF Hist)(S).

[4] Tab A to WD memo (R) WDGAP 210.31 for DCofS USA, 18 Mar 44, sub: Status of Off Repl Pools. AGO Records (R).

officer strength in the ground arms in such a way as to facilitate the provision of replacements.

Wholesale redistribution of officers began in February 1944. Since the Infantry, Field Artillery, and Armored branches were those in which the heaviest replacement needs were anticipated, conversion courses were established in the service schools of these arms.[5] Lasting for eight weeks (ten weeks at the Field Artillery School), the courses retrained company-grade officers—predominantly lieutenants—of the branches in which unusable surpluses existed. Actually, the anticipated replacement needs in the Field Artillery and Armored branches did not immediately materialize. The Armored conversion course was suspended after graduating one class; the Field Artillery course operated at a low level until the fall of 1944. Indeed, more than 1,000 officers of these two branches were converted to Infantry in the summer of 1944.

Initially the conversion program was confined almost entirely to antiaircraft officers, of which there was the most embarrassing surplus. Between February and the end of April, 2,618 antiaircraft officers were ordered to the Special Basic (conversion) Course at the Infantry School. (See Table No. 4.) In April the conversion program was extended to accomplish a general dissolution of surpluses in all the ground arms. It was planned to convert 4,700 officers to Infantry in order to effect a proper distribution of strength. These were to be divided among the other arms as follows: Tank Destroyer, 600; Field Artillery, 1,100; Coast Artillery (harbor defense), 1,200; and Antiaircraft Artillery, 1,800. Since officers in Cavalry and Armored were in relatively short supply, it was not planned to make any conversions from these arms.[6]

On 27 May 1944 the War Department directed that the conversion of officers to Infantry continue at a rate of 1,000 per month.[7] During June this quota was exceeded, 1,604 officers being enrolled in the Infantry Special Basic Course. Substantial inroads having been made on the surplus of antiaircraft officers, conversion of officers in Field Artillery and Armored was accelerated in June and

[5] (1) AGF ltr to CGs, 9 Feb 44, sub: Establishment of Basic Courses to Implement the Conversion of CAC AA Offs to Inf and Armd Comds. 352.11/501. (2) AGF ltr to CG R&SC, 21 Feb 44, sub: Establishment of Special Basic Course at FA Sch. 352.11/4 (FA Sch).

[6] (1) AGF ltr to CG R&SC, 8 Apr 44, sub: Continuation of Prog to Convert Surplus Lieutenants to Inf. (2) AGF ltr to CGs, 7 May 44, sub as in (1). Both in 352/922 (Inf Sch).

[7] WD ltr AGOT-S-WDGAP 352 (24 May 44) to CG AGF, 27 May 44, sub: AGF OCS Quotas. 352/408 (Inf OCS).

TABLE NO. 4

Enrollment of Officers of Other Branches in Officers' Special Basic Course, Infantry School, 1944

Month	Classes	Source of Officers									
		AA	CA (HD)	TD	FA	Armd	Cav	Inf	Vol	Total	Cumulative Total
February...	1–2	405	...	....	...	...	..	..	....	405	405
March.....	3–8	1,180	...	....	...	...	..	..	....	1,180	1,585
April......	9–14	1,033	...	167	...	...	..	..	....	1,200	2,785
May.......	15–20	405	70	433	292	...	..	..	....	1,200	3,985
June.......	21–28	1,000	185	282	...	125	..	12	....	1,604	5,589
July.......	29–32	97	...	70	500	118	..	..	....	785	6,374
August....	33–37	400	...	....	...	...	..	..	400	800	7,174
September.	38–41	350	29	....	...	...	..	..	425	804	7,978
October...	42–45	350	...	150	...	...	..	..	200	700	8,678
November.	45A–49	603	...	75	...	...	..	..	100	778	9,456
December .	50–53	60	...	1	2	...	8	..	50	121	9,577
TOTAL.		5,883	284	1,178	794	243	8	12	1,175	9,577	

Source: Data in Files of Control Div, G–1 Sec, Hq AGF.

July, since it had been estimated that there were 500 officers in each of these arms above replacement requirements.[8]

Although surpluses had by no means been entirely liquidated, it became clear by July that conversion of officers to Infantry could not be maintained at a rate of 1,000 per month. Overhead and training facilities at the Infantry School were badly needed for the expansion, recently ordered by the War Department, of the officer candidate school. In addition, new AGF estimates of officer resources and requirements indicated that the sources of supply were drying up. A study reflecting the officer situation as of 1 July 1944 projected, for the period until 30 June 1945, a net total of only about 800 officers who would be available and qualified for transfer to combat infantry duty. It was felt that precipitate conversions would be imprudent in view of possible shifts in loss requirements among the arms. Army Ground Forces recommended that the 1,000-a-month objective be given up and that excess officers be converted in such numbers as became available. On 25 July the War Department approved the recommendation.[9]

[8] (1) AGF M/S, G–1 to CofS, 13 Jun 44, sub: Continuation of Prog to Convert Surplus Lieutenants to Inf. (2) AGF ltr to CGs, 19 Jun 44, sub as in (1). Both in 352/922 (Inf Sch).

[9] (1) AGF memo (S) for CofS USA, 19 Jul 44, sub: Conversion of Offs to Inf. (2) AGF M/S, G–1 to CofS, 17 Jul 44, sub as in (1). (3) WD 1st ind (S) AGOT–S–A [2] 10.31 (19 Jul 44), on (1) above, 25 Jul 44. All in 352/124 (S).

The calculations underlying this recommendation proved to be conservative. Monthly quotas for conversion were indeed reduced, never again reaching the levels set during the first half of the year, but an average of about 750 a month was maintained from July through November. Of these an appreciable number were volunteers for infantry duty, mainly from outside the Ground Forces. By the end of the year 9,577 officers had been enrolled in the infantry conversion course and 8,590 had graduated. (See Table No. 4.)

Not all officers converted in the Ground Forces attended one of the special retraining courses. Approximately 20 percent of those converted were transferred to another arm directly, learning their new duties on the job. Nor did all the conversions take place in the United States. About 3,000 officers, chiefly Antiaircraft and Tank Destroyer, were converted to Infantry in overseas theaters.[10]

By the branch redistribution of officers during 1944, total officer resources were brought into more realistic adjustment with officer requirements. This change is illustrated by the following comparison of commissioned strengths of the Infantry and Coast Artillery (antiaircraft and harbor defense) in January 1944 and in January 1945:[11]

Date	*Infantry*	*Coast Artillery (AA & HD)*
31 January 1944	80,331	37,383
31 January 1945	91,269	24,835

What was more important in the immediate situation was that converted officers were usable as overseas replacements during the months of low production in the officer candidate schools. The conversion program, which began primarily as a device for eliminating an embarrassing surplus of antiaircraft officers, became an indispensable part of the procurement program during 1944.

The Procurement Situation in Early 1944

Procurement of new officers posed problems during 1944 even more difficult than those of redistribution. One problem was the adjustment of existing production facilities, which had been based on the branch distribution of officer requirements for mobilization, to the distinctly different distribution of requirements for combat replacements. Once the procurement machine was adjusted to its new function it became necessary to recruit candidates in sufficient numbers to keep the machine running at planned capacity.

[10] Statement of Maj W. Meyer, Inf Br, AGF G–1 Sec, to AGF Hist Off, 17 Sep 45.

[11] From statistical reports compiled by Ground Statistics Sec, Hq AGF.

During the first five months of 1944—as final preparations for the assault on the European Continent were completed—the AGF officer candidate system fell to its lowest point of productivity since 1941. The low productive level to which the system had been allowed to sink by June 1944 was in large measure responsible for a continuous crisis in officer procurement that characterized the latter half of 1944 and the early months of 1945. It must be borne in mind that the officer candidate schools were not flexible or quickly responsive to demands for increased production. A minimum of eight months elapsed between a decision to increase output of candidates and the availability of officers for use as overseas replacements: one to two months in publication of quotas and selection and delivery of candidates to school, four months in school, and three months in commissioned service prior to shipment overseas. Once school enrollment dropped to very low levels for a period of four months, sudden large demands for officers had to be met from other sources. Three such sources were available and all were used in 1944. One was the branch pool of surplus officers. Another was the surplus officer personnel of branches who could be transferred to other branches in which demand was heavy. The third source was provided by the appointment of officers overseas. During the earlier part of 1944, when OCS output was insufficient to meet overseas demands, the first two of these sources took up the slack. Later in 1944, when it was discovered that the maximum OCS output obtainable in the United States was too small, increasing reliance was placed on overseas appointments.

Several influences combined to permit production in officer candidate schools to decline sharply between the cessation of output of officer fillers and the resumption of production for replacement purposes. The thinking of those responsible for establishing OCS quotas was doubtless influenced by earlier conditions of officer procurement. Accustomed to gauging officer needs in terms of Troop Basis augmentations, they naturally concluded, late in 1943, that since no additions to the ground Troop Basis were in prospect officer candidate school production should taper off. This carry-over from the period of mobilization was intensified by the existence of a large surplus of officers in late 1943. It was a surplus ample to cover the only current overseas replacement requirement—the pool of 18,500 officers directed by the War Department in March 1943. In addition to the replacement pool, more than 10,000 ground arms officers were surplus in the latter part of the year. With all anticipated replacement requirements more than provided for, and with large calls for replacements still a future concern, it was not unnatural to think in terms of reducing the OCS establishment to a stand-by level. This was all the more natural in view of the severe problems that the officer surplus had generated in 1943, as well as the strong criticism levelled at Army Ground Forces by The Inspector General for its handling of the surplus. The overproduction of officers that had plagued Army Ground Forces in 1943 had to be avoided in 1944. The surplus that had caused so much trouble seemed to provide insurance against overseas demands. Officer strength appeared to be suffering chiefly from maldistribution: there were far too many officers in Antiaircraft and Tank Destroyer, and large cutbacks were current or impending in those branches. Conversion of these officers to arms in which they could be used would build up a backlog against overseas demands and eke out the low production of the officer candidate schools.

In September, since the 1944 Troop Basis gave no indication of further expansion in the ground arms, the Chief of Staff, Army Ground Forces, suggested that the Cavalry, Coast Artillery, Armored, and Tank Destroyer Officer Candidate Schools might be eliminated.[12] No decision was made, but on 26 October, when the December quotas were announced, no personnel were allotted to the Cavalry, Tank Destroyer, or Coast Artillery Schools. The February 1944 quotas were the last for the Antiaircraft School. With the graduation of classes then in session, these four schools closed—Cavalry, Tank Destroyer, and Coast Artillery in March, Antiaircraft in June. The Armored School was scheduled to close in September; its fate will be discussed below. In the schools that remained open, the total monthly quotas dwindled from 1,283 in December 1943 to 986 in May 1944. (See Table No. 3.)

The announcement by the War Department in March 1944 of officer candidate school quotas for the period June–August signalized a major change in admininstrative policy with respect to officer procurement. As noted above, the War Department in March 1943 had granted the three major commands authority to establish OCS capacities and monthly entrance quotas. Thereafter Army Ground Forces set monthly quotas and maintained sufficient capacity to allow for emergency expansion. Without formally revoking this grant of authority, the War Department on 14 March directed Army Ground Forces to admit during June–August a maximum of 550 candidates monthly—500 to the Infantry School and 50 to the Field Artillery School.[13] No such directive had been received from the War Department during the preceding year. In view of the reentrance of the

[12] AGF M/S (C), CofS to G–1, 24 Sep 43, sub: OCS. 352/143 (C).

[13] WD ltr AGOT–S–WDGAP–A 352 (12 Mar 44) to CG AGF, 14 Mar 44, sub: AGF OCS Quotas. AGF G–1 Sec files.

War Department into a province over which it had been supreme, Army Ground Forces understood that its own responsibility for determining the number of candidates to be trained had been terminated.[14]

The role of Army Ground Forces after March 1944 was advisory. The War Department letter of 14 March directed Headquarters, Army Ground Forces, to submit by 1 June "the estimated officer procurement requirements of the Army Ground Forces" to cover losses through 30 June 1945, and to recommend OCS quotas for the last quarter of 1944. The estimates were to be based on War Department loss requirement data. Directives calling for similar studies and recommendations were received from the War Department from time to time in subsequent months. In each case Army Ground Forces was to secure loss requirement data from the War Department, survey present officer strength and future needs, and recommend officer candidate capacities and entrance quotas. Thus after March 1944 Army Ground Forces influenced the program of officer procurement only indirectly.

The War Department gave Army Ground Forces no formal statement of its reasons for resuming direct control. But the change was coincident with the shift in the focus of the procurement program from mobilization to overseas loss replacement. After March 1944 it became increasingly important to bring officer production in the United States into close coordination with officer strength, requirements, and production overseas. Lacking facilities for gathering accurate information on theater loss requirement rates and on officer appointments overseas, Army Ground Forces was not capable of coordinating continental officer production with world-wide officer requirements and resources. It was felt at Headquarters, Army Ground Forces, that, since the War Department was presumably in a better position to relate Zone of Interior officer procurement to overseas demands, reversion to the War Department of control over OCS capacities was a step in the right direction.[15]

Officer Candidate Quotas, February–June 1944

Even before resumption of control by the War Department, Army Ground Forces began a campaign, which was to continue during most of 1944, to lift the ceiling on procurement of officers through the candidate schools. On 2 February 1944 Army Ground Forces submitted to the War Department its recommenda-

[14] AGF M/S (S), G–1 to CofS, 3 Apr 44, sub: AGF OCS Quotas. 352/101 (OCS)(S).

[15] Statement of Col W. S. Renshaw, G–1 AGF, to AGF Hist Off, 11 Sep 45.

tions on officer procurement for the year.[16] The principal officer requirements as fixed by the War Department were for units in the 1944 Troop Basis, for the War Department replacement pool of 18,500 which was to be maintained at that strength throughout the year (presumably in anticipation of 1945 requirements), and for the number of officers who, in accordance with War Department estimates, would be shipped overseas as replacements during 1944. The latter totaled 20,400, of whom 13,700 were in Infantry. The sum of these requirements, balanced against officers on hand, those due to become available out of current OCS commitments, and those available for transfer between arms yielded a net requirement for 1944 of 804 officers in Infantry, all other arms balancing exactly. Under the assumptions used, all schools except that of the Infantry could be closed by 1 June 1944, and a monthly quota of 335 candidates would be admitted to the Infantry Officer Candidate School during June, July, and August.

Army Ground Forces did not believe that the assumptions employed represented a realistic appraisal of the prospects. The War Department estimate of 1944 officer replacement requirements, according to the AGF viewpoint, was approximately 4,000 too low. The distribution of the overseas requirement to the ground arms was thought incorrect: the War Department estimated that 67 percent of the requirement would be in Infantry; Army Ground Forces estimated 76 percent. The replacement pool of 18,500 likewise appeared to be distributed incorrectly, only 49 percent being allocated to the Infantry. A more serious weakness in the calculations seemed to be the failure to include replacement requirements for 1945 in procurement plans for 1944. Army Ground Forces pointed out that it took almost a year to produce an officer replacement; the process of selection and training in the United States required eight or nine months, and three months more elapsed before the new officer was available for active duty at the front. This time factor made it seem unwise on the one hand to close down officer candidate schools merely because there was no immediate demand for officers of certain arms, and imperative on the other hand to begin production early in 1944 to meet the estimated requirements of 1945. Specifically, Army Ground Forces recommended the production by the end of 1944 of a reserve of officers equal to the number to be shipped during 1944. The effect of all these recommendations would have been to increase the officer-procurement objective for 1944 to a net of 24,935 officers, all in Infantry. Army Ground Forces proposed to the War Department that if its recommendations were found

[16] AGF memo (S) for CofS USA, 2 Feb 44, sub: 1944 Off Requirements. 320.2/708 (Str) (S).

unacceptable the War Department should supply an officer-procurement objective for 1945.

No direct action was taken on these recommendations. In March 1944 the War Department, as noted above, resumed its control of officer candidate policy. It also changed the existing system for providing officer replacements. Authorization for officer replacement pools, in effect since March 1943, was withdrawn. Only enough officers were to be retained in each arm to meet anticipated requirements through 31 March 1945; all others were to be transferred to arms in which immediate use for them could be foreseen.[17] The War Department, while continuing in effect the low OCS quotas to which Army Ground Forces had objected in February, increased its previous estimate of officer requirements for 1944 as follows:[18]

Infantry	25,000
Armored	1,600
Field Artillery	4,100
Tank Destroyer	1,100
Cavalry	1,500
Coast Artillery (AA and HD)	2,100
TOTAL	35,400

These estimates remained in effect for planning purposes until August 1944.

AGF headquarters was convinced that the measures taken by the War Department would lead to a severe shortage of officers. On 5 April, bringing together observations on officer procurement gleaned from the experience of the preceding year, Army Ground Forces urged a great increase in OCS enrollment. Its study indicated that quotas now directed by the War Department would result in a shortage of 7,000 infantry officers by November 1944 and—if the low quotas were continued during the last quarter of 1944—a shortage of 9,336 infantry officers by March 1945. To avoid these consequences, Army Ground Forces recommended Infantry Officer Candidate School quotas of 3,800 per

[17] (1) Par 2 of letter cited in n. 13 above. (2) AGF M/S (S), Control Div G–1 to G–1, 14 Mar 44, sub: 1944 Off Requirements. AGF G–1 Sec files (Renshaw) 71. (3) AGF M/S (S), G–1 to G–3, 18 Mar 44, sub: OCS Program. AGF G–1 Sec files (Renshaw) 66.

[18] (1) AGF M/S (S), Control Div G–1 to G–1, 14 Mar 44, sub: 1944 Off Requirements. AGF G–1 Sec files (Renshaw) 66. (2) Table of 1944 Off Repl Requirements from WD G–1. AGF G–1 Sec files (Renshaw) 160.

month during the period from May to August.[19] Since the War Department took no immediate action on this recommendation, Army Ground Forces, in setting quotas for May (the last month for which its responsibility over OCS production extended), followed the spirit of the War Department directive, cutting Field Artillery from 250 to 50 and setting Armored at 136 and Infantry at 800—a total of 986 for the month.[20] June quotas, announced on 3 May in accordance with the War Department directive, eliminated Armored, kept Field Artillery at 50, and cut Infantry down to 510.[21]

Army Ground Forces took steps in another direction to increase the number of officers available for overseas assignment. Since September 1943 Army Ground Forces had required three months of commissioned duty in a tactical unit as a prerequisite to overseas assignment. This was a more stringent requirement than that imposed by the War Department, which called only for three months of commissioned service. By May 1944 it was evident that the number of infantry lieutenants who would become available each month under the AGF service requirement would not satisfy overseas calls at the prevailing level of 2,000 a month. By changing the requirement of Army Ground Forces to the standard set by the War Department it was possible during the months of low OCS production from June through August to supply infantry lieutenants in the necessary numbers.[22]

Meanwhile Army Ground Forces had been preparing a study, ordered by the War Department in March, of officer procurement objectives and school capacities for the last quarter of the year.[23] This study, sent to the War Department on 1 June, was based on the revised 1944 Troop Basis, on War Department estimates of loss replacement requirements from 1 May 1944 through 30 June 1945, and on current strength data. By 30 June 1945, the study indicated, there would be a net shortage of 13,466 officers in the ground arms, concentrated almost entirely in Infantry. Current surpluses in other arms would have to be converted in order to hold the shortage to this figure. Army Ground Forces recommended

[19] (1) AGF memo (S) for CofS USA, 5 Apr 44, sub: AGF OCS Quotas. 352/101 (OCS)(S). (2) Incl to memo cited in (1). AGF G–1 Sec files (Renshaw). (3) AGF M/S (S), G–1 to CofS, 3 Apr 44, sub as in (1). 352/101 (OCS)(S).

[20] AGF ltrs to CGs AA Comd and R&SC, 5 Apr 44, sub: OCS Quotas for May 1944. 352/506 (OCS).

[21] AGF ltr to CG R&SC, 3 May 44, sub: OCS Quotas for June 1944. 352/508 (OCS).

[22] (1) AGF M/S, G–1 to CofS, 13 May 44, sub: Inf Repl Offs. (2) AGF TWX to CGs, 20 May 44. Both in 210.31/27 (O'seas Repl Deps).

[23] AGF memo (S) for CofS USA, 1 Jun 44, sub: AGF OCS Quotas. 352/103 (OCS)(S).

two alternatives. If loss replacement requirements, currently estimated by the War Department at 2,083 per month,[24] were to be met wholly from Zone of Interior OCS production, it would be necessary to increase Infantry quotas to 3,860 per month for the period 1 July to 30 October 1944. If, on the other hand, the disposition to curtail OCS operations indicated in the War Department's March directive remained paramount, the War Department would have to increase the number of direct commissions overseas, thereby reducing loss-replacement demands on the Zone of Interior.

While these recommendations were in preparation the War Department sharply increased Infantry Officer Candidate School quotas for June. On 27 May Army Ground Forces was directed to enter 1,600 Infantry candidates during June, a 100-percent increase over the quota for May. In addition, the War Department directed Army Ground Forces to continue converting officers of other arms to Infantry, at a rate of not less than 1,000 per month.[25]

The receipt, four days after this action, of AGF's prediction of an imminent shortage of officers prompted the War Department to authorize an even greater increase in infantry training capacity. The AGF letter of 1 June urged monthly quotas of 3,860 at the Infantry Officer Candidate School. The War Department ordered the Infantry OCS quotas for the period 1 July to 31 October increased to 3,200 a month.[26] This doubled the monthly input ordered on 27 May for June and increased by 640 percent the quotas set in March for the period June–August. Three reasons were cited by G–1 of the War Department for this abrupt reversal of its earlier position on officer procurement. Combat appointments overseas had proved to be far below the number forecast in March. Replacement shipments had exceeded over-all loss replacement estimates and could not be curtailed until the revised system of personnel accounting recently inaugurated by the War Department became effective. Establishment of the detachment of patients as a Troop Basis accounting device for handling hospitalized personnel had in effect authorized 12,000 additional officers.[27]

[24] (1) AGF memo (S) for CofS USA, 12 Aug 44, sub: AGF OCS Quotas. (2) WD D/F WDGAP 352 OCS to CG AGF, 23 Aug 44, sub: AGF OCS Quotas. Both in 352/105 (OCS)(S).

[25] WD ltr AGOT–S–WDGAP 352 (24 May 44) to CG AGF, 27 May 44, sub: AGF OCS Quotas. 352/408 (Inf OCS).

[26] WD ltr AGOT–S–A 352 (7 Jun 44) to CG AGF, 10 Jun 44, sub: AGF OCS Quotas. 352/105 (OCS)(S).

[27] WD G–1 memo (S) WDGAP 352 OCS of Lt Col Haywood for Gen White, 7 Jun 44, sub: AGF OCS Quotas. WD G–1 files.

The War Department did not at this time make any change in the capacity of the Field Artillery Officer Candidate School; monthly input was to remain at 50 per month, as set in March. But other changes in the replacement system were forecast. Army Ground Forces was directed to submit by 5 September a study on future officer procurement, including recommendations on the Cavalry, Antiaircraft, Tank Destroyer, and Armored Officer Candidate Schools, which the War Department now thought it might be necessary to reopen to meet future replacement requirements. Another change involved officer replacement pools. In March the authorization of a pool of 18,500, in effect since early 1943, had been withdrawn, wholesale conversions being directed to match officer strength with requirements. On 10 June a War Department memorandum directed Army Ground Forces to include a pool of 10,000 officers in future planning. This provision was elaborated on 7 July, when authorized replacement pool capacities were established as follows:[28]

Branch	*1 October 1944*	*1 January 1945*	
Infantry	7,000	7,000	7,000
Field Artillery	3,250	2,250	1,250
Cavalry	1,200	850	450
Coast Artillery (HD)	150	100	50
Antiaircraft	1,500	1,000	500
Armored	1,200	850	450
Tank Destroyer	800	550	300
TOTAL	15,100	12,600	10,000

The immediate effect of the reestablishment of replacement pools was to increase greatly the requirement for officers. Reflecting this increase, the AGF study of officer procurement prepared in September called for another augmentation of the monthly input at the candidate schools. The probable future requirements for officers of all arms which the pool capacities suggested led Army Ground Forces on 7 July to direct that stand-by capacities be maintained at fairly high levels in all officer candidate schools, even in those not operating currently.[29]

While the AGF officer candidate schools closed in the spring of 1944 were not reopened, the Armored Officer Candidate School, previously scheduled to be suspended on 23 September, remained in operation. An interim class was started

[28] WD ltr (R) AGPO–A–WDGAP 210.31 (29 Jun 44) to CG AGF, 7 Jul 44, sub: Establishment of Off Repl Pools. 210.31/355 (R).

[29] AGF ltr (C) to CGs R&SC and AAC, 7 Jul 44, sub: Projected Minimum Capacities of OCSs. 352/305 (C).

in September in order to keep the facilities in operation.[30] Tank Destroyer and Mechanized Cavalry officer candidate training was resumed in November 1944. Anticipated requirements for officers of these two arms being too small to justify maintenance of separate schools, their officer candidate schools were combined with the Armored Officer Candidate School at Fort Knox, each class containing a proportion of candidates of the three branches.[31]

The Search for Candidates, June–December 1944

The establishment of larger officer candidate school quotas was only a necessary preliminary to solution of the replacement problem. The solution itself depended on filling the quotas and training the candidates. Army Ground Forces, having won its campaign for an increase in quotas, now found that candidates were not available in sufficient numbers to fill the quotas. After June 1944 a vigorous publicity campaign was launched—reminiscent in all essentials of the campaign in the autumn of 1942—to find officer candidates. The campaign failed, largely because of the departure from AGF control of units from which candidates could be drawn. It became necessary after September to depend on War Department action to supply candidates from the Army at large in the United States and, increasingly as deployment overseas continued, from the combat theaters.[32]

Difficulties in finding suitable candidates were anticipated as soon as the War Department authorized quotas of 3,200 at the Infantry School for June, July, and August. On 10 June Army Ground Forces instructed its commanders to give the candidate program the widest possible publicity, enjoining them to encourage actively applications even by men whose "work is important or replacement difficult." [33] In view of the scheduled suspension of all except Infantry and Field Artillery Candidate Schools, and of the small quotas for the latter, Ground Forces personnel of noninfantry units were to be encouraged to apply for the Infantry Officer Candidate School.

[30] (1) AGF M/S, CofS to CG, 4 Aug 44, sub: OCSs. AGF G–1 Sec files (Renshaw). (2) AGF memo (C) for CofS USA, 16 Aug 44, sub: Retention of Armd OCS. 352/320 (C). (3) WD 1st ind (C) AGOT–S–A 352 (16 Aug 44), 28 Aug 44, on memo cited in (2). 352/320 (C).

[31] (1) Pars 3 *b* and 5 *b* of AGF memo (S) for TAG, 6 Sep 44, sub: AGF OCS Quotas. 352/105 (OCS)(S). (2) Par 2, WD ltr (R) AGOT–S–A 352 (3 Oct 44) to CG AGF, 11 Oct 44, sub: AGF OCS Quotas and Repl Pool Capacities. 352/7 (OCS)(R).

[32] Statement of Col W. S. Renshaw, G–1 AGF, to AGF Hist Off, 11 Sep 45.

[33] AGF TWX to CGs, 10 Jun 44. 352/411 (Inf OCS).

230-171 O - 66 - 11

This campaign met with only indifferent success. The sources of officer candidates in the Ground Forces were rapidly drying up. Most of the ROTC students had been entered in school by June 1944. The number of candidates returned from overseas, never more than a slender trickle, could not be increased greatly; because of uncertainties of transportation they could not be counted on in any case until they had arrived in the United States. The principal sources of officer material were therefore the replacement training centers and tactical units under AGF control in the United States. Candidates in large numbers could doubtless have been drawn from the replacement centers, but this course was not entirely desirable. During the first six months of 1944 replacement production had passed through a series of upheavals, from which the program was only now emerging. Demands for enlisted replacements overseas were no less urgent than demands for officer replacements; it was not desirable to supply the latter at the expense of the former. A more fundamental objection to using replacement training centers as the chief source for meeting expanded candidate calls was the relative inexperience of men in the centers. In 1944 these men were generally young and had had only four months' training; it was believed that they would be less valuable for training as combat-officer replacements than men of greater maturity and military experience.[34]

The main burden in supplying candidates to fill the swollen quotas after June fell on the tactical units still in the United States. Units, which had been allowed to send only 244 men to the Infantry Officer Candidate School in June, were asked to supply 2,234 candidates in July and a peak of 2,545 in October. (See Table No. 5.) Circumstances less propitious for releasing large numbers of well-trained enlisted men could scarcely have been imagined than those in which units, especially divisions, found themselves during the latter half of 1944. Since late 1943, divisions had been plucked repeatedly to provide enlisted replacements. In March and April they had received infusions of new blood—air cadets, and men from the ASTP and replacement training centers. Forming these recruits into tactical teams was a major preoccupation during the summer of 1944. The experienced men left in the divisions were badly needed to conduct this essential training; they could ill be spared for officer candidate training. It was no wonder that commanders did not respond readily to pleas that even men whose "work was critical or whose replacement was difficult" be sent to officer candidate schools.

[34] AGF M/S (R), G–3 to G–1, 20 Nov 44, sub: OCS Quotas. 352/64 (OCS)(R).

Difficulties connected with training were not the only cause of failure of units to meet quotas. Units were being alerted and shipped overseas in ever increasing numbers in the latter half of 1944. In July the strength of units arriving at ports of embarkation was about 70,000, in August 112,000. Shipments in September totaled 140,000 men in 385 units, including 9 divisions. The peak was

TABLE NO. 5

Distribution of Infantry OCS Quotas Among Major Categories, June 1944–February 1945

Year and Month	T/O Units	RTC's	Overseas Candidates	Adjutant General	Other	Total Infantry OCS Quotas
1944						
June	244	13	29	0	224	510
July	2,234	450	202	0	314	3,200
August	2,339	410	241	0	210	3,200
September	2,230	305	505	0	160	3,200
October	2,545	497	86	0	72	3,200
November	1,200	688	52	0	60	2,000
December	25	525	0	1,390	60	2,000
1945						
January	25	525	0	1,390	60	2,000
February	25	525	0	1,390	60	2,000

Source: AGF quota ltrs in 352 (OCS) diagonals 508, 529, 532, and 539, and in 352 (Inf OCS) diagonals 412, 415, and 429.

reached in October, with the shipment of 150,000 men in 393 units, including 5 divisions.[35] Obviously, when units left the country they were lost to Army Ground Forces as sources of candidates. But the date of shipment was in fact not the date when this loss occurred. It had long been the practice to freeze the personnel of a unit when, usually from one to three months before actual departure, it received orders alerting it for overseas shipment. Army Ground Forces attempted to set this precedent aside on 15 July 1944 when it issued instructions permitting the selection of candidates from alerted units.[36] But this solution, if it ameliorated the situation—and there is no evidence that it did—was merely temporary. A revision of AR 625–5, published on 12 September, forbade selection of candidates

[35] Statistics compiled from AGF Stat Sec Rpt No. 19 (S), "AGF Units Arriving at PE."

[36] (1) AGF ltrs to CGs, 15 Jul 44, sub: Selection of Officer Candidates from Alerted Units. (2) AGF M/S, G–1 to CofS, 10 Jul 44, sub: OCs. Both in 352/520 (OCS).

from alerted units.[37] Army Ground Forces reversed its July instructions.[38] Henceforth men in units were unavailable as candidates during considerable periods before they actually left the country.

By September it was clear that Army Ground Forces could not meet Infantry OCS quotas of 3,200 a month from its own resources. The departure of units from the United States would soon leave the replacement training centers as the principal source of candidates, a source thought undesirable for reasons already stated. Army Ground Forces, in its recommendations of 6 September on future OCS operations, suggested that the pressure be taken off the Zone of Interior in procurement of officers. Two alternative courses were outlined. One was to reduce Zone of Interior monthly OCS quotas to 1,750, for an estimated output of 1,312, and to seek to obtain 2,081 a month by overseas appointment, for a monthly total of 3,393, the number now believed necessary. If this division of production between the Zone of Interior and the theaters should not be feasible, Army Ground Forces recommended that theater commanders be directed to return to the United States their proportionate shares of monthly OCS quotas, based on theater strength.[39]

The War Department had undertaken on 18 August to determine the extent to which the theaters could furnish their own officer replacements. Theater commanders were sounded out on a proposal to curtail, after February 1945, officer candidate schools in the United States to levels which would provide officers for the Zone of Interior only. Overseas replacements would be furnished until March 1945; thereafter theaters would supply their own needs.[40] While reaction from the theaters was being awaited, quotas for November had to be fixed. Those for October, set on 31 August, were the last of the 3,200 series.[41] On 26 September the War Department, recognizing the difficulties of Army Ground Forces in finding candidates, and promising an early increase in the number of overseas appointments, established OCS quotas for November at somewhat lower levels.[42] The Infantry Officer Candidate School was to receive 2,000 candidates; Field Artillery, 150; and Armored (including also Tank Destroyer and Mechanized Cavalry),

[37] Par 9 *d*, AR 625-5, WD, 12 Sep 44.

[38] (1) Par 4, AGF Wkly Dir 42, 17 Oct 44. (2) M/R, C&RD, AGF, 17 Oct 44, sub: Selection of OCs from Alerted Units. 352/536 (OCS).

[39] AGF memo (S) for TAG USA, 6 Sep 44, sub: AGF OCS Quotas. 352/105 (OCS)(S).

[40] WD TWX (C), WARX 89177, 18 Aug 44, to Theater Comdrs.

[41] AGF ltr to CG R&SC, 31 Aug 44, sub: Quotas for AGF OCSs for the Month of Oct 44. 352/529 (OCS).

[42] WD ltr AGOT-S-A 352 (20 Sep 44) to CG AGF, 26 Sep 44, sub: AGF OCS Quotas. 352/532 (OCS).

150. These quotas amounted to 550 more candidates than Army Ground Forces in its memorandum of 6 September had forecast that it could provide.

Army Ground Forces was hard-pressed. There was no backlog of accepted candidates, and procurement was on a hand-to-mouth basis. On 25 September, when informed of the War Department's November quotas, Army Ground Forces still had to obtain 13 Infantry OCS classes, or 2,600 candidates, for entrance in October. The only candidates available were 300 from armored and 100 from field artillery units. Because of the poor response from unit commanders, approximately 40 percent of recent OCS quotas had been filled from the replacement training centers. The high rate of failures in the candidate schools indicated that much of the material uncovered was below standard. An analysis of five recent classes showed that 45 percent of the men enrolled had been relieved.[43] Aside from a lowering of quality, this rate of failure threatened to compromise estimates of output, which had been based on an anticipated failure of 20 percent of each candidate class. Though the causes were somewhat different, the effects were those observed in late 1942: last-minute urgent calls for officers exceeded the available supply of qualified candidates; to fill quotas poor candidates had to be accepted; these failed in large numbers, the original program was only partly fulfilled, units were bereft of good noncommissioned officers, and other units received mediocre officers or disgruntled rejects.

Army Ground Forces again sought to enlist the active support of its subordinate units and installations. On 26 September commanders were directed to give full publicity to the program and to encourage all qualified men to apply, regardless of the arm in which they were serving or the difficulty of replacing them. Commanders were now told to lay less stress on leadership ability as a condition of acceptance. "No application," the memorandum stated, "will be rejected solely because he [the candidate] has not had the opportunity to actually demonstrate leadership ability."[44] This tolerance of lower standards was reminiscent of the decision, taken in a similar crisis in 1942, to award commissions for administrative duty.

But the situation was too far gone to be repaired. By early October Army Ground Forces had decided that after November it should stop providing candidates entirely. On 6 October it recommended to the War Department that the entire December OCS quota be filled by men then serving overseas.[45] Approxi-

[43] AGF M/S (S), G-1 to CofS, 25 Sep 44, sub: OCSs. 352/335 (C).

[44] AGF ltr (C) to CGs, 27 Sep 44, sub: Off Candidate Program. 352/335 (C).

[45] (1) AGF memo (S) for CofS USA, 6 Oct 44, sub: Off Candidate Quotas. (2) AGF M/S, CofS to G-1, 5 Oct 44, sub: OCS Quota for December. Both in 352/107 (OCS)(S).

mately 60 percent of ground combat personnel was overseas, while on the basis of past performance it could be expected that only 6 percent of quotas would be filled from overseas sources. By December it was anticipated that almost all AGF units would be deployed or alerted. Army Ground Forces did not wish to use the replacement training centers as the major source of combat officers.

The War Department could not suspend Zone of Interior production of overseas officer replacements immediately. In August it had proposed to theater commanders that beginning in March 1945 they supply replacement needs from their own resources. Theater commanders had agreed to the proposal on the understanding that replacements would continue to come from the United States until March.[46] In the long run this plan would have put officer procurement on a world-wide basis, utilizing fully the resources of theaters as well as those of the Zone of Interior. But it did not promise the immediate relief that Army Ground Forces, squeezed between high OCS quotas and a dwindling number of troop units, required. The War Department had to ensure a steady flow of replacements overseas through February 1945 and, to guard against unforeseen contingencies, for months thereafter. Sources of officer material remaining in the United States had to be utilized. Monthly quotas for December through February, set by the War Department on 11 October, while well below total requirements for loss replacements, were far above the ability of Army Ground Forces to sustain. The new quotas were somewhat higher than those for November: Infantry, 2,000; Field Artillery, 200; and Armored (Tank Destroyer and Mechanized Cavalry), 250.[47] (See Table No. 3.) Tactical units were still carrying the load; they were given quotas of 1,200 to fill in November.[48] Although less than half the quota assigned to units for October classes, this figure was still far too large. On 28 October, no answer having been received from the War Department to the AGF proposal that all quotas after November be filled from sources outside Army Ground Forces, the Chief of Staff, Army Ground Forces, secured a compromise from the War Department. In the future Army Ground Forces was to supply candidates to the limit of its capabilities, the War Department was to supply an additional number, and the theaters were to

[46] (1) WD TWX (C), WARX 89177, 18 Aug 44, to Theater Comdrs. (2) TWX (C) USAFFE to WD, CM-IN 5663, 7 Sep 44. (3) TWX (C), ComZ ETO to WD, CM-IN 24612, 26 Sep 44.

[47] (1) WD ltr (R) AGOT-S-A 352 (3 Oct 44) to CG AGF, 11 Oct 44, sub: AGF OCS Quotas and Repl Pool Capacities. 352/7 (OCS)(R). (2) AGF ltrs (C) to CGs R&SC and AAC, 5 Oct 44, sub: Off Candidate Capacities. 352/342 (C).

[48] AGF ltr to CG R&SC, 5 Oct 44, sub: Quotas for AGF OCSs for the Month of Nov 44. 352/532 (OCS).

be required to make up the remainder of their requirements.[49] It was estimated that the Ground Forces could provide 700 candidates per month—600 for the Infantry and 50 each for the Field Artillery and Armored Schools.[50] In quota letters issued after 1 November, for classes in December and the months following, commands under AGF control were allotted 700 places in officer candidate schools, of which the majority (600) were given to the replacement training centers. The Adjutant General was assigned the bulk of each quota (1,750) to be filled from continental sources outside the Ground Forces.[51]

The procurement program had thus been brought, so far as the Army Ground Forces was concerned, into balance with resources. Quotas for units dropped from an impossible 1,440 in November to a realistic 50 in December. But the program as a whole continued to be out of balance. The War Department acted to increase overseas appointments, to divert applicants for Army Air Forces and Army Service Forces schools to Ground Forces schools, to increase applications among returning rotational personnel, and to encourage applications among men in inactive theaters.[52] Overseas appointments showed a moderate increase in early 1945. (See Table No. 7.) Other measures taken to recruit candidates outside the jurisdiction of Army Ground Forces brought only the most meager response. Early in December The Adjutant General estimated that he could supply only 300 candidates each month, including those returned from overseas. With monthly input capacity at 2,450, a shortage of 1,450 candidates per month was indicated.[53] The War Department, urged by Army Ground Forces in mid-December to reduce capacities to a level consistent with the anticipated availability of candidates, was reluctant to do so. Army Ground Forces was authorized to employ unused school capacity as it saw fit, but no reduction was made pending more complete information on direct appointments overseas and on the

[49] (1) Memo (S) of CofS AGF for CG AGF, 28 Oct 44, sub: Pers for OCSs. 352/107 (OCS)(S). (2) AGF memo (S), G–1 to CofS, 27 Oct 44, sub: Off Candidate Prog. AGF G–1 Sec files, 352 (Schs)(S). (3) Draft (not used) of AGF memo (S) for CofS USA [27 Oct 44], sub as in (2). AGF G–1 Sec files, 352 (Schs)(S).

[50] (1) AGF M/S (S), G–1 to CofS, 1 Nov 44, sub: Availability of OCS Applicants from Systems under AGF Only. AGF G–1 Sec files, 352 (Schs)(S). (2) AGF M/S (C), G–1 to CofS, 13 Dec 44, sub: OC Prog. 352/372 (C).

[51] (1) AGF ltr to CG R&SC, 10 Nov 44, sub: Quotas for AGF OCSs for the Month of Dec 44. (2) Quota ltrs for Jan 45 (1 Dec 44), and Feb (5 Jan 45). Both in 352/539 (OCS).

[52] (1) WD ltr (R) AGOT–S–A 352 (10 Nov 44) to CG AGF, 15 Nov 44, sub: OCS Quotas. 352/6 (OCS)(R). (2) WD TWXs listed in ltr cited in (1).

[53] AGF M/S (C), G–1 to CofS, 13 Dec 44, sub: Off Candidate Prog. 352/372 (C).

operation of two officer candidate schools being established in England and France.[54] On 29 December 1944 the War Department gave commanders of active theaters virtually unlimited authority to make officer appointments "because of the lack of qualified officer candidates in the United States having the desired experience." [55] The authority was to be used to the maximum extent of theater resources "to meet all theater needs." Commanders of inactive theaters, on the other hand, were enjoined to secure applicants for officer candidate schools in the United States and to make direct appointments sparingly, and then only with the consent of the War Department.[56]

Procurement in 1945

The arrangement put into effect in November 1944, by which Army Ground Forces supplied 700 officer candidates per month and The Adjutant General provided the remainder, continued during early 1945. Overseas theaters, finally convinced that Zone of Interior resources for officer production were limited, began to fill larger proportions of their own requirements.[57] Overseas shipments of officer replacements, after rising to almost unprecedented heights in January and February, largely because of losses in the Battle of the Bulge, receded in March to lower levels than had prevailed in 1944. (See Table No. 6.) Production of officers in the European Theater was facilitated by the establishment of an officer candidate school near Paris, for which Army Ground Forces provided a cadre of instructors from the Infantry School at Fort Benning.[58] In February 1945 appointment of officers overseas rose to 994, the largest for any month since August 1943. (See Table No. 7.)

[54] (1) AGF memo (C) for CofS USA, 19 Dec 44, sub: OCS Quotas. 352/372 (C). (2) WD memo (C) WDGAP 352 OCS for CG AGF, 16 Jan 45, sub: OCS. 352/372 (C). (3) AGF memo for CofS USA, 5 Feb 45, sub: OCSs. 352/566 (OCS). (4) WD ltr (C) AGOT-A-A 352 (14 Feb 45) to CG AGF, 16 Feb 45, sub: Quotas for AGF OCSs. 352/385 (C).

[55] WD ltr AGPR-A-A 210.1 (27 Dec 44) to CGs China Theater, SPA, POA, India-Burma Theater, MTO, and ETO, 29 Dec 44, sub: Authority to Make Appointments. AGO Records, 210.1 (27 Dec 44)(1).

[56] WD ltr, file and sub as in n. 55, to CGs USAF Mid East, Persian Gulf Comd, Alaskan Dept, 29 Dec 44. AGO Records, 210.1 (27 Dec 44)(1).

[57] Cf. Minutes of Meeting to Discuss ETO Repl Situation, held in Washington 23 and 28 December 1944, with representatives of WD, AGF, and ETO. 320.2/173 (O'seas Repls)(S).

[58] (1) Par 9, Summary of Conclusions Reached and Actions Taken with Respect to the ETO Repl Problem (S) WDGAP 322 Repls, 28 Dec 44. (2) TWX, Hq ComZ, ETO, to WD, 3 Jan 45, CM-IN 2673. (3) AGF M/S (R), Off Div to G-1, 6 Jan 45, sub: School and RTC Set-Up for O'seas. (4) AGF M/S (S), CofS to G-3, 29 Dec 44, sub: Establishment of Inf Sch in ETO. All in 354.1/120 (RTCs)(S).

TABLE NO. 6

Overseas Shipments of AGF Officer Replacements, September 1943–August 1945

Year and Month	All Arms		Infantry Only	
	All Theaters	ETO Only	All Theaters	ETO Only
1943				
September	457	147	298	31
October	766	115	480	48
November	1,494	190	776	71
December	1,171	831	598	443
1944				
January	1,814	108	1,117	0
February	1,891	1,032	886	192
March	2,776	1,637	2,192	1,347
April	2,493	1,535	1,919	1,338
May	4,075	3,259	2,164	1,675
June	2,089	1,313	1,714	1,224
July	2,422	2,159	1,607	1,420
August	2,761	2,443	1,684	1,582
September	1,340	1,049	960	855
October	1,186	735	484	314
November	1,779	795	1,387	736
December	2,133	1,172	1,064	500
1945				
January	3,226	2,096	1,898	1,244
February	3,002	1,574	1,942	1,143
March	1,496	785	981	557
April	1,319	676	762	422
May	1,233	10	711	0
June	1,548	11	1,040	0
July	2,005	62	1,032	0
August	5,321	5	2,742	1

Source: **Data from C&RD, Grd AG Sec, Hq AGF.**

By March 1945 it seemed feasible to consider putting the provision of officer replacements by the Army Ground Forces on a standard basis.[59] March had previously been agreed on between the War Department and the theaters as the first month in which the supply of officers from the United States would be reduced to a flat monthly rate, the remainder to be provided within the theaters. The replacement crisis following the Battle of the Bulge had prevented starting

[59] AGF memo (S) for CofS USA, 7 Mar 45, sub: Off Requirements. 210.31/1 (O'seas Rpls) (S).

TABLE NO. 7

Overseas Appointments of Male Officers, September 1942–June 1945

Year and Month	Number Appointed	Year and Month	Number Appointed
1942		1944	
September	79	March	171
October	118	April	499
November	633	May	439
December	1,010	June	642
1943		July	884
January	392	August	833
February	148	September	171
March	811	October	374
April	543	November	291
May	1,305	December	268
June	180	1945	
July	941	January	591
August	1,090	February	994
September	907	March	228
October	937	April	200
November	283	May	464
December	239	June	475
1944			
January	508		
February	936	TOTAL	18,584

Source: The Adjutant General's Office, Machine Records Branch, 26 September 1945.

the system in March as planned. Representatives of G–1, War Department, and of Army Ground Forces now worked out a "Standard Monthly Call" for replacements to be supplied after 20 April:

Infantry	1,000
Armored	200
Antiaircraft	50
Mechanized Cavalry	80
Field Artillery	200
Tank Destroyer	30
TOTAL	1,560

To furnish this monthly call from April through September it was estimated by Army Ground Forces that some readjustments of officer strength would be required. In particular, shortages of officers in Cavalry (75), Tank Destroyer (53), and Armored (426), and excesses of officers in Field Artillery (493) and Antiaircraft (265), were in prospect. After September, when all possible conversions would have been made, it was estimated that monthly calls could not exceed the following anticipated school output:

Infantry	560
Field Artillery	70
Armored	35
Tank Destroyer	10
Cavalry	25
Antiaircraft	0
Coast Artillery (HD)	0
TOTAL	700

On the basis of these calculations, steps were taken immediately to convert surpluses of officers in Field Artillery and Antiaircraft to officers in Armored, Cavalry, and Tank Destroyer. Special Basic Courses were established at the schools of these arms for the purpose.[60] In all, during 1945, conversion courses in the service schools retrained over 3,000 officers of other arms as follows:

Infantry	2,287
Armored	431
Field Artillery	341
Cavalry	77
TOTAL	3,136

The projected standardization of monthly calls for overseas officer replacements was interrupted by the end of the war in Europe. V-E Day found AGF officer candidate schools operating considerably below planned capacity; although 2,000 candidates were scheduled to enter the Infantry Officer Candidate School each month, actual enrollment during the first four months of 1945 was only 1,400 a month, of whom only about 1,000, experience had shown, would

[60] (1) WD ltr (S) AGPO-A-A 210.33 (7 Mar 45) to CG AGF, 13 Mar 45, sub: Off Requirements. 210.31/1 (O'seas Repls) (S). (2) AGF ltr (R) to CG R&SC, 27 Mar 45, sub: Conversion of Offs of Other Arms to Armored. 210.31/1 (O'seas Repls) (S). (3) AGF ltr (R) to CG R&SC, 27 Mar 45, sub: Conversion of AA Offs to Cav. 352/219 (R).

be commissioned. Only ten classes began the Infantry OCS course between 16 March and 9 May 1945, eight projected classes being abandoned for lack of candidates. Of the 2,000 men entering the Infantry Officer Candidate School in this period, 1,107 (55.4 percent) came from AGF replacement training centers, 485 (24.2 percent) were drawn from other Zone of Interior sources, 244 (12.2 percent) were turnbacks, and only 164 (8.2 percent) were from overseas sources.[61]

Two requirements made it desirable to operate the Infantry Officer Candidate School at full capacity: a backlog of replacements had to be built up for the Pacific war, now expected to enter a more intense phase, and a reserve of officers was needed to replace officers discharged during redeployment. On 9 May Army Ground Forces requested the War Department to return 600 candidates per month from inactive theaters—a category in which both the European and Mediterranean Theaters now fell—beginning in June, to bring Infantry Officer Candidate School enrollments up to the authorized 2,000 a month.[62] Although the War Department replied that officer candidates would be returned as rapidly as possible, no candidates from inactive theaters were received or even reported available up to the beginning of July. Officer candidate schools in the European and Mediterranean Theaters were discontinued, and the authority of commanders of those theaters to make unlimited officer appointments was revoked.[63] Army Ground Forces returned to the War Department on 8 July with another plea for expeditious processing and return of candidates from inactive theaters.[64] At the same time, subordinate commanders in the Ground Forces to whom redeployed units were to be assigned were directed to process OCS applications from the moment units arrived from overseas until thirty days prior to their readiness dates for shipment to the Pacific.[65] It was not anticipated that many candidates would be procured from redeployed units; they were to be in the United States for only a very short time, and commanders faced with early combat against the Japanese were not expected to part willingly with good men, especially in view of losses they would have suffered under the point system of discharges.

[61] Classes 470–487; the figures were compiled from reports in 352/513 (Inf OCS).

[62] AGF memo for CofS USA, 9 May 45, sub: Inf OCS. 352/517 (Inf OCS).

[63] (1) WD ltr AGOB–T–A 352 (7 Jun 45) to CG AGF, 12 Jun 45, sub: Inf OCS. (2) AGF M/S, G–1 to G–3, 15 Jun 45, sub: Inf OCS. Both in 352/517 (Inf OCS).

[64] AGF memo for CofS USA, 8 Jul 45, sub: Inf OCS. 352/517 (Inf OCS).

[65] (1) AGF ltr to CGs, 8 Jul 45, sub: OCS Prog. (2) AGF M/S, G–1 to G–3, 15 Jun 45, G–3 to G–1, 20 Jun 45, G–1 to CofS, 5 Jul 45, sub: Inf OCS. Both in 352/517 (Inf OCS).

A full-dress reappraisal of the officer procurement problem was sent to the War Department on 23 July 1945.[66] It surveyed resources and requirements for redeployment and the war in the Pacific to 31 December 1946. In the absence of definite instructions from the War Department, Army Ground Forces planned to discharge 9,307 officers, to convert 6,705 officers of other arms to Infantry—a few going to Coast Artillery (harbor defense)—and to increase monthly enrollment in the Infantry Officer Candidate School to 2,940, a 50-percent increase over the current input. No change was proposed in the capacities of the Field Artillery or the combined Armored–Cavalry–Tank Destroyer Officer Candidate Schools. To implement this plan, Army Ground Forces submitted to the War Department a proposal for meeting the new monthly candidate requirement.[67] The experience of the preceding four months had shown that the shortages noted in May were persistent, as indicated in the following tabulation:[68]

	Infantry	*Field Artillery*	*Cavalry*	*Armored*	*Tank Destroyer*
Monthly Input Recommended by AGF G–1, 28 July 1945 . .	2,940	200	114	100	36
Average Input, Preceding Four Months	1,098	162	51	105	37
Shortage	1,842	38	63	. . .	. .

Army Ground Forces recommended that 2,000 candidates be returned to the United States each month from inactive theaters: 1,875 for Infantry, 50 for Field Artillery, and 75 for Cavalry. It proposed that increments for August and September be returned by air, displacing high-score personnel scheduled to be returned for demobilization.

The ending of the war with Japan, two weeks after these proposals were submitted, threw them into the discard. Officer requirements being immediately reduced, OCS capacities were cut to low levels pending determination of the size of the postwar army.[69]

[66] (1) AGF memo (S) for CofS USA, 23 Jul 45, sub: AGF Off Procurement Objective. (2) AGF M/S (S), G–1 to CofS, 19 Jul 45, sub as in (1). Both in 352/110 (OCS)(S).

[67] (1) AGF memo (S) for CofS USA, 2 Aug 45, sub: Procurement of Accepted OCS Applicants. (2) WD D/F (S) WDGAP 210.1 (S) to CG AGF, 27 Jul 45, sub: AGF Off Procurement Objective. (3) AGF M/S (S), G–1 to CofS, 1 Aug 45, sub: AGF Procurement Objective. All in 352/110 (OCS)(S).

[68] AGF M/S (S), G–1 to G–3, 28 Jul 45, sub: Procurement of Accepted OCS Applicants. 352/110 (OCS)(S).

[69] (1) AGF memo (C) for CofS USA, 5 Sep 45, sub: OCS Capacities. (2) WD D/F (C) 352 OCS (5 Sep 45) to CG AGF, 7 Sep 45, sub: OCS Capacities. (3) AGF ltr to CG R&SC, 14 Sep 45, sub: Capacities and Quotas for AGF OCSs. All in 352/1 (OCS)(S).

IV. Basic Problems of Officer Procurement

The basic problem faced by the Army in procuring officers for World War II, as for all previous wars, was that of drawing from civilian sources an adequate supply to meet a sudden emergency. In World War II that supply had to meet the requirements of a war new in type. The rate at which the supply of officers would have to be maintained to replace casualties was not readily predictable on the basis of previous experience. Furthermore, officers had to be ready to cope with an unprecedented range of technical and administrative problems. In the Army Ground Forces most of them had to be ready to lead troops in combat, and in addition many of them had to be prepared for leadership in organized arms not previously employed by the United States in war: Antiaircraft, Mechanized Cavalry, Armored, and Tank Destroyer.

The Army obtained most of the officers to man its initial expansion either by drawing upon its civilian components—the National Guard and the Officers' Reserve Corps—or by directly commissioning civilians, among whom could be found a number who had had some military training or who had been officers in World War I. Officers of the National Guard were better trained than in 1917, and the Officers' Reserve Corps had been greatly strengthened by the operation of the Reserve Officers' Training Corps. But, in the ground arms at least, it was found that the Army "did not have in fact the great mass of trained officers that were carried on the books." During the initial period of mobilization the officer problem was a problem of quality, inherited from an undernourished peacetime establishment.

During the war years the majority of officers in the Army Ground Forces were procured from the enlisted ranks by means of officer candidate schools. Through this system the Ground Forces obtained the mass of junior officers needed for its rapid expansion in 1942 and 1943 and for the replacement of young officers lost in combat in 1944 and 1945. It was a democratic system. It permitted the Ground Forces to utilize the aptitude for leadership provided by the wide sweep of Selective Service through the youth of the Nation. It provided young leaders who had had experience in the ranks. Army Ground Forces found its OCS graduates better suited for its purposes than graduates of the ROTC. Men graduating from ROTC units had been invaluable, indeed indispensable, in providing the Army with junior officers during the initial period of mobilization, but they necessarily lacked the concentrated training and background of experience of OCS graduates. The officer candidate schools provided such a satisfactory source of junior officers that the efforts of the Ground Forces to procure officers, after the initial period, were concentrated on deriving maximum benefits from the system and overcoming, as far as possible, the conditions that impaired its efficiency.

The main problem was to have graduates of the desired quality in the numbers needed at any given time. By depending on the ranks to furnish officer candidates, the schools were tied in with the current enlisted strength of the Army Ground Forces—until late 1944 with the enlisted strength of the ground combat arms in the Zone of Interior. Thus the number and quality of OCS graduates were affected by the fluctuations in the AGF Troop Basis and the replacement system. The result was that the output of graduates from the AGF officer candidate schools and the demand for them were in fact continuously and seriously out of balance. The consequences of this lack of balance were evident throughout the war.

In 1942 rapid mobilization created a demand for graduates so great that standards were lowered and the quality of junior leadership available to the ground arms declined. In 1943, when mobilization of the ground arms was slowed down and then virtually completed at a much lower level than originally planned, the demand for junior officers fell off sharply, leaving a surplus of men with commissions. In consequence, for a time enlisted men with better qualifications than those previously commissioned were denied officer status, and the Army Ground Forces was deprived of potential leadership. When in 1944 the Army passed from the phase of mobilization to the phase of maintenance, the pendulum again swung in the opposite direction and the demand for junior officers greatly exceeded the supply. At a time when the output of the officer candidate schools had been cut to a minimum, the loss of junior officers in battle, particularly in the Infantry, mounted far above the number that were being provided under the production policies established by the War Department in the spring of 1944. The previous surplus of young officers was quickly consumed. The Infantry Officer Candidate School was greatly expanded after June 1944, but the limited number of enlisted men then available could not supply candidates of adequate quality in adequate numbers, even when standards were once again lowered. An acute crisis ensued which was not completely overcome before the end of the war.

These fluctuations in demand affected adversely the quality of training in the officer candidate schools. When sudden expansion was ordered, facilities and staffs were put under strain and instruction was spread thin. When cuts were ordered, extensive facilities remained idle and experienced staffs were partially dispersed. A few months later, with a new demand, the process of hasty expansion had to be repeated. What the schools accomplished under such conditions was a magnificent example of resourcefulness and devotion to duty.

The lack of balance in demand and supply among the different arms of Army Ground Forces also presented a serious problem. This unbalance could only be corrected by a wasteful process of conversion and retraining. Nevertheless, the conversion of thousands of officers from other branches helped to ease the critical shortage of infantry officers in 1944.

The effect of these difficulties might have been reduced except for the fact that the officer candidate system could not respond quickly to sudden changes in plans. When production had to be curtailed in 1943, months elapsed before the outpouring of candidates could be halted. When the call for more replacements required accelerated production in 1944, months elapsed again between the decision to increase output and the actual increase in officers available. In both cases crises of overproduction or underproduction occurred between the decision for change and its implementation. To select, train, and prepare an officer for overseas duty required a long period, varying from eight to twelve months. Once enrolled in large numbers, candidates would continue to graduate in large numbers until several months later, regardless of intervening changes in requirements. If current output was low, it could not be increased in less than eight to twelve months, no matter how urgent the need for officers became. Such inelasticity was inherent in the system.

Efforts were made to offset this inelasticity, but were largely ineffective or came too late to affect the mass procurement of officers in World War II. One of these efforts was to decentralize the procurement of officer candidates. Since the problems of the OCS system were tied into the Troop Basis, variations in strategy, and the distribution of manpower within the Army as a whole, it was logical that the War Department should control the system. On the other hand, the Army Ground Forces, as the command in control of both the schools and the troops from which the candidates were drawn, might be expected to provide a better adjustment of output to requirements. Both methods were tried, but neither solved the fundamental problem of unbalance.

Another measure designed to help solve this problem was an effort to obtain more accurate and comprehensive information regarding supply and demand. In June 1944, having reassumed control over officer procurement, the War Department established a Strength Accounting and Reporting Office in order to put personnel accounting on a uniform and world-wide basis. Information available on such matters as the number, branch distribution, location, and assignment of officers had been woefully fragmentary and uncertain. In computing officer requirements different sets of figures had been used by the War Department and the Army Ground Forces, and even within the headquarters of Army Ground Forces there was no general agreement on relevant statistical data. Confusion in planning was the greater because the existing system of accounting for officer strength was based on classification by arms which had been superseded. Officers were commissioned only in the four statutory arms, and officers in the Armored, Antiaircraft, and Tank Destroyer arms were detailed from one of these four. Improvised procedures enabled Army Ground Forces to keep track of officers in all of the seven ground arms as long as they were in the United States, but once overseas they could be accounted for only with difficulty because they appeared in strength returns under the branch in which they had been commissioned rather than the one in which they were serving. Too often major decisions had to be based on partial information or delayed while more accurate information was being compiled. The Strength Accounting and Reporting Office was established to reduce these delays and make possible accurate as well as timely planning for the size and composition of the officer corps.

A third attempt to effect a better adjustment of supply to requirements grew out of the difficulties the Army Ground Forces experienced toward the end of 1944 in filling increased quotas for officer candidate schools. The deployment of AGF strength overseas had reduced manpower resources in the United States to levels incapable of supporting a program designed to produce officers to meet world-wide requirements. Under these circumstances the basis for officer procurement had to be extended beyond the Zone of Interior to Army-wide resources. This change in procurement created serious difficulties, which had not been successfully overcome by the end of the war. Production of officers overseas, by direct appointment and by school training, remained low in relation to theater strength. Candidates were returned from theaters in driblets too small to alleviate the shortage in the United States. Consequently, the bulk of candidates con-

230-171 O - 66 - 12

tinued to be recruited from the Army at home, with compromises in experience, training, interest, and ability comparable to those in 1942. A new procurement program of general scope was worked out at the end of 1944. By its terms, overseas theaters were to receive after March 1945 only a limited number of officers from the United States and were to fill remaining needs from their own resources. This program could not be fully implemented because the German offensive of December left many units in Europe extremely short of men and fighting in Europe came to an end before the new program could be fully tested. Still the experience of the Ground Forces had shown that, given the inevitable delay in the reaction of the officer school system to changed demands, it was essential that a sufficient supply of candidates be immediately available when needed to increase output. An Army-wide procurement basis seemed to be the logical solution to this problem.

In the light of the foregoing study it is apparent that changes along the lines projected during the war will not suffice by themselves to produce a well-coordinated program of officer procurement. Throughout, the greatest difficulties were caused by external conditions. The most conspicuous of these were the following:

1. *Initial lack of an officer reserve distributed by branch in proportion to the needs of mobilization.* Few armored, tank destroyer, or antiaircraft officers, Regular or Reserve, were initially available as such. Establishments for training them had to be set up at the last minute.

2. *Necessity for rapid mobilization upon the entry of the United States into war.* The need for men to fill units outran the supply available through Selective Service. Understrength units could furnish officer candidates only by risking their own training or filling their OCS quotas with men of inferior quality.

3. *Rigidity of the ROTC program.* When the War Department decided to induct men in the Advanced ROTC before they had completed the course in college, it felt obligated to enable these men to qualify for commissions after entering the Army. They were therefore sent to officer candidate schools—the bulk of them being enrolled in a period when there was no longer a need for increased officer production. Requirements for officers were so low during late 1943 and early 1944 that OCS quotas were allotted almost entirely to ROTC men, and enlisted men had very little chance of being admitted to officer candidate schools.

4. *Shifts in the AGF Troop Basis.* The deferment of units, for which candidates were scheduled to go to school or were already in training, resulted in 1943 in a surplus of officers above actual Troop Basis needs. This surplus grew as

planned activations were further curtailed and existing units were inactivated during 1943. Heavy cutbacks in certain arms, especially antiaircraft, not only added to the growing surplus of officers but also had the more serious effect of throwing available officer strength out of balance with probable requirements. The conversion of officers in 1944 grew out of this situation.

5. *Shifts in strategic plans.* The demand for replacements which would have resulted from the cross-Channel invasion planned for the spring of 1943, and then postponed, did not materialize. Pending the large-scale invasion of Europe in 1944, it was uncertain how far the surplus of officers would go toward cushioning replacement demands on the OCS system. In the winter of 1943–44, it was believed to be undesirable to add to the surplus by maintaining a substantial volume of OCS output. The expansion of OCS facilities for replacement needs was delayed, and later was not effected in time to avert the crisis in procurement during 1944. In the summer of 1944, when theater demands for replacements were building up to their greatest peak, officer candidate schools had declined to their lowest output since 1941. The immediate crisis had to be met by using up the surplus of officers, including those recently converted from other arms to the Infantry.

Some of the difficulties listed cannot be removed even by the most foresighted plan for officer procurement. They are summarized here to illustrate the type of external factors which planning must take into account.

The Provision of Enlisted Replacements

by

Robert R. Palmer and William R. Keast

Contents

Tables

I. The Replacement System During the Period of Mobilization

The plan for replacements with which the United States Army entered World War II was designed to prevent the hasty and disruptive expedients which had become necessary in World War I. Its distinctive feature was that all replacements were to be produced in the Zone of Interior, in nontactical establishments, in which they were to be properly trained in adequate numbers. These establishments, designated as replacement training centers, were constituted in each arm and service. It was intended to obtain from them enlisted fillers with which to bring to full strength units initially mobilized as well as replacements with which to maintain the fighting strength of units in combat.[1]

In World War I the plan for producing replacements in the combat arms provided for training in depot brigades set up in each divisional cantonment.[2] It failed. All the enlisted men available in 1917 and early 1918 were needed to form the units being whipped into shape for the American Expeditionary Forces. The depot brigades, which were used as reception centers, were completely occupied with this mission.[3] In the spring of 1918, in an effort to cope with the impending need for loss replacements which was soon to become acute, separate replacement training depots were created: six for the Infantry, two for the Field Artillery, and one for the Coast Artillery.[4] Beginning 1 May 1918 these were activated in cantonments vacated by divisions as these were shipped overseas. The exact number of replacements from these centers shipped overseas cannot be determined, but they were only a fraction of the total of 435,285 replacements poured into the combat divisions of the AEF between 1 May and 1 December 1918, or even of the total of 270,444 enlisted men designated as replacements who were landed in France

[1] MR 3–1, 23 Nov 40, "Organization and Training," par 33.

[2] "Replacement of Personnel in the American Expeditionary Forces," Chap. II, pp. 16–18, and Chap. III, *passim*. This monograph was prepared in the Historical Section, Army War College. Typescript copy in Historical Division, WDSS, World War I Branch, file entry 3347. (Pagination is not continuous but by chapters.)

[3] *Ibid.*, III, 4.

[4] *Ibid.*, III, 7.

before 30 October 1918.[5] Training at the centers was thrown into constant confusion by emergency drafts, and the training was poorly conducted. The replacements they turned out received, on the average, less than a month of training.[6] The first combat replacements sent to France had to be used for auxiliary services to meet a need that exceeded all anticipations.[7] When combat began to take its toll and activations were being stepped up to meet the requirements of the 80-division program adopted in July 1918, the replacement system broke down completely. The requisitions of the AEF had to be met by taking men from divisions being trained in the United States, disrupting their preparation for shipment. It finally became necessary, in order to meet the mounting casualties of divisions in the line, to strip the infantry privates from ten divisions which had arrived in France, thus breaking the divisions up or reducing them to skeletons.[8] Consequently, the burden of procuring and training replacements both for combat and specialist duty fell largely on the American establishment in France, which set up an elaborate organization for the purpose. But the strain put on it was so great that many replacements who were inadequately trained had to be thrown into divisions just prior to their commitment to battle or while they were already engaged with the enemy.[9]

Development of the Replacement Program, 1940–42

The prewar replacement plans in effect in 1940 contained various provisions to avoid the experience of World War I. To ensure the proper training of service replacements, provision was made for replacement training centers in the services as well as in the arms. The training was to be sufficiently thorough to qualify individual replacements not only for general duty with their arm or service but also for the military specialties required by each branch. The training programs were tied into the Army classification system and so constituted as to meet requisitions in accordance with military occupational specialties and specification serial numbers. It was thought that by this procedure it might be possible to

[5] *Ibid.*, V, 27 and table at end of Chap. V, prepared by the First Section (G–1), General Staff, Personnel Division, GHQ. For fragmentary figures regarding the number of replacements trained at replacement training depots, see *ibid.*, II, 12.

[6] *Ibid.*, III, 5–6 and 15.

[7] *Ibid.*, II, 10 and *passim.*

[8] *Ibid.*, II, 18–19; V, 9 and 27.

[9] *Ibid.*, V, 7.

minimize the misassignment of replacements. Replacement training centers were not to be used as reception centers but were to devote themselves entirely to their training mission. In general, replacement training was segregated from unit training, was centralized by arms and services from the beginning, and was to be completed in the Zone of Interior. According to the plan, replacements were to be trained in numbers proportionate to the requirements of mobilization and, later, to estimated rates of loss in battle. With a minimum of further preparation they would then be ready for duty with a unit in the United States or for action in a theater of operations. The system was designed to provide a continuous stream of replacements trained in the necessary jobs and delivered where and when needed. The organization of tactical units was adjusted to the existence and proper functioning of such a system. The triangular organization of the infantry division, and the organization of the armored division adopted in 1943, provided an internal reserve that would suffice to maintain the fighting power of the division only through comparatively brief periods of hard fighting; every ounce of fat was cut out of both types by the reductions of Table of Organization (T/O) strength effected in 1943. Once mobilized, combat units depended for their effectiveness very largely on receiving adequate numbers of properly trained replacements.

Prewar mobilization plans contemplated that replacement training centers should be an integral part of the process of mobilization. Actually, because of delays in construction, they were opened only in March 1941, about six months after the establishment of Selective Service. For the remainder of 1941, the newly inducted civilian received his basic training at a replacement training center. As soon as graduates were available, they were used to fill the ranks of divisions and other tactical units that had been mobilized and of new units being activated Freed from having to give basic training themselves, tactical units concentrated on the development of teams up to the division level, on participation in field exercises, and on maneuvers in which, in the summer and fall of 1941, whole corps and armies were engaged.

The system was found eminently satisfactory by those chiefly concerned. "Experience has demonstrated," G-3 of the War Department declared on 27 September 1941, "that the system of supplying all replacements for the ground forces from replacement training centers is far superior to the system of furnishing replacements direct to units or installations from reception centers." [10] Lt. Gen. Lesley J. McNair, then Chief of Staff of GHQ, and in that capacity

[10] WD memo G-3/6457 for TAG, 27 Sep 41, sub: RTCs. AGO Records, AG 341 (4-7-41)(1) Sec 3.

responsible for the tactical training of the ground army, was of the same opinion.[11]

Nevertheless, after Pearl Harbor, when the decision was made to activate thirty-seven new divisions in 1942, the conclusion was reached that a commensurate expansion of replacement training centers was impracticable. Their capacity might be expanded, but the number was not to be increased except for the new centers already authorized, those at Fort McClellan and Camp Robinson for training branch immaterial replacements. The obstacle was new construction, which Gen. George C. Marshall believed it imperative to hold to a minimum.[12] Divisions and most other units activated thereafter received all or some of their initial personnel, except their cadres, directly from reception centers. Units already in training, which would be seriously incommoded by receiving untrained recruits, were to continue to fill their vacancies with graduates of replacement training centers;[13] but actually, in the following years, they frequently received them directly from reception centers. Thus most units activated after Pearl Harbor, and, to an increasing extent, those which had been previously activated, became in effect basic training centers. In time they tended also to become replacement pools. The number of replacement training centers having been restricted, their capacity was subject to only limited expansion. With the rapid expansion of the ground forces, their output was often inadequate to fill even urgent requirements, so that units had to surrender trained personnel on call, receiving in return, often in driblets, men fresh from reception centers. Large units such as divisions found themselves training groups of men at various levels at the same time. The unity of such organizations was broken; they could not pass as teams through the cycles of the unit training program which was designed to have a cumulative effect. Training in teamwork and mutual support was impeded, and readiness for combat was indefinitely delayed.[14] By 1943, as a result of the lag in production of replacements by the replacement training centers, the program of unit training was threatened by a breakdown in the replacement system similar to that which had been so damaging in World War I.

[11] Comment 4a, CofS GHQ, on WD memo G–3/6457–433, for CofS USA, 27 Dec 41, sub: Mob and Tng Plan (revised) 1942. AGO Records, 381 (12–27–41)(2)(S).

[12] Memo (C) of Brig Gen H. R. Bull for G–3, 3 Jan 42, reporting a conference with Gen Marshall on the subject. AGO Records, 381 (12–27–41)(2)(S).

[13] WD memo G–3/6457–436 for CofS USA, 9 Jan 42, sub: Detailed Tr Unit Basis. AGO Records, 381 (12–27–41)(2)(S).

[14] See below, "The Building and Training of Infantry Divisions."

Extent of AGF Authority over the Replacement System

The organization and training programs of replacement training centers had originally been the responsibility of the chiefs of the arms and services. After the activation of these centers in March 1941 they operated under the joint control of these chiefs and of the corps area commanders. As the special service schools were also a responsibility of the chiefs of the arms and services, the training of individuals during the prewar mobilization of the Army was separated from the training of tactical units. The latter was until July 1941 the responsibility of General Headquarters, and after that date was divided between GHQ and the Chief of the new Army Air Forces. Graduates of replacement training centers and schools were assigned to tactical units by The Adjutant General on requisition. With the reorganization of the War Department and the major Army commands on 9 March 1942, the functions of the chiefs of the ground combat arms were vested in General McNair as Commanding General of the Army Ground Forces. The Commanding General of the Army Ground Forces thus became responsible for the training of individuals in the ground combat arms as well as for the training of ground tactical units. To supervise training in the four statutory arms—Infantry, Field Artillery, Coast Artillery, and Cavalry—and the three new quasi arms—Armored, Antiaircraft Artillery, and Tank Destroyer—AGF headquarters acted through three subordinate agencies, the Replacement and School Command, the Armored Force, and the Antiaircraft Artillery Command. School and replacement training in the service branches was vested in the Commanding General of the Services of Supply (later the Army Service Forces). Though many nondivisional service units were activated and trained by the Army Ground Forces, training of replacements for these units was not under AGF control.

On 18 March 1942 the War Department announced that policies and procedures regarding replacements would remain unchanged by the reorganization of 9 March.[15] Authority over the number of replacements to be trained, that is, authority to regulate the capacity of replacement training centers, was retained by the War Department. This was essentially a Troop Basis matter, involving higher policies on the allocation of manpower within the Army. Such authority was fundamental in any replacement system, since success in keeping units at T/O strength depended on the ratio between the number of replacements available and the authorized strength of units. (See Table No. 1.) Procedures of

[15] WD ltr 341 (3–11–42) EC–C–M to CGs AGF, AAF, SOS, 18 Mar 42, sub: Allocation and Distribution of Enl Repls. 322.96/306.

assignment to and from replacement centers remained unchanged (until March 1943). The Adjutant General continued in 1942 to assign inductees from reception centers in numbers sufficient to keep replacement training centers filled to the capacities prescribed by the War Department; he assigned graduates of the centers to units and other installations, according to priorities set by the War Department. Units having the necessary priority requisitioned directly on The Adjutant General, except that armored units requisitioned on the Chief of the Armored Force, who, like the Commanding General of the Army Air Forces, in consequence of an independence won in 1941, controlled the disposition of RTC graduates in his arm.

In 1942 the headquarters of Army Ground Forces was concerned primarily with the activation and training of units, especially infantry divisions, and did not at first give much of its attention to the matter of replacements. Supervision of the centers was willingly delegated to the Replacement and School Command and other commands concerned. Officers from AGF headquarters rarely inspected the centers or visited the Replacement and School Command in 1942.[16] Replacement training proceeded under the impetus given it in 1941 under the chiefs of the arms.

The Army Ground Forces sought no authority over administrative aspects of the replacement system. Shortly after the reorganization of March 1942 the War Department directed Army Ground Forces to submit monthly estimates of requirements for personnel.[17] General McNair believed that this would entail an overlapping with functions already performed adequately by War Department agencies. "The Army Ground Forces," he stated to the War Department on 28 March 1942, "is primarily a training organization and its requirements for personnel are limited solely to those for units to be activated. The actual replacement requirement is limited to that necessary to replace deceased personnel, an almost negligible requirement." [18] Because of turnover within units, this statement with regard to replacement requirements did not prove to be a correct forecast. But on the ground that the War Department already knew what units were to be activated and that, therefore, consolidated estimates by the Army Ground Forces would be a duplication of effort, the War Department rescinded its directive that the Army Ground Forces submit estimates.[19]

[16] AGF M/S (S), Tng Div to G–3, 20 Oct 43, sub: Tng of Repls and AA Units. 353/195 (S).

[17] See n. 15.

[18] AGF memo for G–3 WD, 28 Mar 42, sub as in n. 15. 322.96/319.

[19] WD D/F WDGCT 319 (3–28–42) to CG AGF, 16 Apr 42, sub as in n. 15. 322.96/319.

The Army Ground Forces took the position in 1942 that, while the training of overseas replacements was its function, their movement from its installations to theaters of operations was a function of the Services of Supply.[20] Establishment of overseas replacement depots in the United States for the assembling, temporary storage, and final checking of replacements, pending requisitions from overseas or availability of shipping, had long been foreseen as necessary by the War Department. The Army Ground Forces insisted in 1942 that such depots be operated by the Services of Supply. Though the Services of Supply was directed by the War Department in April 1942 to create two such depots, one on each coast, none was actually set up until January 1943.[21]

Functioning of the Replacement System in 1942

Replacement policy, controlled by the War Department, was geared in 1942 primarily to the needs of mobilization.The proportion of replacements to be trained in each arm or service and in individual jobs within each arm or service corresponded to requirements for the activation of new units, not to probable casualties in various branches and jobs. Filling of vacancies of units in training, not replacement of combat losses, guided the apportionment of RTC capacities. Hence in 1942 the Quartermaster Corps had as large an RTC capacity as the Field Artillery; the Signal Corps a larger capacity than the Armored Force; and the Medical Department half as large a capacity as the Infantry. In the Infantry the number of replacements trained as riflemen, cooks, and clerks corresponded to the number of men in each of these jobs called for in Tables of Organization of infantry units, without allowance for the fact that when battle losses began to occur the casualty rate among riflemen would be higher than among cooks.[22]

This system was well adapted to the early phase of mobilization and to a policy under which all fillers received by units were to have had basic training in replacement centers. The policy, however, was modified by the decisions of

[20] (1) AGF memo for G–3 WD, 10 Apr 42, sub: Repl Depots. 680.1/47. (2) AGF memo (C) for G–1 WD, 7 Jun 42, sub: Plan of Loss Repls for O'seas Forces. 320.2/130 (C).

[21] WD memo (C) WDGCT 320 (3–3–42) to CG SOS, 26 Apr 42, sub: Personnel Repl Depots. 680.1/5 (C).

[22] (1) WD ltr (C) AG 381 (4–1–42) EC–GCT–M to CGs AGF, AAF, SOS, 7 Apr 42, sub: RTC Capacity and Related Matters. 381/27 (C). (2) WD memo (S) WDGCT 320.2 (7–28–42) for CGs AGF, SOS, 28 Jul 42, sub: Allocation of Additional RTC Capacity to be Provided under the Mob Plan, 1943. 320.2/295 (S). (3) AGF 1st ind (S), 5 Aug 42, to G–3 WD on memo cited in (2). 320.2/295 (S). (4) WD ltr (S)AG 320.2 (8–27–42) MS–C–M to CGs AGF, AAF, SOS, 28 Aug 42, sub: Tr Basis, 1943. 320.2/3 (TB 43)(S).

December 1941, which provided that replacement training centers should not be expanded commensurately with the Army and that new units should receive fillers directly from reception centers. With RTC output no longer sufficient to fill all the mobilization requirements of units it was necessary to establish priorities in the assignment of RTC graduates. Units overseas or alerted for overseas movement were given high priority in obtaining RTC-trained personnel. Units forming in the United States were to receive RTC-trained men as these became available in each arm or service after requisitions of higher priority had been filled.

The arms and services varied greatly in respect to the number of RTC-trained men that new units could receive under these circumstances. The War Department announced in July 1942 that new armored, engineer, infantry, and military police units could not expect to receive any RTC-trained men. But new ordnance units could expect to receive 36.1 percent of their personnel in the form of RTC-trained men, new quartermaster units 41.7 percent, and new signal units 48.2 percent. The principle was adopted that service units, requiring a larger number of technically trained men than combat units, should receive a higher proportion of fillers already branch-trained than should units of the combat arms. On 28 July 1942 the War Department authorized an addition in 1943 of 50,000 to the total capacity of all replacement training centers. Some allotment was made to medical, engineer, and military police centers to bring these branches more nearly into line with the other services, but most of the 50,000 were allocated to infantry and armored replacement training centers. This was not, in effect, a departure from the general principle stated above, since existing RTC capacities in the Infantry and the Armored Force were insufficient even for high-priority requirements.[23]

Replacement centers in the ground combat arms were therefore intended in 1942 primarily to fill vacancies in overseas units and alerted units, or for cadres or training installations necessary for expansion. Such replacement needs in 1942, even in overseas units, were generally due to nonbattle causes and tended to occur in all jobs and all arms and services alike. Therefore in that year no particular difficulty was caused by the fact that the proportions of men trained in various arms and various jobs bore no relation to casualties. The main difficulty was that replacements were not numerous enough even for high-priority purposes.

[23] WD memo (S) WDGCT 320.2 Gen (7-28-42) to CGs AGF, SOS, 28 Jul 42, sub as in n. 22 (2). 320.2/295 (S).

It is a paradoxical fact that the output of the AGF replacement training centers was insufficient even for high-priority requirements in 1942, although AGF replacement training centers actually graduated more men in 1942, when virtually no battle losses had to be replaced, than in 1943. (See Table No. 2.) High-priority requirements in 1942 included not only the needs of overseas and alerted units but also the needs of schools and requirements for cadres and RTC trainer personnel. Until September 1942, when a 15-percent overstrength was granted to parent units, AGF units furnishing cadres were authorized to regain their T/O strength by drawing men from replacement training centers. Cadre requirements were very heavy in this period of rapid expansion. Units that were alerted in the summer of 1942 for the projected cross-Channel invasion of 1943 had to be filled with men already basically trained. Some of these units were subsequently de-alerted, but meanwhile a requirement for RTC graduates had been set up. Units preparing for the North African landing had to be filled. A replacement pool to back up this force was likewise created.

The number of RTC graduates available in the ground arms was further reduced when training facilities in the AGF replacement training centers were diverted to meet other needs. With the rapid expansion of service units in 1942 to supply the requirements of BOLERO, the output of SOS replacement training centers, though greater than that of AGF replacement training centers in pro-

TABLE NO. 2

Number of Men Trained at AGF Replacement Training Centers, 1941–45

Arm	1941	1942	1943	1944	1945[a]	Total[a]
Antiaircraft Artillery	....	[b]42,600	85,253	42,474	5,462	175,789
Armored	20,429	51,866	39,841	31,283	28,156	171,575
Cavalry	10,103	26,005	23,289	17,384	10,679	87,460
Coast Artillery	[c]	[c]1,266	7,008	....	....	[c]8,274
Field Artillery	62,403	116,690	95,366	64,981	24,160	363,600
Infantry	108,872	374,804	282,552	[d]457,715	[d]592,759	[d]1,816,702
Tank Destroyer	....	3,102	29,327	10,194	4,849	47,472
TOTAL	201,807	616,333	562,636	624,031	666,065	2,670,872

Source: C&RD, GAG Sec, Hq AGF.

[a] Through 31 August 1945.

[b] Estimated.

[c] Figures for 1941 and part of 1942 unavailable.

[d] Figures for 1944 and 1945 include production of IARTC's.

230-171 O - 66 - 13

portion to T/O requirements, was considered insufficient. To supply RTC-trained men to service units, 16 battalions in infantry replacement training centers, 10 in field artillery, and 2 in cavalry were converted to branch immaterial. Between July and October these 28 battalions trained 80,000 men for assignment to service units.[24] Meanwhile the War Department had begun to induct limited-service men. The 28 RTC battalions which had trained men for the services were, therefore, employed until early in 1943 to give basic training to limited-service men. These were assigned on graduation to defense commands, from which general-service men were assigned in return to the Army Ground Forces.[25]

The insufficiency of RTC graduates in 1942 appears to have been aggravated by faults in administration and by the absence of organized depots or pools. RTC graduates, if not requisitioned for high-priority purposes immediately on graduation, seem to have been disposed of by assignment to any units that might need them. Thus when high-priority requirements occurred at a time not corresponding to graduations at replacement training centers they were filled by drawing upon units as the only available sources.

As early as 28 July 1942 the War Department directed the Army Ground Forces to provide, when RTC output was insufficient, overseas replacements from low-priority units in training.[26] The Army Ground Forces was ordered to submit monthly lists of low-priority units, totaling at least 30,000 in enlisted strength. Activations at this time having proceeded faster than the induction rate, AGF units were chronically understrength. They could hardly supply replacements without further impairing their strength. To fill units earmarked for Task Force A, intended for North Africa, the Army Ground Forces depleted three divisions to below 50 percent of their strength.[27] To fill other earmarked units and to create a replacement pool it would be necessary to strip more units. To avoid stripping divisions and other units at random it was decided that two

[24] WD memo WDGCT 320 (RTC) for CG AGF, 27 May 42, sub: Employment of RTCs. With related papers. 354.1/56 (RTC). See also /69 and /159.

[25] (1) WD ltr (C) AG 220.31 (11–10–42) OC–E–WDGCT to CG AGF, 14 Nov 42, sub: Employment of RTCs for Limited Serv Pers. 327.3/1 (LS)(C). (2) WD ltr (C) AG 220.31 (1–23–42) OC–E–WDGCT to CG AGF, 28 Jan 43, sub as in (1). 327.3/1 (LS)(C). (3) WD ltr (C) AG 220.31 (2–27–43) OC–E–WDGCT to CG AGF, 2 Mar 43, sub as in (1). 327.3/1 (LS)(C). (4) WD memo WDGCT 353 (2–11–43) to CG AGF, 11 Feb 43, sub: Tng of Limited Serv Men in RTCs. 327.3/168 (LS). (5) AGF memo for G–3 WD, 15 May 43, sub: BI Limited Serv Bns at RTCs. 327/185 (LS).

[26] WD memo (C) WDGCT 220 (7–10–42) for CGs AGF, AAF, SOS, 28 Jul 42, sub: Personnel for O'seas Units. 341/12 (C).

[27] AGF memo (S) for OPD, 11 Sep 42, sub: Preparation of Units for O'seas Serv. 370.5/11 (S).

divisions, together with certain smaller units of various arms, should be designated as replacement pools. The 76th and 78th Divisions were so designated.[28] Receiving and temporarily storing RTC graduates pending requisitions, they acted for several months as depots or pools rather than as divisions in training. The raiding of other units for replacements was for a time virtually stopped.

Administrative Changes

Noting that units functioning as pools could not train as units, Army Ground Forces on 9 November 1942 again urged the establishment of Zone of Interior overseas replacement depots.[29] It was still believed by Army Ground Forces that they should be operated by the Services of Supply.[30] Two were established in January 1943, one at Shenango, Pa., and the other at Pittsburg, Calif., for the holding and processing of overseas replacements in all arms and services except the Air Forces.[31] In March the 76th and 78th Divisions reverted to normal training.[32] The handling of overseas replacements seemed to be settled. In fact, it was not.

It was decided at this time to decentralize assignment procedures by delegating authority to the three major commands, effective 1 March 1943.[33] Henceforth the War Department allotted inductees in bulk to the Army Ground Forces, specifying only how many should go to replacement centers. The Army Ground Forces informed The Adjutant General to what particular units or replacement training centers its quota of inductees should be assigned. In practice this con-

[28] (1) Memo of Col Tate, Plans Sec, for DCofS AGF, 21 Sep 42, sub: Rpt of G–3 WD Conference on Pers Matters. AGF Plans Sec file 185 (TB 42). (2) AGF memo (S) for G–3 WD, 23 Sep 42, sub: Activations, Priorities and RTC Pool. 320.2/352 (S). (3) WD memo (S) WDGCT 320.2 Gen (9–25–42) for CGs AAF, AGF, SOS, 25 Sep 42, sub: Repls of Units for O'seas Serv. 320.2/363 (S). (4) AGF ltr (R) to CGs, 2 Oct 42, sub: Repl Pools. 320.2/105 (R).

[29] AGF memo (C) for G–3 WD, 9 Nov 42, sub: Repl Depots. 320.2/222 (C).

[30] Memo of Lt Col Banville, Asst GAG, for Col Hyssong, 2 Feb 43, sub: Conference Relative to Decentralization of RTC Asgmts. 341/1024.

[31] WD Memo S600–1–43, 8 Jan 43, sub: Establishment of Pers Repl Deps. 320.2/5822.

[32] AGF M/S (C), G–3 to CofS, 8 Mar 43, sub: Repl Deps. 320.2/222 (C).

[33] See papers in 341/1024, especially: (1) Memo of Lt Col Banville for Col Hyssong, 2 Feb 43, sub: Conference Relative to Decentralization of RTC Asgmt. (2) WD ltr AG 220.31 (2–5–43) OC–E–WDGAP to CGs AGF, AAF, SOS, 13 Feb 43, sub: Decentralization of Pers Procedure. (3) AGF M/S, C&RD to G–3, 13 Feb 43, sub: Decentralization of Asgmt Procedures. (4) AGF ltr to CGs, 19 Feb 43, sub: Enl Pers Requisitions. (5) AGF ltr to CGs AAC, R&SC, Armd F, 20 Feb 43, sub: Rpts of EM Available for Shipment from AGF RTCs and Schs.

stituted no great innovation. The main innovation was that the headquarters of the Army Ground Forces now assigned graduates of its replacement centers and its schools. AGF units henceforth requisitioned on the headquarters of the Army Ground Forces for personnel from all sources. To implement these new procedures a Classification and Replacement Division was set up in the office of the Adjutant General of the Army Ground Forces. While all higher control remained with the War Department, AGF headquarters was now in a position to gather statistics, codify its needs, plan the distribution of its personnel resources, anticipate difficulties or crises, and recommend action to the War Department. As mobilization approached completion in the summer of 1943, the main work of the Army Ground Forces shifted from the mobilization and training of new units to the maintenance of its own units at authorized strength, to the economizing of manpower by accurate classification and assignment, and to the provision of replacements to units in combat. Under these circumstances the Classification and Replacement Division became one of the most active and important elements of AGF headquarters.

II. The Replacement System and Combat Losses

In the early part of the war, roughly from 1941 to 1943, the primary purpose of the replacement system was to fill the needs of mobilization. From 1943 until the end of the war in Europe, it had to be adapted to the need of supplying replacements for overseas losses. The transition was gradual, running through the year 1943. In the later period the major emphasis was at first on the quality of replacement training—on ensuring that replacements received by overseas forces were properly trained. From the time combat intensified at the close of 1943, the major stress was on quantity—the sending of enough replacements overseas to enable units to continue in combat.

The Question of the Quality of Overseas Replacements

Except for the Philippine campaign of 1941–42, the losses of which could not be replaced, the Army did not engage in large-scale operations requiring many combat replacements until the North African campaign, launched in November 1942. Complaints were received from North Africa early in 1943 that replacements were unsatisfactory. It was reported that combat replacements reaching North Africa included men who had not had the prescribed thirteen weeks of basic training, or had never fired their primary weapons, or were improperly equipped, or were physically unfit, or were disciplinary cases unloaded by units in the United States.[1] The Army Ground Forces directed its observers in North Africa to look into the replacement situation. General McNair and officers of his staff gave it their attention when they visited North Africa in April 1943. In this, as in other matters, the campaign in North Africa was the great experiment from which lessons had to be learned for guidance in the invasion of Europe.

The conclusion reached at AGF headquarters was that the supply of replacements had been unsatisfactory, but that the fault lay not so much in the quality

[1] (1) AGF M/S (S), CofS to G–3, 18 Feb 43, sub: Loss Repls Tng. 354.1/4 (RTC)(S). (2) Memo of Col. L. L. Williams for CG AGF, 14 May 43. AGF G–3 Sec file, Obsrs #35, to which Gen Bull's rpt is atched as Tab B. (3) Obsrs' Rpts in 319.1 (Foreign Obsrs)(S) and (C), for example, the Rpt of Maj Gen W. H. Walker, 12 Jun 43, par 10 in unabridged version. (4) Materials in 353/2 (NATO)(C).

of training as in misconceptions of that training among officers in the theater and in defects of administration in both the United States and Africa. One common misconception was the failure of overseas commanders to understand that replacement centers in the United States were obliged to give in thirteen weeks both basic military training and training for individual jobs, such as those filled by riflemen, antitank gunners, clerks, and radio operators. When questioned in the theater soldiers often stated that they had had only three or four weeks of basic training, while in fact they had had the thirteen weeks prescribed by the War Department but had spent much time during the later weeks in learning their specialties.

Faults in administration lay principally outside the jurisdiction of the Army Ground Forces, which in general had jurisdiction over training only. It was found that medical examination, issue of equipment, and other processing had in some cases been very cursory at the Shenango Replacement Depot and at staging areas through which replacements had passed before that depot was established. The experience of replacements en route tended to destroy their morale and to undo the effects of their training. Shipped without unit organization or strong command, they were passed mechanically from one agency to another—depot, port, transport, and a series of temporary stations in the theater—often spending months before they were assigned to duty with a unit. In this period they became physically soft, their discipline slackened, and their rapidly acquired skills tended to fade out with disuse. What the front-line unit received was not what the replacement training center had produced.

A study of the assignment of replacements in the North African Theater revealed other serious faults in administration. Some men were diverted from the replacement stream to form new units in the theater. It was estimated that by May 1943 17,000 men, most of them intended as combat replacements, had been utilized overseas for the activation of new service units, particularly in quartermaster and military police.[2] Tank replacements were assigned to infantry units. Individual job specialties were not considered in making assignments. Some commanders, eager to get the best men available, were impatient of the aims and procedures of classification. "One division commander," wrote General McNair, "himself told me that when he needed replacements he went to the replacement depot and chose his men individually, regardless of arm or specialty,

[2] Memo (S) of Lt Col H. W. Wilkinson for Mil Pers Div ASF, 28 May 43, sub: Rpt of Visit to O'seas Theaters. 320.2/7 (O'seas Repls) (S).

based primarily on their appearance and actions—somewhat as one would buy a horse."[3]

Misassignment of replacements, whose training had been devoted to individual specialties, was wasteful of training time and of human material. It was not always due to indifference or error, but was frequently made necessary by the fact that depots had a surplus of trainees in some specialties and a shortage in others, usually combat jobs such as infantry riflemen, for which the requirement was heavy. Misassignment in such cases showed that the number of replacements received, the timing of their arrival, and their distribution among arms and individual specialties were not properly geared in Washington to actual theater needs.

Besides revealing defects of administration, the conditions in North Africa threw doubt on the adequacy of replacement training. There had long been a school of thought in the Army which held that replacements should receive more than thirteen weeks of training and that they should be trained, not in somewhat formless "centers," but in units resembling the units to which they would ultimately be assigned. Some of General McNair's staff officers recommended a lengthening of the training program.[4] The Committee on Revision of the Military Program, which in the early summer of 1943 recommended that the ground army be reduced to an 88-division basis, reached an unfavorable judgment on replacement training in the Army Ground Forces. It proposed on 7 June 1943 that replacement training be extended to six months, to include training in units; and that, pending the time when men trained under this longer program became available, replacements should be taken from tactical units, including divisions, many of which could not in any case be shipped until 1944. Since overseas commanders wished almost no noncommissioned officers among their replacements, preferring to promote men already in their organizations, the committee recommended that only privates be taken from AGF units; and to prevent the casting off of undesirables by unit commanders it recommended stripping all privates from the units selected, reducing the units to cadres.[5]

On 13 June G–3 of the War Department, in a strongly worded memorandum

[3] Memo (C) of Gen McNair for CofS USA, 1 Jan 44, sub: "What the Front-Line Infantryman Thinks." 000.7/101 (Inf Program) (C).

[4] (1) See n. 1 (2). (2) Memo (S) of Lt Col Banville for Col Winn, 26 May 43, sub: Loss Repls. 320.2/6 (O'seas Repls) (S).

[5] Memo (S) of Cols Maddocks, Chamberlain, and Carter for CofS USA, 7 Jun 43, sub: Revision of Current Mil Program; Tab C: "Problem: To Improve the Present Repl Tng System." 381/177 (S).

to the Army Ground Forces, declared not only that unfit and untrained men must be eliminated from overseas replacements by firmer administration but also that the training program itself must be reviewed. Following the recommendations of the committee, G–3 invited the Army Ground Forces to consider the establishment of a 6-month replacement training cycle and the setting up of training divisions or similar units, in which officer and enlisted replacements would be trained together and from which they would be shipped together to theaters overseas.[6]

Impact of Overseas Requirements on Training Plans, 1943

The fundamental question was thus raised as to whether replacements should be trained in units, as in the German and British Armies, or in special centers devoted to the production of individual soldiers. Overseas commanders wished individual replacements: for example, if a battalion had been shattered in combat, they preferred to rebuild it with the required number of new officers and enlisted men rather than to have it replaced with a new battalion. Moreover, not wishing to put new men over old, they preferred privates as enlisted replacements and second lieutenants as officer replacements. But overseas commanders also wanted men with specialist training. The specialists in units usually were not privates. To strip all privates from a unit, as proposed, would not produce the necessary specialists. It would produce the men who, after months in a unit, had been deemed least qualified for promotion. Replacement centers, designed to furnish overseas commanders with men who were still privates but among whom there was a normal distribution of ability and specialized training, could meet the demand more adequately than units in training. Officer replacement pools, in which all grades were available, had a similar advantage over training units.

General McNair believed that thirteen weeks of replacement training were sufficient to enable a private to join an established unit, discharge satisfactorily the restricted functions of a private, and learn further soldiering from the more experienced men about him. Thirteen weeks represented far more training than most American replacements had received in World War I.[7] It was obvious that

[6] WD memo (S) WDGCT AG 320.2 Gen (6–12–43) for CG AGF, 13 Jun 43, sub: Loss Repls. 354.1/4 (RTC)(S).

[7] "Replacement of Personnel in the American Expeditionary Forces," III, 9: "With the exception of . . . those taken from divisions in training, the men forwarded as replacements had had, in general, less than one month's training and were in fact recruits and not trained replacements." Typescript in files of Hist Div, WDSS, World War I Br, file entry 3347.

a longer period would have produced a better-trained man, but against the advantages of longer training other considerations had to be weighed. The annual output of replacements depended on two things: the number in training at a given time and the number of training cycles in a year. If the training cycle were lengthened, either fewer replacements would be produced in a given period or more men would have to be kept in training at a given time. An increase in the number of men under training would involve a proportionate increase of overhead. Given the fixed ceiling on manpower adopted in 1943, it would reduce the number of men available for units. The constant need of economizing manpower made necessary the shortest replacement training cycle consistent with military effectiveness.

The Army Ground Forces replied to G–3 of the War Department on 25 June 1943. Three plans for a 6-month training cycle were offered and analyzed, but because of their costliness in manpower they were not recommended. The belief was expressed that difficulties had been caused mainly by misassignment, misuse of replacements in theaters, and other administrative faults, already being corrected, and that the existing training program, recently extended to fourteen weeks, would probably be sufficient if properly carried out. However, a 17-week program, to be given in replacement training centers and to include small-unit training, was offered as a possible substitute for the three plans. It was estimated that to maintain production under such a program an increase in RTC capacity of 75,000 enlisted men would be required. Even with this increase, all RTC graduates would be needed as replacements for overseas or for alerted units; units in the United States, however advanced in their training, would have to fill their losses directly from reception centers. The 17-week program was adopted by the War Department and put into effect in August 1943.[8]

Preparation of Replacements for Overseas Movement

In 1943 the headquarters of the Army Ground Forces assumed increasing administrative responsibilities with respect to replacements, though it had desired only a minimum of such responsibilities in 1942. The establishment of the Classification and Replacement Division was an important step in this development.

[8] For this and the preceding two paragraphs see: (1) AGF memo (S) for G–3 WD, 25 Jun 43, sub: Loss Repls. 320.2/9 (O'seas Repls)(S). (2) Col Winn's comments (S) on recommendations of WD Committee, 9 Jul 43. 381/177 (S). (3) AGF memo (S) for G–1 WD, 20 Aug 43, sub: O'seas Loss Repls. 320.2/14 (O'seas Repls)(S). (4) Gen Lentz's comments when Gen Christiansen first raised the issue of replacement training, AGF M/S (S), G–3 to CofS, 20 Feb 43, sub: Loss Repl Tng. 354.1/4 (RTC)(S).

One administrative correction sought and obtained was a simplification of physical and psychological requirements for replacements. Physically or otherwise unqualified personnel had often slipped through the examining authorities and appeared as replacements overseas. In April 1943 the Overseas Replacement Depot at Shenango, Pa., complained that replacements sent to it had been inadequately screened by AGF replacement training centers. The Army Ground Forces believed that this was not due so much to negligence at replacement training centers as to a divergence of opinion among the various doctors by whom a replacement was examined. There was a tendency for the interpretation of standards to become stricter as nearness to combat increased. Men passed as physically qualified at a replacement training center might be considered unqualified at a replacement depot. Men passed by a replacement depot might be judged unfit by medical officers in a theater. Numerous men were rejected through rigid concepts of dental fitness. In consequence some soldiers threw away dental appliances with which they had been provided in training, in order to avoid overseas service. The Army Ground Forces recommended that dental requirements be clarified at a minimum level, namely, "ability to masticate the Army ration." It recommended further, and likewise in the interest of less subjective judgments, that the term "mentally" be dropped from War Department Circular 85 (1943), in which qualifications for overseas service were stated. Further amendment of Circular 85 was requested on 28 July. Although specific recommendations of the Army Ground Forces were not followed, clarification was achieved with the publication by the War Department, on 1 October 1943, of "Preparation for Oversea Movement of Individual Replacements" ("POR"). This remained the governing document on the subject until quantitative demands in 1944 made it necessary to lower the standards of physical quality.[9]

The Army Ground Forces, at first reluctantly, extended its responsibility over the movement of trained replacements. Reports of mismanagement and poor discipline at Shenango were made by AGF inspectors,[10] and led to a visit of inspection on 17 May 1943 by Brig. Gen. Alexander R. Bolling, G–1 of Army Ground Forces, and other AGF officers. Shocked by their findings, General

[9] (1) AGF memo for G–1 WD, 24 Apr 43, sub: Eligibility of EM as O'seas Repls. 341/1059. (2) AGF 2d ind to TAG, 28 Jul 43, on memo cited in (1). (3) WD pamphlet AG 210.31 (11 Sep 43) OB–S–E–GN–SPGAR–M, 1 Oct 43, sub: Preparation for O'seas Movement of Indiv Repls—Short Title "POR." 370.5/4134.

[10] Memo (R) of members of AGF G–3 Tng Sec for CofS, 12 May 43, sub: Inspection of AGF Repls at Cp Kilmer, N. J., and Cp Shanks, N. Y., May 7–9; Tabs H to N. 333.1/14 (R).

Bolling, who had in the past strongly favored the operation of replacement depots by the Service Forces, recommended that the depot be taken over by the Army Ground Forces.[11] In conference with the War Department it was decided that the Army Service Forces should continue to operate Shenango as a replacement depot for the ASF branches, but that the Army Ground Forces should establish on each coast a depot of its own for overseas replacements in the combat arms.[12]

Depots were therefore organized at Fort Meade, Md., and Fort Ord, Calif., with respective capacities for 18,000 and 7,000 replacements. They were made subordinate directly to Headquarters, Army Ground Forces. Beginning operations in August 1943, they certified that overseas replacements met medical requirements, had done qualification firing of their primary weapons, and were otherwise qualified for overseas duty. The depots reported individuals found deficient, with the names of the replacement training centers or of units from which such deficient individuals came. The Army Ground Forces thus obtained a check on the work of its replacement centers. The depots also issued clothing and equipment as needed, gave inoculations, took blood types, and otherwise processed the men in their charge. A training program was instituted at each depot to prevent deterioration in discipline, morale, and physical condition and to prepare men psychologically for overseas duty. Such training had to be flexible, since men remained in the depots for variable and unpredictable lengths of time, subject to shipment on seventy-two hours' notice from port commanders. Men held in a depot over thirty days were reported to the Army Ground Forces for reassignment.[13]

Improvement in the quality of replacements in the ground arms was soon noted. The Inspector General reported on 30 October 1943 that since the estab-

[11] (1) Memo of Lt Col Banville for Col Hyssong, 2 Feb 43, sub: Conference Relative to Decentralization of RTC Asgmt. 341/1024. (2) See n. 5. (3) Memo (C) of Brig Gen A. R. Bolling for CG AGF, 21 May 43, sub: Visit to Shenango Pers Repl Dep. 353.02/12 (sep file)(C).

[12] AGF M/S, G-3 to CofS, 3 Jun 43, sub: Conference AGF Operating Repl Deps and 15% Pools in RTCs. 354.1/238 (RTC).

[13] (1) WD memo WDGAP 322.96 for CG AGF, 22 Jun 43, sub: O'seas Repl System. 320.2/1 (Repl Deps). (2) AGF ltr (R) to Brig Gen F. B. Mallon, 30 Jul 43, sub: AGF Repl Dep #1, Ft Meade, Md. 320.2/4 (Repl Deps)(R). (3) Same ltr to Gen Lockwood, re Repl Dep #2. 320.2/4 (Repl Deps)(R). (4) AGF ltr (S) to Repl Deps #1 and #2, 16 Aug 43, sub: Rpts from AGF Pers Repl Deps. 319.1/1 (AGF PRD)(S). (5) Rpts from depots in 319.1 (AGF PRD) (C). (6) AGF ltr to R&SC, AA Comd, Armd Comd, 23 Aug 43, sub: Analysis of Shipment of Enl Pers to AGF Pers Repl Depot #1. 220.3/2 (AGF PRD). (7) AGF ltr to Repl Deps #1 and #2, 11 Sep 43, sub: Tng Dir for AGF ZI Repl Depots. 320.2/119 (Repl Deps). (8) Papers in 353/1 (Repl Deps) showing steps taken by AGF to assure performance of qualification firing. (9) Papers in 333.1/1 (Repl Deps) on liaison of R&SC with depots.

lishment of the depot at Fort Meade replacements reached the East Coast staging areas better equipped and clothed than before, and with more confidence and eagerness to go overseas, though a few had still not qualified with their primary weapons.[14] Reports from Italy received through the AGF Board were in general favorable.[15] The Fifth Army found that replacements were better than they had been in the Tunisian campaign and that infantry replacements in particular were good, though some had inadequate knowledge of their weapons. By the time of the Fifth Army reports (November and December 1943) infantry replacements had either benefited from the 17-week program in replacement centers or had come from units well along in their training. The fact that, despite all efforts, some men lacked proficiency with their weapons may be attributed to difficulties in the training and processing of certain types of specialists.

Misassignment of replacements in the theaters could instantly nullify the effects of all training, however thorough, and of all methods of overseas movement and delivery, however much improved. But over such misassignment it was difficult for the War Department, and impossible for the Army Ground Forces, to exercise any direct control. To prevent misassignment the right number of men for each arm, and for each job in each arm, had to be supplied at the right time. The right number depended on the incidence of battle and nonbattle losses; the right time depended on the course of operations. Exact predictions were consequently impracticable, and estimates were all the more liable to error since forecasts had to be made six months in advance to allow for the time that elapsed between calls on Selective Service and receipt of replacements by units in the combat zone.

Reapportionment of RTC Capacity, 1943

In 1942 the apportionment of total RTC capacity among arms and services and among individual jobs in each arm and service had been based on needs for initial filling of units, not on anticipation of combat losses. When, after November 1942, combat developed on a significant scale, the requirements for loss replacements in the combat arms immediately mounted. Replacement needs in the services, except Engineers and Medical, were little affected by combat. In May 1943 the War Department took steps to orient the replacement centers more

[14] (1) TIG memo (C) IG 333.9 Overseas Repl System (AGF) for CG AGF, 30 Oct 43, sub: Caliber of AGF Repls. 320.2/1 (O'seas Repls) (C). (2) AGF memo for CofS USA, 23 Oct 43, sub: Visit to AGF Repl Dep #1. 353.02/249 (AGF) (sep file).

[15] AGF Bd Rpts #86–1, A–89–2, 111–117.

definitely toward the production of combat replacements, estimating that 655,000 replacements would be needed in the ground arms in 1944.[16] At a conference on 18 May between representatives of the War Department G-3, the Army Service Forces, and the Army Ground Forces, it was decided to reduce annual ASF replacement capacity by 140,000 and to increase AGF annual capacity by the same amount.[17] The two commands were instructed to determine the actual capacities—numbers of men in training at a given time—required by each of their respective arms or services to produce the annual totals estimated as necessary for 1944. Immediate compliance was impossible for the Ground Forces since the actual capacity needed to produce a given number of replacements in a year depended entirely on the length of the training cycle, which was then in doubt.[18]

In July, when it was decided to adopt the 17-week training program, the Army Ground Forces submitted a calculation that an actual capacity of 277,800 would be needed to meet the requirements estimated by the War Department.[19] This represented an increase of about 75,000 over the capacity currently in effect. On 25 July Army Ground Forces issued instructions to the Replacement and School Command and to the Armored and Antiaircraft Commands apportioning the new capacity among individual replacement centers of the various arms. It was then decided that replacements returning from preembarkation furloughs should report directly to the new AGF replacement depots instead of to the replacement training centers from which they came. Less housing was thus required at replacement centers, and the figure of 277,800 was therefore cut by the War Department to 220,000.[20] Before corrective orders could be prepared for the field, the War Department produced new estimates adjusted to the revised Troop Basis of 1 July 1943. The new Troop Basis canceled ten divisions from the mobilization program. With fewer units for which to plan replacements, the War Department scaled down its earlier estimates, and on 23 August 1943 it prescribed an actual trainee strength of 203,000 for the AGF replacement centers. ASF centers were drastically reduced to 81,000.[21]

[16] WD memo (S) WDGCT 320 RTC (5-12-43) for CGs AGF, ASF, G-1, G-4, OPD, 12 May 43, sub: Capacity of RTCs. 354.1/4 (S).

[17] WD memo (R) WDGCT 320 RTC (5-20-43) for CGs AGF, ASF, 20 May 43, sub as in n. 16. 354.1/17 (R).

[18] AGF memo (R) for G-3 WD, 15 Jun 43, sub as in n. 16. 354.1/17 (R).

[19] AGF ltr (S) to R&SC, AA Comd, Armd Comd, 25 Jul 43, sub: Increase in RTCs. 354.1/4 (RTC)(S).

[20] (1) WD D/F (S) WDGCT 320 RTC (28 Jul 43), G-3 to G-1, 3 Aug 43, sub: Additional Pers Required for RTCs. 354.1/4 (RTC)(S). (2) WD D/F (S) WDGAP 320.2 (29 Jul 43), G-1 to CG AGF, 7 Aug 43, sub as in (1). 354.1/4 (RTC)(S).

[21] WD memo (S) WDGCT 320 RTC for CGs AGF, ASF, 23 Aug 43, sub: Capacity of RTCs. 354.1/4 (RTC)(S).

With a trainee strength of 203,000, to be in effect by 1 February 1944, the actual capacity set for AGF replacement training centers was almost identical with the actual capacity in effect since the earlier part of 1943. (See Table No. 1.) This capacity, since it turned over fewer times per year under a 17-week than under a 13-week cycle, now was limited to producing annually about 135,000 fewer replacements than before.[22] At the very time when large-scale ground operations were beginning in Europe, and mounting casualties in the ground arms were consequently to be expected, manpower conditions in the United States were such that production of replacements in the ground arms was curtailed. In its directive of 23 August the War Department ordered that replacement center graduates must be used only for combat loss replacements, not for new units, in order "to guard against a breakdown of the replacement system." At the same time theaters were instructed, as a necessary measure of economy, not to carry more than 5 percent of their total strength in replacements.[23] A check was thus placed on the growth of a reserve of replacements, which was a condition prerequisite to accurate assignment. Actually, in 1944 concealed overstrengths of replacements were built up in the theaters.

Restrictions on total numbers made it the more important that the distribution of output among arms and jobs should conform as exactly as possible to the incidence of actual losses. The readjustment of AGF replacement training center capacities in the summer of 1943, while not enlarging total AGF capacity, changed the proportion among the arms to meet anticipated combat losses more closely. The Infantry suffered the highest proportion of casualties. The proportion of AGF replacement trainees in the Infantry, formerly 37 percent, was projected in September 1943 to reach 67 percent by 1 February 1944. (See Table No. 1.) But, since no clear figures on actual casualties incurred to date by each arm were as yet available to the War Department, these projected capacities were subject to further change.

The question of training the right number of men in individual specialties within each arm remained. As early as 12 March 1943 the Army Ground Forces, to clarify replacement planning, had requested the War Department to supply new requirements tables.[24] Such tables showed, for each arm, the number of enlisted men per 1,000 required for each job according to specification serial

[22] Estimate of C&RD, AGF.

[23] (1) WD ltr (R) AG 320.2 (31 Jul 43) PE–A–M–C to CGs AGF, AAF, ASF, theaters, etc., 20 Aug 43, sub: Utilization of Pers. 320.2/255 (R). (2) See n. 21.

[24] AGF memo (S) for G–1 WD, 12 Mar 43, sub: Supply of Loss Repls. 341/104 (S).

numbers. The SSN rates in current tables followed T/O requirements, making no allowance for casualties, since the system had been geared to the needs of mobilization. Replacements were being trained in the various specialties, such as SSN 745, Rifleman, and SSN 060, Cook, without regard to the fact that battle losses were far higher in some specialties than in others. According to the overseas replacement procedure as codified by the War Department on 26 March 1943, theater commanders, in requisitioning enlisted replacements, normally specified only the number required in each arm or service without regard to SSN's.[25] In filling the requisition the War Department included specialists according to rates per 1,000 based on T/O's. Riflemen and cooks were replaced on the same basis. If a theater commander needed more or fewer replacements of certain SSN's than the tables prescribed, and, if he knew his needs, he could specify SSN requirements in his requisition. Under this procedure, however, it was impossible to train in advance the right number of men in the various SSN's.

The War Department was unable to comply with the AGF request of 12 March to supply requirements tables. In June tables were provided for various theaters, but they still took no account of casualties. General McNair believed them inadequate as a guide for replacement center training.[26] On 26 July, in connection with planning the 17-week program, Army Ground Forces again requested new requirements tables.[27] Tables for each theater were desired, together with a weighted consolidated table reflecting the total of overseas needs. Should these not be available, figures were requested on the casualties in infantry and armored divisions in Tunisia, broken down by arm or service and by SSN, and on other aspects of the actual losses in North Africa. It was learned from G-1 of the War Department that such figures were not immediately available.[28]

Up to this time the efforts of Army Ground Forces had been directed entirely toward securing revisions of requirements tables which would reflect differential attrition ratios for the various specialties. In June 1943 it was discovered that the preparation of requirements tables which would be realistic and suitable as a basis for planning replacement training presented another and more fundamental problem. The crucial fact now noted was that AGF replacement centers did not train men in all the specialties listed in unit T/O's. Hundreds of different

[25] WD Memo W600-31-43, 26 Mar 43, sub: O'seas Repl System. 320.2/5990.

[26] (1) AGF M/S (S), 21 Jun and 6 Jul 43. 320.2/10 (O'seas Repls)(S). (2) AGF M/S (S), 5 Aug 43. 320.2/13 (O'seas Repls) (S).

[27] AGF memo (S) for G-1 WD, 26 Jul 43, sub: O'seas Loss Repls. 320.2/13 (O'seas Repls)(S).

[28] WD D/F (S), G-1 to CG AGF, 28 Jul 43. 320.2/13 (O'seas Repls)(S).

specialties (SSN's) occurred in the T/O's of each arm. Only a small fraction of these—the more basic specialties—were trained by replacement training centers. Current requirements tables listed all SSN's used in each arm, giving a percentage requirement for each. Such tables, even if revised to include up-to-date estimates of casualty rates, would be almost useless in planning replacement training because there would be no correspondence between the multifarious categories of demand and the restricted categories of supply.

Although training might have been brought into conformity with unit requirements by instituting RTC training in all specialties found in Tables of Organization, such a complication of replacement training was undesirable and impracticable. The alternative was to bring requirements into conformity with the types of training being conducted, basing requirements tables on the limited number of SSN's trained. This solution required a scheme of translation by which SSN's required overseas, but not taught in the replacement training centers, could be regarded as derivatives from the basic SSN's being taught. After much study, involving both a determination of what training was being conducted and an analysis of all Tables of Organization to determine relationships among specialties, groupings of all SSN's of each arm were evolved. Around each basic SSN taught were grouped all the other SSN's of the arm, not produced by RTC training, into which a man with basic training could be expected to develop after appropriate on-the-job training and experience. Thus SSN 745, Riflemen, taught in the infantry replacement training centers, was parent to the following specialties:

SSN 504, Ammunition Handler
505, Ammunition NCO
521, Basic
566, Duty NCO
585, First Sergeant
590, Laborer
604, Light Machine Gunner
SSN 607, Mortar Gunner
651, Platoon Sergeant
652, Section Leader, Gun
653, Squad Leader
695, Orderly
746, Automatic Rifleman

A demand for an Orderly, SSN 695, or for an Automatic Rifleman, SSN 746, was, as far as the infantry replacement training centers were concerned, a demand for a rifleman. Similar groupings were constructed for all other SSN's.

Preparation of these SSN groupings, or conversion tables, was carried out during the period June–September 1943 by the AGF Classification and Replacement Division, in collaboration with representatives of the Adjutant General's Office. On 29 September Army Ground Forces requested new replacement requirements tables, to be based on the SSN groupings, which were now ready.[29] The Adjutant General's Office declared itself willing to comply but unable for want of personnel.[30] Army Ground Forces detailed one captain, one warrant officer, and six enlisted men to compile data in the Adjutant General's Office.[31] Preparation of requirements tables now became a relatively simple matter. Figures were available showing the rate per 1,000 at which men would be needed for each SSN in a combat arm. Adding together the separate rates for all SSN's in a group and the rate for the basic specialty gave the requirement per 1,000 for training in that basic specialty in the replacement centers. By the end of November new requirements tables for the Infantry were ready. These were soon followed by tables for the other ground arms.[32] The machinery was established for planning replacement training in anticipation of future needs and in conformity with the training system in effect in the centers.

In November 1943 the SSN groupings discussed above were published by the War Department as Circular 283, as a guide to commanders in requisitioning RTC-trained men to fill vacancies in their units.[33]

As a result of the steps taken during 1943 to improve the replacement system—the lengthening of the training cycle from thirteen to seventeen weeks and the introduction of administrative changes to assure that replacements arriving in the theaters would be properly qualified and ready for use—it was anticipated that replacements arriving in theaters would be distributed among arms and jobs in proportion to actual needs. It was hoped also that they would be assigned to positions for which they had been trained. With the adoption of the measures described above, which would be fully in effect by the early months of 1944, replacement production in the ground arms may be said to have shifted from meeting primarily mobilization requirements to meeting combat loss requirements.

On 13 October 1943, after several discussions of the replacement problem

[29] AGF memo for TAG, 29 Sep 43, sub: Computation of Loss Repl Rates. 220.3/1745.

[30] WD ltr (R) AG 220.3 (5 Oct 43) OC–A to CG AGF, 5 Oct 43, sub as in n. 29. With atchd AGF M/Ss. 320.2/1 (Repl Deps) (R).

[31] (1) Memo (C) of Gen McNair for CofS USA, 22 Oct 43, sub: Tng of Repls and AA Units. 353/123 (C). (2) AGF ltr (R) to CG Pers Repl Dep #1, 27 Oct 43, sub: Revision of Allotment of Pers to AGF Repl Dep #1. 320.2/1 (Repl Deps) (R).

[32] AGO memo (R), C&R Branch for Col Banville, AGF, 23 Nov 43, sub: Theater Inf Rqmt Rates. 220.01/2 (R).

[33] (1) AGF M/S, C&RD to G–1, 26 Oct 43, sub: Suggested Dir for Inauguration of New Requisitioning System. 341/1161. (2) Cir 283, WD, 6 Nov 43, sub: EM—Requisition for Repls Trained by AGF.

230-171 O - 66 - 14

with General McNair, General Marshall personally instructed him to concentrate his efforts "for the next two months" on replacement training and antiaircraft.[34] After making a preliminary report on 22 October, General McNair proceeded with Maj. Gen. Harry F. Hazlett, commander of the Replacement and School Command, on a tour of AGF replacement training centers, replacement depots, and ports of embarkation. On 4 January 1944 he reported to General Marshall that he had found the quality of replacements excellent and their training adequate *"within their classifications."*[35] He noted that it was unreasonable to expect them to perform well overseas if misassigned—"which appears to be the prevailing procedure now." On the problem of the length of training he saw no reason why the training period might not be longer than seventeen weeks, but he believed that the cost in overhead required to extend it would be prohibitive. He concluded:

> In my judgment, the most serious aspect of the replacement situation is not in the replacement agencies, but is lack of manpower. Units of the Army Ground Forces today have a net shortage of 56,000 men. . . . Small units have been cannibalized . . . , distressing as such measures are. We now face the necessity of breaking up one or more divisions in order that other units may be made fit for combat. In short, the manpower budget is out of balance. Remedial action in this connection cannot be taken too soon.

In the opinion of General McNair, the replacement issue was settled except for the crucial matter of supplying replacements in adequate numbers.

The Quantitative Crisis in the Fall of 1943

The acceleration of operations abroad, including the landing of the Seventh Army in Sicily in July 1943 and of the Fifth Army on the mainland of Italy in September, coincided with a severe crisis in the production of combat replacements in the Zone of Interior. Replacement training centers were unable to meet overseas demands, especially for infantrymen. This was due only in part to the fact that, through extension of the training cycle without enlargement of capacities, monthly and annual output was reduced. The main causes of the immediate crisis were more transient.

With the lengthening of the training cycle first to fourteen and then to seventeen weeks, trainees already in the centers were held some weeks beyond the

[34] Memo (C) of Gen Marshall for Gen McNair, 13 Oct 43, sub not given. McNair Correspondence with CofS, Historical Records Sec, AGO.

[35] (1) Memo 353/123 GNDCG (C) of Gen McNair for CofS USA, 22 Oct 43, sub not given. Location as in n. 34. (2) Memo (S) of Gen McNair for CofS USA, 4 Jan 44, sub: Tng of Repls. 320.2/10 (O'seas Repls)(S).

dates at which their graduation had been expected. Largely for this reason, the effective output of all AGF replacement training centers fell from about 40,000 in June and July 1943 to about 19,000 in August and September; the effective output of infantry centers dropped from about 20,000 in June and July to less than 8,000 in September.[36] (See Tables Nos. 3 and 4.) These losses due to prolongation of the training of certain individuals could never be made up, but the loss due to extension of the cycle could be made up by increases in capacity in 1944.

In October and November the effective volume of the replacement stream was increased to about 30,000; but the rise was retarded by the fact that the Army Ground Forces had been directed to give basic military training to inductees who had first qualified for the Army Specialized Training Program. To give this training, facilities for 30,000 trainees were set aside at AGF replacement training centers in June and July 1943. Less than a third of this number appeared, and consequently facilities for over 20,000 trainees in replacement training centers stood idle in July and August. Facilities for those ASTP candidates who appeared were used for men who were to be assigned to colleges and hence would not be available as replacements. Had it not been for the requirements of the ASTP, 30,000 more men could have entered replacement training in June and July and been available in October and November to replace battle losses in Italy. Since reconversion of facilities reserved for the ASTP at replacement centers was not completed until December, the net loss in replacements due to the ASTP was estimated, not at 30,000, but at 45,000. In the fall of 1943 room also had to be made at replacement training centers for about 8,000 ROTC students from the colleges, who on completing the RTC course went to officer candidate school, not into the stream of enlisted replacements. Hence 8,000 more potential replacements were lost.[37]

Not only were replacement training centers not being fully used to capacity, but also only 62 percent of the men entering training as replacements actually became available as such at the end of seventeen weeks during the last six months of 1943. This was the period of highest attrition in the entire history of the replacement training centers. In August and September, as noted above, only half of the trainees produced were available for assignment as filler and combat

[36] The term "effective output," as used in the text and in Tables Nos. 3 and 4, means output in terms of the mission of replacement training centers — to supply trained replacements to T/O units in the United States and overseas.

[37] Based on a study made by Lt Col W. S. Renshaw, Control Div, AGF G–1, in Jan 44. AGF G–1 Control Div files.

TABLE NO. 3

Distribution of Output from AGF Replacement Training Centers, March 1943–August 1945

Year and Month	EFFECTIVE OUTPUT			OTHER OUTPUT	
	ZI Depots[a] (Overseas)	T/O Units in U. S.	Total	Parachute and Special Service Schools	Officer Candidate Schools
	(1)	(2)	(3)	(4)	(5)
1943					
March	12,615	37,221	49,836	3,268	3,587
April	13,881	21,565	35,446	3,193	3,227
May	13,536	19,318	32,854	3,218	1,298
June	18,088	20,116	38,204	3,009	1,412
July	11,316	30,962	42,278	2,960	1,774
August	5,779	13,225	19,004	1,313	1,543
September	13,841	5,127	18,968	1,769	1,569
October	15,127	16,641	31,768	2,264	2,299
November	13,742	14,137	27,879	1,836	3,218
December	14,198	17,625	31,823	1,651	467
Total	132,123	195,937	328,060	24,481	20,394
1944					
January	23,077	8,503	31,580	1,306	46
February	24,866	6,304	31,170	1,543	50
March	28,847	12,924	41,771	1,815	100
April	17,371	16,412	33,783	2,466	77
May	20,298	20,063	40,361	2,151	70
June	29,705	13,864	43,569	2,577	353
July	20,170	28,000	48,170	2,722	1,086
August	28,428	25,271	53,699	2,699	476
September	20,407	27,805	48,212	2,430	434
October	22,733	20,893	43,626	2,292	337
November	39,746	4,238	43,984	2,188	605
December	52,196	5,075	57,271	2,713	848
Total	327,844	189,352	517,196	26,902	4,482
1945					
January	45,694	1,545	47,239	....	954
February	43,823	496	44,319	184	643
March	41,535	208	41,743	976	600
April	38,845	312	39,157	2,762	505
May	32,911	222	33,133	2,581	686
June	34,792	1,140	35,932	542	713
July	46,955	1,297	48,252	1,884	670
August	58,140	2,067	60,207	3,346	781
Total	342,695	7,287	349,982	12,275	5,552
TOTAL 1943–45	802,662	392,576	1,195,238	63,658	30,428

TABLE NO. 3—Continued

Year and Month	OTHER OUTPUT				Total Output
	Army Specialized Training Program	Died and Discharged	Other	Total	
	(6)	(7)	(8)	(9)	(10)
1943					
March	48	552	1,213	8,668	58,504
April	403	309	1,454	8,586	44,032
May	2,257	638	854	8,265	41,119
June	4,827	618	707	10,573	48,777
July	7,249	580	975	13,538	55,816
August	4,267	6,604	6,308	20,035	39,039
September	6,648	6,332	2,123	18,441	37,409
October	10,273	6,866	2,388	24,090	55,858
November	7,211	3,853	2,090	18,208	46,087
December	4,370	2,523	2,778	11,789	43,612
Total	47,553	28,875	20,890	142,193	470,253
1944					
January	541	1,956	651	4,500	36,080
February	136	1,990	1,015	4,734	35,904
March	22	1,672	2,685	6,294	48,065
April	6	2,058	1,198	5,805	39,588
May	4	1,892	1,106	5,223	45,584
June	1	2,182	2,205	7,318	50,887
July	....	2,519	2,848	9,175	57,345
August	1	2,852	3,552	9,580	63,279
September	172	4,790	5,061	12,887	61,099
October	854	7,236	4,688	15,407	59,033
November	415	6,646	13,175	23,029	67,013
December	821	6,094	6,298	16,774	74,045
Total	2,973	41,887	44,482	120,726	637,922
1945					
January	469	3,970	4,951	10,344	57,583
February	444	1,494	4,320	7,085	51,404
March	339	1,720	4,722	8,357	50,100
April	399	1,602	3,182	8,450	47,607
May	488	1,968	26,844	32,567	65,700
June	522	2,304	17,493	21,574	57,506
July	503	2,784	23,414	29,255	77,507
August	465	3,182	29,318	37,092	97,299
Total	3,629	19,024	114,244	154,724	504,706
TOTAL 1943–45	54,155	89,786	179,616	417,643	1,612,881

Source: C&RD, GAG Sec, Hq AGF.

[a] Includes shipments sent directly overseas in 1943.

TABLE NO. 4

Distribution of Output from Infantry Replacement Training Centers, March 1943–August 1945

Year and Month	Effective Output			Other Output	
	ZI Depots[a] (Overseas)	T/O Units in U. S.	Total	Parachute and Special Service Schools	Officer Candidate Schools
	(1)	(2)	(3)	(4)	(5)
1943					
March	8,179	19,292	27,471	665	1,384
April	7,510	5,888	13,398	531	1,449
May	7,479	6,031	13,510	656	261
June	12,406	9,792	22,198	1,241	534
July	7,811	11,395	19,206	887	1,170
August	3,438	6,153	9,591	69	924
September	6,689	1,098	7,787	542	925
October	9,729	5,586	15,315	631	1,136
November	9,930	3,433	13,363	549	1,948
December	9,152	3,777	12,929	419	281
Total	82,323	72,445	154,768	6,190	10,012
1944					
January	15,511	2,598	18,109	451	20
February	18,445	1,312	19,757	842	30
March	21,735	4,427	26,162	1,098	51
April	14,980	5,357	20,337	1,383	34
May	19,929	6,764	26,693	1,353	35
June	25,823	4,919	30,742	1,839	249
July	18,646	14,277	32,923	1,852	733
August	27,826	11,910	39,736	2,236	280
September	19,854	14,754	34,608	2,092	237
October	21,721	14,565	36,286	2,175	268
November	33,318	589	33,907	1,858	332
December	45,976	543	46,519	2,392	602
Total	283,764	82,015	365,779	19,571	2,871
1945					
January	41,567	488	42,055	....	793
February	37,239	172	37,411	184	516
March	35,603	5	35,608	839	471
April	33,106	166	33,272	2,588	397
May	23,901	37	23,938	2,356	515
June	28,701	614	29,315	372	589
July	38,108	106	38,214	1,811	595
August	49,490	801	50,291	3,188	586
Total	287,715	2,389	290,104	11,338	4,462
TOTAL 1943–45	653,802	156,849	810,651	37,099	17,345

TABLE NO. 4—Continued

Year and Month	Other Output				Total Output
	Army Specialized Training Program	Died and Discharged	Other	Total	
	(6)	(7)	(8)	(9)	(10)
1943					
March	37	....	489	2,575	30,046
April	170	4	239	2,393	15,791
May	785	....	365	2,067	15,577
June	3,016	185	415	5,391	27,589
July	2,949	84	394	5,484	24,690
August	1,068	2,989	4,591	9,641	19,232
September	4,944	3,545	1,407	11,363	19,150
October	6,393	4,145	1,554	13,859	29,174
November	2,983	1,861	1,412	8,753	22,116
December	1,079	1,674	1,052	4,505	17,434
Total	23,424	14,487	11,918	66,031	220,799
1944					
January	364	1,400	387	2,622	20,731
February	88	1,489	438	2,887	22,644
March	13	1,202	2,017	4,381	30,543
April	5	1,491	1,020	3,933	24,270
May	4	1,381	770	3,543	30,236
June	....	1,688	1,681	5,457	36,199
July	....	2,002	1,716	6,303	39,226
August	....	2,098	2,240	6,854	46,590
September	169	3,463	3,867	9,828	44,436
October	854	5,340	3,628	12,265	48,551
November	415	5,293	7,301	15,199	49,106
December	811	4,554	4,658	13,017	59,536
Total	2,723	31,401	29,723	86,289	452,068
1945					
January	469	3,197	3,363	7,822	49,877
February	444	1,120	3,056	5,320	42,731
March	339	1,231	3,579	6,459	42,067
April	399	1,086	2,155	6,625	39,897
May	487	1,435	25,161	29,954	53,892
June	522	1,768	15,446	18,697	48,012
July	503	2,078	22,098	27,085	65,299
August	465	2,454	27,986	34,679	84,970
Total	3,628	14,369	102,844	136,641	426,745
TOTAL 1943–45	29,775	60,257	144,485	288,961	1,099,612

Source: C&RD, GAG Sec, Hq AGF.

[a] Includes shipments sent directly overseas in 1943.

replacements. Some lost by transfer to service schools or to the ASTP might later become available as replacements, but not before some months had elapsed.

The loss rate at replacement training centers rose in the latter half of 1943 for several reasons. Many trainees of the highest intelligence were transferred to the ASTP—40,018, or nearly 15 percent of the total RTC output. Others went to the Air Forces as aviation cadets. The number discharged for medical reasons mounted rapidly in consequence of War Department Circular 161 of July 1943, which permitted a more liberal policy of discharging physically unqualified men. In addition, about 10 percent of the men being sent to ZI depots by replacement training centers at this time were being disqualified at the depots because they did not meet physical requirements for overseas service.[38]

The War Department, which in August had warned against "a breakdown of the replacement system," took action to control attrition in the replacement training centers. It ordered that not more than 5 percent of RTC graduates should be sent to specialist schools. In November 1943 it was ordered that no trainees should be transferred in the future from replacement centers to the Air Forces or the ASTP.[39] This action came too late to be of much effect, for the ASTP was now recruited to nearly its full strength and could be expected to maintain itself by earmarking men at reception centers; moreover, since 1 August the Air Forces had recruited at the reception centers all men who desired to apply for flying training. The result of such recruiting at reception centers was that, while the losses of the Ground Forces declined, the average intelligence rating of men received by the Ground Forces declined also. The results were the same with respect to physical quality. To stop the wholesale discharges which had followed Circular 161 the War Department issued Circular 293. Discharges at replacement training centers for physical reasons became fewer, but the number of poor physical specimens trained as combat replacements correspondingly increased.

It is difficult to say what constitutes a breakdown of a replacement system. If the purpose of a replacement system is to keep units in combat at full strength without having to deplete other units intended for combat, then this purpose

[38] (1) Additional details on losses at AGF RTC's during July–October 1943 will be found in Tabs A–1 to AGF M/S (S), C&RD to CofS, 11 Nov and 23 Nov 43, sub: AGF RTCs in Relation to O'seas Shipment. 354.1/9 (RTC)(S). (2) AGF M/S, C&RD to G–3, 14 Oct 43, sub: Losses of EM at AGF RTCs during Tng Cycles. G–3 Opns file 800 (Binder 2, 1943). (3) AGF ltr to CGs R&SC and AAC, 29 Mar 44, sub: Non-production of POR Qualified EM in RTCs. 341/1220. (4) AGF M/Ss, CofS to G–1, 3 May 43, G–1 to CofS, 5 May 43, and G–3 to CofS, 14 May 43, sub: Graduates from RTCs. 327.3/472.

[39] (1) WD memo (R) for CGs AGF, ASF, AAF, 14 Aug 43, sub: Utilization of Pers. 320.2/255 (R). (2) WD memo WDGCT 320 (RTC)(15 Nov 43) for CGs AGF, ASF, 15 Nov 43, sub: RTCs. 341/1173.

was not fulfilled in 1943 and the replacement system broke down. At least it broke down in the Infantry. During the last six months of 1943 requirements for combat loss replacements in excess of the number available from replacement training centers were filled by withdrawing trained infantrymen from tactical units of the Ground Forces. In September the War Department had reaffirmed its intention to avoid this practice, but what was rejected as a policy became necessary as an expedient.[40] Demands for replacements increased to such a degree that nondivisional infantry regiments had to be broken up. By January 1944 approximately 26,000 men had also been taken from the infantry regiments of unalerted divisions, leaving most of such divisions, on the average, about 2,000 understrength.[41] By February 35,249 men had been taken from combat units as overseas replacements, and 29,521 had been transferred from low-priority units to fill vacancies in alerted units within the Army Ground Forces.[42] On 31 January 1944, four months before the cross-Channel invasion of Europe, the total net shortage of enlisted men in AGF units was 52,625.[43]

The Problem of 18-Year-Olds

Provision of replacements by the Army Ground Forces in 1944 encountered two major problems. One was created by the need of obtaining replacements in sufficient numbers from an ever dwindling supply, the other by the need of shifting replacements in and out of replacement training centers and tactical units to meet changing rules regarding the length of training and the age of replacements. The former problem troubled the Army Ground Forces throughout the last two years of the war. The latter first became serious in 1944.

At the end of 1943 it was believed at Headquarters, Army Ground Forces, that the taking of replacements from divisions in 1943 represented a temporary measure. It was expected that the policy announced in September of keeping the undeployed tactical forces and the replacement training centers distinct would be followed in principle. It therefore came as a bombshell when, on 19 January 1944, the Office of the Chief of Staff directed the Army Ground Forces to prepare a plan whereby all AGF units not scheduled for early shipment could be used as

[40] WD memo (S), G–1 for CofS USA, 18 Sep 43, sub: O'seas Repls. 320.2/16 (O'seas Repls) (S).

[41] WD Gen Council Min (S), 17 Jan 44.

[42] Memo (S) of Gen McNair for CofS USA, 7 Feb 44, sub: Repl Situation. 320.2/106 (O'seas Repls) (S).

[43] Table, "Comparative Strength of Army Ground Forces, 31 Jan 44," 23 Feb 44. 320.2/102 (Comparative Str) (S).

sources of overseas replacements. The plan was to include a provision that overseas replacements taken from units would be men who had had nine months of training. The vacancies created in units were to be filled with RTC graduates.[44]

In his reply to the Chief of Staff General McNair showed that a nine months' training requirement, if adhered to as a continuous policy throughout 1944, would tie up a large number of infantry divisions in the United States as exclusively training organizations—sixteen divisions according to War Department estimates of requirements for infantry replacements, or twenty-six divisions according to AGF estimates, which at the moment were 50 percent higher than those of the War Department.[45] According to the plan of deployment then in effect, only nine infantry divisions were expected to remain in the United States at the end of 1944. It was obvious that divisions could not be shipped according to the schedule made necessary by the impending invasion of France and at the same time produce replacements in the United States in anything approaching the needed numbers. Faced with this prospect, the War Department modified its instructions. It reduced the minimum training requirement for replacements from nine months to six and gave the Commanding General of the Army Ground Forces a certain discretion in withdrawing personnel from units to prevent divisions needed for prospective operations from being ruined in the process.[46] On 26 February 1946 the War Department ordered that "the greatest practicable proportion of replacements" supplied for overseas service in all the combatant ground arms should be obtained from units not scheduled to be shipped within six months.[47]

Behind this change of policy was a decision not to use as combat replacements the men currently being inducted into the Army. In 1944 half of these men were only eighteen years old; many of the remainder were older men with children, most of whom were known in the administrative language of the day as "pre-Pearl Harbor fathers," whose induction had previously been deferred. The question of the use to be made of young men 18 years old had become a matter of increasing Congressional concern. One of the original objectives sought by the lowering of the draft age in 1942 had been to give the ground combat

[44] (1) WD memo (S) WDCSA 320.2 (16 Jan 44) for CG AGF, 19 Jan 44, sub: Combat Repls. 320.2/105 (O'seas Repls) (S). (2) The surprise at AGF headquarters was reported in a statement of CofS AGF to AGF Hist Off, 2 Mar 44.

[45] AGF memo for CofS USA, 25 Jan 44, sub: Repls. 320.2 (O'seas Repls) (S).

[46] WD memo (S) WDGCT 370.5 (12 Jan 44) for CofS USA, 19 Feb 44, sub: Repls. WD G-3 370.5 (S).

[47] WD memo (C) WDGCT 200 (26 Feb 44) for CG AGF, 26 Feb 44, sub: Repls. 320.2/107 (O'seas Repls) (C).

forces an infusion of youth and physical vigor, and for this reason inductees of ages 18 to 20 inclusive had been assigned when possible to combat units and to the replacement training centers of the Army Ground Forces. In November 1942, when this decision was made, all the ground combat units which needed fillers seemed likely to remain in the United States for a considerable period, and only a small minority of RTC graduates were being sent directly overseas. More of these were sent overseas as operations in North Africa developed, just when the first 18- and 19-year-olds were beginning to graduate.[48]

In May 1943 the Army Ground Forces, to which personnel assignment procedures had recently been decentralized, raised the question whether these younger men should be sent into combat with only the current thirteen weeks' training, in view of the public understanding that teen-age men would receive a year of training. As a solution it was proposed that 18- and 19-year-old inductees be henceforth assigned to units and that inductees assigned to replacement training centers be men of 20 or over.[49] The War Department regarded differentiation in assignment according to age as unworkable, since activation of new units was coming to an end and almost all inductees would have to be assigned henceforth to replacement training centers.[50] Inductees therefore continued to be assigned without regard to age. The problem, however, was raised again toward the end of the year. The mounting severity of the Italian campaign created an increased demand for combat replacements. In December 1943 Gen. Dwight D. Eisenhower, then commanding the North African Theater, suggested, without making an urgent request, that replacements for his theater be obtained from divisions in the United States rather than from replacement training centers, giving as one of his reasons the extreme youth of many of the replacements arriving in that theater.[51]

The War Department was faced with a difficult decision. On the one hand, high casualty rates in the Infantry created an urgent need for combat replace-

[48] (1) WD memo (S) WDGCT 324.71 (11–12–42) for CofS USA, 12 Nov 42, sub: Use of 18–19 Age Gp. AGO Records (S). (2) AGF M/S (S), Enl Div to G–1, 1 Dec 42, sub: Conference—Use of 18 and 19 Year-Olds in Army. 327.3/1 (S). (3) WD ltr (C) AG 327.3 (Drafted Men)(11–12–43) OC–E–WDGCT–M, 5 Dec 42, sub: Asgmt of 18, 19 and 20 Year Old EM. AGF Policy File, 327.3/2 (Drafted Men)(C). (4) WD Gen Council Min (S), 7 Dec 42.

[49] AGF M/S (C), G–1 to CofS, 11 May 43, sub: Advisability of Sending Loss Repls in 18–19 Year Age Gp with 13 Weeks Tng. 341/174 (C). (2) AGF memo (C) for G–1 WD, 4 Jun 43, sub: O'seas Repls within 18–19 Age Bracket. 327.3/9 (C).

[50] TAG 1st ind on above to AGF, 29 Jun 43. 327.3/9 (C).

[51] Rad (S) CM–IN–17276, Eisenhower to Marshall, 29 Dec 43. 320.2/169. (O'seas Repls)(S).

ments; on the other, the sympathy of the American public for pre-Pearl Harbor fathers and teen-age youngsters made it undesirable to use the available trained replacements where they were needed most. To many it seemed unjust to send men in these two groups overseas as individual replacements without the moral support of belonging to an organized unit, while many men who were of the intermediate age levels or without family responsibilities, and who had been inducted two or three years before, remained in the United States in units not scheduled for immediate shipment. It was a question not only of fairness but also of the military value of the men concerned. At this time it was generally believed that the RTC graduate (with the 17-week training cycle now in effect) was sufficiently trained to be a competent soldier. But the opinions of commanders in the theaters were not unanimous on this point. It was not unnatural that some commanders overseas, contrasting their slender resources with the 50-odd divisions still at home, and noting the youth and unavoidable inexperience of their replacements, looked enviously at the personnel of the undeployed field forces in the United States.

On 26 February 1944 the War Department issued a conditional ban against using 18-year-olds as replacements. It directed that the men taken from units were to have had at least six months' service, and that those of longest service be taken first. No 18-year-olds or pre-Pearl Harbor fathers with less than six months' training were to be shipped as replacements as long as men were available from other sources. Men were to qualify for overseas service, not under the high standards for individual replacements established in 1943 ("POR"), but under the less rigid requirements of "Preparation for Overseas Movement" ("POM"), which prescribed requirements for men going overseas as members of units.[52] This relaxation of the standard permitted the sending of somewhat increased numbers of replacements.

Extraction of men with at least six months' service from units in the United States took from them many of their most experienced soldiers and in many cases amounted to stripping them. General McNair believed that resort to such a procedure was not necessary to accomplish the purpose. He considered the current RTC graduates adequately prepared for battle with seventeen weeks of the kind of training that was now being given in AGF replacement training centers. He was strengthened in this conviction by a report made in March 1944 by General Hazlett. During an overseas tour General Hazlett found that commanders generally were satisfied with replacements coming directly from

[52] See n. 47.

replacement training centers with seventeen weeks' training. He stated that RTC graduates were satisfactory if they were assigned to positions for which they had been trained, if the training and physical condition achieved at the replacement training center could be maintained during transit, and if units receiving replacements could absorb them in a continuous small stream instead of having to take large numbers at irregular intervals. There were still many cases in the North African Theater, General Hazlett reported, of misassignment of replacements by arm and job, of diverting them to overhead and service functions, of allowing them to deteriorate physically, and of pouring them into units in indigestible numbers a few days before the unit went into combat.[53] Headquarters, Army Ground Forces, believed that these administrative defects were the real cause for overseas complaints and that the stripping of AGF units to provide replacements with six months' training was not necessary.[54]

The decision, however, to collect replacements from units had already been made, and this policy was applied after February 1944. Since 80 percent of replacements had to be infantrymen, it was mainly infantry divisions and separate infantry regiments that were affected. (See Table No. 8.) Divisions recouped their losses by receiving men graduating from replacement training centers or made available through transfers from the Army Specialized Training Program and the Army Air Forces. In all divisions except those due for earliest shipment, there was generally an almost complete turnover of infantry privates and also a high turnover of infantry noncommissioned officers.[55]

The demand for replacements in the summer of 1944 rose to such a degree that even the drastic stripping of divisions failed to supply sufficient numbers. By June overseas replacements were again furnished in greatest numbers from RTC graduates with seventeen weeks of training. This situation endangered the War Department policy of not sending 18-year-olds into combat as individual replacements. Steps were taken to make the rule against the shipment of 18-year-olds even more rigid. Under the 6-month rule 18-year-olds with less than six months of training could not be used as overseas replacements in any combat arm as long as replacements were available from other sources. On 24 June 1944 it was ordered

[53] R&SC ltr (S) GNRSG 319.1 (S) for CG AGF, 25 Mar 44, sub: Repls in ETOUSA and NATOUSA. 320.2/126 (O'seas Repls) (S). See also 320.2/114 (O'seas Repls) (S).

[54] Statement (C) of CofS AGF to AGF Hist Off, 2 Mar 44.

[55] For the extent and the effects of this stripping of infantry divisions, see below, "The Building and Training of Infantry Divisions."

that no man younger than nineteen should be shipped as an overseas infantry or armored replacement under any circumstances.[56] It was likewise ordered that no inductee younger than 18 years and 6 months should be assigned to an infantry or armored replacement training center.[57]

The age bans adopted in 1944 required a strenuous administrative effort to make ends meet. After June 1944 three-quarters of all men received by the Army from Selective Service were assigned to the Army Ground Forces; half of the new inductees were 18-year-olds; the overwhelming majority of the inductees received by the Army Ground Forces had to be assigned to the replacement training centers of Infantry and Armored to maintain the necessary quotas in these arms. Only the permissive assignment of 18½-year-olds to Infantry enabled Army Ground Forces to find places for the 18-year-olds it was receiving.

The administrative difficulties created by the age rules are illustrated by the problem faced by the Army Ground Forces in June 1944. During that month about 37,000 men, who would be under 19 at graduation, were being trained in infantry and armored replacement centers. It was necessary to store these graduates until they reached the age of 19 or to assign them to units not scheduled for early shipment. Those who were nearest that age, that is, those who on graduation had reached the age of 18 years and 9 months, were stored and given further training as individual replacements. Infantrymen in this group were transferred to certain special nondivisional regiments which had recently begun to train replacements converted from other arms. Men trained for Armored were attached unassigned to the 13th and 20th Armored Divisions, which were expected to be among the last to go overseas. The 22,000 who graduated from replacement training centers while still under the age of 18 years and 9 months were distributed among fourteen infantry and three armored divisions not intended for immediate overseas shipment. To make up the loss to the replacement stream, these divisions gave up an equal number of their own men, who were shipped to the AGF replacement depots.[58]

At the same time the application of the age rules led to a deterioration in the physical quality of infantry and armored replacements. By July assignment had

[56] WD memo (C) WDGCT 370.5 (24 Jun 44) to CG AGF, 24 Jun 44, sub: Repls. 320.2/107 (O'seas Repls)(C).

[57] WD D/F (C) WDGAP 220.3 to Mil Pers Div, ASF, sub: Repls. 320.2/107 (O'seas Repls)(C).

[58] (1) AGF memo (S) for G-3 WD, 21 Jul 44, sub: Inf & Armd Repls under 19 Years of Age. 320.2/142 (O'seas Repls)(S). (2) AGF ltr (R) to CGs, 20 Jul 44, sub: Asgmt of 18-year-old IRTC Grads. 341/208 (R). (3) AGF ltr (R) to CGs, 27 Jul 44, sub: Tng Dir for Sep Inf Regts. 353/101 (Inf)(R).

come to depend almost exclusively on age. Inductees under 18 years and 6 months had to be concentrated in the antiaircraft, field artillery, tank destroyer, and cavalry replacement training centers. Virtually all inductees over 18 years and 6 months, including the oldest inductees and those who were borderline physical cases, had to be used to fill up the infantry and armored replacement centers.[59] The result was a tendency to concentrate youth, alertness, and physical vigor in the artillery branches. The Physical Profile system, recently introduced with the objective of securing the strongest physical types for the Infantry, was rendered ineffective. Infantry and Armored, which needed the men with the highest endurance, had to fill out their ranks with many men least qualified in physique and age for these arduous arms. Moreover, it was no longer possible to withhold pre-Pearl Harbor fathers from the stream of combat replacements.

This deterioration of infantry and armored replacements, together with administrative difficulties, forced a change in policy. On 4 August 1944 the ban on shipping 18-year-olds was rescinded, having lasted less than a month and a half.[60] Eighteen-year-old inductees could again be assigned to infantry and armored replacement centers, from which they began to be shipped as overseas replacements in December.

Meanwhile damage had been done. Discharge rates at replacement centers rose abruptly in September 1944 and remained exceptionally high until the end of the year. This increase in discharges occurred mainly in infantry centers, which in July and August had received numerous men physically unfit for infantry duty. (See Tables Nos. 3 and 4.) Replacement training facilities were thus wasted and the planned flow of replacements reduced at the very time when needed to sustain the offensive in Europe. Moreover, despite these numerous discharges many replacements of low physical quality reached the front.

Within the divisions still in the United States the enforcement of the age rules had caused serious interruption of training and a tremendous turnover in personnel. In April and May 1944, when the initial age rules began to have a substantial effect, approximately 120,000 enlisted men were sent to the AGF replacement depots for shipment overseas. Approximately 72,000 of these came from T/O units and overhead, the latter source supplying only a small propor-

[59] (1) AGF M/S (C), C&RD to G–1, 3 Jul 44, sub: Physically Unfit Trainees. 220.3/3 (Limited Duty) (C). (2) AGF memo, G–1 Enl Div to CofS, 4 Jul 44, sub: Visit to Reception Centers. 220.01/35 (Phys Prof). (3) Papers in 220.01/29 and /33 (Phys Prof).

[60] WD memo (S) WDGCT 370.5 (4 Aug 44) to CGs AGF, ASF, 4 Aug 44 sub: Repls. 320.2/142 (O'seas Repls) (S).

TABLE NO. 5

Enlisted Replacements Withdrawn from AGF Divisions, April–September 1944

Division	Infantry		Field Artillery		Cavalry		Armored		Airborne Infantry		Total
	NCO	Pvt	NCO	Pvt	NCO	Pvt	NCO	Pvt	NCO	Pvt	
13th A/B	......	1,072	.....	....	.....	....	.....	....	.....	580	1,652
8th Armd	......	1,150	40	420	33	207	.....	570	.....	.....	2,420
13th Armd	......	1,800	40	460	9	260	.....	610	.....	.....	3,179
16th Armd	......	1,597	39	475	45	235	15	541	.....	.....	2,947
20th Armd	......	1,459	49	450	20	208	.....	660	.....	.....	2,846
42d Inf	372	3,564	69	771	.....	45	.....	....	.....	.....	4,821
63d	278	3,290	.....	579	5	33	.....	....	.....	.....	4,185
65th	......	5,222	.....	314	.....	45	.....	....	.....	.....	5,581
66th	......	3,999	.....	840	5	38	.....	....	.....	.....	4,882
69th	102	4,312	143	697	5	40	.....	....	.....	.....	5,299
70th	41	2,804	6	474	5	40	.....	....	.....	.....	3,370
71st	......	3,172	36	294	.....	....	.....	....	.....	.....	3,502
75th	......	4,459	70	710	5	40	.....	....	.....	.....	5,284
76th	516	5,730	69	711	5	40	.....	....	.....	.....	7,071
78th	......	4,698	50	730	1	44	.....	....	.....	.....	5,523
86th	......	4,050	50	670	.....	40	.....	....	.....	.....	4,810
87th	......	3,850	38	682	.....	40	.....	....	.....	.....	4,610
89th	......	2,700	.....	360	.....	....	.....	....	.....	.....	3,060
97th	......	5,064	57	279	9	21	.....	....	.....	.....	5,430
100th	125	3,550	.....	....	.....	....	.....	....	.....	.....	3,675
103d	......	2,550	.....	....	.....	....	.....	....	.....	.....	2,550
106th	366	3,859	57	723	.....	45	.....	....	.....	.....	5,050
TOTAL	1,800	73,951	813	10,639	147	1,421	15	2,381	.....	580	91,747

Source: C&RD, GAG Sec, Hq AGF.

tion. From April to September 1944 some 92,000 enlisted replacements were supplied by twenty-two divisions. Every division leaving the United States later than September, except the 10th Mountain and the 14th Armored, underwent heavy stripping. The average loss per division between April and September was 4,170 enlisted men, ranging from 1,652 taken from the 13th Airborne Division to 7,071 taken from the 76th Infantry Division. Seventeen infantry divisions lost, on the average, 3,933 infantry privates per division. Since under the T/O applicable in June 1944 there were only 6,195 privates in the three regiments of an infantry division, two-thirds of the infantry privates in seventeen divisions were replaced by newcomers. In some divisions—the 65th, 76th, and 97th—more than 5,000 infantry privates were exchanged. (See Table No. 5.)

In general, these divisions entered combat with less advanced and thorough training than divisions shipped earlier. The effect on the replacement stream was to supply for a few months overseas replacements who had had at least six months of training instead of four, and who were nineteen years old or over instead of eighteen. The amount of training given to 18-year-olds as replacements was not greatly affected since the policy was of short duration. At best it postponed their combat service as individual replacements by a few months. The principal advantage gained was to allow some 22,000 youngsters to enter combat as members of organized units with which they had had some association in training, rather than in the more difficult role of individual replacements. Whether this advantage offset the disadvantage of committing some twenty divisions to battle with imperfect training is a question that cannot easily be answered.

The Problem of Numbers in 1944

While the Army Ground Forces was struggling with the difficulties created by the age rules, it had to concern itself with the even more fundamental problem of providing overseas replacements in sufficient numbers. General McNair had consistently maintained that inadequacy of numbers underlay the entire replacement problem and on 4 January 1944 he reaffirmed this opinion:[61]

> At no stage in our operations, including the present, has the supply of replacements been adequate. Due largely to this condition, overseas theaters have been forced to distribute incoming replacements without regard to the specialties in which they have been trained. There is no question in my mind that this enforced procedure is the principal cause of dissatisfaction with replacements. . . . Inductions are little more than sufficient to fill replacement training centers, and the latter so far have been unable to meet overseas demands.

In May 1943 the War Department had estimated that 655,000 replacements would have to be produced by the ground arms in 1944 to cover both overseas losses and vacancies in divisions preparing for overseas shipment. In July 1943 the Army Ground Forces had estimated that an RTC capacity of 278,000 would be necessary to produce this number of replacements in a year.[62] The War

[61] Memo (S) of Gen McNair for CofS USA, 4 Jan 44, sub: Tng of Repls. 320.2/101 (O'seas Repls)(S).

[62] (1) WD memo (S) WDGCT 320 RTC (5-12-43) for CGs AGF, ASF, 12 May 43, sub: Capacity of RTCs. (2) AGF ltr (S) to CGs R&SC, Armd Comd, AA Comd, 25 Jul 43, sub: Increase in RTCs. (3) AGF memo for CofS USA, 28 Jul 43, sub: Additional Pers Required for RTCs. All in 354.1/4 (RTC)(S).

Department in September, after reducing the Troop Basis from 100 divisions to 90 and then computing new estimates of losses, had cut this 278,000 to 203,000. This capacity could be expected to turn out an effective production of about 400,000 replacements a year. But in November 1943 the War Department estimated that 431,000 replacements in the ground arms would be needed in 1944 to meet both overseas and Zone of Interior requirements.[63]

Fully as important as total numbers, if replacements were to be used in positions for which they were trained, was the breakdown of these numbers by branch. In its estimates of May 1943 the War Department had anticipated that, of the 655,000 replacements needed in 1944, 380,000, or 58 percent, should be infantry. The Army Ground Forces, in planning a total RTC capacity of 278,000, had accordingly planned a capacity of 161,000 in infantry replacement centers. At the time when total capacity was cut to 203,000 the infantry ratio had been raised, with the result that the capacity to be attained in infantry replacement training centers in January 1944 had been set at 136,900, or 67 percent of the total. (See Table No. 1.) Under a 17-week cycle an infantry capacity of 136,900 could be expected, allowing for attrition, to produce annually in the neighborhood of 275,000 infantry replacements. But the War Department estimate of November 1943 called for 293,000 infantry replacements in 1944, or 68 percent of all ground arms replacements.

As it turned out, the Army Ground Forces in 1944 provided for overseas use alone, not counting replacements assigned to units before sailing, 501,038 enlisted replacements in all arms, of whom 404,446, or 80 percent, were in Infantry. (See Table No. 8.) This was accomplished by raising the capacity of AGF replacement training centers in 1944 and by various supplementary measures.

On 7 February 1944 the Army Ground Forces recommended an increase of AGF replacement training center capacity from 203,000 to approximately 260,000.[64] This was immediately authorized by the War Department. But the increase of monthly output would not occur until July, and in the meantime new demands for overseas replacements made even higher production rates advisable.

As late as December 1943 the War Department had estimated that replacement requirements for all purposes in the ground arms, from March through

[63] Tab A, "1944 Loss Repls by Branch," to AGF M/S (S), C&RD to CG, 16 Dec 43, sub: Tng Rqmts. 341/129 (S).

[64] (1) Memo (S) of Gen McNair for CofS USA, 7 Feb 44, sub: Repl Situation. 320.2/106 (O'seas Repls) (S). (2) WD memo (S) WDGCT 320 RTC (17 Feb 44) for CGs AGF, ASF, 17 Feb 44, sub: Capacity of RTCs. 354.1/102 (RTC)(S).

TABLE NO. 6

Distribution of Replacement Output from Separate Infantry Regiments, March 1944–March 1945

Year and Month	Depots	Divisions	Other	Total
1944				
March	300	....	644	944
April	3,845	....	3,045	6,890
May	....	....	6	6
June	192	....	160	352
July	9,123	891	1	10,015
August	2,368	4,125	483	6,976
September	808	1,466	6	2,280
October	7,490	562	1,002	9,054
November	10,509	517	196	11,222
December	4,780	....	4	4,784
1945				
January	4,120	617	2	4,739
February	3,565	....	52	3,617
March	2,061	....	82	2,143
TOTAL	49,161	8,178	5,683	63,022

Source: C&RD, GAG Sec, Hq AGF.

June 1944, would run to 33,000 a month.[65] In fact AGF replacement training centers produced during this period a monthly average of approximately 40,000 available replacements. But at the same time overseas theaters were taking an average of approximately 48,000 replacements a month, and the European Theater of Operations alone an average of approximately 27,500 a month. This demand not only left no surplus of graduates from which to fill up vacancies in units preparing to move overseas, but also made it necessary to create still more vacancies in units. (See Tables Nos. 3 and 8.) To meet these new demands still more men had to be withdrawn from divisions in the Army Ground Forces. Already men were being taken from divisions to supply replacements with six

[65] "Training Requirements, March, April, May, 1944, 1 Nov 43," incl to WD ltr (S) AG C&R Branch to CG AGF, 29 Nov 43, sub: Tng Rqmts. 320.2/710 (S). (2) "Training Requirements, April, May, June 1944, 1 Dec 43," incl to WD ltr (S) AG C&R Branch to CG AGF, 7 Jan 44, sub: Tng Rqmts. 320.2/710 (S). (3) Estimates made by ETO, as known to the War Department in December 1943, called for an average of less than 20,000 enlisted replacements a month from February through July 1944. See memo (S) SPGAR/200.3 ETO (24 Nov 43) for CG AGF, 8 Dec 43, sub: Pers for ETO. 320.2/150 (ETO)(S).

months' training. Vacancies created by the latter withdrawals were filled with graduates of the replacement centers. To fill the additional vacancies, and to make up shortages from which AGF units had suffered since the earlier stripping in the last months of 1943, the War Department virtually dissolved the Army Specialized Training Program, transferring 73,000 ASTP trainees to the Ground Forces, and assigning to the Ground Forces 24,000 surplus aviation cadets, most of whom had been in the Ground Forces before their selection for flying training. The Army Ground Forces assigned the young men thus obtained chiefly to the infantry elements of depleted divisions. Used in this way as replacements, though not as overseas replacements, they supplemented the output of replacement training centers. Since they were assigned to divisions not intended for overseas movement until August 1944 or later, they had time to acquire or reacquire infantry training.[66]

Meanwhile the War Department had sharply raised its estimates of replacement requirements for 1944. Having estimated in November 1943 that the Zone of Interior would have to produce 431,000 replacements in the ground arms for the whole of 1944, it reached the conclusion in February 1944 that the Zone of Interior would have to produce 352,000 in the last half of 1944 alone. The estimated requirement for Infantry was at the same time raised from 67 to 73 percent of the requirement for all ground arms. This would require the production of 257,000 infantry replacements for the second half of the year, instead of 293,000 previously estimated by the War Department as sufficient for the full year.[67] It became apparent that the increase of RTC output due to begin in July would be insufficient. The Army Ground Forces calculated, on the basis of the new War Department estimates for the last six months of 1944, that RTC production, even with the increased capacities authorized in February, would fall short of requirements by 120,000, and that the shortage of infantrymen alone would be about 67,000.[68] To meet this emergency new sources of replacements had to be found. With divisions approaching their dates for overseas shipment they were no longer an available source after August 1944. Antiaircraft and tank destroyer units therefore had to be inactivated at a more rapid rate than Troop Basis planning had envisaged.[69] Their personnel were for the most part transferred to

[66] See above, "The Procurement of Enlisted Personnel: the Problem of Quality."

[67] Tab B, "Estimate of Loss Replacements, Six Months (Jul–Dec 44)," to AGF M/S (S), C&RD to CofS, 7 Mar 44, sub: Tng Rqmts. 320.2/710 (S).

[68] AGF memo (S) for G–3 WD, 13 Mar 44, sub: Repls. 320.2/114 (O'seas Repls) (S).

[69] WD Gen Council Min (S), 3 Apr 44.

the Infantry. A program of voluntary transfer to the Infantry from other branches was also inaugurated.

For the training of these new men the Army Ground Forces used nine nondivisional infantry regiments obtained by transfer from defense commands or other assignments in which they were no longer needed. Each regiment, reduced to a training cadre, functioned as a small replacement training center specializing in the production of infantry riflemen. Since the transferred personnel were already trained as soldiers, the regiments gave them only eight weeks of infantry retraining—later reduced to six—with some additional training for noncommissioned officers. The regiments were also used, as noted above, to store and give further training to the older group of 18-year-olds graduating from replacement training centers in July and August.[70]

In transferring ASTP trainees and aviation cadets to the Ground Forces, and converting tank destroyer and antiaircraft personnel to infantrymen, the Army was providing replacements from sources within its already existing strength. This policy had to be applied with increasing vigor because the total strength of the Army was over its authorized ceiling. In July 1944, while authorized or Troop Basis strength was only 7,700,000 officers and men, actual strength was approximately 8,000,000. The War Department, intending to cut back to Troop Basis strength, planned to reduce its calls on Selective Service to 60,000 a month. It was becoming difficult in any case, with requirements of the Navy and Marine Corps remaining at a high level, to obtain for the Army more than 60,000 inductees a month who were physically qualified.

This change in the source of AGF replacements made desirable a revision in the capacity of replacement training centers. Set up to train inductees, these centers were not the most suitable agencies for retraining men procured from other branches of the Army. Consequently, in August 1944 the capacity of AGF replacement training centers was reduced from 259,800, the level authorized in the preceding February but not actually attained in terms of output until July, to 241,700, a figure that remained substantially unchanged through December. (See Table No. 1.)

Several other factors also affected the situation. Casualties during the first three months after the landing in Normandy were lighter than had been expected. The European Theater of Operations had a reserve of replacements

[70] (1) AGF ltr to CGs, 16 Apr 44, sub: Tng Dir for Sep Inf Regts. 353.01/112. (2) AGF ltr (R) to CGs, 27 Jul 44, sub as in (1). 353/101 (Inf)(R).

built up since March and was in fact carrying an overstrength in replacements in excess of the authorized reserve. Moreover, the War Department had attempted, through a conference of theater representatives in April and by subsequent directives, to have the theaters provide more fully for their replacement needs from their own resources by converting and retraining as combat soldiers surplus personnel in overhead, service, antiaircraft, and other installations in the theaters.[71] Conversion in the theaters was slow in reaching significant proportions, but it had at least been initiated.

Demand on the Zone of Interior for replacements therefore eased slightly in the late summer and the fall of 1944. It was even thought that RTC output in some arms would exceed immediate needs and that reserve pools might be built up. On 12 October 1944 the War Department instructed the Army Ground Forces to establish "temporary advanced training facilities" for replacements, in addition to facilities in the replacement training centers and the nine separate regiments.[72]

These temporary centers were called infantry advanced replacement training centers (IARTC's). They were intended to give "postgraduate training" to graduates of infantry replacement training centers, similar training to certain numbers of graduates of other AGF replacement training centers except antiaircraft, and infantry conversion training to men converted from other branches under the policy of reducing the Army to Troop Basis strength. It was thought that these temporary centers would disappear as the Army approached its authorized strength of 7,700,000. But this time never came; the Army, instead of shrinking, continued to grow until the defeat of Germany. The temporary centers became an essential feature of the replacement system, and with sudden new demands for replacements their original function was lost sight of.

No pool of RTC graduates ever accumulated. The term "advanced training" proved a misnomer. The new centers concentrated on the retraining of men converted from other branches to Infantry, and their primary aim became the production of infantry riflemen as rapidly as possible.

This mission became most urgent as casualties mounted with the Allied assault on the Siegfried Line in the fall of 1944. To meet the emergency the War Department ordered the Air and Service Forces to transfer physically qualified

[71] (1) WD Gen Council Min (S), 3 Apr 44. (2) WD ltr (S) 320.2 (19 Aug 44) AGOC-E-C to CGs of Theaters, 23 Aug 44, sub: Repls. C&RD files.

[72] (1) WD memo (S) WDGCT 353 (12 Oct 44) for CG AGF, 12 Oct 44, sub: Additional Temporary Repl Tng. 353/218 (S). (2) WD Gen Council Min (S), 15 Oct 44.

men from their Zone of Interior installations to the Army Ground Forces for infantry retraining. About 100,000 men were thus transferred for retraining at IARTC's between November and May 1945.[73] During the first month of their operation, November 1944, IARTC's received most of their trainees from AGF sources. From December through April 1945 most of the trainees were men transferred from the Air and Service Forces. In the six months preceding V-E Day, the IARTC's dispatched approximately 100,000 men to AGF overseas replacement depots, and provided an additional 15,000 replacements to T/O units in the Zone of Interior. (See Table No. 7.)

With the help of the above-mentioned emergency measures the Army Ground Forces was able to meet the sudden and unanticipated demands for enlisted replacements during 1944. The number actually supplied to all the ground arms exceeded the highest forecast previously made—that of the War Department in May 1943 of 655,000. Although the total number of replacements produced for ground combat units overseas and in the Zone of Interior during 1944 cannot be stated exactly, it amounted to approximately 700,000 men, of

[73] See above, "The Procurement of Enlisted Personnel: the Problem of Quality."

TABLE NO. 7

Distribution of Output from Infantry Advanced Replacement Training Centers, November 1944–August 1945

Year and Month	ZI Depots (Overseas)	T/O Units in U. S.	OCS	Prcht Sch	Died and Discharged	Other	Total
1944							
November	8	1,154	58	79	401	2,761	4,461
December	7,752	4,043	5	25	1,084	5,191	18,100
1945							
January	22,461	6,272	98	0	1,802	6,847	37,480
February	27,721	1,503	166	3	484	8,148	38,025
March	25,269	1,520	111	40	679	5,445	33,064
April	16,506	407	99	434	574	5,355	23,375
May	11,689	777	73	506	632	6,198	19,875
June	9,859	782	13	25	1,150	5,265	17,094
July	1,100	34	0	5	335	7,208	8,682
August	15	1	0	3	22	367	408
TOTAL	122,380	16,493	623	1,120	7,163	52,785	200,564

Source: C&RD, GAG Sec, Hq AGF.

whom 501,038 were shipped overseas. The actual provision of infantry replacements in 1944 diverged even more widely from earlier anticipations. In May 1943 the War Department had estimated 1944 requirements at 380,000; and in January 1944 Army Ground Forces estimated that 302,000 infantrymen would be required during the year.[74] The number of infantry replacements actually provided to units overseas and at home was approximately 535,000, of whom 404,446 were shipped overseas.[75]

Further Changes in Replacement Procurement, 1944–45

The War Department on 8 November 1944 notified the theaters that the capacity of the Zone of Interior to furnish replacements was limited and urged them to prosecute their own conversion programs with increased vigor. Each theater was given a specific figure for the number of officer and enlisted replacements it could expect to receive from the Zone of Interior, as shown in the following tabulation:[76]

Monthly Average of Officer and Enlisted Replacements to be Furnished by Zone of Interior

Branch	*European Theater*	*Mediterranean Theater*	*Pacific Ocean Areas*	*Southwest Pacific*	*Total*
All Ground Arms	42,060	7,820	5,410	12,540	67,830
Infantry Only	(35,800)	(7,000)	(4,900)	(11,000)	(58,700)
All Services (except for AAF)	1,530	330	457	810	3,127
TOTAL	43,590	8,150	5,867	13,350	70,957

The War Department estimated at this time that total replacement requirements through April 1945 would amount to 80,000 or 90,000 a month.[77] The difference between these requirements and what the Zone of Interior could produce was to be made up by retraining of rear-area personnel in the theaters of operation.

[74] Tab F to AGF memo (S) 320.2 (O'seas Repls) GNGPS for CofS USA, 25 Jan 44, sub: Repls. This includes a chart comparing AGF with previous WD estimates. WD G–3 Records, 370.5 (S).

[75] These estimates of the number of enlisted replacements actually supplied in 1944 to units of the ground combat arms differ from the figures in Table No. 2; the former include ASTP men and aviation cadets as well as the trainees produced by separate infantry regiments, while the latter include all men trained at replacement centers, irrespective of their ultimate assignment or disposition.

[76] WD ltr (S) 320.2 (30 Oct 44) AGOC–E–C to CGs of Theaters, 8 Nov 44, sub: O'seas Repls. 320.2/166 (O'seas Repls) (S).

[77] WD Gen Council Min (S), 13 Nov 44.

replacement training centers had to be "reprofiled" downward after six weeks of training.[81] This meant that already many men were being retained as combat replacements who were below desired physical standards for their jobs. Under these circumstances the War Department was forced to modify its directive of 12 December. It continued to adhere to the principle of maximum output at replacement training centers but permitted more exceptions to the 95-percent rule.[82] Cases of discharge were to be scrutinized closely. The fact that men discharged on physical grounds would generally have to be replaced by men who were no better was to be given careful consideration. Under the new directive the discharge rate at infantry replacement training centers fell off abruptly.

The German offensive of 16 December 1944 and the ensuing "Battle of the Bulge" came at a time when the replacement system in the Zone of Interior was strained to the utmost. The suddenly increased losses in Europe forced the War Department to raise its commitment for replacements to ETO for January by 20,000. To provide an immediate increase of infantry replacements the training program was shortened to fifteen weeks.[83] It was decided not to take replacements from the few divisions still at home but to ship all remaining divisions to Europe. For a time following the Ardennes offensive preembarkation furloughs of RTC graduates were cut to five days, and men whose homes were more than twenty-four hours distant by rail were shipped by air.[84] The measures taken simply drew on the future to satisfy the present; they did not increase the number of replacements produced. To increase the number, further calls had to be made on the Air Forces for conversion to Infantry, and the Selective Service call was raised to 80,000 for January.[85]

In general, however, it was believed both by the War Department and the headquarters of the Army Ground Forces that the European Theater of Operations would have to meet a large part of its future replacement needs out of its own resources. The G–1 of ETO, who attended conferences in Washington on 23 and 28 December 1944, was told that the Zone of Interior was seriously depleted.[86] Any increase in the shipment of replacements to ETO would have to be made largely at the expense of other theaters. With the Army considerably

[81] WD Gen Council Min (S), 4 Dec 44.

[82] WD memo (S) WDGCT 370.5 (15 Dec 44) for CG AGF, 15 Dec 44, sub: Pers Repls for O'seas Serv. 320.2/168 (O'seas Repls) (S).

[83] AGF M/S (S), G–3 to CofS, 21 Dec 44, sub: WD Conference on Repls. 320.2/172 (O'seas Repls) (S).

[84] AGF memo (C) for G–3, WD, 11 Jan 45, sub: Movement of Inf Repls. 320.2/135 (O'seas Repls) (C).

[85] WD Gen Council Min (S), 26 Dec 44.

[86] Minutes of these conferences are on file in 320.2/173 (O'seas Repls) (S).

overstrength and induction calls therefore subject to restriction, combat soldiers had to be furnished by conversion and retraining within the Army. Since the bulk of the Army was in the European Theater of Operations and the supply in the United States of personnel fit for reassignment to combat duty was disappearing, the process of conversion and retraining would in the future have to be carried on to an ever increasing extent in Europe. Moreover, retraining in Europe would produce quicker results than retraining in the United States, since time spent by replacements in furloughs and in transit would be saved. It was agreed to accelerate the program of combing physically qualified personnel from the communications zone in ETO, retraining them as combat soldiers, and of retraining partially disabled men in the theaters to take over rear-area jobs. Lt. Gen. Ben Lear, transferred in January 1945 from command of the Army Ground Forces to be Deputy Commander of ETO, was charged with the supervision of this retraining program in the theater.

In December 1944, despite the emergency measures in the second half of the month, the number of replacements shipped to ETO turned out to be less than the War Department quota for that month set on 8 November. Thereafter, until the collapse of Germany was in sight, the shipment of replacements to ETO greatly exceeded the commitments of 8 November. On 8 January 1945 commitments of the Zone of Interior to ETO for the period from February to June were revised upward but were largely balanced by corresponding reductions in commitments to other theaters as indicated in the following table:

Monthly Average of Officer and Enlisted Replacements to be Furnished by Zone of Interior

Branch	*European Theater*	*Mediterranean Theater*	*Pacific Ocean Areas*	*Southwest Pacific*	*Total*
All Ground Arms	54,874	6,660	4,000	8,370	73,904
Infantry Only	(48,900)	(6,000)	(3,600)	(7,300)	(65,800)
All Services (except for AAF)	1,142	319	711	805	2,977
TOTAL	56,016	6,979	4,711	9,175	76,881
Commitment of 8 Nov 44	43,590	8,150	5,867	13,350	70,957
DIFFERENCE	+12,426	—1,171	—1,156	—4,175	+5,924

It is evident that, while the gain in replacements for ETO was obtained mainly by curtailment of allowances to other theaters, the Zone of Interior would still have to furnish about 6,000 more replacements each month than had been intended on 8 November. The gain in numbers had to be at the expense of quality. The War Department explained to the theaters in a letter of 8 January that "the present exceedingly large over-all demands for infantry replacements can be satisfied even in part only by use of men who are not fully qualified physically for infantry duty and by waiver of minor training deficiencies."[87]

Actual shipment of officer and enlisted ground arms replacements to ETO allocated on 8 November and 5,723 more than the augmented allocation of 8 November. In February the figure reached 60,597, or 18,537 more than had been allocated on 8 November and 5,723 more than the augmented allocation of 8 January. In March ETO received 58,555 replacements, or 3,681 more than allocated on 8 January; in April, 46,302; in May, with Germany defeated, only 537. All told, from January to April, inclusive, the Zone of Interior supplied 230,005 replacements in the ground arms to ETO, of whom 195,912 were in Infantry. To all theaters, in these four months, the Zone of Interior supplied 309,668 officer and enlisted replacements in the ground arms, about 38,348 more than had been allocated on 8 November. (See Table No. 9.)

It was the IARTC's that made possible the shipment of such large numbers. Other replacement training centers, operating at relatively low levels in December 1944, limited by the number of men received from Selective Service, and requiring in any case at least fifteen weeks to train a replacement, reacted slowly to any emergency. They sent 169,897 graduates to the depots from January to April 1945. (See Table No. 3.) In the same months 101,703 six-week retrainees were sent to the depots, of whom 9,746 were from the separate infantry regiments and 91,957 from the IARTC's, which in January were just beginning to graduate the AAF and ASF men put into them at the end of November. (See Tables Nos. 6 and 7.) In January and February 1945 more than 43,000 AAF and ASF men were put into the IARTC's for conversion into riflemen.

Had severe fighting in Europe been protracted much beyond April 1945 it is difficult to see how the necessary replacements could have been supplied from the Zone of Interior. Possibilities for conversion and retraining in the United States were exhausted. Input into the IARTC's began to decline in January 1945. After December 1944 virtually no infantry retrainees were provided to the

[87] WD ltr (S) 320.2 (6 Jan 45) AGOC–E–C to CGs of Theaters, 8 Jan 45, sub: O'seas Repls. 320.2/174 (O'seas Repls) (S).

TABLE NO. 9

Overseas Shipments of AGF Officer and Enlisted Replacements, by Theaters, September 1943–August 1945

Year and Month	American[a] Theaters		European Theater		Africa–Middle East Theater[b]		Mediterranean Theater[c]	
	Infantry	Other	Infantry	Other	Infantry	Other	Infantry	Other
1943								
September...	....	11	31	1,746	....	....	3,660	840
October.....	28	125	2,211	1,059	....	10	9,553	820
November...	6	537	2,363	2,336	6	....	5,366	1,345
December....	189	7	6,086	4,460	1	1	21	10
1944								
January......	15	12	......	1,208	....	....	6,493	2,558
February.....	639	456	192	8,982	....	....	11,401	391
March.......	644	623	19,889	4,458	....	....	11,711	947
April........	54	44	17,077	6,489	....	....	10,983	2,808
May.........	140	17	30,420	12,944	....	....	2,282	1,024
June.........	416	119	24,680	1,676	....	....	13,733	477
July..........	34	3	25,905	9,817	....	....	11,004	114
August.......	548	135	29,976	2,035	....	....	1,386	8
September...	56	99	29,960	4,288	....	....	1	4
October......	778	123	24,614	3,255	....	2	5,336	459
November...	121	282	23,804	1,527	....	....	9,282	274
December....	63	222	33,212	5,326	....	....	9,034	647
1945								
January......	270	136	57,729	6,822	....	....	3,188	1,502
February.....	60	146	50,970	9,627	....	....	1,170	742
March.......	74	209	48,615	9,940	2	119	6,605	234
April........	143	420	38,598	7,704	....	....	409	9
May.........	58	116	430	107	2	52	......	......
June.........	149	427	673	76	2	200	18	......
July..........	215	4,765	49	25	....	....	......	......
August.......	136	184	4	349	....	....	......	......
TOTAL..	4,836	9,218	467,488	106,256	13	384	122,636	15,213

TABLE NO. 9—Continued

Year and Month	Pacific Theater		Southwest Pacific Theater		Asiatic Theater		Total	
	Infantry	Other	Infantry	Other	Infantry	Other	Infantry	Other
1943								
September...	707	......	......	......	......	203	4,398	2,800
October.....	5,833	1,496	......	......	55	195	17,680	3,705
November...	4,855	1,156	1,844	1,654	50	150	14,490	7,178
December....	2,458	1,451	519	3	184	169	9,458	6,101
1944								
January......	2,114	1,364	5,561	1,336	269	220	14,452	6,698
February.....	5,007	400	965	1,071	20	27	18,224	11,327
March.......	5,668	1,059	3,365	1,753	137	65	41,414	8,905
April........	1,151	216	3,063	1,922	2,937	157	35,265	11,636
May.........	6,051	1,202	3,448	1,985	1	......	42,342	17,172
June.........	910	513	1,869	1,577	2	2	41,610	4,364
July..........	1,154	1,288	308	1,017	......	10	38,405	12,249
August.......	1,816	2,432	922	988	36	718	34,684	6,316
September...	495	446	1,799	1,492	9	621	32,320	6,950
October.....	137	576	1,559	1,931	42	837	32,466	7,183
November...	1,025	364	2,385	2,598	1	20	36,618	5,065
December....	3,195	171	8,261	726	57	1,218	53,822	8,310
1945								
January......	3,777	1,178	6,583	2,385	244	767	71,791	12,790
February.....	8,756	920	10,308	1,494	27	24	71,291	12,953
March.......	543	614	9,292	2,131	238	59	65,369	13,306
April........	107	735	11,143	2,555	8	337	50,408	11,760
May.........	3,395	1,527	34,591	6,457	1	761	38,477	9,020
June.........	14,592	3,118	10,615	9,878	25	3,148	26,074	16,847
July..........	8,449	2,412	22,527	6,116	691	248	31,931	13,566
August.......	68,174	15,463	......	......	......	......	68,314	15,996
TOTAL..	150,369	40,101	140,927	51,069	5,034	9,956	891,303	232,197

Source: C&RD, GAG, Hq AGF.

[a] Includes North American and Latin-American Theaters.

[b] Includes Central Africa.

[c] Includes North African Theater.

IARTC's by AGF units, and after March 1945 virtually none by the Service and Air Forces. At the same time the output of separate infantry regiments used for conversion training tapered off, no graduates being produced after March. It was fortunate that the decline in output from these sources had not come earlier.

Foreseeing the decline of the conversion program in the United States, and anticipating that most replacements furnished by the Zone of Interior after May 1945 would have to come from Selective Service, the War Department in January 1945 raised the monthly induction call for the spring months to 100,000. It also authorized an increase in the capacity of AGF replacement training centers. Their authorized capacity was raised from approximately 246,000 to approximately 366,000—by far the largest increase in the entire history of the war. The capacity of infantry replacement training centers was stepped up from 197,000 to 317,000, or from 80 to 87 percent of the total capacity in the ground arms. (See Table No. 1.) Some IARTC's were converted in February and March to normal infantry replacement training centers; that is, facilities used to give six weeks' retraining in Infantry to men from other branches were directed to give fifteen weeks of infantry training to inductees.[88]

The ensuing increase in RTC output began to make itself evident in May. By that time replacement shipments to Europe had almost ceased. With victory in Europe a new restriction on the use of 18-year-olds was imposed, this time by legislation. The Army was forbidden to send any 18-year-old overseas with less than six months' training. Since half of the incoming inductees were 18-year-olds and virtually all were assigned to replacement centers, this legislation in effect dictated the replacement training program which the Army now had to follow. In May almost half the graduates of replacement training centers were assembled in special centers for the completion of six months' training. The 6-month training requirement for 18-year-olds did not in the long run reduce the number of replacements available, but it did introduce an element of inflexibility into their disposition. It likewise made planning more difficult by requiring that replacement needs be projected further into the future. It had proved hard enough to make advance provision for replacements when only seventeen weeks were needed to produce them. With six months necessary to produce half the replacements obtainable, any accurate forecast of combat requirements was particularly difficult.

[88] (1) WD memo (S) WDGCT 320 RTC (16 Jan 45) for CG AGF, 16 Jan 45, sub: Capacity of RTCs. 354.1/122 (RTC)(S). (2) AGF ltr (S) to CG R&SC, 30 Jan 45, sub: Capacities of IRTCs. 354.1/122 (RTC) (S).

In June 1945 it was believed that replacements would still be needed in large numbers despite the cessation of demands from Europe. Replacement shortages had accumulated in other theaters during the crisis in ETO, and it had to be anticipated that operations in the Pacific would become much more extensive. Moreover, the discharge policies of the War Department were creating many vacancies which had to be filled immediately.

In May 1945 the War Department directed a moderate reduction in the capacity of AGF replacement training centers. Total RTC capacity was reduced from about 366,000 to 291,000, and that of infantry centers from 317,000 to 255,000. (See Table No. 1.) The Redeployment Troop Basis, issued on 15 March 1945, had provided for a sharp cut in RTC capacity to 180,000 after V-E Day. Army Ground Forces, regarding this as a measure likely to reintroduce the vicious cycles in which training and replacement production had been caught during the two-front war, protested against the proposed reduction. In the July revision of the Troop Basis the figure was raised to 245,000.[89] Actual trainee capacity of AGF replacement training centers reached a wartime peak of over 400,000 in June 1945, and declined to about 300,000 in August.[90] V-J Day came too early to furnish any evidence on the efficiency of the replacement system in a one-front war.

[89] (1) WD Redepl TB (S), 15 Mar 45. AGF G–3 Mob Div files. (2) WD Redepl TB (S), 1 Apr 45. 320.2/78 (TUB) (Sep binder) (S). (3) AGF memo (S) for CofS USA, 27 Apr 45, sub: WD Redepl TB. With related papers. 320.2/1 (Redepl TUB) (S). (4) WD Redepl TB (S), 1 Jul 45. 320.2/88 (TUB) (S).

[90] Estimates based on statistics compiled by Historical Section of Replacement and School Command, together with figures for Antiaircraft contained in Table No. 1.

230-171 O - 66 - 16

III. Efforts to Improve Replacement Procedures

The unexpected severity of Infantry combat put grave strains on the replacement system. This severity affected it directly in upsetting estimates of the number of replacements that would be required and their distribution by branch. It was the basic factor in the series of crises described in the preceding pages. After the crisis in the fall of 1943 estimates were readjusted and the capacity of infantry centers was increased, but their output fell far short of the demands imposed by the heavy fighting on the Siegfried Line and the German counteroffensive in the Ardennes.

The unanticipated demands of ground combat also had an indirect effect on the replacement system. Before V-E Day all but two of the divisions in being had to be committed to combat; some of them were kept in line without rotation or relief for periods of unprecedented length. Extended fronts and continuous pressure strained to the limit the normal system of relief and rotation provided in the triangular organization of the infantry division. The burden of maintaining the strength and drive of those committed to action fell upon the replacement system. An adequate flow of individual replacements well enough trained to take their places at once in divisions that were engaged in combat became a crucial factor in the success of ground action. The replacement stream became in effect the reserve of the ground combat forces. The situation was recognized in advance when G–3 of the War Department observed at the beginning of 1944 that, since the United States could deploy only a small number of divisions, "a sound and completely efficient replacement system in operation in all theaters" would be necessary to keep them at fighting strength.[1]

Reports from overseas left no doubt of the heavy impact of combat on the ground forces engaged, especially on infantry elements. As ground forces were increasingly committed in 1943, both in Italy and in the Pacific, it became clear that the infantry soldier, despite additional fire support on the ground and from the air and despite his equipment with the mechanized apparatus of modern

[1] (1) WD memo (S) WDGCT 320.2 (20 Jan 44) for CofS USA, 4 Feb 44, sub: Inf Strength of Inf Divs. (2) WD memo (S) WDGCT 320.2 (19 Jan 44) for CofS USA, 22 Jan 44, sub: Gen MacArthur on Strength of Inf Units. Both in WD G–3 file 320.2, Vol I (S).

warfare, was facing difficulties which put a heavy tax on the strength of the divisions available for employment. For example, American units in the Fifth Army in Italy had an actual strength of about 180,000, of whom 77,000 were in divisions. In January 1944 the American troops, after four months of fighting, had sustained 80,000 casualties, and it was already evident that the Italian campaign was still in its initial stages. Only 24 percent of the 80,000 were killed or wounded. The remainder were cases of sickness, accident, or exhaustion, many of them induced by the grueling conditions to which combat soldiers were subjected.[2]

Shortly after he became senior U.S. commander in the North African Theater, Lt. Gen. Jacob L. Devers analyzed the situation in a letter which he wrote to General McNair on 4 February 1944:[3]

> It has been demonstrated here that divisions should not be left in the line longer than 30 to 40 days in an active theater. If you do this, as has been done in this theater, everybody gets tired, then they get careless, and there are tremendous sick rates and casualty rates. Everybody should know this. The result is that you feed replacements into a machine in the line, and it is like throwing good money after bad. Your replacement system is bound to break down, as it has done in this theater.

The replacement system had not broken down in a literal sense. The 80,000 casualties mentioned above were almost all replaced: 41,000 men had been returned to units from hospitals and 35,000 new replacements had been supplied.[4] But the fact remained that if divisions could be relieved from front-line service after thirty or forty days, casualties would be fewer and fewer replacements would be needed. Less men would be lost through carelessness, fatigue, and overlong exposure to hardship and danger.

About the same time Gen. Douglas A. MacArthur, from the other side of the world, also urged that measures be taken to increase the staying power of infantry. The infantry elements of his divisions were wearing out more rapidly than other divisional elements. Within infantry regiments rifle companies wore out more rapidly than headquarters, service, cannon, or even heavy weapons companies. Hence divisions became useless for offensive action or had to be withdrawn while many of their elements were still capable of further use.[5]

[2] Memo (S) of Gen McNair for CofS USA, 1 Feb 44, sub: Inf Strength in the Inf Div. 000.7/4 (Inf Program) (S).

[3] Personal ltr (S) of Gen Devers to Gen McNair, 4 Feb 44. McNair Correspondence (S).

[4] Par 6, memo cited in n. 2.

[5] Memo (S) of Gen McNair for CofS USA, 19 Jan 44, sub: Gen MacArthur on Strength of Inf Units. 321/100 (Inf) (S).

Additional evidence of the heavy cost of keeping troops continuously in the line was provided by a survey of divisions in the Mediterranean Theater conducted by The Surgeon General during the spring and summer of 1944. He concluded that a substantial proportion of the casualties sustained by divisions in that theater was attributable to psychiatric disorders induced by prolonged exposure to danger. Psychiatric casualty rates of 120 to 150 percent annually were not uncommon in infantry battalions, whereas rates above 3 percent rarely occurred in corresponding units of other branches of service. The front-line soldier, having exhausted the reservoir of pride and devotion to his unit, and having nothing to look forward to but death or wounds, cracked under the strain. It was found that "practically all men in rifle battalions who are not otherwise disabled ultimately become psychiatric casualties." The Surgeon General concluded that the point at which men wore out occurred, on the average, after 200–240 aggregate combat days. Those who broke down before this could usually be rehabilitated in the theater for further combat duty; those who broke down after this maximum period were useless for combat assignment without at least six months of rest.[6]

The Surgeon General's report emphasized that in addition to the physical hazards noted by General Devers there were also mental hazards. Whereas, to reduce these hazards, General Devers recommended rotation of units, The Surgeon General suggested that there should also be rotation of individuals.

Proposals for Unit Rotation

The strain to which divisions in combat were being subjected led to agitation for some form of replacement by unit to supplement the system of individual replacements. Consideration was given to various means of creating a larger reserve of units that could be used to relieve hard-hit units on the line, especially in the fall of 1944 when it had become clear that a costly effort would be required to break the Siegfried Line and that the exhaustion of the existing strategic reserve was in sight. Activation of new divisions could not have given relief in time since approximately a year was required to train a division. Furthermore, as General Marshall pointed out in his *Biennial Report,* the existence of additional divisions, or even their presence in the European Theater, would not have provided relief without logistical facilities that did not exist at the time.[7]

[6] Memo (S) of Office Surg Gen USA SPMC 330.11 for CG AGF, 16 Sep 44, sub: Prevention of Manpower Loss from Psychiatric Disorders. AGF Stat Sec files, 330.11 (S).

[7] *Biennial Report* of CofS USA to the Secy of War, 1 July 1943 to 30 June 1945, pp. 103–04.

Other forms of replacement by units were considered. One was to increase the number of infantry units in the division. Another was to create additional battalions or regiments of infantry to be used for replacement and relief of the hard-hit elements of a division. In connection with the first of these proposals various possibilities were canvassed in the War Department as a means of meeting General MacArthur's recommendations of January 1944. They included an increase in the strength of rifle companies and an addition of a fourth rifle company to the battalion, a fourth infantry battalion to the regiment, and a fourth regiment to the division. The conclusion was reached, General McNair concurring, that these additions if made would result in the occupation of wider frontages, not in the provision of a reserve, so that the whole problem would remain as before or indeed be aggravated since the ratio of artillery and other support to infantry would be less.[8]

Army Ground Forces repeatedly urged the creation of separate battalions or regiments of infantry to replace divisional units withdrawn for rest, rehabilitation, and the integration of replacements. In October 1944 it proposed that eight separate infantry regiments in the Zone of Interior, then being used to train loss replacements, be filled for immediate use in Europe.[9] In November it again urged that individual replacement be supplemented by unit rotation:[10]

> Our whole system of the employment of divisions for long periods and continuous replenishment of these divisions by replacements while they are in action has created a vicious circle with respect to battle fatigue which no system of individual relief can overcome.

There were various objections to the use of replacement units below the divisional level. In January 1944 G-3 of the War Department observed that use of nondivisional regiments to replace exhausted regiments of infantry divisions would conflict with "our national conceptions as to the sanctity of our divisional organization."[11] The overruling objection was that such units could not be created without increasing the authorized strength of the Army as fixed in 1943.[12]

[8] (1) WD memo (S) WDGCT 320.2 (20 Jan 44) for CG AGF, 20 Jan 44, sub: Inf Strength in the Inf Div. 000.7/4 (Inf Program)(S). (2) WD memo (S) WDGCT 320.2 (20 Jan 44) for CofS USA, 4 Feb 44, sub as in (1). WD G-3 file 320.2, Vol I (S). (3) Memo (S) of Gen McNair for G-3 WD, 1 Feb 44, sub as in (1). 321/100 (Inf)(S). (4) WD Gen Council Min (S), 7 Feb 44.

[9] AGF memo (S) for CofS USA, 23 Oct 44, sub: Sep Inf Regts. 320.2/58 (TUB 44)(S).

[10] AGF memo (S) for CofS USA, 13 Nov 44, sub: Prevention of Manpower Loss from Psychiatric Disorders. 330.11/101 (S).

[11] See references cited in n. 1.

[12] (1) AGF memo (C) for G-3 WD, 8 Mar 43, sub: Request for Additional Inf Bns in 1943 Tr Basis. 320.2/10 (TB 43)(C). (2) WD memo (C) WDGCT 320.2 Gen (2-7-43) for CG AGF, 8 Apr 43, sub as in (1). 320.2/10 (TB 43)(C). (3) WD memo (S) WDGCT 320 Tr Basis (23 Oct 44) to CG AGF, 7 Nov 44, sub: Sep Inf Regts. 320.2/58 (TUB 44) (S).

One of the improvements of the replacement system sought in unit rotation and relief was the opportunity it would give the replacement to enter combat with comrades and an organization with which his psychological identification had been previously established. The importance of this sense of identification was strongly emphasized in the report of The Surgeon General. He found that the element chiefly effective in enabling the soldier in combat to overcome the motives for giving way was the strength of the bond between him and his comrades. The newly assigned individual replacement, lacking any strong attachment to other members of his unit, had, according to his report, been found less effective in resisting the strain of combat than the man who entered combat with his unit.[13]

Additional evidence was brought to AGF headquarters by its observers in the theaters and by returning combat veterans that casualties were high among individual replacements who went directly into combat upon joining their units. This was attributed sometimes to lack of training, sometimes to lack of knowledge of how to protect themselves, and sometimes to bewilderment. On occasion, like many unseasoned troops, they would either freeze or would lose their heads the first time under fire. There was also contrary evidence—reports of new men acquitting themselves extremely well upon first going into action. Generally the steadiness and effectiveness of the replacement was in proportion to the amount of time he had spent with his unit before going into combat. During this time he could become acquainted with his fellows, rehearse his role in the team he was joining, and learn from the seasoned men additional tricks of survival. Above all, he would acquire a sense of belonging to and pride in his new outfit.[14]

The creation of new T/O units not having been approved, Army Ground Forces early in 1945 explored the possibility of a plan designed to give individual replacements this desirable sense of comradeship. In December 1944 General Eisenhower had issued an order that the term "reinforcement" be used in the European Theater instead of "replacement," to emphasize the fact that such troops were as vital to success in battle as a reserve regiment in a division. Gen. Joseph W. Stilwell, who in February 1945 became Commanding General of the Army Ground Forces, taking his cue from this order, proposed that units in replacement training centers be designated as training sources for particular divi-

[13] See n. 6.

[14] (1) AGF intelligence documents, Dissemination Division, Hq AGF, particularly Nos. 19562, 21590, 21844, 22260 and 22339. (2) See also Col Elbridge Colby, "Replacements for a Field Army in Combat," in *Infantry Journal,* LX (March 1947), pp. 12–18.

sions overseas. Within these units individuals were to be grouped in platoons, or at least in squads, in which they were to remain throughout their training and while being moved to the scene of combat. He even considered requesting the return to the United States of officers from the respective divisions to escort the groups destined to reinforce them. His argument was that the men would thus be recognized from the outset as "reinforcements" in fact as well as in name.[15] Theater commanders or their representatives, when consulted about this plan, agreed that it would have a good effect but were opposed to its introduction at the current stage of the war. The fundamental objection from the theaters was that it would make the process of replacement too rigid. It would force assignment to particular divisions without regard to the amount of reinforcement that they might need at a given time.[16] In the face of this unfavorable reaction General Stilwell abandoned the plan.[17] Replacements continued to be trained and assigned as individuals, and they were formed into temporary companies during the process of shipment only for disciplinary effect and administrative convenience.

Proposals for More Rapid Individual Rotation

Another form of relief for the severity of infantry combat considered was a more rapid rotation of individuals in front-line units. As early as February 1944 it was suggested that the strain of combat might be relieved by granting periodic 4-day passes to front-line fighters and by authorizing small overstrengths to make such a program possible without loss of fighting strength.[18] A second proposal, indicated above, was that of The Surgeon General who, after making his survey of 1944, recommended that front-line infantrymen, on completing 200 (or 240) aggregate days of combat, be relieved from combat duty for six months and given

[15] (1) GO 131 (R) ETOUSA, 28 Dec 44, sub: Reinforcements. (2) Memo (S) in handwriting of Gen Stilwell to CofS AGF, undated, referring to ETO order cited in (1). (3) Personal ltr (S) of Gen Stilwell to Gen Eisenhower, 21 Feb 45. (4) Personal ltrs (S) of Gen Stilwell to Gens MacArthur (CG USAFE), Richardson (CG USAFPOA), and Sultan (CG CBI), 24 Feb 45. All in 320.2/177 (O'seas Repls)(S).

[16] (1) Personal ltr (S) of Gen Sultan to Gen Stilwell, 9 Mar 45. (2) Personal ltr (S) of Gen J. G. Christiansen (then in ETO) to Gen Stilwell, 11 Mar 45. (3) Personal ltr (S) of Gen Richardson to Gen Stilwell, 19 Mar 45. (1), (2), and (3) in 320.2/177 (O'seas Repls)(S). (4) Rad (S) Gen MacArthur to WD, 4 Mar 45. Rad file CM–IN–4385.

[17] (1) M/R (S) in handwriting of Gen Stilwell atchd to ltr to Gen Richardson cited in n. 16 (3). (2) AGF M/S (S), CofS to G–3, 30 Mar 45, sub: Ltr from Gen Richardson to Gen Stilwell, 19 Mar 45, re Repl System. 320.2/177 (O'seas Repls)(S).

[18] WD Gen Council Min (S), 14 Feb 44.

the option of serving for that period in the United States.[19] The Army Ground Forces, though recognizing the value of these proposals, did not support either of them; it regarded them as palliatives, and in both instances renewed its recommendation that replacement units be created.[20] It was clear that unless a large reserve of replacements was amassed no general system of individual rotation for ground combat soldiers (such as that employed to relieve Air Corps pilots) could be established. The existing ceiling on Army strength made the amassing of a large reserve of replacements as difficult as the creation of new units.

Remedial Measures Adopted

Since it was not regarded as feasible to take measures involving an increase in the size of the Army, the best that could be done to obtain more replacements was to convert into replacements all the men available within the existing strength of the Army, converting into infantry as many men in overhead and in other arms and services as could be spared and could qualify for retraining. This was done. In consequence of General MacArthur's representations a measure was taken to enable divisions to refill their ranks more promptly by improving their means of dropping hospitalized personnel from their rolls. To cover the increased number of men thus charged to hospitals a large figure—eventually 415,000—was set up in the Troop Basis. To meet this figure within the ceiling set on Army strength, Tables of Organization of all units except rifle companies were reduced by 50 percent of their basic privates. The net result was to make it somewhat easier to maintain the fighting effectiveness of rifle units, as long as qualified replacements were on hand in the theater.[21]

Working within the existing replacement system as the best that was feasible (given the situation in 1944–45), the War Department and the Army Ground Forces devoted their efforts to a series of measures designed to make it work effectively and particularly to combat the high rate of casualties that was one of its most severely criticized faults. The main effort was directed toward improving the readiness of the individual replacement for combat. As has been indicated above, much was accomplished by administrative corrections and improvements which resulted in getting the replacement to the point of assignment in a theater

[19] See n. 6.

[20] (1) WD Gen Council Min (S), 14 Feb 44. (2) AGF memo (S) for CofS USA, 13 Nov 44, sub: Prevention of Manpower Loss from Psychiatric Disorders. 330.11/101 (S).

[21] (1) WD memo (S) WDGCT 320.2 (25 Apr 44) for CofS USA, 25 Apr 44, sub: Maintenance of Effective Str of Rifle Companies. WD G–3 file 320.2, Vol I (S).

more promptly, in better physical condition, and with the combat skills he had acquired in training still unimpaired. The efficiency of the two AGF replacement depots established at Fort Meade, Md., and Fort Ord, Calif., in August 1943, contributed to this result; but the effort to improve the individual replacement was vigorously pushed through the whole chain of his processing for assignment, both in the Zone of Interior and in the theaters. On the other hand, his training in replacement centers was extended to include unit training in the field, with the result that he was better prepared to fit quickly into the small battle teams, the squad and platoon, with which he would have his first experience of combat. The Replacement and School Command believed that in 1944 he was better prepared for battle than the ground soldier trained in a tactical unit. In addition, the Army Ground Forces throughout 1944 pressed an effort, which met with some success, to have more rugged men trained as replacements, as part of its general effort to obtain the allocation to the ground arms of men better constituted to meet the exacting requirements of ground combat. Assignment on the basis of the Physical Profile helped to some degree in this effort. The most substantial measure of relief was afforded by the transfer to the Infantry of large numbers of intelligent and able-bodied men from the Air and Service Forces in 1944 and 1945.

The idea of supplementing the system of individual replacements with a reserve of unit replacements, though deemed impracticable while the United States was still fighting a two-front war, was not abandoned. As V-E Day approached, plans were formulated for creating such a reserve for use in the final assault on Japan. The Army Ground Forces in October 1944 had proposed that in long-term planning for operations in the Pacific one separate regiment be provided for every two infantry divisions scheduled for assignment to that theater.[22] In January 1945 it renewed the recommendation, this time proposing a separate regiment for each division and in addition a fixed tour of duty for infantrymen. Since it was understood that only a portion of the ground units then assigned to Europe would be used against Japan, Army Ground Forces believed that after V-E Day a sufficient reserve could be maintained to implement such a plan. One additional regiment for each infantry division deployed against Japan would require a total of 155,000 troops; if regiments were supplied in the ratio of one to every two divisions, only 79,000 would be needed. Adoption of a 120-day tour of combat duty for infantrymen would call for additional replacements

[22] Reference cited in n. 9 above.

totaling 143,000 or 214,000, depending on whether the unit-replacement scheme was adopted as well.[23]

The War Department did not immediately adopt these recommendations, which were again put forward by General Stilwell on 13 March 1945.[24] In May 1945 the War Department accepted the AGF recommendation by approving in principle a plan for unit rotation; it proposed to add a fourth regiment to each infantry division scheduled for redeployment.[25] Army Ground Forces wished to implement the new plan by using the separate infantry regiments that had been employed until March for training replacements, and by adding twenty-nine separate regiments. The 1 June revision of the Redeployment Troop Basis actually made provision for thirty-four separate regiments to implement the unit-rotation plan.[26] But the War Department subsequently disapproved the use of separate infantry regiments for rotational purposes and directed instead that the additional regiments required be taken from the divisions constituting the strategic reserve. The War Department justified this action on the ground that it would cause less disruption than the AGF plan to the supply phases of redeployment, and that regiments taken from reserve divisions would be better fitted for relief missions than units formed from replacement personnel in the United States.[27] In June 1945 the Army Ground Forces noted with concern that the War Department planned to reduce the number of infantry divisions in the strategic reserve to three.[28] The abrupt ending of the Pacific war in August came before the War Department plan for unit rotation could be executed.

Learned-Smith Committee Review of the Replacement System

With the termination of the war against Germany a review of the replacement system was instituted by the Secretary of War. In June 1945 he directed

[23] Memo (C) of Gen Lear for Gen Marshall, 6 Jan 45, sub: Improvement of Inf Fighting Power. Tabs in sep folder. 000.7/121 (Inf Program) (C).

[24] Memo (S) of Gen Stilwell for Gen Marshall, 13 Mar 45, sub: Combat Tour of Infantrymen. Tabs in sep folder. 000.7/12 (Inf Program) (S).

[25] (1) WD D/F (S) WDGCT 322 (10 May 45), 23 May 45, sub: Inf Regts for Rotation. (2) AGF memo (S) for CofS USA, 10 May 45, sub as in (1). Both in 320.2/14 (Redeployment) (S).

[26] WD Redeployment Troop Basis (S), 1 Jun 45, p. 96, line 17M60, "WD Program for Increased Infantry Rotation." 314.7 (AGF Hist).

[27] Memo (S) of Gen J. E. Hull, OPD, for Gen Handy, DCofS USA, 30 May 45, sub: 4th Inf Regt per Div. 322/7 (Divs) (S).

[28] AGF M/S (S), G–3 to CofS AGF, 18 Jun 45, sub: 4th Inf Regt Proposed for Rotation in Inf Divs. 320.2/4 (Redepl TUB) (S).

Dr. E. P. Learned and Dr. Dan T. Smith, civilian advisors to the Commanding General, Army Air Forces, to survey the organization of the War Department and its subordinate commands with respect to the provision of replacements and to recommend improvements that would "make the War Department Personnel Replacement System fully effective in the war against Japan." [29]

In its report to the Learned-Smith Committee the Army Ground Forces reviewed its experience since 1942 and summarized its views on the weaknesses of the system during that period under four headings: (1) deficiency in the quality and often in the supply of men available for replacement training; (2) unduly low levels of RTC capacity, with resultant stripping of units and transfers among branches and commands; (3) fluctuations in policies affecting the program of training and the rate of production, which were reflected in temporary or permanent losses of output and which had made effective long-range planning impossible; (4) the indefiniteness or lack of coordination of policies with respect to replacements.[30]

With reference to the quality and supply of replacements, the Army Ground Forces recommended that, through Selective Service, the procurement of enlisted men be made uniform throughout the armed forces on equal terms; that physical standards for induction be relaxed only in critical cases; and that induction schedules be maintained at predetermined levels. To ensure an adequate and regular output of replacements, it proposed that RTC capacity be set at a high level; that the length of the training cycle be determined once and for all; that training and shipping rates be stabilized over longer periods of time; and that depot capacity and the availability of shipping be brought into conformity with the flow of replacements. To permit definite planning for the Pacific war, it recommended that policy be fixed at an early date on such matters as the training of 19-year-olds, the rotation of limited service and overage cadremen used in training centers, and the critical score for discharge.

In reporting its findings, the Learned-Smith Committee, in conformity with its mandate, directed attention to organizational changes that might correct the faults which had developed in the replacement system. The committee concluded that there had been insufficient long-range planning of personnel requirements and resources; that no single War Department agency had had adequate responsi-

[29] WD memo (R) WDCSA 230 (9 Jun 45) for Dr. E. P. Learned, Dr. Dan T. Smith, *et al*, 9 Jun 45, sub: Review of WD Pers Repl System. 320.2/520 (C).

[30] AGF study (by Col J. H. Banville)(S), 13 Jun 45, sub: The Repl System — EM. 327.3/114 (SS)(S). This study was presented to Dr. Learned and Dr. Smith at a conference with AGF staff officers, 13 June 1945.

bility or authority to ensure an integrated, Army-wide personnel system; that the major commands, particularly the Ground and Service Forces, and also the theaters, had not participated extensively enough in replacement planning; and that in the formulation of strategic plans attention had been given too exclusively to unit requirements, as against replacement requirements, with the result that the Army had been overcommitted. It found that replacements for ground units had been too easily diverted to other uses. Its principal recommendations were as follows: (1) G-1 of the War Department should be designated as the sole War Department agency responsible for personnel planning, its responsibility being concentrated in a personnel resources and requirements branch. (2) G-1 should maintain a long-range master plan embracing all aspects of personnel procurement and distribution. Planning for operations by OPD, G-3, and the Joint Chiefs of Staff should take place within the limitations imposed by this plan. (3) Detailed planning of replacement production should be decentralized by delegation to the three major commands, which should estimate requirements and resources of personnel on a world-wide basis. This would require that they maintain a continuous liaison not only with G-1 of the War Department but also with the theaters. Neither the Army Ground Forces nor the Army Service Forces had had such direct liaison with theaters during the war. The committee recommended that all major changes in personnel policy should be discussed and coordinated with the three commands and the theaters before being put into effect. (4) To ensure greater flexibility in the replacement system the committee recommended that replacements be produced against maximum requirements, and that the Troop Basis limits be maintained by increasing the discharge rate when losses fell below those estimated in planning.[31]

Army Ground Forces agreed with these recommendations except with regard to two points. It favored continuing the existing system of requisitions for replacements based on requirements tables rather than the establishment, at the current stage of the war, of an elaborate statistical control to balance requirements and resources. It also doubted whether the Ground and Service Forces could effectively create, during the remainder of the war, systems of personnel planning extending into the theaters as complete as that which Air Forces had already established. It regarded as the most important recommendation of the committee that made to secure flexibility, namely, the production of replacements against maximum requirements rather than against continually revised estimates of

[31] Memo (C) of Dr. E. P. Learned and Dr. Dan T. Smith for DCofS USA, 20 Jun 45, sub: Review of WD Pers Repl System. Detailed study attached. 320.2/520 (C).

minimum needs. Army Ground Forces expressed the opinion that if this were done, "many of the replacement troubles will disappear." [32]

Recapitulation: the AGF Replacement System in World War II

The procurement and training of replacements to maintain the ground combat forces at effective strength had required tremendous effort and, despite shortcomings, ended with an impressive achievement. By the close of the war approximately 2,670,000 enlisted men had been trained in the replacement training agencies of the ground arms. (See Table No. 2.) This means that the replacement training agencies of the Army Ground Forces had trained a million more enlisted men than were contained in the combat elements of units in the ground arms active on V-E Day, when the Army was at the peak of its strength.[33] The system of replacements used in World War II, thanks to resourceful exertions by all concerned, sufficed to maintain the ground attacks on Germany and Japan at the strength required to obtain unconditional surrender.

The system as contemplated in premobilization plans had had to be abridged at an early date, and the operation of the modified system had been attended by serious faults which were generally acknowledged. Early in the period of mobilization the production of replacements began to lag behind requirements. When casualties began to mount, the output of replacement training centers repeatedly fell short of the number of replacements needed to reinforce even the relatively limited number of ground units in combat. It became necessary to resort to the raiding of divisions in training to make up shortages, a practice so ruinous in World War I. Units earmarked for combat were disrupted even when in advanced stages of training, and the troops withdrawn were replaced with men only partially trained. As a consequence the training goal for World War II of having all divisions prepared to enter combat as thoroughly trained and consolidated battle teams, emerging as such from an orderly progression through carefully planned stages of training, was attained only in part. But the worst evils resulting from replacement shortages in World War I were avoided. The regular training which replacements received was far better in every respect than in World War I, and, with exceptions imposed by the crises and improvisations of 1944, became progressively better as the war advanced. The resort to divisions to fill shortages did not require their conversion into replacement training units

[32] AGF memo (C) for DCofS USA, 29 Jun 45, sub as in n. 31. 320.2/520 (C).

[33] The enlisted strength of such elements was approximately 1,650,000 on 30 April 1945. Strength Reports of the Army (S), Vol II, 30 Apr 45.

except in a few cases and then only for short periods. The detrimental effect of mass withdrawals of infantrymen from divisions in 1944 was alleviated by the physical and mental quality of most of the men who were substituted. Whatever damage the training of divisions suffered, all of those activated in the United States were eventually made ready for combat and shipped overseas. There was no repetition of the bitter experience of having to break up divisions already overseas to obtain individual replacements. The great stream of replacements found to be necessary had been procured from sources within the strength of the Army as fixed in 1943, without dismantling any combat units which were necessary for the execution of strategic plans. The divisions committed were maintained at virtually full strength. All this was a notable achievement.

The principal difficulties in attaining it developed out of failure to calculate correctly the required number of replacements in time to provide them by the established process of training. A basic factor in this failure was the unanticipated severity of combat for ground forces, particularly for infantry units. The resulting crises in the provision of replacements were aggravated by other factors: temporary diversions of replacement training facilities to other purposes; the inevitable lag in the production of center-trained replacements to meet the demands of unforeseen crises; and the desire to protect very young men, who constituted the mass of those immediately available for replacement training in 1944, from the rigors and hazards of replacement duty in combat.

The Army Ground Forces by 1944 found that the provision of replacements had become its principal concern. In 1942 and 1943 General McNair and his staff had given their main attention to unit training. With a comprehensive establishment for training replacements already in operation, General McNair evidently wished to assume only a limited responsibility for a replacement system over which the War Department had retained control of policy following the March 1942 reorganization. Because of his intentness on the thorough training of large units, and his belief that individual training within units in the field was more effective than training in centers, he deplored and resisted the resort to units to obtain replacements. Step by step Army Ground Forces became more deeply involved in replacement problems. In March 1943, with the delegation to it of authority over assignments, its responsibility for the administration of the replacement system was extended. It became further involved during 1943 as the result of criticisms of replacement training in the ground arms, the extension of its jurisdiction over replacement depots, and the disruptive pressure on its unit-training program exerted by the rising demand for loss replacements.

In the crucial matter of anticipating the number of loss replacements that would be needed, Army Ground Forces did not have at its disposal the world-wide data necessary for arriving at correct estimates. Even though its estimates were higher than those of the War Department they fell short of the mark. The reasons why the estimates of the War Department were initially too conservative were not known at Headquarters, Army Ground Forces, at the time. The *Biennial Report* of General Marshall at the end of the war indicates that War Department estimates were affected by excessive optimism regarding the factors that were expected to alleviate the severity of ground combat. To narrow the resulting gap between demand and supply, the Army Ground Forces urged expansion of training center capacities and also the creation of a larger reserve of ground combat units. Meanwhile it intensified the efforts initiated in 1943 to increase the battle-readiness of the graduates of its replacement centers. Training was greatly improved, though the need of haste and resort to improvisations impaired the effort.

The War Department considered the creation of more combat units for replacement purposes to be impracticable within existing limits of time and strength. Adhering to the system of individual replacements, it procured the necessary flow by hasty conversions from overhead and particularly from other arms and branches, including those of the Air and Service Forces. When victory over Germany was achieved, it authorized a larger reserve of ground combat units, together with a liberal allocation of capacity to the AGF replacement training centers. In June 1945 the Army Ground Forces, reviewing its difficult experience with replacements before V-E Day, concluded that these changes, if combined with greater concentration of authority over personnel policies and firmer adherence to policies once established, would enable the replacement system used during the war against Germany to meet the requirements of the intended assault on Japan. The end of the Pacific war came too quickly to permit any conclusive judgment on the effectiveness of the projected improvements.

Service Schools of the Army Ground Forces

by

William R. Keast

230-171 O - 66 - 17

Contents

Tables

I. The Role of Service Schools in AGF Training

The service schools of the Army Ground Forces were agencies for training individuals—officers, officer candidates, and enlisted specialists. Between July 1940 and August 1945 they graduated from their various courses nearly 570,000 officers and enlisted men to fill positions ranging from infantry battalion commander to antiaircraft fire control electrician. Of the eight schools operated under the control of the Army Ground Forces, four, the Cavalry School, the Coast Artillery School, the Field Artillery School, and the Infantry School, had been in existence for many years as the schools of the statutory ground arms and were controlled until March 1942 by the chiefs of those arms. The remaining schools were relatively new, having been established for study and training in new techniques of warfare. These were the Armored, the Antiaircraft Artillery, the Tank Destroyer, and the Parachute Schools.

Although subject to control by Army Ground Forces, the school system was administered through the agencies of subordinate commands. When the Army Ground Forces was established on 9 March 1942, the Replacement and School Command was organized as its agency for supervising the operation of the schools and replacement training centers of the traditional arms. In practice, the Replacement and School Command controlled the conduct of training in the schools of these arms, while Army Ground Forces retained direct control of the methods and techniques employed in training and of the preparation of training literature (field manuals and training circulars) embodying new principles of branch doctrine and special branch techniques. The role of the Replacement and School Command was, therefore, primarily administrative. In the same manner, the schools in the newer arms were administered by subordinate commands. Army Ground Forces controlled their training policies and techniques, but initially, while they were in an early period of development, gave more latitude to the recommendations of these commands regarding programs and methods of instruction. As the newer arms acquired stability in doctrine and techniques, their schools were transferred to the control of the Replacement and School Command—the Tank Destroyer School in July 1942, the Armored School in February 1944, the Parachute School in March 1944, and, after the war had ended, the Antiaircraft School in October 1945.

The Armored School—originally the Armored Force School, later the Armored Command School—was established in October 1940. The Antiaircraft Artillery School developed from the Coast Artillery School, which was responsible until March 1942 for instruction in both seacoast and antiaircraft defense. On 9 March 1942 it passed to the control of the Antiaircraft Artillery Command, which was established to handle the task of activating and training the many antiaircraft units required by the overwhelming air superiority of the Axis at that stage of the war. The establishment of the Tank Destroyer School was directed in November 1941, but its first classes did not begin until May 1942. The Parachute School superseded the Parachute Section of the Infantry School in May 1942.

Mission

The basic principle of the training program of the Army Ground Forces was that every unit should be trained as a unit by its own commander. Such a system had not been entirely possible in World War I, when the scarcity of officers qualified to conduct training had forced the extensive use of vast training centers through which units were rotated to receive instruction from a small corps of experts. AGF training policy, with decentralized responsibility for training, required in each unit a nucleus of officers and enlisted men capable of executing the training programs. The function of the schools in the Army Ground Forces was to contribute to this essential component of trained leaders. Lt. Gen. Lesley J. McNair, Commanding General of the Army Ground Forces, defined the role of the schools in a tribute to the influence of the Field Artillery School:[1]

> The practicability of the system employed in this emergency, with the attendant outstanding success, is due, in my judgment, almost wholly to a single factor—the Field Artillery School. In the World War, we had too few trained officers to permit the system now being used. Since the World War, the Field Artillery School has been pouring forth class after class of officers and enlisted men who not only know their own duties, but who have demonstrated outstandingly that they are able to impart their knowledge to the huge war army now in being, and proving itself so convincingly on the battlefield.

Although General McNair's remarks were confined to the Field Artillery School, the function he described was characteristic of all AGF service schools.

Indispensable as he recognized schools to be, General McNair found it necessary to oppose a strong tendency to multiply school courses. It was not unnatural in a nation addicted to mass education that the remedy for any military deficiency should have been sought in more and bigger schools. But it was impos-

[1] AGF ltr to Comdt FA Sch, 3 Jun 43, sub: Battle Performance of the FA. 330.13/45.

sible, in the view of Army Ground Forces, to create an efficient combat unit by assembling a collection of individuals, however highly trained. Individual proficiency was a prerequisite, but combat efficiency depended more directly on habits of teamwork, more difficult and more time-consuming to develop. Smooth cooperation among diverse elements, adaptation of technique and knowledge to particular situations, discipline, *esprit de corps,* and mutual respect and confidence between leader and men—these were the products of continuous close association under the widest variety of conditions. They could not be developed in the abstract at a school and then transferred to any group in which a man might find himself; they flourished in and were limited to particular groups. Schools, however closely the work they required might parallel that of the individual in combat, were fundamentally unrealistic so far as unit instruction was concerned.

Long established, the schools had traditions, power, and prestige. They were in a strong position in relation to new ground force units. Their recurrent efforts to enlarge the scope of their operations were both natural and laudable, convinced as they were that units would reap direct benefits from more inclusive school training. But extending the domain of the schools meant depriving units of more men for longer periods of time. Such deprivation handicapped unit training directly by forcing the team to practice without all its regular players, and indirectly by denying the absent players the superior form of training that regular work with the team provided.

General McNair protested frequently against excessive schooling. In December 1941, replying to complaints of a brigade commander about the draining of officers and men from units into schools, he said:[2]

> This tendency to start a flock of schools in all echelons is an old one, and caused difficulty in France during the World War. . . . After all, the primary objective of this period is small unit training. Schools are simply a means to that end, and not the end itself. While instruction of officers and noncommissioned officers certainly is necessary, it must be kept within bounds.

"Continuous schooling," General McNair stated in February 1943, "destroys initiative and the necessity for self-help." [3] In February 1944 he replied as follows to a criticism that the Ground Forces had neglected the training of higher commanders in artillery technique:[4]

[2] Personal ltr of Gen McNair to Brig Gen C. P. George, 6 Dec 41. McNair Correspondence.

[3] AGF 3d ind, 17 Feb 43, on 74th FA Brig ltr to Third Army, 22 Jan 43, sub: Tng of Newly Commissioned Officers. 322/35 (74th FA Brig).

[4] Par 16, memo (S) of Gen McNair for ASW, 8 Feb 44. McNair Correspondence (S).

There has been a marked tendency to multiply the number of courses at our service schools until it became a question whether schools or troop training was the object of our home activities. . . . The operations overseas have shown no lack of knowledge on the part of high commanders and their staffs in the employment of masses of artillery. In fact, this subject has been studied in our services for the past twenty-five years. The effort by all means should be to curtail and simplify school courses rather than expand and complicate them by items which can best be characterized as frills. It is a fallacy to assume that when commanders, staffs and troops have witnessed a demonstration they are automatically qualified to execute the features demonstrated. Proficiency comes from execution by the troops themselves.

The mission of the schools as defined by General McNair had two aspects. The schools furnished trained leaders and specialists to units before activation, during training, and in combat. And through their graduates—always a minority in units—the schools standardized procedures common to all units of each arm and disseminated new and improved techniques, tactics, and training methods. Thereby they indirectly raised the proficiency of units and facilitated cooperation among units trained at different times and in different places.

No units were trained at schools—neither regular tactical units nor teams of subunit size, such as gun crews or radar teams.[5] The AGF policy was foreshadowed on this issue by General McNair in the latter days of General Headquarters, the predecessor of Army Ground Forces. The War Plans Division of the War Department had transmitted to GHQ a draft memorandum proposing the establishment of a school for combined arms through which units of various arms would be passed for joint training. General McNair, objecting to the time and manpower such an enterprise would require, based his chief complaint on principle:[6]

In principle, schools are for the training of individuals. . . . For unit training, the instructor of a unit is its commander. Each division and army corps, in turn, with proper leadership, can and should constitute its own combined arms training school.

Individuals were the proper objects of school training, but not all individuals. Among enlisted men, no basic soldiers were trained. No courses were conducted for riflemen, machine gunners, truck drivers, ammunition bearers, cavalry troopers, or tank crewmen. Such men were trained in units or in replacement

[5] This statement requires two minor qualifications. Beginning in 1943 the schools trained teams to operate the odograph and radio-controlled airplane target. In the latter months of 1944 the schools began to conduct courses for instructor teams — small groups, consisting usually of an officer and several enlisted men, selected to introduce new or modified items of equipment to units in the theaters. After arrival in the theaters some of these teams were absorbed as such into units.

[6] GHQ memo for ASW, 12 Feb 42, sub: Sch of Combined Arms. GHQ Records, 352.01/75.

centers; every enlisted student at an AGF school was already a basically trained soldier. No noncommissioned officers of the "leadership" type—that is, rifle platoon sergeants, first sergeants, or tank commanders—were school-trained. Leadership, their principal qualification, was believed to be developed only through the exercise of responsibility and command within units. In permitting the Tank Destroyer School to train enlisted cadremen for new units, Army Ground Forces specifically excepted noncommissioned officers; these men, Army Ground Forces held, "are leaders primarily, whether or not they are technicians; no small part of their qualifications are gained by their experience with troops." [7] In 1943 Army Ground Forces frowned on an Infantry School proposal to train rejected officer candidates as platoon sergeants. The reply of AGF headquarters declared: "No change in the present policy under which service schools for enlisted men are confined to specialists schools is contemplated. General education of and development of leadership in enlisted men remains the responsibility of officers with troop units." [8] In May 1944, after the War Department had expressed interest in a school course for noncommissioned officers, modelled on officer candidate training, Army Ground Forces reiterated its confidence in the training of noncommissioned officers by their own commanders.[9]

Among enlisted men, only specialists were trained at schools. But not all specialists were so trained. The numbers and types of specialist courses varied widely among schools. No single explanation can account for this variety, for no clear policy on the point was enunciated by Army Ground Forces. In general the attempt was made to allow the needs and desires of tactical units for school-trained personnel to determine the nature of courses.

For the training of officers the policy of the Army Ground Forces made somewhat broader provisions. Almost all junior officers were given school training, as were also a proportion of company, battalion, and regimental commanders and staff officers, and a proportion of officer specialists. Junior officers were trained in officer candidate and basic courses, which were substantially the same. Commanders and staff officers were trained in the advanced courses. Training was also given to such specialists as communications and motor officers, battery

[7] AGF 1st ind, 13 Mar 43, on R&SC ltr, sub: Tng of Cadres at TD RTC and Sch. AGF G–3 Schs Br files, RTC binder 1/22.

[8] AGF 3d ind, 19 Mar 43, on R&SC ltr to Comdt Inf Sch, 9 Feb 43, sub: Course for Plat Sgts. 352/740 (Inf Sch).

[9] AGF memo (S) for CofS USA, 12 May 44, sub: Establishment of AGF NCO Schs. 352/113 (S).

executives, and radar, tank maintenance, and cannon officers. The same restrictions were applied to the training of officers in schools as to the training of noncommissioned officers. Leadership was not expected as an outcome of school instruction. The aim of officer training was to give as much technical and tactical knowledge and skill as possible in a brief course and to depend on the exercise of command in a unit to produce or extend the attributes of leadership. Officers' courses, however "advanced," were always preliminary to further training in the unit.

The missions—and consequently the operations—of the Antiaircraft Artillery and Tank Destroyer Schools (and to a more limited extent of the Armored School) differed appreciably from those of the older service schools. The difference arose from the problems of expansion. When new units of the older arms were to be formed, trained cadres of officers and enlisted men were drawn from existing units. Initially no tank destroyer and only a few antiaircraft units were available as a backlog; activations had to start from scratch. It fell to the Antiaircraft Artillery and Tank Destroyer Schools to train and supply officers and enlisted men for both command and technical positions in new units.[10] Although some armored divisions existed when rapid expansion began in 1942, they were not numerous enough to furnish all the cadres necessary for new armored units without severe depletion that would have hampered training. The Armored School also took on something of the character of an activation agency.

In view of this special addition to their missions the Antiaircraft and Tank Destroyer Schools, during the period of expansion, offered courses having no counterpart in the older schools. The Tank Destroyer School operated an Enlisted Weapons Course designed to train personnel for new units in tank destroyer armament, an Enlisted Pioneer Course on demolitions, engineering, camouflage, etc., and an Officers Pioneer Course. The Antiaircraft School conducted an Officers Cadre Course—in effect a basic course slanted particularly at the problems of unit formation and training—from which 7,530 officers had been graduated by January 1944, when the course was discontinued. Both schools conducted special orientation and refresher courses to indoctrinate officers lacking unit experience. Not until 1944, when activations had ceased and AGF school policy had been more definitely formulated, were the newer schools brought into conformity with the general pattern, confining their training to subjects that could not be effectively taught in units.

[10](1) AGF M/S (S), G–3 to CofS, 11 Nov 43, sub: Capacity of Courses of Instruction for AAA Pers. 352/72 (S). (2) AGF 1st ind, — Mar 43, on R&SC ltr, — Mar 43, sub: Tng of Cadres at TD RTC and Sch. AGF G–3 Schs Br files, RTC binder 1/22.

Conditions Influencing School Programs

Reference has been made above to the lack of uniformity among schools in the numbers and types of courses offered. The tables at the end of this study show the relative stability of courses at the Infantry and Cavalry Schools and the fluctuations of those at the Antiaircraft, Armored, Coast Artillery, Field Artillery, and Tank Destroyer Schools. They indicate also the comparatively small number of the courses given at the first two schools, and the much greater extensiveness of the offerings of the other five.

For the general training of officers the schools maintained substantially equivalent programs. The only important variations appeared in the range of specialist instruction. Since specialist training at the schools was normally a direct reflection of the needs of tactical units, the explanation of the variations lies in differences among the arms served by the schools. Differences were notable in three respects: proportion of technical positions, rate of technological development, and relative maturity. The Infantry and Cavalry Schools served old and relatively nontechnical arms; the Field and Coast Artillery Schools operated for old arms with large and fluctuating technical requirements; the Antiaircraft, Armored, and Tank Destroyer Schools served new establishments whose needs for technicians were great and ever changing.

The proportion of technical positions in units of an arm influenced its school program directly. Branches using the largest and most complex weapons, vehicles, and communications equipment—primarily the artillery branches—had the highest ratio of specialists per unit and the greatest requirement for school training.

The rate of technological development within the arm—that is, the rate at which new items of equipment, or significant modifications of old, were introduced—influenced its school program. The rate of technological development depended in part on the technical level of the arm: the more the equipment, the greater the modifications which were possible; the more complex the technical problems of the arm, the greater the pressure for the development of machines adequate to meet them. The rate of obsolescence and invention in the more technical arms was spectacular. With science and industry mobilized on behalf of the military machine, new developments appeared in astounding numbers and were rapidly available for use in the field. The schools, mediating between the sources of supply and the users, had to respond quickly to constantly changing demands for training. In January 1945 antiaircraft units were using only one item of the major equipment—weapons, vehicles, communication devices—with which they had entered the war; every item then standard except the .50-caliber machine gun was a wartime development.[11] It is not surprising, therefore, that the Antiaircraft School conducted such an abundance of courses or that such large numbers of men were graduated from them.

The age of the arms also exerted an influence that was reflected in their school programs. Aside from technical demands the traditional arms tended to be more conservative in matters of doctrine, organization, and equipment than the newer arms. Since the latter—Armored, Antiaircraft, and Tank Destroyer—had had no previous combat experience and very limited peacetime experience, they had to proceed gropingly at first and later to adjust and refine original decisions in the light of combat lessons. A greater degree of change was inherent in their situation than in that of the traditional arms, and it was reflected in the operations of their schools. A further consequence of the youth of these three branches was, as already noted, the lack of units from which cadres for activation could be drawn; the schools, acting in place of units in supplying cadremen, had to extend their operations even further.

Decentralization of Technical Training

A distinctive feature of AGF school policy designed to relate school training more directly to the needs of units was the duplication of technical courses. The school of each arm, for example, conducted motor and communications courses for officers and enlisted men, and an enlisted radio repairman's course; artillery mechanics were trained at four schools and odograph teams at five. To some extent, of course, this duplication was made necessary by differences of equipment among the arms. But extensive similarities in materiel, maintenance procedures, and techniques might have justified centralized technical courses for all arms, at considerable saving of overhead. The decentralized procedure followed in Army Ground Forces arose from the desire to give technical training a tactical slant. Radio operators and vehicle mechanics, to be of maximum value to their organizations, needed to practice their technique under tactical conditions similar to those they would encounter in the field. It was believed that this need could be met only by a course in the school of the arm, where contact could be retained with related activities peculiar to the arm. It was desired, moreover, to localize

[11] Statement of Col H. S. Johnson, AGF G–3 AA Br, to AGF Hist Off, 18 Feb 45.

responsibility for maintenance and materiel in the using organizations. This would be accomplished most easily by developing within the arm a body of doctrine and a tradition of competence through instruction in the branch school.

No serious inroads were made upon the policy of decentralized technical instruction until 1944, when it was modified owing to the stringency of the personnel situation. A proposal to centralize all training in mechanized reconnaissance at the Cavalry School, instead of conducting separate courses there and at the Armored and Tank Destroyer Schools, had been considered early in 1942, but nothing came of the idea because Army Ground Forces was not convinced that improvement of training or economy of personnel would result.[12] In May 1944 the Armored School recommended that tank mechanics for all organizations using tracked vehicles—including armored, cavalry, field artillery, and tank destroyer units—be trained at the Armored School. The Armored School espoused the principle that "the type of vehicle issued to the organization [should be] the determining factor in deciding what service school will give this type of training." Tracked vehicles were preponderant in armored organizations, but training of tank mechanics was not centralized at the Armored School. The older principle that each arm should be responsible for its own maintenance and maintenance instruction continued to govern policy.[13]

Within the limits imposed by this principle, some standardization of courses took place. If it was true that each arm had distinctive material to teach motor mechanics and radio operators, it was also true that large areas of purely technical similarity in the work of such men demanded fairly uniform treatment. In June 1944, AGF inspectors noted striking variations in the content, scope, and emphasis of motor courses at the service schools—variations that could not be justified on grounds of varying branch tactical employment.[14] The Replacement and School Command thereupon produced outlines for standardized officers' and enlisted men's motor courses. The standard courses went into effect in November 1944. The purpose of each course was prescribed, as was also the general allotment of time to subjects:

[12] (1) R&SC ltr 352 Cav Sch to CG AGF, 23 Apr 42, sub: Centralization of All Mecz Rcn Tng for the AGF at the Cav Sch, Ft Riley, Kan. With related papers. 352/53 (Cav Sch).

[13] (1) Armd Sch ltr 353 GNRUB to CG AGF, 22 May 44, sub: Tng of Tank Mechanics in Arty and Cav Units. With related papers. 352.11/24 (Armd Comd Sch).

[14] AGF ltr to CG R&SC, 15 Jun 44, sub: Inspection of Motor Courses at Serv Schs, R&SC, 22 May 44 to 4 Jun 44. 353.02/560.

Subject	*Hours*	
	Officer Course	*Enlisted Course*
Orientation	3	1
Engine	142	142
Chassis	90	90
Maintenance	176	210
Operations	117	85
Reserved	48	48
TOTAL	576	576

The reserved time was to be used for specific branch subjects. Each school continued to give its maintenance and operations training a tactical orientation appropriate to the requirements of the arm. But all schools now distributed time and emphasis on a sounder basis.[15]

The Quota System

The determination of Army Ground Forces to subordinate school operations to the needs of troop units appeared also in the provisions for school attendance. It was a cardinal principle of AGF school policy that assignment of men to school courses should be discretionary with the unit commander and that no commander should be required to fill quotas if he did not wish to. It had not always been so. Before 9 March 1942 the chiefs of branches, who were then responsible for the conduct of schools, followed established peacetime practices in keeping schools filled. In peacetime each branch chief had been responsible for the education of officers and key enlisted men at the branch school. Each year the chief had detailed, through the chief of staff, a quota of men to attend the service school; the detail was compulsory, and unit commanders were forced to get along without assigned personnel. This system was not objectionable in peacetime: education at schools was a paramount concern; units were small and training was not urgent. The system was disastrous when applied to units recently mobilized or expanded, chronically short of officers and specialists, and training intensively for combat. Operating independently of each other and having no responsibility for the orderly progress of unit training, the branch chiefs expanded their school capacities rapidly and detailed officers and enlisted men from units to attend a bewildering variety of courses. Harassed unit commanders often found them-

[15] (1) R&SC ltr 353.02 GNRST to Comdts Serv Schs, 23 Aug 44, sub: Revision and Standardization of Motor Course. R&SC files, 352.11 (Gen). (2) R&SC ltr 353.02 GNRST to Comdts Serv Schs, 6 Nov 44, sub: Standardized Motor Course. R&SC files, 352.11 (Gen).

selves required to send so many key men away to school that training could proceed only with the greatest difficulty. The commander of the 9th Division, for example, wrote to General McNair early in 1942 that 103 officers —roughly one-eighth of those authorized for the division—were absent attending seventeen school courses.[16] It was an open question whether schools existed to serve units or units existed to supply schools with students.

General McNair made it an early item of business in the Army Ground Forces to rectify this condition. As far as possible, officers were to go to school before joining units.[17] The practice of establishing quotas and of detailing officers to schools was stopped. Army Ground Forces announced the principle that "requests for the detail of officers to attend courses of instruction at schools of the Army Ground Forces must originate within the tactical unit concerned, and have the approval of the unit commander." [18]

Under the procedure set up to carry out the new policy, the school commands notified unit commanders of the number of vacancies in school courses available to their units; the commanders could fill the vacancies or not.[19] In effect these notifications were the unit's quota allotment. Quotas were allotted at first directly to regiments, later to divisions, and still later to armies and separate corps. These changes were occasioned by the discovery that personnel turnover in lower units was too rapid for the allotting school command to follow. Quotas were more likely to be assigned where needed if a higher headquarters apportioned a bulk allotment among its subordinate units.

The new system was effective in getting men to school. Unit commanders rarely failed to fill quotas allotted to them, partly because there was sometimes an overstrength that could be spared, and partly because the prospect of having to furnish cadres at a later date prompted commanders to prepare themselves by sending men to school. But the procedure did not implement effectively the principle of command responsibility. A quota allotment issued by a higher headquarters even when accompanied by a general statement that filling quotas was not mandatory, savored of command. To tell a commander in a quota allotment how many school vacancies were available to him was to tell him how many men

[16] Personal ltr of Maj Gen R. E. D. Hoyle to Gen McNair, 24 Apr 42. McNair Correspondence.

[17] AGF Tng Div memo for Gen McNair, 29 Mar 42, sub: Attendance of Off Filler and Loss Repls at Serv Schs Prior to Joining Units. 210.63/265.

[18] (1) AGF ltr to CGs, 10 Apr 42, sub: Off Pers. 210.63/265. (2) AGF ltr to CGs R&SC and AA Comd, 7 Apr 42, sub: Discontinuance of Quotas for Special Serv Schs. 352/70.

[19] R&SC 1st ind, 20 Apr 42, on AGF ltr cited in n. 18 (2). 352/70.

an outside agency thought he should send. The system needed overhauling to place the commander effectively in control.[20]

There was another cause for dissatisfaction with the existing arrangement. In allotting quotas to armies and separate corps, the Replacement and School Command was guided by the number of units of a given branch assigned to each command. No account was taken of the status of training of units, and consequently of their relative needs for school training. Even though armies and separate corps could apportion quotas among their units according to need, it was felt that allotment of quotas by the school command did not take sufficient account of varying needs. Some relatively old, stable, and well-trained units were provided with more school vacancies than they could use, while newer units were given fewer than they needed. A unit with an early readiness date was assumed to have the same school requirements as a nonalerted unit, despite the fact that the former could probably not spare any men from the final phases of unit training. A fairer basis of dividing school facilities among units was needed.

Rectification was sought in a radical revision of procedure instituted in June 1944. Henceforth no quotas or lists of vacancies for school courses were published. Instead the Replacement and School Command published to the field a monthly list of the starting dates of school courses. Armies and separate corps canvassed their subordinate units to determine the number of men each wanted to send to school, consolidated the requests, and submitted them to Replacement and School Command, which allotted the full quotas requested or, if course capacities were too small, a percentage of them. Unit commanders were now in full control and could use school facilities as the progress of training dictated. There was no danger that changes in needs would be disregarded. The school command, regularly informed of the demands for school courses, could undertake revision of course capacities promptly when demand increased or slacked off.[21]

Determination of School Capacities

Capacities of schools and of individual school courses presented a knotty problem. Course capacity had two meanings. It referred on the one hand to the number of men who could be trained in a course at one time, either in a single class or in several classes running simultaneously. The capacity of the officer can-

[20] This paragraph is based on statements of Lt Col H. S. Schrader, AGF G–3 Sec, to AGF Hist Off, 20 Apr 45.

[21] AGF ltr to CGs Second and Fourth Armies, III & XVIII Corps, R&SC, 10 Jun 44, sub: Allotment of Quotas for Courses of Instruction at Inf, FA, Cav, Armd, TD, and CA Sch. 352/761.

didate course at the Infantry School in September 1942 was 15,400: that number of candidates was being trained simultaneously, in 77 concurrent classes of 200 men each in different stages of advancement. Course capacity also meant the number of men who could be trained in a course in a year, calculated by multiplying capacity in the first sense by the quotient of 52 weeks divided by the length of the course. In the example cited above the annual capacity was 15,400 times 4 (the course at the time being 13 weeks long).

The ideal in establishing course capacities was to provide training for enough men but not for too many, avoiding wasted facilities and excessive diversion of men from units, and to maintain fairly even capacities and output over extended periods, avoiding sharp increases or decreases, which caused confusion and wasted effort in the schools. Another object was to produce the required numbers when they were needed, neither so early that they accumulated in pools, losing skill from inactivity, nor so late that units were handicapped by their absence.

The task of determining capacity for a given course entailed estimating the number of men per unit who needed school training; the number of men who had already attended the course; the number of replacements who would become available and the percentage of these who should be school-trained; the number of units active; the number of units to be activated during the planning period; the dates of activation of these units; the physical limitations of school plant, personnel, and equipment; and the probable demand for the course from the field. Most of these factors could not be controlled.

Wide fluctuations in capacity marked the history of the schools after 1940 and illustrated the difficulty of operating institutions almost wholly dependent on external conditions for a regular supply of students.[22] The capacity of the Infantry School, for example, rose to a peak of 18,810 in November 1942, dropped nearly 50 percent to 9,388 in May 1943, and remained fairly stable until June 1944, when it jumped from 10,991 to a new high of 19,455. The rise and fall in the capacity of the Antiaircraft Artillery School were even sharper. In terms of strength figures as an index (strength paralleled capacity closely until 1944), this school rose from a moderate size of approximately 1,700 in March 1942 to nearly 15,000 in July 1943. By December of the same year the school had shrunk almost to its original size, 2,700. The major cause of these rapid changes in school size was the officer candidate program, the vicissitudes of which are traced above in "The Procurement of Officers." [23] Capacities of other courses were much more

[22] AGF G–3 Schs Br study, 1 Mar 45, sub: Capacities of AGF Schs and RTCs. 314.7 (AGF Hist).

[23] See "The Procurement of Officers" in this volume.

stable. If officer candidate capacities are subtracted, the curve of school size flattens out considerably. Without officer candidates, the capacities of the Infantry School were as follows: November 1942, 4,310; May 1943, 5,788; and June 1944, 6,655. Officer candidate training in all schools in 1942 and 1943 (and at the Infantry School in 1944) received the highest priority. As officer candidate school capacity increased, the remaining courses were crowded into the slack left between candidate requirements and the limit of school facilities. When the candidate schools contracted, other courses were increased, but never to the limit of previous candidate operations. Large amounts of plant and equipment were simply left unused or were converted to noninstructional functions; instructors were relieved; and school troop units were assigned elsewhere. When the next burst of production was ordered, reconversion and retraining had to be undertaken at great expense of time and effort and with considerable loss of efficiency.

The Parachute School

The Parachute School, in a strict sense, was not a service school. The airborne establishment never achieved the status of a combat arm, but airborne operations presented peculiar problems, for which special training had to be provided. The Parachute School was established to conduct this training. In contrast to the schools of the recognized arms, it was not the agency of a single arm; it cut across branch lines, training all prospective members of parachute units—infantrymen, field artillerymen, medical aid men, and chaplains. It conducted a common course for all students, officer and enlisted, regardless of branch or assignment—the basic jump or basic parachute course. Beyond this course its program included only enlisted technician subjects peculiar to parachute operations. It did not conduct basic or advanced officer courses, nor did it duplicate the facilities of branch schools for technical instruction presenting no problem peculiar to airborne operations. Whereas the regular schools trained only a fraction of the men assigned to units of the branch, the Parachute School trained—in the basic courses, at least—every man in every parachute unit. Whereas the other schools trained only a small percentage of total replacements—the most technical—the Parachute School trained all parachute replacements. It was, then, a combined school, activation agency, and replacement center, without specific branch affiliation, and limited to instruction in a technique of transportation and in the technical problems created by drop landing.

II. Development of the AGF School Program

The mission of the special service schools before 1940 had been to provide competent leaders for all units of an arm or service, to qualify instructors for the various regular and civilian components of the Army, and to develop and perfect arm or service technique and arm tactics. To perform the last of these functions each school engaged in research and experimentation. The first two constituted the teaching mission.

The curricula of the special service schools on the eve of mobilization were the end products of a series of developments beginning in 1920, when the educational system of the Army was formalized. Under the original plan for officer training, a career officer attended, at intervals between tours of duty, three successive courses at the School of his arm—a Basic Course, a Company, Troop, or Battery Officers Course, and a Field Officers Course. These courses averaged nine months in length. Special service school courses were preliminary to the Command and General Staff School and Army War College, which constituted the officer's "higher" education. The three-course scheme proved impractical. It cost more than meager appropriations would sustain. It kept officers away from troops too much of the time. It deferred until too late in an officer's career his readiness for the general service schools and for higher command or general staff assignment.

In 1922 the number of regular officer courses at special service schools was reduced to two. The Basic Course was dropped from the schools and was conducted for all new officers in troop schools of the units to which they were initially assigned. This plan was followed until 1936, when need for further economy forced another reduction in the number of regular courses for officers. The two existing courses were combined to make a single regular course, which was taught until 1940.[1]

In addition to the regular course for officers, each school taught a National Guard and Reserve Officers Course, an abridged version of the regular course, usually lasting three months; a short refresher course for senior officers of the

[1] G–3 Study, "Course at the Army War College, 1939–1940," Rpt of Committee No. 2, sub: Mil Education, pp. 84–87. AWC Records.

arm; and such advanced specialist courses as the Tank Course at the Infantry School, the Advanced Equitation Course at the Cavalry School, an Advanced Course in Motors at the Field Artillery School, and the Advanced Technical Course at the Coast Artillery School.

For enlisted men, both general and specialist courses were also provided. The general courses were for noncommissioned officers. Such courses were designed either, as in the Cavalry School's Regular Army NCO Course, to develop unit instructors, extend the training of noncommissioned officers, and prepare them for duty with civilian components of the Army, or, as in the Infantry School's Refresher Course for Sergeant Instructors on National Guard Duty, to review the duties of noncommissioned officers and bring them up to date on recent developments in the arm. The specialist courses were more numerous and more important. Such subjects as tank maintenance, communications, saddlery, and motor maintenance were covered in specialist courses conducted for both Regular Army and National Guard enlisted men. These courses were the principal means by which the school disseminated to the branch at large the innovations and refinements of technique produced by the research of its staff.[2]

The Schools in 1940–41

With the beginning of mobilization in 1940 the War Department authorized service schools to conduct, as contemplated in Mobilization Regulations, four types of courses: (1) refresher courses for selected officers of all Army components; (2) a special basic course for newly commissioned officers; (3) specialist courses for selected officers; and (4) specialist courses for key enlisted personnel.[3] The 9-month regular course, the National Guard and Reserve Officers refresher courses, and the refresher courses for senior Regular Army officers were discontinued.[4] All courses were short, none longer than twelve weeks, in conformity with the War Department principle that " it is . . . out of the question to expect the Army School system to complete the individual instruction of any personnel prior to arrival at his organization." [5]

[2] AR 350–200, 350–400, 350–600, 350–700.

[3] (1) WD ltr AG 352.01 (7–26–40) M–C to Chiefs of Br, 31 Jul 40, sub: Courses at Spec Serv Schs. (2) TAG memo AG 352.01 (6–11–40) M–C to CofInf, 15 Jun 40, sub as in (1). AGO Records.

[4] (1) WD ltr AG 352.01 (7–27–40) M–M to CGs and Comdt FA Sch, 1 Aug 40, sub: Courses of Instruction at the FA Sch. (2) WD ltr 352.01 (6–18–40) M M–C to Chiefs, 18 Jun 40, sub: Courses for Regular Offs at Spec Serv Schs, 1940–41. AGO Records. At the Infantry School the Special Refresher Course for Senior National Guard Officers was not discontinued until January, 1941.

[5] TAG 1st ind AG 352.01 (6–18–40) M–C, 22 Jun 40, on CofInf memo for TAG, 18 Jun 40. AGO Records.

Provision of both officers refresher and officers basic courses proved unnecessary. So few Regular Army officers were available to guide the mobilization that none could be spared for refresher courses; most of the Reserve officers called to duty were in the company grades and in need of basic training. Basic and refresher instruction were merged in courses variously called Basic, Company Officers, Battery Officers, and Rifle and Heavy Weapons Company Commanders Courses. Advanced courses for battalion or similar unit commanders and staff officers were not established until 1941 except at the Infantry and Field Artillery Schools, where such courses began in November 1940. Specialist courses for both officers and enlisted men were few in number at this stage, and the offerings of the various schools were fairly uniform.

Training of enlisted specialists had three purposes: to provide replacements for specialists sent from units in cadres; to augment the number of specialists provided to new units, and to furnish existing units with additional specialists for use in later cadres.[6] The core of instruction for specialists was constituted by motor and communications courses for both officers and enlisted specialists, given at all the schools. Courses in such specific branch subjects as tank maintenance, horseshoeing, gun maintenance, and height-finder operation were also given. No school gave more than eight courses for enlisted specialists, and one, the Infantry School, gave only two.

Additions to school programs were not numerous in 1941. The Coast Artillery School added several officers specialist courses, and the Field Artillery School instituted a course for Field Officers. The Cavalry School increased its enlisted specialist program by starting horseshoeing, saddlery, motors, communications, and armory courses. The training of full-track vehicle mechanics was begun at the Field Artillery School, of motor and radar operators at the Coast Artillery School, and of blacksmiths and sheet metal workers at the Armored School. No officer or enlisted courses were added in 1941 at the Infantry School. The most significant addition to the school program in 1941 was the officer candidate courses, although quantitatively they were of only minor importance before Pearl Harbor.

The major effort of the schools during the preliminary mobilization period from September 1940 to December 1941 was directed toward training as many as possible of the 100,000 National Guard and Reserve officers who had been called to active duty. Most of the Reserve officers, as already noted, were in the

[6] WD ltr AG 200.63 FA Sch (6–17–40) E to CGs, 18 Jun 40, sub: Enl Specialists Courses, FA Sch. AGO Records.

company grades; they were to be the primary agents in carrying out training programs in units and replacement centers. The needs of an inexperienced officer in preparing for this task were as follows: (1) information to pass on to his men and knowledge of where to find additional information; (2) reasonable skill in the subjects to be taught, to enable him to demonstrate them and to recognize good and bad performance among his men; (3) familiarity—and, if possible, proficiency—with the most effective methods of conducting training in each subject; (4) knowledge of army administration to enable him to command a unit efficiently; and (5) a conviction of the importance of leadership in training and combat. The officers basic courses took shape from these needs, of which the first three were paramount at the moment. It would have been desirable to give each officer an opportunity to teach a school unit at least some of the subjects for which he was to be responsible, after he had acquired some skill in the material himself. Limitations of time and facilities made this impossible. The procedure adopted was to instruct the officer in a basic subject and simultaneously to demonstrate to him how he should teach it to his men. Each subject was made as similar as possible, in scope, sequence, and method of presentation, to the courses which the officers were later to teach. School instructors repeatedly directed the attention of the officer students to the methods being used on them and to the value of these methods in their later service. The officers were told that learning the subject and learning how it should be taught were of equal importance. This procedure was a compromise and inevitably had its disadvantages. Officers did little or no instructing; there was a wide gap between knowledge of a good instructional practice and facility in its use. The need to attend at the same time to a subject and to the technique being used to present it was undoubtedly confusing. Moreover, a class of officers was not the same as a class of enlisted men; the pressure of time frequently formed the use of methods—heavy reliance on the lecture is but one example—which the officers could not employ in a unit without loss of effectiveness. Despite these disadvantages the procedure adopted did produce officers who knew their subjects, had a model of good teaching practice, and approached their tasks in fairly uniform ways.

As a result of the attempt to reproduce for students approximately the training they would later conduct, programs of instruction for the basic courses paralleled rather closely the training programs for small units and replacement centers. Such purely operational subjects as administration and military law were given relatively little time.

By no means all Reserve and National Guard officers attended the basic course of their arm. By the end of 1943 approximately 40,000 officers had been graduated from them. Many Reserve officers, of course, were of higher rank and ineligible to attend. Others were so urgently needed for training that they could not be spared until they had been promoted past the appropriate rank for the course. Of the 40,000 officers graduated from basic courses, the bulk were trained in 1940 and 1941 and played a role of great importance in the early phases of mobilization.

Expansion, 1942

The great expansion in the AGF school program occurred in 1942. Existing school facilities grew enormously, largely to accommodate the thousands of officer candidates who had to be trained for the hundred divisions and the multitude of other units which it was planned to activate in 1942 and 1943. Basic courses for commissioned officers were continued, but the numbers enrolled in them steadily declined. Training masses of candidates while continuing to operate officers basic courses was greatly simplified by the use of common programs of instruction for both. Whether a student was a candidate about to take up his duties for the first time, or an officer of little or no experience, it was assumed that the same basic instruction was required, with principal attention given to weapons, materiel, small-unit tactics, and methods of instruction, administration, and leadership. More emphasis, to be sure, was placed on leadership in the course as given to officer candidates, and they were also held to more rigorous standards of conduct and achievement. But the two courses were substantially identical, and this facilitated the preparation and use of instructors, the assignment of areas, buildings, and ranges, and the use of school troops. However, as more and more officers came to the basic courses, not directly from Reserve status or brief duty with troops but from extended tours in units or training centers, it became increasingly clear that the background and requirements of such men and of officer candidates were too different to be dealt with satisfactorily by a common course. Officers tended to resent being given the same training as enlisted men who were not yet officers. Many, having conducted unit or individual training for a period of time, felt they could gain little from a course designed to teach them just that. These attitudes, whether or not justified, interfered seriously with instruction.[7]

During 1942, 54,233 candidates were trained and commissioned in the AGF officer candidate schools, nearly forty times the number who were graduated in

[7] Statement of Col P. H. Kron, Sec Inf Sch, to AGF Hist Off, 7 Mar 45.

1941. By the end of 1942 the training of junior leaders had been substantially completed in the officers basic courses. A survey conducted at the end of the year showed that in four arms only a comparatively small number of officers remained who had not attended either an officer candidate or an officers basic course.

An important addition to the curriculum of some of the schools in 1942 was a course for officers assigned to units scheduled for activation. Early in 1942 General Headquarters worked out a plan for the activation of infantry divisions.[8] Key officers of the various branch components of the division attended a special course at their respective service school prior to the activation date. The Infantry School organized, and began to operate in January 1942, a 4-week course for the infantry component, consisting of the assistant division commander, regimental commanders and staffs, battalion commanders and their executives, and company commanders—ninety-two officers in all. Similarly, the officers of the artillery component attended a preactivation course at the Field Artillery School. These courses were designed to familiarize key members of command and staff with the activation plan, to make available to them the lessons learned by earlier cadres, to assist them in drawing up training programs and schedules, to permit them to become acquainted with each other and with the policies of the commander, and to prepare them for the many difficult problems they would encounter during the early stages of training. Special instruction was conducted for regimental and battalion staffs as a whole and for members of the individual staff sections.[9] The schools followed closely the progress of each division as it was activated, in order to correct their teaching and increase the help they could give cadres of later divisions. A total of 3,746 officers attended the New Division Course at the Infantry School from January 1942 until July 1943, when, with division activations coming to an end, the course was no longer needed. One class per month had been conducted in 1942—except in March, November, and December—and during the first six months of 1943.[10]

Formulation of a Policy for Officer Training, 1943

The tremendous production of officer candidates, which had occupied the major attention of AGF schools in 1942, had eliminated the officer shortage by the end of that year. To prevent a wasteful production of new officers in excess of

[8] See below, "The Building and Training of Infantry Divisions."

[9] Personal ltr of Gen McNair to Gen Parks, 27 Mar 43. McNair Correspondence.

[10] Study, "Authorized Course Capacities for All Courses at the Infantry School, 1940–1945." Files of Inf Sch, Ft Benning, Ga.

anticipated requirements for the coming year, the War Department on 15 December 1942 directed a severe cut in officer candidate school capacities. Amounting to approximately 50 percent of capacities currently devoted to training candidates, the cut released facilities for training 18,000 more officers and enlisted men each quarter than were currently enrolled in schools.[11] Although the War Department revised downward slightly its limits on officer candidate training, so that an additional capacity of only 14,410 became available, Army Ground Forces was still presented with an opportunity to make general readjustments in its school program.[12]

It was decided late in 1942 to use part of the available facilities for a "major expansion" of advanced courses for officers. Large numbers of officers—products for the most part of the officer candidate program—had accumulated in pools and in unit overstrengths toward the end of 1942; the graduation of candidate classes in session in late 1942 would augment this stock. Of these officers many had already served for several months with troops and during 1943 many more would complete a tour of troop duty. It was considered essential to return a proportion of them to school for advanced training.[13]

As the question of how best to employ the available school facilities was explored in Headquarters, Army Ground Forces, and as the schools and school commands sent in their recommendations, it became clear that a general policy for the training of officers was needed. Little consistency was apparent in the handling of officer schooling in the several arms. Events had moved so rapidly, and the schools had expanded so quickly to meet varying requirements, that the only fixed policy had been to get as many officers as could be spared from units to some sort of school course. General McNair directed his G–3 in February 1943 to "take stock and determine what should be our goal in the education of officers" and to evolve "a basic program for future schooling of officers." [14] He proposed for consideration a total of six months' schooling for officers, believing the three months given in candidate and basic courses too little. He suggested that G–3 consider extending the basic courses, although he felt that the OCS course need

[11] WD memo (S) WDGAP 352 OCS for CG AGF, 15 Dec 42, sub: Quarterly Capacities of AGF OCSs. 352/12 (OCS)(S).

[12] Tab N, AGF G–3 study (S), 26 Feb 43, sub: AGF Schs. AGF G–3 Schs Br files.

[13] (1) AGF ltr (S) to CGs R&SC, AA Comd, and CofArmd F, 19 Dec 42, sub: Quarterly Capacities of AGF OCSs. (2) AGF memo (S) for ACofS USA, 31 Dec 42, sub as in (1). Both in 352/12 (OCS)(S).

[14] AGF M/S, CofS to G–3, 20 Feb 43, sub: Utilization of Facilities Made Available by the Reduction in OCS Capacity. In Tab P of AGF G–3 study (S), 26 Feb 43, sub: AGF Schs. AGF G–3 Schs Br files.

not be lengthened except in Antiaircraft and Field Artillery. In this he differed from his G–1, who had suggested in December that available capacity should be absorbed in part by extension of the OCS course.[15] While recommending six months as a desirable figure to use in planning officers' school training, General McNair did not believe it necessary to adopt a uniform standard for all arms. Study might reveal, he thought, that an infantry officer should go to school for five months, a field artilleryman for six, and an antiaircraft officer for some other period.

Working along the lines suggested by General McNair, G–3, Army Ground Forces, produced a study of the school problem and a set of recommendations that formed the basis for subsequent AGF policy.[16] G–3 recommended that courses should be extended "reluctantly"; preferably, it was suggested, students should be returned to school for subsequent courses after serving with troops. With this view General McNair agreed. "It is better," he said, "to return students for the advanced course than to lengthen the basic course." But it did not seem likely that all officers could return to school for advanced instruction. At the time the study was made, school capacities were large enough to provide advanced training for only 34 percent of the officers in AGF units, or 25 percent of all AGF officers. In General McNair's opinion it was unnecessary to send all officers to the advanced course; he wrote that "perhaps as few as one third will answer our needs."[17]

Changes in the school program followed. Expansion of officers basic courses at the Infantry and Field Artillery Schools, which had been recommended by the schools and the Replacement and School Command, was disapproved, even though Army Ground Forces had reported to the War Department in February, before the G–3 study was made, a decision to make such an expansion. The study had revealed that only 8,301 officers of the four traditional arms lacked basic schooling of some sort. These could easily be trained in the current basic courses or, in view of the extended experience of many of the officers, in advanced courses.

It was the advanced courses, both general and specialist, that received the principal increase, as had been planned in December. The change of emphasis can best be shown by a comparison of the facilities for advanced training of offi-

[15] AGF M/S (S), G–1 to G–3, 17 Dec 42, sub: Quarterly Capacities of AGF OCSs. 352/12 (OCS)(S).

[16] AGF G–3 study (S), "Army Ground Force Schools," 26 Feb 43. AGF G–3 Schs Br files.

[17] AGF M/S, CG to G–3, 27 Feb 43, sub: Utilization of Facilities Made Available by the Reduction in OCS Capacity. Tab P of AGF G–3 study cited in n. 16. AGF G–3 Schs Br files.

cers at the time the G–3 study was made (February 1943) and those available in April 1943:

School	*Total Officers with Troop Units (Including 1943 Augmentation)*	*Annual Capacity for Advanced Schooling*		*Percentage of Officers for Whom School Capacity was Available*		*Officer Secondary School Capacity per Unit (Regt or Similar Hq or Bn)*	
		Feb	*Apr*	*Feb*	*Apr*	*Feb*	*Apr*
Inf	33,415	7,788	12,588	23	38	9.6	15.5
FA	17,189	6,488	9,640	38	56	11.1	16.4
AA	18,499	7,948	13,481	43	73	12.6	21.4
CA	2,771	655	655	24	24	5.0	5.0
Cav	3,518	932	932	26	26	9.3	9.3
Armd	13,031	3,900	8,140	30	62	8.4	23.7
TD	5,896	4,320	3,013	73	51	27.8	17.7
TOTAL	94,319	32,031	48,449	34	51	11.2	17.5

Source: AGF G–3 study (S), sub: AGF Schs. AGF G–3 Schs Br files.

While capacities were being increased, the advanced courses were changed. They had been designed for field officers and senior captains. The names given the courses—Field Officers, Battalion Commanders and Staff Officers, Squadron Commanders and Staff Officers, and Squadron Commanders—had reflected this intention. In all schools, graduation from a basic or officer candidate course had been a prerequisite for admission to an advanced course. Major emphasis had been placed on tactics and staff procedures. Readjustments were made to meet the new conditions. The officers for whom increased advanced schooling was to be provided were largely of company grade, and their need for training could not wait upon the uncertainties of promotion. Numerous officers with considerable troop experience, of both company and field grades, had not attended a basic or officer candidate course; to prevent commanders from sending them to advanced courses because of the current entrance requirement would deny schooling to those who needed it most—officers without recent school training. Moreover, if the courses were to be thrown open to officers who had been away from school for some time, advanced courses had to be made more general. Weapons, the tactics of units smaller than the battalion, and the technique of troop leading had to be stressed.

The principle on which advanced schooling had been provided was therefore changed. General courses for officers were established not in terms of rank, as formerly, but in terms of qualification, based in turn on recency of school training and amount of duty with troops. Army Ground Forces directed that courses be renamed: Field Officers, Battalion Commanders, and Squadron Commanders Courses became simply Officers Advanced Courses.[18] They were opened to any officer above the grade of second lieutenant whom a commander considered qualified to attend; no other school course was a prerequisite.[19] The Infantry and Field Artillery Schools were directed to lay particular emphasis on technique. The purpose of the Infantry School Advanced Course was announced as "the development of field commanders of battalions and companies." The Advanced Course at the Field Artillery School, extended from eight to twelve weeks, was to review the Basic Course and to train officers for duty in battalion, group, and corps artillery headquarters.[20] When the Field Artillery School requested permission to reinstitute an old special Advanced Course for higher commanders — discontinued in 1941 for lack of qualified students — Army Ground Forces disapproved. Maneuvers, Army Ground Forces believed, were the best school for teaching tactical employment of artillery; "the entire resources of the school," the AGF reply stated, "should be devoted to building up sound technical training at this time."[21] When the Tank Destroyer School proposed an Advanced Tactical Course, Army Ground Forces directed that the name be changed to Officers Advanced Course because "it is desired not to stress too much tactics." The primary purpose of the course, the school was told, was to develop practical field leaders of battalions and companies.[22] The advanced course at the Coast Artillery School was lengthened from four weeks to eight. Army Ground Forces defined its purpose as "to instruct potential battery and battalion commanders in the technique of seacoast artillery. Theoretical instruction including

[18] AGF ltr (S) to CG R&SC, 1 Mar 43, sub as in M/S cited in n. 17. 352/17 (OCS)(S).

[19] (1) AGF ltr to CG R&SC, 22 Apr 43, sub: Qualifications for Offs Advanced Courses. 352/610. (2) AGF 1st ind (S), 17 May 43, on AA Comd ltr (S) to CG AGF, 23 Mar 43, sub: Expansion of AAA, Cp Davis, N. C. 352/12 (OCS)(S). (3) AGF 2d ind, 8 Feb 43, on FA Sch ltr to CG R&SC, 7 Jan 43, sub: Increase in Fld Offs Course. 352/17 (OCS)(S).

[20] (1) AGF 1st ind (S), 26 May 43, on R&SC ltr (S) to CG AGF, 1 May 43, sub: Utilization of Facilities Made Available through the Reduction of OCS Capacity in the Inf Sch. 352/17 (OCS)(S). (2) AGF 2d ind, 8 Feb 43, cited in n. 19 (3) above.

[21] AGF 2d ind, 1 Mar 43, on FA Sch ltr to R&SC, 30 Jan 43, sub: Resumption of Advanced Course (Special)(FAS). 352/687 (FA Sch).

[22] AGF 3d ind (C) to R&SC, 10 Feb 43, on TD Sch ltr, 29 Dec 42, sub: Offs Tactical Advanced Course at the TD Sch, and atchd AGF M/S, 3 Feb 43, sub: Offs Tac Advanced Course at TD Sch. 352/65 (C).

command and staff should be kept to a minimum." [23] Major revisions were incorporated in the Cavalry School's Advanced Course to deemphasize tactics, command, and staff procedure and to stress the technique of reconnaissance.[24] At the Antiaircraft School a new Advanced Course was set up, combining the Officer Cadre and Officer Refresher Courses previously given. Although the need for officers for new units limited this course to six weeks—only half the standard recommended in the G–3 study—it was still two weeks longer than the courses it replaced.[25]

The Armored School was an exception to the new trend. Instead of a single course for all officers above the grade of second lieutenant, the Armored School instituted a Company Commanders Course and a Battalion Commanders Course, eight and six weeks long respectively, to replace the Basic Tactical and Advanced Tactical Courses.[26] This arrangement continued until late in 1943. By that time it had become clear that to obtain a rounded course of advanced instruction an officer would have to return to the Armored School two or even three times. This was contrary to the policy of returning an officer only once for advanced training. The Company and Battalion Commanders Courses overlapped seriously, with about 185 hours of common material. Both were too theoretical, 64 percent of the time in the Battalion Course being given over to theory, as against 23 and 39 percent in the Infantry and Field Artillery Advanced Courses, respectively. Practical instruction in such subjects as gunnery was left largely to special courses. Early in 1944 both courses were abolished, and in their place an Officers Advanced Course of thirteen weeks was initiated. Like other AGF advanced courses, it was open to officers of all grades above second lieutenant. Theoretical instruction was reduced; tactics was minimized; gunnery and the technique of implementing tactical decisions were stressed.[27]

Army Ground Forces also refused to permit a three-level system of officer schooling when the Tank Destroyer School proposed in August 1943 to institute a Company Officers Course. The new course, according to the school, would

[23] AGF 1st ind, 5 May 43, on R&SC ltr to AGF, 13 Apr 43, sub: Revision of Offs Advanced Course, CAS. With atchd AGF M/S. 352/514 (CAS).

[24] Cav Sch ltr to CG R&SC, 26 Mar 43, sub: Revised Programs, Offs Advanced Course, and atchd inds and M/Ss. 352/50 (S).

[25] AGF M/S (S), G–3 to CG, 11 Mar 43, sub: AA Schs. 352/12 (OCS)(S).

[26] Armd F ltr to CG AGF, 9 Feb 43, sub: Increase in Intake of Tactical Courses, Armd F Sch, and AGF 1st ind, 1 Mar 43. 352/12 (OCS)(S).

[27] (1) AGF ltr to CG Armd Comd, 28 Sep 43, sub: Tng Programs — Bn Comdrs and Co Offs Courses. 352/269 (Armd F Sch). (2) AGF M/Ss and inds in same file.

"provide instruction of a grade and quality higher than that given to officer candidate classes." It was the view of Army Ground Forces that the inauguration of an "intermediate" course would produce less desirable results than extending the Tank Destroyer Advanced Course, then only six weeks long, to include the review of basic subjects and information on new developments desired by the school. The longer advanced course that emerged from the discussion was similar in scope and length to those given at the other schools.[28]

A detailed statement of AGF policy on school training, foreshadowed in the February study on schools, was issued to the field in July 1943. As a preface to a catalogue of school courses then available, a number of principles were laid down. Two types of courses comprised an officer's schooling: basic courses (officer candidate or regular basic) and advanced courses (regular advanced or specialist—motor, communication, etc.). At least four and preferably six months should elapse between attendance at a basic and attendance at an advanced course, except when an advanced specialist course was very short. An officer might attend two advanced courses, regular and specialist. A statement that every officer should normally have six months' schooling, which appeared in the draft of the directive, was deleted because facilities were too limited for so ambitious a program, even had it been desirable. But for the officers who could be given the full school program, six months continued to be the general limit applied by Army Ground Forces.[29]

The importance of advanced officer schooling in 1943 can be gauged from the number of graduates of the officers' advanced courses or their predecessors at four service schools during the period 1941–44:

School	*1941*	*1942*	*1943*	*1944*
Antiaircraft Artillery	. . .	1,347	5,816	[a] 1,241
Cavalry	. . .	155	363	652
Field Artillery	173	455	1,068	1,678
Infantry	1,504	1,025	3,242	3,713
TOTAL	1,677	2,982	10,489	7,284

[a] To 30 September 1944.

[28] TD Sch ltr to CG R&SC, 12 Aug 43, sub: Co Offs Course. With atchd inds and M/Ss. 352/240 (TD Sch).

[29] (1) AGF ltr (R) to CGs, 19 Jul 43, sub: Courses at AGF Spec Serv Schs. With atchd M/S. 352/48 (R). (2) AGF M/S, G-3 to CofS, 30 Apr 43, sub: Increase in Length of OC Courses. 352/440 (OCS).

While taking steps to make advanced training more generally available and more suitable to the needs of line officers, Army Ground Forces consistently opposed efforts to extend school training upward to include higher commanders. The Antiaircraft School, in February 1943 and again in June, urged the establishment of a Special Observers Course to indoctrinate commanders of other arms in the proper employment of antiaircraft artillery. Army Ground Forces viewed the project with disfavor; it also disapproved a similar scheme, emanating from the Cavalry School, to operate a brief orientation course for higher commanders and staffs in employment of mechanized cavalry reconnaissance. The grounds for disapproval were the same in both cases: the best school for higher commanders was maneuvers; when errors were made in employment of a given arm they could be corrected on the spot, when the correction would do some good. This was a realistic judgment, since a school course for higher commanders, because of limitations of troops, ammunition, and areas, was bound to be largely theoretical.[30]

As advanced schooling for officers was expanded, the basic courses were reduced. In the middle of 1943 basic courses were extended to seventeen weeks as a consequence of the extension of the officer candidate courses, which they duplicated.[31] By 1 September 1943 there remained only 4,550 officers in the four basic arms who had had no schooling; many of these had been on duty so long that they were beyond the basic course stage.[32] During the following year, therefore, officers basic courses were discontinued.[33]

Retrenchment and Readjustment, 1944–45

Until late 1943, the mission of AGF service schools was to supply adequate numbers of trained officers and enlisted men, including requirements for cadres, to a rapidly expanding army. As expansion gave way to stabilization, deployment overseas, and retrenchment at home, the mission changed. From late in 1943, the task of the schools was "the raising of standards of education generally,

[30] AA Comd ltr (C) to CG AGF, 23 Feb 43, sub: Establishment of Spec Observers Course at the AAA Sch, Cp Davis, N.C., for Selected Pers of Other Arms. With atchd papers. 352/108 (C). (2) R&SC ltr to CG AGF, 26 Feb 43, sub: Initiation of Course on Mecz Cav Rcn at the Cav Sch, Ft Riley, Kan. With atchd papers. 352/293 (Cav Sch).

[31] AGF ltr to CG R&SC, 4 Jun 43, sub: Increase in Length of Offs Basic Course. With atchd M/Ss. 352/619.

[32] AGF G–3 study (S), 1 Sep 43, sub: AGF Schs. AGF G–3 Schs Br files.

[33] For dates, see Tables Nos. 4, 6, and 7 below.

the improvement of training, and the maintenance of the level of personnel requiring school training in units." [34]

It had become obvious by late 1943 that the school system needed overhauling. Commanders were less interested than formerly in sending qualified men to school, as was indicated by complaints from schools about the receipt of unqualified students.[35] The schools varied greatly in the relation of their capacities to the needs of units. Using as an index the number of battalions plus the number of headquarters companies in each arm, a study in November 1943 revealed the following variations among schools in their ability to provide training:[36]

Annual Rate of Graduates Per Unit

School	*Officers Courses*	*Enlisted Courses*
Infantry	15.4	13.9
Field Artillery	20.5	31.8
Antiaircraft	27.4	36.1
Coast Artillery	4.2	18.5
Cavalry	19.7	45.9
Armored	39.8	110.2
Tank Destroyer	24.5	100.1

It was not possible or feasible, of course, to establish a uniform unit-rate for all schools: the legitimate needs of various arms differed. Furthermore, some graduates of replacement centers were given further training in schools, swelling the total for those arms having a high proportion of technicians in the replacement stream. But even by the most flexible standard, the productive capacities of the Tank Destroyer and Armored Schools, at least, were vastly in excess of any reasonable demand.

In October 1943 the capacity of the Tank Destroyer School was cut 33 percent for officers courses and 47 percent for enlisted courses.[37] Field commanders were canvassed to determine what courses were desired and how large they should

[34] AGF ltr (R) to CGs, 9 Nov 43, sub: Courses at AGF Spec Serv Schs. 352/69 (R).

[35] See papers in 352/735 and /740 (FA Sch); 352/251, /254, /286, /263, /283, /288, /294, and /299 (Armd Sch).

[36] Tab G to AGF M/S (C), G-3 Misc Div to G-3, 29 Nov 43, sub: Reduction in Stu Caps at TD Sch. 352/140 (C).

[37] AGF ltr (C) to CG R&SC, 31 Oct 43, sub: Reduction in Stu Caps at TD Sch. With atchd papers. 352/140 (C).

be.[38] School capacities were modified on the basis of this survey to fit the demands of the field and the requirements for postgraduate training of replacements. Modifications were generally downward, a reduction of 1,000 each being made in the capacities of the Infantry, Field Artillery, Cavalry, Armored, and Tank Destroyer Schools. At the same time some courses for which there was no longer a need were eliminated. The Pioneer Courses for officers and enlisted men and the Enlisted Weapons Course at the Tank Destroyer School were discontinued. They had been justified when the activation rate was rapid and cadre specialists in these categories were not available in established units. But in a mature establishment these subjects were the proper concern of units, not of service schools. The Armored School was directed to stop operating courses for Enlisted Machinists and Enlisted Radiator, Body, and Fender Repairmen, because these were properly Ordnance Department subjects, and also to discontinue courses for Enlisted Blacksmiths and Welders, because enough had been trained to meet all demands.[39]

Concurrently, steps were taken to establish definitely the percentage of replacement center graduates who would be sent to service schools for further training. In August 1943 the War Department had directed that no more than 5 percent of all AGF replacements be given further schooling; but no apportionment of that fraction was made by Army Ground Forces, even though a September study revealed considerable variations in the percentages of men sent to school from replacement training centers of the various arms and even from different replacement training centers of a single arm.[40] Definite allotments of the number of RTC graduates who might be school-trained were finally made in February 1944, each arm being given a fixed percentage based on the technical requirements of its training.[41]

These efforts to bring school activities more closely into conformity with current needs resulted also in reducing the overhead personnel used to operate the schools. The need for channeling all possible manpower into combat forces was so urgent that reduction of overhead became a separate concern. Staffs of

[38] AGF ltr (R) to CGs, 9 Nov 43, sub: Courses at AGF Spec Serv Schs. 352/69 (R).

[39] (1) AGF ltrs to CG R&SC and CG Armd Comd, 26 Jan 44, sub: Adjustments in Capacities of Courses at AGF Schs. 352/706. (2) AGF G–3 study, undated [— Jan 44], sub: Proposed Adjustments in Capacities of Courses. AGF G–3 Schs Br files.

[40] (1) WD memo (R) for CGs AGF, ASF, AAF, 14 Aug 43, sub: Utilization of Pers. 320.2/255 (R). (2) AGF G–3 study (S), 1 Sep 43, sub: AGF Schs. 314.7 (AGF Hist)(S).

[41] AGF ltr to CGs R&SC, Armd Comd, 3 Feb 44, sub: Sch Tng for RTC Specialists. 352/712.

230-171 O - 66 - 19

schools and replacement centers represented the principal sources in Army Ground Forces of men not in combat units and available for such assignment. Owing largely to their relatively decentralized and unsupervised growth, the schools were overstaffed. While school capacities and enrollments had fallen steadily, school overhead had declined only slightly. At the peak of school operations, capacities had been 60,378, and overhead, including school troops, 30,486—a ratio of approximately 2 students to 1 overhead. By 1 December 1943 an enrollment of 24,094 was using an overhead of 22,819, a ratio of almost 1 to 1. The overhead authorized for the schools was considerably higher than necessary, and the overhead actually used was 3,600 above that authorized. It was estimated that, in all, 10,000 officers and men could be withdrawn from the schools without injury to their operations.

The schools were directed in February 1944 to eliminate their overstrength at once and to achieve by 1 May a ratio of 1.5 students (capacity) to 1 overhead. Because requirements for administrative personnel were relatively inelastic, not falling proportionately with decline in students, it was not considered feasible to set the ratio at 2 to 1, the ratio attained in 1943.[42] It was much easier to order such a reduction than to achieve it. The schools, believing that their efficiency derived in no small measure from the use of small instructional groups, protested strongly against a measure which they feared would increase the size of classes. Because regular rotation of instructors continued in force, more teaching per instructor was required from men who were on the whole less expert than those they replaced. As there was always a chance that new courses or new increases of capacity would become necessary, the schools were afraid that they would be left without means to cope with a new expansion.[43] Reductions were made despite these objections. With infantry divisions being stripped to supply replacements, the demand for savings in overhead became ever more urgent. Fortunately, actual enrollment in the schools proved to be lower than had been forecast, except at the Infantry School, where officer candidate training rose sharply. By working instructors harder, by conserving transportation, by curtailing such luxuries as enlisted assistants to display charts, and by similar economies the schools managed to survive on a slimmer diet.

These economies were only a foretaste of what was to come. While Army Ground Forces was squeezing a 10,000-man surplus out of the schools, the War

[42] AGF ltr (C) to CGs, 16 Feb 44, sub: Reduction in Overhead of Schs. 352/222 (C).

[43] For the attitude of the schools see memo of Col Jeter for AGF G-3, 11 Mar 44, sub: Obsn during Visit to R&SCs. AGF G-3 file 333.1/99 (1944).

Department, in February 1944, directed the elimination of 25,000 men from AGF overhead, which included operating personnel for schools as well as replacement centers, depots, and headquarters, during the second half of the year.[44] This was to be accomplished by curtailing officer candidate schools and by reducing overhead in the Airborne, Antiaircraft, and Armored Commands, in the Infantry, Cavalry, and Field Artillery Schools, and in the Tank Destroyer Center. A stay was granted in the accomplishment of this directive, in view of the recent expansion of replacement training centers and depots, the probable increase in officer candidate production, and the likelihood that schools would have to expand in 1945 to provide advanced training for the additional replacements and candidates produced in 1944. It was desirable to maintain a level of overhead sufficient to handle these anticipated requirements.[45] In June 1944 the War Department, believing that the limit of economy in the use of overhead had not been reached, directed Army Ground Forces to consider the elimination or consolidation of the Cavalry, Coast Artillery, Armored, and Tank Destroyer Schools and of certain replacement centers.[46] A committee of officers of the G–3 Section, Army Ground Forces, appointed to study these and related economies, recommended in July that the Armored, Cavalry, and Tank Destroyer Schools be consolidated, that new ratios of overhead to students be applied, and that numerous revisions be made in the school programs. Among the latter were proposals to reduce the length of officers advanced courses, to eliminate pack artillery training at the Field Artillery School, to combine four officers advanced courses at the Antiaircraft School into one, and to discontinue certain specialist courses at the Antiaircraft, Coast Artillery, and Infantry Schools. The committee's recommendations, it was anticipated, would save 8,184 in overhead. Further savings, the committee believed, could be effected by adopting standard organizations for such comparable types of installations as schools and replacement centers.[47] G–3, Army Ground Forces, adopted these recommendations only in part. The proposals to reduce advanced courses, eliminate pack training at Fort Sill, and establish new ratios of students to overhead, were accepted. But G–3

[44] WD memo (S) WDGCT 220 (24 Feb 44) for CG AGF, 24 Feb 44, sub: Reduction of ZI Establishments. 320.2/33 (TUB 44)(S).

[45] (1) AGF memo (S) for CofS USA, 10 Apr 44, sub: Reduction of ZI Establishments. 320.2/33 (TUB 44)(S). (2) WD memo (S) WDGCT 220 (24 Feb 44) for CG AGF, 6 May 44, sub as in (1). Both in 320.2/33 (TUB 44)(S).

[46] WD D/F (S) WDGCT 220 (24 Feb 44) to CG AGF, 13 Jun 44, sub: Reduction of the Bulk Allotment to the AGF. 320.2/33 (TUB 44)(S).

[47] AGF G–3 Sec memo (S) for G–3, 22 Jul 44, sub: Committee Rpt. 314.7 (AGF Hist).

did not favor consolidating the Armored, Cavalry, and Tank Destroyer Schools. Consolidation would inevitably produce confusion that might interfere with meeting theater requirements for trained personnel. The schools were going concerns, capable of adjusting to changed needs. Future needs were indeterminate, and flexibility in meeting them might be sacrificed under a highly centralized school system. Finally, elimination of schools would imply a preliminary judgment in respect to the survival of Cavalry, Tank Destroyer, and Armored as separate arms; the time was not ripe, G–3 believed, for such decisions.[48]

In August and again in September 1944 the War Department renewed its drive for economy. In August consolidation of service schools and reduction in the number of school courses were recommended, together with consolidation and elimination of certain replacement training centers and officer candidate schools.[49] The September memorandum specifically directed Army Ground Forces to consolidate the Tank Destroyer and Cavalry Officer Candidate Schools with the Armored Officer Candidate School at Fort Knox and to combine the Tank Destroyer School and Armored School at Fort Knox, at the earliest practicable date.[50] Officer candidate training for the three branches was concentrated at Fort Knox, the first combined class starting in November. The consolidation of the Tank Destroyer and Armored Schools, which the G–3 committee had recommended in July, was not carried out. Further study showed that at Fort Knox artillery ranges were inadequate and tactical training areas too small; fire and movement problems required for tank destroyer and mechanized cavalry instruction would be impossible. The saving of overhead that could be achieved by combining the schools would not be large, and the cost of the move was estimated in the millions. Loss of efficiency in instruction was probable. The War Department decided not to require consolidation.[51]

While the question of consolidation and elimination of schools was being studied, reductions were made in activities within the schools. The July G–3 study had recommended reduction in the length of officers advanced courses. It soon

[48] AGF M/S (S), G–3 to CofS, 26 Jul 44, sub: Committee Rpt. 314.7 (AGF Hist).

[49] WD memo (S) WDGCT 353 (19 Aug 44) for CG AGF, 19 Aug 44, sub: Consolidation of Tng Activities. 353/215 (S).

[50] WD memo (R) WDGCT 352 (16 Sep 44) for CG AGF, 16 Sep 44, sub: Consolidation of Certain AGF Schs. 352/176 (R).

[51] (1) AGF memo (R) for CofS USA, 5 Oct 44, sub: Consolidation of Certain AGF Schs. 352/176 (R). (2) AGF memo (S) for CofS USA, 3 Oct 44, sub: Consolidation of Tng Activities. 353/215 (S). (3) WD D/F (R) to CG AGF, 9 Oct 44. 352/176 (R).

became apparent that most courses were longer than necessary. AGF units were being deployed more rapidly than had been anticipated when courses were originally planned. It was found that unit commanders confronted with early readiness dates could not afford to permit their men to be absent at schools for long courses. It was thought at Headquarters, Army Ground Forces, that tactical courses for officers could be reduced from three months to six weeks, and that technical courses for both officers and enlisted men could be reduced to about eight weeks without impairment of standards.[52] Recommendations on reduction of courses were submitted by the schools, the Replacement and School Command, and the Antiaircraft Command. Almost without exception the schools held out for less drastic reductions than those proposed by Army Ground Forces, insisting that standards could not be maintained if curtailment were too severe.[53]

Actually courses were not reduced; they were eliminated. By the time the replies were tabulated, in late September 1944, the conditions that had called forth the original proposals for reduction had changed. The bulk of AGF units had left the United States or were about to leave.[54] The demand for school training for personnel assigned to units was nearing the vanishing point. During the six months from May to October 1944, requests from units for officers course quotas decreased 66 percent. Actual attendance during the same period had averaged only 60 percent of the authorized capacities of all school courses, modest though these were by earlier standards. These facts caused G-3, Army Ground Forces, to remark in October that "our service schools were dying a natural death due to a lack of students." [55] Except at the Infantry and Field Artillery Schools, demands for attendance at existing officers courses were so small that their continuance could not be justified. It was decided to eliminate all officers courses at these schools; officers in need of training currently given would be accommodated in similar enlisted courses.[56] Aside from the need to continue specialist courses for infantry and field artillery officers, one general requirement for officer training remained. Each arm contained a number of officers who had not yet been over-

[52] (1) AGF ltr, 24 Aug 44, sub: Reduction in Length of Courses at Serv Schs. (2) AGF M/S, G-3 to CofS, 19 Aug 44, sub as in (1) above. Both in 352.11/511.

[53] (1) Recommendations by Schools, R&SC, and AA Comd in 352/357 (C). (2) AGF M/S, G-3 to CofS, 23 Sep 44, sub as in n. 52 above. 352.11/511.

[54] AGF Stat Sec Rpt (C), 19 Mar 45, sub: Comparison of Enl Strengths of AGF — By Months, Troop Units (C). AGF Stat Sec files.

[55] AGF M/S, G-3 to CofS, 25 Oct 44, sub: Courses in Serv Schs. 352.11/518.

[56] AGF ltr to CGs and R&SC, 16 Nov 44, sub: Changes in Capacities of Courses at Serv Schs. 352.11/518.

seas, who would probably go in the near future, and who had not recently attended a general advanced course. They needed some refresher work before being assigned overseas. In October Lt. Gen. Ben Lear, Commanding General of Army Ground Forces, directed such training for infantry officer replacements. Replacement pools contained some officers for whom no assignment existed and for whom some useful employment had to be found. Officers without recent troop duty needed up-to-date training in combat tactics and technique. The existing advanced courses were not suitable for officers in these categories. They were too long. Their treatment of many subjects, especially administration, training management, and weapons, was too detailed for purposes of review. They were generally too diffuse to give officers the required over-all view of their arm. It was decided, therefore, to institute in the service schools an 8-week Officers Refresher Course, open to any officer of the arm, regardless of rank, who had not attended an advanced course within the past year. The refresher courses were designed as a "broad, intensive summation of the essentials of tactics, technique, and weapons of the arm." Existing advanced courses in the schools were discontinued.

The new courses, which began in most schools early in 1945, had a tactical emphasis, the amount of the emphasis varying with the complexity of the weapons and material which had to be covered as a preliminary to tactical instruction. The proposed allotment of hours to subjects showed general similarity among the schools, except that the Infantry School concentrated far more heavily on tactics than did the others:[57]

Allotment of Hours in Officers Refresher Courses, 1945

	Inf	*FA*	*Cav*	*TD*	*CA*	*Armd*
Weapons, Gunnery	16	157	85	157	132	132
Tactics	284	144	192	165	112	154
General Subjects	53	9	2	14	15	...
Communication	12	24	33	24	...	24
Automotive	4	20	48	24	...	24
Physical Training	1	...	...	...	...	...
Materiel	...	14	...	...	88	...
Orientation	...	...	8	...	...	...
Submarine Mining	...	...	...	...	12	...
Tank Maintenance	...	...	...	...	...	20
Reserved	14	16	16	...	25	30
TOTAL	384	384	384	384	384	384

[57] Schedules in 352.11/518.

The refresher courses were not intended merely to provide review instruction for officer replacements or officers without recent school or troop experience. They were projected with redeployment training in mind. Increasing numbers of officers were returning from overseas late in 1944. It was anticipated that after the defeat of Germany large numbers of officers would need some retraining in the United States in preparation for duty in the Pacific. The experience gained by the schools in conducting the refresher courses between January 1945 and V-E Day would equip them, it was believed, to meet the needs of such redeployment instruction. The refresher courses, emphasizing tactics, in which it was expected the returnees would be weakest, would be in operation and ready for any necessary expansion when restaging began. Special provision was made in some of the course programs for subjects pertinent to operations in the Pacific: the Infantry School Refresher Course, for example, contained instruction in Army-Navy cooperation and in the conduct of landing operations.[58]

Courses for enlisted men were not overhauled so drastically. Although units were disappearing rapidly as sources of enlisted students for school courses, the output of replacement training centers provided a steady flow of men to be given advanced training. It had long been the practice to send a percentage of RTC graduates in certain specialities, such as mechanics and radio operators, to service schools for advanced training before assignment as replacements. The number of such men had not been large in proportion to the total volume of replacements—never more than 5 percent in the aggregate—but by the end of 1944 they made up the bulk of students in the enlisted courses at the schools. Enlisted courses had to be kept in operation to train these men, as well as the driblets still coming from units and overhead installations. No reductions were made in the length of the specialist courses in view of their technical nature, the relative inexperience of the students, and the demand for large amounts of practical work.[59] At the time the revisions of capacity were made it was hoped to increase the proportion of RTC graduates sent to schools for advanced training. This would have improved the quality of replacements and permitted more economical operation of courses. But the need for replacements became so acute late in 1944 and early in 1945 that no more than 5 percent could be diverted from the replacement stream.[60]

[58] AGF 2d wrapper ind, 25 Dec 44, on R&SC 1st wrapper ind, 15 Dec 44, to CG AGF. 352.11/518.

[59] See footnotes 55 and 56.

[60] Statement of Lt Col H. S. Schrader, AGF G-3 Sec, to AGF Hist Off, 10 Apr 45.

The major addition to the school program in a year characterized chiefly by curtailment was the Special Basic Course for officers, established in February and March 1944. Operated at the Infantry, Field Artillery, and Armored Schools, this course was designed to facilitate the conversion to those branches of surplus officers of other arms. By the end of 1944, 9,270 officers had been retrained under the program: 8,590 at the Infantry School, 642 at the Field Artillery School, and 38 at the Armored School.[61]

Impetus for establishing the Special Basic Courses came initially from the existence of a large surplus of officers in the Antiaircraft establishment. During early 1943, output of the Antiaircraft Officer Candidate School was building up a surplus of officers even over requirements then contemplated. The modification of the 1943 Troop Basis in October, cutting the Antiaircraft strength by 112,000 men, lowered officer requirements from 24,350 to 18,845. In December the surplus of antiaircraft officers was variously estimated at from 5,000 to over 10,000. Congregated in officer pools and in large-unit overstrengths, these men were not usefully employed and were steadily losing professional skill. It was expected that in 1944 and 1945 shortages of officers would develop in other arms, principally in the Infantry. Antiaircraft officers were encouraged to transfer voluntarily to other arms. By February 1944 it became necessary to reduce the surplus by nonvoluntary block transfers. The Infantry, Armored, and Field Artillery arms were selected as those into which the antiaircraft officers would be transferred.

Except for a core of common basic subjects, such as first aid, military law, small arms, and administration, the training required for an infantry, field artillery, or armored officer differed fundamentally from that which the surplus antiaircraft officers had received. Organization, weapons, technique, and tactics of the arms were dissimilar. The transferees would be of little value in their new arms without retraining. Such retraining could not be conducted easily or uniformly in the units and training centers to which they would be assigned. The Infantry and Armored Schools in February 1944, and the Field Artillery School in March, organized Special Basic Courses to provide centralized conversion training. The courses at the Infantry and Armored Schools lasted eight weeks, that at the Field Artillery School ten weeks. Each was an abbreviated version of the school's officer candidate course, eliminating subjects covered in the Antiaircraft Officer Candidate Course, from which the convertees, all second lieutenants, had been graduated.[62]

[61] See Tables Nos. 3, 6, and 7 below.

[62] (1) AGF ltr to CGs, 9 Feb 44, sub: Establishment of Basic Courses to Implement the Conversion of

Although the largest and most unmanageable surplus of officers was in Antiaircraft, excesses were not confined to this arm. Pools and unit overstrengths held surpluses in most branches. Once some headway had been made against the large backlog of antiaircraft officers, the conversion program was used as a means of achieving a balanced officer strength in all ground arms. Beginning in April, excess tank destroyer, field artillery, and coast artillery officers were detailed and retrained as infantry officers.[63] By the end of the year the Infantry School had enrolled officers of all ground arms in its Special Basic Course in the following numbers:[64]

Antiaircraft Artillery	5,883
Coast Artillery	284
Tank Destroyer	1,178
Field Artillery	794
Armored Force	243
Cavalry	8
Infantry	12
Volunteers (all branches)	1,175
TOTAL	9,577

The Special Basic Course at the Armored School was discontinued after one class because of a prospective surplus of armored officers. The Field Artillery School Conversion Course ran through the year, although on a small scale. By January 1945 this course too was slated for suspension in view of the pressing need of the Infantry for available surplus officers.[65] The Infantry School course remained throughout 1944 the principal vehicle for conversion and branch reapportionment of officers, even though the conversion rate at the Infantry School was reduced after July, owing to the decline in the available surplus and to an increase in the Infantry officer candidate program.[66]

CAC AA Offs to Inf and Armd Comd. 352.11/501. (2) AGF ltr to CG R&SC, 21 Feb 44, sub: Establishment of Special Basic Course at FA Sch. 352.11/4 (FA Sch).

[63] (1) AGF ltr (S) to CG R&SC, 8 Apr 44, sub: Continuation of Program to Convert Surplus Lieutenants to Inf. 352/922 (Inf Sch). (2) Statement of Lt Col W. S. Renshaw, AGF G–1 Sec, Control Div, to AGF Hist Off, 25 Apr 45.

[64] See Table No. 4 in the preceding study, "The Procurement of Officers."

[65] AGF 2d ind, 30 Jan 45, on FA Sch ltr to CG R&SC, 26 Dec 44, sub: Offs Spec Basic Course. 352.11/53 (FA Sch).

[66] (1) AGF memo (S) for CofS USA, 19 Jul 44, sub: Conversion of Offs to Inf. (2) AGF M/S, G–1 to CofS, 17 Jul 44, sub as in (1). Both in 352/124 (S).

By the end of 1944 the AGF schools, after a year of slump and general overhauling, had returned to the pattern of 1943. Basic training for officers continued to be given, but now in special basic courses designed for convertees, which had replaced the regular basic courses designed for Reserve and National Guard officers. Advanced officers schooling continued: shorter refresher courses, with primary emphasis on tactics, replaced regular advanced courses. Specialists training for both officers and enlisted men was still given; the courses, however, were smaller, and the subjects somewhat altered by obsolescence and innovations in equipment. Some officer candidate courses were still in operation. A major change was in the shift of emphasis among branches: schools of the more active and populous arms—Infantry, Field Artillery, and Armored—retained fairly full programs; programs of the other schools had been curtailed more or less severely.

In the last year of the war the Army Ground Forces gave the Replacement and School Command a broader administrative control over the schools than had previously been delegated. In the execution of certain functions related to doctrine and broad policy questions, the schools had been authorized from the beginning to carry on direct communication with AGF headquarters. Because it was difficult to draw the boundary line of such functions the schools had often taken directly to AGF headquarters matters which the Replacement and School Command felt to be within its province. Considering that this made its administration and control of the schools difficult, the Replacement and School Command had repeatedly protested. In early 1945, when Gen. Joseph W. Stilwell became Commanding General of the Army Ground Forces, he announced that the Replacement and School Command was considered to be in full charge of the schools. The policy of requiring all correspondence with schools to be processed through the Replacement and School Command was not, however, officially implemented until Gen. Jacob L. Devers assumed command of the Army Ground Forces.[67]

The instructional pattern which the schools had acquired by the end of 1944 was retained with relatively little modification until the end of active hostilities. Between January 1945 and V-E Day, the new courses opened were principally refresher courses for officers and specialist courses for both officers and enlisted men in types of equipment in which innovations were frequent, such as radar. After the conclusion of active hostilities in Europe, the schools began revising their programs to provide for the redeployment training directed by Section VII

[67] Interview of R&SC Hist Off with Brig Gen J. W. Curtis, CofS R&SC, 4 Dec 45.

of AGF Training Memorandum No. 1, published 1 June 1945. This section instructed the schools to continue training under current mobilization training programs but to adapt them, wherever practicable, to combat against the Japanese. It specified a number of subjects in current instruction that should be stressed. Topics particularly pertinent to the war in the Far East included Japanese tactics and techniques, identification of Japanese weapons, materiel, uniforms, and insignia, and effective means of employing American weapons against the Japanese. It was possible to achieve these emphases in instruction within the framework of existing curricula, but special directives on the details of implementation were needed and were in process of preparation in the schools throughout the summer of 1945. To a degree the adaptation of the programs to warfare against the Japanese was effected in this period by means of changes in training aids, such as conversion of sand tables to Japanese landscapes.

During the summer of 1945 the service schools were also concerned with planning for the redeployment training of officers who would be returned from the European Theater. It had been hoped to use the refresher courses for this purpose but it was later realized that their length would prevent this adaptation. Instead it was decided to institute so-called "short courses," and on 15 May Army Ground Forces directed the Replacement and School Command to prepare these courses. On the day before V-J Day a number of these courses were started in the Field Artillery, Infantry, and Tank Destroyer Schools. (See Tables Nos. 6, 7, and 8 below.)

During the spring and summer of 1945 the Replacement and School Command was less concerned with innovations in the curriculum of the schools than with the problem of keeping instruction up to the desired pitch of realism. Its inspectors reported slackness in this regard, in part attributable to the withdrawal of experienced officers and their replacement by instructors of lower quality. Various corrective measures were taken, one of which was to encourage the schools to send key officers to observe instructional methods at the replacement training centers, then at a high peak of efficiency in realistic training.

It was in the decline of output and in the reorientation of the mission which the schools were performing that the year 1945 brought the greatest changes from the pattern characteristic of their earlier war history. In 1945 the average monthly output of the Infantry School, for example, was 1,846, as compared with 2,759 in 1944 and 3,191 in 1943. The year 1945 brought accentuation of the trend which, as noted above, began in 1944: the shift from the provision of a large volume of leaders and specialists required by a rapidly growing Army to emphasis upon more qualitative improvements in specialist training. With nearly all units of the ground arms deployed overseas by the end of 1944, only a small proportion of the output of the schools was sent to units in the Zone of Interior. Even though operating on a reduced level, the schools supplied trained specialists sent directly to overseas units and also provided instructors to maintain the level of teaching proficiency in AGF replacement and school training installations in the United States. The chief use to which it had been planned to put the schools—the expansion of training during redeployment of the Army against Japan—did not materialize because the war against Japan ended too quickly for the units returned from Europe to receive further training.

III. The Schools in Operation

Although it was common to distinguish between general and technical (specialist) courses, all service school courses—even the general advanced or command courses for officers and the officer candidate courses—were essentially technical. Officers courses were not differentiated by the abilities fostered but by the kind of object to which the technique was to be applied. Broadly speaking, the general courses and the command and officer candidate courses taught the technique of managing men in units; the specialist courses taught the technique of handling equipment. Procedures for using materiel figured in the general courses, but primarily as a necessary foundation for the management of men. The technique of handling men was introduced into specialist courses, but largely as a byproduct; officers who attended specialist courses were assumed to possess ability in handling men, but enlisted students were to be merely operators.

Although all school instruction was concerned fundamentally with technique—with the right execution of the functions the student was preparing to undertake—important differences in school courses arose from the varying degrees to which the functions in prospect could be anticipated. Functions that were the objects of instruction in the general courses (Officer Candidate, Officers Basic, Advanced, Special Basic, and Refresher) could not be particularized as neatly as those to which specialist instruction was directed. The question "What should a battery commander or regimental S–2 know and be able to do?" permitted a greater diversity of answers than the question "What should a communication officer or radio repairman know and be able to do?" The specialist, by and large, was concerned with a particular machine or group of machines: the M10 director, the recording odograph, the motor vehicles used in the infantry regiment, the M5A1 tank, the SCR 584, and so forth. Technicians were trained, not to repair radios, but to repair the particular radios used in particular units. So far as possible, the aim in the planning of specialist courses was to eliminate all material not having direct pertinence to the particular skills it was desired to produce.

With the general courses, exclusively for officers, the opposite was true. Officer candidate schools trained platoon leaders, not rifle platoon leaders or antitank platoon leaders or motor platoon leaders. Advanced courses were even less specialized; graduates of an advanced course, to name but a few of the possibilities, might be company commanders, battalion commanders, or regimental S–3's. Planners of the general courses had to avoid committing the program to any more specific direction than that implied by the general level of command for which its graduates were intended.

The effects of this difference between the functions for which the two types of courses prepared were noticeable in the determination of the curriculum, in the sequence of instruction, and in its effectiveness.

The training of specialists was dictated by the nature of the machine. The machine—a weapon, vehicle, radar set, or gun director—had a determinate function, a single mode of operation, a finite number of parts arranged in a definite order, and a correct mode of employment. The content of a course of instruction in its operation or maintenance could be deduced directly from an analysis of the machine and its work. Determination of the content of the course to train infantry company officers was far less direct. Since the objects of a company officer's actions were many—men, weapons, paperwork, mess halls, vehicles, health, to name but a few—and since they were not bound together by any single organizing principle, as were the parts of a machine, a general course had inevitably a more miscellaneous content.

Because the material in a typical specialist course was selected with reference to a highly specific objective, it could be arranged in a more coherent order than could the miscellany of a general course. A motor course for enlisted infantry specialists affords an example. The objective of the course was to train specialists to perform first- and second-echelon maintenance on the wheeled vehicles of the infantry regiment under field conditions. The sequence of instruction was four weeks of study and work on engines, three weeks on the chassis, and five weeks on field driving, inspections, and maintenance, during which the skills acquired in the first seven weeks were refined, applied, and tested under field conditions.[1] Each item in the course, essential in itself, occupied a position clearly dictated by its dependence on material previously presented or the dependence on it of material to be introduced subsequently. Pedagogy here was largely supplanted by physics.

The variety of subjects included in a general course presented a problem of order inherently more difficult. Within the major subdivisions of a course, as in weapons, tactics, materiel, or communications, the problem of order was fairly easy to handle; each of the subdivisions was a specialist course in brief. In a

[1] Program of Instruction, Enlisted Motor Course, Inf Sch, 10 Jan 45. AGF G–3 Schs Br files.

subcourse in tactics, organization logically preceded tactical employment, problems in small-unit tactics preceded those involving larger units, problems confined to one arm preceded those in combined arms. But even within a subcourse there could not be the smooth unfolding of subject matter possible in a more restricted field. Instruction in tactics in the Officer Refresher Course at the Infantry School, for example, included the following diversity of topics:[2]

- Organization of Infantry
- Combat Orders
- Motorized Detachment on a Zone Reconnaissance
- Protection of a Motorized Column
- Outposts
- Combat Intelligence
- Estimate of the Situation
- Staff Functions
- Map Maneuvers
- Defense of Rear Areas
- Operation and Situation Maps
- Associated Arms
- Offensive Combat
- Defensive Combat
- Field Engineering

Although the bulk of the time was spent on Offensive and Defensive Combat, topics which could be arranged in an orderly manner, the integration of the remaining topics was a problem.

In training men for work they were to do, the specialist courses were generally more effective than the general courses. Members of specialist classes were more homogeneous in experience, ability, and probable assignment after graduation than members of general courses. The immediately usable proportion of the content of a specialist course was greater than that of a general course, since—provided assignments were properly made—all graduates of a specialist course performed the same work while graduates of a general course might do a dozen different jobs. Motivation for specialist training was stronger because of the greater clarity of objectives and the more obvious pertinence of the material to the student. More realistic practical work was possible: a tank mechanic could be put to work repairing tanks; a battalion commander could scarcely be given a battalion of troops to lead. The specialist subjects, by and large, were easier to teach. Equipment was its own best teacher. Intervention of the instructor between the student and his work was less frequent, less prolonged, and—since performance was always available as a check—less important than in courses where the instructor had to act as umpire. Specialist training, on the whole, was also easier for the student to grasp. Manual dexterity for qualified students—and all specialist students had to possess certain minimum qualifications—is easier to develop

[2] Program of Instruction, Offs Refresher Course, Inf Sch, 10 Jan 45. 314.7 (AGF Hist).

than the understanding of general principles and procedures and the ability to apply them. Work done or seen by the specialist student was identical with the work he would do after graduation. Problems solved by or demonstrated for students in general courses stood in no such relation to subsequent problems. They were merely archetypes from which it was hoped the student would absorb generally useful principles. Abstraction, and skill in adjusting to similar but by no means identical cases, were required. On-the-spot check of the student's ability could not, in the nature of the case, be as valid when the test case was merely similar to future cases as it could be when the test case was identical with them.

Conduct of Training

Classes at the service schools were generally small, though their size varied considerably among schools and within schools. In July 1943 the average sizes of officer and enlisted classes in the AGF schools were as follows:

School	*Officers Classes*	*Enlisted Classes*
Antiaircraft Artillery	103	81
Armored	104	78
Cavalry	46	29
Coast Artillery	36	36
Field Artillery	41	52
Infantry	132	150
Tank Destroyer	61	87

Specialist classes, because they required more supervision over practical work and because the amount of equipment available for student use was limited, were smaller, on the whole, than classes in general courses. The size of officers advanced classes at the Antiaircraft Artillery School was 350; of officers stereoscopic height-finder classes, 12. At the Armored School, 320 enlisted radio operators were trained per class, while 4 men made up an enlisted machinist class. Large classes were handled in either of two ways. In most schools each class was split up into a number of small sections of from 25 to 35 men each. The section was the unit for instruction, except for the infrequent special lectures and demonstrations, for which the entire class was brought together. This arrangement was dictated in some cases, as at Fort Sill, by the small size of the classrooms available. It ensured relatively close contact between instructor and student, but it required a sizeable group of instructors and more supervision to ensure uniform instruction. The other way of handling large classes was to teach them as units. At the Infantry School the normal size of candidate, basic, and advanced classes was 200. All lectures, demonstrations, and practical work periods, and all classrooms and problem areas, were arranged for groups of this size. For field work the class was normally broken down into four platoons of 50 men each, with an officer instructor in charge. Considerable saving of instructors was effected. In a school as large as the Infantry School the demands of a small-class scheme for classrooms, equipment, and personnel would have been prohibitive. Holding the attention and interest of 200 men in a large classroom was not easy. Such expedients as public-address equipment, assistant instructors, and ample practical work reduced the chances of failure.

Instruction was conducted by means of conferences, demonstrations, and practical work. Officially, no lectures were given at service schools; programs of instruction announced conferences, not lectures. A strong prejudice against lectures was noticeable. They were regarded as largely a waste of time, producing no sure results and deferring or curtailing really beneficial practical work. This attitude was doubtless in part defensive. Lecturing was a difficult art, not to be acquired in a quick course in the technique of instruction. It was easier to decry lecturing than to improve it. In part, also, the attitude sprang from a determination to limit the pronounced tendency of many instructors to talk interminably, and from a desire to maximize, in short courses, the amount of practice a student could be given. No amount of listening to lectures on how to fire a rifle would enable a man to fire it skillfully. But lectures were not avoided, they were merely disguised. They appeared as conferences. A conference—according to official training doctrine—was a directed discussion, with the students taking the initiative and the instructor confining himself to the modest role of moderator. Conferences required three conditions rarely present in service school courses: experience and adroitness in the instructor; experience and aggressive interest in the students; and ample time. Ability to stimulate thinking, to arouse questions, to encourage shy or backward students, to keep free discussion flowing surely toward an objective, and to deal spontaneously with an unpredictable range of questions and problems—these required on the part of the instructor much practice, a warm personality, great self-restraint, and a very detailed knowledge of his subject. Like most students, those at service schools were reluctant to ask questions or to offer independent views, preferring rather to be fed than to feed themselves. And time was the most precious commodity used at the

230-171 O - 66 - 20

schools. Conferences could not be rushed without losing much of their value; the flow of information per minute in a conference was small—a lecturer could cover twice the ground in half the time. Conferences therefore tended to become lectures. The chief tribute paid to the doctrine of conferences consisted of questions asked by the instructor. These served to keep students awake (no small problem on a summer afternoon in Georgia or Texas), to maintain interest, and to inform the instructor of the readiness of students to proceed to more advanced work.

The lectures were kept as brief as possible, although 2- or even 3-hour lectures were not uncommon in the larger schools, where one instructor had to do the work of ten. Wherever possible they were preceded and followed by demonstrations and sessions of practical work. In a typical arrangement for teaching marksmanship, the class would be assembled to hear a 10-minute talk on the prone position, during which the position would be demonstrated fully; then the class would practice for twenty minutes. This would be followed by a lecture and a demonstration of the kneeling position, after which the class would practice it. Rapid alternation of short periods of different types of instruction provided variety, sustained interest, and enabled students to put knowledge to use before it had been forgotten or submerged.

Lectures were profusely illustrated. Charts, blackboards, models, and actual items of equipment were used to minimize the uncertainty of reliance on hearing and thought. Students had been conditioned through movies, comic strips, advertisements, and illustrated magazines to depend heavily on pictures for intelligibility. Most students at service schools were without recent educational experience, and only a minority were skilled in listening and in extracting meaning from what they heard. It was a stock military judgment that "one picture is worth 10,000 words." Charts and kindred visual aids were a great help to the instructor. He was relieved to some extent of the necessity for lucid speech by the availability of a picture or object to which he could point. He could use the chart or model as notes for his talk, taking his cues from the aspects of the visual aid. The topics of most school lectures lent themselves to some form of visual representation, since lecture subjects were rarely abstract. Such topics as types of electrical circuits, channels of communication, characteristics of weapons, echelons of command, routes of deployment, formations for patrols, and nomenclature of equipment predominated. Instructors tended, when no objective representation could be found, to prepare charts that gave a verbal condensation of the main points of the presentation. In teaching target designation, for example, a chart might be shown that read:

TARGET DESIGNATION

DISTANCE
DIRECTION
DESCRIPTION OF TARGET

The instructor would display the chart during his talk, pointing to the proper word when he came to discuss the point it stood for. If the student derived nothing else from the period, he would remember—he would certainly have in his notes—the words on the chart. When the instructor wanted to discuss several topics in sequence and to keep his class with him at every step, he could "strip-tease" a chart—fasten strips of paper over each line and remove each when the proper time came. The weakness of word charts as compared to charts representing objects or relations or processes, or to the objects themselves, was that words on the chart were so meager a proportion of what the student was supposed to learn. When a student was shown a diagram of the recoil mechanism of the Browning automatic rifle, the content of the diagram was almost exactly the content it was hoped the student would absorb from the instruction. When he was shown a word chart, he was all too likely to memorize the words and forget the context in which they stood, the relations and processes they symbolized.

Service school demonstrations were abundant, carefully planned and staged, and, usually, perfectly executed. Each department had regularly assigned to it a number of enlisted assistants who performed the smaller demonstrations. Many of these men were Regular Army soldiers of much experience who often knew far more about their subject than the instructors did. Running through the same demonstrations day after day for months, even years, they developed great skill. They were able to demonstrate at any rate of speed, always with precision, snap, and accuracy, and could be counted on to deliver on the claims the instructor made for his weapon or instrument. They made any operation look easy, and they provided students with an indispensable requirement of rapid learning—a finished model to imitate.

Larger-scale demonstrations were executed by troop units assigned to the school. Demonstrations illustrating tactical principles, troop-leading procedures, message-center organization, river-crossing techniques, march organization, and artillery firing required large numbers of men. To each school were assigned regular tactical units whose primary duty was to furnish details to assist the faculty in presentation of instruction. Units or their component teams sometimes functioned as such; sometimes individuals from the units served as assistant instructors and individual demonstrators. The magnitude of school operations can be gauged from the number of troops on such school duty. In July and August 1944, when the War Department Manpower Board surveyed the schools, the strength of demonstration and other special units assigned to AGF schools was 35,699, nearly 11,000 of whom were at the Field Artillery School and 9,000 at the Infantry School.[3] Tactical units were not detailed permanently to schools but were rotated regularly, using the time available between school assignments to train for combat.[4] Late in 1944 troop units were replaced at schools by detachments made up of limited-assignment personnel.[5] This step was taken to save men—the detachments being considerably smaller than the units they replaced—and to make available for combat the maximum number of tactical units. The change had in addition the good effect of clarifying the mission of school troops. Not always without conflict, units had served two masters—the demands of the school for assistance and the demands of impending combat training. School detachments had no independent status, existed exclusively for the school, and had no other duty than to serve it.[6]

Practical work by students occupied much of the time in every school course, the actual proportion ranging from 50 to 80 percent. Heavy emphasis on practical work sprang from the conviction that theoretical understanding could be reached only after much experience and training, and from the corollary conviction that the proper function of schools was to graduate men immediately capable of skillful performance. Practical work took many forms. The simplest was that around which most specialist courses were built—performance of the duties for which men were being trained. Motor mechanics disassembled and assembled engines, located troubles, and replaced defective parts; radio operators sent and received code and voice messages. Specialists normally worked in small groups under

[3] Exhibit B of "Summary of WDMB Surveys of AGF Schools," atchd to WD memo for CG AGF, 27 Oct 44, sub: Pers Allotments for ZI Establishments of the AGF. 320.2/7035.

[4] (1) AGF ltr (C) to CG R&SC, 8 Jan 43, sub: Sch Trs. With related M/Ss and ltrs. (2) AGF M/S (C), CG to G-3, 29 Dec 42, sub: Sch Trs. With later M/Ss. 320.2/10 (TB 1943)(C).

[5] AGF ltr (R) to CG R&SC, 24 Jan 45, sub: Repl of T/O Sch Trs by an Allotment of Pers on Tables of Distribution at Inf Sch, Ft Benning, Ga. 320.2/59 (R&SC)(R). See same file for similar letters to all other schools.

[6] Statements of Col P. H. Kron, Sec Inf Sch, to AGF Hist Off, 7 Mar 45; of Col H. J. McChrystal, CO Sch Det, TDS, 14 Mar 45; of Col A. S. Johnson, Chief OD&T Sec, Armd Ctr, 22 Mar 45; and Lt Col C. J. Hay, Dir of Tng, Cav Sch, 24 Mar 45.

close supervision by the instructor and his assistants. A typical organization for practical work would include several groups of four students and one enlisted instructor. Each group might be found around a tank engine; the students, after listening to a discussion of the work they were to do, solved problems set by the assistant. Other forms of individual practical work included paper problems, in which, for example, students might be required to enter data correctly on a morning report form; map exercises, in which tactical plans were drawn up, orders were formulated, or routes of advance for ammunition and supplies were selected; terrain exercises; and terrain walks and rides. Group practical work was common even though group organizations in school courses were temporary. The class might be divided into gun crews for firing, with members rotating duties during the period; several regimental and battalion staffs might be formed for a map maneuver, with each student playing the part of a commander or staff officer; the class might be organized as one or more tactical units, with students taking all roles in a field exercise from private to commander. In general, practical work done individually or in small groups was the most beneficial, because supervision was closer and because all students received equivalent instruction. When practice groups became too large some students were inevitably slighted: an officer in an advanced course who, as a private in a tactical problem, had to lug the base plate of a mortar doubtless learned something about the feelings of mortar crewmen but little about how to command a heavy weapons company. But through rotation of duties each student had several opportunities to fill all positions, getting experience which was rounded in general even if limited in particular assignments.

Testing

Tests were an important part of the school program. They were relied upon not only to determine success or failure but also to indicate weaknesses in the instruction and to aid in reviewing and consolidating materials for the student. In a typical course such as the Officers Advanced at the Field Artillery School, 21 of the 576 hours of instruction were given to examinations on 11 subjects.[7] Tests were given on every major subject and on as many minor subjects as their importance and the time available would justify.

Tests of all types were used. In general courses written tests were most common, while in specialist courses performance tests in which the student executed an assigned piece of work were more often used. There were several reasons

[7] Program of Instruction, Offs Advanced Course, FA Sch, 11 Nov 44. 314.7 (AGF Hist).

for this difference. One was the smaller size of the specialist classes, which permitted performance tests, usually more time-consuming than written tests, to be completed in a shorter total time. Another was the relative abundance of equipment and facilities for smaller specialist groups. Again, it was easier to devise test performances for men being trained for a highly specific job, such as radio repair. To compensate for the absence of actual performance most schools, in the testing program of general courses, devised schemes for assessing the student's practical work during regular instruction, determining his grade in the course partly from his test score and partly from his work record.

Although written tests both of essay and objective or short-answer types were used, essay examinations were held to a minimum, because they required much time to score and because scoring was too unreliable where success or failure in a course was involved. Essay tests found their widest use in tactical subjects, which were the most difficult to reduce to black-and-white alternatives.

In one institution, the Infantry School, the volume of test scoring was so great that electrical scoring machines were introduced and tests adapted to the use of separate answer sheets. Great savings were thereby made in the time of instructors, and increased amounts of training could be conducted by a smaller corps of teachers.

Although in early 1942 it had been intended to establish a uniform system of grading examinations in all AGF schools, this was never done; each school developed its own methods.[8] The grading system used in most schools involved weighting test grades, totaling them, and determining success or failure on the basis of an aggregate score. Each subject to be tested was assigned a weight factor, the sum of all weight factors equalling 100 or 1,000. The weight given a subject was generally proportionate to the number of hours allotted the subject in the course, and therefore indirectly proportionate to its relative importance. The student's raw or derived score on the test, multiplied by the weight factor, gave the numerical rating in the subject. The sum of all these was the aggregate score. Seventy was commonly set as the minimum aggregate score necessary for graduation.[9]

[8] (1) AGF ltr to CG R&SC, 20 Mar 42, sub: Method of Grading at Serv Schs. (2) Memo of Lt Col L. L. Lemnitzer, ACofS Plans Div, for CofS AGF, 20 Apr 42, sub: Coordination of Policies within Schs and RTCs of the AGF. Both in 352/56.

[9] (1) Statement of Maj E. R. Bryon, Adj Armd OCS, to AGF Hist Off, 22 Mar 45. (2) "Sub-Course and Subject Weights" (Armd OCS Class No. 70). 314.7 (AGF Hist). (3) "Academic Record, Field Artillery School — Officers' Communication Course; Officers' Motor Course." 314.7 (AGF Hist). (4) Statement of Lt Col D. F. Sellards, S-3 AAA Sch, to AGF Hist Off, 16 Mar 45.

As a rule tests were listed in the program of instruction and announced a week in advance on the course schedule. Instruction "writs" or "pop quizzes"—short, informal tests covering a day's work or a small unit of material—were given to students without warning from time to time at some schools. Although they were scored, relatively little weight was attached to them in comparison with that given to formal scheduled examinations. The testing system employed at the Command and General Staff School, in which no tests were scheduled but certain regular problems were selected for grading after the students had completed work on them, was not used in AGF schools. A single, limited exception was the Officers Refresher Course introduced in January 1945 at the Infantry School. In this course no tests were scheduled. For each class a different set of regular written exercises was selected for grading after the students had completed them without forewarning that they were to be used as examinations. The chief disadvantage of this scheme was the difficulty of finding regular instruction problems broad enough to represent the content of an entire subject. Advantages were heightened alertness and seriousness among students during all instruction, and greater likelihood of discovering the student's permanent gain as distinguished from what he had crammed into his head for test purposes only.[10]

The purpose to which tests were put complicated the testing program. Tests were designed both as a measure of the student's achievement and as a means of instruction. To have instructional value the tests had to be returned to the students or correct answers had to be read in class or posted on the company bulletin board. In all schools to some extent, but especially in the Infantry and Field Artillery Schools, where many classes were in session simultaneously and were examined in each subject on successive days, publication of test and answers to one class meant that succeeding classes had ready access to the information. For measuring achievement, a test once given and published diminished rapidly in value. A sizable group of different tests on each subject had to be prepared and administered in turn to successive classes so that "G–2-ing," even if not eliminated, would be less reliable. The use of several tests on the same body of material for different classes, all judged according to the same criteria, raised the question of standardization. Until a number of classes had been subjected to a new test, it was hard to be sure that the test maintained the same standard as those in current use. Comparable tests were standardized largely by estimation; only the

[10] Statement of Col P. H. Kron, Sec Inf Sch, to AGF Hist Off, 7 Mar 45.

Armored School had a regularly organized test section equipped for the statistical work needed to standardize tests on a sounder basis.

Except at the Armored School, testing programs were highly decentralized. The chief of each department was allotted time for testing in his subject. The departments set their own standards, wrote and revised their own examinations, established their own grading systems, and reported student grades to the school secretary. Standards, tests, and grading systems were governed by broad school policies and checked by the director of training or the assistant commandant. But, except at the Armored School, no central agency was set up to review all tests, to establish common scoring procedures, and to lend the statistical assistance necessary in a coordinated program. In view of the fact that the use to which test scores were put assumed them to be comparable, the absence of central control was a major weakness. The test section at the Armored School, staffed with personnel experienced in testing, did not originate test materials. That function remained with the departments. But it gave advice on the construction of test questions and problems, reviewed tests for ambiguity, comprehensiveness, and difficulty, compared tests submitted by different departments for relative difficulty, maintained statistics on the basis of which revisions could be made, and calculated standard test scores.[11]

Faculty Organization

School faculties were organized in groups according to subject matter. Variously called departments, committees, and sections, these groups were normally responsible for all instruction given in the school in their subject. Instructional groups corresponded to the major subjects taught in the school. The faculty of the Infantry School consisted of five sections: Weapons, Tactics, General Subjects, Automotive, and Communications. At the Field Artillery School there were departments of Gunnery, Materiel, Motors, Communications, Combined Arms, Observation, and Air Training. The faculty as a whole was under the direct supervision of an assistant commandant charged with responsibility to the school commandant for all matters pertaining directly to instruction. The administrative and supervisory staff of the assistant commandant varied among the schools. Each had a secretary who maintained academic records; some had executives, and some directors of training, inspectors of train-

[11] Statements of Lt Col G. E. Holloway, Classification Off, Inf Sch, to AGF Hist Off, 8 Mar 45, and of Maj S. C. Carpenter, Dir, Instructor Tng Dept, Armd Sch, 21 Mar 45.

ing, and coordinators of training. The internal organization of faculty departments varied also, two systems predominating. In some schools departments were divided, still in terms of subject matter, into subgroups. Thus the Department of Tactics at the Cavalry School was comprised of four sections—Reconnaissance; Organization, Command, Staff, and Logistics; Pioneer and Map Reading; and Associated Arms and Services. Such subgroups, if the subject matter was complex, might be split still further. The General Committee of the General Section at the Infantry School, for example, was made up of three groups—Training Management, Administration, and Leadership. The fractioning process rarely went beyond this point. An instructor in such a department taught only the subjects falling within the sphere of the smallest subgroup to which he was assigned. In the General Committee an instructor taught administration or training or leadership, but not more than one of these. Although their range was limited their coverage was broad: these small subgroups taught their subject to all types of classes—officers, enlisted, and candidate. This plan of intra-departmental organization had the merit—in one view—of intense specialization. Each instructor was responsible for a very limited field, which he could master more rapidly than a broader one. When school staffs were relatively inexperienced and subject to regular rotation, this was an undeniable advantage. Some relief from the monotony of the instructor's life came from contact with different types of classes. Considerable flexibility was possible in the use of instructors since they were practiced in presenting their material in different packages to different audiences. One marked disadvantage was a loss of continuity. Extreme compartmentalization entailed committing students to a succession of instructor groups as they progressed through a major subject. Unless liaison between groups was regular and detailed, the students were likely to finish without a clear notion of the direction and purpose of the course and of the relation of its parts.

The Field Artillery School, instead of using distinctions of subject matter to form subordinate instructor groups, grouped instructors within departments according to the courses in which their students were enrolled. Gunnery appeared in the program of many school courses. Gunnery training was given to officer candidates and battery executives, also to officers in Advanced, Refresher, and Special Basic Courses, to name but a few. In the Department of Gunnery, therefore, one group of instructors taught the subject to candidate classes, another group to battery executive classes. For each major course in which gunnery training figured, a separate group of instructors was set up in the department. Each course group was further subdivided into class teams, the aim being to give each class the same instructors for all their work in the subject. Under this arrangement instructors were specialized in administering a given type of instruction. An instructor did not face a class of enlisted men one day, a class of officer candidates the next, and a class of officers the next. On the other hand, the instructors were less intensively specialized. Each one taught—this was at least the aim—most or all of the material in the entire department; he was not confined to a narrow corner of a large field. Among the advantages of this organization were continuity and integration within a department through the continuous presence of the same instructors for a given class. Instructors could more easily judge the progress and difficulties of students since they saw them over a longer period of time; grading of practical work was more reliable; and there was greater variety in what they taught since there was no chance of giving the same lecture several days in succession.[12]

Aside from differences in detail, faculties in AGF schools were organized on the same principle. All training in a major subject given at a school was the responsibility of a single group of instructors under a single command. Instruction in weapons at the Infantry School, whether given to officers, enlisted men, or officer candidates, was conducted by the Weapons Section. An alternative to the principle was tried at the Antiaircraft Artillery School and found completely impracticable. The principle adopted in the original organization of this school was to establish departments on the basis of students rather than of subjects. Three departments were set up—Officer, Enlisted, and Officer Candidate. Each department was subdivided into subject-matter sections. Since many subjects were common to courses for all three types of students, considerable duplication among departments was inevitable: all three had sections teaching map reading, communications, motor maintenance, gunnery, and so forth. A corollary to this wasteful duplication of effort, equipment, and facilities was lack of coordination among faculty groups teaching the same subjects. As there was little or no direct contact between departments, supervision and standardization had to trickle down from the highest levels. Doctrines and procedures taught by members of one department were contradicted or ignored by their opposite numbers in others. Officer and enlisted graduates of the school found, when they joined units, that they had little in common. After a year of such mutual confounding the school was reorganized and the normal functional division of faculty was instituted.[13]

[12] Statement of Lt Col Otto Kerner, Exec to Asst Comdt, FA Sch, to AGF Hist Off, 26 Mar 45.

[13] AGF Historical Section, The Antiaircraft Command and Center, Chap. XII.

A vestige of the earlier Antiaircraft Artillery School plan remained at certain schools. Most specialist courses consisted entirely of instruction within a single department. In some, programs included brief treatments of material for which other departments were normally responsible. Some map reading, usually taught by a tactics department, might be included in a communications course. Enlisted sound and flash rangers were given a brief orientation on fire direction. It was the practice in certain schools—notably the Field Artillery School—for the department conducting the bulk of instruction in a specialist course to give also the related work in the fields of other departments. Such excursions into related subjects were in any case brief and very elementary. Concentrating all instruction in the hands of a single department avoided frittering away the faculty strength of other departments. All material could be presented from the point of view of the specialty.[14]

Scheduling of Instruction

Instruction in AGF schools was scheduled under what was known as the "block system." Under this system each major subject occupied the student's entire time until it was completed, in contrast to the usual civilian practice of scheduling several subjects concurrently. In operation, all instruction given by a Weapons Department, for example, might be concentrated into a 6-week period, followed by a 3-week interval containing all the training offered by a Tactics Department. Within the block of time allotted to the Weapons Department, shorter blocks were scheduled for each weapon. At the end of each block an examination tested the student's command of the subject covered. There his responsibility for the material ended, as did also his opportunity to practice it, except incidentally as the subject figured in subsequent phases of the course.

The widespread use of the block system testified to the marked advantage it brought to high-speed mass instruction. Many of these advantages were administrative. The block system saved time and transportation by reducing the amount of ground a class had to cover during a day's instruction. Allotment of an unbroken series of periods to a single subject-matter committee promoted flexibility in revising or rearranging instruction given by the committee. Such rearrangements could be made without interfering with the schedules of other committees. The normally vexing question of which committee was to have claim to the student's study time was quickly resolved when only one subject

[14] Statement of Lt Col Otto Kerner, Exec to Asst Comdt, FA Sch, to AGF Hist Off, 26 Mar 45.

was taken up at a time. Most important, especially when personnel and facilities were critically short, were the economies made possible by the block system. Fewer instructors were needed. The schools were able to get along with less equipment and other training aids. The block system made it easy to turn back students to repeat that portion of the course in which they had been found deficient, whereas concurrent scheduling of several subjects would have forced the student to repeat during the same period a good deal of material he had already mastered.

The block system also had educational advantages. For most students learning was probably speeded by concentration on one subject at a time. Men who lacked recent educational experience—a category which included most students at service schools—were not forced to keep three or four subjects in mind at once, with attendant risk of confusion. The intensity of the application to each subject probably resulted in greater immediate proficiency. But on the educational side the block arrangement of subjects was also open to serious criticism. Precautions had to be taken to avoid monotony. Slow students were handicapped by the necessity of mastering a subject in a few days of concentrated work rather than in weeks or even months of more leisurely application, as under the traditional organization of instruction. Special attention had to be given to the relation between subjects occurring early in the course and those given late. Since each major subject was taught by a different committee, continuity and integration could be obtained only with difficulty. Inasmuch as each subject was formally completed within the block of hours devoted to it, the student, immediately occupied with a new subject, was not likely to perceive the relationships between subjects. Furthermore, although the intensive treatment of each subject was undoubtedly productive of great immediate skill, it was likely that the lack of continuous practice and the regular piling-on of new subjects would outweigh the short-term benefits. Another problem raised by the block system was the handling of minor subjects. Every course contained, in addition to such large subcourses as weapons, tactics, motors, or communications, a miscellany of topics bearing no obvious relation to one another, each scheduled for but a few hours time, not enough to form a true "block." Among these were first aid, discipline, training management, administration, military law, and censorship. These subjects were a universal headache. Consisting mostly of indoor work, presented by lectures and paper problems, they were too varied to be allotted a collective block of hours. The alternative was either to sandwich them into the joints between major blocks or to concentrate them in a block allotted to one of the major subcourses. In the former case continuity was usually lost. When a few hours of first aid were spread over six or eight weeks, the instructor was forced to address his class with "Now you will recall last month when we discussed fractures. . . . " Much time and training were wasted in introductory reviews under this scheme. When, on the other hand, the miscellaneous general subjects were crowded for convenience into one of the major blocks, the sequence of instruction in the major subject was interrupted and the student might be confronted with such an anomaly as a lecture on mess management in the middle of a tactics course.

Mitigating these disadvantages were the special conditions surrounding the wartime programs of the schools. Courses were short, so that the carry-over of material covered and dropped early in the course was not excessively long. Regular practice of all the techniques taught was somewhat less necessary in view of the immediate use to which they would be put upon completion of the course. Provided a good foundation of principle, fact, and fundamental habits had been laid, the renewed application of knowledge and skills would not be difficult. Monotony was offset on the one hand by the strong motivation with which most students approached the work, and on the other by the variety inherent in practical activity and field training, as distinguished from lectures and demonstrations. As for the slow learners, they could be turned back to repeat the course if they showed promise. If not, there was no obligation to slow up an entire class to keep them from falling by the wayside.[15]

Selection and Training of Instructors

The efficiency of any training program depends in the last analysis on the quality of the instructors who administer it. On the whole, instruction at service schools was the best available in the Army Ground Forces. Instructors were carefully selected and trained, a high degree of specialization was practiced, and facilities and equipment were abundantly, if not lavishly, provided. This is not to say either that instruction at the schools was perfect or that a high level of efficiency was consistently maintained. Actually the quality of instruction, after reaching its peak in 1942, declined steadily thereafter.

[15] (1) Dr. James Grafton Rogers, civilian representative of CofS USA, "Notes on the Fort Sill Artillery Officer Candidate School," 22 Oct 42. (2) R&SC 1st ind, 1 Dec 42, on AGF ltr, 18 Nov 42, sub: Visit of Dr. James Grafton Rogers to FA Sch. (3) FA Sch 2d ind, 1 Dec 42, on AGF ltr above. All in 095/41 (Rogers, J. G.). Statement of Lt Col Otto Kerner, Exec to Asst Comdt, FA Sch, to AGF Hist Off, 26 Mar 45.

Problems of instruction were complicated by the rotation policy. Throughout the period of greatest expansion it was the policy of Army Ground Forces to restrict tours of duty at service schools to one year. Although the schools used a wide variety of arguments, pretexts, and dodges to alter the rule, delay its application, or minimize its force, the rule was not modified. Temporary exceptions for key personnel were provided for in the policy, but otherwise the staffs of service schools underwent a regular turnover.

The schools began operations in 1940 with a small corps of Regular Army officers, many of whom had taught at the schools in peacetime. They were largely responsible for getting the expanded program under way: organizing courses, preparing problems, devising tests, and training new instructors. In 1940 and 1941 the augmentation of the teaching staffs came largely from Reserve officers called to active duty and recently graduated from school courses. Some had had no duty with troops. Others were drafted from the units that had sent them to school. It was this practice of raiding units for suitable instructors that prompted the Army Ground Forces, when it became responsible for the schools in March 1942, to direct that an officer sent to school from a unit should return to his unit at the end of the course. The schools had to depend thereafter chiefly upon unassigned officers as the source of additions and replacements for their staffs. The greatest source of unassigned officers was the officer candidate schools, from which during 1942 and 1943 the bulk of instructors at the AGF service schools were drawn. Since the schools had the candidates under prolonged scrutiny and were free of competition for their services from other agencies, they were able to select from graduating classes the new lieutenants best qualified as instructors. As the output of OCS courses fell in 1944, the candidate schools dwindled as a source of instructors, but they continued to supply limited numbers of junior instructors except at the Infantry School, where the assignment of candidates as instructors was prohibited in August 1944 because of the shortage of infantry lieutenants.[16]

Beginning in 1943 and continuing thereafter at a constantly accelerating pace, officers who were returned from overseas under the rotation policy or because of wounds, illness, or other reasons were assigned to teach at the schools. Such assignment was considered necessary because schools were among the principal users of overhead personnel, a category to which returnees were restricted for a minimum of six months. In addition, it was hoped that these assignments would infuse new life and realism into school instruction. Such

[16] Statement of Maj W. Meyer, AGF G–1 Sec, Inf Div, to AGF Hist Off, 27 Apr 45.

instructors would document their teaching out of their own experience; their know-how would be available for other instructors to draw on; being keenly alive to the requirements of combat, they would help direct instruction into the most useful channels; the authority of experience would lend weight to the veteran's words; students would attend more closely and benefit in greater measure from the instruction. Some of these expectations were fulfilled. Many were not. It was the consensus of responsible school authorities early in 1945 that despite increasing numbers of combat veterans on their staffs the quality of instruction had declined noticeably in late 1943 and 1944.

A number of factors contributed to this result. With the decline of candidate courses as the principal source of personnel, schools depended increasingly on sources outside their control. Combat returnees, the major source in 1944 and 1945, were assigned to the schools—those of company grade by the Replacement and School Command, those of field grade by Headquarters, Army Ground Forces. Assignments by these two headquarters were limited by the qualifications of arrivals from the theaters. Neither eligibility for rotation nor injury in combat was a guarantee of ability to teach. Among the officers available, the two headquarters had only qualification cards as guides. Despite great care, some officers were inevitably detailed whose paper promise surpassed their actual abilities.[17] The schools themselves simply took what was sent. Though they were permitted to report officers as unsuitable after a period of trial, it was not easy to testify that an officer was unsuitable for any assignment in the installation, and it was not unlikely that if he were given the boot his replacement would be still less qualified. The schools found it easier to struggle along with mediocre instructors than continually to requisition and train replacements for them.

Among the early arrivals from overseas in 1943 the schools found few suitable instructors. During this period, before the rotation policy began to operate generally and equitably, overseas commanders were prone to send incompetent officers home rather than to reclassify them. The better officers tended to remain in the theaters. After rotation became effective on a large scale, returnees were a much fairer cross section of officers as a whole. But the schools discovered that a greater number of potential instructors would not be found among a hundred combat veterans than among a hundred officers of any other category. Combat experience did not make a man a teacher. The power to convey information clearly, enthusiastically, and forcefully seemed to be unrelated to the qualities of a battle leader.

[17] *Ibid.*

So far as service school duty was concerned, some officers were even handicapped by their combat background. The battle experience of most officers, while intense, had been restricted to a particular theater or portion of a theater, to specific units and specific duties within units. Their work as teachers tended to reflect these limitations. Schools had to stress techniques adapted to combat generally, and undue emphasis on one theater would handicap students who might be sent to another. It was necessary to encourage returnees to take a broader view. As one director of training said, "I got my instructors together and told them to quit fighting the Battle of Sicily in class." Some officers, having had occasion to "throw the book out the window" in combat, were inclined to offer students their private solutions for battle problems in lieu of the orthodox principles the schools had to teach. Close supervision was necessary to prevent sabotage of official doctrine. Some officers were not interested in teaching school. A few thought their work had been completed when they were returned from overseas.

Those officers who had both combat experience and instructional ability were strong additions to the schools. In them, although they were not numerous, the expectation of greatly improved training was fulfilled. The only complaint of the schools was that there were not enough of them.[18]

Few instructors at service schools were professional teachers, and these generally had had little experience in handling demonstration crews, using elaborate training aids, or supervising practical work. All instructors needed indoctrination and training. Although it was a traditional point of view in the Army that an officer was by definition an instructor, this was found to be an impractical, not to say hazardous, assumption. All schools conducted some form of training for new instructors. The training took the form of relatively brief orientation courses on teaching technique, followed by supervised study and rehearsal in the committee to which the instructor was assigned.

One of the earliest and certainly the most elaborate and carefully planned of these courses was the Instructor Training Course at the Armored School. The course, set up in February 1942 under civilians experienced in industrial education, was at first considered a conspicuous failure. Running for three months, meeting one hour each day, it was heavily theoretical; psychology, statistical pro-

[18] Statements to AGF Hist Off of Brig Gen J. W. Curtis, CofS R&SC, 9 Jan 45; Col W. E. Shallene, G-3 R&SC, 6 Jan 45; Col P. H. Kron, Sec Inf Sch, 7 Mar 45; Lt Col G. E. Holloway, Classification Off, Inf Sch, 8 Mar 45; Lt Col S. W. Luther, G-3 Schs Br, AA Comd, 17 Mar 45; Maj S. C. Carpenter, Dir, Instructor Tng Dept, Armd Sch, 21 Mar 45; Col A. S. Johnson, Chief OD&T Sec, Armd Ctr, 22 Mar 45; Col J. B. Thompson, Asst Comdt, Cav Sch, 24 Mar 45; and Lt Col C. J. Hay, Dir of Tng, Cav Sch, 25 Mar 45.

cedure, job analysis, and kindred mysteries constituted the bulk of the fare. Instead of working within the framework of Army teaching procedure as set forth in FM 21–5, with which all the instructors had at least a speaking familiarity, those responsible for the course insisted upon the use of training techniques to which they had become professionally attached in civil life. Constant friction and resentment between the course staff and the instructors who were being trained largely nullified whatever value the course might have had.

In March 1943 the program was completely revised. A Reserve officer who had been a teacher in civil life was appointed to direct the course, which was recast to conform to the needs of school instructors, not to an educational theory. Practice teaching was the heart of the new course, which ran four hours a day for two weeks. Each student was required to plan and present to the class a short lesson (ten minutes) and a long lesson (forty minutes), to evaluate and suggest improvements on the lessons taught by the seventeen other members of the class, to conduct a critique on two lessons presented by other students, and to plan a test on the content of the lessons he taught. All practice lessons were required to be typical of those the instructor would later conduct in the assigned department. This practical work occupied two-thirds of the time of the course or three-quarters in the enlisted instructor's course. The remainder was spent on conferences and a final examination. The conferences were designed to set forth standard military teaching procedures and to give directions on planning and presenting instruction at the school. The student's grade in the course was derived partly from the final written examination but chiefly from the quality of his performance in the practice lessons. Ratings on each instructor were sent to the assistant commandant. Any instructor rated merely "Satisfactory" was relieved from the school as soon as a replacement could be found. Those rated "Very Satisfactory" were put on probation in their departments.

After completion of the Instructor Training Course, instructors at the Armored School were monitored from time to time by members of the course staff. The monitor—assigned to one department to acquire familiarity with its doctrine and problems—conferred with the instructor immediately after the class was over, giving a precise criticism of his performance. Later the monitor sent a detailed report to the instructor and to his department chief. In the early days of the course the monitoring system failed to accomplish its purpose because instructors regarded the course faculty as pedagogues, reformers, and spies. Diligent effort to be as helpful as possible and to deal openly and frankly with

230-171 O - 66 - 21

instructors enabled the course staff to make the monitoring a valued service.[19]

Other schools conducted comparable courses. Not all were as successful as the one at the Armored School became. At some schools the attendance of the new instructor was optional with the department chief. The benefits of standardized teaching procedure were lost to some extent under this practice. Frequently instructors were not detailed to attend the course until after they had been teaching for some time. The value of courses explicitly designed for beginners was largely lost on such men. The proportion of time devoted to practice lessons was low in some courses, with the result that the instructor received too little of what he needed most—rehearsal under expert scrutiny. In few schools was the rating in the course given as much weight by the authorities as at the Armored School. Some courses, notably that at the Infantry School, were conducted by members of the faculty in addition to their regular duties in a department. Because of the double demand on their time, these officers could not plan or revise their courses carefully nor conduct them often enough to hold classes down to manageable size.[20]

Courses for instructors did not teach a subject matter. They dealt only with techniques. The new instructor learned his subject on the job with his department. The normal practice was to assign an instructor to a team that taught an integrated subcourse in the department—for example, antitank gunnery in a weapons department. He observed for a time to become aware of the layout of the course as a whole—its objective, sequence, contents, and methods in general. Next he was assigned a particular period of instruction to conduct, usually a fairly elementary period. He prepared himself by listening through the period as taught by one or more experienced instructors, by assisting in minor ways during instruction, by studying the outline or lesson plan for the period. When he thought he had mastered the material and could put it across clearly and convincingly, he went through a trial performance before his team chief, department head, and any other members of the hierarchy who happened to be responsible or available. In this trial effort he taught exactly as he meant to teach before his first class, using the regular training aids, demonstrations, questions, and practical work. If the audience approved, he became eligible for the final test that would qualify him for the role of instructor. If they did not, he returned to his

[19] Statements of Col A. S. Johnson, Chief OD&T Sec, Armd Ctr, to AGF Hist Off, 22 Mar 45, and Maj S. C. Carpenter, Dir, Instructor Tng Dept, Armd Sch, 21 Mar 45.

[20] Statements to AGF Hist Off of Lt Col Robert Franks, Dir, Instructors Tng Course, Inf Sch, 8 Mar 45; Lt Frank Gary, Instructors Course, AAA Sch, 16 Mar 45; Lt Col C. S. Hampton, Sec Cav Sch, 24 Mar 45; and Lt Col C. R. Yates, Dir, Technique of Instruction Course, FA Sch, 26 Mar 45.

observations, his manuals, and his "poop sheets." Highly standardized teaching was ensured by this system; unprepared instructors were rare; class time was used to maximum advantage; instructors, if they were not all inspired, were at least competent.

Supervision of instructors was constant and was carried on at all levels of command. The team chief supervised members of his team, the subcourse chief the instructors in his subject, the committee chairman the men under him, the department head all members of the department. At the top were the directors of training, inspectors or coordinators of training in some schools, the assistant commandant, and the commandant. The instructor did not lack critics to point out his mistakes. Supervision was more expert and useful on the lower levels where the critics had more time to give to each instructor and more detailed knowledge of the subject. Supervisors on the middle and upper levels—department heads, directors of training, assistant commandants—were the repositories of school standards and policies, the guardians against inefficiency, contradiction, loss of time, duplication, and major errors in doctrine. They were the key men in the organization. When they were lost through rotation, the continuity of instruction suffered greatly.

Students are generally more or less vocal critics of the training they receive. Some of the schools put the critical disposition of students to use in the interest of improved instruction. At the Infantry School, for example, students in officers advanced and basic classes were asked to fill out, just before graduation, a questionnaire on which they answered such queries as the following: "What subjects would you delete (add) (devote more/less time to)?" "Is the course too easy (hard)?" "What periods were outstandingly bad (good)?" Students were encouraged to add comments on anything they thought pertinent. Although such questionnaires were for many students a medium for airing purely personal discontent, and although students could not judge accurately such questions as the best length for the course, much of value was gained from the questionnaires. The majority of students took them seriously, their comments on instruction were often searching, and they made many suggestions for improvement. As a supplement to other forms of supervision, student reports gave insight into the reactions of the ultimate consumer, often a valuable guide and corrective to an exclusively faculty view.[21]

[21] Statements of Lt Col G. E. Holloway, Classification Off, Inf Sch, to AGF Hist Off, 8 Mar 45, and of Maj W. B. Anderson, Sec TD Sch, 13 Mar 45.

TABLE NO. 1

Total Output of AGF Service Schools, by Branch, 1940–45

School	Officers	Officer Candidates	Enlisted Men	Total
Antiaircraft	18,671	25,191	15,717	59,579
Armored	12,110	11,615	67,657	91,382
Cavalry	6,506	3,489	13,267	23,262
Coast Artillery	2,005	1,989	6,966	10,960
Field Artillery	34,314	25,598	37,752	97,664
Infantry	51,856	62,968	25,618	140,442
Tank Destroyer	5,526	5,281	17,211	28,018
Parachute	7,119	....	110,959	118,078
TOTAL	138,107	136,131	295,147	569,385

Sources: (1) R&SC 1st ind, 10 Sep 45, on AGF ltr to CG R&SC, 18 Aug 45, sub: Information on Output of AGF Service School Courses. (2) AAC 3d ind, 11 Sep 45, on AGF ltr to CG AAC, 18 Aug 45, sub: Information on Output of Courses at the Antiaircraft Artillery School. (3) Incl 2 to AGF 1st ind, 20 Aug 45, on TAG ltr AGOC–S–A 220.01 (29 May 45), 12 Jul 45, sub: Description of the Curricula and Courses in the Army's Training Program for Use in Separation Classification and Counseling. All in 352.11/526.

TABLE NO. 2

Courses and Output at the Antiaircraft Artillery School, 1942–45

Name of Course	Length In Weeks	Date of Opening	Date of Closing [a]	Number of Graduates	
				Off	EM
Officers					
Refresher	8	14 Mar 42	29 Jul 42	124	....
AA SC Tactics Special	2	13 Apr 42	31 Oct 42	55	....
40-mm. Special	4	8 Jun 42	12 Mar 43	555	....
Cadre	4–6	15 Jun 42	— Jan 44	7,530	....
90-mm. Special	4	3 Aug 42	27 May 43	164	....
Automatic Weapon Airborne Machine Gun	2	6 Oct 42	21 Oct 42	140	....
Marine Automatic Weapon Special	2	6 Oct 42	21 Oct 42	63	....
Searchlight and Communication Special	3	13 Oct 42	23 Apr 43	117	....
Automatic Weapons Special	4	13 Oct 42	7 May 43	149	....
OQ2A Radio-Controlled Target Plane	3	28 Oct 42	18 Mar 44	92	....
Field and Staff Special	4	13 Nov 42	7 May 43	38	....
Radar Course for Gun Cadre Officers	4	4 Jan 43	23 Apr 43	54	....
Methods of Teaching Aircraft Recognition	12 days	4 Jan 43	24 Apr 43	172	....
West Point	12	1 Feb 43	15 Aug 45	128	....
Radio Detection	3	22 Feb 43	28 Aug 43	78	....
Heightfinder	3	2 Mar 43	4 Aug 44	376	....
US Navy 90-mm. Special	3	15 Mar 43	9 Apr 43	19	....
US Navy Automatic Weapon Special	3	15 Mar 43	9 Apr 43	47	....
Automotive	8	29 Mar 43	31 Mar 45	1,656	....
Communications	8–12	1 May 43	17 Mar 45	704	....
Target Recognition	10 days	10 May 43	31 Dec 43	1,872	....
Automotive (108th Group) Special	5	24 May 43	2 Jul 43	117	....
Weiss Sight Group No. 1	27	27 Aug 43	17 Mar 44	107	....
Radar 545	3	30 Aug 43	21 Nov 43	34	....
Radar 584	5	13 Sep 43	4 Dec 43	115	....
Harvard MIT	3	13 Sep 43	23 Jun 44	243	....
Air Officers	5 days	30 Nov 43	15 Aug 45	1,417	....
Special Observers	4	— Dec 43	— Jan 44	36	....
Advanced (Guns)	15	3 Jan 44	16 Sep 44	207	....
Radar General (Fire Control)	10–24	3 Jan 44	15 Aug 45	77	....
Advanced (General)	12	21 Jan 44	16 Sep 44	167	....
Advanced (Searchlight)	12	21 Jan 44	16 Sep 44	122	....
Advanced (Automatic Weapons)	10	31 Jan 44	16 Sep 44	378	....
Radar Operational (Guns)	4	7 Feb 44	13 Jan 45	243	....
Radar Operational (Searchlight)	4	14 Feb 44	30 Dec 44	126	....
IFF	10 days	20 Mar 44	31 Mar 44	7	....
Advanced	14	15 Oct 44	17 Mar 45	37	....
Gun	4	22 Oct 44	15 Aug 45	257	....
Automatic Weapons	4	30 Oct 44	15 Aug 45	347	....

Table No. 2—Continued

Name of Course	Length In Weeks	Date of Opening	Date of Closing	Number of Graduates	
				Off	EM
Officers					
Flak Analysis	4	2 Mar 44	14 Jul 45	168	....
Searchlights	4	6 Nov 44	15 Aug 45	82	....
Refresher	4	29 Jan 45	15 Aug 45	242	....
AN/TPL-1	4	5 Mar 45	31 Mar 45	9	....
Special Gun Instruction Teams	3	5 Mar 45	31 Mar 45	[b]	....
TOTAL	....	....	....	18,671	
Enlisted Men					
Fire Control	12	9 Feb 42	14 Sep 42	....	172
Master Gunner	12	9 Feb 42	— Jul 43	....	675
Communications	10–12	9 Feb 42	15 Aug 45	....	2,392
Searchlight Electrician	6–14	9 Feb 42	15 Aug 45	....	1,143
Radio Detection	12	9 Mar 42	14 Sep 42	....	[b]
Automotive	12	9 Mar 42	15 Aug 45	....	1,765
Radar Repairman	12	— Mar 42	— Sep 42	....	199
Stereoscopics	12	20 Apr 42	14 Sep 44	....	920
Fire Control (Guns)	9–18	13 Jul 42	15 Aug 45	....	1,412
Fire Control (Automatic Weapons)	6–16	13 Jul 42	15 Aug 45	....	2,042
Radio Detection (Guns)	4–12	10 Aug 42	3 Jan 44	....	1,346
Radio Detection (Searchlights)	4–12	10 Aug 42	7 Feb 44	....	1,403
OQ Radio-Controlled Aerial Target	3	2 Feb 44	17 Apr 44	....	35
Master Gunner (Automatic Weapons)	12	14 Jun 43	15 Aug 45	....	344
Master Gunner (Guns)	12	14 Jun 43	15 Aug 45	....	390
Radio Repairman	13	4 Oct 43	15 Aug 45	....	890
Radio Operator	9	18 Oct 43	17 Jan 44	....	103
Basic Electricity	9	25 Oct 43	21 Feb 44	....	193
Radar Repair (Guns)	12	3 Jan 44	15 Aug 45	....	133
Radar Repair (Searchlights)	12	3 Jan 44	15 Aug 45	....	116
IFF	2	20 Mar 44	3 May 44	....	14
AN/TPL-1 (Special)	4	— Mar 45	— Jul 45	....	30
TOTAL	....	....	....	....	15,717
TOTAL Officers and Enlisted Men	....	....	....	18,671	15,717
TOTAL Graduates [c]	....	....	....	34,388	

Sources: See Table No. 1.

[a] Or date of last graduation before 1 Sep 45.

[b] No record of graduations.

[c] Exclusive of officer candidates.

TABLE NO. 3

Courses and Output at the Armored School, 1940–45

Name of Course	Length In Weeks	Date of Opening	Date of Closing [a]	Number of Graduates	
				Off	EM
Officers					
Communication	12	4 Nov 40	31 Mar 45	748	....
Tank Maintenance	12	4 Nov 40	18 Aug 45	2,259	....
Motor	12	4 Nov 40	7 Jul 45	1,139	....
Basic Tactics	8	9 Feb 42	22 Apr 43	595	....
Special Division Cadre	4	7 Sep 42	5 Jun 43	343	....
Advanced Tactics	6	1 Apr 43	30 Nov 43	145	....
Company Officers	8	26 Apr 43	12 Feb 44	968	....
Battalion Commanders	6	21 Jun 43	5 Feb 44	194	....
USMA Graduates	8	— Jul 43	30 Sep 44	53	....
Advanced Tank	13	17 Jan 44	3 Mar 45	375	....
Advanced Armored Infantry	12	7 Feb 44	2 Dec 44	130	....
Basic Gunnery	6	14 Feb 44	20 Jan 45	281	....
Advanced Gunnery	3	14 Feb 44	30 Dec 44	361	....
Special Basic (FA Conversion)	8	13 Mar 44	10 May 45	469	....
Armored Refresher	8	15 Jan 45	7 Apr 45	35	....
Cavalry Officers Conversion	4	12 Mar 45	7 Apr 45	18	....
TOTAL	....	....	....	8,113	....
Enlisted Men					
Tank Mechanics	12	4 Nov 40	18 Aug 45	2,165	17,110
Motor	12	4 Nov 40	18 Aug 45	....	14,717
Radio Repairman	14	4 Nov 40	25 Aug 45	....	3,427
Motorcycle Operators	2	4 Nov 40	31 May 41	....	232
Motorcycle Mechanics	8	4 Nov 40	22 Jul 43	....	1,289
Cryptographer	14	4 Nov 40	24 Jul 41	....	142
Clerical	8	4 Nov 40	22 Jul 44	....	4,151
Communications	12	4 Nov 40	25 Aug 45	....	12,832
Blacksmith & Welders	7	5 Nov 41	27 May 44	....	492
Radiator & Sheet Metal	8	5 Nov 41	9 Feb 43	....	154
Special Typing	6–10	3 Aug 42	5 Nov 43	....	378
Machinists	7	15 Jan 43	1 Apr 44	....	207
Radiator, Body, & Fender Repair	7	15 Jan 43	8 Apr 44	....	283
Airborne Tank	3	8 Nov 43	18 Dec 43	....	33
Amphibious Vehicle Mechanics	3	15 May 44	18 Aug 45	....	152
Armorer & Artillery Specialists	9	12 Jun 44	18 Aug 45	....	691
Replacement Motor	9	12 Jun 44	25 Aug 45	....	609
Replacement Communication	9	12 Jun 44	25 Aug 45	....	655
Replacement Clerical	9	12 Jun 44	25 Aug 45	....	535
Amphibious Communication	1	4 Jun 45	23 Jun 45	....	15
Amphibious Radio Repairman	1	2 Jul 45	21 Jul 45	....	10
TOTAL	....	....	....	2,165	58,114

Table No. 3—Continued

Courses and Output at the Armored School, 1940–45

Name of Course	Length In Weeks	Date of Opening	Date of Closing [a]	Number of Graduates	
				Off	EM
Composite					
Instructor Training	2–12	2 Mar 42	1 Jul 43	30	2,006
Radio-Controlled Airplane Target	3	28 Feb 43	25 Sep 43	33	162
Odograph	2	22 Nov 43	27 Jul 44	59	108
Special Medium Tank Maintenance FA Personnel	4	31 Jan 44	4 Apr 44	15	129
Overseas Instructors M24–M26	3	8 Jan 45	2 Jun 45	11	574
Night Vision Instructors	2	10 May 45	7 Jul 45	72	48
Gun Mechanics	4	4 Nov 40	1 Jul 44	1,612	6,516
TOTAL				1,832	9,543
TOTAL Officers and Enlisted Men				12,110	67,657
TOTAL Graduates [b]				79,767	

Sources: See Table No. 1.

[a] Or date of last graduation before 1 Sep 45.

[b] Exclusive of officer candidates.

TABLE NO. 4

Courses and Output at the Cavalry School, 1940–45

Name of Course	Length In Weeks	Date of Opening	Date of Closing [a]	Number of Graduates	
				Off	EM
Officers					
Basic Horse and Mechanized Cavalry	12	7 Aug 40	23 Dec 43	1,414	....
Special Reconnaissance Troop Commanders....................	4	26 Jan 42	21 Feb 42	3	....
Troop Commanders (Horse and Mechanized)....................	12	6 Apr 42	27 Jun 42	38	....
Staff Officers and Squadron Commanders..........................	6	6 Apr 42	18 Mar 43	1,201	....
Communications..................	12	28 Sep 42	21 Dec 44	544	....
New Unit Officers................	4	11 Jan 43	2 Jul 43	137	....
Tank Maintenance................	4	1 Feb 43	9 Dec 44	138	....
U.S. Military Academy............	12	8 Feb 43	8 Sep 44	16	....
Advanced........................	6–12	29 Mar 43	27 Jan 45	1,198	....
Special Mechanized Reconnaissance.	8	10 Apr 44	2 Dec 44	64	....
Motor............................	12	1 May 44	6 Jan 45	645	....
Gunnery..........................	6	8 May 44	2 Dec 44	117	....
Refresher for Cavalry Commanders..	2	19 Jun 44	30 Jun 44	37	....
Pack.............................	6	31 Jul 44	2 Jun 45	711	....
Refresher (Mechanized)...........	8	29 Jan 45	11 Aug 45	60	....
Basic Cavalry (Horse).............	6	5 Feb 45	28 Apr 45	29	....
Special Basic......................	8	23 Apr 45	11 Aug 45	77	....
TOTAL..........................	....	....	....	6,429	....
Enlisted Men					
Advanced Communications.........	12	31 Aug 40	26 Sep 42	....	535
Advanced Motor...................	12	31 Aug 40	4 May 44	....	640
Noncommissioned Officers Regular and National Guard.............	12	16 Dec 40	23 Dec 41	....	400
Horseshoers.......................	12	6 Jan 41	7 Jun 45	....	1,054
Saddlers..........................	12	6 Jan 41	21 Jul 45	....	740
Communications..................	12	17 Mar 41	28 Jul 45	....	3,653
Motor............................	12	17 Mar 41	18 Aug 45	....	3,166
Armorers.........................	6	20 Oct 41	9 Aug 45	....	787
Radio-Controlled Airplane Target...	3	4 Jan 43	4 Jan 44	....	112
Tank Maintenance................	4	8 Feb 43	4 Aug 45	....	709
Radio Repairman..................	8	18 Dec 43	4 Aug 45	....	277
Truck Company Maintenance.......	8	10 Apr 44	2 Dec 44	....	434
Pack.............................	6	13 Nov 44	18 Aug 45	2	641
TOTAL..........................	....	....	....	2	13,148
Composite					
Operation and Maintenance of Recording Odograph..............	10 days	22 Nov 43	24 May 45	75	119
TOTAL Officers and Enlisted Men..........................				6,506	13,267

TOTAL Graduates [b]......................................19,773

Sources: See Table No. 1.

[a] Or date of last graduation before 1 Sep 45.

[b] Exclusive of officer candidates.

TABLE NO. 5

Courses and Output at the Coast Artillery School, 1940–45

Name of Course	Length In Weeks	Date of Opening	Date of Closing [a]	Number of Graduates	
				Off	EM
Officers					
Stereoscopic Heightfinder (AA)	4	10 Nov 40	2 May 42	[b]	69
AA Refresher	12	23 Nov 40	11 Apr 42	[c]	....
AA Replacement Center	4	7 Dec 40	7 Feb 41	183	....
Seacoast Replacement Center	4	4 Jan 41	8 Feb 41	79	....
Submarine Mining	10	3 Feb 41	25 Nov 44	232	....
Seacoast Refresher	12	15 Feb 41	23 Jun 45	[c] 96	....
Radar SCR 268 (AA)	10	24 Feb 41	4 Apr 42	50	....
WO's (JG) Army Mine Planter	10	19 May 41	28 Nov 42	64	....
AA Field Officers	4	15 Nov 41	7 Mar 42	61	....
Artillery Engineer	12	12 Jan 42	6 Apr 42	....	5
Special Equipment	12	8 Aug 42	10 Feb 45	284	....
Seacoast Battery Officers	10	7 Sep 42	13 Mar 43	268	....
M1 Data Computer	4	21 Sep 42	1 Jan 44	68	....
Radio-Controlled Airplane Target	3	28 Dec 42	26 Feb 44	30	....
Seacoast Field Officers	12	4 Jan 43	6 Jan 45	291	....
Radio-Controlled Target Boat	5	11 Oct 43	18 Nov 44	6	....
M9 Director	2	19 Feb 44	25 May 44	....	70
Identification Friend or Foe Equip.	2	17 Apr 44	10 Jul 44	6	22
M8 Gun Data Computer	4	15 Jan 45	23 Jun 45	90	....
Special Radar Course for R A Officers	8	12 Mar 45	7 Jul 45	7	....
Mine Property Officers	10 days	17 Mar 45	11 May 45	32	....
TOTAL	....	....	....	1,847	166
Enlisted Men					
Clerical	10	15 Sep 39	7 Dec 40	....	61
Electrical	12	4 Mar 40	7 Jul 45	....	2,090
Communications	12	16 Sep 40	29 Sep 45	....	581
Master Gunner	12	16 Sep 40	30 Jun 45	....	489
Radar Set SCR 268	10	24 Feb 41	9 May 42	....	50
Motor	12	7 Apr 41	30 Jun 45	....	769
Submarine Mine Maintenance	14	2 Feb 42	19 May 45	....	145
Special Equipment Maintenance	20–22	13 Jul 42	9 Jun 45	158	724
Radio-Controlled Target Boat	5	24 Aug 42	18 Nov 44	....	98
M1 Seacoast Data Computer	4	21 Nov 42	17 Oct 42	....	122
Special Equipment Operators	20	14 Dec 42	23 Sep 44	....	1,083
Radio-Controlled Airplane Target	3	28 Dec 42	16 Jan 43	....	152
Radio Repairman	6	3 Jul 44	1 Aug 45	....	41
Diesel	10	10 Apr 44	18 Aug 45	....	209
Stereoscopic Range Finder Observers	6	3 Oct 44	9 Jun 45	....	36
M8 Data Computer	12	18 Dec 44	23 Jun 45	....	150
TOTAL				158	6,800
TOTAL Officers and Enlisted Men				2,005	6,966
TOTAL Graduates [d]				8,971	

Sources: See Table No. 1.

[a] Or date of last graduation before 1 Sep 45.

[b] No record of officer graduates.

[c] Graduates of AA Refresher included in Seacoast Refresher Course.

[d] Exclusive of officer candidates.

TABLE NO. 6

Courses and Output at the Field Artillery School, 1940–45

Name of Course	Length In Weeks	Date of Opening	Date of Closing [a]	Number of Graduates	
				Off	EM
Officers					
Motor	12	1 Aug 40	18 Aug 45	2,276	....
Horsemanship	12	1 Aug 40	4 Jul 42	89	....
Communications	12	1 Aug 40	25 Aug 45	2,361	....
Basic (Battery Officers)	12	15 Aug 40	30 Sep 44	8,544	....
Advanced	12	14 Nov 40	21 Feb 42	2,736	....
Field Officers	8	10 Jul 41	8 May 43	734	....
New Division Officers	4	26 Jan 42	3 Jul 43	1,980	....
Full-Track Vehicles	4	23 Feb 42	18 Aug 45	1,003	....
Sound- and Flash-Ranging	4–8	15 Jun 42	26 Aug 45	615	....
Pack Artillery	4–12	3 Aug 42	26 Aug 44	250	....
Battery Executive	4	22 Dec 42	14 Jul 45	1,767	....
Survey	4	11 Jan 43	26 May 45	3,652	....
Officers Advanced	12	12 Apr 43	24 Feb 45	3,606	....
New Unit Officers	4	27 Sep 43	8 Apr 44	559	....
Special Basic	10	13 Mar 44	4 Aug 45	983	....
Refresher	8	29 Jan 45	11 Aug 45	256	....
Field Artillery Pilot Short Course	2	13 Aug 45	31 Aug 45	12	....
Refresher Artillery Intelligence	3	13 Aug 45	....	[b]	....
Battery Officers Short Course	2	13 Aug 45	....	[b]	....
Field-Staff Officers Short Course	2	13 Aug 45	....	[b]	....
TOTAL	....	....	....	31,423	....
Enlisted Men					
Horsemanship	12	10 Jul 40	29 Aug 42	....	373
Artillery Mechanic	8–12	10 Jul 40	28 Jul 45	....	5,049
Saddlers	12	10 Jul 40	6 May 44	....	387
Horseshoers	12	10 Jul 40	23 Sep 44	....	397
Communications—Radio I and II	12	10 Jul 40	25 Aug 45	....	9,421
Motor	12	10 Jul 40	18 Aug 45	....	8,577
Full-Track Vehicles	4	17 Nov 41	18 Aug 45	....	3,177
Packmaster	4–12	3 Jul 42	23 Sep 44	....	522
Field Artillery Air Mechanic	5–10	17 Aug 42	18 Aug 45	....	2,269
Radio Repairman	4	15 Dec 42	25 Aug 45	....	4,322
Survey	4	24 May 43	11 Aug 45	....	850
Flash-Ranging	4	21 Jun 43	11 Aug 45	....	546
Sound-Ranging	4	21 Jun 43	25 Aug 45	....	560
Sound-Ranging Equipment Repair and Maintenance	2	5 Jun 44	4 Aug 45	....	178
Instrument Repair and Maintenance	2	5 Jun 44	18 Aug 45	....	312
Radar Preparatory	4	19 Feb 45	23 Jun 45	....	377
Field Artillery Air Mechanic Short Course	2	20 Aug 45	31 Aug 45	....	19
TOTAL					37,336

Table No. 6—Continued

Name of Course	Length In Weeks	Date of Opening	Date of Closing [a]	Number of Graduates	
				Off	EM
Composite					
Field Artillery Pilot	7–14	3 Aug 42	7 Jul 45	2,754	15
Radio-Controlled Airplane Target	4	28 Dec 42	28 Mar 45	7	253
Odograph	11 days	22 Nov 43	27 Jul 45	120	108
Meteorological Team Training	12	5 Feb 45	28 Apr 45	10	40
TOTAL				2,891	416
TOTAL Officers and Enlisted Men				34,314	37,752
TOTAL Graduates [c]				72,066	

Sources: See Table No. 1.

[a] Or date of last graduation before 1 Sep 45.

[b] No graduates reported before 1 Sep 45.

[c] Exclusive of officer candidates.

TABLE NO. 7

Courses and Output at the Infantry School, 1940–45

Name of Course	Length In Weeks	Date of Opening	Date of Closing [a]	Number of Graduates	
				Off	EM
Officers					
Special Refresher Senior National Guard Officers	12 days–3 mos	14 Aug 40	25 Jan 41	510	....
Communications	12	21 Aug 40	24 Apr 45	3,847	....
Basic	13–17	— Oct 40	10 Mar 44	15,106	....
Advanced	13	— Nov 40	22 Mar 45	9,710	....
Motor	12	20 Nov 40	13 Mar 45	3,720	....
New Division Officers	4	24 Jan 42	2 Jul 43	3,746	....
Cannon	4–6	30 Aug 42	5 Dec 44	1,376	....
Radio Airplane Target	3	29 Dec 42	31 Aug 45	502	....
Air Force Weather Officer	4	24 Nov 43	25 Jan 44	82	....
Special Basic	8	27 Feb 44	25 Aug 45	10,877	....
Air Liaison Officer	4	25 Mar 44	30 May 44	39	....
US Military Academy Basic	8–12	8 Jul 44	4 Sep 45	557	....
Radio Countermeasure Training	2 days	8 Aug 44	9 Aug 44	10	....
Refresher	8	10 Jan 45	10 Aug 45	696	....
Professor of Military Science and Tactics	3	5 Jun 45	30 Aug 45	289	....
Field Officers Short Course	2	13 Aug 45	....	[b]	....
Company Officers Short Course	2	13 Aug 45	....	[b]	....
TOTAL	....	....	....	51,067	....
Enlisted Men					
Radio Repairman	6	23 Feb 45	28 Aug 45	....	831
USMA Preparatory	12	1 Apr 45	28 Jun 45	....	398
Pre-Officer Candidate Course	4	5 Mar 45	31 Aug 45	....	1,162
Bayonet Instructors	1	26 Jun 45	5 Jul 45	....	63
TOTAL	....	....	....	....	2,454
Composite					
Motor Mechanics	12	10 Jul 40	21 Aug 45	14	13,719
Communications	12	14 Oct 40	12 Aug 45	4	7,863
Operation and Maintenance of Recording Odograph	10 days	22 Nov 43	26 Jul 45	158	159
Artillery Mechanics	15 days	24 Nov 43	24 Nov 44	313	502
Gun Instructors	3–4	27 Jan 45	29 Aug 45	36	283
Sound Locating	4–6	25 Feb 45	14 Aug 45	55	377
Explosives, Mines, and Booby Traps	2	17 Mar 45	10 Jun 45	155	200
Special Light Machine Gun Instructors	3 days	4 Jun 45	13 Jun 45	39	18
Canadian Army Instructors	2	30 Jun 45	16 Jul 45	15	43
TOTAL				789	23,164
TOTAL Officers and Enlisted Men				51,856	25,618
TOTAL Graduates [c]				77,474	

Sources: See Table No. 1.

[a] Or date of last graduation before 1 Sep 45.

[b] No graduates reported before 1 Sep 45.

[c] Exclusive of officer candidates.

TABLE NO. 8

Courses and Output at the Tank Destroyer School, 1942–45

Name of Course	Length In Weeks	Date of Opening	Date of Closing [a]	Number of Graduates	
				Off	EM
Officers					
Advanced Orientation	4	3 May 42	6 Feb 43	686	....
Basic Tactical	12	15 Aug 42	25 Jun 43	788	....
Pioneer	6	15 Aug 42	29 Apr 44	690	....
Motor	12	15 Aug 42	13 Jan 45	1,032	....
Basic Orientation	4	7 Nov 42	2 Jan 43	146	....
Advanced	12	6 Feb 43	6 Jan 45	644	....
Advanced Tactical	6	8 Feb 43	7 Feb 44	71	....
Communications	9½	27 Mar 43	27 Sep 44	305	....
New Unit Officers	6	1 May 43	3 Sep 43	208	....
US Military Academy Graduates	3	26 Jun 43	30 Sep 44	26	....
Full-Track Vehicles	4	4 Sep 43	23 Jun 45	238	....
Gunnery	9	6 May 44	10 Feb 45	194	....
Refresher	8	6 Dec 44	28 Apr 45	34	....
Indirect Fire	4	3 Feb 45	4 Aug 45	62	....
Field Officers of Other Arms	4	17 Mar 45	14 Apr 45	10	....
Company Officers of Other Arms	6	17 Mar 45	28 Apr 45	25	....
Officers Short Course	2	13 Aug 45	....	[b]	....
TOTAL	....	....	....	5,159	....
Enlisted Men					
Pioneer	6	15 Aug 42	29 Apr 44	....	2,031
Weapons	8	29 Aug 42	3 Mar 44	....	6,095
Radio Electrician and Technician	8	5 Sep 42	31 Dec 43	....	3,480
Motor	12	19 Sep 42	18 Jun 45	....	3,048
Full-Track Vehicles	4	4 Sep 43	23 Jun 45	....	825
Artillery Mechanics	6	25 Sep 43	10 Feb 45	....	356
Communications	12	13 Nov 43	18 Aug 45	....	624
Radio Repairman	6	18 Dec 43	7 Jul 45	....	352
TOTAL	....	....	....	....	16,811
Composite					
Diesel Maintenance	4	3 May 42	10 Jul 43	65	78
Odograph	2	20 Nov 43	13 Jul 44	78	79
Demolitions, Mines, and Booby Traps	2	24 Mar 45	2 Jun 45	224	243
TOTAL				367	400
TOTAL Officers and Enlisted Men				5,526	17,211

TOTAL Graduates [c] 22,737

Sources: See Table No. 1.

[a] Or last date of graduation before 1 Sep 45.

[b] No graduates reported before 1 Sep 45.

[c] Exclusive of officer candidates.

TABLE NO. 9

Courses and Output at the Parachute School, 1941–45

Name of Course	Length in Weeks	Date of Opening	Date of Closing [a]	Number of Graduates	
				Off	EM
Enlisted Men					
Parachute Artillery	4	20 Nov 44	25 Aug 45	....	778
Parachute Medical	4	20 Nov 44	26 Aug 45	....	329
Advanced Parachute Jump	2	4 Dec 44	25 Aug 45	....	12,916
TOTAL	....	....	....	....	14,023
Composite					
Basic Parachute Jump	4	19 Mar 41	25 Aug 45	5,995	82,949
Parachute Communication	3–9	2 Mar 42	25 Aug 45	323	5,563
Parachute Demolition	2–3	16 Mar 42	25 Aug 45	338	[b]4,787
Parachute Riggers	4–5	20 Jul 42	25 Aug 45	198	3,182
Parachute Camouflage [c]	5	8 Mar 43	18 Dec 43	....	....
Jumpmaster	1	20 Mar 44	22 Apr 44	....	[d]116
Machine Maintenance	2	....	9 Dec 44	....	[d]337
Parachute Infantry [c]	2–4	— Mar 44	....	....	....
Parachute Engineers [c]	4	— Apr 44	....	....	....
Airborne Orientation	1	11 Dec 44	19 May 45	665	2
TOTAL				7,119	96,936
TOTAL Officers and Enlisted Men				7,119	110,959
TOTAL Graduates				118,078	

Sources: See Table No. 1.

[a] Or date of last graduation before 1 Sep 45.

[b] This figure probably includes some officers.

[c] No other information available.

[d] No breakdown between officers and enlisted men available.

The Training of Officer Candidates

by

William R. Keast

230-171 O - 66 - 22

Contents

Chart

I. The Role and Organization of Officer Candidate Schools

The training of officer candidates, and their selection for commissions, in the service schools of the Army Ground Forces were integral parts of the officer procurement program, the more general aspects of which have been dealt with in a preceding study in this volume, "The Procurement of Officers." The mission of the officer candidate schools (OCS) was to convert enlisted men into combat officers to meet mobilization requirements for commissioned personnel in the company grades, in excess of the available supply of Regular, Reserve, and National Guard officers. In courses varying from twelve to seventeen weeks in length, the schools trained enlisted men and warrant officers in the basic duties of a junior officer of an arm, determined their possession of leadership qualities and other traits desirable in an officer, and recommended their commission, if qualified, as second lieutenants in the Army of the United States. This mission was extended in 1942 to include the training of members of the Reserve Officers' Training Corps who left college campuses to enter the Army before completing the full ROTC course; such men—numbering about one-tenth of all OCS graduates from AGF schools—received Reserve commissions after graduating from officer candidate school.

Officer candidate training was a mobilization procedure. Production of officers in peacetime was limited to the Military Academy, the Reserve Officers' Training Corps, the National Guard, and extension courses conducted by service schools. From these sources it was anticipated that enough officers would be available to meet the requirements of the first 120 days of mobilization. Thereafter, additions to officer strength were to come—except for civilian specialists commissioned directly—from the officer candidate schools, the operations of which were to begin on M Day.

Plans for officer candidate training were embodied in Mobilization Regulations and in mobilization plans drawn up before 1940.[1] Mobilization plans in 1938, for example, called for 225,000 officers during the first year of mobilization, to command an Army of 3,000,000. Of these officers 128,000—Regular, Reserve, and National Guard—were expected to be available on M Day. The officer candi-

[1] MR 1–4, 17 Oct 38, 25 Oct 39; MR 3–1, 3 Apr 39, 23 Nov 40.

*Graduation of Officer Candidates from AGF Service Schools, 1941–45**

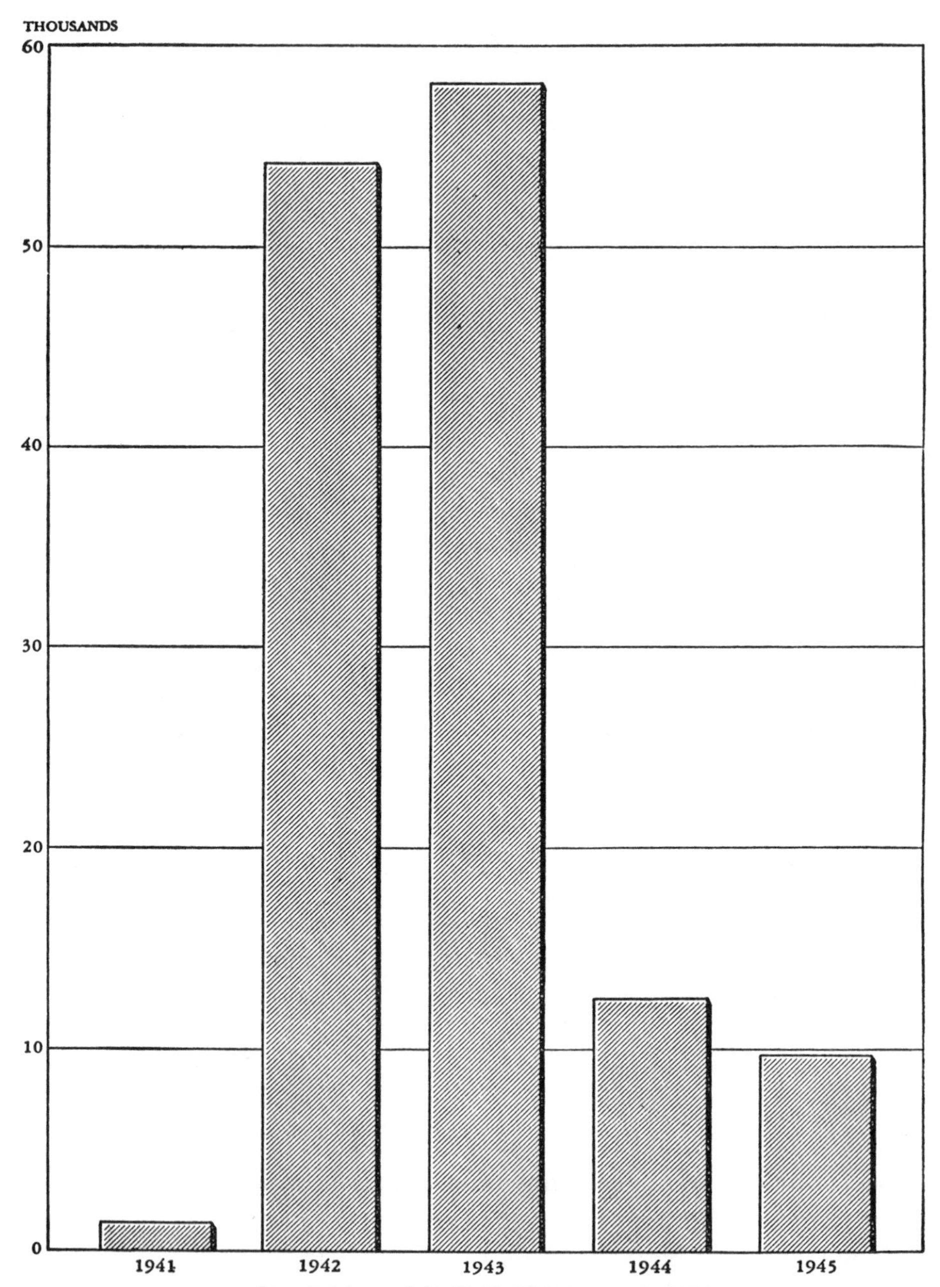

Source: Statistics compiled in Hist Div, WDSS, from records of AGO.

*Through August 31, 1945.

date schools were to supply the remainder, training monthly increments varying from 25,000 to 1,500 during the first nine months and none thereafter.[2]

Mobilization of the Army after 1940 did not proceed according to the schedule envisaged in prewar plans. Before Pearl Harbor mobilization was much slower than had been anticipated. As a result of the slow pace of early mobilization, requirements for officers in excess of those who could be supplied from the Regular, Reserve, and National Guard components did not appear until after Pearl Harbor. Accordingly, large-scale officer candidate training was deferred until the beginning of 1942, by which time the Army had attained a strength of approximately 1,600,000 men. By the end of 1941 only 1,389 officer candidates had been commissioned in the ground arms.

During 1942 mobilization was very much more rapid and extensive than had been anticipated, and the officer candidate schools were forced to expand to unforeseen dimensions. More than 112,000 officer candidates for the ground arms alone were graduated during the peak mobilization years, 1942 and 1943. For the war period as a whole, the ground arms received more than 136,000 graduates from the schools. (See the accompanying chart.)

Although the mission assigned to officer candidate schools in prewar planning was that of supplying urgent officer requirements, and while they actually performed that mission after 1941, they were not established primarily for such a purpose. In the early fall of 1940, when Gen. George C. Marshall directed his staff to study the feasibility of opening officer candidate schools during December, there was an abundance of officers. The statutory size of the Army was 1,400,000, including an annual increment of 900,000 selectees. Reserve officer strength was judged sufficient for an Army of 2,000,000. G–1 and G–3 of the General Staff saw no need for officer candidate training. The Chiefs of Infantry, Cavalry, Field Artillery, Coast Artillery, and Signal Corps—the only branches concerned in the early planning—were "unanimous in opposing the project, stating that no necessity existed therefor." The Chiefs preferred not to expand the Officers' Reserve Corps—to which originally it was intended to assign officer candidate graduates—unless the need became urgent. The War Department G–3 conceded that officer candidate schools might have some morale value, but urged that the number of candidates be kept at a minimum.[3] General Marshall,

[2] Army War College Study (R), 1 Nov 38, sub: Procurement of Off Pers. See also AWC Study (R), 2 Nov 39, same sub. AWC Records.

[3] WD memo of Brig Gen F. M. Andrews for CofS USA, 7 Sep 40, sub: OCSs. AGO Records, 352 (9–19–40) (1) Sec 1, Part 1.

over the opposition of his staff, directed that plans be drawn to provide officer candidate schools for trainees during the last months of their year of training. Although they were not required in the near future, it was believed that officer candidate graduates might be useful a year hence when most of the 50,000 Reserve officers on extended active duty would return to civilian life. Since 4,500,000 men were to pass through the Army during the succeeding five years, the War Department was confident that the "cream of the crop" would make good officers for the National Defense Program.[4]

Five officer candidate schools for the ground arms—Infantry, Field Artillery, Coast Artillery, Cavalry, and Armored—were accordingly established in July 1941. Until March 1942 the Coast Artillery School trained both seacoast and antiaircraft officer candidates. When the Antiaircraft Artillery Command was established as a part of the Army Ground Forces in March 1942, training of antiaircraft officers was transferred from the Coast Artillery School to the new Antiaircraft Artillery School at Camp Davis, N. C. Until October 1942, new officers for tank destroyer units were detailed from the other arms; then an Officer Candidate Department of the Tank Destroyer School was established and henceforth trained junior officers for tank destroyer units.

Selection of Candidates

The War Department delegated the authority to select men who were to attend officer candidate schools to designated commanding generals to whom quotas for the several schools were allotted. These commanders in turn appointed boards of officers to interview applicants and recommend those best qualified for officer training. All selection boards were guided in their examination of applicants by standards laid down in War Department regulations and circulars. Although these standards were changed in detail from time to time to meet changing conditions, they always involved age, physical condition, military service, capacity for leadership, learning ability, citizenship, character, and education.

Standards of learning ability, education, and leadership produced the greatest practical difficulties. Learning ability was measured by the Army General Classification Test (AGCT). To qualify for officer training, an applicant was required to have a minimum score of 110. Originally it was not intended to use

[4] WD memo G-3/25445 for CofS USA, 19 Sep 40, sub: OCSs. AGO Records, 352 (9-19-40) (1) Sec 1, Part 1.

AGCT scores in selecting candidates but to develop an educational test and a leadership ability test for the screening of applicants. The Army General Classification Test was decided upon only as a temporary expedient pending completion of these tests.[5] Since only one of the projected tests was developed, however—and this test was not ready for general use until the end of 1944—the Army General Classification Test remained the principal instrument for selection.

No formal educational requirement was ever specified for OCS applicants. War Department directives suggested that for certain technical schools—for example, Engineer, Ordnance, and Finance—academic degrees would be desirable, but they were not held to be essential. The educational standard was merely the possession of "such education or civil or military experience as will reasonably insure . . . satisfactory completion of the course." [6]

The most important requirement for selection as an officer candidate was proven leadership ability. No definition of leadership was ever provided by the War Department and no test of leadership ever devised. Each selection board was left to draw up its own specifications. Consequently, candidates chosen from different sources and at different times displayed the greatest variation in this respect. Other standards, such as age, physique, citizenship, and learning ability, were susceptible of fairly precise determination. When demands for candidates rose above the supply of men clearly qualified for training, it was the leadership requirement that was most frequently neglected. Then, instead of getting men who had "demonstrated high qualities of leadership" [7] from whom they would select the best, the schools had to devote much time and effort to clearing the rolls of men almost completely lacking in leadership ability.

In general the requirements for admission to officer candidate school were so loosely drawn that the schools were forced to develop their own means of eliminating men who should never have been selected.

General Organization of the Schools

The operation of officer candidate schools was complicated by their twofold mission—training and selection. School instruction, which occupied the major portion of time, was designed to provide the technical and tactical knowledge needed by a platoon leader. Concurrently the schools carried on a thorough

[5] WD AG memo for G-1 WD, 6 Jun 41, sub: Selection of Trainees for OCS. AGO Records, 352 (9-19-40) (1) Sec 1, Part 1.

[6] Par 6 *h*, Cir 126, WD, 28 Apr 42.

[7] Par 10, Sec II, Cir 48, WD, 19 Feb 42.

screening process to determine which candidates should become officers and which should be returned to enlisted status. The two functions of training and selection were performed by separate groups of officers. Regular instruction and academic examinations were the responsibilities of a faculty of instructors. Selection of candidates for commissions was the primary responsibility of the "tactical officers," to whose charge the men were assigned during the course. This double structure of training and selection contrasted with the scheme used in training officers during World War I, when the same officers taught the candidates and judged their suitability for commissions. When candidate schools were established in 1941, it was thought that more efficient instruction and more reliable judgment of suitability would result if each function were performed by specialists.[8] The work of instructors and tactical officers overlapped to some extent: academic grades supplied by instructors were the chief academic basis for selection of candidates; tactical officers conducted instruction in drill, discipline, and physical training and, in some schools, in such basic subjects as military courtesy, first aid, and administration.[9] The gap between instructors and tactical officers was bridged by the Faculty Board, a group of officers normally containing representatives of the instructional departments and of the officer candidate school staff, responsible to the school commandant for final selection, rejection, or turnback of candidates. At regular intervals each candidate class was screened by the Faculty Board, which based its decisions on academic records and recommendations of tactical officers, supplemented by its own observations.

Academic Training

Except at the Antiaircraft Artillery School, officer candidates were given only general training. That is, no attempt was made to prepare officers to fill specific types of assignment within the branch. A graduate of the Field Artillery School might become a platoon leader in a battery firing any one of several kinds of weapons; he might be assigned to training duty at a replacement training center or to duty in an artillery staff section; or he might become an instructor or tactical officer at the Field Artillery School. A single curriculum was designed to prepare him for any of these duties. Training was not quite as generalized as a

[8] Statements of Col R. R. Coursey, WD G–1 Div (formerly Director of OCs, Inf Sch) to AGF Hist Off, 2 Mar 45; of Col Waine Archer, G–3 Div Hq ETOUSA (formerly Coordinator of Tng, Inf Sch), 7 May 45.

[9] Until 1943, for example, at the Tank Destroyer OCS; statement of Maj W. B. Anderson, Sec TD Sch to AGF Hist Off, 13 Mar 45.

list of possible branch assignments might indicate. The focus of the curriculum was on eventual duty as a combat platoon leader. The great majority of graduates were so assigned; to have built a program on a wider range of probable assignments would have resulted in an unintegrated course. The test applied to each subject suggested for inclusion in OCS programs was the question: "Will this material help produce an officer who can train troops and lead them in battle?" Subjects that could not pass this test—even though they might be adapted to some possible officer assignments in the branch—were omitted in favor of subjects that could.

The policy of giving only general training in officer candidate schools rested in part on the assumption—fundamental in Army doctrine—that every officer should be qualified to fill any position commensurate with his rank. It rested also on the conviction in the Army Ground Forces that service in a troop unit provided the best training for an officer, and that officer candidate courses should be kept short and basic in order not to delay unduly the beginning of an officer's troop duty. After a period of service in a unit, during which habits of leadership had been developed, officers destined for higher command, staff, or technical assignments could be returned to school for more specialized instruction.

From the generalized character of OCS training it followed that programs had to include familiarization work in preparation for a number of combat assignments, with concentration on the one which the majority of graduates would probably be given. Thus the Infantry OCS course included training in all infantry weapons and tactical exercises involving all elements of the infantry regiment, but more time was devoted to the rifle and to tactics of the rifle company than to the rest. At the Field Artillery School the candidate was given a brief orientation in each field artillery weapon, but firing problems and tactical exercises used only the 105-mm. howitzer, which was the basic piece and the one with which the new officer would most probably be concerned.

After January 1943 the Antiaircraft Artillery School deviated from the policy of conducting only general training. During its first year of operation this school, like the others, had trained men to fill any second lieutenant's position in any type of antiaircraft unit. By late 1942, when a considerable number of graduates had reached units in the field, the school received reports that they were unqualified. They had been given a smattering of work on antiaircraft guns, automatic weapons, and searchlights, but the 12-week course had been too brief to qualify them fully for duty in a unit equipped with any one of the three. It was decided to lengthen the course to thirteen weeks and to divide each class into three groups for specialized instruction on guns, automatic weapons, and searchlights during the latter part of the course. The time was divided as follows: one week of organization, orientation, physical hardening, and basic subjects; seven weeks of common instruction in individual weapons, tactics, motors, communications, etc.; four weeks of specialized instruction in one of the three groups mentioned above; and during the final week a field exercise in which the class was again brought together. After March 1943, when the Antiaircraft Artillery School received permission to lengthen its officer candidate course to seventeen weeks—chiefly because the specialized training had been found to require more time than was available in the 13-week cycle—ten weeks were devoted to common instruction and seven to specialization.

Division of the class into three groups for specialized instruction was carried out primarily on the basis of class standing and the difficulty of the specialty. Gun instruction was regarded as the most difficult, searchlights as the next most difficult, and automatic weapons as the easiest. After the number of officers required in each specialty had been determined, the men ranking highest in the class academically were assigned to instruction in guns, the middle portion of the class was assigned to searchlights, and the bottom group was assigned to automatic weapons. Specialized OCS instruction had great immediate benefits. Officers assigned to units were much more proficient initially than their more broadly trained predecessors had been. This immediate advantage was counterbalanced by serious long-run defects. Transfers were more difficult because officers were qualified only in one type of equipment. As the war progressed and the antiaircraft establishment shrank, necessitating extensive reassignment of officers, it was found that much retraining had to be conducted in order to broaden their knowledge and skill. Such retraining was expensive and time-consuming.[10]

The program of instruction for the officer candidate course was substantially identical at all schools with that for the Officers Basic Course, but candidates were required to attend a study period four or five nights a week and were held to somewhat more rigid academic standards than commissioned officer students. The principal difference between instruction as conducted for candidates and instruction as conducted for officer students in the basic course lay in the use of regular training as a source of information about the candidate's leadership ability.

[10] (1) Statement of Lt Col D. F. Sellards, S–3 AAA Sch, to AGF Hist Off, 17 Mar 45. (2) Statement of Lt Col S. W. Luther, G–3 Schs Br, AA Comd, to AGF Hist Off, 17 Mar 45.

Officer candidates were judged not only on their academic record but also on their attitude in class, their force, initiative, and other qualities not directly related to academic performance. Tactical officers accompanied their men to classroom and field to observe them. The candidate had to learn the subject and at the same time to demonstrate that he possessed leadership qualities of more general applicability.

Use of regular training as a basis for selection, while necessary in view of the limited time available to decide upon the candidate's fitness, compromised the quality of instruction. The candidate had to think both of the work at hand and of the kind of impression he was making on his judges. Often candidates were reluctant to ask questions for fear they would appear stupid or slow; they preferred not to hazard answers unless they were sure of themselves; they tried to avoid responsibility and conceal initiative, for with these went the possibility of blundering before the class and the tactical officers. Although a good, honest mistake is frequently the quickest and surest method of learning, candidates were impelled by the instinct of self-preservation to play safe and remain in the background, in the hope that avoidance of error might be construed as positive merit.[11] These results of the system may throw some light on the frequent complaints that junior officers hesitated to accept responsibility, to take risks, and to carry on in the absence of specific directions from above.

The union between training and selection in some schools produced what came to be known as the "Hockey Team." The Hockey Team was a group of unfortunate candidates occupying the limbo between the possibilities of graduation and failure. To support a definite judgment of these doubtful men, tactical officers needed more information than regular methods provided. They arranged that instructors call on such men frequently in class and assign them positions of responsibility in training problems. Assignment to the Hockey Team was a severe blow to a candidate's morale, and the heavy load of assignments and unrelenting public attention subjected him to more exacting standards than those to which his more fortunate colleagues had to conform. Indirectly, the other candidates suffered also. Largely exempted from accountability for work assigned, they had less incentive to study and fewer opportunities to put their knowledge into practice.

Estimates of the candidates by instructors took the form of examination grades, supplemented by written reports on class or field performance and by informal conferences with tactical officers. A candidate failed if his average

[11] See unpublished MS by Cpl Henry G. Fairbanks, "A Candidate's Critique of Infantry OCS," on file in Office of the Secretary, Inf Sch.

grade on tests fell below a designated level. In some schools the grades were weighted in proportion to the importance of the different subjects. Each man's academic standing was made available to his tactical officers and was included in records submitted to the Faculty Board.

Training in Leadership

The officer candidate schools tried to influence and to hasten the development of leadership ability in men who were potentially possessed of it. They tried to weed out those who lacked a capacity for leadership and those who might become leaders only after too long a period of training. Training in leadership took two forms, direct or theoretical and indirect or practical.

The indirect, practical training occurred during regular instruction and daily drill. Each candidate was put in as many situations as possible—as squad leader, platoon sergeant, or company commander in the company organization; as patrol leader, platoon leader, company commander, tank commander, or gunnery officer, during school problems—in which he would have to exercise command, express his ability as a leader, act on his own responsibility, and direct a group in carrying out an assignment. School problems were designed primarily to teach a subject and to demonstrate to the candidate how he could teach it to his men. But through rotation of assignments, each man had in addition a series of opportunities to demonstrate his leadership ability and to improve it.

A notable example of leadership training was that given in the technique of instruction. In learning to teach a group of men the candidate was actually learning to perform one of the basic continuing functions of military leadership. At the Armored School, and to a lesser extent at the Cavalry School, this fact was recognized and exploited in the curriculum. Each candidate was required to prepare and teach his classmates one or more extended lessons on basic military subjects. The candidate's ability to capture and hold the attention of the class, to organize and transmit his material clearly, and to deal with unexpected questions and problems gave him experience and provided a basis for judgment of his potential value as an officer.

Direct or theoretical instruction in leadership took place in the classroom. It usually consisted of lectures, case studies, and conferences designed to make clear to the candidate the ingredients of leadership and to indicate the ways in which leadership problems might arise. The candidate was required to analyze hypothetical situations that might confront him and decide what he would do to meet them, so that he would begin at once to assume the combat officer's burden of responsibility and go into battle with a capacity for any problem that might arise. At the Infantry School, where this system of teaching leadership was developed by Lt. Col. Samuel I. Parker (winner of the Congressional Medal of Honor in World War I), six hours were devoted to the subject.[12] During this time the qualities fundamental to leadership were distinguished and analyzed, several actual cases of combat leadership were discussed by the instructor, each student was required to prepare and present his analysis of a real or hypothetical combat situation involving a problem in leadership, and the students were introduced to a scale for rating themselves and others with respect to leadership. The instructors in the course were, whenever possible, officers decorated for heroism in World Wars I or II. To supplement the regular course in leadership, lectures on combat experiences were given from time to time by officers recently returned from overseas.

It is impossible to assess precisely the effectiveness of these devices for improving the leadership ability of the candidates. In the practical exercise of command during routine instruction, classes were too large for any man to receive more than a limited number of opportunities to control a unit. The scarcity of occasions was balanced to some extent by the vividness of each. Knowing he was on trial, observed by classmates, instructors, and tactical officers, the candidate probably learned each lesson in leadership more thoroughly.

Selection for Commissions

The selection system used in the officer candidate schools, as well as that used for selecting candidates, had to be evolved in the face of the absence of an objective standard of leadership ability. No way was discovered during the war of accurately defining, measuring, or detecting leadership ability in individuals. Each school, within a framework of generalized attributes thought to be indicative of leadership, amassed from as many sources as possible a collection of independent judgments on each candidate's leadership ability. The consensus was taken as the nearest practical approximation to an objective measure. The schools frankly recognized the impossibility of reducing the judgment of leadership to an exact formula. Each observer was directed to work out for himself a criterion by which to assess the individuals under his observation. No substitute

[12] The course is outlined in the Infantry School *Mailing List*, Vol. XXVI (1943), Chap. 7, Vol. XXVII (1944), Chap. 1.

for human judgment could be invoked. In appraisal the essential question was: "Would I be willing to follow this man in battle?" [13]

Despite wide variation in details, all AGF officer candidate schools followed the same basic plan in screening candidates for commissions. The purpose of screening was to determine as early as possible, first, the candidates manifestly unqualified for commissions, so that they could be relieved and more time spent on the remaining men; second, the candidates obviously fit to become officers, so that time would not be wasted in observing them extensively; and, finally, the borderline candidates needing assistance, extra practice, and careful scrutiny before final determination of their suitability could be made. Usually three screenings occurred during the 17-week cycle. At each screening the Faculty

[13] Unless otherwise indicated, this section is based on the following documents, located in 314.7 (AGF Hist), except those of the TD School, which were in TD Sch files:

Antiaircraft Artillery School
- Candidates' Class Record, 6 Apr 43.

Armored School
- Orientation for the Officer Candidate of the Armored Officer Candidate School, Jul 43.
- Standing Operating Procedure for the Rating of Officer Candidates, undated.
- The Armored Officer Candidate School—General Regulations and Information, 2 Oct 43.
- Memo of Col A. S. J. Stovall, Jr., Director Armd OCS, for New Members of AFOCS Status Board, 22 Apr 43.

Cavalry School
- Instruction Circular for Officer Candidates, Oct 43.
- OCS Information Bulletin No. 1, Apr 43.
- OCS Memo, Classification and Final Selection of Officer Candidates, undated.

Field Artillery School
- Handbook for Officer Candidates, 15 Mar 44.
- Handbook for Officer Candidates, 15 Mar 45.
- Rating Form for Use of Interviewers and Oral Examiners, 22 Jan 45.
- Rating and Observation Report on Officer Candidates, 16 Jan 45.

Infantry School
- Hq 3d Student Tng Regt memo, 21 Dec 43, sub: Guide for Officers of the OCS.
- Leadership Rating Scale, 1 Jul 44.
- Leadership—How to Use the Rating Scale, 1 Jul 44.
- Memo of Capt J. J. McGrath for Asst Comdt, undated [1942], sub: OC Failures—Some Obsns.
- Guide for Tactical Offs of the Tng Brig, 9 Nov 42.
- Regulations Governing the Opns of the Faculty Bd for OC Classes, 24 Mar 44.

Tank Destroyer School
- Candidate Rating Sheet, undated.
- Consolidated Efficiency Report, undated.
- Officer Candidate Characteristics, 1 Jun 43.
- OCS Dept memo for CO OCS Regt, 12 Dec 42, sub: Reports on OCs.
- TD Sch memo for all OCs, 12 Nov 42, sub: Academic and Leadership Standard.

Board met and reviewed the record of each candidate recommended to its attention by the tactical officers.

The first screening of the class (after the OCS course had been extended to seventeen weeks) occurred during the fifth or sixth week of the course. At this time men who were failing academically or who lacked aptitude or basic education were relieved or were turned back to a later class in the hope that they might do better on a second try. Candidates were not usually relieved for lack of leadership ability at the first board meeting; it was felt that a candidate had not yet had enough time to demonstrate his capacity for leadership. At the second screening, usually carried out during the twelfth or thirteenth week, men put on probation at the first board meeting were reinstated or disposed of, and academic failures since the last board meeting were relieved. The principal function of this screening was to weed out men weak in leadership. The final board, meeting usually during the sixteenth or seventeenth week, dealt with any men who had recently fallen from grace, decided what to do with men put on probation by the second board, and recommended for commissions the men considered qualified.

The decisions of the Faculty Board—whether to relieve the candidate, to turn him back, to place him on probation, to allow him to continue in good standing, or, if it was a final screening, to commission him—were based on the candidate's academic record, on the ratings made by tactical officers and fellow candidates, and, if necessary, on the board's own opinion of the man based on an interview with him. The function of the school faculty in supplying evidence of academic ability has already been discussed; ratings by tactical officers and fellow candidates remain to be considered.

For information on each of the thirty to one hundred men assigned to him the tactical officer depended on several sources. Information as to the candidate's AGCT score, civilian education and occupation, and previous military service was available from records. Early in the course, at most schools, each candidate prepared a brief autobiography, from which the tactical officer drew inferences about his character. The platoon leader interviewed each man early in the course and at intervals thereafter, to obtain a more direct and personal impression of his personality. Before the course was well under way the tactical officer had begun to analyze his men and to mark those who looked especially good and especially poor. But the chief sources of information became available during the course. One of these, the candidate's performance during regular academic instruction, has already been mentioned. The other major sources were the candidate's

230-171 O - 66 - 23

performance of assigned company duties, his skill in conducting drill and physical training, his demerits or "gigs," and the ratings made of him by his fellow candidates.

Except for routine administration, messing, and supply, each officer candidate company or section was staffed by the candidates. The duties of company commander, executive, platoon leader, and so on down to assistant squad leader were performed by the men, who were rotated in these assignments weekly or semiweekly. Tactical officers were present at all formations, during all movements of the company, and during all instruction, but they remained in the background as observers, letting the candidates run the show. Regular rotation of company duties put each candidate in some kind of command position several times during the course. During these assignments he was on his own, making decisions, giving commands, maintaining discipline, making corrections, anticipating problems, and coping with emergencies. The tactical officers had an excellent opportunity to assess the candidate's capacity for command. Some form of efficiency report was maintained on each candidate during the command assignments and was incorporated in his record.

In all schools daily periods of drill and physical training were conducted by the candidates themselves. Normally four or five men in each platoon or section were detailed, two or three days in advance, to prepare instructions covering designated paragraphs of FM 22–5, Infantry Drill Regulations, or FM 21–20, Physical Training. Each man took the group for ten or fifteen minutes, explaining the drills or exercises, demonstrating them, conducting practical work by the other candidates, and criticizing the performance. These assignments required the candidate to display his ability to give clear directions and forceful orders, his command over the men, and the quality of his voice and appearance. The value of assignments was diminished somewhat by the amount of warning the candidates received and by the care the candidates took to protect each other. Knowing they would be in the same position later, they did their best to execute drills and exercises with a precision that would reflect credit on the candidate in charge.

Candidates were held to severe standards of dress, conduct, bearing, obedience to orders, and police of quarters and equipment. Infractions of the many rules were punished by demerits or delinquencies, commonly called "gigs" or "skins." Daily lists or "gig sheets" were posted showing the names of offenders and the nature and severity of their offenses. Gigs were graded according to gravity, and each candidate was permitted to accumulate a certain number of delinquencies during a week or during the course. After the limit was passed, or after a major offense was committed, disciplinary action, probation, or even relief from the school ensued.

Actions or omissions judged to be delinquencies varied greatly from school to school. In most schools the candidates learned the exact list of crimes by their own transgressions or those of their classmates. Only the Armored School went so far as to publish a list of punishable delinquencies—an elaborate catalogue of sins ranging from "Abrasives, using on rifles" to "Yelling, or cheering, or allowing same, in disapprobation of published orders." [14]

Although the gig sheets were universally disliked by the candidates, they were useful in the quick conversion of civilians into officers. The system of allotting definite penalties for even the most minor violations of orders promoted alertness, precision, foresight, and responsibilty. It subjected the candidate to a regimen more rigorous than he would impose upon his men, but it gave him a standard toward which to guide his unit. The system aided tactical officers in judging the candidates. The man who left dust upon his book shelf, appeared in formation without his name tag, or failed to get all the powder foulings out of his rifle might be habitually careless; the tactical officer would confirm or deny this judgment in later observation.

Tactical officers were as nearly ubiquitous as possible. But they could not watch the candidate in his informal moments, few though these were. An artful candidate might conceal disqualifying habits and attitudes from the tactical officer. But he could not hide them from the men with whom he lived. As a check on the reliability of the tactical officer's judgment and as a source of additional information, the candidates were required to rate each other at intervals during the course. Each candidate rated the members of his platoon or section two or three times during the 17-week cycle. The most common procedure was to require the candidate to list his classmates in the order of their suitability as combat leaders and to supply a brief comment on each man justifying the rating he was given. A rating scale or a list of important attributes was usually furnished as a guide. When consolidated, the candidate ratings gave each man a relative position in the composite judgment of the group.

Three purposes were served by the intra-platoon ratings. They gave a fairly reliable measure of each man's ability to command the respect and confidence of his fellows, a signal attribute of a successful leader. They gave some insight

[14] Armd F OCS pamphlet, "Demerit and Punishment Procedure." 314.7 (AGF Hist).

into each candidate's ability to judge others, also important to an officer. Finally, the intra-platoon ratings corrected each other and the judgments of the tactical officers. If half the men put a candidate near the top of their lists and half placed him near the bottom, something was wrong and investigation might turn up evidence that would permit a fairer judgment of the man. If the platoon leader rated a candidate high and the men rated him low, investigation might disclose error, collusion, or some other flaw in the system.

The system of class ratings did not work perfectly. Knowing that he was to be rated, a candidate might try to put on a new character for seventeen weeks. He might try to ingratiate himself with the other men in order to win their favor. The whole thing might at times take on the aspect of a popularity contest. Cliques might develop and turn into mutual commendation societies. It was in recognition of these weaknesses that the candidate ratings acquired the derisive name of "Buddy Sheets." Purely personal feelings were difficult to divorce from the sober estimates required. Comments supplied by the candidates to justify their ratings of each other were often mechanical—and therefore worthless—repetitions of the vocabulary furnished by the prescribed rating scale. Remarks such as "A little weak in leadership," "Has military knowledge," and "Plenty aggressive" were too brief and too general to give a clear definition of a man's qualities. Many candidates did not know what leadership was nor how to recognize its presence in an individual. The candidate ratings were often misused by tactical officers having access to them. The tactical officers based their own judgments of the men on those of the candidates; independence of judgment was thereby lost, and the value of having several sources of data on each man largely nullified. Most schools, when they found candidate ratings abused in this manner, required tactical officers to rate their men before the candidate ratings were turned in, but it was difficult to secure complete independence.

On the whole, however, the men took their responsibilities seriously and tried to rate each other honestly. In the nature of things some variation was inevitable. But there was a high degree of concordance among the estimates made by the candidates and between their estimates and those made by the tactical officers. Used cautiously, with recognition of their limitations, and in combination with ratings and measures from other independent sources, class ratings were a valuable part of the selection scheme.

Of the three principal ratings made on each man—academic rating, tactical officer's rating, and fellow candidate's rating—the last two carried the greater weight because they were based on the candidate's leadership ability. A man whose leadership ability was high but whose academic average was low would probably be commissioned. A man whose grades were high but whose leadership was thought mediocre or poor would probably not be commissioned.

Several schools experimented with supplementary or substitute techniques for selecting candidates. At the Armored School a military psychologist interviewed and rated each incoming candidate and predicted his chance of success in officer candidate school. Ratings were made on (1) ability, including general ability, reading, arithmetic, and mathematical comprehension; (2) personality, including emotional stability, test-honesty, and pattern (a psychological term used to sum up such an observation as "aggressive and fairly self-confident"); and (3) totals for the first two, and over-all suitability. [15] The predictions were formulated in the light of standards prevailing in the school, with the result that it is impossible to judge whether the psychologist and standards were correct or whether the psychologist was merely able to anticipate what the tactical officers would do. The school made no use of these ratings except to watch more closely a candidate who emerged from the interview with low marks. [16]

Late in 1943 the OCS Department at the Tank Destroyer School experimented with a Combat Adaptability Test developed by Dr. Ernest M. Ligon, Expert Consultant to the Secretary of War, with the purpose of discovering a reliable and objective method of selecting successful combat officers. [17] The approach involved an analysis of the "job elements" of the combat leader's work; among these were ability to instruct his men in their mission, to reach his objectives, to get his men to cooperate, to keep his head when things went wrong, and to foresee what the enemy would be likely to do. A rating scale was developed to record the judges' estimate of the candidate's possession of these traits, and the candidate was placed in several test situations in which, presumably, the traits or their absence would be revealed. The candidate was first interviewed for ten or fifteen minutes by a group of four or five judges who studied and rated him. On the basis of his answers to a list of questions—all questions were the same for all candidates—the judges rated some of the desired "job elements." Thus ability to get men to cooperate was inferred from the subject's

[15] Study, Armd Sch, Office of the Military Psychologist, "Report of Psychological Examinations of OCs (based on tentative Norms) OC Class #68," 20 Jun 44. Armd OCS Dept files.

[16] Statement of Col T. E. Winstead, Dir OCS Dept, Armd Sch, to AGF Hist Off, 21 Mar 45.

[17] Study (R), TD Sch Classification Dept, 20 Dec 43, sub: Pers Research Rpt—Experiment in Combat Adaptability. 3 Parts. TD Sch files.

response to such a question as "How would you deal with stubborn subordinates." After the interview the candidate was given a short time in which to prepare and deliver a 2-minute talk to an imaginary platoon about to go into battle for the first time. This performance was designed to reveal something about the candidate's performance under stress, his power of expression, and his ability to command attention. For more direct evidence on the candidate's ability to work under pressure he was placed in two "stress situations." Against time, he was required to solve a map problem and to translate two different codes transmitted alternately by two senders. As he worked he heard a battle-noise recording through an earphone, felt periodic shocks applied through a shock device strapped to one wrist, had his chair violently shaken by a vibrator, and breathed with difficulty through the partially closed intake of the gas mask he wore.

The Combat Adaptability Test was given to the last three officer candidate classes at the Tank Destroyer School. No relationship was discovered between the test ratings and the regular OCS rating scale, or between the test and AGCT scores, age, height, weight, or education. A slight correlation was noticed with scores on the Officer Candidate Test, which was being given experimentally at this time. Since the Tank Destroyer School closed soon after the experiment was undertaken, no complete findings or revisions were possible.

Selection and Training of Tactical Officers

As the principal judge of the candidate's potential value, the tactical officer was the key figure in OCS training. He was in close daily contact with his men and was to a considerable extent the model they imitated. He had the most opportunities to observe, assess, correct, and assist the candidate. Above all, his recommendation was in the normal case tantamount to final selection or relief from the school. It followed from his strategic position that the tactical officer had to be chosen with great care. As the Infantry School's "Guide for Tactical Officers" stated:[18]

> Every man is inclined to judge others by the values he places upon himself. This makes it vital that those officers called upon to pass judgment be themselves of the highest caliber, as well as mature in judgment. Too much stress cannot be placed upon this point. . . . Since the platoon leader is the basic judge at the school, it is imperative that he be selected with care and be constantly supervised and trained.

[18] Ltr, 9 Nov 42, sub: The Rating of OCs. Infantry School *Mailing List*, XXVI (1943), 202.

Early plans for officer candidate training, which contemplated very limited operations, provided for the assignment of Regular Army men as tactical officers whenever possible. In the first five classes at the Infantry School, for example, Regular Army majors commanded candidate companies, and Regular and Reserve captains acted as platoon leaders.[19] Detail of Regular Army officers to such duty could not be continued after 1941 because of the more urgent need for them in tactical units. After 1941 the chief sources of tactical officers were the Officers' Reserve Corps and the officer candidate schools themselves, particularly the latter. To staff the greatly increased numbers of classes during 1942, hundreds of graduating candidates were detailed. One week they were being judged, the next week they were judges. The schools were careful to pick tactical officers from among the best men in a graduating class. They tried to select mature men with civilian and military experience. But there was no way of maintaining the standard originally contemplated. Maturity and experience came to repose more and more in members of the Faculty Board, who were usually older Regular Army officers with combat records in World War I. Not until 1944, when officers began to return from overseas, did the schools have large numbers of tactical officers who combined judgment and maturity with fresh knowledge of what combat required in an officer.

Little formal training for tactical officers was conducted. Since most of them were recent OCS graduates, they had a detailed familiarity with the operation of the selection system. The new tactical officer was normally assigned for a time as a supernumerary in a candidate company, to peer over a veteran's shoulder as he made out reports, listen as he interviewed candidates, and trail along as he observed the men in class and field. After this period of observation the novice was given a platoon, whenever possible in a "strong" company whose commander had a reputation for correct application of the school's standards. In addition to this on-the-job training, regular, if informal, training was administered by battalion and regimental commanders and members of the Faculty Board or OCS Department. These men, oldest at the game and the ultimate custodians of selection standards, directed the tactical officers both through regular supervision and inspection of records, procedures, and class conduct and through the criteria they applied in recommending candidates for commission. It was natural for tactical officers to build up a case for or against a candidate in terms acceptable

[19] Statement of Col R. R. Coursey, WD G–1 Div (formerly Dir of OCs, Inf Sch), to AGF Hist Off, 2 Mar 45.

to the board of officers before whom they were to present it. Finally, from time to time, tactical officers were brought together for orientation or for discussion of current problems. On the whole it does not appear that the training of tactical officers was as thorough as was called for by their general inexperience and the importance of their mission.

Factors Determining Success and Failure

Only about three-fourths of the men detailed to officer candidate schools were commissioned there. The mortality rate of 25 percent represented a heavy cost—in disappointment to men who failed and, of greater practical significance, in time, money, effort, and facilities largely wasted on men who might never have been selected for training had the conditions of success been better understood. Unfortunately, though material for investigation was ample, no comprehensive study was ever made of the causes of failure at the schools or of the relevance of standards used in the field in selecting applicants.

The principal causes of relief from officer candidate school, however, were apparently academic deficiency and lack of leadership. A few men were relieved for misconduct. Miscellaneous causes of relief included resignation, failure to meet physical standards, receipt of direct commissions, hospitalization, and death. No close comparison can be made among schools, for with the possible exception of the category "Conduct" no common definitions or standards for the categories of failure were applied at the schools. "Other Causes" was a particularly ambiguous classification. Until April 1942, failures were not classified at all. After April 1942 the category of "Other Causes" included such a diversity of cases as to preclude any precise definition. Furthermore, few failures were attributable to a single cause; they were reported in terms of the predominant cause, but methods of weighing the causes for relief varied widely.

In general, schools of those arms using a considerable amount of complex equipment and requiring mathematical ability for the solution of gunnery problems were more difficult academically; in the arms in which the platoon leader was more often required to direct the combat action of small mobile units the schools placed heavier emphasis on leadership. In the artillery schools especially, the technique of handling equipment occupied a larger proportion of time than at the Infantry and Cavalry Schools, where tactical training predominated. In a course involving a high proportion of mathematics, specific educational deficiencies, as distinguished from deficiencies in general intelligence, could more often cause failure. The strong tactical emphasis of such a course as that at the Infantry School, on the other hand, provided more opportunities for the candidate to be revealed as lacking in force, resolution, initiative, and responsibility.

In addition to the reservation made above—that no two schools defined leadership or academic proficiency in the same way—a further qualification must be made. Academic deficiency could be proved more easily than lack of leadership; it was a matter of test scores, about which argument was difficult. Some schools apparently preferred to keep a weak candidate in school and allow him to fail academically rather than to relieve him for poor leadership. In this manner they protected themselves against the complaints from families and friends that inevitably followed the relief of certain candidates.

No definitive listing can be given of the immediate causes of academic or leadership failure. Even if the schools had attached equal importance to the same qualities, a multitude of deviations from the standard would defy easy classification. Some indication of the reasons advanced for failure at one school can be given. Approximately 9,000 failures in 200 classes at the Infantry School were analyzed by the school authorities. The following deficiencies were found to be the chief causes of relief of these men:[20]

Academic Failures

1. Insufficient preparation: lack of basic education, insufficient basic training, administrative rather than military experience.

2. Inadequate application: laziness, carelessness, lack of interest.

Leadership Failures

1. Inadequate power of self-expression: lack of personal force, colorless personality.

2. Insufficient force and self-assurance: lack of self-confidence, lack of initiative, inability to make quick decisions, unwillingness to assume responsibility, timidity, lack of poise under stress.

3. Attitude: lack of effort, inattention, lack of perseverance, indifference.

4. Incapacity for teamwork: intolerance, lack of adaptability.

5. Military appearance: untidiness, lack of cleanliness, lack of coordination, stamina, and endurance.

6. Speech: crudity of speech, lack of volume and authoritative tone.

[20] Inf Sch pamphlet, undated [23 Oct 43], sub: The Selection System of the OC Course, The Inf Sch, and An Analysis of OC Failures. 314.7 (AGF Hist).

In general, men with high AGCT scores were more likely to be graduated from officer candidate school than men with low scores. Evidence on this point is clear, but it loses some of its significance because tactical officers were influenced in their judgments by the candidate's AGCT score, and because success depended in considerable measure on test grades, which were usually higher for men with higher AGCT's. In two groups of classes at the Infantry School, AGCT scores and failures were correlated as follows:[21]

AGCT Score	*Percentage of Failures*	
	Classes 253–281	*Classes 329–338*
110 or less	61.3	70
111–115	49.2	59
116–120	39.6	42
121–125	32.1	33
126–130	23.9	31
131–135	21.6	30
136–140	17.4	24
141 and over	18.4	21

Age was another factor that governed the likelihood of graduation. Most candidates during the period before mid-1944 were in their twenties. Younger candidates came to predominate in the later months of 1944, when men were drawn principally from the replacement centers. One would expect both the youngest and the oldest candidates to fail more frequently than those in the middle bracket—the youngest largely from lack of experience in dealing with men, the oldest from greater difficulty in standing the physical strain and from lack of recent educational experience. Available evidence confirms this judgment. The Infantry School reported 1,465 failures in Classes 253–281, distributed in three age groups as follows:[22]

Ages	*Percentage of Failures*
25 and under	33.5
26–30	29.7
31 and over	37.0

Chances of success or failure varied also with the sources from which candidates were drawn. In general, candidates from within the branch were more

[21] (1) Incl to personal ltr of Col Thornton Chase, Inf Sch AG, to Lt Col W. S. Renshaw, AGF G–1 Sec, 9 Aug 43. 314.7 (AGF Hist). (2) Inf Sch Classification Sec study, Jul 44, sub: OC Performance Related to AGCT Scores. Inf Sch files.

[22] See n. 21 (1).

successful than those from other branches; candidates from replacement training centers more successful than those from troop units. ROTC students were generally more successful than volunteer officer candidates (VOC's); VOC's more successful than regular enlisted candidates. These generalizations, like those above, are based, to be sure, on only partial data.

The fullest study that has been made concerns the operation of the Antiaircraft Artillery School. During its span of operation this school received 33,195 candidates, of whom 25,220 graduated. Performance by component was as follows:[23]

Component	*Graduated*		*Relieved*	
	Number	*Percent*	*Number*	*Percent*
ROTC	1,564	85.2	271	14.8
VOC	2,292	79.5	591	20.5
Enlisted	21,364	75.0	7,113	25.0
TOTAL	25,220	76.0	7,975	24.0

Men from different sources performed as follows:

Source	*Graduated*		*Relieved*	
	Number	*Percent*	*Number*	*Percent*
ROTC	1,564	85.2	271	14.8
CA Units not Stationed at AATC's	4,109	82.0	907	18.0

In classes 253–281 at the Infantry School, failures were distributed according to the source of candidates as follows: [24]

Source	*Graduated*		*Relieved*	
	Number	*Percent*	*Number*	*Percent*
ROTC	237	75.8	76	24.2
Infantry	2,139	72.3	820	27.7
ASF	303	53.7	262	46.3
AAF	231	50.2	229	49.8
Other Branches in AGF than Infantry	66	45.8	78	54.2
TOTAL	2,976	67.1	1,465	32.9

[23] (1) AAA School, OC Div Final Statistical Rpt, 15 Jun 44. AA Comd files. (2) These figures differ slightly from those shown in the chart in this study, and in Table No. 2 of the study, "The Procurement of Officers," in this volume. The figures in the chart and table were compiled from reports by classes of EM graduates and from the monthly reports of ROTC graduates in the files of the Adjutant General's Office.

[24] Incl to personal ltr of Col Thornton Chase, Inf Sch AG, to Lt Col W. S. Renshaw, AGF G–1 Sec, 9 Aug 43. 314.7 (AGF Hist).

A survey of another block of students at the Infantry School (1,419 men in Classes 294–300, September 1943) showed that 60.7 percent graduated, 31.9 percent failed, and 7.4 percent were turned back. Of the men from infantry divisions and replacement training centers, 70.9 percent were graduated, as compared with only 44.2 percent of men from other branches (including 42.3 percent of those from Army Air Forces). In this group, ROTC students as a whole fared much better than men from all other sources—74.3 percent graduating as against 60.5 percent from other sources.[25]

ROTC candidates showed a higher rate of graduation than did men without ROTC training. A tabulation made in May 1944 by the Office of the Executive for Reserve and ROTC Affairs disclosed that, during the period from 1 June 1942 to 21 April 1944, of 9,261 ROTC candidates entering AGF officer candidate schools, 7,565, or 81.7 percent, graduated. During the comparable period, June 1942 through April 1944, 137,513 candidates from other sources (exclusive of turnbacks) entered AGF officer candidate schools; of these, 103,602, or 75.3 percent, graduated.[26]

Among ROTC candidates those from the Junior Division (from preparatory schools and junior colleges) were less likely to graduate than those from the Senior Division. In Classes 128–335 at the Infantry School, 646 candidates from the ROTC Junior Division entered; 263, or 40.7 percent, graduated with their class, and 48, or 7.3 percent, were turned back. In these same classes, 5,905 candidates from the ROTC Senior Division entered; 4,103, or 69.8 percent, graduated with their class, and 240, or 4.1 percent, were turned back.[27]

Although superior in academic performance, ROTC candidates were more likely to fail for lack of leadership qualities than men drawn from other sources. In the period from June 1942 through April 1944, approximately 12.0 percent of the ROTC candidates who entered AGF officer candidate schools failed for lack of leadership, whereas only 6.7 percent of the candidates from other sources failed for this reason.[28] This higher rate of failure among ROTC candidates in meeting tests of capacity for leadership is traceable to several causes. ROTC

[25] Inf Sch Classification Sec study, Dec 43, sub: Study of OCs. Inf Sch files.

[26] (1) Table, WD Office of the Executive for Reserve and ROTC Affairs, sub: Comparative Mortality among OCs, 29 May 44. 314.7 (AGF Hist). (2) Figures compiled in Hist Div, WDSS, from Consolidated Reports of Officer Candidate Schools, Grd Stat Sec, Hq AGF.

[27] Report of ROTC graduates and nongraduates, OC Cl 128 through OC Cl 335 (21 Sep 42–4 Jul 44), Infantry School. AGF G–3 Sec files.

[28] Sources cited in n. 26 above.

candidates as a group were younger than regular enlisted candidates and were penalized for their "immaturity." It was somewhat illogical to admit immature candidates to officer candidate school and then hold their lack of experience against them. ROTC candidates had on the whole received less practical military experience than enlisted candidates, even though most had gone through a replacement training center. Leadership had been a critical factor in the selection of enlisted candidates to attend officer candidate school, but ROTC men had not been screened for leadership to the same extent or on the same basis during their ROTC course.

Candidates from replacement training centers were in general more successful at the officer candidate schools than were men sent from units. The regular turnover of personnel in the replacement training centers ensured a constantly refreshed supply of representative selectees, with a relatively fixed proportion of men in the various intelligence brackets. If a large number of candidates was assigned to school, new arrivals at the replacement training center would replenish the supply of qualified men before another quota had to be met. In units, after considerable numbers of candidates had been sent, as in 1942, the quality of the remaining men was not so easily made up. Some fillers came from replacement training centers, and these had already been screened for officer candidates. Unit commanders, looking toward combat, were naturally reluctant to send their best men off to school and face the prospect of training inadequate substitutes.

The superior record of candidates from replacement training centers was due also to more efficient screening methods used there. The large quotas available to replacement training centers enabled them to convene selection boards at regular and frequent intervals. Officers assigned to these boards became experienced in selection; with much practice, interviewing and rating procedures were refined. With smaller quotas more irregularly allotted, units did not have an opportunity to develop as much skill in selection. A third factor contributing to the success of RTC candidates was the special preparatory schools operated in most centers from late 1942 until the spring of 1943. The results of these differences were striking. At the Field Artillery School, for example, the record of candidates in Classes 23–32 was as follows:[29]

Source	*Total Enrolled*	*Failures*	*Percentage Failing*
RTC's	1,118	71	6.35
Units	3,778	626	16.53

[29] AGF M/S (C), G–1 to CofS, 8 Mar 43, sub: OCSs. 352/60 (C).

In the first sixty-four classes at the Infantry School (approximately 13,000 men), only 6 percent of candidates from infantry and branch immaterial replacement training centers failed to graduate; the average percentage of failure for classes as a whole—most of the remaining men were from units—was 17 percent during this period.[30]

[30] Memo of Col Thornton Chase, Inf Sch AG, for Col C. K. Krams, R&SC G–1, 25 Sep 42. R&SC files, OCS Gen #1.

II. Modifications of the Officer Candidate Program, 1942-45

The tremendous expansion of officer candidate schools in 1942, and a resulting sharp decline in the quality of candidates, confronted the schools with a dilemma. The selection of inferior candidates for officer training forced the adoption of special measures to weed out the undesirable and unfit. But since demand was great and supply of even poorly qualified candidates none too abundant, the schools had to seek ways of squeezing the maximum number of graduates from the material at hand. Among the devices used to eliminate the obviously unfit were retests on the Army General Classification Test and various locally prepared qualifying examinations. The chief measures used to qualify weak or inexperienced candidates were the preparatory schools and the turnback policy.

Introduction of Tests

In the fall of 1942 it became a regular practice at the Infantry School to administer the AGCT to all incoming candidates, even though their records showed that they had previously achieved a score of at least 110 on the test. The school was convinced that the test was often improperly administered in the field and that scores were being juggled to get men into officer candidate school.[1] Although many men scored less than 110 on the retest, Army regulations prevented their relief before one-third of the course had been completed. Tactical officers and the Faculty Board watched such men more closely, and they were usually relieved from the school. Other schools administered AGCT retests only when they suspected the authenticity of a candidate's recorded score.

Several schools developed screening tests designed to locate candidates whose educational qualifications were insufficient to enable them to complete the course or to perform satisfactorily as officers. No general educational quali-

[1] Statement of Maj F. C. Ash, AGF G-1 Sec (formerly Inf Sch AG Sec), to AGF Hist Off, 20 Feb 45.

fication was ever set by the War Department or by Army Ground Forces. In practice the schools faced a hard fact: many candidates lacked the educational equipment to cope with the material—especially the mathematics—of the courses. The Field Artillery School developed an Arithmetic Qualifying Examination designed to screen out men with too little mathematical ability.[2] In the fall of 1942 the Infantry School adopted a basic education test, covering reading, grammar, spelling, geography, and arithmetic, given in the reception unit when the candidate arrived. Although the test was extremely simple, the number and type of errors made by candidates cast doubt on the ability of many men to extract meaning from field manuals, formulate and issue orders, conduct clear instruction, and solve the mathematical problems that a platoon leader would encounter.[3] Deficiencies in arithmetic revealed by the test were so striking that a mathematical examination, called the Platoon Leader's Computations Test, was made a regular part of the Infantry OCS course in 1943. The Armored School in 1942 adopted a basic education test embracing grammar, geography, and current events.[4]

By use of such tests the schools protected themselves against extreme variability resulting primarily from the absence of measures to eliminate unfit candidates at the source. The schools were not permitted to relieve candidates merely on the basis of failure to pass an educational screening test. But the adoption of such tests reflected a disposition to unload at the earliest opportunity men who could not pass them. Such candidates were watched more closely and it was usually found that their subsequent performance tallied with their low screening test scores. In effect, the same result was achieved as if candidates had been subjected to similar screening in units. Had this been done, the time and expense of sending educationally unqualified men to school might have been saved, and greater uniformity might have been achieved through use of a single test prepared by experts.

Preparatory Schools

Officer candidate schools in 1942 were handicapped not only by basically inferior candidates but also by the presence of men who were merely inexperi-

[2] FA Sch 2d ind, 1 Dec 42, on AGF ltr to CG R&SC, 18 Nov 42, sub: Visit of Dr. James Grafton Rogers to FA Sch. 095 (Rogers, J G).

[3] Inf Sch study, Tabulation of Performance of Candidates on the TIS Test, 1943. Filed in Office of the Secretary, Inf Sch.

[4] Statement of Maj Combatalade, Chief Gen Tng Sec, OCS Dept, Armd Sch, to AGF Hist Off, 21 Mar 45.

enced, slow, immature, or lacking in basic training. To conserve and ultimately to commission as many of these man as possible, two special devices were employed—preparatory schools and the turnback policy.

When, in 1942, RTC commanders were authorized to retain OCS applicants up to 15 percent of training center capacity for thirty days to receive special instruction, OCS preparatory schools were established in the replacement training centers of each arm.[5] During a 4-week course the applicants were taught weapons, small-unit tactics, map reading, drill, and other subjects stressed in officer candidate school. Special attention was given to inspections and to practice in giving commands. Men who failed the course were not selected for officer candidate school. In December 1942 the commandants of the Infantry, Cavalry, and Tank Destroyer Schools were authorized to send to the preparatory schools at the nearest replacement training center candidates from other branches who lacked basic training in their new arm. This measure enabled potentially good candidates from other branches to compete at officer candidate school on equal terms with men from within the branch served by the school.[6]

The candidate schools conducted their own preparatory instruction. Before preparatory courses were started at replacement training centers the Field Artillery School, in September 1942, inaugurated a Salvage School for candidates reporting to officer candidate school with inadequate artillery training and for men encountering difficulty during the regular officer candidate course. The Salvage School course, lasting four weeks, taught basic mathematics, gun drill, fire control instruments, and fire direction procedure. It was found that by putting through this course transferees from other branches, together with candidates from artillery units whose duties had been largely administrative, the pace of instruction in the regular officer candidate course could be maintained and a higher proportion of graduates ensured.[7] At the Antiaircraft Artillery School a Special Training Battery was set up to give two weeks of drill, discipline, and basic training to men deficient in command ability. Men were normally detailed to this battery after their weaknesses had been revealed in the regular course.[8]

[5] AGF 1st ind, 24 Nov 42, on R&SC ltr, 18 Nov 42, sub: Instructor Pers for Offs' Pool Sch and OCS Preparatory Sch, FA RTC. 352/108 (FA OCS).

[6] (1) R&SC ltr to CGs, 31 Dec 42, sub: Preliminary Tng for OCS. R&SC files, OCS Gen. (2) WD Memo W350-56-43, 13 Mar 43, sub: Guide for OCS Applicants and OCS Examining Bds, pars 24, 32, 38, 57. 352/424 (OCS).

[7] "History of the Field Artillery School," n. 832. Draft copy in files of FA Sch.

[8] Statement of Lt Col D. F. Sellards, S-3 AAA Sch, to AGF Hist Off, 17 Mar 45.

230-171 O - 66 - 24

After April 1943 the OCS program was greatly curtailed and it seemed no longer necessary to give special attention to the preliminary training of candidates. Preparatory schools at the replacement training centers were closed down.[9] But they had served a useful purpose. Maj. Gen. Harold R. Bull, Commanding General of the Replacement and School Command, summarized the benefits that had been derived from the preparatory schools as follows: "... men are better prepared to undertake the course, have a uniform background, and those weak in leadership are weeded out, thus protecting school capacity."[10]

The Turnback Policy

During 1941 and the early months of 1942, when the need for officers was not acute and the supply of applicants for officer candidate school far exceeded training capacities, a candidate judged lacking in academic or leadership ability was relieved, and he was not given a chance to redeem himself. So many applicants were waiting for the opportunity to enter officer candidate school that it was both unnecessary and unfair to nurse along a weak candidate. As the demand for officers mounted and the supply dwindled, it appeared that some deficient candidates might be salvaged if they were given a chance to repeat all or part of the course. Some men lacked experience, others lacked basic training, and some men had been away from school for so long that they could not keep up with the class. The principle followed by the schools in regard to such men was enunciated by the Chief of Field Artillery in January 1942: no man who showed "reasonable prospect" of developing into a satisfactory officer should be dismissed prior to completion of the prescribed course.[11]

The number of turnbacks became tremendous.[12] At the Antiaircraft Artillery School 5,847 students, 23.6 percent of the enrollment, were turned back in 1943; at the Field Artillery School, 3,694, 22.1 percent of the enrollment; and at the Infantry School, 2,683, 8.6 percent of the enrollment. The numbers turned back

[9] (1) R&SC ltr to CGs RTCs, 27 Apr 43, sub: Discontinuance of OC Preparatory Schs. R&SC files, 352 (Sch Gen) #1. (2) R&SC ltr to TAG, 30 Apr 43, sub: Change on WD Memo W350–56–43. 352/424 (OCS).

[10] R&SC 1st ind, 1 Dec 42, on AGF ltr to CG R&SC, 18 Nov 42, sub: Visit of Dr. James Grafton Rogers to FA Sch. 095/41 (Rogers, J G).

[11] Office CofFA ltr to Comdt FA Sch, 8 Jan 42, sub: Turnback of OCs. R&SC files, OCS Gen #1. See also par 11 (3), Cir 126, WD, 28 Apr 42.

[12] Statistics in this paragraph were derived from Consolidated Reports of Officer Candidate Schools, AGF Statistics Section. They do not include ROTC candidates.

were smaller at the other schools, where the demand for quantity production was less acute. Between July 1942, when a separate account began to be taken of turnbacks, and January 1945, about 15 percent of the candidates enrolled were turned back as indicated below:

School	*Number of Turnbacks*	*Enrollment (Less Turnbacks)*
Antiaircraft Artillery	8,158	28,244
Armored	923	7,902
Cavalry	180	2,475
Coast Artillery	57	1,751
Field Artillery	4,351	23,076
Infantry	4,417	52,979
Tank Destroyer	400	5,954
TOTAL	18,486	122,381

It is impossible to determine what proportion of these 18,486 men were commissioned after their second (or, in some cases, third) try at the course. Detailed figures are available only from the Infantry School. There it was found that the proportion of turnbacks graduating was generally similar to the proportion of all graduates in classes leaving the school in the same period. Candidates turned back in Classes 10–300 graduated as follows:[13]

Class Number	*Percentage of Graduates*
10 – 38	80.5
39 – 67	92.4
68 – 85A	93.5
89 – 116	81.4
119 – 139	69.6
140 – 162A	80.8
163 – 186	66.6
187 – 206	69.0
207 – 227	82.3
229 – 249	53.2
251 – 276	50.7
277 – 300	53.2

Three classes at the Infantry School consisted entirely of turnbacks. Class No. 273, made up of 254 turnbacks, graduated only 30.3 percent, the lowest percentage in the history of the school. Classes 290 and 293 graduated 58.3 and 44.4 percent respectively.[14]

[13] Incl 3 to Inf Sch ltr to CG R&SC, 10 Aug 44, sub: Selection of OCs. AGF G–1 Sec files (Renshaw).

[14] Analysis of Inf Sch OC Classes 1–408. 314.7 (AGF Hist).

If 50 percent of the candidates turned back were commissioned, the Army gained 9,000 officers who would have been lost had there been no turnback policy and had no better candidates been available. The crux of the matter was in the availability of suitable material. When good candidates were plentiful the turnback policy was wasteful, expensive, and discriminatory. It prolonged candidate training by from one to four months; it greatly increased the cost of producing a second lieutenant; it absorbed facilities that might have been devoted to training a first-rate candidate; and it did not ensure the graduation of even a majority of those turned back. The policy was justified only by sheer necessity.

Proposed Revision of Procedures for Selecting Candidates

The deterioration in the quality of officer candidates during 1942 had effects more far-reaching than the institution of the correctives discussed above. Because of the officer shortage, the prevailing theory of officer recruitment was modified to permit the commissioning of volunteers from deferred classes under Selective Service and of candidates regarded as suitable for the performance of administrative duties only. In this way large officer demands were more nearly met.

Recommendations for major changes in the procedures used in selecting candidates were put forward by The Inspector General in January 1943. Inspection of nine schools, of which five were in the combat arms, had led The Inspector General to the conclusion that "during recent months, there has been a definite decline in the quality of candidates." The success of school operations was being compromised by the low quality of candidates as reflected in increasing percentages of failures and turnbacks. The Inspector General noted that "a substantial portion" of failures and turnbacks consisted of men whose AGCT scores were only a few points above the 110 minimum; that the educational requirement was too loosely drawn, since the mere possession of a college degree—in art appreciation, for example—did not promise likelihood of success in a candidate course; that men sent to a school of another branch were severely handicapped by lack of proper basic training, as were also men whose experience within their own branch had been mainly clerical; and that many candidates were given no opportunity to develop and demonstrate leadership ability before they went to school. In view of these conditions, The Inspector General recommended several methods of raising the quality of candidates and tightening the selection process. The minimum AGCT score was to be raised to 115.

"Substantiating examinations" were to be prepared at each school to measure, in borderline cases, "the minimum adequacy of candidates' educational (or equivalent) background." All schools were to establish preparatory courses to give basic instruction to candidates who had had no basic training in the branch. Commanders were "to take active steps" to ensure that potential candidates had ample opportunity to develop and demonstrate leadership qualities.[15] Some of these measures, as already indicated, had been adopted piecemeal at certain schools.

Army Ground Forces opposed all The Inspector General's recommendations. Raising the AGCT score requirement, it was felt, might eliminate many candidates with good leadership qualities but little education. School tests were held unnecessary, not only because borderline cases could be rejected without further examinations, but also because such tests would place an additional administrative burden on the schools. Army Ground Forces no longer favored preparatory schools for candidates lacking proper basic training. The number of men who would fall in this category was not expected to be large enough under greatly reduced candidate quotas to justify the time, expense, and overhead for such special training. New pressure on unit commanders to select candidates who had demonstrated leadership was thought unnecessary in view of the great reduction in the number of candidates that units were now required to furnish; the selection standards would be self-correcting under conditions of severe retrenchment.

As an alternative to the policy recommended by The Inspector General, which would have improved the quality of candidates by refining the selection system, Army Ground Forces advocated improving the officer material available to the ground arms. Headquarters, Army Ground Forces, believed that it was essential for the ground arms to receive a larger share of Class I and Class II men (those whose AGCT scores were 110 or higher), in order to provide ample leadership not only in commissioned but also in noncommissioned and enlisted specialist positions. The diversion of high intelligence inductees to the Air Forces, together with the siphoning of Class I and Class II men out of the Ground Forces into the Army Specialized Training Program, made it necessary to take steps to obtain the allotment of sufficient numbers of high-quality personnel to the ground arms.[16] Nothing came of The Inspector General's

[15] TIG memo (C) IG 352.4 (OCS) (1–26–43) for ACofS G–1 WD, 26 Jan 43, sub: OCSs. 352/60 (C).

[16] (1) AGF memo (C) for ACofS G–1 WD, 14 Mar 43, sub: OCSs. (2) AGF M/Ss, G–1, G–3, AG, various dates, Feb and Mar 43, sub as in (1). Both in 352/60 (C).

recommendations. The War Department issued special instructions to ensure every candidate's completing basic training before going to school.[17]

Extension of the OCS Course to Seventeen Weeks

Instead of adopting The Inspector General's recommendation, an effort was made to improve the quality of graduates by lengthening the OCS course. The proposal to extend the course came from Army Service Forces, which recommended a 4-month (17-week) period.[18] The War Department looked with favor on the proposal, as did also the Replacement and School Command.[19] Headquarters, Army Ground Forces, opposed the extension because of its inveterate view that, beyond minimum technical training in the schools, officers were best trained in units, where responsibilities of troop training would develop whatever leadership qualities the officer had. Army Ground Forces agreed that the school training of officers would be improved by a longer course and that initially the new second lieutenant might be a better qualified instructor in certain subjects. But it viewed with disfavor a plan that would delay the moment when the officer would be thrown upon his own resources in a unit. Furthermore, it saw no reason why all OCS courses should be of the same length. Since their mission was primarily to give basic technical and tactical training, they might reasonably vary in length as the subject matters of the several arms varied in difficulty. The antiaircraft officer candidate course had already been extended to seventeen weeks, and proposals for a similar increase in armored officer candidate training were under consideration. Army Ground Forces saw an additional reason for rejecting the 4-month plan in the fact that the officer candidate course was not the whole of an officer's schooling. After a suitable period of troop duty the officer would be returned to school, if he was qualified, for an advanced general or technical course.[20] On 18 May 1943 the War Department decided in favor of the original ASF proposal and directed that all OCS courses be extended to a minimum of four months by 1 July.[21]

[17] WD Memo W625–4–43, 13 Apr 43, sub: OCS Applicants. 352/434 (OCS).

[18] WD SOS memo SPTRS 352.11 (OCS) (23 Apr 43) to ACofS G–3 WD, 23 Apr 43, sub: Increase in Length of OC Course. 352/440 (OCS).

[19] (1) WD memo WDGCT 352 OCS (4–23–43) to CG AGF, 24 Apr 43, sub: Increase in Length of OC Courses. (2) AGF M/R, Tab C, tel conv between Col Shaw, AGF, and Col Shallene, R&SC, 29 Apr 43. Both in 352/440 (OCS).

[20] (1) AGF memo for CofS USA, 9 May 43, sub: Increase in Length of OC Courses. (2) AGF M/S, G–3 to CofS, 30 Apr 43, sub as in (1). Both in 352/440 (OCS).

[21] WD memo WDGCT 352 OCS (4–23–43) for CGs, 18 May 43, sub as in n. 20 (1). 352/440 (OCS)

Seeking to salvage as much of its original scheme as possible, Army Ground Forces directed its school commands to draw up courses that would emphasize practical instruction and technique and reduce theoretical instruction to a minimum.[22]

The programs of instruction submitted by the schools to cover the extended training period revealed considerable variation, both in total length and in treatment of common general subjects. Courses varied in length from 782 hours (Coast Artillery) to 852 hours (Tank Destroyer). Army Ground Forces directed that all courses be 816 hours in length, the correct total for seventeen 48-hour weeks. The following tabulation indicates the wide variety of ways in which certain subjects common to all branches were treated in the programs submitted:

	Schools					
Subject	*TD*	*Cav (M)*	*Cav (H)*	*FA*	*CA*	*Inf*
Administration	31	17	16	7½	30	17
Military Law	10	5	5	4½	0	0
First Aid	8	4	4	3	6	6
Defense against Chemical Attack	7	9	9	0	7½	3
Methods of Instruction	6	18	14	7	0	13
Safeguarding Military Information	0	4	4	0	0	0
Reserved Time	47	73	71	Indef.	Indef.	50

It was unlikely on the face of it that a tank destroyer officer needed four times as much instruction in company administration as did a field artillery officer. If a cavalry officer required some instruction in military law, so too did an infantry officer. While some Reserved Time was useful in giving the program flexibility, it was doubtful that the cavalry course needed nearly twice the flexibility required by the tank destroyer course. Army Ground Forces directed that all programs be reviewed to equalize the time spent on such common courses as those listed above.[23] The Replacement and School Command worked out a list of common subjects and directed their inclusion in the programs of all officer candidate schools under its control. The list totaled 140 hours, or approximately one-sixth of the course:[24]

[22] AGF ltr to CG R&SC, 28 May 43, sub as in n. 20 (1). Same ltr to Armd F. 352/440 (OCS).

[23] (1) AGF M/S, G–3 to CofS, 26 Jun 43, sub: Increase in Length of OCS Courses. (2) AGF 2d ind, 27 Jun 43, to CG R&SC on programs of instruction submitted 12 Jun 43 by R&SC. (3) 17-week OCS programs. All in 352/440 (OCS).

[24] R&SC ltr to Comdts Inf, Cav, FA, CA, and TD Schs, 6 Jul 43, sub: Increase in Length of OCS Courses. AGF G–3 Schs Br files, OCS Gen/46.

Subject	*Hours*
Classification Procedure	1
Company Administration (including Mess Management)	16
Defense against Chemical Attack	4
Elementary Map and Aerial Photograph Reading (including Foreign Maps)	30
Leadership and Morale	2
Methods of Aircraft Identification	1
Methods of Armored Vehicle Identification	1
Methods of Instruction	10
Military Censorship	2
Military Courtesy and Discipline (including Customs of the Service)	3
Military Law (including Court-Martial Procedure)	4
Military Sanitation and First Aid	8
Mines and Booby Traps (except at Coast Artillery School)	16
Organization of the Army	1
Physical Training	34
Safeguarding Military Information	2
Special Service Activities	1
Training Management	4

Proposals for a 6-Month OCS Course

While the schools were getting under way with the new 17-week course, a proposal to extend officer candidate training to six months was being studied. Put forward by G–1 of the War Department and concurred in by Army Service Forces, which wished part of the 6-month training to be conducted at a single basic school for candidates of all branches, the proposal was strongly opposed by Army Ground Forces. An AGF study was produced for the War Department to show that probable additions to the 17-week programs would not improve the quality of new officers. The study indicated that adding two months to the course would result in increasing by one-third the subjects adequately covered in the current programs (tactics and weapons), and in adding physical drill and open time to keep the candidate in condition; no new subjects would be added since all those pertinent to officer training were already included in the courses. Army Ground Forces reiterated its views on officer training: to a minimum of technical instruction should be added service with troops, where the habits of leadership and command could be developed. Comments of overseas commanders on the performance of junior officers were cited to show that technical training had not been criticized. Only leadership, which Army Ground

Forces felt could not be improved by lengthening school courses, had been questioned.[25]

Army Ground Forces had barely finished its rebuttal of this proposal when it was invited to consider another scheme for amplifying officer candidate training. G–1 of the War Department put forward on 1 September 1943 a detailed plan for giving six months' training: the first thirteen weeks in a basic course for candidates of Air, Ground, and Service Forces to be conducted at Fort Benning; the remainder in specialized branch courses at the existing candidate schools. G–1 believed that such a program would produce better-qualified officers by increasing instruction in common basic subjects, subjecting all candidates to more uniform standards, and enhancing the candidate's readiness for specialized instruction. The basic course was to include the following:

Subjects	*Hours*
Weapons: Technique	144
Tactical Employment	78
Tactics: Company and Higher Units, including Staff Procedure	87
General Subjects Common to all Branches	231
Administration: Processing, Boards, Organization, Graduation	48
Unscheduled Time	52
TOTAL	640

To meet the AGF objections to six months of training for candidates, G–1 pointed to the fact that "no emergency exists at present which would require the shortening of officer candidate school courses."[26]

Army Ground Forces sought once more to make clear its views on the education of officers. General McNair stated to G–1 that candidate training in wartime "should be as brief as practicable, and limited to sound basic training and technical and tactical training sufficient to enable the young officer to join a training unit and render reasonably effective service." The training of any officer did not cease with his graduation from a candidate school; it continued while the officer performed his regular duty in a unit. Indeed, this schooling on the job was the most important part of his education because it was practical.

[25] (1) AGF memo for CofS USA, 11 Aug 43, sub as in n. 24. 352/20 (OCS)(S). (2) AGF M/S, G–3 Misc Div to G–3, 30 Jul 43, sub: Conference at WD Concerning Extension of OCS Course to Six Months. (3) AGF memo for CofS USA, undated, but about 6 Aug 43, sub: Increase in Length of OCS Courses. Not Sent. Both (2) and (3) in AGF G–3 Schs Br files, OCS Gen/47.

[26] WD D/F WDGAP 352 OCS (C) to CG AGF, 4 Sep 43, sub: Plan for Centralized Basic OC Tng at the Inf Sch, Ft Benning, Ga. With incls. 352/21 (OCS)(S).

Refresher and advanced training followed after the officer acquired enough experience to benefit from it. General McNair found the proposed scheme undesirable on other grounds also. The mobilization of the Army was nearly complete and it seemed fruitless to revise radically the plan for officer training at so late a date. The proposal would increase overhead, already absorbing more than 80,000 officers and enlisted men in Army Ground Forces. Curtailment, not expansion, was in order. He believed that most candidates in 1944 would be drawn from the ROTC: the few enlisted men would be more carefully screened than ever before. Expanded training was therefore less necessary than in the past.[27]

No action was taken by the War Department, but the extension scheme remained a live issue. By the end of November 1943 the Acting Chief of Staff of the War Department had tentatively approved a plan similar to that put forward in September: three months of basic officer training at the Infantry School and three months of branch training. The attitude of Army Ground Forces had not changed. The plan was considered undesirable for the following reasons: It would divide the responsibility for officer training between the Infantry School and the branch schools; it would increase the number of men to be trained at Fort Benning without corresponding reductions elsewhere, thereby increasing overhead requirements; and it would throw all candidates into a common pool from which Army Ground Forces might have difficulty getting its own men back. Since mobilization was "over-complete" in officers, of whom approximately 30,000 were now surplus in the ground arms alone, it seemed futile to embark on a new plan for officer training. "The crying need," General McNair observed, "is to improve the officers already available in superabundant numbers."[28]

Developments in 1944–45

The increased officer requirements resulting from accelerated operations in Europe during 1944 were not uniformly distributed among the ground combat arms. They were concentrated primarily in the Infantry and, to a lesser extent, in the Field Artillery. Beginning in October 1944 the Infantry School substantially expanded its enrollment of officer candidates; during the first

[27] (1) AGF memo (S) for CofS USA (G–1 Div), 10 Sep 43, sub as in n. 26. 352/21 (OCS)(S). (2) AGF M/S (C), G–1 to G–3, G–3 to CofS, 6–9 Sep 43, sub as in n. 26. 352/21 (OCS)(S). (3) Draft, AGF memo for CofS USA, undated, but about 4 Sep 43, sub as in n. 26. AGF G–3 Schs Br files, OCS Gen/52.

[28] AGF memo (S) for CofS USA, 11 Dec 43, sub: OCS. 352/21 (OCS)(S).

eight months of 1945 the Infantry School graduated 8,521 candidates, more than twice the number graduated in the corresponding months of 1944. The Field Artillery Officer Candidate School continued to operate until the end of the war, although on a reduced level. On the other hand, the requirements for antiaircraft, coast artillery, cavalry, and tank destroyer officers were so low in relation to the supply available that the officer candidate schools of these arms were suspended in the spring of 1944. It was anticipated that armored officers would be needed in somewhat larger numbers, but suspension of the Armored Officer Candidate School was planned for September.

By September 1944 the estimates of officer requirements made earlier in the year had been found too low. Future needs for armored officers were too great to permit closing the Armored School, and it became necessary to resume the production of cavalry and tank destroyer officers. The numbers required were too small to justify the expense and overhead necessary to reopen the Cavalry and Tank Destroyer Officer Candidate Schools. Since the Armored School was in operation and since the training of armored, mechanized cavalry, and tank destroyer officers had so many common features, it was decided to train officers of all these arms at the Armored School. The consolidated program went into effect in November 1944. Candidates of the three arms were admitted in the following proportions: Armored, 40 percent; Tank Destroyer, 15 percent; and Cavalry, 45 percent.[29] The program provided for twelve weeks of common training and five weeks of branch instruction. The breakdown of hours was as follows:[30]

Subject	*Common Training*	*Branch Training*
Drill and Discipline	99	...
General Subjects	52½	...
Tactics	129	108
Communications	42	...
Motors, Wheeled	50	...
Motors, Full Track	...	46
Gunnery	136	94
Instructor Training	33	...
Orientation	17	...
Reserved Time	9½	...
TOTAL	568	248

[29] (1) AGF memo (S) for TAG, 6 Sep 44, sub: AGF OCS Quotas. 352/105 (OCS)(S). (2) WD ltr (C) AGOT–S–A 352 (20 Sep 44) to CG AGF, 26 Sep 44, sub: OCS Capacities. 352/342 (C).

[30] R&SC "Program of Instruction for OCS (Consolidated Mechanized Cav, Armd, and TD)," 20 Oct 44. 314.7 (AGF Hist).

An important development in the officer candidate system was a change in the method of selecting candidates for admission. The educational test proposed in 1941 was developed by the Personnel Research Section of the Adjutant General's Office. Known as the Officer Candidate Test, it was first given experimentally at the Tank Destroyer, Armored, and perhaps other schools in the fall of 1943. In the summer of 1944 the test was ready for general use. An Army Regulation of 12 September 1944 required that it be administered at replacement training centers and elsewhere to candidates for admission whenever possible; but it was not until February 1945 that the test came into universal use in the selection of candidates.[31]

No substantial changes were made in the conduct of officer candidate instruction during the last year of the war. The quality of instruction suffered somewhat from accelerated rotation and the inexperience in teaching of instructors who had been returned from overseas. Deterioration in instruction, however, was offset by standardization in method and by the system of schools for instructors which was introduced into the service schools. While no important changes in courses were made, certain emphases were introduced in the officer candidate school courses, as in others, in response to the current needs of the war. Thus additional stress was placed on physical hardening in view of the severe combat conditions experienced by junior officers in the field, and in the spring and summer of 1945 training was oriented more and more toward the war against Japan.

Despite continued agitation by Army Service Forces for an extension of the OCS course to six months, the length of the course was limited until V-J Day to seventeen weeks. Army Ground Forces maintained consistently the position that officer candidate schools provided only the initial and individual phase of officer training; the final and perhaps decisive training experience came only with the assignment of OCS graduates to unit command. While AGF officer candidate schools fulfilled an indispensable mission, becoming the main source of junior officers, it was the combination of school and unit training that produced the successful junior officer for the ground combat arms in World War II.

[31] (1) AR 625-5, 12 Sep 44. (2) Sec III, Cir 468, WD, 13 Dec 44.

The Training of Enlisted Replacements

by

William R. Keast

Contents

Table

I. The Initial Role and Organization of Replacement Training Centers

At the beginning of 1940 the only establishments in the U.S. Army providing military training for individuals over any considerable period were the General and Special Service Schools, small organizations designed to furnish advanced and specialist training to a limited corps of key individuals, enlisted and commissioned. The much larger task of providing basic military training for all soldiers on their induction into the Army was handled by units of the field forces. In 1940 the War Department adopted a revolutionary plan for the conduct of basic training: the establishment of special training organizations, known as replacement training centers. [1]

For the anticipated large influx of citizen soldiers, mass production was to be attained by rotating them in successive cycles through replacement training centers which would be devoted solely to individual basic and basic specialist military training. The mission of these training centers was to provide a steady flow of trained men to tactical units, relieving such units during mobilization of the burden of conducting individual training and enabling them to remain effective during combat despite large losses.

The center system of training was put into effect in March 1941. Twelve centers began operation: 3 Coast Artillery, 1 Armored, 1 Cavalry, 3 Field Artillery, and 4 Infantry. During the remainder of 1941 they trained over 200,000 replacements for the ground arms. [2]

After the declaration of war in December 1941 two requirements would have to be met if the replacement centers were to fulfill their intended mission. One was to supply fillers (often called "filler replacements") to occupy initial vacancies in units being activated or brought to war strength. The other was to

[1] A more detailed discussion of the origin and development of the replacement training centers will be found above in the study "The Provision of Enlisted Replacements."

[2] For statistics of AGF replacement production, see the tables in "The Provision of Enlisted Replacements."

230-171 O - 66 - 25

provide loss replacements for units already in training and for units engaged in combat. But after Pearl Harbor, the replacement centers were not expanded to capacities sufficient for the conduct of basic training for both purposes. The limited capacity of replacement centers was reserved primarily for the training of loss replacements, cadres, and cadre equivalents. The normal method of filling up newly activated units was to assign inductees to them directly from reception centers, giving them their basic training after they had joined their unit.[3]

Control of Replacement Training Centers

Both types of individual training organizations—the special service schools and the replacement training centers—were controlled originally by the separate chiefs of branches in the War Department. The chiefs of the four statutory ground arms and the Armored Force were responsible for the activation and constitution of their respective replacement centers and for the preparation and supervision of their training programs. For direct supply and administration the installations were served by the corps area where they were located. Final action on the allotment and assignment of overhead personnel and capacities, and on the allocation and shipment of trainees and students, was effected by the War Department through The Adjutant General on the basis of recommendations made by the offices of the chiefs of arms.

When, on 9 March 1942, the Army Ground Forces was created as the major command responsible for the preparation of the ground forces for combat, it fell heir to most of the functions of the Chiefs of Infantry, Field Artillery, Cavalry, and Coast Artillery,[4] and in addition was given the responsibility for replacement training in the new quasi arms—Armored, Antiaircraft Artillery, and Tank Destroyer. Major decisions of policy with respect to the number of replacements to be trained, the branch distribution of RTC capacity, and the assignment of personnel to and from the centers remained with the War Department. Army Ground Forces made no effort to enlarge its power over replacement matters, insisting that its function should be limited to training and that the War Department or the Services of Supply (later called Army Service Forces) should handle all other aspects of the replacement system.

[3] (1) WD G–3 memo (S) G–3/6457–433 for CofS USA, 27 Dec 41, sub: Mob and Tng Plan (revised), 1942. (2) WD ltr (S) AG 381 (4–1–42) EC–GCT–M to CGs, 7 Apr 42, sub: RTC Capacity and Related Matters. Both in AGO Records, 381 (12–27–41)(S).

[4] Cir No. 59, WD, 2 Mar 42.

Headquarters, Army Ground Forces, concerned itself with the formulation of the basic policies to prevail in replacement training centers and with such general supervision as was necessary to ensure their execution. It established in its G–3 Section a Schools and Replacement Training Branch and, through this branch, sent out inspection teams to the Replacement and School Command and to the centers. AGF headquarters supervised training in the seven arms and quasi arms through three subordinate agencies. The chief of these was the Replacement and School Command, provided for in the reorganization of March 1942 as a headquarters directly subordinate to Headquarters, Army Ground Forces. It was at once given control of the replacement centers and the schools of the four statutory arms, and in the summer of 1942 it acquired control over replacement training in the new tank destroyer establishment, which it exercised through the commander of the Tank Destroyer Center. The second subordinate agency was the Armored Force, whose chief was made directly responsible to Headquarters, Army Ground Forces, in all his functions. When the Armored Force was reorganized, finally emerging in February 1944 as the Armored Center, its replacement training center, at Fort Knox, Ky., passed to the control of the Replacement and School Command. The third supervisory agency, also provided for in the reorganization, was the Antiaircraft Artillery Command, located in Richmond, Va., which was given charge of antiaircraft artillery training, formerly under the Coast Artillery Corps. Personnel from the offices of the former Chiefs of Infantry, Cavalry, Field Artillery, and Coast Artillery were distributed among the headquarters of the Army Ground Forces, the Replacement and School Command, and the Antiaircraft Artillery Command.

The Replacement and School Command

Maj. Gen. Courtney H. Hodges, Chief of Infantry when that office was absorbed into Army Ground Forces, became the first commanding general of the Replacement and School Command. The initial statement of the mission of the Replacement and School Command, contained in an advance directive to its commanding general, vested in the Command control over the replacement training centers of Infantry, Coast Artillery, Field Artillery, and Cavalry, and of two branch immaterial replacement training centers which had been established on 15 January 1942. The duties and responsibilities of the Commanding General of the Replacement and School Command were stated by Army Ground Forces to include the following:[5]

a. Activation of such units as are directed by this headquarters.

b. Unit training of all units under his command, and the individual training of personnel assigned to the various schools . . . and replacement training centers under his command.

Of these two responsibilities, that for "the individual training of personnel" easily took precedence in the training of replacements. Tactical units were assigned to the command only to perform the function of school troops at the various service schools. The mission of activation was reflected chiefly in the subsequent establishment of new replacement training centers, of which fourteen were activated by the command in the course of the war. Within each installation the activation of additional training units to expand capacity was a frequent occurrence, while the activation of tactical units as school troops was comparatively rare.

The Replacement and School Command carried out its mission of replacement training entirely through the agency of replacement training centers. It was the mission of the Headquarters, Replacement and School Command, to provide the centers with training programs and to supervise their execution; to study, improve, disseminate, and direct the practice of the best possible techniques and methods of training; to facilitate the conduct of training by administrative procedures designed to effect the best and most economical organization of the installations for training; to provide the installations with at least the minimum of personnel adequate to carry out their missions; to control the flow of trainees and students through the installations, in accordance with capacities prescribed by the War Department and (after March 1943) by Army Ground Forces; and to provide the centers with equipment, ammunition, and supplies sufficient to accomplish their training mission.

Training Program of Replacement Centers

Replacement training centers trained newly inducted enlisted men in basic military subjects and in elementary specialist techniques of the arm to which they were assigned. Since at the time they were established, before the war, the immediate object of replacement training was to supply filler replacements, the training system adopted originally reflected this purpose. Only privates were produced, the higher grades being available to units in cadres initially and

[5] AGF ltr 320.2/1 (R&SC) (3-9-42) to Maj Gen C. H. Hodges, CofInf, 9 Mar 42, sub: Advance Directive, Actvn of R&SC. R&SC Records, 320.2, binder 1, #4.

through upgrading later. Training was conducted only in a limited number of the commonest military occupational specialties (MOS's), since many MOS's were limited to grades above private and since schools were available to conduct training in the rarer, more technical, and more difficult specialties. In general only individual training was given, training in teamwork being reserved largely for tactical units. Training was standardized, to permit units to base advanced training on a common foundation. It was desirable to centralize instruction in order to use the limited number of experienced instructors to the maximum and to enable inexperienced instructors to concentrate on a few subjects. The system had to be economical of overhead personnel and training facilities. It had to be flexible, permitting the speediest possible adjustment to changing demands for replacements of different branches or of different specialties within a branch.

All men in an RTC company were trained for identical jobs, in contrast to the T/O unit which was characterized by the variety of functions which its members performed. Replacement training was in this sense specialized, in contrast to the diversified training in many military occupational specialties conducted in a unit during its individual training period. But the identical training in one MOS received by all recruits in the RTC company was broader and less specialized than training in that MOS in a unit. For example, riflemen in an RTC company were trained in light machine-gun and mortar firing and in the tactics of the squad and section of the weapons platoon of a T/O rifle company. In contrast, during basic training the men in a rifle company of a unit were instructed only in the weapons and the tactics of the particular squad or section to which they were assigned. Thus upon completion of training in the same MOS all men in the RTC rifle company were assigned the same specification serial number or SSN (in this case 745, Rifleman) and were considered ready to take their place in any basic position of the rifle squads or weapons sections of a T/O rifle company.

This specialization of training allowed for flexibility of production by MOS. In time of peace, because losses occurred in units by reason of natural death, disability, or discharge—causes affecting all positions in a T/O unit equally—units organized on a T/O basis could be utilized for replacement training, though only by sacrificing the training advantages inherent in the functional organization of RTC training units. The occurrence of casualties in combat did not correspond to the occurrence of T/O positions in a unit: a greater proportion of riflemen needed replacement than cooks. Hence a T/O unit which trained combat replacements would soon produce a surplus of cooks and a shortage of riflemen. A replacement training center, on the other hand, produced as great a proportion of replacements with a particular MOS as the number of companies training men for that MOS bore to the total number of companies in the center. A change in loss replacement requirements for a given MOS was met simply by increasing or decreasing the number of companies which trained recruits for that MOS.

Specialization of training in a replacement training center by company also allowed cadre instructors to specialize in a single broad type of instruction, that is, all the basic military and technical subjects of the training given to replacements of one particular MOS. Such specialization avoided the extreme which characterized instruction at the special service schools, where instructors taught only one or a few of the subjects of a training program. It was equally in contrast to the extreme found in the T/O unit during basic training, when cadre instructors were required to be "Jacks-of-all-trades" in their units.

Special functions and programs were envisaged for two branch immaterial replacement training centers which, on 14 January 1942, were established at Fort McClellan, Ala., and Camp Robinson, Ark.[6] The function of these centers was to provide basically trained individuals, in excess of the number that could be supplied by branch centers, to meet emergency requirements in all arms and services. They were established with initial capacities totaling 26,400 trainees to train for an 8-week period under a new MTP, 20–2, which outlined a course that consisted essentially of infantry rifle training but which included also tactical training of the individual soldier and of the rifle squad.[7] Under this program a large number of men were trained and assigned to whatever branch needed them most urgently.

Organization of Centers [8]

Although in March 1942 replacement training centers were just emerging from the experimental stage, and were to undergo extensive changes in the fol-

[6] (1) WD ltr (R) AG 353 Repl Ctrs (12–29–41) MSC–C–M to CofInf, 21 Dec 41, sub: RTCs at Ft McClellan and Cp Robinson. (2) WD ltr (R) AG 353 (12–19–41) MSC–C–M to CGs 4th and 7th CAs, 21 Dec 41, sub as in (1). Both (1) and (2) in AGO Records, 353 RC (12–19–41)(R). (3) WD ltr AG 320.2 (12–24–41) MR–M–AAF to CGs, 31 Dec 41, sub: Constitution and Activation of RTCs at Ft McClellan, Ala, and Cp Robinson, Ark. AGO Records, 320.2 (10–4–40)(2) Sec 13.

[7] MTP 20–2, WD, 31 Dec 41.

[8] The remaining portion of this chapter is based in part on the history of the Replacement and School Command prepared by its Historical Section.

lowing three and a half years, their basic organizational characteristics were fixed. The replacement training center was organized with reference to instructional rather than tactical functions. It consisted of a center headquarters and a number of training units, organized by regiment, battalion (squadron), and company (battery or troop). The center headquarters performed the bulk of administrative duties and those housekeeping duties not discharged by the post commander, thus freeing the training units for the primary function of training. The RTC regiment consisted of a small headquarters, sufficient for adequate supervision and scheduling of training, but unencumbered with the personnel and supply functions of a T/O regiment. Similarly, the battalion was a training headquarters, performing only a supervisory training function. Trainees were assigned to companies on the basis of the type of training they were to receive. All riflemen were grouped in rifle training companies, all cooks in cook companies, all truck drivers in truck companies, and so forth. Regiments and battalions consisted of subordinate units of the same kind, on the principle that efficient supervision depended on specialization by regimental and battalion officers in only one type of training.

The list of specialties varied among arms, but it always included specialists of two broad categories. Combat specialists were trained to man the combat weapons of the arm—riflemen, tankers, gunners, troopers. Administrative specialists were trained to perform unit administrative, supply, and maintenance functions—those of cooks, clerks, radio operators, mechanics, truck drivers, linemen, observers, buglers, etc. Men of both categories were specialists in the strict sense; that is, all were trained in a military occupational specialty and were given a specification serial number to designate their skills. In practice it was customary to refer to combat specialists in replacement training centers as "line" soldiers or "basics" and to confine the term "specialist" to men training in an administrative specialty.

The number of companies of each type depended on requirements for the various specialties. Originally, training capacity was distributed in Table of Organization proportions. A T/O infantry regiment, for example, contained 9 rifle, 3 heavy weapons, 1 antitank, 1 service, and 1 headquarters companies; infantry replacement training centers contained the same ratios of rifle, heavy weapons, antitank, service, and headquarters training companies.

The standard training company (battery, troop) contained from 200 to 240 trainees, grouped in 4 platoons, each of which consisted of 4 squads. For simplicity in administration, supervision, and use of equipment and personnel, training companies of a given type were organized into training battalions and, when numerous enough, into training regiments. Four companies made up a battalion; four battalions, a regiment.

Each company was allotted a permanent trainer group of officers and enlisted men, called a cadre. A rifle training company of 240 trainees, for example, used a cadre of 6 officers and 30 enlisted men. Eighteen of the enlisted men and all the officers were instructors; the ratio of trainers to trainees was 1:10. In specialist companies, where instruction had to be conducted in smaller groups, the ratio was higher: 1:8.6 in an infantry radio company; 1:5.8 in a motor mechanics company.

Organization of replacement centers on this basis had important advantages for training. It greatly simplified the planning and scheduling of instruction, since only one type of training was conducted in a company. It permitted the massing of facilities, equipment, and specially trained instructors for each major variety of training. It simplified supervision by company and by higher commanders and staff officers, who could concentrate on a single program and a single set of standards and requirements. It facilitated the maintenance of training records within the companies. It increased uniformity of instruction. It economized on trainer overhead by reducing the number of instructional groups into which a unit had to be divided. The number of men being trained in one specialty could be changed without changing the numbers trained in other specialties, simply by adding or subtracting units of one type.

The physical organization of the training centers was adapted as far as possible to the requirements of training, with a resulting increase in training efficiency. Barracks and messes were larger than those provided in tactical unit training, with the consequence that housing and messing costs were lower in the centers in proportion to trainee strength. Whenever possible, training areas were assigned to each training regiment, since this arrangement reduced movement, saved training time, facilitated planning, and permitted trainer cadres to become intimately familiar with their assigned areas. Even more important, regimental training areas encouraged the development of permanent training aids in which a regimental cadre had an exclusive interest. The long period of time spent in constant repetition of basic training by an RTC regiment, in contrast to the short span of the single basic training cycle of a T/O regiment, ensured the continuous development of training aids since repetition of training under close supervision revealed defects and stimulated improvement in their use.

Guides for RTC Training

The ultimate authority for the training conducted at a replacement center was the appropriate Mobilization Training Program (MTP) published by the War Department. The first replacement MTP's were written in the offices of the chiefs of arms in 1940, specifically for the new centers which began operations under their jurisdiction in March 1941.[9] The MTP consisted of two sections: one was devoted to general provisions regulating replacement training; the other consisted of a detailed breakdown of the programs applying to a particular branch, specifying the subjects, total number of hours for each subject, and the breakdown of these hours by week of the cycle. The training cycle in all MTP's except that of Cavalry was divided into two stages: a shorter period of basic training, of variable length and content, and a longer period of technical and tactical training designed to qualify the replacement for a particular military occupational specialty.

Before the end of 1941, revised MTP's had been issued for the replacement training centers of the Cavalry, Coast Artillery (including Antiaircraft), and Infantry, and a new MTP had been published to guide Armored replacement training.[10] There was a good deal of disparity among the prescribed programs. The training cycles were not all of the same length: Infantry and Armored were 13 weeks; Cavalry, Coast Artillery, and Field Artillery were 12. There was an even greater difference in the allotment of time to basic or general training. In Field Artillery all replacements received identical basic training for 2 weeks; in Coast Artillery basic training lasted 4 weeks for line replacements, 4 weeks for some specialists, and 8 for others; in Infantry the basic training period was 5 weeks for all; and in Cavalry replacement training there was no distinct separation between basic and technical training. In all the programs some specifically "branch" subjects, such as rifle marksmanship, gunner's instruction, and vehicle driving, were started early in the cycle in order to allow the longest possible time for formation of habits. On the other hand, some "basic" subjects, notably drill, physical training, inspections, and marches, occurred throughout the cycle, since their effect depended largely on daily or weekly repetitions.

While the MTP afforded a general guide for the conduct of training, a more specific guide was found in the Subject Schedules. Subject Schedules were

[9] (1) MTP 2-2, WD, 12 Nov 40. (2) MTP 4-1, WD, 5 Sep 40. (3) MTP 6-1, Sec III, WD, 25 Jul 40. (4) MTP 7-1, Sec III, WD, 26 Sep 40.

[10] (1) MTP 2-2, WD, 22 Jul 41. (2) MTP 4-1, WD, 2 Oct 41. (3) MTP 7-3, WD, 1 Mar 41. (4) MTP 17-1, WD, 3 Oct 41. (5) The first MTP to guide Tank Destroyer replacement traing. MTP 18-2, was not published until 31 December 1942.

written and revised periodically by the service schools under the direction of the Replacement and School Command, which became responsible for the revision of MTP's for those arms under its jurisdiction. In them could be found the current and approved methods of instruction and a guide for instructors in planning their presentation. Subject Schedules were of necessity general; for local application each replacement center issued training schedules and training memoranda which related the provisions contained in Subject Schedules to the training areas and local conditions of each installation. These training schedules and memoranda were submitted to Headquarters, Replacement and School Command, for review to ensure that local directives conformed to approved doctrine, and to aid in the dissemination to all replacement centers of improvements in training methods.

MTP's were also implemented by specific directives from Army Ground Forces and the Replacement and School Command. These directives ranged from minor revisions of previous directives to complete and detailed specifications for the conduct of training in a particular subject.

Methods of Instruction

Training conducted at replacement training centers was of two types. One type comprised subjects requiring personal supervision and intimate contact with the trainee or affording opportunity for the development of leadership, discipline, or morale in the training unit. Company trainer cadre conducted the instruction in this type of training; it was exemplified in the teaching of dismounted drill, physical training, marches and bivouacs, inspections, and extended order drill.

The other type of training consisted of instruction which was technical in nature, requiring elaborate training aids, the pooling of weapons, or the coordination of limited facilities. Training of this character was conducted by battalion, regimental, or center committees. A battalion or regimental committee was a group of trainer cadre drawn from the companies of the organization for the purpose of preparing and presenting instruction in a particular subject. Membership on a battalion or regimental committee was on a part-time basis. During periods when instruction was not being prepared or presented the personnel were on duty with their companies. In contrast, the center committee was a permanent organization. It was very small and the bulk of its work consisted of supervising instruction presented by company cadre or battalion committees. The RTC committee system, a modification of that common in the service schools, was developed by the Replacement and School Command. It allowed specialization of instructor personnel without unduly sacrificing the benefits of discipline, supervision, and personal contact with the trainee which training by company cadre afforded. Typical battalion committee subjects were map reading, mines and booby traps, hand grenades, and mortar and machine-gun field firing. Regimental and center committees presented or supervised instruction in such subjects as chemical warfare training, tactical exercises, and battle courses.

Instructor personnel were subject to rotation at the end of a year's service. A newly appointed officer was considered to be in the status of an assistant instructor during his first cycle at a replacement center, during which time his work was under the immediate supervision of more experienced officers. At the end of his tour of duty the RTC instructor supervised the work of his replacement during the period of overlap allowed under the rotation system. This supervision made for continuity of teaching methods and the improvement of training efficiency. Instructor personnel profited also from the repetition of training arising from the extension of the tour of duty over three or more training cycles.

Special schools which emphasized the techniques of instruction were held regularly between cycles in the RTC program; in addition, cadre schools were conducted during the training cycle by battalions, regiments, and the RTC headquarters. While these schools gave instructor personnel additional instruction and review in the technical and tactical subjects of the MTP, their main purpose was to improve and standardize techniques of instruction by providing practical demonstrations of correct pedagogy and to give company officers an opportunity for trial teaching before the other instructors and their superior officers.

One of the most significant developments in RTC methods of instruction was the widespread use of visual training aids, comprising not only charts, training films, and enlarged working models of weapons and equipment but also training areas, battle courses, and dramatic skits illustrative of instruction. Because of their permanence, replacement training centers were able to develop training aids to a high peak of efficiency, particularly in the infantry centers.

II. Development of the RTC Program, 1942-43

Army Ground Forces, on assuming responsibility for the training of replacements in March 1942, inherited a going concern, whose organization, distribution of capacity, system of training, and programs of instruction had taken definite form under the chiefs of the ground arms. The replacement centers, having been in operation a year when Army Ground Forces was organized, had evolved a system of training that appeared to be satisfactory. Continuity was ensured by assigning experienced personnel from the offices of the chiefs of the arms to the two new agencies set up under Army Ground Forces to handle replacement training, the Replacement and School Command and the Antiaircraft Artillery Command. With the administrative aspects of the replacement system in the hands of the War Department and with replacement training under the immediate supervision of its subordinate commands, Army Ground Forces in 1942 devoted its attention mainly to the activation and training of units, especially infantry divisions.

Army Ground Forces found it increasingly necessary, however, to concern itself with certain broad questions of policy with respect to replacement training, and, by the end of 1943, some of these problems had engaged its most careful consideration. There were three principal reasons why AGF headquarters became involved in replacement training problems. One was the fact that the replacement system had developed separately under the chiefs of the arms and, after the outbreak of the war, required coordination and standardization in the light of the common requirements of the ground combat arms. Another was the necessity of adapting the military training programs of the replacement centers to the needs of the current war as revealed by the combat experience that had been acquired. The most important factor that raised policy issues was the circumstance that changes in emphasis developed in the use to which replacement training centers were put.

As previously noted, the original mission of the replacement training centers had been to give basic training to all newly inducted enlisted men prior to their assignment to tactical units. During 1941 most RTC graduates were assigned as fillers to newly activated or understrength units. In December 1941 this mission had been altered by a decision that henceforth, in principle, newly activated units would ordinarily receive the bulk of their enlisted men directly from reception centers, instead of securing them as fillers from replacement training centers. Although some units received fillers from replacement centers as late as 1944, the principal function of the replacement system after the beginning of 1942 was the provision of loss replacements to established units in the United States and in active theaters of operations. Loss replacements, as distinguished from filler replacements, were those provided to fill vacancies in units caused by transfer, discharge, hospitalization, or death.

The transition from the training of fillers for new units to the training of loss replacements for established units created certain qualitative problems in the training of replacements. The training given fillers was relatively simple. Since fillers received additional training after joining a unit, RTC programs for their training could be confined to essential individual instruction; and since fillers were produced for specific job assignments in units, it was desirable not to aim at too much versatility but to restrict their training within fairly narrow limits in order to establish their skills. In training loss replacements, on the other hand, it was desirable to avoid narrow specialization and to produce versatile replacements capable of satisfactory performance no matter where they were assigned. If they joined an established unit in the United States, loss replacements needed considerable unit training if they were not to delay the unit's progress; if they joined a unit in combat, they needed even more skill in teamwork in order not to impair the unit's effectiveness. The problem was to provide replacements sufficiently well trained so that they could be placed in units without unduly disrupting either the training or the combat efficiency of the unit involved. The solution to this problem was to be sought in the lengthening of the RTC training cycle, in the introduction of greater realism into replacement training, and in the increasing emphasis in the replacement system on unit as opposed to individual training.

A second major transition occurred as mobilization approached completion and as the intensity of combat increased. Henceforth the greatest need was for combat loss replacements in active theaters of operation, rather than for replacements to fill and maintain at full strength units in training in the United States. This change introduced problems that were primarily quantitative in character. The requirements for filler replacements could be predicted with reasonable accuracy, on the basis of fixed Tables of Organization which listed the number of men in each military occupational specialty in each kind of unit, and the forecasts provided by the Troop Basis and the activation schedule. Loss replacements in the Zone of Interior did not require any particular deviations in a replacement system that had been designed primarily to provide filler replacements, because nonbattle losses occurred roughly in T/O proportions. But combat losses did not correspond proportionately to T/O strength, being heaviest in the fighting elements of combat units. A replacement system geared to the production of men in different specialties in T/O proportions was, therefore, inadequate to meet combat needs. Furthermore, since battle losses were heaviest in Infantry and Armored, combat loss requirements were felt soonest and most sharply in those arms. The quantitative problems that arose because of this shift in the primary function of the replacement system produced crises in procurement that have been discussed above in the study "The Provision of Enlisted Replacements"; but they also affected the replacement training programs of the various ground arms. The list of specialties trained had to be revised to provide the flexibility of assignment essential to an efficient combat-loss replacement system. The allotment of training capacity among arms and among specialties had to be adjusted to battle loss rates. Even the concept of the training center, central to the whole replacement scheme, did not escape critical scrutiny.

Standardization of the Length of Training

The period 1942–43 witnessed a series of attempts to set a standard length for the training cycle. By the fall of 1943 it had, except for special programs, become fixed at a 17-week period, which, with one interruption, remained standard during the remainder of the war.

Replacement training centers, as first constituted under the chiefs of the arms, were operated on a 12- or 13-week training cycle. Immediately after Pearl Harbor many of the replacement center programs were cut drastically to eight weeks. Fillers for units to be activated and for overseas garrisons were needed at once and in greater numbers than could be supplied by the existing centers, operating on longer cycles. The War Department directed that training be curtailed in all replacement training centers except those of the Armored Force, the Infantry, and the Signal Corps, which, it was believed, could not reduce training without a dangerous loss of efficiency.[1] The revision of training programs was carried out wherever possible by reducing the time spent on sub-

[1] (1) WD ltr AG 320.2 (12–17–41) MT–C to CGs, 19 Dec 41, sub: Reduction in Length of Tng Programs at RTCs. (2) WD G–3 M/R, 17 Dec 41. Both in AGO Records, 320.2 (10–4–40)(2) Sec 1–A.

jects rather than by eliminating subjects; the subjects eliminated were selected from those, such as team training on crew-served weapons, that could be taught with greatest ease in the units to which the trainees were to be sent.

By February 1942, after it was decided to send recruits directly to units for basic training, pressure on the replacement centers was somewhat relieved. In that month the War Department directed that the field artillery and cavalry replacement centers, in order to return to a normal period of training, should stagger enlisted men in training, and that all enlisted men should receive full training after 15 July.[2] This was the situation when Army Ground Forces received control of the replacement training centers in March 1942. By 15 July all replacement training centers except those of the Antiaircraft Artillery Command were on the longer schedule. Because of continuing heavy demands for replacements to man new antiaircraft units, the Army Ground Forces received permission to continue the curtailed program in antiaircraft centers. Not until the end of November 1942 had the situation been sufficiently eased to permit them to return to the normal cycle.[3]

A special problem was presented by the training cycle for the two branch immaterial replacement training centers (BIRTC's), which had been established concurrently with the reduction of the training cycle to eight weeks. From July through December 1942, these centers were used in part to assist in the training of 84,000 men for Services of Supply for whose training SOS training center capacity was insufficient. For these men the training period was cut in May 1942 to six weeks.[4] The two branch immaterial centers were also used to train limited-service personnel. But even when their product was available, it was not of maximum use to Army Ground Forces because the training had been too brief. Most BIRTC graduates assigned to Army Ground Forces were assigned to the Infantry, and the War Department had decided in early 1942 that the infantry training cycle should not be curtailed. If these BI men were to be used, they would have to receive more training.

In March 1943 the War Department, noting that products of the branch immaterial centers were not considered suitable for immediate shipment over-

[2] WD ltr AG 320.2 (2–3–42) EC–C–M to branch chiefs, 28 Feb 42, sub: Increase in Period of Tng at RTCs. AGO Records, 320.2 (10–4–40)(2) Sec 1–A–1.

[3] (1) AGF memo for G–3 WD, 2 May 42, sub: Tng Period of AA RTCs. (2) WD ltr AG 320.2 (5–2–42) EC–C–M to CG AA Comd, 9 May 42, sub as in (1). Both (1) and (2) in AGO Records, 320.2 (10–4–40)(2) Sec 1–A–1. (3) AGF ltr to G–3 WD, 30 Nov 42, sub as in (1). AGO Records, 353 (3–14–42)(1) Sec 1.

[4] WD G–3 memo WDGCT 320 (RTC) (5–27–42) to CG AGF, 27 May 42, sub: Employment of RTCs. 354.1/56 (RTCs).

seas, placed the issue before Army Ground Forces.[5] AGF headquarters recommended that trainees in these centers receive the standard infantry RTC course and that the training cycle be extended to thirteen weeks. This change was authorized, and henceforth branch immaterial training was infantry training.[6]

As early as the fall of 1942 it was becoming apparent that the 13-week training cycle was not sufficient to train a replacement to fulfill properly his assignment as a loss replacement. In September an observer from the Replacement and School Command at the VIII Corps maneuvers in Louisiana reported that "it was the general opinion that the thirteen weeks training period could not provide sufficient time simultaneously to physically harden the individual soldier, give the necessary basic and technical instruction, and provide sufficient practice in the tactics and techniques of small units, to enable him to function efficiently in a combat team engaged in actual combat operation." [7] With the development of the campaign in North Africa it became still more evident that the 13-week training period was inadequate to produce well-trained loss replacements. On 11 June 1943 Army Ground Forces extended the training period for all infantry and armored replacements from thirteen to fourteen weeks. The additional week was to be used exclusively for tactical training in the field, which, it was felt, had not been adequately emphasized.

At the same time the War Department was receiving criticisms of replacements from overseas. Most reports indicated the need for unit training to supplement the individual training currently received in the replacement centers. The War Department directed Army Ground Forces to submit recommendations on a training program of six months' length. Army Ground Forces submitted three plans to provide replacements with six months' training, but recommended a compromise plan that would extend the RTC training cycle to seventeen weeks. On 13 July the War Department adopted the recommendation for a 17-week program.[8]

Army Ground Forces directed[9] the Replacement and School Command to establish a 17-week training cycle in all replacement training centers, effective

[5] WD G–3 memo WDGCT 320 (BIRTC) (3–8–43) to CG AGF, 8 Mar 43, sub: BIRTCs. 354.1/146 (BIRTCs).

[6] AGF memo for G–3 WD, 28 Mar 43, sub and location as in n. 5.

[7] AGF ltr of Maj S. R. Harrison to CG R&SC, 11 Sep 42, sub: Rpt of Observer Attending VIII Corps Maneuvers. R&SC Records, 354.2/49 (Maneuvers).

[8] WD memo (S) WDGCT 320.2 Gen (6–12–43) to CG AGF, 13 Jul 43, sub: Loss Repls. 354.1/4 (RTC)(S).

[9] AGF ltr to CG R&SC, 25 Jul 43, sub: Increase in RTCs. R&SC Records, 354.1/01 (S).

8 August 1943. The added weeks of instruction were to be devoted to small-unit training up to and including company, battery, and troop, including at least two weeks of continuous field exercises.[10] The improvement in training made possible by the 17-week program was reflected in the lessening of criticisms of replacements received by the War Department from overseas commanders.[11]

Standardization of Programs

Army Ground Forces was concerned in 1942 not merely with the standardization of the training cycles in the replacement training centers of the various arms but also with the standardization of programs. Uniformity was desirable only with respect to those basic subjects which were common to all MTP's for replacement training. Since the training programs currently in use had been produced in the offices of the various branch chiefs, with only slight coordination, these common subjects exhibited wide variations. The subject matter was treated differently in different MTP's and not even the titles of subjects were the same; what appeared as a single subject in one MTP might be listed as two or even three subjects in another. In particular, in the initial MTP's there were wide divergencies in the allotment of time to subjects common to all programs, as the following examples indicate:

Subject	*Hours*			
	MTP Cav (2–2)	*MTP CA (4–1)*	*MTP FA (6–1)*	*MTP Inf (7–1)*
Courtesy, Discipline, Articles of War	3	5	3	2½
Sanitation, Hygiene, First Aid	4	9	4	5½
Interior Guard Duty	2	5	3	2
Physical Training	24	8	16	15
Equipment, Clothing, Tent Pitching	5	9	5	3

As the war advanced it became important, particularly for the purpose of securing greater flexibility of assignment, to effect greater uniformity in the subjects basic to all replacement training. By October 1942 Army Ground Forces had

[10] R&SC ltr 353 GNRST to CGs RTCs, 30 Jul 43, sub: Extension of Tng Period in RTCs to 17 Wks. R&SC Records, 353/155.

[11] R&SC ltr 319.1 (S) GNRSG, Gen Hazlett to CG AGF, 25 Mar 44, sub: Rpt on Repls in ETOUSA and NATOUSA. R&SC Records, 319.1/1 (Rpts) (S).

230-171 O - 66 - 26

evolved a list of subjects common to all MTP's for replacement training and had standardized them in nomenclature and time allotment as follows:[12]

Subject	*Hours*
Military Courtesy and Discipline, Articles of War	6
Orientation Course	7
Military Sanitation, First Aid, and Sex Hygiene	10
Defense against Chemical Attack, individual	12
Practice Marches and Bivouacs (minimum hours)	20
Dismounted Drill	20
Equipment, Clothing, and Shelter Tent Pitching	7
Interior Guard Duty	4
Hasty Field Fortifications and Camouflage	8
Elementary Map and Aerial Photograph Reading (minimum hours)	8
Physical Training (minimum hours)	36
Inspections	18
Protection of Military Information	3
Organization of the Army	1

The time allotted to the various subjects in the training programs reflected the impact of actual warfare. The amount of time devoted to physical conditioning was steadily increased; marches, night training, chemical warfare instruction, safeguarding of military information, and individual tactics were all emphasized more strongly in revisions of the training programs made during 1942. Subjects predominantly related to garrison duty, such as dismounted drill, ceremonies, and inspections, suffered repeated cuts to provide time for material more directly relevant to combat. On the other hand, the broad Orientation Course, which had been absent at the outset, was gradually introduced into the various MTP's of replacement centers during 1942.

As indicated above in the study "The Provision of Enlisted Replacements," a major achievement in the administration of the replacement program during 1943 was the preparation of conversion tables by means of which types of training demanded overseas could be translated into the types of training given in replacement centers. These tables, embodied in War Department Circular 283, 6 November 1943, also had the effect of standardizing further the types of training in the centers through setting up the SSN's for which courses had to be given.

[12] (1) AGF 1st ind to G–3, WD, 30 Oct 42, on CofOrd ltr 00 352.11/7703 to TAG, 13 Oct 42, sub: MTPs. 461/9 (MTP). (2) R&SC 2d wrapper ind to CG AGF, 18 Nov 42, on R&SC ltr to CG AGF, 24 Oct 42, sub: Coast (Seacoast) Arty MTP (MTP 4–1). 461/5 (MTP).

Introduction of Greater Realism into Training

Even before the extension of the replacement training cycle to seventeen weeks, a major revision of the training programs was undertaken with a view to preparing replacements for immediate entrance into combat. In February 1943, special battle courses were added to RTC training.[13] The infiltration course, the close combat course, and a village fighting course were introduced to prepare the trainee psychologically for experience with live ammunition and to accustom him to use his weapon under conditions more realistic than those of the range. These battle courses became one of the most characteristic features of replacement centers, the training aids *par excellence* of these establishments. Battle courses were conducted in carefully prepared and highly organized training areas, each designed to introduce the trainees to some phase of the sound and fury of actual combat. For this reason they were often referred to as "battle inoculation" courses. Although used by tactical units in their basic training, the courses developed at the replacement training centers were ordinarily far better constructed and organized, and more stress was placed on their proper use.

Among the battle courses the infiltration course [14] was distinctive in that it did not lend itself readily to realistic tactical training or a tactical situation. The purpose of this course was primarily to accustom men to overhead fire and to the noise and effect of near-by explosions.[15] Stress was laid on the proper techniques of moving forward under fire and negotiating barbed-wire entanglements. In the summer of 1943 handling and care of the rifle under the adverse conditions of the course were added to counteract the tendency of trainees to neglect their weapons during the excitement.[16] In September 1943, the Replacement and School Command directed that all trainees run the infiltration course at night as well as during daylight.[17] Further refinements heightening the realism of the course were introduced in 1944 and 1945.

[13] AGF ltr to CGs, 4 Feb 43, sub: Special Battle Courses. 353.01/61.

[14] (1) Incls 1 and 2, "Street Fighting," and "Infiltration," to TDC 1st ind, 24 Feb 43, on R&SC ltr 353 GNRST to CG TDC, 17 Feb 43, sub: Orgn of Infiltration and Combat in Cities Crses. R&SC Records, 353/4 (Tank Destroyer). (2) Incl, Subject Schedule, "Battle Conditioning," prepared by TDRTC, to 1st ind TDRTC, 6 Jul 43, on R&SC ltr 353 GNRST to CG TDRTC, 19 Jun 43, sub: Battle Conditioning Crse. R&SC Records, 353/9 (TDRTC). (3) Subject Schedule No. 11, Battle Courses, 10 Dec 43. (4) MTP (7-3) Subject Schedule No. 11, "Mental Conditioning Course," 1 Mar 45.

[15] AGF ltr 353.01/61 GNGCT to CG R&SC, 4 Feb 43, sub: Special Battle Crses. R&SC Records, 353/68.

[16] (1) R&SC ltr 474 GNRST to CGs RTCs, 13 Jul 43, sub: Handling and Care of Weapons on Infiltration Crse. (2) Gen Hazlett's personal ltrs to all CGs of Inf, Cav, and BIRTCs, 14 Jul 43. Both in R&SC Records, 353/125.

[17] R&SC memo, Gen Hazlett to Gen Curtis, 29 Sep 43. R&SC Records, 353/149.

The close combat course,[18] included in the MTP by direction of Army Ground Forces in February 1943, was evolved out of the quick-firing reaction course and the so-called "blitz" course used in replacement training in 1942. The quick-firing reaction course consisted of lanes containing surprise targets which were engaged by the trainees, but it did not involve the negotiation of obstacles. The blitz course had no targets and required no firing by the trainee, but contained obstacles, explosives, and, during certain stages, overhead fire. The close combat course contained elements of each of these earlier courses. Its purpose was to teach men to fire small arms with speed and accuracy at surprise targets while negotiating a broken terrain. Explosions and overhead fire were excluded. Before the end of 1943 the close combat course, which had usually been only 100 yards long, was lengthened, and the series of obstacles was made less artificial. Several further improvements in the direction of realism were made in 1944, including the introduction of explosions. In its final form the close combat course was a highly realistic tactical problem, complete with a tactical situation involving a dozen or more separate actions, and based on the so-called "buddy system" in which several trainees paired off in two groups moving forward with mutual support and "leap-frog" tactics.

The village fighting course [19] had a threefold purpose: first, to train the individual soldier to work efficiently and to fire accurately at fleeting targets amid the noise and confusion of battle; second, to train the individual soldier in the proper techniques of street fighting, entering and clearing houses, jumping from roofs and scaling walls, and avoiding booby traps; and, third, to train the individual soldier to operate as a member of a team in the tactics of a small unit in clearing a village.[20] The course ultimately provided for trainees going through a complete tactical problem involving all the techniques of village fighting and the application of the principles of mutual support, cover, and movement. There was a profuse expenditure of live ammunition, including flanking and overhead fire, augmented by explosions and simulated mortar fire, while the noise and confusion of battle reached its climax with the introduction of tank support in the final stages of the "battle." To stress realism, the cadre control was made wholly

[18] See n. 14.

[19] (1) See n. 14. (2) Pars 30–31, MTP (7–3), Subject Schedule No. 81, "Tactics of the Rifle Squad and Platoon," 1 May 45. R&SC Hist Sec files.

[20] (1) AGF ltr 353/52 (Tng Dir) GNGCT to CGs . . . R&SC, 19 Oct 42, sub: Tng Dir effective 1 Nov 42. R&SC Records, 353/1 (AGF Tng Dir). (2) See n. 15. (3) AGF ltr 353/29 (Assault) GNGCT to CGs . . . R&SC, 8 Feb 43, sub: Construction of "Mock Villages" for "Combat in Cities" Tng, and incls. R&SC Records, 353/69.

tactical, and the only safety precautions were those inherent in normal tactical control.

In June 1943 AGF headquarters instituted another important battle course—overhead artillery fire.[21] While it had been used previously at the field artillery replacement training center, AGF headquarters now directed that one field artillery battery be stationed at each infantry center to expose infantry trainees to overhead artillery fire.[22] The purpose was to demonstrate what a concentration of artillery fire actually was, to build confidence in trainees in their own artillery, and to convince them that artillery fire need not be feared. By the fall of 1943 several replacement centers had developed tactical problems, centering on the action of a squad as part of the platoon or company, organized tactically, and based on a situation which called for close artillery support. The problem was essentially a company attack on a fortified position. All infantry weapons were employed, and, in addition to artillery fire, trainees were subjected to overhead and flanking mortar and machine-gun fire.

The basic battle courses and other courses reflecting the trend toward greater realism had by September 1943 become common to the MTP's of all branches. By that month the list of these common subjects, standardized by Army Ground Forces in nomenclature and number of hours, was as follows:[23]

Subject	*Hours*
Organization of the Army and [Branch]	2
Military Courtesy and Discipline, Articles of War	5
Military Sanitation and First Aid	
Personal and Sex Hygiene	3
First Aid	9
Field Sanitation	2
Equipment, Clothing, and Tent Pitching	4
Interior Guard Duty	4
Chemical Warfare Training	6
Protection against Carelessness	2
Combat Intelligence and Counter-Intelligence	
Protection of Military Information	2
Enemy Information	3
Antitank and Antipersonnel Mines and Booby Traps (including Improvisation)	8

[21] See n. 14, (3) and (4).

[22] R&SC ltr 322 GNRST to CGs Inf and BIRTCs, 18 Jun 43, sub: Ovhd Arty Fire. R&SC Records, 320.2/13.

[23] R&SC wrapper ind to CG AGF, 18 Sep 43, on MTPs. 461/64 (MTP).

Subject	*Hours*
Grenades	
Hand Grenades (including Improvisation)	8
Battle Courses	
Infiltration Course	2
Close Combat Course [not included in CA and FA programs]	2

Field Training

An important feature of the revised 13-week MTP in force during the first six months of 1943 was its prescription of a 3-day period of field exercises.[24] Lack of field training had been one of the major weaknesses of the replacement training programs. In general the trainee was taught to perform his individual job under more or less ideal conditions. It was assumed that once he had mastered his trade he could learn to operate under field conditions after joining a unit. By 1943 most replacements could not be given a "shakedown" period in a unit; they had to be able to practice their trades under the worst conditions immediately upon joining. Field training formerly given in units now had to be given in the replacement centers.

In March 1943 the Replacement and School Command prescribed a 3-day field period for all infantry trainees except specialists, to come at the end of the training cycle.[25] It included a 20-mile march, squad and platoon exercises, and enforcement of ration and water discipline. Further increase in the amount of field training was thought necessary by Army Ground Forces. Brig. Gen. John M. Lentz, G–3, Army Ground Forces, noted that "after all, [replacements] are supposed to go straight into battle. Cables from overseas state they are not ready." [26] He singled out combat firing, transition firing, night patrolling, and field work as subjects in which individual replacements were especially weak. Study of the content of the training programs led officers of the G–3 Section to raise the question: "If the purpose is to fit men for battle—why should not replacements be exposed to actual physical hardships?" They recommended a 2-week field training period, during which night marches, patrolling, combat firing, and battle courses would be stressed, and an extension of the training cycle to four-

[24] R&SC memo, Col Shallene to CofS, 2 Jun 43, sub: Field Exercises. R&SC Records, 853/5.

[25] Inf Tng Prog for Inf Repls at RTCs, 1 Mar 43. R&SC Records, 353/41 (Inf RTC).

[26] Record of tel conv between Gen Lentz and Gen Hazlett, R&SC, 31 Mar 43. AGF G–3 Schs Br files, R&SC–RTC binder 1/66 (S).

teen weeks.[27] It was estimated that the 2-week period would give the replacement one-third of the field experience gained by a soldier on maneuvers with a unit.

When the Replacement and School Command produced a plan to extend the training cycle one week and add a 10-day field training period, Army Ground Forces renewed its recommendation to the War Department to extend the training cycle.[28] The extension was approved for infantry and armored centers, and on 11 June Army Ground Forces directed that in the new 14-week cycle the field training be increased to ten days for all trainees, including specialists. Experience with replacements of the other arms had not been extensive, and drastic changes in the other programs were not believed to be necessary.

When the War Department on 13 July 1943 approved the extension of the RTC training cycle to seventeen weeks, it directed that the training programs be "modified to include additional small unit training and at least two weeks of continuous field exercises." [29] Programs embodying these changes went into effect in August. The 2-week field period, occurring in the fifteenth and sixteenth weeks, comprised a series of tactical problems during which the trainees, under conditions simulating those of combat, were called upon to apply the skills acquired earlier in the course. Although altered from time to time in specific content, the field period remained a standard feature of replacement training and was generally regarded as one of its most notable developments.

The Problem of Tactical Training

The stipulation of "additional small unit training" in the July directive of the War Department touched on an important issue—the question of how large a unit was desirable in RTC training. The words of the directive did not make clear the size of the unit which was envisaged. The question of tactical training of small units had concerned the Replacement and School Command from the beginning, and it had at times differed with AGF headquarters as to the most desirable solution.

Tactical training of small units played a relatively minor role in the original

[27] AGF M/S, G–3 Tng Div to G–3, 15 Apr 43, sub: Increase of MTP 7–3 to 14 Wks. AGF G–3 Schs Br files, R&SC–RTC binder 1/66 (S).

[28] (1) R&SC ltr to CG AGF, 14 Apr 43, sub: Increase in Length of Tng Period of Inf Loss Repls from 13 to 14 Wks. (2) AGF M/S, G–3 to CofS, 9 May 43, sub: Increase in Length of Tng of Loss Repls from 13 to 14 Wks. Both in 354.1 (RTC).

[29] (1) WD memo (S) WDGCT 320.2 Gen (6–12–43) to CG AGF, 13 Jul 43, sub: Loss Repls. 354.1/4 (RTC) (S). (2) AGF ltr to CG R&SC, 25 Jul 43, sub: Increase in RTCs. 354.1/4 (RTC) (S).

replacement training programs. Tactical problems for the squad had been standard in replacement training centers since 1941, but for the first few months after Pearl Harbor the rapid turnover of company officers placed the main burden of tactical training on platoon sergeants, who were not available in sufficient numbers to make that training worthwhile. The Replacement and School Command was not satisfied with the situation, and on 1 May 1942 it directed each of the infantry centers to prepare for review tactical problems for each type of exercise called for in the various Subject Schedules.[30] Reviewed and to some extent standardized, these problems provided for each center a corpus of approved tactical exercises designed to enable inexperienced instructors to conduct sound tactical training. In a general training directive of 21 November 1942 the Replacement and School Command placed great stress on tactical training and declared that "the team in which the soldier is trained is ordinarily the . . . squad." [31] While admitting the value of platoon problems insofar as they enhanced the tactical setting of squad operations, the Replacement and School Command specifically forbade the expansion of these exercises into company or battalion problems. Its main reason was that the nontactical organization of replacement centers made realistic unit tactical exercises difficult; this difficulty was more pronounced in the case of larger units because of the discrepancy between the variety of assignments in a T/O unit and the uniformity of personnel in an RTC organization.

These views on the level of tactical training appropriate to the replacement center were not shared by Headquarters, Army Ground Forces. Criticism of replacements in 1943 rested largely on the insufficiency of their unit training, and the War Department had pressed Army Ground Forces to train replacements in regularly organized units. It was not unnatural, therefore, that Army Ground Forces should construe the instructions given it to include "additional small unit training" as calling for training in tactics of the company. This was "additional" in the sense of being new to replacement training. AGF headquarters directed that field problems be conducted from the company point of view, in order to accommodate tactical training of specialists in combined exercises.[32] The revised, 17-week programs called for a week of company training for combat specialists.

[30] R&SC ltr 320.2 Inf RTC to CGs Inf and BIRTCs, 1 May 42, sub: Standardization of Tactical Tng. R&SC Records, 353/12.

[31] R&SC ltr 353 GNRST to CGs Inf and BIRTCs, 21 Nov 42, sub: Tng Policy. R&SC Records, 353/49.

[32] (1) M/R tel conv between Gen Curtis and Col Shaw, AGF, 24 Jul 43. (2) AGF ltr 353/2220 (S) GNGCT to CG R&SC, 25 Jul 43, sub: Increase in RTCs. 354.1 (S), # .01.

The object of tactical training was to teach the soldier to apply his knowledge of weapons and his individual tactical training to his duties as a member of a unit in offensive and defensive combat, and to train him to work as a member of a team. During this tactical training the men were conditioned gradually for the shock of battle by being subjected to overhead flanking fire, to the noise and confusion of combat, and to realistic attacks by actual or simulated tanks and aircraft. All problems were drawn with the purpose of emphasizing the duties of the individual within the squad while introducing the principle of coordination with other squads in the accomplishment of a common mission.[33] Except for a brief orientation period preceding each exercise, and a thorough critique following it, all tactical training was practical. In the course of these exercises every basic weapon of the unit involved was employed, with profuse expenditure of ball and blank ammunition. All leaders in the presence of troops were required to act tactically. Safety officers were all but eliminated, and every effort was made to make the conduct of training realistic.

[33] MTP (7-3) Subject Schedule No. 81, "Tactics of the Rifle Squad and Platoon," 1 May 45. R&SC Hist Sec files.

III. Proposals to Change the Basic Pattern of Replacement Training, 1942-43

None of the changes made in the replacement training centers during 1942–43 altered the basic pattern of replacement training as Army Ground Forces found it on assuming control. But during 1942 and 1943 various proposals were made both within the Army Ground Forces and by the War Department which would have transformed replacement training, giving the replacement centers a different function or allocating a share in such training to some other agency. While none of these plans was adopted, all were seriously debated and the views developed tended to influence the less radical adjustments that were actually made. The issues discussed fell under two main heads—the question of the relative merits of specialization and general proficiency, and the problem of unit versus center organization of replacement training. Repeated proposals of drastic change compelled Army Ground Forces to enter into a thoroughgoing study of replacement training. But in the second half of 1943 the demand for quantity production of combat loss replacements became so urgent that any basic reorganization of replacement training, whatever its merits, seemed impracticable. The pressure of quantitative requirements had been felt from the beginning of the war. At no time after December 1941 was RTC capacity adequate to meet demands for replacements, and crises caused by low capacity were recurrent. This prevented the solution of training problems on their merits; availability of manpower was a controlling factor in all discussions. Compromise was continually necessary between the course considered best from the point of view of training alone and the course least likely to reduce output.

The Issue of Branch Immaterial Training

From May 1942 to April 1943, G–1, Army Ground Forces, pressed a proposal to place all RTC training on a branch immaterial basis, that is, to limit such training to a common basic course. Later, a similar proposal was made by the Armored Force. The background of these proposals is to be found in the inadequacy of RTC output, which had occasioned serious concern even among those not favoring so drastic an expedient. Output of the replacement centers during 1942 was insufficient to fill even high-priority requests.[1] Repeatedly expedients had to be adopted to raise production or to make RTC output available when needed. During the first half of the year all AGF replacement training centers except those of the Infantry and the Armored Force operated on a curtailed training cycle of eight weeks. As already noted, two branch immaterial centers were established to furnish basically trained men for general-purpose use. To provide men urgently needed for activation of service units, twenty-eight training battalions in AGF replacement training centers were converted to an 8-week branch immaterial program in 1942. It was clear not only that RTC capacity was insufficient to support all the demands made on it, but also that its distribution among branches was not geared to requirements.

It was essential that RTC training in view of its scarcity value should not be wasted through misassignment. But misassignment was an acute problem throughout the year, resulting repeatedly in waste of training carried on in the centers. In June 1942 the AGF G–1 estimated that at least 50 percent of the personnel in the fifteen most critical occupational specialties were misassigned.[2] In the same month the 45th Division reported the following discrepancies between replacements requisitioned on 30 April and those received:[3]

Type of Training	*Requisitioned*	*Received from IRTC*
Rifle	3,217	1,082
Heavy Weapons	866	1,413
Headquarters	383	701
Service	50	671
Antitank	158	559

The over-all inadequacy of RTC output was not the only factor responsible for misassignment. Commanders had not yet become generally aware of the importance of proper classification and placement. Facilities for proper assignment were lacking. Moreover, the expert advice of classification officers was rarely available. The Classification and Replacement Division, Headquarters, Army Ground Forces, whose subsequent influence on assignment policies and proce-

[1] See above, "The Provision of Enlisted Replacements."

[2] AGF M/S, G–1 to G–3, 17 Jun 42, sub not given. 333.1/1 (Classification Inspection).

[3] 45th Div 3d ind to CG AGF, 25 Jun 42, on personal ltr of Pvt Thomas D. Milewski, 180th Inf Regt, to TAG, 25 May 42. 341/265.

dures was very great, had not yet been established. There was no common basis for training and requisitioning personnel: commanders were permitted to call for men in any specialty needed, even though replacement centers trained men in but a small fraction of the specialties included in Tables of Organization. Training in the replacement centers had not yet been organized to ensure that even in each category of specialty men would become available at regular and frequent intervals. A large number of cooks would be available during one week and none for thirteen weeks thereafter. There were no facilities available for holding cooks in the meantime. Unless they were requisitioned at the time they completed their training, cooks would be dispersed and probably assigned to other jobs than cooking. Requisitions for cooks received before the next group was trained would go unfilled or would be filled with men not specifically trained for the work. Though much effort was directed toward regulating the output of replacement training centers on an even weekly basis, no solution was found until 1943.[4]

The G–3 Section of Army Ground Forces saw the problem as primarily one of attaining maximum production. Attempts were made to secure additional capacity and to reduce losses from replacement training centers to officer candidate schools, air training, and special training units for illiterates.[5] The G–1 Section believed more radical action to be necessary and proposed to place all replacement training on a branch immaterial basis, giving all inductees assigned to Army Ground Forces a common basic course. Such specialist training as was required would be conducted in schools or in units after assignment. The first proposal made by G–1 called for eliminating branch training in replacement training centers altogether. When G–3 objected on the ground that replacements could not be assimilated in units without some branch training, G–1 recommended that all trainees be given a common program for six weeks, followed by branch training for the remainder of the cycle.[6] G–1 contended that either of these measures would add flexibility to the training system.[7] Output could be

[4] This paragraph is based on an interview by AGF Hist Off with Col J. H. Banville, C&RD, AGF, AG Sec, 20 Nov 45.

[5] See, for example, AGF G–3 memo for CofS AGF, 28 Sep 42, sub: Visit to Repl Cen, Cp Robinson, Ark, 25 Sep 42. With attached M/Ss. 354.1/142 (RTC).

[6] AGF M/S, G–1 to CofS, 29 Sep 42, sub: RTCs. 354.1/142 (RTC).

[7] Background for this paragraph was provided by statements of Brig Gen Edward Barber to AGF Hist Off, 26 Nov 45. For the G–1 arguments, see the following AGF M/Ss in 314.7 (AGF Hist)(S): (1) G–1 to DCofS, 12 Jun 42, sub not given. (2) G–1 to CofS, 3 Aug 42, sub not given. (3) G–1 to G–3, 21 Oct 42, sub: Bl Tng in Inf, FA, and Cav RTCs. (4) G–1 to G–3, 28 Dec 42, sub: Requirements for EM in 1943 Augmentation of AGF. (5) G–1 to CofS, 4 Jan 43, sub as in (4).

easily diverted to meet emergency requirements. Misassignment would disappear or be greatly reduced, since the categories of classification would be less restrictive. Effective production would be increased, since capacity would no longer have to be diverted for special purposes. G–1 believed that greater flexibility would also be achieved in relating replacement production to overseas needs. Accurate prediction of battle losses, in the opinion of G–1, could not be based on a long list of specialist categories; prediction by total numbers would be difficult enough. Branch immaterial training would be adaptable to prediction on an over-all basis. Since replacements would go to established units, there should be time enough for specialist training after the soldier had joined a unit. Especially would this be true if greater advantage were taken of the civilian skills of inductees. In several categories of skill, such as clerk and truck driver, RTC training was largely a duplication of training already received in civilian life. On 28 December 1942 the G–1 case was stated as follows:[8]

> . . . our RTC's have placed too much emphasis upon training specialists. If this is continued when the mission is changed to that of furnishing loss replacements only, we will find ourselves critically short in some categories and over-produced in others. This leads to forced misassignments and lowered morale. The loss replacements in the general case should be a well-trained individual soldier who can be expected to join any kind of a unit and function effectively. The current British practice follows this ideal in that only basically trained individual soldiers are charged to theaters of operation as loss replacements. G–1 believes that training of the bulk of loss replacements should be limited to that required to produce a basically trained soldier capable of firing any of the individual weapons with which he may be armed. The additional training he may require as for example a cannoneer, chauffeur, clerk, etc., can be acquired very rapidly after he joins a unit in the theater.

The G–3 Section consistently opposed these proposals.[9] Its view was that only a full program of branch training would prepare a replacement to take his place in a unit, old or new. Specialist training had to be continued in order to produce men who would be effective from the moment of joining. G–3 believed that the remedy for misassignment and low production was to be sought in resisting demands for diversion of RTC facilities to special purposes (such as training illiterates and limited-service men, supplying officer candidates, ASTP students, air cadets, and the like) and in pressing for increases in RTC capacity.

The last round of the debate took place early in 1943, with General McNair acting as umpire. By this time it was clear, if it had not been a year before, that the primary mission of the replacement training centers was to supply overseas

[8] See n. 7 (4).

[9] (1) AGF M/S, G–3 to CofS, 30 Sep 42, sub: RTCs. 354.1/142 (RTC). (2) See n. 5.

loss replacements. Misassignment in the theaters had now been added to misassignment at home. Severe criticisms had been made of the quality of replacements sent to units in combat. The question of how to coordinate training of replacements with theater requirements, in respect to both quantity and quality, was receiving wide attention.

G–1, Army Ground Forces, once more proposed a general revision of the replacement training system.[10] The existing system had been designed "primarily with a view to the creation of new units" and only secondarily with a view to supplying loss replacements. Efficiency in the latter task demanded "a maximum of simplicity and flexibility," which, in the opinion of G–1, the existing system did not possess. It was proposed, therefore, that all RTC training be branch immaterial, so planned as "to produce an individual fighting man capable of self-sufficient action in any arm or service as a basic replacement," that specialist training be concentrated in service schools and be branch immaterial, and that school graduates, the large floating Army population unassigned at any moment, and RTC graduates be pooled in depots for assignment.

G–3 agreed that the mission of the replacement training centers was to furnish battle-loss replacements. But it contended that "replacements should be able to fight when they join." Branch immaterial training "would be inadequate for Antiaircraft, Field Artillery, Tank Destroyer, and Armored Force replacements. Therefore replacement training centers should continue branch training." G–3 would concede only that specialist training within branches might be poorly distributed and that there should be more basic and less specialist training.[11]

The principle that each combat arm should be self-sufficient in the training of specialists organically assigned to its units was an important element in AGF training policy. General McNair's view expressed this prevailing theory of the Army Ground Forces:[12]

> The question of whether training should be by branch or by specialty is not new. For example, the Quartermaster Corps in the past has tried to take over the operation of all army messes; the Ordnance Department has tried to take over the supply of ammunition to include the front line, and the Signal Corps has tried to take over signals to include the infantry regiment. The decision uniformly has been that the integrity of the arms should be preserved in the interest of teamwork and unity of command, even though it was realized fully that such a policy would not permit mass production and probably not result

[10] (1) AGF memo (C), G–1 for CofS, 13 Apr 43, sub: Supply of Repls. (2) AGF M/S (C), G–1 to CofS, 6 May 43, sub as in (1). Both in 341/257 (C).

[11] AGF M/S, G–3 to CofS, 29 Apr 43, sub: Supply of Repls. 341/257 (C).

[12] AGF M/S (C), CG to CofS, 18 May 43, sub and location as in n. 10 (1).

in maximum economy. Just as combat units are built by arm, so I believe should the training of replacements for such units be by arm. The specialists of an arm should be trained in that arm basically before they become specialists in order that they may fit into the picture to the best advantage.

The long debate over the form of replacement training had no immediate outcome, except perhaps to focus attention in the headquarters on fundamental issues. The basic question was the relative weight which should be given, in determining the form of the replacement training system, to flexibility of assignment and to perfection of training. The extreme positions taken by G–1 and G–3 reflected the natural bias of their dominant interests.

Temporarily G–3 won the debate. No action was taken on the proposal to institute common branch immaterial training in the centers and to confine specialist training to the service schools. It remained standard practice to train replacement specialists of the more common types in replacement training centers and to reserve schools for the rarer, more advanced, and more complex specialties.

A modification of the rejected G–1 proposal was introduced into the training of armored replacements. It was put forward by the Armored Command (formerly the Armored Force) in November 1943. Because the school and the replacement center of the Armored Command were both at Fort Knox the practice had been to give specialists five weeks of basic replacement training and then enroll them in appropriate school courses for the remainder of the training cycle. With a view to improving the quality of specialist replacements and to fitting them for broader assignment, the armored replacement training center in November 1943 began giving all trainees, whether or not destined for further specialist training, the full 17-week program of training as tank replacements. On completion of the course trainees were screened for aptitude and sent to the Armored School for specialist instruction. The result was to produce specialist replacements who, regardless of military occupational specialty, were trained tankers. The result was also to extend the training period for specialist replacements to as much as twenty-eight weeks.[13]

In August 1943 the War Department, in order to increase the availability of replacements at a time when demand was high and output unusually low, had fixed a limit of 5 percent on the number of RTC graduates who could be sent to service schools for further training.[14] The Armored Command policy violated

[13] AGF M/S, G–3 to CofS, 13 Nov 43, sub: Specialist Tng of Repls. 353/523 (Armd F).

[14] WD memo (R) for CGs AGF, ASF, AAF, 14 Aug 43, sub: Utilization of Personnel. 320.2/255 (R).

this ruling and Army Ground Forces directed that the policy be discontinued.[15] General McNair, personally answering the request of Maj. Gen. Alvin C. Gillem, Commanding General of the Armored Command, for reconsideration, admitted that the War Department limitation might be appealed, but added that he thought it sound. The question came down, as did so many questions that appeared to relate only to training, to the scarcity of manpower:[16]

> It would be desirable, of course, to train replacements for twice 17 weeks or even more, but the point is that the procedure, if applied widely, would be terrifically costly in manpower. We have studied this question from many angles up to a period of replacement training as great as six months. The period of 17 weeks was adopted as a compromise between the conflicting considerations of thorough training and the crying need of economizing manpower.

General McNair even saw a certain value in not training replacements too completely before they were handed over to a unit commander:[17]

> Of course armored unit commanders would like very highly trained replacements, as would other commanders, but there is much to be said in favor of requiring a unit commander to assume a certain responsibility for training his own unit, including the individuals composing it. It seems to me that 17 weeks is a very reasonable period by way of helping a fighting commander in building and maintaining a trained unit.

Perhaps this observation would have had greater force a year earlier, when fewer replacements were being sent directly into combat, but the fact remained that over-all insufficiency in the number of replacements did not permit the luxury of so finished a training program as that urged by the Armored Command.

However, the pressure of events in the remainder of 1943 and in 1944 was to modify the established system in the direction desired by G–1, broadening the categories of specialist training and laying greater emphasis on general proficiency within each branch.

The Issue of Unit versus Center Organization of Training

Discussion of the theory of replacement training during 1943 was also concerned with another pair of alternatives, the center versus the unit as the most

[15] AGF ltr to CG Armd Comd, 30 Sep 43, sub: Visit to Ft Knox, Ky, 17–18 Sep 43. 353.02/233 (AGF).

[16] (1) Personal ltr of Gen Gillem to Gen McNair, 9 Nov 43. (2) Personal ltr of Gen McNair to Gen Gillem, 15 Nov 43. Both in 353/523 (Armd F).

[17] See n. 16 (2).

effective vehicle for training. In analyzing complaints about the training of replacements, officers in Army Ground Forces, as early as February 1943, defined the problem in terms of concepts which were to become basic in these discussions. The AGF G–3 noted that criticism of replacements had not been very specific "but that in general the weakness is in lack of unit or team training, not in individual training." [18] The replacement was skillful enough at his specific job, but he had not acquired habits of cooperation with other members of a military team which would enable him to take the place of a man who had been an integral part of a smoothly functioning unit. The problem, G–3 acknowledged, was "a tough one," since the replacement training centers had been organized to provide individual training only, in contrast to the British and German systems of maintaining regular units to train replacements for specific units in combat. For the performance of its original mission of providing fillers for new units, the emphasis of the replacement system upon merely individual training had been appropriate. It had been planned that the trained individual would learn teamwork after he joined a unit, not while he was in the replacement center. Combat loss replacements, however, had to be more completely qualified for immediate duty. A unit in battle had no time to give training in teamwork to the replacements it received. It must have men who could fit into the established pattern of cooperation in the shortest time and with a minimum loss of unit effectiveness. The view of G–3, Army Ground Forces, was that such men could best be trained in regularly organized units, not in functionally organized centers. A major reorganization and expansion of the replacement training centers—undesirable during the pressure of war—would be required to convert them to a unit basis. As an alternative, after receiving individual training in existing centers replacements might go through training units set up especially for the purpose or through elaborate overseas depots organized on a unit basis. The latter plan seemed preferable since it would not divert tactical units to a training mission and also would acclimate men to the specific conditions of the combat theater.

Officers in Headquarters, Army Ground Forces, and in the War Department recommended the establishment of units in which replacements could be trained after graduation from replacement centers. It was reported that a similar revision of the existing system was favored by the G–1 and G–3 of the North African Theater and the G–1 and G–3 of the European Theater.[19]

[18] AGF M/S (S), G–3 to CofS, 20 Feb 43, sub: Loss Repl Tng. 354.1/4 (RTC)(S).

[19] (1) Memo of Lt Col Banville, AGF, for Col Winn, AGF, 26 May 43, sub: Loss Repls. 320.2/6 (O'seas Repls)(S). (2) Memo of Col L. L. Williams for CG AGF, 14 May 43. AGF G–2 Sec file, Observers #35.

230-171 O - 66 - 27

In May 1943 a committee of officers of the Plans, G–1, and G–3 Sections of AGF headquarters studied the replacement system with a view to improving the processing of replacements from the centers to the theaters. On 29 May the committee submitted a report which strongly recommended the establishment of replacement depots under AGF control.[20] Changes in training were also proposed. The committee noted that "the basic organization" of the replacement training centers and the 13-week training period were both adapted to the conduct of recruit training and the preparation of men "to start unit training in a peacetime army." No change had been made in these plans and no distinction had been made between "the training of a battle loss replacement and a training loss replacement." Overseas demand was for a replacement able to join a unit engaged in combat. The conclusion of the report was that training currently conducted in replacement training centers was not adequate for this purpose. In addition to establishment of AGF depots and other administrative improvements, the committee recommended a 4-week extension of replacement training, to be conducted in provisional units organized in the depots and shipped together overseas. G–3 of the Army Ground Forces did not believe additional small-unit training should be conducted in depots.[21] If unit training was to be given, G–3 maintained, it should be done either by designating divisions as replacement divisions or by reorganizing the replacement training centers into units and extending their training period. But G–3 did not favor immediate change in the existing plan of training. General McNair was asked to decide the two fundamental questions thus raised—whether the training of replacements should be increased, and where additional training, if provided, should be conducted.[22] General McNair's decision was delayed by the entrance of the War Department into the discussion.

On 7 June 1943 the War Department Committee on the Revision of the Military Program presented an unfavorable report on the replacement system. The committee recommended a plan similar to that put forward by the AGF committee: an extension of training to six months to include unit training.[23] On 13 June G–3 of the War Department, in a memorandum severely critical of the replacement system, called for the comments of Army Ground Forces on a plan,

(3) WD memo (S) of Lt Col H. W. Wilkinson for Director MPD, 28 May 43, sub: Rpt of Visit to O'seas Theaters. 320.2/7 (O'seas Repls) (S).

[20] Draft of Rpt (C), G–1, G–3, and Plans Sec for CofS AGF, 29 May 43, sub: Loss Repl System. 354.1/11 (Camps) (C).

[21] AGF M/S (C) to CofS, 29 May 43, sub: Repl System. 354.1/11 (Camps) (C).

[22] AGF M/S (C), Plans to CofS, 31 May 43, sub and location as in n. 21.

[23] Memo (S) of Cols Maddocks, Chamberlain, and Carter for CofS USA, 7 Jun 43, sub: Revision of Current Mil Prog, Tab C. 381/177 (S).

substantially the same as that of the War Department Committee: to give replacements six months' training, three months of which would be devoted to unit training, combined training, and field exercises, and to organize training divisions or similar units in which both officer and enlisted replacements would be trained together and from which they would be shipped together overseas.[24] The War Department did not intend to discard the individual replacement system for a system of replacement by units, though the maximum value of its proposals seemed to depend on such a change. But it hoped that by shipping replacements overseas in the units in which they had been trained a greater degree of discipline, morale, physical fitness, and general training efficiency might be preserved than under the method of individual shipment then prevailing.

General McNair agreed with the proposal to provide six months' training for replacements, favoring a combination of the existing RTC system and of assignment to regular units as overstrength for the last three months. He did not favor setting up training divisions, feeling that training in them would lack realism: men in such organizations would know they were not going to fight as units but would be broken up on arrival overseas. The program would furnish, consequently, little incentive to genuine unit training. General McNair was convinced that, regardless of reforms, no system of training would be effective unless replacements were requested on the basis of losses rather than of T/O strength, were correctly assigned overseas, and were used to replace losses and not to activate new units.[25]

In commenting on the War Department proposals, General McNair had restricted himself to their merits from the standpoint of training and to the administrative obstacles to effective training. The reply of Army Ground Forces to the War Department memorandum, while embodying certain of the views of General McNair, was based on a broader view of the replacement problem and concluded with a recommendation which General McNair had not originally put forth.[26] Three plans for providing six months' training were put forward. Plan I involved doubling the length of training in replacement training centers, which would require great increases in center capacity, equipment, and housing. Under this plan Army Ground Forces thought it would be advisable to form special units in the replacement centers for the unit and field training phase,

[24] WD memo (S) WDGCT 320.2 Gen (6-12-43) to CG AGF, 13 Jun 43, sub: Loss Repls. 354.1/4 (RTC)(S).

[25] AGF memo (C), CofS for G-3, 18 Jun 43, sub: Loss Repls. 314.7 (AGF Hist)(C).

[26] AGF memo (S) for CofS USA, 25 Jun 43, sub: Loss Repls. 320.2/9 (O'seas Repls)(S).

rather than to reorganize existing RTC units for combined individual and unit training. Plan II would have continued the regular thirteen weeks' RTC training, to which would have been added thirteen weeks' training in existing tactical units —substantially the plan suggested by General McNair. This would not have increased overhead requirements, but unit strengths would have had to be increased, as would also RTC capacities to train reception center men whom the units could no longer absorb. In Plan III, existing replacement center training would have been continued, with thirteen weeks added in special units—a replacement regiment with each division in training. Of the three, Plan II was recommended as likely to produce the best unit-trained replacement, but it was thought undesirable because of the prohibitive burden of administration and training that it would place on divisions training for overseas service. Plan III, it was believed, would afford the next best unit training. All factors considered, Plan I seemed best to Army Ground Forces if six months of training had to be given. But since a major increase in personnel, housing, and equipment overhead would be entailed by all three plans, Army Ground Forces opposed resorting to any of them until "all other methods" had failed. Two other plans were put forward, which Army Ground Forces felt "no compelling reason to believe at present . . . would fail to produce replacements meeting all reasonable requirements." The first of these, Plan IV, would have continued the current system of training without change but would have eliminated the administrative deficiencies in the use of replacements overseas. Plan V was a compromise, increasing the training period to seventeen weeks, by which, it was held, the present course "could be improved greatly and unit training included." Army Ground Forces recommended adoption of Plan V.

While the War Department's suggestions were under consideration in Headquarters, Army Ground Forces, the Armored Force put forward a concrete plan for training replacements which was similar in all essentials to that outlined by the War Department. The Armored Force was convinced that training given in the replacement training center produced a replacement "fully prepared to take his place *as an individual in* . . . vehicular crews," but it believed that before the trainee could be considered a suitable loss replacement for an armored unit he needed "further training as a member of the crew, platoon, and company teams." General Gillem proposed that all RTC graduates be sent to the 20th Armored Division, which had been used to train cadres and to store replacements, for a unit training period of four weeks.[27]

[27] Personal ltr of Gen Gillem to Gen McNair, 21 Jun 43. 353/515 (Armd F).

In view of its recommendation that training be extended to seventeen weeks in the replacement training centers, Army Ground Forces disapproved the Armored Force plan. General McNair, replying to General Gillem, summed up the attitude of the headquarters on the use of divisions to train replacements:[28]

> One of the points at issue is whether combat divisions should be utilized for the advanced training of replacements, or whether such training should be given by replacement training centers. If this former system were applied generally, it would take out of circulation a formidable number of divisions now being trained for combat, and set them aside primarily and practically entirely as replacement divisions. The wisdom of such a course is doubted.

Opportunity to test the value of the Armored Force proposal was not provided. On 13 July the War Department approved the AGF recommendation to extend training in replacement centers to seventeen weeks without use of other training units.[29] The new program went into effect on 8 August 1943. The 20th Armored Division was ordered to prepare for a combat assignment.

The considerations weighing most heavily in support of simple extension of the existing training cycle pertained not to training but to production and economy of manpower. The "small-unit training" which Army Ground Forces proposed to include in the extended program was not the kind of unit training that had been repeatedly urged since February as meeting criticism of replacements. What had been urged was training as a member of a tactical unit. What Army Ground Forces proposed to put into the 17-week program was instruction in unit tactics to be given to men who were members not of units but of nontactical RTC organizations.

The extension of the training cycle, together with the increase in field training and greater emphasis on tactics, did not finally dispose of questions concerning the appropriate form of replacement training. For the time being, the War Department was satisfied with the improvement in replacement training made possible by the extension of the training cycle to seventeen weeks. In Army Ground Forces, however, the discussion continued. In November, after an inspection trip to replacement centers, Brig. Gen. John M. Lentz, G-3, reported to General McNair:[30]

[28] Memo of Gen McNair for Gen Gillem, 5 Jul 43, sub not given. 353/515 (Armd F).

[29] WD memo (S) WDGCT 320.2 Gen (6-12-43) to CG AGF, 13 Jul 43, sub: Loss Repls. 354.1/4 (RTC)(S).

[30] AGF M/S, G-3 to CG, 2 Nov 43, sub: Items as Result of Inspection Trip (Last Week). AGF G-3 Schs Br, RTC Policy File, Tab L (S).

I now believe that the replacement training centers would do better to organize on a straight unit basis, i.e., each battalion in infantry replacement training centers to be a standard infantry battalion. Such an organization does not provide for special requirement rates and is therefore wasteful. On the other hand, trainees at present show faulty unit training, are not prepared to take their place in a regular unit. While individual training at replacement training centers is superior to that in new divisions, the new divisions turn out better platoon problems.

Other officers of the G-3 Section, after visiting replacement centers, came to the same conclusion.[31] It was reported that infantry light machine gun and 60-mm. mortar replacements, trained primarily as riflemen and only secondarily as gunners, were not receiving enough training to qualify them.[32] The organization of the centers prevented realistic tactical training: "A heavy weapons battalion cannot conduct logical field exercises by itself. Within the units platoons are organized as training units and must therefore reorganize along tactical lines for field work. This must result in confusion in the minds of the trainees." [33] Members of the G-3 Section recommended that a study be made looking toward reorganization of replacement training centers on a Table of Organization basis.[34] Brig. Gen. Francis B. Mallon, Commanding General of AGF Replacement Depot No. 1 and formerly the commander of the infantry replacement training center at Camp Robinson, expressed the same view.[35] On 26 November 1943 the substance of these proposals was presented to the Replacement and School Command. In concluding a summary of a recent inspection of replacement centers General McNair raised the general question of reorganization: "Although well trained individually it is questionable that replacements are being prepared fully to take their places in a T/O unit. Organization on a T/O basis might serve to correct this defect." Such a method of organization would eliminate, he suggested, the confusing dual platoon organization—4-squad platoons for training, 3-squad platoons for tactical exercises. It would facilitate a more logical grouping of combat and administrative specialists for field exercises. In rifle companies better-trained individuals might result from the concentration of each trainee on a particular job—rifleman, light machine gunner,

[31] See G-3 Schs Br Inspection Rpts in 314.7 (AGF Hist) (S).

[32] Memo (S) of Col R. M. Shaw for G-3 AGF, 18 Nov 43, sub: Visit to R&SC and AA Comd. 314.7 (AGF Hist) (S).

[33] Memo (S) of Col L. L. Williams for G-3 AGF, 8 Nov 43, sub: Visit to Cp Fannin, Cp Wolters, Cp Hood, and Cp Hulen, 3-5 Nov 43. 314.7 (AGF Hist) (S).

[34] See n. 31.

[35] AGF M/S, G-3 to CofS, 13 Nov 43, sub: Tng of Repls. AGF G-3 files, 353/382 (Tng Gen, 1943).

mortar man. The Replacement and School Command was asked for comments and recommendations on "the advisability of organizing battalions or regiments along T/O lines." [36]

In a long reply Maj. Gen. Harry F. Hazlett, Commanding General of the Replacement and School Command, presented a variety of arguments against unit reorganization. A T/O plan, he held, would increase the enlisted and commissioned overhead required, principally because a T/O company was much smaller than an RTC company. Housing would be complicated, because most replacement center construction had been designed for 240-man companies: to fit smaller T/O companies into present housing would result either in waste of housing and loss of capacity or in overlap of companies in barracks and messes, difficult to administer and operate. The Replacement and School Command believed that the training of specialists would present serious difficulties under a T/O scheme. Headquarters and service specialists were currently segregated in companies adjacent to their schools, shops, and code rooms, with special instructional staffs assigned to them. If specialists were dispersed in T/O units throughout a training center, this centralization of instruction would be impracticable because of the loss of time required to move men to the training areas and also because of the administrative difficulty involved in maintaining training records on men drawn from many units. On the other hand, to conduct specialized training by regiments or smaller units would waste special instructors and training equipment by dispersion. Great difficulty was anticipated in keeping RTC output adjusted to requirements. The existing organization permitted rapid and easy increase or decrease in any category of trainee, whereas the fixed T/O system would necessitate the wasteful addition of men in all SSN's of the unit merely to increase the production of men in one or two SSN's. Even if they could be trained in the proper numbers, trainees produced under the proposed organization would be still more liable to misassignment than those currently produced. Trained in a single weapon or job category, a soldier, though better qualified in his specialty than a replacement more broadly trained, could not be shifted to another weapon or job in the same type of company without almost complete waste of skill.[37]

The only advantage—and in the opinion of the Replacement and School Command a qualified one—that might be expected under a T/O organization was "a more comprehensive picture of military organization" for the trainee.

[36] AGF ltr to CG R&SC, 26 Nov 43, sub: Inspection of RTCs. 353.02/263 (AGF).

[37] R&SC ltr to CG AGF, 9 Dec 43, sub: Orgn of RTCs on T/O Basis. 354.1/301 (RTC).

Pointing out that a general picture was already given of units up to the company, General Hazlett declared that, while a demonstration of the battalion and its attachments could be included in the training program, an understanding of echelons higher than the company was not essential to proper training of the replacement unless the mission of the replacement center was to be changed. General Hazlett concluded that the existing organization of the centers best accomplished the mission of replacement training centers and was the most economical in use of overhead.[38]

There the matter rested. General Lentz believed that the Replacement and School Command's reply involved a "major fallacy" in assuming a regular tactical organization instead of an organization "along T/O lines" as intended by Army Ground Forces. "Our thought," General Lentz reported to the Chief of Staff, "was that RTC battalions still would consist of four 250-man companies with one of these companies heavy weapons and one platoon in rifle companies a light weapons platoon." But he pointed out that "change from one system to another, no matter how superior, may not be advisable at this date," especially if additional overhead would be needed and if recent reports of the improved quality of replacements were borne out. He therefore recommended that the Replacement and School Command should not be required to change the organization of replacement training.[39]

[38] *Ibid.*

[39] (1) AGF M/S, G-3 to CofS, 28 Dec 43, sub: Orgn of RTCs on T/O Basis. AGF G-3 Schs Br files, RTC Binder 1/169 (S). (2) AGF M/S, G-3 to CofS, 31 Dec 43, sub as in (1). 354.1/301 (RTC). (3) AGF ltr to CG R&SC, 5 Jan 44, sub as in (1). 354.1/301 (RTC).

IV. Adjustments to Theater Requirements, 1944-45

A number of important changes in the training program for replacements were made during 1944-45 in response to developments in the pattern of theater requirements, both quantitative and qualitative. In general, these changes were in the direction of emphasis on broad general training and the development of basic combat skills, as distinguished from excessive specialization and inclusion of what, under conditions of emergency, were regarded as "frills." Such emphasis not only appeared to meet the principal needs revealed by combat experience but also permitted a flexibility of assignment which the quantitative needs of the ground combat troops rendered necessary. The required changes were made in the training program without drastic alterations in the organization of replacement training centers. While for a time common branch immaterial training was established, it was carried on only during the first six weeks of training and was later abandoned in favor of a program combining branch immaterial with branch training. The proposal of 1943 to place replacement training on a unit rather than individual basis was dropped from consideration with the decision that the replacement centers should develop basic combat skills rather than tactical training on the higher level. When the question of training for the Pacific war became uppermost, this stress on basic combat skills, with appropriate modifications to meet the special conditions of the war, was given particular emphasis.

Criticisms of Company Tactical Training

By the spring of 1944, when replacements trained under the 17-week program were arriving in overseas theaters, it began to appear that the new program, while producing men better trained than formerly, had serious weaknesses. For these the inclusion of company tactical training was believed to be chiefly responsible. Overseas commanders and AGF observers, as well as RTC officers, agreed that training in the tactics of the company—adopted largely as a means of removing deficiencies in unit training which had occasioned so much agitation in 1943 —was not necessary for the individual replacement, was too advanced for him fully to grasp, and was conducted at the expense of time that could be spent to greater advantage on more urgently needed "basic" instruction.

As early as March 1944 General Hazlett, who had opposed the inclusion of extensive company tactical training in the 17-week Mobilization Training Program, concluded, in a report on a 2-month inspection tour of the European and North African Theaters of Operations, that "unit training and instruction in the tactics of units higher than a platoon are not essential for Infantry replacements." [1] Officers interviewed overseas agreed with the comment of Maj. Gen. Charles W. Ryder, Commanding General, 34th Division:[2]

> The tactics of the Patrol (Infantry Rifle Squad) is all that is necessary in the way of tactical training. All that replacements need to know about attack and defense of units, they will know if they are proficient in scouting and patrolling. Unit training is not essential.

In March also Brig. Gen. Eugene W. Fales, commanding the infantry replacement training center at Camp Blanding, expressed to General McNair the opinion that it was unwise to spend time on company problems and urged limiting the 17-week course to squad and platoon exercises.[3] However, Brig. Gen. Leo Donovan, G–3, Army Ground Forces, believed at this time that training in tactics of the company should be continued: "Company problems," he wrote, "introduce the principles of mutual coordination with other platoon teams of the company in the accomplishment of a common mission." They introduced the trainee to the idea of supporting fire and to the supply, mess, and administrative set-up necessary in an efficient organization; squad and platoon problems would not illustrate these points. Moreover, General Donovan suggested that, "since specialists should apply their specialties in their normal T/O positions," company problems were needed, because few specialists were found in squads and platoons.[4]

By May 1944 it had become increasingly clear that these advantages of company training could be obtained only at the sacrifice of more essential instruction. After a visit to Camp Blanding, G–3 of the War Department reported to General McNair that "the importance of squad and platoon training for replace-

[1] R&SC ltr (S) to CG AGF, 25 Mar 44, sub: Repls in ETOUSA and NATOUSA. 320.2/126 (O'seas Repls) (S).

[2] *Ibid.*

[3] (1) AGF M/S, CG to G–3, 31 Mar 44, sub: Items Resulting from Inspection Trip. AGF G–3 files, 333.1/118 (1944). (2) Memo of Lt Col J. L. Hines, AGF, for G–3 AGF, 22 May 44, sub: Obsns during Trip. 314.7 (AGF Hist) (S).

[4] AGF M/S, G–3 to CG, 4 Apr 44, sub: G–3 Items Resulting from Trip, 29–30 Mar 44. AGF G–3 files, 333.1/118 (1944).

ments has been emphasized in reports from all theaters; however, suggestions that company training be materially reduced, if not entirely eliminated, appear to merit consideration."[5] On 13 May 1944 the War Department, in a memorandum to the Army Ground Forces, asked for comments on eliminating company tactics and recognition of aircraft, in order to devote more time to basic subjects, particularly mines, booby traps, weapons, and tactical training of the individual soldier.[6]

Further Revision of Mobilization Training Programs

The War Department's suggestion coincided with plans already under way in the Army Ground Forces looking toward major revisions of the Mobilization Training Programs. Readjustments of hours and subjects, and particularly the reduction of time spent on company training, had been considered recently in discussions between Headquarters, Army Ground Forces, and the Replacement and School Command. Shortly after the War Department's views were received, the concept of revision was broadened. "There is more time given to a variety of subjects than is thought practical," declared an AGF representative. "It is better," he maintained, "to eliminate some subjects and put more time on basic work." The Replacement and School Command agreed. The revision now undertaken, it was concluded, should be "more radical than anything else so far."[7]

The shape of this radical modification of the program became apparent late in May—less than two weeks after the War Department's memorandum—when the Replacement and School Command requested permission to publish changes pending the printing of revised MTP's.[8] The rifle trainee, for example, was no longer to receive 4 hours' training in aircraft recognition or 44 hours in tactics of the rifle company. Instead, he was now to get 4 hours of mental conditioning under overhead artillery fire; 8 additional hours—making a total of 16—on

[5] WD G-3 memo (C) to CG AGF, 12 May 44, sub: Rpts of Visit to the IRTC at Cp Blanding, Fla. 333.1/120 (C).

[6] WD memo WDGCT 353 (13 May 44) to CG AGF, 13 May 44, sub: MTPs for Enl Repls. 461/119 (MTP).

[7] (1) Record of tel conv (C) between Col Porch, AGF, and Col Shallene, R&SC, 16 May 44. (2) Record of tel conv, as in (1), 18 May 44. Both in 333.1/120 (C).

[8] (1) R&SC ltr (R) to CG AGF, 24 May 44, sub: Revision of Branch MTPs. 353/109 (R). (2) Memo of Col S. E. Faine, AGF, for G-3 AGF, 3 Jun 44, sub: Conference at R&SC, 30 May-1 Jun, on Revision of RTC MTPs. AGF G-3 files, 353/463 (Tng Gen, 1944).

antitank and antipersonnel mines and booby traps; and increases in several other basic combat subjects:

Subject	*MTP Old 7–3*	*MTP New 7–3*
Bayonet	16	18
Automatic Rifle:		
Mechanical Training	8	12
Firing at Field Targets	8	12
Tactical Training of the Individual Soldier:		
Concealment and Camouflage	4	8
Hasty Fortification	4	8
Scouts, Observers, and Messengers	8	12
Operation of Patrols	40	48

Changes similar to these were made in the four other MTP's for replacement training, and were approved by Army Ground Forces on 1 June 1944. Their effect was "to augment and emphasize training in mines and booby traps, weapons, and individual and squad tactical training."

But this was only a beginning; the major reduction of the "variety of subjects" came on 15 July, when the Replacement and School Command submitted to the Army Ground Forces drafts of five completely revised MTP's.[9] Continuing the policy of standardization that had received persistent attention during the past two years, the Replacement and School Command had equalized the number of hours allotted to subjects common to all programs where the same degree of proficiency was desired, and it had also standardized the nomenclature for all common subjects. But the major shift in policy was omission from the new programs of a number of subjects, among them some venerable titles that had been on the list since the earliest programs were prepared. The object in view, agreed upon by General McNair and General Hazlett, was "to reduce the total number of subjects and to emphasize training of the individual to fit him in the smallest tactical unit." The following subjects were eliminated, to be combined as concurrent instruction with other subjects or to be taught during the pre-cycle orientation period: Military Discipline; Articles of War; Equipment, Clothing, and Tent Pitching; Protection against Carelessness; and Recognition Training.

Recognition Training had been eliminated from the programs in June. Discipline, it was decided, could not be implanted in the soldier in a 4-hour course; it was a pervasive requirement of action, "beginning with the orientation talk of the commanding general and extending through all phases of

[9] R&SC ltr to CG AGF, 15 Jul 44, sub: Revision of MTP 7–3, 6–3, 2–2, 17–1, 18–2. 461/121 (MTP).

training throughout the training cycle." Protection against Carelessness was similarly reappraised: the best way to develop an awareness of the need for care was to insist upon it at all times in all types of training. Equipment, Clothing, and Tent Pitching—an old stand-by dating back to the 1935 MTP's—had always been taught largely through concurrent training during Inspections, Marches, and Bivouacs. The new programs formalized this practice and provided that inspections would henceforth specifically include training in Care and Wearing of Equipment and Clothing, and that Marches and Bivouacs would include Tent Pitching. The Articles of War were put in the same category with information about bond allotments, the Soldiers' and Sailors' Relief Act, and free mail service—administrative matters to be taken up during the trainees' pre-cycle week of orientation to Army life.

Other changes reflected the same determination to abolish frills and to concentrate on subjects of practical importance to the individual soldier. The subject "Organization of the Army" was changed to "Organization of the Battalion or Regiment": the trainee was no longer required to become familiar with so large a picture. "Combat Intelligence and Counter-Intelligence" was superseded by a new title with a more limited range: "Prisoners of War; Protection of Military Information and Military Censorship." The course was reduced from five hours to two in the transformation.

The hours allotted in the 1944 MTP 7-3 to several infantry rifle subjects show numerous increases over those of 1943:[10]

Subject	*Hours*	
	MTP 7–3 (1943)	*MTP 7–3 (1944)*
Bayonet	16	20
Extended Order	6	8
Marches	24	28
Antitank and Antipersonnel Mines and Booby Traps	8	18
Hand Grenades	8	12
Operation of Patrols	40	48
Tactics of the Rifle Squad and Platoon	82	94
Tactical Training of the Individual Soldier	20	31
Battle Courses (Mental Conditioning)	10	12
Automatic Rifle	36	48
Light Machine Gun	48	62
Mortar, 60-mm.	42	60

[10] (1) MTP 7-3, WD, 9 Dec 43. (2) MTP 7-3, WD, 4 Nov 44.

On the other hand, a few important subjects were cut:

Rifle Marksmanship	126	103
Tactics of the Light Machine Gun Squad and Section	34	20
Tactics of the 60-mm. Mortar Squad and Section	34	20

These cuts were due primarily to the institution of six weeks of common branch immaterial training in all replacement training centers. A record course with rifle was prescribed for everyone; it could not be given as much time as the regular infantry rifle training without crowding out other necessary basic subjects. The time for Rifle Marksmanship in MTP 7-3 therefore had to be reduced to bring it into line with the other branch programs. The use of the first six weeks to teach all the basic subjects meant, on the other hand, that specifically branch subjects, such as Tactics of the Light Machine Gun Squad, were all thrown into the last eleven weeks. Here they competed for the limited time available, which it seemed more important to give to technique than to tactics. It was for this reason that the time given to some of these subjects was reduced.

The 1944 revision of the replacement training programs had the effect of bringing instruction into closer conformity with the needs of overseas theaters, while in effect carrying out the War Department's July 1943 directive "to include additional small-unit training and at least two weeks of continuous field exercises." The field exercises remained, and "small unit tactics" was now construed, as it had been until 1943, as tactics of the squad and platoon; nonessential subjects that dissipated precious time and energy were cut out. It was generally agreed that these were the best programs that had been produced.

Revision of Training Rates

During 1944 great changes in the RTC program were brought about by revisions of training rates, that is, rates issued by the War Department fixing the proportions of men trained in each specialist category in each branch. The rates originally established for replacement centers were based roughly on Tables of Organization: the infantry regiment contained 9 rifle companies, 3 heavy weapons companies, 1 antitank, 1 service, and 1 headquarters company—15 in all. Infantry centers trained 60 percent riflemen, 20 percent heavy weapons crewmen, and 6.66 percent each of antitank, service, and headquarters specialists.

It had long been anticipated that heavy combat would increase the demand for combat specialists, such as riflemen, tankers, troopers, and tank destroyer crewmen, and would decrease the demand for technical and administrative specialists—cooks, clerks, mechanics, and the like. The extent of the difference in requirements for these two types of specialists was not appreciated in advance, and changes in training rates were made late and hesitantly.[11] No general revision of the rates originally in effect was made until February 1944; thereafter rate changes were directed at frequent intervals. The fluctuations in infantry rates from 1941 through 1945 are shown in the accompanying table.

Frequent revisions of training rates had undesirable effects on training. Each change required a major reorganization of replacement centers, transfer and retraining of instructors, and reapportionment and procurement of equipment, all of which disrupted the established system of training for some time. Changed rates were not reflected in RTC output until at least five months after they were made. Training rates had to be based on fairly accurate long-range prediction of losses and had to remain stable for at least five months in order to be effective. Neither condition was satisfied during 1944.[12] The immediate effect of rate changes was to complicate training and to impair considerably its efficiency.

The training of specialists was greatly complicated by revisions of rates during 1944. From the beginning it had been standard practice to organize full companies of specialists of a single type. Training and administration were simplified and equipment, facilities, and instructor personnel were economized under this system, which was made possible by the need for specialists in all categories in considerable numbers. Successive changes in training rates during 1944 greatly reduced the numerical requirement for most types of specialists. It was no longer possible, without overproduction, to form complete companies of specialists of a given type. Training by platoon and even section groups became necessary. There were only two ways in which companies could be formed: either by grouping specialists of one type in different stages of training, or by grouping different types of specialists in the same stage of training. Either method presented disadvantages: supervision was difficult under the first plan; effective use of special instructors was difficult under the second. In some instances the number of specialists of a given type to be trained fell so low that all training in the specialty had to be concentrated in one or two replacement centers in order to form groups of economical size. This expedient wasted potential specialists

[11] AGF study (S) (by Col J. H. Banville), 13 Jun 45, sub: The Repl System—EM. 327.3/114 (SS)(S).

[12] See above, "The Provision of Enlisted Replacements."

Training Rates for Infantry Replacement Training Centers, March 1941–October 1945

(Percentage Distribution)

Type of Training	Original Rates Mar 41[a]	In Effect Mar 43	In Effect Feb 44	Directed 8 Mar 44	Directed 4 Aug 44	Directed 17 Nov 44	In Effect 31 Mar 45	Directed 11 Oct 45
	(1)	(2)	(3)	(4)	(5)	(6)	(7)	(8)
Rifle (SSN 745).......	60.0	60.1	58.0	61.9	74.25	77.67	87.32	42.40
Heavy Weapons (SSN's 1605, 812)..	20.0	18.9	19.9	13.8	16.00	10.55	5.49	16.60
Antitank (SSN 610)...	6.7	6.8	6.7	4.1	4.75	3.54	2.17	9.90
Cannon (SSN's 9531, 844)...............	....	....	2.1	0.9	0.25	1.00	0.58	4.90
Headquarters Specialists (SSN's 636, 761, 641, 667, 776).....	6.7	7.4	6.8	7.3	1.91	3.60	2.23	7.40
Service Specialists (SSN's 014, 060, 213, 345, 405, 511, 729, 803)......	6.7	6.8	6.5	12.0	2.84	3.64	2.21	18.80
TOTAL........	100.0	100.0	100.0	100.0	100.00	100.00	100.00	100.00

Source: Col. 1: CofInf ltr to TAG, 21 Oct 40, recorded in Logbook of Brig Gen J. W. Curtis, CofS R&SC.
Col. 2: AGF G–1 study (S), Mar 43, sub: Repl Tng Centers—Capacities and Types of Tng. 341/104 (S). Apparent discrepancy in original records corrected on basis of personnel reported.
Cols. 3 and 4: AGF ltr (S) to CG R&SC, 8 Mar 44, sub: Revision of RTC Capacities and Tng Rates. 354.1/101 (RTC) (S).
Col. 5: (1) WD memo (C) WDGCT 320 RTC (31 Jul 44) for CG AGF, sub: Tng MOS's for Inf Repl Tng Cens. 220.01/101 (C&R) (C). (2) AGF ltr (C) to CG R&SC, 4 Aug 44, sub: Revision of Tng Rates in Inf Repl Tng Cens. 220.01/101 (C&R) (C).
Col. 6: AGF ltr (S) to CG R&SC, 17 Nov 44, sub: Tng Rates, AGF Repl Tng Cens. 354.1/112 (RTC) (S).
Col. 7: AGF G–3 Sec, Schs and Repl Tng Br, Tng Rates Binder (S).
Col. 8: AGF ltr (C) to CG R&SC, 11 Oct 45, sub: Tng Rates, AGF Repl Tng Cens. 354.1 (RTC) (C).

[a] Components do not add to 100.0, due to rounding.

assigned to the centers from which specialist training had been withdrawn, since men were screened for special training within the center, not within Army Ground Forces or the branch as a whole. Thus a potential field lineman assigned to a center where no field linemen were trained might arbitrarily be made into a rifleman or cannon crewman.[13]

Besides creating these difficulties for training, revision of training rates by the end of 1944 had worked vast changes in the replacement system. By that time,

[13] This paragraph is based on (1) AGF memo (S) of Lt Col Hines to G–3 AGF, 22 May 44, sub: Obsns during Trip. 314.7 (AGF Hist) (S). (2) AGF memo (S) of Lt Col Hines to G–3 AGF, 13 Jun 44, sub: Brief of Rpt of Inspection to Ft Riley, Kans, and Reply by CG R&SC. 314.7 (AGF Hist)(S). (3) R&SC ltr (S) to CGs RTCs, 22 Mar 44, sub: Orgn for Sp Tng. AGF G–3 Schs Br files, RTC Binder 1/262 (S). (4) R&SC ltr to CGs IRTCs, 16 Aug 44, sub as in (3). AGF G–3 files, 353/521 (Tng Gen, 1944).

as far as numbers were concerned, training was overwhelmingly concentrated on a very small array of combat specialties. In most branches, one or two types of training predominated. The two most common specialties in each branch accounted for the following proportions of its RTC training:

Branch	*Percent*
Antiaircraft	65.49
Armored	85.54
Cavalry (Mechanized)	83.66
Cavalry (Horse)	97.92
Field Artillery	47.07
Infantry	88.22
Tank Destroyer	87.94

The other specialties, ranging from three in Horse Cavalry to fourteen in Antiaircraft, took up the remaining capacity.[14]

Institution of Branch Immaterial Training

Branch immaterial training had been strongly recommended by the G–1 Section of Army Ground Forces during 1942 and 1943, largely as a way of gearing replacement production to overseas requirements. Rejected in 1942 and 1943 as unlikely to produce replacements ready for battle, branch immaterial training was adopted in 1944 for reasons very similar to those offered in 1942 and 1943. Under the plan adopted in August 1944, all replacements, regardless of branch, received a common course of instruction during the first six weeks of the training cycle. Branch training for specific military assignments was confined to the last eleven weeks.

Adoption of branch immaterial basic training was the result of two developments, the Physical Profile plan and the intensification of combat. Under the Physical Profile plan introduced in February 1944 it was contemplated that all trainees assigned to AGF replacement training centers would be "reprofiled" at the end of the sixth week of training.[15] The 3,500 men of lowest profile in infantry centers were then to be exchanged for an equal number of high-profile trainees in other branch centers. Continuity of training could be maintained for men so transferred only if the first six weeks of training were identical in all

[14] AGF ltr (S) to CGs R&SC and AA Comd, 17 Nov 44, sub: Tng Rates, AGF RTCs. 354.1/112 (RTC) (S). There was no Coast Artillery RTC production in 1944.

[15] WD Gen Council Min (S), 31 Jan 44, 21 Feb 44, 28 Feb 44.

230-171 O - 66 - 28

centers. In the summer of 1944 the intensification of combat in Europe put an increasing emphasis on broad training.[16] Assignment overseas, none too precise in any event, was more subject to error the more specialized the replacement was and the more complicated the provision of large numbers of replacements to many units became. Since it was difficult to anticipate precisely either the numbers or types of replacements needed, pools had to be maintained, and for flexibility it was essential that replacements in pools be as generally useful as possible. In addition, radical revisions were being made in the estimated requirements for replacements in the several arms. Infantrymen were at a great premium; production of antiaircraft artillerymen, tank destroyer crewmen, and cavalrymen tapered off sharply. The possibility was ever present that men might have to be transferred from one branch to another before their training had been completed or immediately thereafter. Transfer, if it was not to involve uneconomical retraining, had to be based on a common military background.

In earlier developments of the RTC programs precedent was not lacking for the adoption of common basic training. It had always been assumed that every soldier needed training in certain basic subjects; common recruit training had long been a standard peacetime practice. The original MTP's for training replacements, giving general expression to this custom, had provided a 2-week basic training period common to all branches and designed to prepare each trainee for emergency use in any unit. In all branch MTP's common subjects had been included from the beginning; among these were such basic subjects as first aid, drill, equipment, clothing, tent pitching, physical training, and courtesy and discipline. Through successive revisions of the branch programs, this list of common subjects had been lengthened, and their names and the allotment of hours to each had been standardized. From early in 1942 until April 1943 two branch immaterial replacement training centers had conducted basic training for men who might be assigned to any military branch. The value of common training had been demonstrated in the availability of men for variable assignment to meet emergency requirements.

Concomitant developments in the MTP's, on the other hand, militated against setting aside six weeks for branch immaterial training. The most important of these was the long and growing list in each arm of subjects which had been demonstrated by combat experience to be necessary. Adjustment of branch programs to the demands placed upon loss replacements shipped overseas had

[16] Record of tel conv between Col Porch and Lt Col Schrader, AGF, and Col Shallene, R&SC, 8 Aug 44. AGF G-3 files, 341.6/145 (RTC, 1944).

entailed great increases in specific branch subjects, especially in the technique of weapons and in individual and small-unit tactical training. The time required to develop combat proficiency in these branch subjects could not easily be concentrated into the last eleven weeks of the program. It was feared that to reduce the time for these subjects in order to set up a uniform 6-week basic program might lower the quality of replacements. Here again was the familiar dilemma of versatility versus specialization: better gunners could be produced by starting gunnery instruction early in the training cycle; soldiers who might be shifted among branches when necessary could be better produced by deferring gunnery instruction until a rounded basic training had been given.

For a period of several months the Army Ground Forces, lukewarm on the proposal and anxious to defer action on it at a time when exceptionally heavy demands for replacements had to be met, managed to postpone its application to AGF replacement centers.[17] Tentative branch immaterial programs were prepared calling for six weeks of training, closely similar to the first six weeks of rifle training under the current MTP 7-3.[18] They provided for qualification firing with the rifle in infantry centers and with the carbine at centers where the long ranges necessary for the rifle were not available. By August 1944 the adoption of the branch immaterial program could be postponed no longer.[19] The program of 28 April was revised to provide rifle qualification firing for trainees in all replacement centers and to facilitate their conversion into infantrymen, the most likely eventuality.[20] In line with the 1944 policy of eliminating subjects from the program whenever possible, some subjects, notably Personal Adjustment and Articles of War, were deleted and placed in the pre-cycle week of training.[21] Training under the branch immaterial program began in late September and

[17] (1) WD ltr AG 220.01 (11 May 44) SPGAP–MB–M to CG AGF, 19 May 44, sub: MTPs at RTCs. 461/116 (MTP). (2) AGF M/S, CofS to G–3, 24 May 44, sub and location as in (1). (3) WD ltr AGOC–E–A 220.01 (26 May 44) to CG AGF, 27 May 44, sub and location as in (1). (4) Record of tel conv between Lt Col Schrader, AGF, and Col Smith, AA Comd, 10 Aug 44. AGF G–3 files, 341.6/145 (RTC, 1944).

[18] (1) AGF memo (R) for CofS USA, 20 Mar 44, sub: Six Weeks Branch Immaterial MTP under Physical Profile Plan. 353/106 (R). (2) WD D/F WDGCT 353 (20 Mar 44) to CG AGF, 25 Apr 44, sub as in (1). 353/106 (R). (3) Proposed 6 Wks BI Tng for all Inductees (Rev 28 Apr 44). AGF G–3 files, 341.6/163 (RTC, 1944).

[19] See n. 16 and n. 17 (4).

[20] (1) R&SC ltr to CG AGF, 11 Aug 44, sub: BI Tng Programs. With AGF 1st ind, 21 Aug 44. 353/113 (R&SC). (2) R&SC ltr to CGs RTCs, 8 Sep 44, sub: 6 Wks BI Tng Prog. AGF G–3 files, 341.6/163 (RTC, 1944).

[21] R&SC ltr to CG AGF, 16 Sep 44, sub: 6 Wks BI Tng Prog. 354.1/304 (RTC).

early October. Concurrently, branch programs for the period from the seventh to the seventeenth week of training were put into effect.

The branch immaterial course being essentially infantry rifle training, the change in instruction entailed by its adoption was least marked in infantry centers. Many subjects in the branch immaterial program had been previously taught to trainees of noninfantry branches, but the changes, though small in number, were significant. Basic training during the early part of the program in gun and howitzer batteries in the field artillery centers, for example, had included 56 hours on the carbine and 16 hours on the .50-caliber machine gun. The carbine was now reduced to 8 hours, the machine gun omitted (to be taken up later in the cycle), and 71 hours of rifle marksmanship substituted. More significant, basic subjects in all programs had previously been spread over all 17 weeks of the cycle; now they were to be completed in 6 weeks. As a result, branch technical and tactical training had to be removed entirely from the first 6 weeks. Formerly, gun and howitzer trainees had been given a total of 87 hours of technical training during the first 6 weeks. This was no longer possible. On a mere hourly basis, the amount of basic-training time taken out of the last 11 weeks and the amount of technical-training time removed from the first 6 weeks were about equal. But the difficulty came in interrupted continuity of instruction: skill in technical and tactical subjects was dependent not merely on a total of hours but also on repetition of practice over as extended a period as possible. This kind of habituation was curtailed by several weeks under the new scheme. For these reasons the plan met with opposition from those who had to schedule and conduct the training, despite the favor with which it was regarded by those who were responsible for assigning its products.

The Tendency toward Broader Categories of Training

Increased flexibility of assignment had been the primary objective of the inauguration of branch immaterial training. The same end was sought in a simplification of specialist training in 1944. As noted above, the replacement centers had from the beginning trained only a fraction of the types of specialist found in Tables of Organization—the types of most common occurrence. The principle was implicit in the original scheme of training that a replacement would be grounded in a particular specialty and would develop skill in related assignments after joining a unit. This principle had been explicitly recognized in War Department Circular 283, issued in 1943, for the preparation of which Army Ground

Forces was largely responsible.[22] In fixing the categories of training to be conducted in replacement centers, the breadth of the categories had always been an open question. At one extreme all training might be identical, leaving all specialist skills to be developed after assignment to a unit—the plan recommended by G–1, Army Ground Forces, in 1942–43. At the other extreme RTC training might be conducted in all specialties to which privates were assigned in Tables of Organization, higher specialties growing out of these after assignment to a unit. Between these extremes lay a great range in possible definitions of training categories. The tendency during 1943 and 1944 was to move away from a large number of narrow specialist categories in the direction of a smaller number of broad specialties. The culmination of this trend was the publication, on 30 June 1944, of War Department Circular 267, which announced as War Department policy the doctrine that "broad general training which will produce a worker capable of development through on-the-job training in a number of directions should be substituted for narrow training which produces a specialist designed to be used at a highly specific occupation." Training in thirty specialties then conducted in AGF replacement training centers and schools was eliminated under Circular 267 and made derivative from twelve specialties of broad application. The extent of the shift in AGF replacement training between 1943 and 1945 can be gauged by comparing the list of specialist training categories in War Department Circular 283, 6 November 1943, and that in Circular 39, 1 February 1945:[23]

Number of Types of Training Conducted in AGF Replacement Training Centers, 1943 and 1945

	Cir. 283, 1943	*Cir. 39, 1945*
Antiaircraft	26	20
Armored	25	12
Cavalry	16	8
Field Artillery	39	16
Infantry	16	16
Tank Destroyer	17	9

The transition from narrow to broad categories of training derived impetus from the policy of training crewmen capable of filling any position in a gun or

[22] Par 4, Cir 283, WD, 6 Nov 43.

[23] Cir 39 corrected errors in Cir 267.

tank crew instead of training specialists for each position in the crew. This policy, originating at the armored replacement training center in 1943, had been extended by early 1944 to the training of tank destroyer and field artillery replacements.[24] Under the provisions of Circular 267 the crew training policy was carried a step further. Crewmen had been trained for each kind of artillery weapon —for example, 105-mm. howitzer, 155-mm. gun, 4.5-inch gun, 8-inch howitzer. Under Circular 267 the types of artillery weapons were grouped in four classes, pack, light, medium, and heavy, and crewmen were trained for each class of weapon. The four categories of crewmen listed in the preceding sentence were combined in one—Gun Crewman, Medium Artillery.

Special Expedients to Increase Infantry Replacement Production

In addition to the measures taken to maintain the production of replacements in general at the highest level, various special expedients were resorted to during 1944 and the first half of 1945 in order to supplement normal sources of infantry combat-loss replacements. These expedients exercised considerable influence on training.

In April 1944 nine nondivisional infantry regiments were reduced to cadre strength and filled with men transferred to the Infantry from inactivated antiaircraft and tank destroyer units and volunteers for Infantry from other branches. Already basically trained, these men were given a brief course, originally of eight and later of six weeks, to fit them as riflemen. The training program was a modification of the standard infantry rifle course, with emphasis on weapons and tactical training.

The rifle-training capacity of these regiments was augmented in October 1944 by a number of infantry advanced replacement training centers. Operating under the program used in the regiments, these centers converted transferees from Army Service Forces and Army Air Forces, as well as from other AGF branches, to Infantry. Although intended originally to be advanced training, the course was advanced only in the sense that the trainees, being soldiers already, were not receiving basic training. It was an accelerated 6-week course in the rudiments of infantry weapons and tactics.

The replacement crisis which necessitated these additional training facilities also brought about changes in the normal training of riflemen. To increase the

[24] (1) Statements of Col J. H. Banville to AGF Hist Off, 22 Nov 45; of Col H. R. Matthews, 23 Nov 45. (2) Par 9, memo of Lt Col J. L. Hines to G-3 AGF, 13 Mar 44, sub: Rpt of Visit to R&SC. 314.7 (AGF Hist).

number of riflemen available to replace losses sustained during the Battle of the Bulge, the course was reduced from seventeen weeks to fifteen. It was raised again after V-E Day.

A new restriction on the use of 18-year-old soldiers was enacted by Congress after V-E Day. It was directed that no 18-year-old be sent to a combat unit until he had received six months of training. The men affected, constituting about half of all those received for training, were assigned to the infantry advanced replacement training centers after graduation from the regular centers and given a course emphasizing weapons and tactics.[25]

Abandonment of Branch Immaterial Training

As mentioned above, a common branch immaterial basic course of six weeks had been introduced into the replacement training programs of all arms in August 1944. Intended primarily to facilitate transfers to and from the Infantry under the Physical Profile plan, branch immaterial training had also been intended to provide a cushion against emergency interbranch transfers in the United States or in the theaters. The advantages anticipated for the plan were largely administrative. So far as the quality of training was concerned there had been little enthusiasm for the plan in Army Ground Forces during the discussions leading to its adoption, and even less enthusiasm in subordinate operating headquarters.

After five months of trial the Replacement and School Command recommended, on 9 February 1945, that branch immaterial basic training be discontinued and that full programs of branch training be resumed.[26] It was the opinion of that command and of all RTC commanders that a trainee completing a full branch course was "much better prepared as a combat replacement" than a trainee completing a combination branch immaterial and branch program, and that trainees transferred from one branch to another after the 6-weeks branch immaterial course were "not materially better prepared to complete training in the new arm" than trainees whose first six weeks had been under a regular branch program. An elaborate bill of particulars was drawn up to support these views. In some arms trainees received instruction under the branch immaterial program which had no bearing on their ultimate combat assignment: field artillerymen,

[25] For a more detailed discussion of these special expedients see above, "The Provision of Enlisted Replacements."

[26] R&SC ltr to CG AGF, 9 Feb 45, sub: Six Wks BI Tng Prog. 353/1 (BI).

for example, were trained on the rifle although they were armed with the carbine. Training did not always proceed in logical sequence: infantry trainees ran the grenade course before receiving bayonet instruction, the latter not being included in the branch immaterial program. Specialist training, crowded into the last eleven weeks of the program, had to be given in larger doses than could be assimilated: seven hours a day of code practice were required although five hours were believed the effective maximum. For all trainees except those of the Infantry the formation of good habits of operation and maintenance of equipment was confined to an 11-week period although it was well known that longer periods of practice produced firmer habits and greater skill.

These disadvantages in training would perhaps have been outweighed if the original purpose of branch immaterial training, administrative flexibility, had been fulfilled. But transfers between branches during the training period had been few, largely because other personnel policies prevented full application of the Physical Profile plan and because demand for infantrymen was so great that men not qualified for infantry duty had to be accepted for infantry training. Only 4,726 men qualified for infantry training were transferred to infantry replacement training centers under the Physical Profile plan. In contrast, 17,400 men not qualified for infantry duty had to be sent to infantry centers during the same period.[27]

Army Ground Forces concurred in the recommendations of the Replacement and School Command and petitioned the War Department for resumption of full branch training.[28] On 17 March 1945 the War Department authorized Army Ground Forces to initiate "*modified* branch training," stipulating that the "identical training idea" would be adhered to wherever possible, and that new programs should vary from those currently in effect "only where experience indicates that unsatisfactory results have been obtained." [29]

In the programs as revised in April 1945 certain elements of the branch immaterial plan were retained.[30] An extensive list of subjects was standardized as to content and length in all branch programs:

[27] AGF M/S, G-3 to CofS, 15 Feb 45, sub: Six Wks BI Tng Prog. 353/1 (BI).

[28] AGF memo for CofS USA, 20 Feb 45, sub and location as in n. 27.

[29] WD memo WDGCT 353 (20 Feb 45) for CG AGF, 17 Mar 45, sub: Mob Tng Programs at RTCs. 353/1 (BI).

[30] (1) R&SC ltr to CG AGF, 2 May 45, sub: Revisions to MTPs. With attached programs. (2) AGF 1st ind on above, 22 May 45. (3) R&SC ltr to CG AGF, 8 May 45, sub: Revisions to MTPs. With attached programs. All in 353/130 and 131 (R&SC).

Subject	*Hours*
Military Courtesy	3
Military Sanitation and First Aid	
Personal and Sex Hygiene	3
First Aid	9
Field Sanitation	2
Malaria Control	4
Scrub Typhus	1
Dismounted Drill	12
Interior Guard Duty and Combat Sentry	4
Marches and Bivouacs	16
Chemical Warfare Training	8
Prisoners of War; Protection of Military Information and Censorship	3
Organization of the Branch Battalion	1
Mines, Booby Traps, and Demolitions	18
Elementary Map and Aerial Photo Reading	12
Infiltration Course	4
Orientation Course	17
Japanese Small Unit Tactics and Technique	5
TOTAL	122

In addition, certain subjects common to all branch programs were retained but not standardized in length:

Tactical Training of the Individual Soldier
- Concealment and Camouflage
- Cover and Movement
- Hasty Fortifications

Combat Formations
Defense against Aircraft and Mechanized Vehicles
Hand Grenades
Launcher, Rocket, Antitank, and Rifle Grenades
Overhead Artillery Fire
Physical Training
Inspections

Except for training in rifle and carbine, included in the branch immaterial program but not in all the new branch programs, the roster of subjects in the revised MTP's included all the subjects prescribed in the branch immaterial program. Aside from differences in time allotments, the most noteworthy deviation of new programs from old was in the removal of the barrier separating the first six weeks of training from the last eleven. With this barrier removed the time allotted to subjects common to all branches was spread over the entire training period, although their elementary character confined them predominantly to the earlier weeks. The same loosening of the division between basic and advanced training permitted early initiation of branch specialist subjects hitherto deferred. Abandonment of branch immaterial training did not mean reversion to completely diverse branch programs. Common elements in all programs still assured substantial similarity in the basic training received by all replacements. Similarity, however, was not identity, and the completion of common training could no longer be fixed at a definite point in the training cycle. Branch immaterial training was now intermingled with branch instruction in an effective sequence of subjects.

Adjustment of Training Programs to the War in the Pacific

Revision of MTP's undertaken in March and April 1945 to eliminate formal branch immaterial training also embodied substantial changes designed to improve the training of replacements destined for use in the Pacific. Two conditions shaped the revisions: the special characteristics of combat in the Pacific war, and the fact that replacements, at least for several months, would be used not only to make up for combat losses but also to refill units depleted during redeployment.[31]

Combat against the Japanese had emphasized the use of flame throwers, demolitions, and rockets, the assault of pillboxes and other prepared fortifications, and the tactics of the smallest units. Marked increases in the time given these subjects were made in the new programs. A course in Japanese small-unit tactics and technique was put into effect for all trainees, and instruction was begun in the prevention and control of scrub typhus, a major health hazard in the Pacific combat areas. Compensatory cuts were made in subjects which in view of the special conditions foreseen were thought less essential—minor tactics, especially of the section and platoon, and defensive operations.[32]

Redeployment posed further problems. It was anticipated that units would lose so many men under the point system that it would no longer be possible to

[31] The following three paragraphs are based primarily on statements of Col J. K. Bush, Chief, Tng Div, G–3 Sec, AGF, to AGF Hist Off, 29 Nov 45.

[32] (1) MTP 7–3, WD, 4 Nov 44. (2) MTP 7–3, WD, 11 Jul 45.

bring replacements in on the lowest, most basic level and train them in the unit to fill more specialized assignments. Replacements might be assigned initially to jobs calling for more skill than had been required when the replacements of battle losses only had been involved. Riflemen had always been given enough machine gun and mortar instruction to enable them to fill a subordinate crew assignment on either weapon. Now it was entirely possible that a rifleman would be assigned at once as a light machine gunner or mortar gunner. Very large increases were therefore made in subjects related to the replacement's main specialty, amounting in the case of riflemen to almost 50 percent more time on the secondary weapons.

The general effect of the 1945 revisions was to continue the trend, begun in 1944, away from higher tactics and a multitude of subjects and to produce programs which emphasized more strongly than did any previous programs the basic disciplines, skill with weapons and equipment, and competence in individual and squad tactics.

The revised MTP's were put into effect in most centers during June. The only further changes in replacement training prior to V-J Day were those called for by AGF Training Memorandum No. 1, issued 1 June 1945, on redeployment training. This memorandum did not stipulate adding new courses but merely directed that, within the framework of existing MTP's, the replacement training centers adapt instruction to the special needs of combat against the Japanese. The fact that the revised MTP's gave added stress to the weapons, tactics, and techniques of such combat facilitated the adaptation required by the Training Memorandum. Among the problems given particular emphasis in replacement training were assault on jungle positions and jungle villages, jungle patrolling, attack on Japanese command posts, and identification of Japanese uniforms and equipment. To provide realism, new training aids were installed and those used in training for the war against Germany were modified to represent Japanese terrain features and villages. The Replacement and School Command obtained some Japanese-American intelligence teams to assist in the training.

In the summer of 1945 RTC training was, to a greater extent than ever before, infantry training. Out of a total output of 258,496 during June, July, and August, 224,465 were infantry replacements.[33]

By the end of active hostilities Army Ground Forces had reason to believe that replacements leaving its training centers were the best-trained combat

[33] See Tables Nos. 3, 4, and 7 in the study "The Provision of Enlisted Replacements."

replacements so far produced. Criticism of particular aspects of replacement training had persisted, often on grounds identical with the unfavorable comment of 1943. Reports of overseas observers continued to reflect dissatisfaction with physical training, battle indoctrination, discipline, skill with weapons, and proficiency in individual tactics.[34] But whereas in 1943 such criticisms had formed the basis for a generally unfavorable judgment of replacement training, they were outweighed in 1945 by the opinion of overseas commanders that replacements were, on the whole, satisfactorily trained for their combat assignments. As early as March 1944 General Hazlett found commanders in Europe impressed with the superiority of replacements trained under the 17-week programs over those trained under the 13-week programs.[35] This reaction continued. A running file of overseas comments on replacements, maintained in the Schools and Replacement Training Branch, G–3 Section of Headquarters, Army Ground Forces, showed criticisms diminishing in number and severity and favorable comments increasing throughout the year.[36] During December and January 1944–45, General Donovan, G–3, and Maj. Gen. Clyde L. Hyssong, G–1, of Army Ground Forces, visited the European Theater of Operations to investigate the replacement situation. General Hyssong reported that he had heard no complaints about replacements supplied by Army Ground Forces,[37] and General Donovan observed that "the state of training of . . . replacements was most satisfactory despite lack of opportunity in many instances to integrate rifle company replacements into units prior to their entry into combat." [38] Despite continuing difficulties with the administrative phases of the replacement system, the training of replacements had improved greatly since the days of North Africa and Sicily.

[34] See, for example, the comments of division commanders in MTO, in AGF Bd Rpt (MT) No. 271, 16 Jan 45, with 14 incls. AGF G–2 Sec file A–271.

[35] R&SC ltr (S) to CG AGF, 25 Mar 44, sub: Repls in ETOUSA and NATOUSA. 320.2/126 (O'seas Repls) (S).

[36] (1) Digest of Overseas Rpts — Basis of Monthly Trend Rpt. AGF G–3 Schs and Repl Tng Br files. (2) AGF G–3 Schs & Repl Tng Br file 319.1 (Observers Rpts).

[37] Memo (C) of Gen Hyssong for CofS AGF, 15 Jan 45, sub: Obsns in ETO. 319.1/113 (ETO)(C).

[38] (1) AGF memo (S) for CofS USA, 15 Jan 45, sub: Rpt of Obsns in ETO. 319.1/154 (ETO)(S). (2) Detailed notes of General Donovan and other members of the AGF party in binder Report of Observations, ETO, Maj Gen Leo Donovan. AGF G–3 files.

The Building and Training of Infantry Divisions

by

Bell I. Wiley

Contents

Tables

Charts

I. Activation Procedure

When the Army Ground Forces was created on 9 March 1942, 29 infantry divisions were in existence. Of these, 10 were Regular Army, 18 were National Guard, and 1 was Army of the United States.[1] The Regular Army divisions had been constituted and activated prior to September 1940, while the National Guard divisions had been inducted into Federal service during the period from September 1940 to November 1941. Both the Regular Army and the National Guard units were commonly referred to after 1941 as "old divisions" in contrast to "new divisions" activated in 1942 and 1943.[2]

The conversion of the old divisions from the square to the triangular organization had, with one exception, been completed when the Army Ground Forces came into being, though triangularization of the National Guard units had not been effected until the early weeks of 1942. A few of the divisions were stationed at posts outside the United States, and others had been assigned to defensive missions along the country's borders. Nineteen were in various stages of training. Most of the divisions that had taken part in the 1941 maneuvers were engaged in a 4-month program designed to remove deficiencies revealed in the GHQ exercises of the previous fall.[3]

Thirty-six divisions of all types had been activated before the end of 1941. The outbreak of war led to the launching of a program of expansion for the armed forces which provided for the creation of 35 new divisions during 1942, of which 26 were to be Infantry. As a result of subsequent modifications of the mobilization program, a total of 38 divisions—9 Armored, 2 Airborne, and 27 Infantry—was activated in 1942. Seventeen more divisions, of which eleven were

[1] The AUS Division was the 25th, activated in Hawaii, 1 October 1941.

[2] Much information on the activation and training of divisions was obtained from Unit History Data Cards, Organization & Directory Section, Operations Branch, Operations and Training Division, AGO, and from the "Division Book" kept by the AGF Deputy Chief of Staff. The Division Book contains key information gleaned from records of the various staff sections and the War Department about each division, including the following: date of activation; date of reorganization; commanding general, assistant commander, and artillery commander; date of completing major phases of training; inspections by AGF; graphic representation of strength; and remarks, telling of unusual circumstances or events. Activation dates of the 1st, 2d, and 3d Infantry Divisions were furnished by the Historical Section, Army War College. Office files of Gen Mitchell, DCofS, AGF.

[3] (1) Speech of Gen McNair to West Point Graduating Class, 5 May 42. Army War College Library, Collection of McNair Speeches. (2) GHQ ltr to Army Comdrs and CofAF, 30 Oct 41, sub: Post-Maneuver Tng. GHQ Records, 353/652 – C.

230-171 O - 66 - 29

Infantry, were created in 1943.[4] This brought the total number of divisions activated before or during World War II to 91, of which 67 were Infantry.[5]

Initial AGF Activation Procedure

When the Army Ground Forces on 9 March 1942 was given responsibility for supervising the creation and training of divisions, it adopted a procedure for activation that was already well developed. This was operated mainly by the G–1 and G–3 Sections of AGF headquarters. The selection and assembly of personnel for a new division were coordinated and supervised by the G–1 Section. The commander, assistant commander, and artillery commander were designated by the War Department. G–1, Army Ground Forces, compiled a list of officers eligible for these positions (listed in the order of their general efficiency ratings) from which Lt. Gen. Lesley J. McNair, Commanding General of the Army Ground Forces, made his nominations to the War Department. The Commanding General of the Army Ground Forces chose the general staff heads of the new division. His G–1 designated, subject to his approval, these and the other key officers for whose appointment the Army Ground Forces was responsible. It coordinated with the appropriate branch chiefs of the Army Service Forces the designation of special staff heads and other key service officers. Subordinate commands were responsible for designating other personnel. G–1 checked with them to see that action was taken as ordered, and it also set up and supervised the flow of personnel to schools and thence to the division's home station.

Each new division had a "parent" unit, responsible for furnishing it with a trained cadre. The G–3 Section, mainly through its Mobilization Division, designated this unit and fixed the date by which the parent unit should initiate cadre training. It specified the army or other subordinate agency to which the new division was to be assigned, and charged it with the execution of formal activation. The G–3 Section also designated the camp at which the division was to be stationed. G–3, in collaboration with G–1 and other interested sections, prepared for War Department publication a letter officially ordering activation of the division and instructing all interested agencies in their respective duties. This letter provided for delivery by the service commands, without requisition, of enlisted fillers from reception centers on a schedule to be worked out by the

[4] Unit History Data Cards. Files of Orgn and Directory Sec, Opns Br, Opns and Tng Div, AGO.

[5] For the classification, activation, and shipment of divisions, 1917–45, see the tabulation at the end of this study.

division and the service command. In addition, G–1 prepared for issuance as a War Department memorandum full instructions for the selection, schooling, and assignment of commissioned personnel of the division.[6]

At the time of the establishment of the Army Ground Forces, new divisions were created and trained in accordance with a system developed by General Headquarters, U.S. Army. The plan for bringing new infantry divisions into existence was promulgated in January 1942 and was applied, insofar as circumstances permitted, to divisions activated prior to June.[7] This plan, which Brig. Gen. John M. Palmer called the "finest piece of large-scale planning" that he had seen in fifty years of army service,[8] provided for construction of each new division around a cadre of 172 officers and 1,190 enlisted men drawn from a parent division. It was set forth graphically in a chart captioned "Building an Infantry Triangular Division" (see Chart No. 1). The plan provided for systematic schooling of an officer and enlisted cadre chosen from two to three months in advance of the activation date. The principle of building units around trained nuclei had been applied in 1940–41, but intensive schooling of cadres prior to activation was an innovation. Enlisted cadremen, selected by the commander of the parent division, were promoted to the positions which they were to fill in the new unit and given preliminary training by officers of the parent division. Further preparatory training was given by cadre officers after the men arrived at their new camp.[9]

The division commander, the assistant division commander, and the division artillery commander were designated by the War Department not later than seventy-eight days prior to activation and were brought to General Headquarters for a week of orientation. The division commander then went to Fort Leavenworth for a month of special instruction at the Command and General Staff School; the assistant division commander took a special course at the Infantry School; the division artillery commander, at the Field Artillery School. The General and Special Staff officers, also designated by the War Department, joined the division commander at Fort Leavenworth for the special Command and General Staff School course. Forty-four key officers of the infantry, artillery, engineer, quartermaster, medical, signal, and cavalry components were desig-

[6] Statements of Col E. C. Bergquist, AGF G–4 Sec (originally in G–1 New Divisions Division), and of Col W. W. Johnson, AGF G–3 Sec, to AGF Hist Off, 7 Mar 46.

[7] General McNair credited his Deputy Chief of Staff, Brig. Gen. Mark W. Clark, with the development of this plan. Personal ltr of Gen McNair to Gen John M. Palmer, 25 Mar 42. McNair Correspondence.

[8] Personal ltr of Gen John M. Palmer to Gen McNair, 24 Mar 42. McNair Correspondence.

[9] For this and the following two paragraphs, see WD ltr AG 320.2 (1–4–42) OP–A–M to CGs, 6 Jan 42, sub: Commissioned Pers of the 77th, 82d and 90th Inf Divs. AGF G–1 Records Sec files.

nated by the War Department, on the recommendations of the chiefs of their respective branches and services, and sent to appropriate branch or service schools for special courses, taken concurrently with those of the commander and his staff at Fort Leavenworth. The remainder of the officer cadre, designated by an army commander, followed the same procedure.

The commander and the principal officers of his staff arrived at the division camp thirty-seven days before activation. A week later they were joined by the remainder of the officer cadre and all the enlisted cadre. During the next few days the complement of 452 officers, provided by the War Department from graduates of officer candidate and service schools and the officer replacement pool, reached the camp. On D Day the division was formally activated. During the next fifteen days the enlisted filler, consisting of 13,425 men (authorized strength), arrived from reception centers. In the meantime the division would, under optimum conditions, have received about 50 percent of the training equipment authorized by Tables of Basic Allowances (T/BA's). Immediately after arrival of the last installment of fillers, the division was ready to begin the routine of training.

Modifications after March 1942

When the Army Ground Forces superseded GHQ, five infantry divisions scheduled for activation in March and May were already in process of formation.[10] The new AGF G–1 Section, which was actually an abbreviated edition of G–1, GHQ, in collaboration with the AGF G–3 Section,[11] entered busily upon the task of preparing other units for activation. One of the first steps was the setting up in G–1 of a New Divisions Division, which was given the task of coordinating and supervising all personnel activities connected with the creation of new divisions.[12]

One of the first matters requiring attention was revision of the activation procedure. Some changes came as a result of the War Department reorganization of March 1942; others were suggested by experience gained in building the first new divisions. Modifications made in March for the June divisions—the first to be tailored from start to finish by the Army Ground Forces—provided that only the division commander and his two principal assistants should be designated by the War Department. Henceforth, key infantry and artillery officers, previously

[10] No infantry divisions were scheduled for activation in April 1942.

[11] Designated as "Divisions" until 12 July 1942.

[12] Information furnished AGF Hist Off by WO R. P. Grahamer, AGF G–1 Sec Offs Div, from files of Offs Div.

selected by the War Department, were named by the Army Ground Forces; the principal officers in service components were designated by the Army Service Forces. The size of the officer cadre was increased from 172 to 185 to provide new divisions with a larger nucleus of leaders specially schooled for their duties. The remainder of the officer cadre was designated by army or corps, and the officer complement was provided by the Army Ground Forces and the Army Service Forces instead of the War Department. Among additions to the cadre were antitank officers, who "preferably should have had experience and knowledge of antitank operations and defense," and an assistant G-4 charged with the supervision of automotive affairs. The former were sent to Fort Leavenworth for the special command and staff course, and the latter was sent to the Quartermaster Motor Transport (QMMT) School at Holabird, Md., for instruction in automotive maintenance. Other changes provided that housekeeping elements of the enlisted cadre should reach camp at about the same time as the command and staff, in order to prepare the way for the coming of the remaining cadre and the filler.[13]

The activation procedure was modified further in the spring and summer. The most significant changes were those relating to motor maintenance. In April the policy was initiated of requiring the division commander, the assistant division commander, and the division artillery commander to attend the Quartermaster Motor Transport School for a 5-day "refresher course" in automotive maintenance before proceeding to the Command and General Staff School. The G-4 automotive officer, instead of being ordered to the QMMT School as formerly, was sent to an older division for practical instruction by officers in charge of motor maintenance.[14] In June the practice was modified further to provide for his attending the short course at Holabird with the division commander before beginning the division motor course. Another change made in June provided for selection of that portion of the officer cadre not designated by the War Department, the Army Ground Forces, or the Army Service Forces, by the parent division instead of by army or corps.[15]

The tendency toward larger cadres continued throughout the summer of 1942. By autumn the officer cadre had increased to 216, and the enlisted cadre had

[13] WD ltr AG 320.2 (3-6-42) OD-A-M to CGs concerned, 11 Mar 42, sub: Commissioned Pers for the 76th, 79th and 81st Inf Divs. AGF G-1 Records Sec files.

[14] WD ltr AG 210.31 (4-8-42) OD-M to CGs concerned, 8 Apr 42, sub: Commissioned Pers for the 80th, 88th and 89th Divs. AGF G-1 Records Sec files.

[15] WD ltr AG 210.31 (6-20-42) SPXOD-TS-M to CGs concerned, 21 Jun 42, sub: Commissioned Pers for the 84th and 92d Inf Divs. AGF G-1 Records Sec files.

grown from the March figure of 1,190 to 1,460. The latter included an augmentation of 98 clerks, stenographers, and mechanics to meet a deficiency in such workers; an ordnance maintenance platoon to assist with the ever pressing problem of automotive upkeep; and a postal section provided by The Adjutant General. Additions to the officer cadre included an assistant G–4, a division chaplain and assistant, and a special service officer.[16]

A significant change made in the fall of 1942 was the provision that divisions be given an overstrength of 15 percent, to offset cadre and attrition losses, at the time they received their enlisted fillers.[17] Army Ground Forces had been aware of the desirability of this arrangement for some time,[18] and General Lear of the Second Army had recommended it,[19] but limitations of available manpower and the difficulty of revising activation schedules had hitherto prevented its adoption. Under the old procedure, it had been necessary for divisions to receive a cadre increment of some 1,200 men about three months after activation and to fit the newcomers into the training program.[20] The new plan proposed to make it possible for a division to run the gamut of training without this interruption.

The impression that the building of divisions was approaching a routine basis prompted consideration in late 1942 and early 1943 of the possibility of abolishing the New Divisions Division and delegating activation matters to armies and corps. When the Third Army was queried in December as to its ability to furnish general staff officers for its proposed allotments of 1943 divisions, the response was not hopeful. Investigation in January and February of other phases of the question indicated that loss of the coordination and guidance customarily provided by the New Divisions Division would result in confusion and inefficiency.[21] One phase of the decentralization scheme—the proposal that army commanders designate chiefs of special staff sections and other officers previously chosen on recommendation of heads of the various services—aroused opposition

[16] WD Memo W605–3–42, 28 Aug 42, sub: Commissioned Pers for the 86th and 87th Inf Divs. AGF G–1 Records Sec files, 210.31 (Asgmt–Offs).

[17] AGF ltr (R) to CGs, 25 Sep 42, sub: Policies Concerning Mob. 320.2/80 (R).

[18] AGF 1st ind, 5 Aug 42, on WD ltr WDGCT 320.2 Gen (7–28–42), 28 Jul 42, sub: Allocation of Additional RTC Capacity to be Provided under the Mobilization Plan, 1943. AGF G–1 files, stayback file of Gen Edward Barber.

[19] Personal ltr of Gen Lear to Gen McNair, 11 Sep 42. Personal files of Gen Lear.

[20] (1) AGF ltr (R) to CGs, 23 Apr 42, sub: Cadre Pers for New Divs. (2) AGF ltr to CGs, 10 Sep 42, sub: Cadre Pers for New Divs. Both in 320.2/9 (Inf) (R).

[21] AGF M/S, New Divs Div to G–1, 1 Feb 43, sub: Decentralization of Activation of New Divs. AGF G–1 New Divs Div Policy file.

from those whose appointive prerogatives were threatened.[22] Because of these and other considerations the idea of decentralizing activations was dropped.[23]

An important change in divisional organization was made in late 1942 as a result of the transfer of automotive maintenance from quartermaster to ordnance jurisdiction. A light ordnance maintenance company was added to the divisional Table of Organization, and the quartermaster battalion was replaced by a company. About the same time the procedure was adopted of activating ordnance and quartermaster companies separately and requiring them to report to divisional camps four weeks before activation day. Henceforth the division commander, the assistant division commander, the artillery commander, and the G–4 together with the chief of staff, who was added to the group in November, went to the Ordnance Automotive School at Holabird for eight days' instruction, and then to the Ordnance School at Aberdeen for a 3-day course in half-track vehicles and small arms, before proceeding to their respective courses at Fort Leavenworth, Fort Benning, and Fort Sill.[24] It was increasingly appreciated that motor maintenance, which had been a sore spot in both the 1941 and the 1942 maneuvers, was primarily a responsibility of command.[25] It was hoped that this instruction in vehicular maintenance would make the division commander and his principal assistants more motor-minded than they had been in the past.[26]

Early in 1943 steps were taken to improve the selection and training of officer cadres with a view to raising the quality of leadership. In January seven field artillery liaison officers were added to the cadre and sent to Fort Benning for four weeks of schooling in infantry tactics and technique.[27] The following month saw the initiation of a policy making it mandatory that all General Staff appointees be graduates of the regular Command and General Staff School course; in choosing special staff heads and assistant G's, preference was to be

[22] AGF memo for chiefs of admin and supply agencies, SOS [undated, but evidently late Dec 42], sub: Decentralization of Off Cadre Selection, and 2d ind thereto by Mil Pers Div, SOS, 14 Jan 43. AGF G–1 New Divs Div Policy file.

[23] Statement of WO R. P. Grahamer, G–1 AGF, to AGF Hist Off, 25 Nov 43.

[24] WD Memo W605–24–42, 22 Nov 42, sub: Commissioned Pers for the 97th Inf Div. AGF G–1 Records Sec files.

[25] Memo of Capt Robert P. Cotter, Dept of Motor Transport, FAS for Comdt FA School, 30 Oct 42, sub: Observer's Rpt on La Maneuvers, Cp Polk, La, 28 Sep–4 Oct 42. 354.2/252 (La 42).

[26] Statement of Maj H. Conner, Ord Sec AGF, to AGF Hist Off, 26 Nov 43.

[27] WD ltr (R) AG 210.31 (1–26–43) PO–A–GNGAP–M to CGs concerned, 30 Jan 43, sub: Commissioned Pers for the 69th Inf Div. AGF G–1 Records Sec files (R).

given to Command and General Staff School graduates.[28] In March completion of the regular course at Leavenworth was made a requirement for assistant G's. At the same time four field artillery battalion assistant S–2's, graduates of the field artillery survey course at Fort Sill, were added to the cadre.[29]

AGF headquarters continued to check closely the selection of enlisted cadres, with good results.[30] But occasionally there were complaints. A regimental commander of the 97th Division wrote as follows to a friend at AGF headquarters in the spring:[31]

> My cadre officers were about fifty per cent castoffs as were my cadre NCO's. . . . Lots of men [were] pulled out of [the] guard house and sent to us. . . . One corporal [was] sixty-one years old. Another corporal above 50. . . . In other words, we got the undesirables of many posts, camps, and stations. We are even having to teach master and tech sergeants how to do right and left face, proper military courtesy, how to roll a pack, etc.

The requirement that commanding officers select cadres from among their best men put them to a severe test. The feeling of most of them must have approximated that expressed by a regimental commander to a close friend in March 1943: "I will have to furnish a cadre and I want that to be a good one, but I do not intend to send to it my best officers or non-commissioned officers if I can avoid it." [32] When this attitude—an entirely human one—is taken into consideration, it appears remarkable that the Army Ground Forces was able to obtain the selection of a very high percentage of superior personnel as nuclei for the new divisions.

Efforts of the Army Ground Forces to provide competent command for divisions were substantially aided by two steps initiated in the spring and summer of 1943 by the War Department. The first was the practice of choosing division commanders, assistant commanders, and artillery commanders from officers who had successfully filled command positions in a theater of operations.

[28] WD ltr (R) AGF 210.31 (27 Feb 43) PO–A–GNGAP–M to CGs concerned, 17 Feb 43, sub: Commissioned Pers for the 63d and 70th Inf Divs. AGF G–1 Records Sec files (R).

[29] WD ltr (R) AG 210.31 (30 Mar 43) PO–A–GNGAP–M to CGs concerned, 30 Mar 43, sub: Commissioned Pers for the 42d Inf Div. AGF G–1 Records Sec files (R).

[30] AGF memo, G–3 for CofS, 13 Mar 43, sub: Obsns During Visit to Cp Atterbury, Ind, 10–11 Mar 43. 353.02/119 (AGF). This memorandum explained and highly commended the methods used by the commanding general of the 83d Division in choosing and training a cadre for the 75th Division.

[31] Undated extract inclosed in memo of Col Burns Beall, Asst G–3 AGF, for G–3 AGF, 2 Apr 43. AGF G–3 Tng Div files, 333.1 (97th Div).

[32] Confidential ltr of a regtl comdr to the col of a newly activated regt, 22 Mar 43. AGF G–1 New Divs Div Policy file.

Between 1 June and 22 October 1943 five AGF divisions received commanders from overseas as follows:

Division	*Commander*
10th (Light)	Lloyd E. Jones
71st	Robert L. Spragins
87th	Eugene M. Landrum
91st	William G. Livesay
104th	Terry de la Mesa Allen

During the same period the following divisions received brigadier generals from overseas as assistant division commanders or division artillery commanders:[33]

Division	*Brigadier General*
10th (Light)	Frank L. Culin, Jr.
35th	Edmund B. Sebree
69th	Robert V. Maraist
77th	Edwin H. Randle
79th	Frank U. Greer
89th	George Honnen
93d	Leonard R. Boyd

The second change was the requirement that the division commander and his two principal assistants serve an apprenticeship of two or three months in the respective grades of brigadier general and colonel before becoming eligible for promotion to the rank authorized by Tables of Organization.[34] In July 1944, because of the poor showing made by some division commanders in their baptism of fire in Normandy, the Chief of Staff, U.S. Army, directed that, in the case of brigadiers commanding divisions in training, promotions be withheld until they had proved their qualifications in combat.[35]

The ultimate of refinement attained in the activation procedure was exemplified by the 65th Infantry Division, last of the divisions created in World War II, activated at Camp Shelby on 16 August 1943. The plan followed in the building of this division is set forth in Chart No. 2.

[33] AGF memo (C) for CofS USA, 22 Oct 43, sub: Battle Experienced High Comdrs. 211.311/524 (C).

[34] Statement of Lt Col R. H. Booth, Asst G–1 AGF, to AGF Hist Off, 18 Dec 43.

[35] (1) Memo (C) of CofS USA for CG AGF, 6 Jul 44, sub: Gen Offs. McNair Correspondence. (2) Statement of G–3 AGF to AGF Hist Off, 19 Feb 45.

II. The Training of Infantry Divisions

Initial AGF Training Program

New infantry divisions activated prior to November 1942 followed a training schedule promulgated by the G–3 Section of GHQ on 16 February 1942. This schedule established a program designed to train divisions within a period of forty-four weeks after the date of activation. The training period was divided into three definite phases—individual training, unit training, and combined-arms training—and a training guide was set up for each. For the guidance of the division commander and his staff, the directive of 16 February included three charts covering respectively each of the three periods of training. These charts showed at a glance the week-by-week routine to be followed by each major component of the division. The period of individual training was set at seventeen weeks. During this period, War Department Mobilization Training Programs (MTP's) were used as guides. The MTP's were drawn on a 13-week basis, but the framers of the new division schedule deemed it wise to allow four weeks of extra time to offset delays in the receipt of fillers and equipment, and to permit a thorough testing at the end by higher command. The period of unit training was to last for thirteen weeks; of combined training, for fourteen weeks.[1]

The new training schedule offered a sharp contrast to previous plans, which had been designed to fill and train Regular Army and National Guard divisions during peacetime. The former training program had set no specific period for the attainment of combat readiness. Furthermore, it had not clearly differentiated between individual and unit training and it had not provided any detailed guide for training similar to that included in the February directive.

A feature of the new training plan was the requirement that schools for both commissioned and noncommissioned officers be conducted concurrently with other activities during each period of training. The primary purpose of these

[1] GHQ ltr to CGs and incls 1, 2, and 3, 16 Feb 42, sub: Tng of Newly Activated Inf Divs. GHQ Records, 353/21 (Inf–H).

schools was to refresh instructional personnel in subjects that they were scheduled to teach in the immediate future. It was provided that schools would normally be held at night to prepare instructors for their duties of the next day. General McNair consistently opposed schools "so extensive as to deprive units unduly of officers and non-commissioned officers needed for troop training." [2] The schools operated by the division headquarters stressed methods of instruction, leadership, technical proficiency, and the ability of cadremen to do well themselves the things which they were to teach the fillers. Particular stress was placed on subjects which were to be taught during the period of individual training. Courses conducted by division headquarters were paralleled by those in schools operated by regiments and other components. These offered courses in such subjects as mess management, communications, administration and supply, preventive maintenance, and physical training.

The February directive for new divisions made specific provisions for the administering of tests that had been introduced earlier in the GHQ period. MTP tests, prepared by army or corps, were to be given to the entire division in the last week of individual training. During the unit training period infantry and cavalry platoons were to take platoon combat-firing proficiency tests prepared by GHQ, and artillery units were to be given GHQ battery and battalion tests. Infantry battalion field exercise tests, prepared by GHQ, were prescribed for the combined training period.[3]

It was contemplated that infantry divisions, on completion of the three periods of training prescribed in the directive of 16 February, would participate in large-scale maneuvers directed by a higher headquarters. On 23 April the Army Ground Forces issued a training directive outlining the 1942 maneuvers. This directive, which placed primary emphasis on air-ground and infantry-mechanized phases of training, stated that all divisions completing the maneuvers would be considered ready for combat. An additional directive was issued in July to provide for training in staging areas, so that divisions would not lose in fighting trim while awaiting overseas shipment.[4]

[2] GHQ ltr to CGs, 16 Feb 42, sub: Tng of Newly Activated Inf Divs. GHQ Records, 353/21 (Inf–H).

[3] (1) Copies of the platoon and battery tests may be found as inclosures 1 and 2, GHQ ltr to Army Comdrs and CofAF, 30 Oct 41, sub: Post-Maneuver Tng. GHQ Records, 353/652–C. (2) The artillery battalion tests are in GHQ ltr to Army Comdrs, 5 Sep 41, sub: Field Arty Firing. GHQ Records, 353.4/3–C (Firing Tests). (3) For the infantry battalion field exercise tests, see incl 3, GHQ ltr to Army Comdrs and CofAF, 30 Oct 41, sub: Post-Maneuver Tng. GHQ Records, 353/652–C.

[4] (1) AGF ltr to CGs, 23 Apr 42, sub: Tng Dir for the Period Jun 1–Oct 31, 1942. 353/1043. (2) AGF ltr to CGs, 10 Jul 42, sub: Tng Dir for Units during the Period from Arrival at Staging Areas to Departure for Ports of Embarkation. 353/1515.

Training Program at the End of 1942

On 19 October 1942 the Army Ground Forces issued a training directive which was, in the words of Col. John B. Sherman, a "directive to end all training directives." It became effective 1 November 1942.[5] Previously the practice had been followed of issuing directives periodically, for stipulated intervals or phases. The new directive had no terminal limits but was designed to guide all existing and future units through the complete cycle of preparation for combat. Leaving basic principles and general outlines unchanged, it was a codification of experience acquired to date, adapted to the great task that was still ahead: training for imminent combat a large force of combined arms and services, built around divisional teams. The training period for divisions was reduced from 44 to 35 weeks, with allotments for the various phases as follows: individual or basic, 13 weeks; unit, 11 weeks; and combined, 11 weeks.[6] Reduction of the basic phase from 17 to 13 weeks seemed feasible in view of the belief that accelerated draft inductions would make possible the filling of divisions and the beginning of training immediately after activation. Shortening of the training cycle as a whole was considered necessary because of the likelihood of heavy requirements in 1943 for overseas operations. General McNair thought it better to hurry divisions through an abbreviated cycle than to take a chance of having them snatched away before completing one of greater duration: if more time should be available, it might be devoted to review of weak points.[7] A significant provision of the new training directive was the extension of the testing program. A physical training test was added to unit training, and an infantry battalion combat-firing test to combined training. Both tests were prepared by the Army Ground Forces.[8] With the issuance of this new directive, the training of infantry divisions assumed a pattern which was expected to be stable and which, in fact, was not radically altered later. Each major phase—individual or basic, unit, and combined—of this pattern of training which had developed by the close of 1942 is briefly described in the following pages.

The individual training period of thirteen weeks was allotted to basic and small-unit training up to the battalion. During this period War Department Mobilization Training Programs were, as already indicated, used as guides.

[5] Statement of Col John B. Sherman, Plans Sec AGF, to AGF Hist Off, 12 Oct 43.

[6] AGF ltr to CGs, 19 Oct 42, sub: Tng Dir Effective 1 Nov 42. 353/52 (Tng Dir).

[7] Personal ltr (C) of Gen McNair to Gen Lear, 19 Sep 42. Personal files of Gen Lear.

[8] Par 7, AGF ltr to CGs, 19 Oct 42, sub: Tng Dir Effective 1 Nov 42. Copies of the tests, except the MTP test, are attached to this letter as inclosures. 353/52 (Tng Dir).

During the first few weeks all elements of the division concentrated on such basic subjects as military courtesy, discipline, sanitation, first aid, map reading, individual tactics of the soldier, and drill—the idea being that an individual must learn to be a soldier before he can become a specialist. Lectures, films, and practical demonstrations were the principal means used to teach these fundamentals.[9]

After the first month, the emphasis shifted to technical subjects and training became more diverse. Infantry lieutenants took their platoons out to the ranges to teach them to shoot; ran the men over obstacle courses to toughen their muscles; lined them up on grenade courses to show them the technique of pin-pulling and tossing; marched them to parade grounds and turned them over to squad leaders who showed them how to take their weapons apart and put them together again; and led them to bayonet courses and demonstrated to them the principles of parry and thrust, then set them to charging straw-packed effigies of Hitler and Tojo. Engineer officers loaded their men into trucks and took them out to near-by streams to build fixed and floating bridges; the men were marched to open country for demonstrations and practice in building roads, constructing fortifications, erecting road obstacles, blowing up bridges, and planting and clearing mine fields. Signal officers set up schools for the training of cryptographers and radio specialists, and conducted practical exercises in stringing wire and operating message centers. Other elements of the division likewise blended technical instruction with practical demonstration. The John Dewey principle of "learn by doing" had a wide application throughout infantry, artillery, and specialist components.

During the last month of the basic period, emphasis in training turned more and more to tactical subjects, and the locale of activities shifted increasingly from camp to ranges and fields. Infantry units concentrated on completion of qualification firing at fixed targets with the principal weapon, familiarization firing with other weapons, execution of squad problems in attack and defense, and squad combat firing. Other components of the division performed tactical marches and appropriate exercises, including bivouacs. Each field artillery battalion, for instance, marched out to a range, occupied a position, executed a firing

[9] This paragraph and those which follow, describing training during the individual, unit, and combined training periods, are based on the following: (1) AGF ltr to CGs and inclosures, 19 Oct 42, sub: Tng Dir Effective 1 Nov 42. 353/52 (Tng Dir). (2) Interviews of AGF Hist Off with Div Staff Offs and Unit Comdrs, 65th Inf Div, Cp Shelby, Miss, 30 Mar–10 Apr and 8–17 Jul 44. (3) An analysis of current MTPs as follows: (a) MTP 7–1 (Inf Regt) 1 Jul 42, (b) MTP 6–1 (FA Unit Tng Program) 15 Feb 42, (c) MTP 5–1 (Engr Units) 19 Dec 41, (d) MTP 8–1 (Med Units) 18 Feb 42, (e) MTP 11–1 (Sig Units) 13 Jan 42, (f) MTPs 10–1, 10–2, and 10–3 (QM Units), and (g) MTPs 9–2, 9–3, and 9–4 (Ord Units).

problem, returned to a bivouac area, concealed their guns under trees and camouflage nets, posted guards, prepared and served chow, and late at night returned to camp under blackout conditions.

The last few days of the basic period were spent in a rapid review of training in anticipation of the MTP tests to be given by the corps or army commander. These tests covered all subjects included in the 13-week program of individual training. Limitations of time and personnel made it impossible to test all units in all subjects, but enough units and individuals were tested in each to assure a fair gauge of the division's proficiency. Except in tactical problems involving squads, the standard unit tested was the platoon. Each platoon was tested in several subjects.

The second period consisted of eleven weeks of progressive unit training, from the squad to the regiment, inclusive. The purpose of this phase, as defined in the February directive, was "to develop each unit into a fighting team capable of taking its place in the division team and fulfilling its own particular role in battle." At some time during the thirteen weeks, infantry and cavalry platoons and field artillery battalions were tested in combat-firing proficiency by the corps or army commander. Field exercises were stressed; troops found themselves living more in the field during the unit training period. Although emphasis shifted from the training of the individual to the development of platoons, companies, battalions, and regiments into teams, actually there was no sharp break. The creation of teams on the squad level had figured prominently in basic training, and in unit training the development of the individual fighter proceeded concurrently with the molding of larger teams.

Highlights of unit training included AGF Platoon Combat Firing Proficiency Tests for infantry components and the reconnaissance troop; AGF Special Battle Courses and Physical Fitness Tests for all units; AGF Battery Tests for the field artillery; and Attack of a "Mock-up" Fortified Area by infantry platoons and companies. As a general rule these activities were staggered so as to permit maximum utilization of range facilities. Night operations were also emphasized throughout the unit training period. Each component of the division devoted a minimum of sixteen hours a week to night training.

Infantry units concentrated on tactical training, progressing from platoon problems in the first few weeks to regimental exercises at the end of the period. The artillery program consisted mainly of service practice, motor marches, battery and battalion field exercises, difficult traction expedients, and battalion firing in preparation for the AGF tests slated for the early portion of the combined training period. The engineers, working mainly by companies, devoted the major portion of unit training to such activities as constructing field fortifications, building fixed and floating bridges, laying mine fields, erecting road blocks, gapping and removing enemy mine fields, and building roads. In the medical battalion, the quartermaster company, the ordnance company, and the signal company troops were given practical training in their specialist roles and taught to work together in platoons and companies. Medical technicians, for example, gave enemas and blood transfusions, and medical companies spent considerable time in the field evacuating casualties across rivers, setting up battalion aid stations, and moving casualties back from collecting stations to clearing stations. Ordnance personnel usually spent the first half of the day on military subjects, including tactical training by platoon and company, while afternoons were devoted to maintenance work in shops. On account of the inability of post ordnance authorities to meet fully the division's requirements in heavy maintenance, the ordnance company was called on to perform a considerable amount of fourth-echelon maintenance. Both ordnance and quartermaster companies devoted much time to motor marches and bivouacs.

Tests given during the period of unit training comprised the following: (1) a physical training test, by the corps or army commander; (2) an infantry (and cavalry) platoon combat firing test, by the division commander; (3) a field artillery battery test, by the corps or army commander; and (4) a field artillery battalion test, by the corps or army commander.

Unit training was followed by eleven weeks of combined-arms training, the purpose of which was, in the words of the February directive, "to weld the several units of the division into a division team capable of acting as a concerted whole and maintaining itself under any and all battle conditions." A chart accompanying the directive of 19 October 1942 outlined three series of problems: regimental combat team exercises, which culminated in field maneuvers; division exercises and maneuvers; and command post exercises. The combined training period began with the regimental combat team exercises, in which a battalion of field artillery functioned in support of an infantry regiment, and ended with free maneuvers of one division against another. Command post exercises were held in preparation for both regimental combat team exercises and those of divisions. All except the combat team exercises were directed by the next higher commander. The exercises comprised both night and day operations. They were given in wooded as well as open terrain and, in their latter phases, emphasized the use of supporting units. All were followed by a thorough critique.

Time not consumed by scheduled exercises was devoted to preparation of all units for prescribed combined training exercises, correction of unit deficiencies disclosed in combined training, subjects currently prescribed by higher authority, and technical training.

Combined-arms training culminated in tests of two types: infantry battalion (horse squadron) field exercise tests; and infantry battalion (horse squadron) combat firing tests. Both tests were given by the corps or army commander. In short, the eleventh week was devoted to review.

Improvements in Training, 1943–44

The training of infantry divisions steadily improved in 1943 and 1944 in spite of continued personnel problems and shortages of equipment. Of the many factors contributing to this improvement, three were outstanding. The first was the inclusion in the training program of lessons learned from American experience in combat theaters. AGF headquarters kept close check on the battle performance of ground units, at first through observer teams made up in part of personnel of subordinate headquarters, and later through observer boards. Moreover, participants returning from theaters were sometimes brought to the War College for personal interviews. Important lessons from these reports and conferences were disseminated to subordinate commanders by means of letters and conferences. On 1 June 1943 a training letter, supplementing the directive effective 1 November 1942, was issued for the guidance of AGF components approaching combat readiness. This directive was based almost exclusively on lessons learned in battle. It provided for approximately two months' training after maneuvers in mine removal, scouting, patrolling, night fighting, infiltration, physical hardening, small-unit leadership, and progressive field exercises from the squad to the division. This program was interspersed with frequent tests. Further utilization of battle experience was secured by employment of overseas personnel as officers and cadremen in training units.[10]

The second important factor which improved the preparation of divisions in 1943 was the infusion of greater realism into the training program. The directive which became effective 1 November 1942 laid the basis for this improvement by suggesting that obstacle courses be made to "resemble the battlefield rather than the gymnasium" and by providing training in such tactical problems as attack

[10] (1) AGF ltr to CGs, 7 Jun 43, sub: Supplement to Tng Dir Effective 1 Nov 42. 353/52 (Tng Dir). (2) Telg of Gen McNair to CG IRTC, Cp Wheeler, Ga, 29 Sep 43. 220.3 (106th Div).

on fortified areas, combat in cities, and infiltration.[11] These general requirements were incorporated in specific directives covering each of the prescribed activities. On 5 January 1943 a letter was issued outlining a schedule of divisional exercises which had as their objective "the production of trained infantry-artillery-engineer teams capable of operating effectively with other arms as a task force in the attack of fortified localities." The training was to include attack by combat teams composed of divisional units, supported where practicable by tank, tank destroyer, antiaircraft, and chemical battalions, on defensive installations featuring replicas and mock-ups of pillboxes. At least one battalion of each infantry regiment participating in the assault was to use live ammunition in all its weapons. To ensure sufficient time for these exercises the combined training period was extended from eleven to twelve weeks.[12]

On 4 February 1943 the Army Ground Forces issued a lengthy letter laying down requirements for exercise in infiltration, close-combat firing, and combat in cities. These exercises were designed to subject the trainee "to every sight, sound, and sensation of battle," and to train him "to act calmly with sound judgment regardless of noise, confusion, and surprise." The infiltration exercise required that troops crawl about 100 yards over ground traversed by wire entanglements and dotted by bomb craters and slit trenches, with machine-gun bullets whistling closely overhead and explosive charges throwing up dirt about them. The close-combat firing course, designed "to teach men to fire small arms with speed and accuracy at surprise targets and while negotiating broken terrain," provided for the advance of troops over a considerable expanse of rough, wire-traversed terrain, with explosives going off about them and with targets, controlled by pulleys, bobbing up unexpectedly at ranges varying from five to fifty yards. The combat-in-cities exercise consisted of small units moving through mock villages and clearing streets and houses of hostile forces simulated by pulley-controlled dummies, some of which were made to appear suddenly on stairways or to jump from closets. Sketches of the various types of courses, based mainly on installations already in use by some training units, were attached to the letter prescribing battle-course training. The unit training period was extended from eleven to twelve weeks to allow time for these newly scheduled

[11] AGF ltr to CGs, 19 Oct 42, sub: Tng Dir Effective 1 Nov 42. 353/52 (Tng Dir).

[12] AGF ltr (R) to CGs, 5 Jan 43, sub: Tng in Opns against Permanent Land Fortifications. 353/2 (Assault)(R). A course in operations against permanent land fortifications was established at the Engineer School, Fort Belvoir, Va., to train selected officers as unit instructors in assault operations. Each division was given a quota of about twenty students for this course.

230-171 O - 66 - 30

activities. The letter outlining these special battle courses also directed coordination of other phases of training so that artillery practice might be utilized for accustoming infantrymen to overhead shell fire. Another activity prescribed was the overrunning of infantrymen in slit trenches by tanks.[13] In April 1943 four light tanks were issued to each division to facilitate this training.[14]

Experience revealed that the gap between firing under ordinary conditions and shooting amidst the hurly-burly of simulated combat was too wide for soldiers to take in one leap. Men who performed creditably in qualification and familiarization firing tended, when they came to combat courses, to make flagrant mistakes in assuming position, adjusting sights, and taking aim. The result was a low percentage of hits and a waste of ammunition. To remedy this situation the Army Ground Forces on 28 April 1943 issued a directive requiring all troops to complete a course in transition firing, outlined by the War Department, before attempting combat exercises. The transition course involved adjusting sights and firing at silhouettes that were made to appear in quick succession at varying distances. A fourteenth week was added to the individual training period to afford ample time for the transition program.[15]

Realism in divisional training was further promoted by the conversion of the California–Arizona Maneuver Area to a model theater of operations. This arrangement permitted divisions, after they completed regularly scheduled maneuvers, to devote thirteen weeks to "post-graduate" training under a play of influences bearing the closest possible resemblance to combat conditions.

The third salient factor in the production of better-trained divisions in 1943 was the improvement of AGF supervision. Inspections became more thorough if not more frequent. New tests were prepared and old ones were revised to secure a more satisfactory check on the quality and progress of training. Furthermore, as the headquarters command and staff obtained more experience in their duties, there was a tendency for the Army Ground Forces to become more positive and exacting in its relations with its major components. This was apparent in such forceful correctives[16] as the "Conduct of Training" letter of 1 January 1943, as well as in a letter to the commanding general of the Second Army, dated

[13] AGF ltr to CGs, 4 Feb 43, sub: Special Battle Courses. 353.01/61.

[14] Par 14, AGF Wkly Dir 15, 13 Apr 43.

[15] (1) AGF ltr to CGs, 26 Apr 43, sub: Tng Ammunition, Marksmanship Courses, Familiarization and Combat Firing. 471/1719. (2) Training Circular 30, WD, 10 Mar 43.

[16] (1) AGF ltr to CGs, 1 Jan 43, sub: Conduct of Tng. 319.22/22. (2) AGF ltr to Second Army, 1 Apr 43, sub: Inf Bn Firing Tests. 353.02/121 (AGF).

1 April 1943, criticizing severely the manner in which III Corps tested 80th Division units in battalion combat firing.

On 4 December 1943 Brig. Gen. John M. Lentz, G–3 of the Army Ground Forces, wrote to an assistant division commander as follows: [17]

> Combat firing . . . is our major weakness. It is the one phase about which I am discouraged. . . . Officers with years of background and peacetime safety concern simply will not cut loose with realistic combat firing as a general thing. There are so damn many flags and umpires and control they no more resemble a battlefield than a kindergarten.

Headquarters, Army Ground Forces, concentrated attention on the problem. In February 1944 it directed commanders "at every opportunity" to conduct combat-firing exercises for squads, platoons, companies, battalions, and regimental combat teams. The directive sought to loosen the control to which firing exercises had been subjected. Umpires and safety officers were ordered to permit units to advance in uneven lines as on the battlefield, to restrict the use of flags, and, in advanced training, to eliminate them altogether. Artillery and mortars were not to be restricted to the delivery of prepared fires but were to engage unforeseen targets on call of supported units and forward observers. Ammunition in unprecedentedly generous quantities was made available to further the new program.[18]

The Army Ground Forces also revised the Infantry Battalion Combat Firing Tests. The new tests required a battalion to attack a defensive position prepared by another battalion rather than by its own troops and, in general, were far more realistic than the old.[19]

Recurrently in 1944 the Army Ground Forces issued directives providing for participation of artillery, tanks, and tank destroyers with infantry in combat firing. Commanders were urged to bring into play every weapon at their disposal and to use an abundance of live ammunition in both organic and supporting elements.[20]

[17] Personal ltr of Brig Gen John M. Lentz to Brig Gen Marcus B. Bell, 81st Inf Div, 4 Dec 43. Lentz Correspondence.

[18] AGF ltr to CGs, 11 Feb 44, sub: Combat Firing. 471/1907.

[19] (1) AGF M/S, G–3 to CofS, 26 Feb 44, sub: Inf Bn and Horse Cav Sq Combat Firing Test. 353/52 (Tng Dir). (2) Memo of Lt Col B. A. Ford for G–3 AGF, 7 Jun 44, sub: Obsn during Visit to Cp Howze, Tex; Cp Swift, Tex; Cp Van Dorn, Miss, 29 May–3 Jun 44. AGF G–3 files, 333.1/33 (Inspections by AGF Staff Offs).

[20] (1) AGF ltr to CGs, 11 Feb 44, sub: Combat Firing. 471/1907. (2) AGF ltrs to CGs, 14 Jun 44, 16 Aug 44, and 17 Aug 44, sub: Combined Tng for Tanks and Tank Destroyer Units with Inf Divs. 353/2311. (3) Record of tel conv, Col S. E. Faine, AGF, and staff offs of Second Army, Fourth Army, and XXII Corps, 21 Aug 44. AGF G–3 files, 333.1/338 (Inspections by AGF Staff Offs).

In the fall of 1944 the close-combat course as operated since February 1943 was replaced by a more realistic exercise which featured the "buddy system." The new scheme provided for running of the course by teams of three or four men, each of whom filled alternately the roles of the soldier moving forward and the soldier providing cover.[21]

As General Lentz had observed in December 1943, many unit commanders were reluctant to "let go" in combat firing to the extent desired. Inspecting officers noted squeamishness in the use of live ammunition, particularly by supporting tanks, and failure to bring all weapons into play; they also found control officers still hovering too closely over men running close-combat courses. At a conference following inspection of the 86th Division in October 1944, Lt. Gen. Ben Lear, Commanding General of the Army Ground Forces, said:[22]

> Yesterday I saw a Close Combat Course. It started out by having a 2d lieutenant in charge, cautioning four men. A little later on I found a captain attempting to caution them. A second or two later a couple of sergeants were trying to influence the team, and when they got about two-thirds of the way through, there was a field officer up on the hill controlling it.

On another occasion General Lear observed control personnel in a close-combat exercise with their hands on the backs of the men running the course. Such instances of excessive control became less frequent as time went by. On the whole, combat firing was much more realistic in the latter part of 1944.[23]

The intensification of AGF supervision improved divisional training in 1944. The stepping up of overseas movements reduced the number of divisions in training and made possible more frequent visits to those remaining under AGF control. Supervision was brought closer by changes in inspection procedure instituted by General Lear after he assumed command of the Army Ground Forces. Beginning in September 1944, the size of the Commanding General's inspection party was practically doubled by the addition of a second planeload of officers to each trip. As a rule, occupants of the first plane, consisting of the Commanding General and higher-ranking members of his staff, attended ceremonies and sought to obtain an over-all picture of the division's problems and activities, including discipline and housekeeping, while the other group of officers, some of whom dubbed themselves the "second team," made a

[21] AGF ltr to CGs, 6 Oct 44, sub: Special Battle Courses. 353.01/61.

[22] Transcript of Notes on Conference of CG AGF and Staff at 86th Inf Div, 28 Oct 44. AGF G-3 files, 333.1/461 (Inspections by AGF Staff Offs).

[23] (1) Statement of Gen Ben Lear to AGF Hist Off, 20 Dec 44. (2) Statement of Col J. K. Bush, G-3 Sec AGF, to AGF Hist Off, 7 Feb 44.

more detailed inspection of personnel, equipment, and training. The second group consisted usually of representatives of the Infantry and Artillery Branches of G–3, the Maintenance and Supply Divisions of G–4, and the Engineer, Signal, Ordnance, and Quartermaster Sections. This system made it possible for the AGF party to give a division a comprehensive examination in two or three days.[24]

At some time during the inspection visit, General Lear assembled the junior officers and noncommissioned officers of the division and talked to them about their responsibilities as leaders. The purpose of the talks was to impress on small-unit leaders the importance of their work and to stimulate determination and aggressiveness.[25]

Prior to the summer of 1944, AGF inspectors followed the practice of withholding their findings, other than those which concerned minor deficiencies corrected on the spot, until their return to Washington, where comments were consolidated, edited, and transmitted through channels in an official letter. In August 1944 General Lear instituted a new procedure. After each inspection he assembled the division commander, the principal officers of the division staff, and the regimental commanders, and gave them a full oral report of observations, both favorable and unfavorable. General Lear himself presided over the conference. After a very brief statement of the purpose of the meeting, he introduced in succession the members of the AGF party, each of whom gave a succinct summary of his observations and made suggestions for the correction of deficiencies. General Lear concluded with a statement of his own impressions. Stenographers made a shorthand record of the conference, copies of which were usually mailed by the Army Ground Forces to army, corps, and division.[26]

The tenor of these oral comments differed little if any from that of the written communications which they superseded. But there can be little doubt that a prompt face-to-face presentation of the inspection report in a meeting presided over by the Commanding General of the Army Ground Forces made a greater impression on the division commander and his staff than did the delivery of a written report through channels after a lapse of several days.[27]

[24] Statement of Lt Col D. I. Davoren, AGF Gen Staff Secretariat, to AGF Hist Off, 8 Feb 45.

[25] Statement of Brig Gen Leo Donovan to AGF Hist Off, 19 Feb 45.

[26] This description of inspection procedure is based on (1) a study of transcripts of inspection conferences in AGF G–3 files, 333.1 (Inspections by AGF Staff Offs), (2) statement of Brig Gen Leo Donovan, G–3 AGF, to AGF Hist Off, 19 Feb 45, and (3) personal observations of the AGF Hist Off.

[27] (1) Statement of Brig Gen Leo Donovan to AGF Hist Off, 19 Feb 45. (2) Statement of Col J. K. Bush, G–3 Sec AGF, to AGF Hist Off, 8 Feb 45.

Between 21 July 1944, the date when the new plan was initiated, and 5 December 1944, General Lear and members of his staff applied the team-conference method of inspection to 19 infantry divisions, 5 armored divisions, and 1 airborne division. These inspections covered all the infantry divisions activated in 1943.[28]

It thus becomes evident that the AGF program for training divisions was refined and intensified with experience, though well established as a process for creating and training large units while General McNair was still Chief of Staff of GHQ. The principles were rooted in prewar planning, and they had been tested and elaborated during the initial mobilization. They were defined and implemented by GHQ in February 1942, on the basis of a peacetime field experience, culminating in the great maneuvers of 1941, such as the U.S. Army had never had before. The GHQ program thus defined was the program which General McNair applied as commander of the Army Ground Forces. To it the best efforts of his headquarters were directed during the summer of 1942, when the program was receiving a further test in the maneuvers of the older divisions and in the construction and initial training of the new—those activated after Pearl Harbor. The final results were codified in the great training directive of 1 November 1942, which governed unit training by the Ground Forces for the rest of the war. It centered in the perfecting of the division as a closely knit team of combined arms which would enter combat with a maximum of field experience. In the division the Army Ground Forces sought to achieve its masterpiece, its main contribution to what it regarded as its broad mission—the preparation "of a large force for combat."

After 1 November 1942 the program was continually refined and improved. The main effort was directed toward making it realistic, on the basis of the experience in combat which the ground forces began to acquire on a large scale with the launching of the offensive in North Africa. Further experience with training seemed to indicate that, to make it effective under the conditions existing in 1943, more tests were needed, and these were introduced. At the same time the headquarters staff under General McNair and his successors, Lt. Gen. Ben Lear and Gen. Joseph W. Stilwell, while hewing to the principle of a lean headquarters and decentralized responsibility as essential to good training, exercised an increasingly close watch and check on the results of training in the field. The main object continued to be realism. Only battle could produce battle-wise divisions: of this General McNair was thoroughly convinced after his visit to

[28] Information compiled from AGF G–3 files, 333.1 (Inspections by AGF Staff Offs).

the Tunisian front, in April 1943. But he devoted strenuous efforts to ensuring that no division should be "green" when delivered to a theater commander. As will presently appear, his ideal was most difficult to achieve and, in the case of the last divisions shipped, was unattainable. But the results achieved were reflected in the performance of new divisions in battle, beginning with the 85th and 88th Infantry Divisions on the bitterly contested Gustav Line in Italy, and in the exclamation which many soldiers were quoted as making when thrown into battle: "This is no worse than maneuvers."

III. Obstacles to Effective Training, 1942-43

The training of both old and new divisions encountered many obstacles during the period of mobilization in 1942 and 1943, when expansion of the armed forces was proceeding at a breath-taking pace. While obstacles were to be expected in any enterprise as full of imponderables as the training of a large force in a short time, the difficulties encountered were sufficiently great and persistent to imperil the combat effectiveness of the infantry divisions produced by the Army Ground Forces.

Training Difficulties in 1942

One of the most serious difficulties in 1942 was the shortage and obsolescence of equipment. Revised Tables of Organization issued in April 1942 listed improved types of weapons and vehicles for divisions, including Browning Automatic Rifles, .50-caliber machine guns, carbines to replace most of the service pistols, and ¼-ton trucks, or "jeeps."[1] Current regulations authorized the outfitting of divisions with about 50 percent of the equipment prescribed in Tables of Basic Allowances. But inspection reports and correspondence of officers in the field indicated a wide divergence between the amount of equipment authorized and that actually provided. Deficiencies could be attributed not only to the inability of industry to keep pace with the rapid expansion of the armed forces but also to the effort to provide arms and other equipment for the Allied Powers, particularly Russia. The increase in the number of units alerted for overseas movement during the summer of 1942 was also a factor, for these units had to be fully equipped regardless of the consequences to those in less advanced stages of training. After a visit of inspection to seven division camps at the end of July, G-4 of the Army Ground Forces observed: "The shortage of equipment in new units is becoming more critical with each month's new activations."[2] About a

[1] T/O 7, Inf Div, 1 Aug 42. This was a recapitulation of T/O's of division components published 1 April 1942.

[2] AGF memo, G-4 for CofS, 5 Aug 42, sub: Rpt of G-4 Inspection Trip, 26 Jul-1 Aug 42. 333.1/1250 (sep file).

month later, after inspecting four other divisions, G–4 wrote that his observations "showed a continuance of the tightening up of equipment." [3]

AGF headquarters tried to remedy this situation by (1) prescribing a rotative system which permitted successive groups of trainees to use the same equipment, (2) redoubling efforts to prevent deterioration of equipment on hand, (3) requiring strict economy in the expenditure of ammunition, and (4) encouraging improvisation on the part of subordinate commanders.[4] But these efforts met with only partial success.

Personnel deficiencies were as serious as those of equipment. A major cause of the shortage of manpower for divisions during the summer and fall of 1942 was the attempt to meet unanticipated requirements of task forces for Europe and the Pacific and, at the same time, to maintain the schedule of activations. Divisions in advanced stages of training suffered more during this period than those activated in 1942.[5] Some of the old divisions not only were required to furnish several cadres but also were subjected to repeated strippings to fill alerted units. On 30 June 1942 the 27 infantry divisions under AGF jurisdiction reported an understrength of 4,150 officers and 42,880 men.[6] Later the situation became even worse. General McNair informed General Lear on 31 July that "thousands" of service units not in the Troop Basis were being formed and that old divisions would probably have to supply some of the men for them.[7] His apprehension proved to be well-founded. Three National Guard divisions, the 30th, 31st, and 33d, became virtual pools for the Army Service Forces. The 30th declined from a strength of 12,400 in June 1942 to 3,000 in August; the 31st, from 15,200 to 7,200; and the 33d, from 13,200 to 8,400. The 35th, 38th, and 44th suffered losses almost as great.[8] General Lear pointed out to General McNair in August that some of the National Guard units were "low in their minds," since recurrent depletions to fill other units meant continuous postponement of the opportunity for combat.[9] Even when replacements were received promptly,

[3] AGF memo, G–4 for CofS, 8 Sep 42, sub: Rpt of G–4 Inspection Trip, 31 Aug–4 Sep 42. 333.1/1355.

[4] (1) Par *6b*, AGF ltr to CGs, 19 Oct 42, sub: Tng Dir Effective 1 Nov 42. 353/52 (Tng Dir). (2) AGF ltr to CGs, 4 Feb 42, sub: Special Battle Courses. 353.01/61.

[5] See "Mobilization of the Ground Army" in *The Organization of Ground Combat Troops*.

[6] Incl 2 to memo (S) of Gen McNair for the CofS USA, 3 Aug 42, sub: Pers and Tng Status of Units of the AGF. 320.2/283 (S).

[7] Record of tel conv between Gens McNair and Lear, 31 Jul 42. Personal files of Gen Lear.

[8] (1) "Division Book" of DCofS AGF. (2) Record of tel conv between Gens McNair and Lear, 31 Jul, 11 Aug, 20 Aug, 1942. Personal files of Gen Lear.

[9] Record of tel conv between Gens McNair and Lear, 11 Aug 42. Personal files of Gen Lear.

which was usually not the case, the effect on training was disruptive. Some divisions had to maintain several programs concurrently to accommodate replacements received at various stages of training. This practice seriously strained instructional personnel, already sparse from repeated turnover. Most of the older divisions adopted the plan of segregating replacements in special training units until they reached a level that made admixture with other troops practicable. But some were so much reduced that they had to go through the entire training cycle again.[10]

General Lear repeatedly urged AGF headquarters to desist from piecemeal robbing of divisions. "If you have to take men," he said, "take large numbers from a few units rather than a few men from many units, and take them in hunks rather than in driblets." Units that were reduced to cadres, he added, could begin their training over again, while the others could proceed without interruption.[11]

General McNair admitted the soundness of General Lear's advice but was doubtful of its practicability under existing circumstances. "It is very difficult to shape and to stick to a policy," he remarked, "since the demands made are entirely at variance with what we have been told previously would be the situation."[12] In August he finally prevailed upon the War Department to postpone activation of one of the December divisions. As he wrote to General Lear, there was obviously "no sense in building new units while old ones sit around in a mangled condition."[13] In the fall of 1942 the 30th, 31st, and 33d Divisions were promised immunity from further stripping, and two new divisions, the 76th and 78th, were allotted an overstrength of 33⅓ percent and earmarked as replacement pools.[14]

A third deterrent to divisional training during the early AGF period was the scarcity and inexperience of officer personnel. The problem of division command was not as great as during the GHQ period; nevertheless, responsible

[10] (1) Personal ltrs of Brig Gen J. F. Brittingham, 89th Div, to Col Edmund W. Searby, Asst G-3 AGF, 3 Feb, 12 May, 1943. (2) Memo of Col Burns Beall, Asst G-3 AGF, for G-3 AGF, 7 Feb 43, sub: Obsns on Tng Activities, 3-5 Jan 43. Both in AGF G-3 Tng Div files, 333.1.

[11] (1) Record of tel conv between Gens McNair and Lear, 11 Aug 42. Personal files of Gen Lear. (2) Personal ltr of Gen Lear to Gen McNair, 11 Sep 42. McNair Correspondence.

[12] Personal ltr of Gen McNair to Gen Lear, 19 Sep 42. McNair Correspondence.

[13] Personal ltr of Gen McNair to Gen Lear, 20 Aug 42. McNair Correspondence.

[14] (1) Statement of Gen Ben Lear to AGF Hist Off, 14 Oct 43. (2) AGF ltr (R) to CGs, 2 Oct 42, sub: Repl Pools. 320.2/105 (R).

authorities found it necessary to replace a number of general officers because of defective qualifications for leadership.[15] Most of those affected belonged to National Guard organizations. In political circles the charge was revived that National Guard officers were being victimized by the prejudice of the Regular Army group. The War Department felt constrained to allay this feeling by attempting to search out the most capable National Guard colonels for promotion to brigadiers.[16] When the request for recommendations was passed down the line, it elicited a cool response. General Lear observed that the matter reduced itself to one of recommending the advancement of National Guard officers to positions of command over Regular Army officers who were their superiors in ability, and this he refused to do.[17]

The rapid expansion of the Army created a demand for trained staff officers that was considerably greater than the supply. During the early months of 1942 it was sometimes necessary to designate for high staff positions persons who had not taken the regular course in the Command and General Staff School and whose background for the responsible duties required of them was utterly inadequate. The results were disruptive and unfortunate.[18] There was also a dearth of competent regimental and battalion commanders and of other field grade officers. But the situation with regard to junior and noncommissioned officers was even more disturbing. Reports of AGF inspections of divisions were filled with such judgments as "hesitant uncertain leadership by platoon and squad leaders," "poor troop leadership by junior commanders," and "squad and platoon leaders were lax in correcting errors." [19]

[15] (1) Statement of Lt Col R. H. Booth, AGF G–1 Sec, to AGF Hist Off, 25 Nov 43. (2) Personal ltr of Gen McNair to Gen Lear, 10 Apr 42; Gen Lear to Gen McNair, 17 Apr 42. McNair Correspondence.

[16] (1) Memo (C) of Gen McNair for Gen Lear, 11 Aug 42, sub: Promotion of Natl Guard Offs. McNair Correspondence (C). (2) Memo of Gen Lear for Gen McNair, 18 Aug 42, sub: Promotion of National Guard Offs. McNair Correspondence. (3) For evidence of persistence of the feeling that the War Department discriminated against National Guard generals, see speech of Senator Clark, 20 May 43, *Congressional Record,* LXXXIX, 4745.

[17] Memo (C) of Gen Lear for Gen McNair, 18 Aug 42, sub: Promotion of Natl Guard Offs. Personal files of Gen Lear (C).

[18] (1) AGF M/S of G–1 FA Br, Offs Div, to Misc Div, 13 Feb 43, sub: Notice for Wkly Dir. (2) AGF memo, ExO G–1 to New Divs Div, 30 Nov 42, sub: Policy to be Followed in Selecting Gen Staff Offs. Both in G–1 New Divs Div Policy file.

[19] (1) 90th Div ltr to AGF, 14 Oct 42, sub: Plat Combat Proficiency Tests. (2) IV Corps ltr to AGF, 28 Jun 43, sub: Bn Combat Firing Test of 91st Inf Div. (3) VIII Corps ltr to Third Army, 7 Dec 42, sub: Rpt of Inspection, 95th Inf Div, Cp Swift, Tex. All in AGF G–3 Tng Div files, binders for 90th, 91st and 95th Divs, respectively.

The deplorable state as to officers to which some of the old divisions were reduced was recorded in a Third Army inspection report of the 28th Division in late July 1942:[20]

> There is an acute shortage of officers; of the 706 authorized by the T/O, the division has 440 assigned, and of this number 106 are on special duty and detached service, several of the companies and most of the platoons are commanded by non-commissioned officers: many of the best officers have been sent on cadres. This has left company officers who are inexperienced, and at present incapable of properly instructing their men. Over eight hundred non-commissioned officers have been sent to Officers Candidate Schools, many have been sent on cadres, and those who are left are below the desired standard . . . . some of the battalion commanders are over age . . . . the spirit of the division has showed a lack of objective and the will to do.

Personnel shortages were aggravated by the failure of service commands to provide adequate station complements. This made necessary the detail of officers and men from tactical units to perform security and housekeeping functions that were the responsibility of the post commanders.[21]

A few of the divisions had their administrative burdens multiplied during the early AGF period by the attachment of nondivisional "spare parts" for supervision. In April 1942 Col. Hammond M. Monroe of the Army Ground Forces listed the following units as attached by Second Army to the 6th Division at Fort Leonard Wood:[22]

72d Field Artillery Brigade
Two tank destroyer battalions
Hq & Hq Detachment, 56th QM Regiment
3d Battalion, 56th QM Regiment
Hq & Hq Detachment, 87th QM Battalion
Three companies of the 87th QM Battalion
1st Battalion, 49th QM Regiment
Two engineer battalions
An engineer company
An evacuation hospital
A medical sanitary company
Hq & Hq Detachment, 42d Ordnance Battalion
Three ordnance companies
162d Signal Photo Company Detachment

[20] Third Army ltr to AGF, 17 Aug 42, sub: Rpt of Inspection, 28th Inf Div. AGF G-3 Tng Div files, 333.1 (28th Div).

[21] AGF ltr to CGs, 31 Jan 43, sub: Interferences with Tng. 353.02/78 (AGF).

[22] Memo of Col H. M. Monroe, Asst G-3 AGF, for CofS AGF, 7 Apr 42, sub: Visit to Ft Leonard Wood, Mo — the 6th Div and the 72d FA Brig. AGF G-3 Tng Div files, 333.1 (6th Div).

Colonel Monroe commented as follows:

These attached units throw a heavy burden of paper work and inspection on the G–3 Section of the 6th Division. Army reviews all training memoranda and then calls on 6th Division for correction. 6th Division has to inspect all cadres from these units in minute detail. Consequently, G–3, who has no additional help to take care of these units, is tied to his desk constantly.

The provision by Army Ground Forces in May 1942 of headquarters and headquarters detachments, special troops, relieved divisions of "spare parts" responsibilities,[23] but excessive paper work overburdened most of them throughout 1942. This difficulty was, in part, of their own making. The 6th Division, for example, issued 27 numbered and 22 unnumbered training memoranda in the first 6 weeks of the year. Additional paper was issued by higher headquarters. The mass of material was passed on down to regimental and other commanders —already encumbered with a plethora of responsibilities—to be digested and applied. In the early part of 1942 the 6th Division artillery was operating under an accumulation of 77 training directives or memoranda.[24] There was a tendency for paper to beget paper; many of the directives issuing from higher headquarters called for the preparation of tests and the making of reports.

A considerable portion of the instructional material, tests, and reports showered upon divisions and their components was necessary or helpful. But there was too much overlapping and duplication by the various headquarters in the chain of command. A part of the excess was due to an effort by staff officers to substitute the mimeograph for personal visits; a part, in the words of General McNair, was attributable to the fact "that some individual feels that he can write a better manual than the War Department publication." [25]

Early in 1942 a battalion commander wrote:[26]

We are actually swamped with typed and mimeographed literature. More than 90% of it is utterly useless. Trite exhortations and repetition of much of the information found in field and technical manuals. Each general and special staff officer all the way down the line, tries to amplify and expand his own department. It would take me 6 to 8 hours a day to read and digest all the stuff that reaches this battalion. The ——— Army and the ——— Army corps are shoving it out by the ream, and this division shoves it on down . . . . we have training programs, master schedules, weekly schedules, progress charts, and so on ad

[23] See below, "The Training of Nondivisional Units."

[24] Memo of Lt Col John M. Lentz for G–3 GHQ, 23 Feb 42, sub: Obsns at Ft Leonard Wood, Mo, 19–21 Feb 42. AGF G–3 Tng Div files, 333.1 (6th Div).

[25] Ltr of Gen McNair to CGs, 1 Jan 43, sub: Conduct of Tng. 319.22/22.

[26] Quoted in AGF ltr to CGs, 25 Jun 42, sub: Paperwork. 312.11/82.

infinitum. I have had 6 clerks busy day and night since we received our typewriters. The field manuals and the unit training program put out by GHQ are all we need to turn out a good battalion. But we don't have time to read the former, and the latter is so bastardized when the staffs get through changing that it is useless.

The paper menace eventually reached such proportions that General McNair personally prepared a stinging letter on the subject: staff officers who tried gratuitously to improve upon War Department manuals were sharply rebuked; armies and corps were enjoined from sending their training literature to units lower than divisions; and division commanders were reminded of the fact that they and their staffs were within daily reach of their unit commanders and that personal instruction was preferable to written communication. General McNair directed further that "periodic, written, training-progress reports will not be required of units lower than the division." He also ordered a curtailment of the number and elaborateness of tests.[27] The results of General McNair's philippic were immediately apparent.[28]

Difficulties of less frequent occurrence, involving mainly the first groups of new divisions, included inadequacy of post facilities, particularly of housing, and inclusion of undesirables in cadres. GHQ and its successor, the Army Ground Forces, spared no effort to assure selection of the highest type personnel as nuclei for the new divisions. But the temptation to use cadres as dumping grounds for substandards and misfits sometimes proved irresistible. The designation of some unsatisfactory officers, especially battery and company commanders, for the March divisions was the subject of a critical letter from Gen. George C. Marshall to General Lear in which the Chief of Staff said: "I have directed GHQ to make arbitrary selections of officers on duty with units of your army in the event that there is a recurrence of the apparently perfunctory attention to this matter in the future." [29]

Difficulties in the spring of 1942 might have been less had the Army Ground Forces been able to exercise a close supervision over the affairs of its components. But the excessive accumulation of activities which came in the wake of the transition from GHQ to the Army Ground Forces made intensive checking for a time impossible. In May General Lear asked that AGF staff members send him informal reports of their visits to Second Army units, remarking that he had not received any comment for some time. When this request was passed on

[27] AGF ltr to CGs, 1 Jan 43, sub: Conduct of Tng. 319.22/22.

[28] Personal ltr (C) of Gen Lear to Gen McNair, 11 Jan 43. Personal files of Gen Lear (C).

[29] Personal ltr (C) of Gen Marshall to Gen Lear, 20 Feb 42. Personal files of Gen Lear (C).

to Col. Lowell W. Rooks, Chief of the AGF Training Division, he observed:[30]

> General Lear has heard little from this headquarters of late . . . for the reason that few visits of inspection have been made . . . . the press of business here in the office has been such that I have been loath to recommend any extensive activity along that line. However, just as for any other commander, I believe our job is only half done with the issuance of orders. We must get out and see that they are faithfully executed.

At the time of Colonel Rooks' comment a checklist was being prepared by the AGF G–4 from data submitted by the various general staff sections. The result was a standard form, carried by AGF officers on their field trips, which covered information on points of prime interest to headquarters as a whole as well as to the section making the inspection.[31] In the summer and fall AGF officers, with General McNair often in the vanguard, appeared with increasing frequency at the stations which dotted the far-flung training domain to observe tests, maneuvers, and routine activities, together with equipment and camp facilities. Reports improved in both form and content.[32]

Despite the shortage of equipment, the fluctuations and depletion of enlisted personnel, the scarcity and inexperience of officers, the overburden of paper work, the drag of "spare parts," abuses in cadre selection, and initial deficiencies in AGF supervision, the divisions as a whole made discernible progress during 1942. Old divisions gave a good account of themselves in the 1942 maneuvers.[33] Of the new March divisions, General McNair said in November: "The President, the Secretary of War, and the Chief of Staff of the Army have all pronounced you good, at least so far as you have gone. After over seven months of training you are well on your way toward fitness for battle." [34] Many deficiencies remained, which General McNair did not fail to specify, but the shortcomings that persisted appeared less serious than those that had been overcome.

Equipment and Personnel Problems in 1943

Despite the general improvement of conditions affecting the activation and training of divisions in the latter part of 1942 and the early months of 1943, short-

[30] Memo of Col Lowell W. Rooks, Chief of Tng Div AGF, for Gen McNair, 21 May 42, sub: Comment on Ltr of Gen Lear, 18 May 42. AGF G–3 files.

[31] *Ibid.*

[32] This statement is based on a study of numerous inspection reports in the 333.1 files of the AGF G–3 Section (some of which are in the central files of the G–3 Section and some in the files of the G–3 Training Division) and of the AGF AG Section.

[33] Statement of Gen McNair on maneuvers of AGF, 12 Oct 42. AWC Library, McNair Speeches.

[34] Radio speech of Gen McNair on the "Pass in Review" Program, Mutual Network, 10 Nov 42. AWC Library, Collection of McNair Speeches.

ages of equipment, particularly of ammunition and late-model automatic rifles, persisted. Reports from division artillery commanders protested against the meagerness of the ammunition allotment and the system by which it was meted out to them. A corps artillery commander called the plan of annual allowances an absurdity and urged adoption of distribution by training periods, with reserve supplies available at all times at training camps. "It is discouraging," he wrote, "to be forced to postpone certain types of training for a month or six weeks awaiting the shipment of ammunition." [35] The artillery commander of the 90th Division expressed the view that existing allowances should be increased from three to six times. "I do not believe," he wrote, "that sufficient ammunition is provided for either the Infantry, or the Artillery, or the others to become really proficient with their weapons." [36] An AGF staff officer replied: "We are of course in entire agreement with you on ammunition. We keep after the War Department all we can and will get every round they will let us have." [37]

The Commanding General of the 94th Division, Maj. Gen. Harry J. Malony, summarized training problems that his division had encountered, mainly in 1943, as follows:[38]

Small Arms—Our rifles and carbines (approximately 11,367) were issued initially on a 25% and 20% basis. Of necessity they were rotated between and among units. The very important sense of individual responsibility was not established in the first instance and it became very difficult to establish later, in view of the fact that many men were fully aware that they were carrying arms not combat serviceable, and rejected by the 8th Division for that reason, which would be replaced before they went into combat.

Mortars—The mortars are worthy of special mention, since the 45% initially received were in such bad shape as to be of very limited value. Mortar ammunition and rocket launcher ammunition were late and scarce.

. . . .

Deficiencies

1. We never had enough practice mines. As a result, again we had to keep shuttling the material in inadequate amounts between units.

2. We lacked enough explosive to carry out all the jobs for which it was required. The allowances in AR 775–10 are too small.

[35] Personal ltr of Arty Off III Corps to Lt Col John C. Oakes, Asst G–3 AGF, 9 Apr 43. AGF G–3 Tng Div files, 333.1 (98th Div).

[36] Personal ltr of Arty Comdr 90th Div to Brig Gen John M. Lentz, G–3 AGF, 12 Apr 43. AGF G–3 Tng Div files, 333.1 (90th Div).

[37] Personal ltr of Lt Col John C. Oakes, Asst G–3 AGF, to Army Comdr 90th Div, 30 Apr 43. AGF G–3 Tng Div files, 333.1 (90th Div).

[38] Personal ltr of Maj Gen Harry J. Malony, CG 94th Div, to Maj Gen John P. Lucas, CG Fourth Army, 22 Jul 44. 322/30 (94th Div).

3. By reason of never having received the equipment, our Artillery had no practical training in Net Sets, Camouflage, No. 2. Our Engineers had some experience with Shop, Motorized, General Purpose, but when it went out of the T/O, we turned it in and when it was restored to the T/O we could not get it back. It was never again supplied. We never received our Engineer Diesel engine tractors nor the Semi-trailers, 20-ton.

Radio—We were able to train with the radios and radio substitutes, but when during maneuvers we were confronted by divisions completely equipped with better radio equipment, we were badly handicapped in communications.

Flame Throwers—We should have had more flame throwers available.

After inspection of an armored division in February 1943, an AGF staff officer observed: "The general shortage of equipment is a serious handicap to training. . . . Groups working on single weapons were so large that individuals were receiving scant instruction." [39] Two weeks later another staff member reported observing a lieutenant of an infantry division conducting a bayonet exercise in which "sticks were used in the absence of rifles." [40] Such conditions were exceptional, but as late as July 1943 training equipment was still not available in the quantity needed.[41]

Tragic consequences of persistent shortages in training material were manifested on the field of combat. Elements of the 45th Division, which was activated in September 1940 and left the United States in May 1943, met with disaster in an engagement near Persano, Italy, on 13 September 1943. In commenting on this action to AGF observers in November, the commanding general of the division said:[42]

During our training period . . . there was a definite lack of training ammunition for the antitank rifle grenade and bazooka. The men did not have the ammunition or proper targets, such as old German tanks, at which to fire in order to give them the necessary confidence that is vital in repelling a tank attack. I believe that the lack of this confidence in the antitank rifle grenade and the bazooka was a determining factor in the fight near Persano.

There was considerable improvement in the ammunition situation after the spring of 1943. On 30 July the War Department published a revision of AR 775–10, increasing allowances for training purposes and providing for allocation on a monthly basis.[43] But at the same time, on the ground of the greater urgency

[39] Incl 19 to AGF ltr to CGs, 21 Oct 43, sub: Inspection Comments. 333.1/1505.

[40] Incl 24, to ltr cited in n. 39.

[41] AGF ltr (S) to Procurement Review Board, 31 Jul 43, sub: Status of Equip in the AGF. 401.1/25 (S).

[42] Incl 4 to AGF Bd ltr (S) to CG AGF, 21 Nov 43, sub: Rpt 82, AGF Bd, AFHQ–NATO. 319.1 (NATO)(S).

[43] (1) AR 775–10, 30 Jul 43. (2) AGF M/S, G–3 to CofS, 10 Nov 43, sub: Marksmanship Courses for Tactical Units and Repl Deps. 471/1790.

230-171 O - 66 - 31

of building up stock piles in Great Britain, OPD rejected General McNair's renewed plea that the equipment allotment of divisions be raised from 50 to 100 percent at the end of the sixth month of training.[44]

Personnel problems, though they had seemed to be nearing solution in the latter part of 1942, also continued to hamper training. In the early part of 1943 some of the recently activated divisions complained of receiving their fillers in driblets, thus necessitating training on several levels at the same time. An AGF G-3 officer wrote sympathetically in February 1943 to a division artillery commander who was struggling with four echelons of training: "The delay in filling our draft requirements played hell with the training program. We understand your predicament. It is tough having to contend with men in several stages of training and still meet the program."[45] The filler situation grew worse in the summer and fall. The 63d Division, activated on 15 June, had received only about half of its T/O strength by mid-September; the 65th Division, activated on 16 August, was short 10,000 men on 30 November.[46]

Officer candidate schools were turning out an adequate number of junior officers by the spring of 1943, and after a period of seasoning the great majority of them were making excellent platoon leaders; but there was a persistent shortage of competent officers of field grade. Demands for cadre and for overseas loss replacements produced, in some units, a rate of turnover that was disruptive. An AGF staff member reported on 25 May 1943 after an inspection trip to Fort Jackson and Camp Forrest:[47]

> In both the 80th and the 100th Divisions the turnover of personnel has been one of the chief obstacles to training. In the 80th Division the officer losses have mounted to 450 in six months. Although many field officers have been taken, the replacements have been second lieutenants. . . . Over a period of 10 months, each of two of the infantry regiments had had three regimental commanders and the third had had four. Changes in battalion commanders have been even more frequent.

Part of the turnover was due to the apparently common practice of "stealing" officers who attended Command and General Staff School. Several division com-

[44] (1) Memo (S) of Gen McNair for CofS USA, 3 Jul 43, sub: Policies Governing Issues of Equip. (2) OPD memo 400 (19 Jun 43) for CG AGF, 26 Jul 43, sub: Pre-Shipment. Both in 320.2/22 (TUB 43)(S).

[45] Personal ltr of Arty Comdr 89th Div to Col Edmund W. Searby, Asst G-3 AGF, 3 Feb 43, and reply of Col Searby, 22 Feb 43. AGF G-3 Tng Div files, 333.1 (89th Div).

[46] (1) Personal ltr of Arty Comdr 63d Div to Col John C. Oakes, Asst G-3 AGF, 18 Sep 43. AGF G-3 Tng Div files, 333.1 (63d Div). (2) Master Card for 65th Div, dead files. AGF C&RD files.

[47] AGF memo of Lt Col R. L. Baughman, Asst G-3, for ACofS G-3, 25 May 43, sub: Inspection Trip to Ft Jackson and Cp Forrest, 20-22 May 43. AGF G-3 Tng Div files, 333.1 (100th Div).

manders complained that "there is no use trying to educate and train a young staff officer by sending him to Leavenworth for that is the surest means of losing him." [48]

Some commanders were reluctant to requisition replacements in field grades from other units for fear of having undesirables unloaded on them. The commanding general of the 44th Division wrote to General McNair, 27 February 1943:[49]

> My commissioned personnel problem is quite difficult of solution. I have the vacancies. In fact, if I promote to fill all vacancies of colonels and lieutenant colonels . . . I would need fifteen infantry majors. . . . I can now get officers from divisions nearby but such a selection would be officers that the current division commanders are willing to lose. I will do better struggling along with what I have, rather than import men "selected out" of other combat units.

It was at the field grade level that divisions could least afford to lose officers. The commanding general of the 84th Division wrote to General McNair in March 1943:[50]

> We have the best company officers we have ever had in time of war, but they have their shortcomings. They are splendid technicians. They really know their technique. They are less well-qualified in minor tactics, but they are passable in that department. However, as to handling men in the mass—in leadership, their ignorance is abysmal.
>
> The majors and lieutenant colonels (the battalion echelon) comprise the weakest strata in an army today. Their development into satisfactory commanders is the division commander's biggest problem. He can expect, and will get, very little help from them in improving the quality of his company officer group. This is particularly true in the field of leadership.

The unsatisfactoriness of the situation was reflected shortly in theaters of operations. In December 1943 the commanding general of the 45th Division stated:[51]

> The battalion commander problem is serious. It is our weakest link. The replacements for them are nil. The only way a senior captain can get training as a battalion commander is by being put in as a battalion executive, and that job is usually held by some deadhead, some major who has been promoted because he is good company or something like that. My battalion executives are no good.

[48] *Ibid.*

[49] Personal ltr of Maj Gen James I. Muir to Gen McNair, 27 Feb 43. AGF G–3 files.

[50] "Notes on Training" by Maj Gen J. H. Hilldring, incl to ltr of Gen Hilldring to Gen McNair, 29 Mar 43. McNair Correspondence.

[51] Statement of Maj Gen Troy H. Middleton, incl I to AGF Bd AFHQ–NATO Rpt 91 (S), 9 Dec 43. 319.1 (NATO)(S).

Despite continued efforts of the Army Ground Forces to keep officers with their units, there were occasional complaints in 1943 of heavy inroads on commissioned personnel for nontraining functions. A Third Army testing team, reporting on an inspection of the 84th Division in July, observed:[52]

> Some platoons were found to have poor discipline. . . . An incomplete investigation revealed that the greater portion of these platoons were without a commissioned leader most of the time. . . . Most companies have the proper number of officers assigned but so many of them are detailed on special duty by higher headquarters and sent away to schools that normally there is not more than two or three for duty with the company. In some instances companies had to borrow officers to witness the pay.

Both new and old divisions were adversely affected by the Army Specialized Training Program. Trainees selected for this program were the choicest of the enlisted group, and the loss of so many intelligent men from personnel already picked over by the Air Corps and depleted by cadre and officer candidate school drafts reduced noncommissioned officer sources to disastrously low levels—not to mention the disruption produced by replacing these men in the midst of the training program. An assistant G–3 at AGF headquarters estimated that ASTP losses suffered by the 75th Division just after completion of the MTP Test had set back training from four to six months.[53] The 104th Division faced the prospect of losing 767 men to ASTP in June 1943; more than 300 of them had been trained as cadremen.[54]

The loss of men to the ASTP was felt the more keenly as many of them had been trained as specialists. The surgeon of the 44th Division reported in August 1943 that technical training had been set back seriously "when practically all the trained medical, surgical, and dental technicians were lost to ASTP." [55] The commanding general of the 94th Division stated about the same time that, because of the withdrawals of trained artillery specialists to the ASTP, "survey teams and fire direction centers have had to be reorganized as many as 5 times." [56]

[52] Third Army Testing Team ltr for CG Third Army, 19 Jul 43, sub: Rpts of Combat Bn Firing Tests, 84th Inf Div, Cp Howze, Tex. AGF G–3 Tng Div files, 333.1 (84th Div).

[53] Memo of Lt Col Carl H. Jark, Asst G–3 AGF, for G–3 WD, 31 Jul 43, sub: Obsns During Visit to Cp Phillips, Ft Leonard Wood, and Cp Campbell, 27–30 Jul 43, inclusive. AGF G–3 Tng Div files, 333.1 (94th Div).

[54] Memo of Col Jark for G–3 WD, 2 Jun 43, sub: Rpt of Obsns on Inspection Trip, 23–30 May incl. AGF G–3 Tng Div files, 333.1 (104th Div).

[55] Memo of Col Wm. E. Shambora for G–3 AGF, 31 Aug 43, sub: Inspection Rpt of Units at Ft Lewis, Bend [Maneuver Area], Cp Adair, Cp White, Cp Beale, and DTC. AGF G–3 files, 333.1/44 (Inspections by AGF Staff Offs).

[56] M/S of Lt Col W. S. Renshaw for G–3 AGF, 2 Aug 43, sub: G–1's Rpt of Inspection Trip made 27 Jul–30 Jul 43. AGF G–3 files, 333.1/37 (Inspections by AGF Staff Offs).

Recruiting officers of the Army Air Forces took away other choice personnel. The commanding general of the 75th Division complained in July 1943 that "there are two officers of the Air Corps stationed at Camp Leonard Wood whose duty is to proselyte and procure Air Corps cadets." [57] After a visit to the 104th Division in August 1943, G-1 of the Army Ground Forces stated:[58]

> It was reported that the Air Forces attempt to recruit enlisted personnel assigned this division when men go on pass to Portland, Oregon. I directed the division to disregard requests from Air Forces to have men report for physical examinations unless the individual concerned made application for air crew training.

The transfer to reduced Tables of Organization after 15 July 1943 improved the divisional manpower picture for a time. But the growing need for trained men to replace overseas losses resulted in heavy drafts on the older organizations. By late fall many divisions in advanced stages of training had fallen considerably below authorized strength.[59]

In spite of these persistent equipment and personnel problems, the divisions which reached the end of the AGF production line in the latter part of 1943 were better prepared for battle than their predecessors. General Lentz, G-3 of the Army Ground Forces, in a personal letter to Brig. Gen. Marcus B. Bell of the 81st Division, summarized this improvement in the following terms:[60]

> While we have many weak spots and a hell of a lot remains to be done, yet in general, I am convinced that we have been turning out soundly trained and well trained divisions. Some of them, I believe sincerely, equal anything the Germans ever turned out, at least so far as training is concerned. Lacking the necessity for defending our homes and [having] a certain national softness that does not develop a keen desire to fight, our individual fighting spirit may not be too hot, but I still think the training is there.

[57] *Ibid.*

[58] Memo of Brig Gen C. L. Hyssong for G-3 AGF, 31 Aug 43, sub: Rpt of Inspection. AGF G-3 files, 333.1/44 (Inspections by AGF Staff Offs).

[59] (1) AGF M/S, G-3 to Tng Div, 10 Sep 43. AGF G-3 Tng Div files, 333.1 (97th Div). (2) DCofS's "Division Book."

[60] Personal ltr of Brig Gen John M. Lentz to Brig Gen Marcus B. Bell, 4 Dec 43. Lentz Correspondence.

IV. Effects of Overseas Requirements Upon Training, 1944-45

Benefits accruing from refinement of the training program, provision of more generous allotments of ammunition, and intensification of higher supervision were in large measure offset, particularly in 1944, by the disruption resulting from unforeseen requirements of units and individuals for overseas theaters.

Overseas Calls for Units

In April 1944, mainly because heavy drafts for overseas operations left an insufficient number of service units for support of divisions in the field, the California–Arizona Manuever Area was closed.[1] Discontinuance of this graduate school of combined training was a serious blow to the divisional program. Of the 64 infantry divisions trained in the United States, only 13 had received training in the California–Arizona Maneuver Area, and, of the 26 activated after July 1942, only 1; of the 87 divisions of all types activated in the United States, only 20 received such training.[2]

Urgent calls for units overseas necessitated discontinuance of maneuvers in Tennessee in March 1944 and of those in Louisiana in April. Plans were made for resumption of the Louisiana maneuvers in the summer, but they had to be abandoned in view of the advancement of the readiness dates of the divisions scheduled for participation.[3] A few divisions received, in lieu of the canceled maneuvers, a month of exercises at or near their home stations, with each division, less a combat team, maneuvering against the detached team. These exercises, however, were a poor substitute for "big maneuvers."[4]

[1] AGF memo (C) for CofS USA, 24 Dec 43, sub: CAMA. 320.2/104 (CAMA) (C).

[2] (1) Information from DCofS's "Division Book." (2) AGF G–3 Chart, "AGF Maneuvers," dated 13 Apr 44. 314.7 (AGF Hist). The divisions having tours in C–AMA were:

Infantry: 6th, 7th, 8th, 33d, 77th, 79th, 80th, 81st, 85th, 90th, 93d, 95th, and 104th.

Armored: 3d, 4th, 5th, 6th, 7th, 9th, and 11th.

[3] (1) Statement of Brig Gen Leo Donovan, G–3 AGF, to AGF Hist Off, 19 Feb 45. (2) AGF memo (S) for CofS USA, 24 Aug 44, sub: Maneuvers, 1944. 354.2/101 (S). (3) AGF ltr (C) to CGs, 21 Sep 44, sub: Maneuvers for Divs at Home Stations. 354.2/105 (C).

[4] Divisions receiving a month of maneuvers at or near their home stations, in lieu of division-versus-division maneuvers, were the 86th, 66th, and 69th. The 63d had a week of maneuvers at home station. Information compiled from Status Rpts of Divs, AGF G–3 Shipment files, Nos. 0288, 9550, 9615, and 0960 (S).

Of the eleven infantry divisions activated in 1943, only four participated in maneuvers against other divisions.[5] Four noninfantry divisions activated in 1943 and two divisions activated prior to that time were also denied participation in division-versus-division exercises. This meant that commanders of thirteen of the eighty-seven divisions of all types trained in the United States took their commands overseas without ever having had the opportunity of maneuvering them as a unit in the field.[6] The loss of training in staff functioning, logistics, maintenance, supply, teamwork with supporting units, and large-scale tactical operations under higher command was incalculable.[7]

In the fall of 1944, as the struggle of the armies in the European Theater was intensified, it became necessary to alert seven divisions whose training had been planned on the assumption that they would not be moved from the United States until after June 1945.[8] Not only were some of the youngest of these denied experience in maneuvers, but other phases of their training were also curtailed. The 42d and the 65th Divisions, activated respectively in July and August 1943, received no combined training of regiments with their supporting battalions of field artillery.[9]

Overseas Calls for Individual Replacements

The War Department was obliged not only to take divisions from the strategic reserve in the United States but also to send overseas individual replacements, particularly infantrymen, far in excess of the output of replacement training centers and officer candidate schools. This necessity imposed the most serious difficulties experienced by divisions in late 1943 and 1944. To meet these calls

[5] Infantry divisions activated in 1943 and participating in division-versus-division maneuvers were the 97th, 106th, 71st, and 75th. Those not participating were the 42d, 63d, 65th, 66th, 69th, 70th and 76th.

[6] The thirteen divisions of all types not participating in division-versus-division maneuvers were:

Infantry: 10th, 40th, 42d, 63d, 65th, 69th, 70th, and 76th.

Armored: 16th and 20th.

Airborne: 13th.

Cavalry: 2d.

[7] Statement of Brig Gen Leo Donovan, G–3 AGF, to AGF Hist Off, 19 Feb 45.

[8] (1) The seven divisions affected were the 42d, 63d, 65th, 69th, 70th, 71st, and 89th. WD Troop Basis (S), 1 Jan 44. (2) Statement of Lt Col S. L. Weld, Task Force Div G–3 AGF, to AGF Hist Off, 24 Feb 45. (3) AGF memo (S), G–3 for CofS, 14 Jul 44, sub: Earmarking of Major Units. AGF G–3 Task Force files (Earmarking, Large Units) (S). (4) AGF M/S (S), G–3 to DCofS, 13 Oct 44, sub: Move-up for Shipment of Inf Divs to ETO. AGF G–3 Task Force files (Earliest Dates for Divs) (S).

[9] Status Rpts, 65th and 42d Divs. AGF G–3 Shipment files, Nos. 4848 and 0629 (S).

lower-priority divisions were stripped and replenished repeatedly, becoming in effect replacement training centers.

Inroads on the immediately available supply of enlisted infantry personnel began in the fall of 1943. By the end of the year 24,541 enlisted men had been withdrawn from fourteen infantry divisions for transfer either to overseas replacement depots or to alerted units.[10] (See Table No. 1.) In January 1944 the average infantry strength of these divisions was approximately 2,000 below that prescribed in Tables of Organization.[11] A second major draft on divisions for overseas enlisted replacements occurred in February 1944. The 63d Division lost about 3,200 men and the 70th about 3,000; losses were also suffered at this time by seven other infantry divisions.[12] The heaviest inroads on infantry divisions for overseas replacements came in the spring and summer of 1944. Between April and September, seventeen divisions lost 78,703 enlisted men.[13] (See Table No. 2.) In addition to this total, which includes only withdrawals directed by Headquarters, Army Ground Forces, for overseas loss replacements, many other enlisted men were withdrawn from divisions to fill high-priority units, to meet officer candidate and parachute school requirements, and for various other purposes. The withdrawals were often made in driblets, aggravating the disruption of training. For example, there were 14 separate withdrawals, involving from 25 to 2,125 men at a time, of enlisted men for overseas replacements from the 106th Division between September 1943 and August 1944.[14]

The aggregate of withdrawals for all purposes was tremendous. The 94th Division, from activation to departure for port of embarkation, lost 8,890 enlisted men; the 65th Division, 11,782; the 106th Division, 12,442; and the 100th Division, 14,787.[15] The 69th Division, which apparently had the greatest turnover of any

[10] Incl to personal ltr (S) of Gen McNair to Maj Gen E. P. Parker, CG 78th Div, 20 Dec 43. McNair Correspondence (S).

[11] Memo (S) of Gen McNair for CofS USA, 4 Jan 44, sub: Tng of Repls. 320.2/101 (O'seas Repls)(S).

[12] (1) Statement of Col Earle G. Wheeler, CofS 63d Div, to AGF Hist Off, 6 Jul 44. (2) Memo of Lt Col Ralph W. Zwicker for G–3 AGF, 26 Feb 44, sub: Visit to Cps Adair, White and Beale, 18–23 Feb 44. AGF G–3 files, 333.1/75 (Inspections by AGF Staff Offs). (3) The seven other divisions stripped in February 1944 were the 10th (Light), 42d, 75th, 76th, 78th, 84th, and 92d. (Information from DCofS's "Division Book.") Evidence of the stripping of the 76th Division in February was found in the status report on that division in AGF G–3 Shipment file No. 8912 (S). Figures on February losses, except for the 63d and 70th Divisions, could not be found.

[13] Figures furnished by AGF AG Sec, C&RD.

[14] Information from Lt Col B. V. Bryant's "Division Book," AGF G–3 Mob Div files.

[15] (1) 94th Div memo, G–1 to CG, 14 Jul 44, sub not given. 314.7 (AGF Hist). (2) Statement of G–1 65th Div to AGF Hist Off, 3 Nov 44. (3) TIG memo (R) for DCofS USA, 29 Sep 44, sub: Overseas Readiness Status of the 106th Inf Div. (4) TIG memo (R) for DCofS USA, 29 Sep 44, sub: Overseas Readiness Status of 100th Inf Div. Both (3) and (4) in 353/992 (Readiness) (R).

TABLE NO. 1

Withdrawals of Enlisted Men from Fourteen Infantry Divisions, September–December 1943

Division	Withdrawn for Overseas Replacements		Withdrawn for Transfer to Alerted Divisions			Total Number Withdrawn
	Number	Month	Number	Month	Division	
66th	3,300	Sep	191	Sep	28th	3,491
69th	3,000	Oct	....	....	....	3,000
75th	1,870	Sep	191	Sep	28th	2,061
78th	1,100	Dec	....	....	....	1,100
83d	....	....	820	Oct	4th	820
84th	300	Oct	500	Oct	85th	800
86th	750	Sep	1,700	Sep	88th	2,450
87th	2,583	Sep	....	....	....	2,583
94th	1,700	Oct	....	....	....	1,700
97th	1,234	Sep	509	Sep	8th	1,743
99th	....	....	1,180	Oct	85th	1,180
100th	500	Oct	....	....	....	500
103d	....	....	357	Oct	88th	357
106th	1,800	Sep	956	Sep	28th & 31st	2,756
TOTAL	18,137	....	6,404	....	....	24,541

Source: Incl to personal ltr (S) of Gen McNair to Maj Gen E. P. Parker, CG 78th Div, 20 Dec 43. McNair Correspondence (S).

TABLE NO. 2

Withdrawals of Enlisted Men for Overseas Replacements from Seventeen Infantry Divisions, April–September 1944

Division	Infantry	Field Artillery	Cavalry	Total
42d	3,936	840	45	4,821
63d	3,568	579	38	4,185
65th	5,222	314	45	5,581
66th	3,999	840	43	4,882
69th	4,414	840	45	5,299
70th	2,845	480	45	3,370
71st	3,172	330	....	3,502
75th	4,459	780	45	5,284
76th	6,246	780	45	7,071
78th	4,698	780	45	5,523
86th	4,050	720	40	4,810
87th	3,850	720	40	4,610
89th	2,700	360	....	3,060
97th	5,064	336	30	5,430
100th	3,675	....	....	3,675
103d	2,550	....	....	2,550
106th	4,225	780	45	5,050
TOTAL	68,673	9,479	551	78,703

Source: C&RD, Ground AG Sec, 26 Jun 45.

division activated during the AGF period (except possibly those specifically designated as replacement divisions in 1942, for which complete figures on turnover are not available), lost 22,235 enlisted men.[16]

Officer losses were insignificant in the early months of 1944, but beginning in the late spring they became increasingly heavy. The turnover was greatest among infantry officers, particularly among leaders of companies and platoons. An experience typical of a number of regiments was summarized as follows by the commanding officer of the 260th Infantry, 65th Division, a few weeks before that unit moved to port:[17]

> The turnover of commissioned personnel in this regiment since activation has been about 150 percent. The turnover has been heaviest among junior officers, principally among the lieutenants. Some companies have had as many as seven commanders and some platoons have had sixteen leaders. Battalions have had as high as five commanders. The regiment has had two commanding officers.

In June 1944 General Malony, Commanding General of the 94th Division, reported that there was not a second lieutenant in his command who had been on duty with the division in maneuvers seven months before. The infantry officer of a low-priority division who stayed with his unit longer than three months during the period April–September 1944 was an exception. Losses of medical officers, engineers, and chaplains also were unusually heavy—often more than 100 percent of the T/O allotment. The 94th Division during the whole of its training period, but mainly in 1944, lost 54 medical officers (T/O 52), 32 engineers (T/O 27), and 16 chaplains (T/O 13).[18] Officer losses in all categories totaled 873 in the 94th Division, 1,088 in the 65th Division, 1,215 in the 106th Division, and 1,336 in the 69th Division.[19] Distribution of officers transferred from the 65th Division is shown in Table No. 3 by branch and rank.

[16] Information furnished AGF Hist Off by AG 69th Div, 2 Nov 44, at Cp Shelby, Miss. To put it another way, the staff of the 69th Division (activated in May 1943) trained almost enough enlisted personnel to man three divisions. The 31st Division, inducted in November 1940, had a slightly larger loss of enlisted personnel than the 69th (22,511 as against 22,235), but the 31st's losses extended over a considerably longer period (38 months as against 17 months). Officer losses of the 31st and 69th Divisions were 1,453 and 1,336 respectively. For figures on the 31st Division see personal ltr of Maj Gen John C. Persons for Gen McNair, 31 Jan 44. 353/45 (31st Div).

[17] Statement of Col Frank Dunkley, CO 260th Inf Regt, 65th Inf Div, to AGF Hist Off, 1 Nov 44.

[18] Maj Gen Harry J. Malony, "Unit Commander's Six Month Report to Higher Headquarters," 20 Jun 44. Excerpt in 314.7 (AGF Hist).

[19] (1) Personal ltr of Maj Gen Harry J. Malony, CG 94th Div, to Maj Gen John P. Lucas, CG Fourth Army, 22 Jul 44. 322/39 (94th Div). (2) Statement of G–1 65th Div to AGF Hist Off, 3 Nov 44. (3) TIG memo (R) for DCofS USA, 29 Sep 44, sub: Overseas Readiness Status of 106th Inf Div. 353/992 (Readiness) (R). (4) Information furnished AGF Hist Off by AG 69th Div, 2 Nov 44.

TABLE NO. 3

Turnover of Officers in 65th Division,
16 August 1943–31 October 1944

Branch	General	Colonel	Lt Colonel	Major	Captain	1st Lt	2d Lt	Total
Inf	1	4	9	17	64	219	407	721
FA	1	1	3	6	20	43	70	144
QMC	....	....	1	1	3	4	7	16
CE	....	....	1	....	3	3	26	33
SC	....	....	1	....	....	6	14	21
GSC	....	....	1	....	....	....	....	1
MC	....	....	....	3	24	60	....	87
JAGD	....	....	....	1	....	1	4	6
MAC	....	....	....	....	2	2	9	13
DC	....	....	....	....	2	8	....	10
Ch	....	....	....	....	12	7	1	20
IGD	....	....	....	....	2	....	....	2
Cav	....	....	....	....	....	3	6	9
Ord	....	....	....	....	....	....	3	3
CMP	....	....	....	....	....	....	2	2
TOTAL	2	5	16	28	132	356	549	1,088

Source: Data furnished AGF Hist Off by G–I, 65th Div, 3 Nov 44.

Quality of Replacements

Officers and men going out from divisions were replaced by personnel from various sources and of diverse backgrounds. Sometimes the replacements came in large quantities, but more often they came in driblets. A substantial number of the enlisted replacements were from replacement training centers, with basic training completed in their arm. Others came from service installations, antiaircraft battalions, and tank destroyer organizations, with basic training completed but not in the arm of the unit to which they were being assigned. Further diversity was offered by men from the ASTP, some of whom had had only basic training, and men sent back from overseas garrisons whose training had become somewhat obsolete.[20]

Difficulties arising from the repeated trading of seasoned riflemen for men with little infantry training were enhanced by concurrent exchange of experi-

[20] Statements in this paragraph are based on personal interviews by the AGF Historical Officer with officers of the 86th, 84th, 63d, 65th, 69th, and 94th Infantry Divisions in June–July 1944, and officers of the 65th and 69th Infantry Divisions in October–November 1944. This source will be cited hereafter as "Interviews wih div offs." Notes of the interviews are in 314.7 (AGF Hist).

enced officers for those with meager infantry background. Officer replacements frequently were "retreads" from antiaircraft and tank destroyer units, or instructors from replacement training centers who had grown rusty in broad infantry knowledge as a result of specialization for long periods in a few subjects. Occasionally divisions received, as replacements for company commanders or battalion executives, officers who had risen to the grade of captain or major as mess supervisors or in other administrative capacities, and who had had little or no experience in unit command. Sometimes the newcomers were able after a few weeks to overcome the handicap of inexperience by observing subordinates and taking refresher courses under the supervision of regimental or battalion commanders. In many instances, however, they had to be reassigned or reclassified. In either case there was a considerable time when the unit concerned suffered from ineffective leadership.[21]

Some division commanders thought that the majority of replacements whom they took to port were inferior to those men who had been lost, not only in training but also in stamina and other qualities essential to combat effectiveness.[22] This was not true of replacements received from the ASTP and the Air Corps, who generally were recognized as superior in all respects save training to the men whom they replaced. The typical division subjected to large-scale stripping in 1944 received about 3,000 replacements from these sources, but in some instances a portion of this choice personnel had shortly to be given up to nondivisional units.[23]

Newcomers from replacement training centers were for the most part men inducted into the Army late in the mobilization period, when the stock of first-class manpower was running low. This disadvantage was offset to some extent by the discontinuance of the preferred status enjoyed by the Air Forces in initial assignment of selectees. Some of the personnel converted from other branches compared favorably with the men they replaced, but others were men deficient in soldierly qualities who had been pushed about from one organization to another. In February 1944 the commanding general of the 94th Division observed to G–3 of the Army Ground Forces: "The quality of this personnel we are getting

[21] Interviews with div offs.

[22] (1) Statement of Maj Gen Harry J. Malony, CG 94th Div, to AGF Hist Off, 18 Jul 44. (2) Statement of CofS 69th Div to AGF Hist Off, 16 Jul 44. (3) Statement of Maj Gen S. E. Reinhart, CG 65th Div, to AGF Hist Off, 3 Nov 44.

[23] (1) Interviews with div offs. (2) Tabulation, "Status of Divisions" (dated 23 Sep 44) in Lt Col B. V. Bryant's "Division Book." AGF G–3 Mob Div files. This table shows a total of 14,700 ASTP trainees removed from 36 divisions and given to nondivisional units.

is awful. Busted down parachutists, guard house addicts from McClellan and Bragg and various other replacement training centers. Less than 50 percent are physically qualified." [24]

Particularly disappointing were the men who came into divisions as infantry volunteers. Some of these volunteers proved to be incompetents and trouble-makers, who had been forced out of their units on threat of loss of ratings. Others came to the Infantry in the hope of getting soft jobs in headquarters.[25]

Some divisions received as replacements considerable numbers of men returned from overseas. A portion of these troops proved to be of great value to units in training, particularly as instructors and as speakers at orientation sessions. But others, taking the attitude that they had already done their part in the war effort, or that overseas service gave them a privileged status, particularly with reference to uniform regulations, fatigue duties, and routine matters of discipline, were an unwholesome influence. Soldiers with battle experience were as a rule less troublesome than those whose overseas service had consisted mainly of non-combatant duties.[26]

A substantial portion of the men transferred into divisions as replacements for privates and privates first class were noncommissioned specialists. This resulted in the piling up of a large surplus of noncommissioned officers in most divisions. In July 1944 seven divisions reported NCO surpluses averaging 454 men.[27] At the beginning of July the 76th Division had an excess of 1,228 NCO's, distributed as follows:[28]

Rank	*Number*
Master Sergeants	6
First Sergeants	8
Technical Sergeants	12
Staff Sergeants	31
Sergeants	112
Corporals	377
Technicians, 3d Grade	9
Technicians, 4th Grade	96
Technicians, 5th Grade	577

[24] Record of tel conv, Gen Malony and Gen Lentz, 15 Feb 44. AGF G–3 files, 000/37 (Tel Conv 44).

[25] Interviews with div offs.

[26] *Ibid.*

[27] AGF M/S, C&RD to G–3, 7 Aug 44, sub: Disposition of Surplus Inf NCO's. 220.3/9 (NCO's).

[28] AGF memo, G–1 for G–3, 10 Jul 44, sub: Inspection Trip to Cp Carson and Cp McCoy, 6–8 Jul 44. AGF G–3 files, 333.1 (sep binder).

The influx of noncommissioned officers had an unfortunate effect on the morale of old-timers who, after working long and hard for advancement, found promotion blocked by the presence of men possessed of many stripes but of little if any experience in infantry positions. Demoralization was also rife among the newcomers, whose specialist ratings did not prevent their being required to serve in the ranks as riflemen, frequently under men who wore fewer stripes. The NCO situation in the 63d Division in July 1944 was summarized by its G–3 as follows:[29]

> The transfer to us of so many men with chevrons — particularly from the Army Air Forces — has given us a heavy surplus of NCO's. The surplus NCO's wear the chevrons and draw NCO pay, but they have to perform all the duties of privates. The newcomers kick about having to do KP. We have so many men wearing chevrons that we had to devise some way of distinguishing those who actually filled the T/O positions from those who were surplus. We had a quantity of orange dye on hand. So we made up a large number of orange bands for the T/O NCO's to wear on the arms of their fatigue clothes. A corporal leading a squad frequently has T/4's serving as riflemen under him and sometimes, though rarely, he commands staff sergeants.

After a period of orientation the noncommissioned newcomers were usually given a trial in infantry positions corresponding to their specialist ratings. Some of them made good and were able to retain their chevrons. A larger number, being unable to make the transition, had to forfeit their stripes. "This has played hell with their morale," stated a division G–3, "and they haven't made good riflemen. It's too much to expect us to take mavericks and make doughboys out of them in three months." [30]

There was apparently an increase in venereal cases, absence without leave, and other disciplinary offenses in 1944.[31] The rise in venereals and AWOL's can be attributed in part, no doubt, to the unusually large number of furloughs granted in anticipation of overseas movement. It seems probable, however, that other factors were the hasty conversion of men and officers of other arms and services into infantrymen and the scraping of the manpower barrel for inductees.[32] The increase of court-martial cases and of venereals was especially marked in the 65th Division, youngest in the Army Ground Forces (activated in August

[29] Statement of G–3 63d Div to AGF Hist Off, 6 Jul 44.

[30] Statement of G–3 65th Div to AGF Hist Off, 3 Nov 44.

[31] Interviews with div offs.

[32] Memo of Maj G. H. Murphy, G–1 Sec AGF, for G–3 AGF, 8 Sep 44, sub: Rpt of Visit of Inspection to 75th Inf Div and to Hq & Hq Dets Sp Trs, Second Army, Cp Breckenridge, Ky. AGF G–3 files, 333.1 (Inspections by AGF Staff Offs).

1943 but not filled until January 1944). In commenting on the court-martial cases the division judge advocate declared:[33]

> Our court-martial rate remained consistently low until near the end of unit training. Up to that time training had proceeded intensively without interruption, and there had been little turnover of personnel. Then the stripping of the division began. There was much repetition of training until the division was alerted. Morale was adversely affected by recurrent rumors that ours was a replacement division. As the men lost hope of going overseas there was an increasing tendency for them to get into trouble. But if there is any single factor that accounts for the climb of the court-martial rate more than any other, it is the quality of the replacements that we received — many were culls from other outfits. Men coming to us from Central American bases and from Alaska have had a particularly high court-martial rate. Those coming from the paratroopers also have been frequent offenders.

The following observation made by a regimental commander of the 65th Division near the end of its training period is also pertinent:[34]

> The quality of enlisted replacements has not been as good as that of the original fillers. The AGCT is up a bit, but physical quality and attitude toward soldiering is down. Some of the recently received replacements have been in as many as six divisions prior to coming to us. They have gone through a culling process. The decline in the quality of our enlisted personnel has enhanced our disciplinary problem immensely. We've had an increase of AWOL and of cases involving moral turpitude — theft, robbery, etc. Many men brought before the courts-martial were previous offenders; some had been through rehabilitation centers.

Adjustment of Training to the Replacement Problem

The continual coming and going of men and officers made it extremely difficult for the divisions affected to develop unit spirit and teamwork. The Army Ground Forces from the beginning attached great importance to unit integrity and to the training of the members of fighting teams in their normal associations as against the mass production of individuals and small units in training centers. The division was viewed somewhat in the light of the ideal team, and from the beginning the perfection of this team was the focal point of the AGF training program.

The development of unit pride and of effective teamwork required that officers know their men and that the men know each other. Infantrymen needed to develop confidence in teammates of other branches—in the artillerymen to place supporting fire in the right place at the right time, in the quartermaster company to get supplies to them, in the engineer battalion to clear roads for their advance,

[33] Statement of Judge Advocate, 65th Div, to AGF Hist Off, 2 Nov 44.

[34] Statement of Col Dunkley, CO 260th Inf Regt, 65th Inf Div, to AGF Hist Off, 1 Nov 44.

in the ordnance company to keep their weapons in fighting condition, in the signal company to maintain the flow of communications, and in the medics to treat their wounds. This confidence could come only from long acquaintance and from working together on various levels from individual training to large-scale maneuvers.

Various means were adopted to bring the miscellany of replacements received by divisions to something approaching a common denominator of training. In some divisions the newcomers were segregated in special training units varying in stages of advancement, and were given intensive instruction according to the committee plan used in replacement training centers; meanwhile the division's old-timers reviewed earlier training or proceeded at a retarded tempo. In other instances the replacements were thrown into their companies immediately on reaching the division and the level of training was adjusted to meet the needs of the majority.[35]

On 27 April 1944 the Army Ground Forces issued a special directive for the guidance of twenty-two divisions (of which seventeen were infantry) designated to bear the principal burden of stripping and replenishment. This directive, based on a careful computation by General McNair of the maximum stripping which divisions could stand,[36] provided for the adjustment of training on the basis of

[35] Interviews with div offs.

[36] AGF M/S (S), CG to CofS, 7 Mar 44. 353/206 (S). General McNair's computation included this statement:

It is manifest that the more completely a division is stripped, the greater the time required to retrain the division as a unit. The following graduated scale of training is established:

Percent of Maximum Stripping	*Weeks of Retraining*	
	RTC Graduates	*Inductees*
100	32	49
90	29	46
80	26	43
70	23	40
60	20	37
50	17	34
40	14	31
30	11	28
20	8	25

As an example, let us assume that a division has 23 weeks remaining before its readiness date. Then its infantry may be stripped of 70% of its maximum and the division refilled with RTC graduates. The maximum of course is all privates plus 5% NCO's. If RTC graduates were not available the division might be stripped only by 20% of the maximum, since it would be refilled by inductees.

the division's readiness date and the sources of its filler replacements. The following "typical distribution of training time" was suggested:

1. Six weeks of individual training time and tests for replacements received from other units or replacement training centers of an arm or service other than that to which assigned.
2. Thirteen weeks of individual training and tests for replacements received from reception centers.
3. Five weeks of unit training.
4. Four weeks of combined training.
5. Seven weeks of maneuvers.
6. Six weeks of post-maneuver training.

The directive also stated: "The periods indicated will be adapted to the time available so as best to meet training needs. Where total time available is insufficient, maneuvers will be either curtailed or omitted. Individual and small-unit training must not be slighted." [37] Supplementary instructions provided that divisions were to initiate this "modified" or "retraining" program as soon as they had obtained 80 percent of their authorized enlisted strength.[38] Subsequent events prevented the attainment of the full course of training outlined in this directive by any of the twenty-two divisions.[39] Each of the seventeen infantry divisions, with one exception, received increments of fillers after being alerted, varying in round numbers from 1,000 to 4,000. Requirements of Preparation for Overseas Movement (POM) and limitations of time made it impossible for division commanders to give the eleventh-hour replacements very much in the way of either unit or combined training.

On the eve of their departure from the Army Ground Forces these seventeen divisions, which included all but one of the infantry divisions activated after November 1942 and which were about the last divisions to go overseas, contained a considerable portion of personnel that had not progressed far beyond the level of basic training. (See Table No. 4.)

While all the divisions turned out by the Army Ground Forces had a year or more in training, the younger divisional organizations were hardly more than

[37] AGF ltr to CGs, 27 Apr 44, sub: Supplemental Tng Dir for Specially Designated Divs. 353.01/114.

[38] Statement of Gen Leo Donovan, G–3 AGF, to AGF Hist Off, 19 Feb 45.

[39] This and the following two statements are based on a study of the status reports of all the divisions concerned. Status reports are filed in AGF AG Records, G–3 Shipment files (S). These reports give a summary of the divisions' training from activation until date of the report, which usually is within a month of movement to port.

230-171 O - 66 - 32

loose frames in which successive installments of infantrymen were processed for service overseas as individual replacements. When they finally were sent overseas these divisions, far from being groups of individuals welded by a year's collaborative training into smoothly functioning teams, were to a regrettable extent crazy-quilt conglomerations hastily assembled from sundry sources, given only a minimum of training, and loaded on transports.

Experience of the 65th Division

Men of the 65th Division began to board trains at Camp Shelby, Miss., for movement to the New York Port of Embarkation on Christmas Eve, 1944, at the moment when von Rundstedt's drive through the Ardennes was at its height. Since the 65th was the last division to be activated and one of the last to move overseas, its experience may be used to illustrate the impact of personnel changes on the final group of divisions produced by the Army Ground Forces.[40]

The 65th Division was activated on 16 August 1943. But because at that time inductions were lagging behind mobilization requirements, the complete quota of fillers was not received until the end of the year.[41]

Individual training began early in January 1944. The division made a good showing on its Mobilization Training Test, given by the IX Corps the first week in April.[42] During the first few weeks of the unit period, training proceeded satisfactorily. Personnel turnover was inconsequential, equipment was plentiful, morale was good, and squads and platoons were beginning to take shape as teams.

In the latter part of May, while infantry units were engaged in company exercises and taking the AGF Platoon Proficiency Tests, an order came down from higher headquarters to begin furloughing infantry privates in preparation for their movement to overseas replacement depots. Even though furloughs were staggered over a period of several weeks, the disruption to training was great. One battalion was so badly depleted that some of its platoons numbered only fifteen or twenty men when they took the platoon tests.[43] The heaviest losses of

[40] The summary of the experience of the 65th Division, unless otherwise indicated, is based on statements of division staff officers and unit commanders to the AGF Historical Officer on three visits to the 65th Division in 1944, 30 March–10 April, 8–17 July, and 31 October–3 November.

[41] Master Card, 65th Inf Div, AGF AG Sec, C&RD files.

[42] This statement is based on observations of the MTP Test of the 65th Division by AGF Historical Officer (including attendance of final critique), 3–7 April 1944.

[43] Statement of Lt Col R. J. Hunt, CO 2d Bn, 259th Inf Regt, 65th Inf Div, to AGF Hist Off, 15 Jul 44.

enlisted men occurred during June and July. By the end of July the division had lost about 7,000 men, the bulk of whom were sent to replacement depots to fill overseas requirements.[44]

Officer losses for overseas replacements during the period April–July inclusive exceeded 250.[45] These and other withdrawals almost cleaned out the division's infantry lieutenants and captains. In mid-July the commander of an infantry battalion remarked:[46]

> We didn't keep platoon leaders very long. We have had about four complete turnovers since January. In one of my companies the 2d Platoon has had three commanders and the 1st Platoon has had six. In another company two platoons haven't had an officer for two months; platoon sergeants have been in command.

About the same time the division G–1 reported a 100-percent turnover in regimental and battalion commanders since activation, and a 50-percent turnover in general staff officers. "In one of the regiments," he noted, "one battalion is commanded by a major, in another, two, and in the third, all three." [47]

Shipping out of men and officers was interspersed with the reception of replacements. The processing of incoming and departing men placed a heavy burden on the dwindling corps of experienced officers and NCO's. Lights frequently burned far after midnight in the offices of the division G–1 and adjutant general, and regimental personnel staffs worked in shifts on a 24-hour basis. Platoon and company leaders spent many extra hours at night and on Saturday afternoons to get outgoing men through prescribed firing courses, to complete immunizations, and to clear the vast pile of paper which Preparation for Oversea Replacements (POR) laid on their desks. They had to find time also for the interviewing and assignment of new men received in their units.

The first large batch of replacements was the 1,100 Air Corps cadets who came to the division in May. These were bright, brawny youngsters, and, after a period of adjustment, most of them made excellent soldiers. In July the division received a thousand-odd 18-year-olds from replacement training centers in exchange for a like number of soldiers of age nineteen and over which the division sent to a replacement depot. These boys were somewhat inferior to the Air Corps cadets. About 3,000 other replacements from miscellaneous sources trickled

[44] Tab A to AGF M/S (S), G–3 Mob Div to G–3 Opns Div, 13 Oct 44, sub: Status of Pers in Divs. Lt Col B. V. Bryant's "Division Book," AGF G–3 Mob Div files.

[45] Tab B to M/S cited in n. 44.

[46] Statement of Lt Col C. G. Cooper, CO 3d Bn, 261st Inf Regt, 65th Inf Div, to AGF Hist Off, 15 Jul 44.

[47] Statement of Lt Col D. H. Arp, G–1 65th Div, to AGF Hist Off, 14 Jul 44.

into the division in June and July, bringing the total influx of enlisted men during the period May–July to something over 5,000.[48]

A substantial portion of the miscellaneous group came from disbanded antiaircraft artillery and tank destroyer units. About 700 were men sent back from overseas. Of these the assistant division commander remarked: "Some are a definite benefit to the division, others are a detriment. The majority come within the former category. But if I had my choice of 700 of our original fillers and the 700 replacements that have come to us, I should take the original fillers." [49] The division G–1 took a less favorable view: "Overseas commanders send their 'eight-balls' to us under the rotation plan. Most of the men are very bitter. They feel like they have done their share. They are a bad influence on the other men." [50] More than 300 of the replacements were "infantry volunteers." Of these the G–1 observed:[51]

> In every case . . . [they] have been men who were dissatisfied in other branches — men who did not like their commanding officers, who wanted a change of station, or who were falling down on their jobs. In some instances pressure has been put on them to volunteer. . . . An officer will say to a misfit or ne'er-do-well: "You're apt to lose your rating if you stay here. You've got a good chance to keep your stripes by joining the doughboys. My advice is for you to take it."

Because the division was overstrength when the ASTP was curtailed, it did not receive an allotment of this choice personnel.[52]

Of replacements in general, except those from the Air Forces, the Division G–1 reported: "As they come along the line they are picked over. When they get to us they're a sorry lot." [53] The division commander made the comment: "Replacements have been inferior in quality to the original fillers. Some of them have been kicked about from unit to unit. We did not have an opportunity to indoctrinate them as we did the original fillers, to imbue them with the spirit of the organization." [54] The division commander observed that the replacements

[48] (1) Statement of Lt Col D. H. Arp, G–1 65th Div, to AGF Hist Off, 14 Jul 44. (2) This exchange resulted from the War Department's decision to discontinue sending 18-year-old men overseas as individual replacements. (3) Tab A to AGF M/S (S), G–3 Mob Div to G–3 Opns Div, 13 Oct 44, sub: Status of Pers in Divs. Lt Col B. V. Bryant's "Division Book," AGF G–3 Mob Div files.

[49] Statement of Brig Gen John E. Copeland, Asst Div Comdr 65th Div, to AGF Hist Off, 11 Jul 44.

[50] Statement of Lt Col D. H. Arp, G–1 65th Div, to AGF Hist Off, 14 Jul 44.

[51] Statement of Lt Col D. H. Arp, G–1 65th Div, to AGF Hist Off, 16 Jul 44.

[52] Statement of Lt Col D. H. Arp, G–1 65th Div, to AGF Hist Off, 14 Jul 44.

[53] *Ibid.*

[54] Statement of Maj Gen S. E. Reinhart, CG 65th Div, to AGF Hist Off, 3 Nov 44.

as a group were younger than the original fillers, but he deemed this a doubtful gain: "Our original fillers had a considerable sprinkling of older men, 'PPHP's' [Pre-Pearl-Harbor-Papas] we called them. These older men had a stabilizing influence on the youngsters—helped to keep them out of trouble." [55]

Enlisted losses in the Artillery and the special units, except the Engineers, were small in comparison to those in the Infantry, but such turnover as was experienced resulted usually in the exchange of novices for trained technicians.

When they first came to the division, replacements were given a test in basic subjects to determine their level of training. Those who demonstrated a passable knowledge of individual training were sent immediately to their units. Others were organized into special training groups under regimental supervision and trained in fundamentals until they were able to pass an MTP Test prepared by the division.

An attempt was made to continue the regular program of unit training concurrently with the process of POR for departing men and the instruction of replacements. But the depletion of personnel and the heavy burden of running a multi-level program made progress difficult. Unit training was completed after a fashion early in July, but some of the battalion exercises were held with less than 200 men, and the few regimental problems that were undertaken were not deserving of the name.

In July the Infantry and Artillery went through the motions of combined training for a period of approximately two weeks, but strength was so low and many of the officers so inexperienced that the regimental combat team exercises bore little resemblance to the real thing. The operations were so limited, indeed, that when, later, the division's final status report was submitted none of the personnel was credited with any combined training.

Late in July, having reached approximately 80 percent of its T/O strength, the division initiated the 6-week program of modified individual training directed by the Army Ground Forces. Under this plan, the new men and the old-timers were lumped into the units and given an intensive "refresher course" in basic training. Special schools were set up under the division G–3 to train the new officers, an increasing number of whom were coming from units of other arms.

Even after retraining was initiated the division continued to lose men. Withdrawals of infantrymen were lighter than formerly, but drafts on specialists of other branches were heavier. Enlisted losses in all categories during August totaled 1,173.[56]

[55] *Ibid.*

[56] Information furnished AGF Hist Off by G–1 65th Div, 3 Nov 44.

From 3 September to 14 October the division participated in modified unit training. During the fourth week of this period word came from Second Army that the division had been placed on alert status with readiness dates of 3 January 1945 for equipment and 18 January 1945 for personnel.[57] This news came as a bombshell, for until the alert the division had no indication that overseas movement was likely before the summer of 1945. On the other hand, the alert gave a definite lift to morale. Efforts to meet individual and unit POM requirements were intensified immediately.

The alert, together with the change about the same time of War Department regulations concerning physically deficient personnel, made it possible for the division to drop about a thousand "cripples." The worst cases were discharged. Those considered capable of service in noncombat capacities were transferred to the Air Forces or the Fourth Service Command.[58] The division was pleased to be relieved of this dead weight, but the postponement of housecleaning until the eleventh hour gave another setback to the development of teamwork. All in all, the division received more than 2,000 replacements in the three months preceding embarkation. The prior training of many of the last-minute replacements left much to be desired. Moreover, a considerable number of men originally received in response to emergency requisitions were disqualified by physical defects.[59] This caused additional disruption and delay.

Another startling bit of news came on 13 October in the form of a telephone call from the Second Army stating that, because of pressing overseas needs, the division had to prepare its infantry regiments for movement to port by 13 November. Organizational equipment was to be ready by 28 October and packing was to begin immediately.[60]

This notice prevented the beginning of modified combined training. In the regiments efforts were concentrated on training late arrivals and on putting the battalions through infantry-tank exercises as previously directed by the Army

[57] AGF ltr (R) to CG Second Army, 20 Sep 44, sub: Preparation of Unit for Overseas Serv (Alert Instructions). 353/729 (Int Tng)(R).

[58] TIG memo (R) for DCofS USA, 15 Dec 44, sub: Overseas Readiness Status of the 65th Inf Div. 353/1220 (Readiness)(R).

[59] Statement of Capt Robert Farber, Classification Off 65th Div, to AGF Hist Off, 2 Nov 44. Captain Farber stated that about half of a shipment of 400 men transferred to the 65th Division by the 71st Division on 22 October 1944 (they were supposed to be POR–qualified) had to be sent back to the 71st Division because they could not meet physical or other requirements for overseas service.

[60] (1) *Ibid.* (2) WD ltr (R) 370.5 (15 Oct 44) OP–S–E–M to CGs, 15 Oct 44, sub: Movement Orders Shipment 4848. 370.5/1054 (MO)(R).

Ground Forces. Other components lent a hand to help the infantrymen in their packing.

On 24 October the regiments completed the packing of their organizational equipment and began to load the boxes on freight cars. The next day a telephone call from Second Army directed that all loading cease as the movement order had been temporarily suspended. Several days later, instructions were received moving the personnel readiness date back to 24 December and the equipment date to 10 December. The revised instructions also provided that infantry regiments should move with other parts of the division, except for the usual advance detachment.[61]

The division staff, in telephone conferences with higher headquarters, worked out an interim training program designed to fill in major gaps without making heavy demands on organizational equipment. Mortars, heavy machine guns, and other essential equipment were borrowed in considerable quantities from nondivisional units stationed at Camp Shelby, but, in spite of such emergency measures, the division had to go through the heartbreaking task of unpacking some of the equipment that had been so carefully processed and stored away in the shipping boxes.[62] The highlights of the interim training were battalion field exercises, in which each infantry battalion was supported by elements of a 4.2-inch chemical mortar battalion and division artillery, and battalion combat firing exercises, with each infantry battalion supported by infantry cannon artillery and chemical mortars.[63]

The last element of the division left Camp Shelby on New Year's Eve.[64] If the plans for the building and training of this division had been carried out as originally laid down by General McNair and his staff, the 65th when it moved overseas in 1945 might have been the most battleworthy of the long line of divisions produced by the Army Ground Forces. For into the planning of the organization, training, and equipment of this unit was poured the accumulated experience of four years' intensive effort. But, mainly because of personnel exigencies the control of which lay beyond the jurisdiction of the Army Ground Forces, the 65th was about the least ready for combat of all divisions trained in

[61] (1) Memo (C) of Lt Col J. S. Hardin, G-4 65th Div, for Lt Col J. A. Hanson, G-4 Task Force Div, AGF, 31 Oct 44, sub not given. AGF G-4 Movement Orders, Shipment 4848 (C). (2) AGF memo (R) to CofS USA, 6 Nov 44, sub: Amendment to Movement Orders, Shipment 4848. 370.5/1366 (MO)(S).

[62] Statement of Maj H. B. Dominick, G-4 Task Force Div, to AGF Hist Off, 24 Feb 45.

[63] 65th Div Status Report (C) (prepared by Second Army), dated 7 Dec 44. AGF G-3 Shipment file 4848 (S).

[64] Information furnished AGF Hist Off by G-4 AGF Task Force Div, 24 Feb 45.

World War II. Its regiments had never worked with their supporting battalions of artillery in field exercises. The division commander had never maneuvered his command as a unit; in fact, the division had never been together, except for reviews and demonstrations, and its composition had changed greatly from one assembly to another. In the infantry regiments only one man in four had been with the division for a year, and almost every fourth man had joined his unit in the past three months.[65] The division was more of a hodge-podge than a team.

Near the end of the training period the division commander observed to an AGF staff officer:[66]

> The Division that I gave basic training to is no longer here. . . . The last time I checked up on personnel turnover, this Division had furnished over 10,000 men for other duties and had sent out enough officers to fill one and one-half divisions. . . . Personnel turnover prevented the making of a team out of this Division. Our situation is comparable to that of a football coach who has to turn over his team to other institutions a few weeks before the playing season starts. He wires for replacements. He gets two players from one college, three from another, and so on down the line. The pickings are so bad at this late date that he gets a miscellany of misfits and culls. He has to put backfield men in the line and linemen in the backfield. He can't be expected to make a team under such circumstances.

This general's lament was very much like that which had come from divisions in 1942. But such complaining was usually the obverse of a splendid morale. While the commanders protested often to higher headquarters against the misfortunes that befell them and sometimes exaggerated, the overwhelming majority did not use their tribulations as pretexts for evasion of command responsibilities. Because their minds were set on having battleworthy organizations, these leaders, in the best tradition of the Army, rebuilt their broken teams with the material at hand as often as was necessary and, in spite of enormous difficulties, took them to port in far better condition than seemed possible when the flood of stripping was at its height.

That so much could be accomplished in the face of such great difficulties was a tribute not only to the commanders but also to their officers, to the men in the ranks, and to the ability of higher headquarters to make all the adjustments required by shortages of industrial production, deficiencies in the inflow of manpower, and changes in operational requirements.

[65] AGF M/S (S), G–3 for CofS, 17 Oct 44, sub: Pers Status of Certain Divs. 320.2/760 (S).

[66] Statement of Maj Gen S. E. Reinhart, CG 65th Div, to AGF Hist Off, 3 Nov 44.

U.S. Army Divisions in World War II

Number, Classification, and Dates of Activation and Movement to Port of Embarkation[a]

Division	*Classification*	*Date of Activation*	*Date of Movement to Port of Embarkation*[b]
(Infantry)			
1	Regular Army	May 1917	Jun 1942
2	RA	Sep 1917	Sep 1943
3	RA	Nov 1917	Sep 1942
4	RA	Jun 1940	Jan 1944
5	RA	Oct 1939	Apr 1942
6	RA	Oct 1939	Jul 1943
7	RA	Jul 1940	Apr 1943
8	RA	Jul 1940	Nov 1943
9	RA	Aug 1940	Sep 1942
10(Mtn)	Army of the United States	Jul 1943	Dec 1944
24[c]	RA	Feb 1921	....
25[d]	AUS	Oct 1941	....
26	National Guard	Jan 1941[e]	Aug 1944
27	NG	Oct 1940[e]	Mar 1942
28	NG	Feb 1941[e]	Sep 1943
29	NG	Feb 1941[e]	Sep 1942
30	NG	Sep 1940[e]	Jan 1944
31	NG	Nov 1940[e]	Feb 1944
32	NG	Oct 1940[e]	Apr 1942
33	NG	Mar 1941[e]	Jun 1943
34	NG	Feb 1941[e]	Jan 1942
35	NG	Dec 1940[e]	May 1944
36	NG	Nov 1940[e]	Apr 1943
37	NG	Oct 1940[e]	May 1942
38	NG	Jan 1941[e]	Dec 1943
40	NG	Mar 1941[e]	Aug 1942

Division	*Classification*	*Date of Activation*	*Date of Movement to Port of Embarkation*[b]
41	NG	Sep 1940[e]	Mar 1942
42	AUS	Jul 1943	Nov 1944
43	NG	Feb 1941[e]	Sep 1942
44	NG	Sep 1940[e]	Aug 1944
45	NG	Sep 1940[e]	May 1943
63	AUS	Jun 1943	Nov 1944
65	AUS	Aug 1943	Dec 1944
66	AUS	Apr 1943	Nov 1944
69	AUS	May 1943	Nov 1944
70	AUS	Jun 1943	Nov 1944
71	AUS	Jul 1943	Jan 1945
75	AUS	Apr 1943	Oct 1944
76	Organized Reserves	Jun 1942	Nov 1944
77	OR	Mar 1942	Mar 1944
78	OR	Aug 1942	Oct 1944
79	OR	Jun 1942	Mar 1944
80	OR	Jul 1942	Jun 1944
81	OR	Jun 1942	Jun 1944
83	OR	Aug 1942	Mar 1944
84	OR	Oct 1942	Sep 1944
85	OR	May 1942	Dec 1943
86	OR	Dec 1942	Feb 1945
87	OR	Dec 1942	Oct 1944
88	OR	Jul 1942	Nov 1943
89	OR	Jul 1942	Jan 1945
90	OR	Mar 1942	Mar 1944
91	OR	Aug 1942	Mar 1944
92	AUS	Oct 1942	Sep 1944
93	AUS	May 1942	Jan 1944
94	OR	Sep 1942	Jul 1944
95	OR	Jul 1942	Jul 1944
96	OR	Aug 1942	Jul 1944
97	OR	Feb 1943	Feb 1945
98	OR	Sep 1942	Apr 1944
99	OR	Nov 1942	Sep 1944

Division	*Classification*	*Date of Activation*	*Date of Movement to Port of Embarkation*[b]
100	OR	Nov 1942	Sep 1944
102	OR	Sep 1942	Sep 1944
103	OR	Nov 1942	Sep 1944
104	OR	Sep 1942	Aug 1944
106	AUS	Mar 1943	Oct 1944
Americal[f]	. . .	May 1942	. . . .
(Cavalry)			
1	RA	Sep 1921	Jun 1943
2 (1st)[g]	RA	Apr 1941	. . . .
2 (2d)	RA	Feb 1943	Feb 1944
(Armored)			
1	RA	Jul 1940	May 1942
2	RA	Jul 1940	Sep 1942
3	RA	Apr 1941	Sep 1943
4	RA	Apr 1941	Dec 1943
5	AUS	Oct 1941	Feb 1944
6	AUS	Feb 1942	Feb 1944
7	AUS	Mar 1942	May 1944
8	AUS	Apr 1942	Oct 1944
9	AUS	Jul 1942	Aug 1944
10	AUS	Jul 1942	Sep 1944
11	AUS	Aug 1942	Sep 1944
12	AUS	Sep 1942	Sep 1944
13	AUS	Oct 1942	Jan 1945
14	AUS	Nov 1942	Oct 1944
16	AUS	Jul 1943	Jan 1945
20	AUS	Mar 1943	Jan 1945
(Airborne)			
11	AUS	Feb 1943	Apr 1944
13	AUS	Aug 1943	Jan 1945
17	AUS	Apr 1943	Aug 1944
82[h]	OR	Mar 1942	Apr 1943
101	AUS	Aug 1942	Aug 1943

Summary of Activations, by Year

Year	*Infantry*	*Cavalry*	*Armored*	*Airborne*	*Total*
1917–1940	20	1	2	0	23
1941	9	1	3	0	13
1942	27	0	9	2	38
1943	11	1	2	3	17
TOTAL	67	3	16	5	91

Summary of Movements to Port of Embarkation, by Year[i]

Year	*Infantry*	*Cavalry*	*Armored*	*Airborne*	*Total*
1942	12	0	2	0	14
1943	11	1	2	2	16
1944	37	1	9	2	49
1945	4	0	3	1	8
TOTAL	64	2	16	5	87

[a] Information concerning the classification of divisions was obtained from the Organization and Directory Section, Operations Branch, Operations and Training Division, AGO. Activation dates, except for the 1st, 2d, and 3d Infantry Divisions, were obtained from Unit History Data Cards in the Organization and Directory Section, Operations Branch, Operations and Training Division, AGO. Information concerning the activation of the 1st, 2d, and 3d Infantry Divisions was furnished by the Historical Section, Army War College. Dates of movement to port of embarkation were compiled from the files of the Statistics Section, and of the Mobilization Division, G–3 Section, Army Ground Forces.

[b] The month given is that in which more than half of the personnel of the division arrived at the port or staging area.

[c] When activated in 1921 (in the Hawaiian Department) the 24th was known as the Hawaiian Division. In August 1941 the Hawaiian Division was broken up; parts of it were redesignated as the 24th Infantry Division; other elements became the nucleus for the 25th Infantry Division.

[d] Organized in Hawaii.

[e] Date of induction into Federal service.

[f] Organized in New Caledonia from miscellaneous AUS and NG units.

[g] The 2d Cavalry Division, activated in April 1941, was partially disbanded in July 1942 and fully reactivated in February 1943.

[h] The 82d Airborne Division was activated originally as an infantry division and redesignated as airborne 15 August 1942. Actually the personnel and equipment of the 82d were distributed evenly to the 101st Airborne Division, activated on 15 August 1942, and the 82d, redesignated as airborne on the same day. AGF ltr (R) to CGs Third Army and Airborne Command, 30 Jul 42, sub: Activation of 82d and 101st Airborne Divisions. 320.2/9 (Airborne) (R).

[i] For the explanation of differences in figures and totals, see *c, d, f,* and *g* above. Eighty-seven divisions shipped overseas, plus 3 activated and trained overseas, total 90 divisions in theaters of operations prepared for employment in combat. Actually only 89 were available for such employment, the 2d Cavalry Division having been inactivated after its arrival in the Mediterranean Theater. Only two divisions made available for employment in combat were not committed: the 13th Airborne Division, stationed in France at the close of the European conflict; and the 98th Division, stationed in Hawaii, 1944–45.

The Training of Nondivisional Units

by

Bell I. Wiley

Contents

Chart

230-171 O - 66 - 33

I. The Jurisdiction of Army Ground Forces over Activation and Training

Nondivisional units activated and trained by the Army Ground Forces were of two types: combat and service. Combat units consisted of antiaircraft, cavalry, coast artillery, field artillery, infantry, tank, and tank destroyer organizations. Service units included machine records, medical, military police, ordnance, and quartermaster organizations. Chemical, engineer, and signal units were in one or the other of these two classes, according to their functions and associations. The ratio of combat to service units in the Army Ground Forces varied from time to time. In 1942 the total strength of the former was roughly twice that of the latter; subsequently the relative strength of combat units increased. Throughout 1944 and the early months of 1945 approximately three-fourths of the nondivisional troops were in combat units.[1]

The actual enlisted strength of AGF nondivisional units in the United States on 30 June 1942 was about 300,000. Six months later the figure had passed the half-million mark, and on 30 June 1943 it was about 800,000, the highest point attained during the war. On 31 December 1943 nondivisional enlisted strength had fallen to about 650,000; on 31 July 1944 the figure was 520,989; on 31 December 1944, 191,122; and on 31 March 1945, 92,397.[2]

In 1942 the strength of these "spare parts" [3] with the Army Ground Forces was considerably less than that of divisions, but early in 1943 the gap began to close, and in 1944 the strength curve of divisions fell below that of nondivisional units. In the aggregate the strength of spare parts trained by Army Ground Forces exceeded that of divisions. On 31 March 1945 the Table of Organization strength of AGF-type nondivisional units active in the Troop Basis in the United

[1] This statement is based on a study of reports, "Comparative Strength of the Army" and "Uniform Strength of the Army," prepared by the AGF Statistics Section and filed in 320.2 (Comp Str)(S), and for the period June–December 1942 on occasional comparative strength reports filed in the records of the AGF Statistics Section (S). Training units, such as those of schools and replacement centers, are not included in the category of nondivisional units.

[2] *Ibid.*

[3] "Spare parts" was a term applied to nondivisional units.

States and abroad was 1,468,941 officers and men, while that of divisions was only 1,194,398, a ratio of approximately 5 to 4.[4]

AGF Jurisdiction over Activation

Army Ground Forces was responsible for the activation of nondivisional units, in categories and quantities necessary to meet requirements established by the War Department. Basic requirements were laid down in War Department Troop Bases, but modifications to meet changes in strategic plans and other exigencies were frequent and sometimes great. Army Ground Forces had to adapt activation as well as training schedules to successive revisions of requirements. Its problem was complicated by the failure of the War Department to adjust the flow of inductees to the various changes in mobilization requirements.

The G–3 Section of Army Ground Forces exercised general supervision over activation, but administration of details was delegated to special staff sections and subordinate commands. The Mobilization Division of G–3 determined activation schedules, designated "parent units," and prescribed activation procedures. This division also, in coordination with other interested divisions of G–3 and appropriate special staff sections, drafted activation letters for guidance of the army or other subordinate command charged with actual activation. Policies for the procurement and assignment of personnel were formulated by the Officer, Enlisted, and Assignments Divisions of G–1. Details of assignment were executed by the Adjutant General's Section, acting (after March 1943) through its Classification and Replacement Division. Army Ground Forces issued the activation letter unless the activation procedure called for action by the chiefs of technical services or other outside agencies, in which case it was issued by the War Department.

Because of the higher priority of large units, and other considerations, Army Ground Forces did not at the outset draw up a systematic scheme for the activation of spare parts similar to the well-charted procedure adopted early in 1942 for the building of divisions. The procedure established even before the creation of Army Ground Forces for the activation of divisions provided for the designation of key officers two or three months prior to date of activation; these were then sent to special preactivation courses at appropriate schools and, together with enlisted cadremen chosen and trained ahead of time by parent units, channeled into camps for further training before the arrival of fillers. Officers for nondivisional units were sometimes designated and given special training prior to the

[4] Troop Basis, 1 April 1945 (S).

activation of such units, but there was no provision for the systematic schooling of either commissioned or enlisted cadre.[5] It was usual for nuclei to be hastily selected from miscellaneous sources, such as unit overstrength and replacement training centers, and assembled in camp at the time of activation without prior training in cadre duties. It was not uncommon for the cadre and some of the fillers to arrive simultaneously on activation day.

Personnel shortages and the mad scramble for units produced by the plan for a cross-Channel invasion of Europe in the spring of 1943 would doubtless have vitiated any *a priori* scheme for building nondivisional units, but its existence might have forestalled some of the confusion. No chart for building nondivisional units was published until 18 March 1943. The effects of its adoption were not apparent until summer because initial steps in the creation of units had to be taken three months prior to date of activation.

The War Department suggested in August 1942 that a plan comparable to that for divisions be developed for spare parts.[6] Headquarters, Army Ground Forces, responded that such a system would be futile unless the War Department adhered more rigidly to the Troop Basis in the future than it had in the past, pointing out that the haphazardness of the current procedure was attributable to shortage of personnel, which in turn was due to activation of units far in excess of the number stipulated in the 1942 Troop Basis.[7] Nevertheless, in order to carry out the War Department's suggestion, G–4 of Army Ground Forces on 20 November 1942 submitted to other AGF staff sections for comment a new plan for the activation of nondivisional units.[8] Objections were offered by the G–1 and G–3 Sections, but the Plans Section, noting that the current easing of the personnel problem promised to reduce deterrents to orderly activation, recommended that the G–4 scheme be adopted and given a fair trial.[9] When the entire discussion was laid before Lt. Gen. Lesley J. McNair in late December 1942, he wrote: "I feel definitely that G–4's proposals are excellent, and I hope that they can be put into effect. Even though substantially this procedure has been fol-

[5] AGF M/S (S), G–3 to Plans, 4 Dec 42, sub: Activation of Nondivisional Units. 320.2/283 (S).

[6] WD memo (S) WDGCT 320.2 Gen (8–3–42) to CG AGF, 7 Aug 42, sub: Pers and Tng Status of Units in the AGF. 320.2/283 (S).

[7] Memo (S) of CG AGF for CofS USA, 9 Sep 42, sub as in n. 6. 320.2/283 (S).

[8] AGF memo (S) of G–4 for all staff secs, 20 Nov 42, and replies thereto, sub: Activation Plan for Nondiv Units. 320.2/283 (S).

[9] AGF M/S (S), Plans to DCofS, 19 Dec 42, sub: Visit to Maneuvers and to Cp Hood, Tex, May 27–30, 1943. AGF G–3 Tng Sec files, 333.1 (93d Div).

Building a Nondivisional Unit: AGF Plan Published 18 March 1943

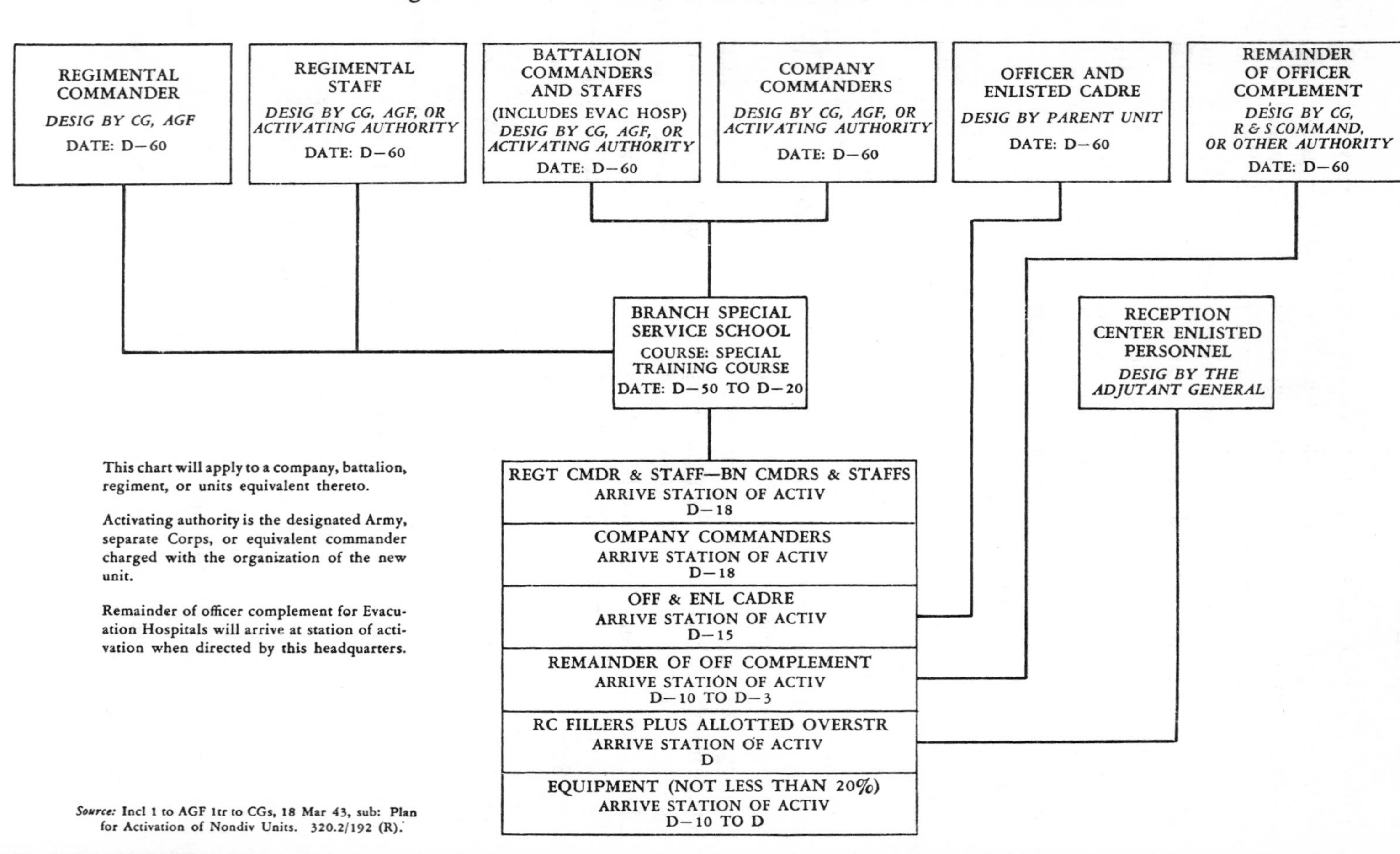

Source: Incl 1 to AGF ltr to CGs, 18 Mar 43, sub: Plan for Activation of Nondiv Units. 320.2/192 (R).

lowed in the past, it is helpful to regularize the matter, and especially to obtain War Department approval." [10]

During the early weeks of 1943 the G–4 scheme was subjected to further refinement and revision, but the plan published on 18 March 1943 did not differ materially from that brought forward four months before. The procedure which it prescribed for the activation of nondivisional units was along the same lines as that drawn up for divisions at the beginning of 1942. This procedure provided that preliminary steps should be initiated ninety days prior to the activation of a unit. Officers and enlisted men of the cadre were to be designated two months before D Day and given special instruction for their prospective duties. Key officers were to attend a 30-day course at the school of the appropriate arm or service. Commissioned personnel and enlisted men were to reach camp prior to activation date, according to a schedule. (See Chart, "Building a Nondivisional Unit.") Fillers and allotted overstrength were to arrive on D Day. A minimum of 20 percent of the equipment was to be on hand at the time of activation.[11]

The plan for building nondivisional units was followed rather closely during the first few months after its adoption. But the dwindling of the manpower supply in the latter part of 1943 made rigid observance impossible. Activations reverted far too frequently to the old catch-as-catch-can basis of 1942.[12]

AGF Jurisdiction over Training

Subject to the general supervision of the War Department, Army Ground Forces had complete jurisdiction over the training of AGF-type nondivisional units. Initially, AGF-type service units followed mobilization training programs prepared by chiefs of the technical services, but this was for the sake of expediency and convenience; from the beginning, preparation of training programs for ground units was an AGF prerogative. Army Ground Forces was responsible for training all personnel of the ground arms, but, since the technical services had jurisdiction over the schooling of their respective officers and enlisted specialists, the Ground Forces had to look to the Service Forces for officers of service branches and for the training of such enlisted technicians as could not be provided within the units.

[10] AGF M/S (S), Gen McNair to CofS, 28 Dec 42, sub: Activation Plan for Nondiv Units. 320.2/283 (S).

[11] AGF ltr (R) to CGs, 18 Mar 43, sub: Plan for Activation of Nondiv Units. 320.2/192 (R).

[12] Statement of Lt Col W. W. Johnson, AGF G–3 Activation and Cadre Br, Mob Div, to AGF Hist Off, 29 Jan 44.

The G–3 Section of Army Ground Forces exercised general supervision over training but, as in the case of activation, delegated administrative details to special staff sections and subordinate commands. The infantry, field artillery, and other branches in the Training Division of G–3 prepared general training programs and directives for guidance of nondivisional units of the arms and made occasional inspections to see that armies and other subordinate commands complied with them. After the reorganization of the AGF headquarters staff on 12 July 1942, similar functions were performed for ground service units by the special staff sections set up by that reorganization. These sections were coordinated by G–4, which maintained liaison with War Department supply agencies to see that units were provided with equipment as specified in Tables of Equipment and other applicable regulations. G–4 also established policies for maintenance of equipment and, in coordination with G–3, prescribed and supervised training in maintenance and in maintenance discipline. Preparation of tests, except for unit tests for Field Artillery and certain units of other arms, was usually delegated to subordinate commands.

For a considerable time, and especially in the first few months after Army Ground Forces was created, there was no clear delimitation of the jurisdiction of Army Ground Forces over nondivisional service units. In the War Department reorganization of 9 March 1942 the responsibility for training service units was not clearly fixed as between the Services of Supply and the Army Ground Forces. In April, and again in May, the Chief of Staff, Army Ground Forces, requested clarification of this troublesome matter.[13] On 30 May the War Department laid down the principle that in general "the using command will train a unit." In elaboration of this policy the following rules were set forth: (1) The Commanding General, Army Air Forces, would train all units serving with the Air Forces. (2) The Commanding General, Services of Supply, would train units organized to operate installations and activities controlled by him and those units organized in the United States solely for SOS installations and activities in overseas garrisons, bases, and theaters. (3) Commanding generals of defense commands would be responsible for the training of units assigned to them. (4) The Commanding General, Army Ground Forces, would be responsible for the training of all units not falling in the above categories. (5) By mutual agreement the Commanding Generals of the Army Air Forces, Army Ground Forces, and

[13] Memo of CofS AGF for G–3 WD, 9 Apr 42, sub: Agency or Agencies to Activate Units. 320.2/1915 (Str). (2) Memo of CofS AGF for G–3 WD, 9 May 42, sub: Responsibility for Tng. 353/1267.

Services of Supply might transfer among each other the responsibility for training certain units.[14]

This declaration of policy was helpful as far as it went. But it left unsettled the responsibility for training those types of units, such as the quartermaster truck regiments and engineer general-service regiments, which might be used in either the combat or the communications zones. Both the Services of Supply (later called Army Service Forces) and the Army Ground Forces claimed authority to train these borderline types and intermittently urged their cases on the War Department. To settle this dispute, G–3 of the War Department proposed early in June to publish "a list of units peculiar to Services of Supply" to be activated and trained by Services of Supply only. Both Army Ground Forces and Services of Supply, at the War Department's request, recommended units for inclusion in the proposed list, which was published on 20 June. But this effort at compromise was not satisfactory to either headquarters.[15]

During the latter part of 1942 and the early months of 1943 the War Department took steps to clarify the responsibility for training service units. The principle laid down in the spring of 1942, that the using command would train a unit, had produced confusion and controversy as to those types of units which might ultimately be used either in combat zones or in the Zone of Interior. This situation, and the conviction that service organizations were not being adequately prepared for the discharge of their missions, caused the War Department in November to direct The Inspector General to conduct a fact-finding survey of the training of service units. Visiting eleven stations where considerable numbers of various service-type organizations under the Army Ground Forces were located, The Inspector General found many instances of personnel and equipment shortages as well as some cases of inadequate supervision. But evidence that both standards and methods were "steadily improving," and apprehension as to the disruption and expense that might result from a large-scale redistribution of units among the principal commands, caused him to recommend that no major changes be made in existing training policies.[16]

[14] WD memo WDGCT (5–30–42) for CGs AGF, AAF, ASF, 30 May 42, sub: Responsibility for Tng. 353/1389.

[15] (1) Memo of Opns AGF for G–3 WD, 11 Jun 42, sub: Responsibility for the Activation of Units. 320.2/4488. (2) WD memo WDGCT 320.2 (6–20–42) for CGs AGF, AAF, SOS, 20 Jun 42, sub: Responsibility for the Activation of Serv Units. 320.2/4733. (3) The list was extended on 15 Jul 42, WD memo WDGCT 320.2 (7–2–42) for CGs, 15 Jul 42, sub: Guide to Responsibility for Activation of Certain Units. 320.2/473.

[16] Memo (S) of G–3 WD for CofS USA, 30 Dec 42, sub: Tng Serv Units. 353/163 (S).

Studying the problem with The Inspector General's report in hand, G-3 of the War Department considered the possibility of grouping all service units at unit training centers under SOS control for basic and technical training, and then transferring those destined for combat support to Army Ground Forces for instruction in tactical functions. But this proposal was ruled out, not only on grounds of the cost and confusion that it would entail, but also because of the obvious improvement made by Army Ground Forces in methods and plans for the building and training of service organizations.[17]

On 30 December 1942, the War Department announced that no fundamental change would be made in existing arrangements for the training of service units. At the same time, however, it reduced the confusion which had prevailed as to responsibility for training "borderline" organizations by specific apportionment of units to each of the two commands. This definite information enabled both commands to plan more effectively with regard to schedules of activation and programs of training. The new procedure meant, however, that units of the same general type could be allotted to both commands for training, and thus entailed some duplication of efforts and facilities. For example, of nine quartermaster truck regiments scheduled for activation in 1943, five were to be activated and trained by Army Ground Forces and four by Services of Supply; Army Ground Forces was to train all quartermaster supply companies, and Services of Supply was to train all quartermaster laundry companies.[18]

In January 1944 the War Department abandoned the scheme of allotting units of the same type to both commands for training, and adopted the practice of specifically designating in each revision of the Troop Basis those units that were to be activated and trained by the Army Ground Forces and those that were to be activated and trained by the Army Service Forces.[19] Thus quartermaster truck companies, which in 1943 had been activated and trained in considerable numbers by both the Army Ground Forces and the Army Service Forces, were in 1944 made the responsibility of the Army Ground Forces alone; on the other hand, quartermaster service battalions, likewise formerly divided, were all given to the Army Service Forces.[20]

The argument over responsibility for training which had reached such a high pitch in late 1942 was revived apparently in only one instance between 1 January

[17] *Ibid.*

[18] *Ibid.*

[19] WD memo WDGCT 353 (6 Jan 44) to CGs AAF, AGF, ASF, 6 Jan 44, sub: Responsibility for Tng of Serv Units. 353/2301.

[20] This statement is based on study of the 1944 Troop Basis and various revisions thereof. 320.2 (Tr Basis) (S).

1944 and V-E Day. This was in reference to signal photographic companies. In January 1945 the Chief Signal Officer, Army Service Forces, complained that these units, trained by the Army Ground Forces, were not satisfactorily meeting overseas publicity requirements for still and motion pictures because of deficiencies in technical training. Taking the position that only the Chief Signal Officer had proper facilities for the required technical training, and that the agency which had the responsibility for preparing publicity pictures for release should also have jurisdiction over the selection and training of photographic personnel, he recommended that authority for training photographic signal companies be transferred from the Army Ground Forces to the Army Service Forces. The Army Ground Forces disapproved the recommendation on the ground that the securing of photographs for news and historical purposes was only a secondary function of these units, that their primary mission was the taking of pictures for combat intelligence, and hence they should be trained by a combat command. Responsibility for the training of signal photographic companies remained an AGF responsibility.[21]

[21] (1) ASF memo SPSHP 353 Gen, CSigO ASF for CG ASF, 18 Jan 45, sub: Integration of Photographic Tng with WD Pictorial Reqmts. (2) AGF ltr to CG ASF, 26 Feb 44, sub: Tng of Sig Photographic Cos. Both in 353/304 (Sig).

II. The Organization of Training

Higher supervision of the training of spare-parts organizations was at first left by Army Ground Forces almost wholly to armies, corps, commands, and centers. This situation, which did not make for the most effective control and coordination, was due to three principal causes. First, the AGF staff was too much absorbed in setting up headquarters organizations and procedures for its rapidly expanding strength to give close attention to field activities; inspections had to be held to a minimum. Second, divisions were accorded a higher priority than spare parts on the assumption that the latter could be trained in less time and with less difficulty than the former. Third, supervision of service units was impeded by the fact that, as already indicated, the initial AGF organization did not provide special staff sections for such units (except for military police).[1]

During the spring and summer of 1942 it was increasingly apparent that some method had to be devised for improving the supervision of nondivisional training. The 700-odd nondivisional units scattered about the country were assigned principally to armies, but army staffs were not large enough to permit them to exercise a close control over the numerous regiments, battalions, and companies dotting their far-flung commands. It was not unusual in 1942 for separate companies to go for months without being tested by representatives of higher echelons, and sometimes the intervals between visits of inspection were unduly long. The Inspector General's report of 11 December 1942 emphasized this point as the following excerpts indicate:[2]

1. Camp Edwards, Mass., 663d Engineer Company, activated prior to 31 May 1942. "No training tests . . . have been made by higher headquarters."

2. Fort Meade, Md., 229th Signal Operations Company. "The unit commander stated that visits from higher headquarters were made monthly but were of very little help in training. No training tests have been made by higher headquarters."

[1] (1) Memo of Col Lowell W. Rooks, Chief of AGF Tng Div, for Gen McNair, 21 May 42, sub: Comment on Ltr of Gen Lear, 18 May 42. McNair Correspondence. (2) Memo (S) of Brig Gen W. S. Paul, G–4 AGF, for Sec GS, 28 Jun 42, sub: TUB 42. 320.2/283 (S). (3) Memo (S) of Brig Gen W. S. Paul to CofS AGF [undated, but early Jul 42], sub: Condition of Nondiv Serv Units. 320.2/283 (S). (4) AGF memo (S) for CofS USA, 3 Aug 42, sub: Pers and Tng Status of Units of AGF. 320.2/283 (S). (5) Statement of Col J. B. Hughes to AGF Hist Off, 29 Jan 44.

[2] Memo of Brig Gen Philip E. Brown for CG AGF, 11 Dec 42, sub: Sp Survey of AGF Serv Units other than Divisional. 333.1/1415 (Insps, Fld Forces).

3. Fort Devens, Mass., 206th Military Police Company. "No test of training has been made by higher headquarters."

Lack of intensive direction was particularly unfortunate during the early period of AGF jurisdiction because of the dearth at that time of satisfactory manuals, detailed training programs, and other literature for guidance of unit commanders.[3]

Army commanders attached many of the spare parts to corps, but corps were not able to give any more effective supervision than armies. The accumulating burden of spare parts threatened to convert corps headquarters from the lean, tactical organizations they were supposed to be into bulky administrative organizations. In April 1942 Inspector General Virgil L. Peterson reported that the Third Army had attached 83 separate units, aggregating 30,000 troops, to the IV Corps for administration and training, and that the IV Corps had added 25 more officers to its headquarters than were authorized by current Tables of Organization.[4] Later in the spring the III Corps was swamped with 60,000 nondivisional troops which Army Ground Forces had received from the First Army and the Eastern Defense Command.[5]

In some instances separate units were attached to divisions and even to regiments; in other cases army commanders, without the formality of attachment, merely directed division commanders to give an eye occasionally to spare parts stationed in the vicinity of their headquarters. These arrangements were definitely not satisfactory.[6] Division commanders, harassed as they were in 1942 by formidable difficulties, and knowing well that their reputations rested on the showing made by organic troops in tests, inspections, and maneuvers, gave scant heed to the stepchildren dumped on their laps by higher headquarters. Moreover, the frequent stationing of small separate units at the same posts as divisions placed commanding officers of the former at a decided disadvantage with respect to

[3] General Brown's report included the statement: "Cp Blanding. 33d Chem Decon Co, activated Aug 10 1942, and 25th Chem Decon Co activated March 25 1942—There is a complete lack of coordinated information and training literature on decontamination subjects." 333.1/1415 (Insps, Fld Forces).

[4] Memo of TIG for Gen George C. Marshall, CofS USA, 20 Apr 42, sub: Hq Third Army. 322/4 (Third Army).

[5] Statement of Gen Ben Lear, former CG Second Army, to AGF Hist Off, 14 Oct 43.

[6] (1) Personal ltr of Gen Ben Lear to CG 9th Div, 16 Jun 42. Second Army files, AG 353.01–2 (Inf). (2) Statement of Col J. W. Younger, Gd QM (formerly QM Second Army), to AGF Hist Off, 25 Jan 44. (3) Personal ltrs of Lt Gen H. J. Brees, CG Third Army, to Gen McNair, 7, 11 Jan, 4 Feb 41. GHQ Records, 353/7 (Third Army). (4) In one instance at least, some service units were attached to a corps area for supervision. See memo of Lt Col E. V. McAtee, G–4 AGF, to CofS AGF, 6 Apr 42, sub: Rpt of Visit to the 82d Div, Hq Third Army, and 90th Div. 333.1/748 (Insps, Fld Forces).

equipment and services provided by post authorities. When post commanders received simultaneous requests for training aids from the captain of a signal company, who was apt to be young and inexperienced in military procedure, and the major general of a division, there was a strong tendency to favor the stars over the bars. In view of the scarcity of equipment in 1942 the result was frequently a failure to fill the requisitions of low-ranking commanders.[7]

Shortly after Inspector General Peterson's report on the unsatisfactory situation in April 1942 with respect to nondivisional troops in the IV Corps and Third Army, General McNair, in conformity with a suggestion of Gen. George C. Marshall,[8] directed his staff to work out a solution for the spare-parts problem. Common to all the schemes considered was the plan of setting up small supervisory headquarters under corps or army jurisdiction at stations where considerable numbers of nondivisional troops were located.[9]

Headquarters and Headquarters Detachments, Special Troops

On 21 May 1942, Army Ground Forces, in letters sent to the commanders of the Second Army, Third Army, II Corps, and VII Corps, authorized the creation by each of an experimental headquarters and headquarters detachment, special troops, at some undesignated station. The objective was twofold: first, to intensify supervision of nondivisional units; second, to curb the increasing tendency of corps toward administrative functions. Two types of headquarters were authorized: Type A, consisting of 5 officers and 16 enlisted men, for stations where nondivisional troops totaled from 2,000 to 5,000 troops; and Type B, consisting of 8 officers and 31 enlisted men, where spare-parts personnel exceeded 5,000.[10] Commanding officers of both types of headquarters were to have the rank of colonel. Army and corps commanders concerned were directed to report to Army Ground Forces "as soon as the measures taken have been tested sufficiently to warrant conclusions." [11]

[7] Statement of Col J. B. Sherman, Plans Sec AGF, to AGF Hist Off, 8 Jan 44. Col Sherman was formerly in the G-3 Sec, Hq Second Army.

[8] Memo (C) of Gen Marshall for Gen McNair, 25 Apr 42, sub not given. 333/2 (C).

[9] AGF M/S (C), CofS to G-3, 23 Apr 42, sub: Administration in Army Corps. 322/1 (Hq and Hq Det Sp Trs) (C).

[10] In October 1942 the authorized strength of Type A headquarters and headquarters detachments was increased to 6 officers and 20 enlisted men, and of Type B to 8 officers and 32 enlisted men. AGF ltr (R) to CGs, 20 Oct 42, sub: Orgn of Comd of Army and GHQ Trs. 322/4 (Hq and Hq Det Trs) (R).

[11] For copies of these letters see binders for Second Army, Third Army, II Corps, and VII Corps in 322 (Hq and Hq Det Sp Trs) (C).

The first response to this directive came from Lt. Gen. Ben Lear on 29 May.[12] The Second Army commander, on the basis of his own difficulties with spare parts,[13] had already instituted remedial procedures at two stations along the same lines as those advocated by Army Ground Forces. On 29 December 1941 he had designated ten miscellaneous units at Fort Knox, Ky., as Special Troops, Second Army, and placed them under a small provisional headquarters commanded by Lt. Col. Ben Stafford.[14] He had made a similar disposition of separate units stationed at Fort Custer, Mich., with Col. George Byers in command.[15] These two experiments had convinced him that the supervisory detachment scheme was practicable. His recommendation to Army Ground Forces on 29 May, therefore, was that Type A headquarters be immediately established at eight Second Army Stations, including Fort Custer and Fort Knox.[16]

In June and July ten headquarters and headquarters detachments, special troops, were activated by the Second Army, and one each by the Third Army, II Corps, and VII Corps. In ensuing months others were added and by 31 December 1942 the number totaled 29, distributed as follows: 13 in the Second Army, 8 in the Third Army, 7 in corps, and 1 in the Armored Force. The number of these headquarters reached a peak of 49 in July 1943, with 15 assigned to the Second Army, 16 to the Third Army, 13 to corps, 1 to the Armored Command, and 4 to the California–Arizona Maneuver Area.[17] The action initiated in July 1943 for placing all nondivisional combat units under corps, together with the decline of the strength of AGF service units as a result of overseas movement, made possible the inactivation of several headquarters, special troops, in late 1943 and early 1944.

The functions of special troops headquarters varied somewhat in the different commands, but directives of Army Ground Forces and subordinate headquarters placed primary stress throughout on the supervision of training. General Lear was particularly insistent that priority should be given to such training. In a

[12] Telg of Gen Lear to Gen McNair, 29 May 42. 322/1 (Hq and Hq Det) (Second Army).

[13] As early as December 1940 the commanding general of the 5th Division, burdened with the task of supervising spare parts not only at his own station but at three other stations as well, requested General Lear's permission to set up a small headquarters for supervision of small Army units located at Fort Knox, Ky. The request was disapproved because of lack of officers.

[14] Second Army ltr AG 322–43 (F) to Lt Col Ben Stafford, 29 Dec 41. 314.7 (AGF Hist).

[15] Second Army ltr to Col George Byers, 18 Apr 42. Second Army Records, correspondence of Col Byers.

[16] Telg of Gen Lear to Gen McNair, 29 May 42. 322/1 (Hq and Hq Det) (Second Army).

[17] These figures are from compilations "AGF Units" in AGF G–3 Mob Div files.

personal letter written to each officer placed in command of a detachment he indicated the general nature of the supervisory duties:[18]

> I desire that you assure compliance with provisions of training directives and memoranda from headquarters, and that you will coordinate the use of training aids, facilities, and equipment, in the best interest of all units. I desire that you supervise preparation of training schedules and that you follow through full compliance with them.
>
> It is particularly important that you assure yourself by inspections and conferences with unit commanders, and in instructions to them, that proper attention is being given to matters affecting the discipline, morale, soldierly bearing, and appearance of personnel. I desire also that you supervise carefully the conditions of barracks, messes, and equipment.

Lest there be some question as to the extent of the commanding officer's authority, General Lear added: "You are my personal representative at Fort —— and orders issued by you to members of your command have my full sanction."

In addition to training duties, the commanding officers of headquarters detachments had a number of administrative responsibilities. They exercised special court-martial jurisdiction, and took final action on requests for leaves and furloughs and on transfers of enlisted men between units under their command. Through their offices passed (1) recommendations for promotions, reclassification, and reassignment of officers, (2) board proceedings for selection of enlisted personnel to attend officer candidate school, (3) assignment of officers to units ordered overseas, (4) investigation and charges for trial by general court-martial, and (5) discharge of enlisted men prior to expiration of term of service. They were also responsible for preparation of units for movement overseas or to other stations. In many cases the headquarters staffs devoted considerable attention to instructing the inexperienced officers of units under their supervision in administrative procedure.[19]

Detachment commanders were assisted in their supervisory duties by visits and communications of the staffs of the higher headquarters to which they were immediately responsible. Nevertheless, the responsibilities were most onerous. The shortage of personnel caused a tendency on the part of higher commands to hold staff personnel of special troops detachments to reduced levels.[20] Type A headquarters often had to supervise units totaling considerably more than 5,000 troops, and some Type B headquarters were required to supervise from 50 to 60

[18] Ltr (C) of Gen Lear to Col Wm. H. Wilbur, 24 Jun 42. 322/11 (Hq and Hq Det Sp Trs)(C).

[19] Memo (C) of Col Clyde L. Hyssong for Gen McNair, 16 Sep 42, sub: Inspection of Hq and Hq Det Sp Trs, Second and Third Armies. 322/11 (Hq and Hq Det Sp Trs)(C).

[20] Memo of Col Hyssong for Gen McNair, 13 Apr 43, sub: Inspection of Adm and Repl Matters. 353.02/142 (AGF).

units with a strength of from 10,000 to 15,000 men. Sometimes units under jurisdiction of a special troops headquarters were located at widely separated stations. In September 1942 Col. Clyde L. Hyssong of Army Ground Forces reported that the 1st Headquarters and Headquarters Detachment, Special Troops, Second Army, was supervising some units located at its home station, Fort Bragg, others at Camp Davis, 125 miles to the east, and still others at Camp Sutton, 100 miles to the west. A Third Army headquarters and headquarters detachment was charged with the supervision of units scattered at four Louisiana stations.[21]

The creation of many additional headquarters and headquarters detachments in late 1942 and early 1943 reduced the necessity of assigning excessive numbers of spare-parts personnel to any one commander. The practice of extending supervision to several stations was curtailed by the provision made late in 1942 for setting up reduced versions of Type A headquarters at posts where nondivisional personnel fell short of two thousand, but where as many as four units were located.[22]

As the number of nondivisional units remaining in the Zone of Interior declined in 1944 and the early months of 1945, inactivation of headquarters and headquarters detachments, special troops, proceeded rapidly. The number and distribution of these supervisory organizations by quarters were as follows:[23]

	31 Mar 44	*30 Jun 44*	*30 Sep 44*	*31 Dec 44*	*31 Mar 45*
Armies	27	25	15	14	10
Corps	13	9	4	..	..
C–AMA	3	..	..	..	..
AGF	..	..	1	1	1
TOTAL	43	34	20	15	11

The decline in the number of these headquarters was paralleled by an increase in both their size and their responsibilities. In the latter part of 1943 the Second Army charged headquarters and headquarters detachments, special troops, with the preparation for overseas movement (POM) of nondivisional units assigned to corps. Early in 1944 the Army Ground Forces approved this step, and in the following months the plan was applied to other AGF com-

[21] Memo cited in n. 19.

[22] AGF ltr (R) to CGs, 15 Oct 42, sub: Hq and Hq Det Sp Trs Army and Corps. 322/4 (Hq and Hq Det Sp Trs) (S).

[23] Compiled from AGF file 320.2 (Comp Str) (C).

230-171 O - 66 - 34

mands.[24] In one instance, at least, a headquarters and headquarters detachment was called on to act as the representative of an army in supervising the POM of a division.[25]

The great increase in the rate of overseas movements for the invasion of Europe multiplied the duties which the headquarters and headquarters detachments, special troops, had to perform in connection with the final processing of their own units. Because group headquarters usually were shipped apart from their battalions and frequently in advance of them, it became necessary to place the principal burden of preparing battalions for shipment on the special troops headquarters rather than on the group.[26]

The various measures instituted in 1944 for a more effective utilization of manpower, together with the large turnover of personnel after the beginning of the year, placed an unprecedented volume of personnel administration on armies and other major commands. In February 1944 an AGF staff officer stated:[27]

> Within divisions where a regularly assigned classification officer has been provided, operation of the personnel classification system has for the most part been efficient. . . . On the other hand, the nondivisional units have not kept pace in this regard. Army classification officers do not have the time, facilities or personnel to handle all of the separate units in addition to the corps and divisions for which they are responsible. The lack of "on the ground" personnel to direct, supervise, and administer the classification system within nondivisional units has resulted in limiting the ability of personnel sections of such units to comply with either the intent or the letter of the various regulations and directives aimed at proper utilization of the personnel assigned. Over 400,000 men with the Army Ground Forces are without direct classification supervision. Approximately two-thirds of this number are in organizations attached to special troops headquarters.

To meet this situation a classification officer was added to each headquarters and headquarters detachment, special troops, in March 1944.[28]

In part to meet the increasing volume and complexity of responsibilities, and in part to provide greater flexibility with reference to nondivisional strength at

[24] AGF M/S, CofS to CG, 11 Feb 44, sub: POM Functions. With related papers. 370.5/4202.

[25] Memo of Col S. E. Rall for G–4 AGF, 11 Jul 44, sub: Rpt of Visit to 104th Inf Div and other AGF Units, Cp Carson, Colo. AGF G–3 Sec files, 333.1/40 (Inspections by AGF Staff Offs).

[26] (1) AGF M/S (R), G–3 to CofS, 13 Mar 45, sub: Asgmt and Atchmt of AGF units. 321/78 (R). (2) AGF memo, G–1 to G–3, 1 May 44, sub: Rpt of G–1 Representative on Gen McNair's Inspection Trip, 23–29 Apr 44. 353.02/599 (AGF).

[27] AGF M/S (R), C&RD to G–1, 11 Feb 44, sub: Almt of Classification Offs in Hq and Hq Dets Sp Trs. 322/103 (Hq and Hq Det Sp Trs) (R).

[28] AGF ltr (R) to CGs, 24 Mar 44, sub: Reorgn of Hq and Hq Dets Sp Trs, Army and Sep Corps. 322/103 (Hq and Hq Dets Sp Trs) (R).

the various posts, Army Ground Forces in July 1944, on the recommendation of the Second Army, authorized two new types of headquarters and headquarters detachments, special troops. At this time Type A headquarters, for stations having a nondivisional strength of from 2,000 to 5,000 men, had an authorized strength of 7 officers and 20 enlisted men, and Type B headquarters, for those housing over 5,000 men, of 9 officers and 32 enlisted men. The system instituted in July 1944 authorized a Type C headquarters of 11 officers and 35 enlisted men at posts where nondivisional strength was 2,500–7,500, and a Type D headquarters of 16 officers, 1 warrant officer, and 49 enlisted men where nondivisional strength exceeded 7,500. All A and B headquarters not scheduled for inactivation in the near future were to be converted to C and D types. In calculating the strength of units to determine the appropriate type of headquarters for a given post, one-third of the corps troops were counted; this was because of the responsibilities which the headquarters and headquarters detachments bore for the POM of these units. The most striking difference between the composition of the Type D headquarters and that of the B Type which it superseded was that the former had greater strength in administrative and supply personnel.[29]

In the fall of 1944 the size and the functions of the headquarters and headquarters detachments, special troops, were again increased. This change was brought about mainly by the prospective movement overseas of all the corps headquarters. When the III Corps departed in August 1944, a miscellany of nondivisional units was left on the Pacific Coast without benefit of close supervision. To fill in the gap the Army Ground Forces set up at Fort Ord a "super" headquarters and headquarters detachment, special troops, called it 1st Headquarters and Headquarters Detachment, Special Troops, Army Ground Forces, gave it general courts-martial jurisdiction, and placed some 42 units, with a strength of over 10,000 men, under its supervision for administration, supply, and training. The new headquarters, consisting of 28 officers (commanded by a brigadier general), 4 warrant officers, and 90 enlisted men, was charged with "all the functions and duties, normally discharged by an army or separate corps commander." [30]

The success of the experimental headquarters at Fort Ord naturally sug-

[29] AGF ltr (R) to CGs, 6 Jul 44, sub: Reorgn of Hq and Hq Dets Sp Trs, Army and Corps. 322/106 (Hq and Hq Dets Sp Trs) (R).

[30] (1) WD ltr (R) AG 322 (29 Jul 44) OB–I–GNGCT–M to CG III Corps, 1 Aug 44, sub: Reorgn and Redesignation of the Hq & Hq Det Sp Trs III Corps. 322/1 (Hq and Hq Dets Sp Trs AGF) (R). (2) AGF ltr (R) to CGs III Corps, 1st Armd Div, and 1st Hq and Hq Det Sp Trs AGF, 12 Aug 44, sub: Release and Reasgmt of III Corps Units. 321/48 (R). (3) Statement of Maj W. W. Wells, AGF G–1 Sec, to AGF Hist Off, 10 May 45.

gested filling in the gaps left by removal of other corps with similar organizations. In October 1944 the seven principal headquarters and headquarters detachments remaining in the Army Ground Forces were designated as S (Special) Type, with an authorized strength of 30 officers, 5 warrant officers, and 88 enlisted men. To permit adaptation of the headquarters and headquarters detachments to variations in local needs, army commanders were authorized to depart, at their discretion, from the branch allocation of officers set forth in the published Table of Distribution. For example, the published Table of Distribution provided for 2 ordnance officers and 1 signal officer, but if a given headquarters had no ordnance units attached and had many signal units the army commander could delete the ordnance officers and add 2 signal officers. All of the Type S headquarters were assigned to armies, but their functions were comparable to those prescribed in August for the headquarters at Fort Ord.[31] One AGF staff officer said of the new organizations: "Special troops headquarters act as a branch army headquarters in dealing with all army units." [32] Another said that these headquarters were recognized "as administrative as well as training agencies of the armies." [33]

In Type S headquarters, for the first time, specific provision was made for the inclusion in headquarters and headquarters detachments, special troops, of officers of the various services. This removed a major criticism levelled at these organizations from the time of their inception: namely, their inability to furnish expert supervision for technical training.

As the headquarters and headquarters detachments, special troops, declined in number and were reorganized into new types, they were able to dispense with their less capable officers. At the same time they received a larger admixture of combat-experienced personnel from the ever increasing flow of returnees pouring into the United States. By V-E Day the headquarters and headquarters detachments, although far from perfect, were considerably better adapted to their supervisory functions, from the standpoint both of organization and of leadership,

[31] (1) Statement of Maj C. C. Clark to AGF Hist Off, 9 Apr 45. (2) AGF ltr (R) to CGs, 7 Oct 44, sub: Almt of Pers for Hq & Hq Dets Sp Trs, Army and Sep Corps. 322/110 (Hq and Hq Dets Sp Trs)(R). Personnel for the headquarters and headquarters detachments were placed in a bulk allotment by this letter. (3) AGF ltr (R) to CGs, 29 Oct 44, sub: Revised Almt of Pers for Certain Hq & Hq Dets Sp Trs. 322/111 (Hq and Hq Det Sp Trs)(R).

[32] AGF M/S (R), G-3 to DCofS, 13 Mar 45, sub: Asgmt and Atchmt of AGF Units. 321/78 (R).

[33] AGF M/S (R), G-3 to CofS, 19 Dec 44, sub as in n. 32. 321/78 (R).

than during their pioneer days in 1942. On the whole their contribution to the training of the ground army was a valuable one.[34]

An appraisal of headquarters and headquarters detachments, special troops, reveals, however, several defects and shortcomings. The policy sometimes followed of choosing as commanders men who, because of advanced age or other handicaps, were not deemed suitable for more active duty had unfortunate consequences. As one AGF staff member bluntly expressed it: "You didn't often get effective command from a worn-out colonel who had failed to make good in some other capacity." [35]

A second deficiency resulted from the failure to staff the special troops headquarters in such a way as to provide competent supervision for all the specialties represented in units under their jurisdiction.[36] The five officers comprising a Type A headquarters in 1942 might be an infantry colonel, a lieutenant colonel of engineers, an infantry major, and a captain each of ordnance and the quartermaster corps. This staff might be charged with supervision of a miscellany made up of artillery, chemical, engineer, ordnance, quartermaster, and signal units. The infantry colonel and major would have little knowledge of the intricacies of artillery practice, and less of the technical functions involved in training the service organizations. The ordnance units might be of three distinct types and yet be required to look for advice and instruction to a young captain who recently had been a "straw boss" in an automobile factory. The signal and chemical units, being unrepresented on the headquarters staff, would have to fend for themselves, with particularly unfortunate consequences if, as was likely, the commanders of both units were young and inexperienced. This deficiency could have been remedied by including on the headquarters staff an officer of each arm or service represented among attached units. While Army Ground Forces was aware of the desirability of such an arrangement, two factors prevented its adoption prior to

[34] This statement is based on interviews with various officers of AGF headquarters by the AGF Historical Officer, 1943–45, and on a survey of inspection reports of AGF officers filed in 353.02 (AGF) (Visits of AGF Staff Offs).

[35] Statement made to AGF Hist Off, — Jan 44.

[36] Interviews by AGF Hist Off with heads of AGF Special Staff secs, Jan 44. This source will be cited hereafter as "Interviews with Special Staff heads, Jan 44." The following AGF officers were interviewed on the dates indicated:

Maj F. P. Bonney (for Chem Off), 1 Feb 44
Col J. B. Hughes, Engr Off, 29 Jan 44
Lt Col G. J. Collins (for Med Off), 28 Jan 44
Lt Col A. P. Thom (for Med Off), 29 Jan 44
Lt Col E. J. Gibson (for Ord Off), 27 Jan 44
Lt Col L. H. Harrison (for Ord Off), 28 Jan 44
Maj R. E. Peters (for Ord Off), 28 Jan 44
Col Garland C. Black, Sig Off, 26 Jan 44
Col J. W. Younger, QM Off, accompanied by Lt Col H. H. Rodecker and Maj C. A. Brown of the QM Sec, 25 Jan 44

1944. First was General McNair's consistent opposition to the concentration of more than two or three units of the same type at any one station. Second was the scarcity of officers of all arms and services. The supply of officers improved in 1943, but there were still serious shortages in some categories, particularly in medical and engineer units.

The Second Army attempted to cope with the deficiency of specialist supervision in detachment staffs by making temporary details, in cases of the most urgent need, from its own headquarters personnel. For example, if railhead and gas supply companies were assigned to a special troops headquarters detachment having no quartermaster officer on its staff, the army quartermaster sent one of his own assistants to aid the special troops commander, for a period not exceeding two months, in supervision of the quartermaster units. But Headquarters, Army Ground Forces, disapproved this procedure as an undesirable use of army staff.[37]

A third shortcoming of the headquarters, special troops, was a tendency on the part of some officers to sacrifice training to administration and to substitute memoranda for personal contact in the supervision of attached units. In September 1942 Colonel Hyssong reported that some detachment commanders were preparing directives that should have been issued by armies, and that others, instead of merely initialing papers addressed by higher headquarters to units under their supervision—all that was expected of them—were transmitting them by formal indorsement.[38] Of one special troops headquarters General McNair, to whom overuse of the mimeograph was ever a *bete noire,* wrote to General Lear:[39]

> The Headquarters is definitely administering when it should be training. Those headquarters should not even be in the administrative channel. The commander should be out with the units every day, all day. His administration consists solely of spot checks in the units themselves. . . . [The commanding officer] is getting entirely too much mail.

Despite their handicaps and shortcomings, the headquarters and headquarters detachments, special troops, filled a vital need and served a useful function in the supervision of nondivisional training. They provided supervision and an articulate guardian for hundreds of small units. The colonels who commanded the headquarters were men of broad experience and acquaintance. When they asked post commanders for services and equipment, their requests were more apt

[37] (1) Statement of Col J. W. Younger, AGF QM, to AGF Hist Off, 25 Jan 44. Col Younger was QM of Second Army from Jan 42 to Dec 43. (2) Memo (C) of Col Hyssong, AG, for Gen McNair, 16 Sep 42, sub: Inspection of Hq and Hq Det Sp Trs, Second and Third Armies. 322/11 (Hq and Hq Det Sp Trs)(C).

[38] See n. 37 (2).

[39] Personal ltr of Gen McNair to Gen Lear, 9 Feb 43. Personal files of Gen Lear.

to be honored than those made by low-ranking and inexperienced leaders of small separate units. Colonels also were able to deal more effectively with the staffs of armies and corps.[40] The headquarters, special troops, also facilitated administration on the part of higher commands. Army staffs found it much easier and more effective to deal with and hold responsible one officer at a given station than to attempt direct supervision of many separate and uncoordinated parts. At various times General McNair, the Inspector General's Office, and army commanders noted with approval the salutary results which these headquarters had produced in the training of small units.[41] At the end of his career as Second Army commander, General Lear, whose knowledge of the work of the special troops headquarters was particularly intimate, wrote to General Marshall: "The organization of these detachments for training and administration is sound." He stated further that it would be desirable to place brigadier generals in command of some of the larger headquarters—a practice which the Third Army had already adopted and which was carried further by Army Ground Forces in 1944.[42]

Flexible Attachment to Headquarters

A second important development in the organization of nondivisional training was the extension to service-type units in 1943 of the flexible attachment plan of organization, adopted for combat units in 1942.[43] This plan provided for the grouping of companies under administratively self-sufficient battalion headquarters, of battalions under group headquarters, and of groups under brigade headquarters. The new type of headquarters, while designed primarily to facilitate tactical operations, served also a useful function in the supervision of training.

From the standpoint of training, the group headquarters was of the greatest benefit, particularly in respect to service units. In general the regiment, which the group replaced in all but infantry organizations, had provided satisfactory supervision for units of the arms. But in many cases small units of the services had not

[40] Statement of Col J. B. Sherman, AGF Plans Sec, to AGF Hist Off, 8 Jan 44.

[41] (1) Memo (C) of Gen Lear for Gen Marshall, 1 Jun 43, sub: Inspection of 1st Det Hq Sp Trs Third Army; 74th FA Brig, Cp Shelby, Miss. 333.1/66 (Insps, Fld Forces)(C). (2) Memo of Brig Gen Philip E. Brown, Dep of TIG USA, to CG AGF, 11 Dec 42, sub: Special Survey of AGF Serv Units Other Than Divisional. 333.1/1415 (Insps, Fld Forces).

[42] (1) Memo (C) of Gen Lear for Gen Marshall, 1 Jun 43, sub: Inspection of 1st Det Sp Trs Third Army; 74th FA Brig, Cp Shelby, Miss. 333.1/66 (Insps, Fld Forces)(C). (2) On 30 April 1943, the CO 5th Hq and Hq Det Sp Trs Third Army was promoted to brigadier general, and on 15 September the CO 9th Hq and Hq Det Sp Trs Third Army was promoted to brigadier general.

[43] For details of the plan for flexible grouping of battalions and companies, see "Reorganization of Ground Troops for Combat," in *The Organization of Ground Combat Troops.*

been formed into regiments because frequently service troops were not required in blocks as large as a regiment; if organized as regiments they often were scattered at various stations apart from the parent headquarters, with no supervision immediately at hand save in the form of occasional visits by officers of the headquarters and headquarters detachment, special troops.[44] The group plan provided for bringing together varying numbers and types of these orphaned service units, of the same branch, under an officer of sufficient rank and experience to give effective supervision. Concerning the practical value of the group as an intermediate agency the AGF medical officer in January 1944 stated:[45]

> Because of the scarcity of medical officers many of the lieutenant colonels who command battalions are men in their early thirties. They do not have enough age and experience to exercise control over the training of units attached to battalion headquarters. Commanding officers of the group headquarters, on the other hand, are full colonels, old and experienced enough to carry considerable authority.

The group organization was not only better adapted to supervision of training than the regimental system which it replaced in the tactical scheme, but it was also more economical with respect to overhead personnel in that it could accommodate a greater number of battalions. One advantage of the flexibility afforded by attaching units to a group rather than making them organic in a regiment was that a single headquarters could train several installments of battalions. Under the group plan units could be shifted, when convenience might be better served by the change, from one headquarters to another while in process of training.

Another advantage of the group plan was its partial answer to AGF objections to large Negro units. General McNair had sought to reduce the size of Negro units, especially of the combat types, to achieve greater flexibility in their tactical employment.[46] The group plan, stressing flexible attachment of battalions to group headquarters, gave Army Ground Forces and its arms an opportunity to request the elimination of Negro group headquarters and headquarters companies so that Negro or white battalions or both might be attached to any group.[47]

[44] Interviews with AGF Special Staff heads, Jan 44.

[45] Statement of Lt Col Alfred P. Thom to AGF Hist Off, 29 Jan 44.

[46] AGF memo (S) for WD G–3, 11 Nov 42, sub: Negro Personnel TB 43. 322.999/1 (Cld Trs)(S).

[47] (1) AGF memo for CofS USA, 23 Jan 43, sub: Orgn of Gp Hq and Sep Bns. 320.2/254 (C). (2) AGF memo for CofS USA, 2 Feb 43, sub: Gp Hq in 43 TB. 320.2/12 (TUB)(C). (3) AGF memo for CofS USA, 17 Mar 43, sub: Orgn of Gp Hq and Sep Bns. 320.2/254 (C). (4) AGF memo for CofS USA, 26 Mar 43, sub: Orgn of Hq and Hq Co, TD Gp. 320.2/31 (C). (5) As further justification these requests indicated that the transfer of Negro personnel from group headquarters companies to the battalions would fill a distinct need for high-caliber personnel in the battalions.

While the War Department did not authorize the complete substitution of white for Negro group headquarters, the number of Negro group headquarters in the Troop Basis was reduced substantially.[48] For supervision of training, service units, especially quartermaster and ordnance, were primarily affected. A group headquarters which proved especially effective in the training of Negro troops could be left undisturbed as successive increments of units came under its supervision and passed on to a port of embarkation. In the theaters the group system made it possible to attach Negro or white units to a group headquarters as needed or desired. Negro units especially gained in strength, usefulness, and experience by the operation of this plan.[49]

The group was designed as a predominantly tactical organization: General McNair wished the group staff in training to concern itself only incidentally with paper work and to spend its time primarily in the field supervising attached units. He insisted that the bulk of administration should be left to the battalion and to the army, both of which were provided with administrative personnel.[50]

In December 1942 group headquarters numbered only 27; by 31 March 1943 the figure had increased to 121, distributed as follows:

Armored	10	Field Artillery	45
Tank Destroyer	14	Air Base Security	3
Antiaircraft	41	Combat Engineer	8

The fullest development of the group came in the summer and fall of 1943, following extension to service units of the plan of flexible attachment. On 31 December 1943 group headquarters under the Army Ground Forces totaled 170 with the following distribution:

Armored	13	Combat Engineer	25
Tank Destroyer	20	Medical	12
Antiaircraft	43	Ordnance (Base)	2
Field Artillery	43	Quartermaster	12

[48] (1) WD memo, G–3 for CG AGF, 26 Jan 43, sub: Orgn of Gp Hq and Sep Bns. 320.2/254 (C). (2) WD memo, G–3 for CG AGF, 23 Mar 43, sub: Orgn of AA Gp Hq and Sep Bns. 320.2/254 (C). (3) WD D/F, 27 Mar 43, sub: Orgn Hq and Hq Co, TD Gp. 321/4 (TD Units)(C). G–3 cited the War Department policy of providing some Negro units of each type and of providing opportunities for promotion of Negro officers up to the grade of colonel, where possible; though admitting the desirability of eliminating Negro group headquarters, he concluded that complete elimination would "subject the War Department to a justifiable accusation of discrimination."

[49] For an example of the tactical use of the plan as it affected the flexible attachment of Negro and white combat units under Negro or white group headquarters, see After Action Reports, 333d Field Artillery Group, FAGP–333, and After Action Reports, VIII Corps Artillery, 208–33.4, in Operations Reports, Historical Records Section, WD Records Branch, AGO.

[50] AGF ltr to CGs, 24 Jan 44, sub: Administrative Functioning of T/O Orgns. 320.2/7005.

Chemical, military police, and signal units were not formed in groups, because ground operations did not require a massing of these organizations. The flexible attachment of groups to brigades was limited in practice to combat units, principally to antiaircraft organizations. In medical, ordnance, and quartermaster organizations separate companies were attached to battalions in the same manner as in the attachment of battalions to groups. In the combat arms and in the chemical, engineer, military police, and signal branches, companies remained organic in battalions.[51]

Enlargement of Group and Brigade Headquarters

The group and brigade headquarters provided for by the general reorganization of 21 July 1943 were intended by Army Ground Forces to be primarily tactical organizations; but like the corps these organizations, particularly the group, in actual practice manifested a chronic tendency toward administration. This tendency sprang mainly from the unwillingness of higher commanders to bypass the brigade and the group in dealing with battalions.[52]

When the Antiaircraft Command in early 1944 asked for enlargement of the group headquarters to meet administrative demands, General McNair personally wrote a directive "to educate higher commanders and group commanders" in the appropriate functions of the group headquarters. The AGF Commanding General admitted the responsibility of the group for the administrative efficiency of attached units but stated that this was to be achieved by instruction and by correction of faults. "The group commander and his staff should devote their time and energy to the troops," he added, "and should be freed to the utmost from routine administrative duties." [53]

General McNair's admonition may have brought improvement for a time, but, as the months passed, groups, and to a lesser extent brigades, found themselves burdened with an increasing load of administrative and supply functions. Group commanders seemed unable to avoid entanglement in the mass of paper produced by such activities as the processing of replacements and the distribution

[51] (1) Compilation, "AGF." AGF G–3 Mob Div files. (2) Interviews with AGF Special Staff heads, Jan 44.

[52] (1) AGF M/S, CG to G–1, 10 Jan 44, sub: Request for Add T/O Adm Pers for AA Gp. 320.2/7005. (2) Penciled notes [undated] of CofS on AGF ltr (R) (draft) to CGs, 20 Mar 45, sub: Asgmt and Atchmt of AGF Units. 321/78 (R).

[53] AGF ltr to CGs, 24 Jan 44, sub: Adm Functioning of T/O Orgns, and accompanying papers. 320.2/7005.

of supplies sent from higher headquarters.[54] In theaters of operations there was a similar tendency of group commanders to become entangled in administrative routine. In August 1944 the War Department, noting that "recent reports from observers in the Zone of Interior and the theaters indicate that . . . [brigade and group] headquarters are required to perform administrative functions," directed the Army Ground Forces and the Army Service Forces to restudy Tables of Organization and Equipment and other pertinent publications with a view to providing adequate administrative and supply personnel.[55]

In reply to the War Department, Army Ground Forces expressed opposition to the addition of personnel for administrative functions to groups and brigades but stated that, if enlargement of these headquarters were decided upon by the War Department, an administrative staff should be added as follows:

1. S–1 Section:
   - 1 Captain, Adjutant and S–1
   - 1 Master Sergeant (Sergeant Major)
   - 1 Clerk-typist, T/4
   - 1 Stenographer, T/3
2. S–4 Section:
   - 1 Captain, Assistant S–4
   - 1 Clerk, record, T/4
   - 1 Clerk-typist, T/4

The reply of Army Ground Forces stated further that a total of 906 captains and 2,305 enlisted men would be required for enlarging brigade and group headquarters under AGF control.[56]

The War Department did not consider favorably the AGF nonconcurrence in the proposal to enlarge group and brigade headquarters for administrative functions. It directed the immediate revision of Tables of Organization and Equipment to provide the additional staff outlined in the AGF memorandum.[57]

In the final months of 1944 and the early months of 1945, new Tables of Organization were published for all brigades and groups under AGF control. In most cases the revision provided for the addition of an administrative and supply section, consisting of an officer who was to be both adjutant and S–1, an

[54] Statement of Lt Col R. T. Jones, AGF Rqmts Sec, to AGF Hist Off, 10 May 45.

[55] WD memo (S), G–3 for CGs AGF and ASF, 9 Aug 44, sub: Inclusion of Adm and Sup Functions in Brig and Gp Hq. AGF Rqmts Sec files, 320.3/A (S).

[56] AGF memo (S) for CofS USA, 13 Sep 44, sub and location as in n. 55.

[57] WD memo (S), G–3 for CG AGF, 14 Sep 44, sub and location as in n. 55.

S–4, an assistant S–4, and from five to eight enlisted men, to the brigade and group headquarters.[58]

This modification did not contemplate placing administrative duties in the group or brigade to anything like the same extent as in the regiment. The group S–4, for example, was "to plan for, process papers, and supervise [but not physically handle] . . . supplies, maintenance of equipment, salvage, . . . evacuation of personnel, and traffic control." The duties of the S–1 were likewise mainly of a planning and supervisory character.[59] In short, the group remained, in the AGF view at least, predominantly a tactical organization with administration restricted largely to supervisory and processing functions of a general nature; the bulk of administration remained with the battalion.

The concept of the group as a predominantly tactical organization, made up of self-sustaining and easily removable parts, was not as firmly held by the War Department as by the Army Ground Forces. This was attributable in part, it seems, to differing reactions of the two headquarters to overseas opposition to the group, particularly the artillery group. An observer in the Southwest Pacific Theater wrote in February 1945 as follows:[60]

> Group Headquarters exercises no administrative control, but from administrative control stems uniformity in training. The term "flexibility" as applied to the separate battalion organization can frequently be translated "confusion." The indications are that the desirability of a return to the corps field artillery brigade and to regimental organization within the corps brigade is under consideration.

Earlier in 1944 Maj. Gen. John A. Crane, Chief of Artillery, Allied Forces Headquarters, had written in the *Military Review* as follows:[61]

> Separate battalions and separate group headquarters are a nuisance. They work under a decided handicap and constitute an uncoordinated mass of administrative chaff in an otherwise well-organized system. . . . There is no need whatsoever to break up organic corps artillery into separate battalions and separate headquarters like headless bodies and bodyless heads.

General Crane was also critical of the effect on morale and discipline of substituting the group for the regiment:[62]

[58] Statement of following offs of AGF Rqmts Sec to AGF Hist Off, 10 May 45: Lt Col W. V. Hungerford, Maj N. R. Richardson, Lt Col E. B. Hall, Maj M. T. Edmonds, Maj I. F. Belser, and Lt Col R. T. Jones.

[59] AGF memo (S) for CofS USA, 13 Sep 44, sub: Inclusion of Adm and Sup Functions in Brig and Gp Hq, and accompanying papers. AGF Rqmts Sec files, 320.3/A (S).

[60] AGF Obsrs SWPA Rpt (S) B–211, 11 Feb 45, sub: FA in the Leyte Campaign, 20 Oct–31 Dec 44. 314.7 (AGF Hist).

[61] Maj Gen J. A. Crane, "What Makes Our Army," *Military Review*, XXIV (September 1944), pp. 3–7.

[62] Personal ltr of Maj Gen J. A. Crane to Gen McNair, 22 May 44. McNair Correspondence.

A great letdown is beginning to manifest itself in matters of an administrative nature, sanitation, personal appearance, discipline, etc. It seems to be due to a lack of any feeling of loyalty to the group commander. He comes around to inspect. He finds something wrong. The troops say, "He don't know what we have been through, anyhow we will probably only be with him a week longer so we should worry . . . ."

General McNair apparently thought that much of the criticism of the group was due to its newness, and that as commanders became accustomed to it their aversion would subside. In reply to General Crane's comments he observed: "Flexibility is the big object of the present organization. Admittedly the loss of the old regimental traditions is regrettable, but I feel not a dominant consideration." General McNair went on to state that he would not oppose recommendations for change based on war experience.[63] His attitude in the summer of 1944, when he left the Army Ground Forces, was one of wait and see. His successors shared this view and on V-E Day the opinion still prevailed at Headquarters, Army Ground Forces, that evidence from overseas was not such as to warrant any considerable modification of the original functions of the group.[64]

As early as August 1944 sentiment in the War Department, reacting more positively to adverse reports from the theaters on discipline and morale in the group, had come to favor a change in its organization and function. After conferences with representatives of the Army Ground Forces and the Army Service Forces, the War Department in November 1944 issued a circular stating that "normally three or four battalions . . . will be *assigned* to a group, and that additional battalions might be attached as required." Furthermore, the group was redefined as "an *administrative* and tactical unit." [65]

Headquarters, Army Ground Forces, interpreting the provision for assignment of units to groups as optional, and deeming attachment preferable to assignment for both the training and the shipment of the group and its elements, elected to continue the existing scheme of flexible organization.[66]

When the functions of the group were defined in July 1943, the attachment of groups to headquarters and headquarters detachments, special troops, was forbidden. This prohibition sprang from the fact that at that time no group head-

[63] Personal ltr of Gen McNair to Maj Gen J. A. Crane, 29 May 44. McNair Correspondence.

[64] Statement of Col A. L. Harding, AGF G–3 Sec, to AGF Hist Off, 10 May 45.

[65] (1) Cir 439, WD, 14 Nov 44. Italics author's. (2) M/R attached to WD memo WDGCT 320.3 (31 Oct 44) for TAG, 31 Oct 44, sub: Change to WD Cir 256, 1943. Italics author's. AGO Records, 322 (12 Oct 43), case 2.

[66] (1) AGF ltr (R) to comdrs concerned, 20 Mar 45, sub: Asgmt and Atchmt of AGF Units. With related papers. 321/78 (R). (2) Statement of Col A. L. Harding to AGF Hist Off, 10 May 45.

quarters for service units had been activated in the Army Ground Forces and that planners were thinking solely in terms of combat units which were to be assigned exclusively to corps. Extension of the group organization to service units, which normally were assigned to armies, made it only common sense to provide a link between the group and the army's subagency, the headquarters and headquarters detachment, special troops. This arrangement was authorized in July 1944. In March 1945 the Army Ground Forces gave subordinate commanders authority, in exceptional cases where more effective training supervision was indicated, to attach combat-type group headquarters to headquarters and headquarters detachments, special troops.[67]

The Issue of Concentration in Training Centers

While the practice of flexible grouping was being extended, the question of concentrating service units of the same branch for training came up for discussion at Headquarters, Army Ground Forces. It was generally admitted that concentration of like units had proved desirable and practicable in antiaircraft, armored, and tank destroyer organizations. Cognizance was taken of the fact that Services of Supply had adopted the training center idea on a large scale. The Second Army had assembled a considerable number of signal units at Camp Crowder, and the Third Army had grouped certain medical organizations at Fort Sam Houston. Some circles of Army Ground Forces, particularly at army headquarters, felt rather strongly that the principle of concentration was sound and that training conditions required its extension to all the services.[68]

The question was brought to the attention of Headquarters, Army Ground Forces, in September 1942 by a request of the Third Army to adjust station assignments in such a way as to effect a widespread concentration of units by branch for basic and technical training. In response Army Ground Forces, while admitting the desirability of grouping some types of units, declined to authorize general application of the practice.[69] When the Third Army asked permission in

[67] (1) *Ibid.* (2) AGF ltr (R) to CGs, 13 Jul 44, sub: Functioning of Med, Ord, and QM Gp Hq Dets. 320.2/234 (R). (3) AGF ltr (R) to CGs, 20 Mar 45, sub: Asgmt and Atchmt of AGF Units. 321/78 (R).

[68] (1) AGF memo, Ord to G–3, 14 Jan 43, sub: Concentration of Units for Tng. (2) M/S of Gen McNair for G–3 AGF, 8 Jan 43, sub as in (1). Both in 353/2129. (3) Third Army ltr AG 320.2 (Gen) GNMCD–2 to CG AGF, 14 Sep 42, sub: Concentration of Serv Units by Branches. 322.11/253 (Third Army). (4) Second Army ltr 370.5–405 (GNMBF) to CG AGF, 31 Dec 42, sub: Transfer of Chemical Units. 353/2129.

[69] Third Army ltr AG 320.2 (Gen) GNMCD–2 to CG AGF, 14 Sep 42, and AGF 1st ind thereto, 30 Sep 42, sub: Concentration of Serv Units by Branches. 322.11/253 (Third Army).

November to transfer some engineer units from Camp Maxey to Camp Swift on the ground that the latter afforded better training facilities for the type of units concerned, the request was disapproved.[70] But this action did not represent the unanimous opinion of Headquarters, Army Ground Forces; both the engineer officer and G–4 favored approving the request.[71]

The issue of concentration was raised again on 31 December 1942 when the Second Army sought authority to transfer thirteen chemical units to Camps Rucker and McCain with a view to facilitating their training. After a canvass of the staff sections on the general subject of concentration of units for training, the Second Army's request was disapproved. In the round robin which preceded this action, the engineer and the signal officers and G–1 registered approval of the practice of grouping service organizations for basic and unit training.[72]

Advocates of concentration supported their position with the following arguments: (1) Concentration gave new units the opportunity to profit from the counsel and example of old units of the same type. (2) It made possible the pooling of equipment and instructional personnel and thus mitigated the greatest obstacles to training. (3) The economy achieved by pooling permitted the release of equipment to alerted units. (4) Branch grouping facilitated and improved supervision by higher headquarters. An army headquarters staff could visit quartermaster units concentrated at two or three stations more frequently, and with far less expenditure of time and travel, than it could the same number of units dispersed over the army's entire area of jurisdiction; moreover, the headquarters, special troops, at the two or three centers could be staffed completely with expert quartermaster personnel, thus providing vitally needed specialist supervision.[73]

The principal argument of those who opposed large-scale concentration of service units was that such a practice created an unnatural situation. They held that the *raison d'etre* of Army Ground Forces service units was the support of

[70] Third Army ltr AG 370.5 Engrs–GNMCR to CG AGF, 19 Nov 42, and AGF 1st ind, 10 Dec 42, sub: Concentration of Serv Units by Branches. 370.5/407 (Engrs).

[71] AGF M/Ss, Engr and G–4 for CofS, 2 and 4 Dec 42, respectively, sub: Concentration of Serv Units by Branches. 370.5/407 (Engrs).

[72] (1) Second Army ltr AG 370.5–405 (GNMBF) to CG AGF, 31 Dec 42, sub: Transfer of Cml Units. (2) See M/Ss by heads of the various staff secs during Jan 43. All in 353/2129.

[73] (1) *Ibid.* (2) AGF M/S (S), G–1 to Plans, 16 Dec 42, sub: Activation of Nondiv Units. 320.2/283 (S). (3) AGF M/S, Engr and G–4 to CofS, 2 and 4 Dec 42, respectively, sub: Concentration of Serv Units by Branches. 370.5/407 (Engrs). (4) Statement of Col J. W. Younger, AGF QM, to AGF Hist Off, 25 Jan 44.

combat organizations. These units should, therefore, have from the very beginning as close an association as possible with the fighting elements which they were designed to service. At the very earliest opportunity, the argument continued, ordnance companies should begin to service weapons of infantry and artillery units near them; quartermaster companies should likewise begin to perform subsistence and sanitary functions for combat troops; chemical units should provide smoke screens for them; and medical organizations should have infantry soldiers on whom to practice first aid and evacuation.[74] Another objection to concentration was that it might deprive unit commanders of the responsibility for training the troops whom later they were to lead in battle.[75]

Proponents of concentration countered this argument with the statement that they advocated grouping only during the first stages of training, that during this period service units were not far enough advanced "to support anything," and that normal relations with combat organizations could be established during combined training, after graduation from the primary courses offered by the centers. G–1, Army Ground Forces, emphasized that concentration had been approved for antiaircraft, armored, and tank destroyer elements, and contended that "if the idea is sound for these three, it is certainly sound for nondivisional [service] units." [76]

It was General McNair who finally settled the discussion. He took the position that large-scale concentration could be justified only in instances where training was so highly specialized that technical considerations outweighed the value of normal association. This, he believed, was the case in antiaircraft, armored, tank destroyer, and certain types of service units and also with units extremely short of training equipment.[77]

The ultimate of concentration for service units that General McNair favored was the arrangement known as the "sponsor" or "buddy" system.[78] In its original and most widely applied form, this system meant the stationing of a new unit near an older one of the same type, in order that the latter might share with the former its equipment, its instructional staff, and its experience. A modification provided for the grouping of three units as "buddies"—the first in an early stage

[74] (1) M/S of Gen McNair for CofS AGF, 8 Oct 42, sub: Concentration of Units for Tng. (2) AGF ltr to CGs, 31 Jan 43, sub as in (1). Both in 353/2129.

[75] Memo of Col John C. Oakes for G–3 AGF, 1 Jun 43, sub: Visit to Maneuvers and to Cp Hood, Tex, May 27–30, 1943. AGF G–3 Tng Sec files, 333.1 (93d Div).

[76] AGF M/S (S), G–1 to Plans, 16 Dec 42, sub: Activation of Nondiv Units. 320.2/283 (S).

[77] (1) AGF M/S, Gen McNair to CofS, 8 Oct 42, sub: Concentration of Units for Tng. (2) AGF M/S, Gen McNair to G–3, 8 Jan 43, sub as in (1). Both in 353/2129.

[78] (1) See n. 77 (2). (2) AGF M/S (S), Gen McNair to CofS, 28 Dec 42, sub as in n. 77. 320.2/283 (S).

of training, the second in an intermediate stage, and the third in an advanced stage. The "buddy" system was first used by ordnance units, and during 1942 it was also employed on a large scale for quartermaster, signal, and engineer units.[79]

Collaboration with Army Service Forces

In 1944–45 there was a marked trend toward closer collaboration of the Army Ground Forces and the Army Service Forces in matters pertaining to the training of service units. Harmony between the two commands was promoted by the War Department's adoption in January 1944 of the practice of assigning types of service units specifically to one command or the other, instead of to both, for activation and training. Personalities constituted another factor in closer cooperation between the Army Ground Forces and the Army Service Forces. Turnover in each of the headquarters resulted, in most cases, in the arrival in key positions of officers who proved to be congenial with their opposites in the other. Closer collaboration was evidenced by the sending of various AGF units to ASF installations for advanced functional training. In 1944 AGF chemical depot companies were sent to the Chemical Warfare Depot at Huntsville, Ala., for advanced on-the-job training; AGF signal depot companies and signal repair companies to ASF depots at Sacramento, Calif., Holabird, Md., San Antonio, Tex., Atlanta, Ga., and Lexington, Ky.; AGF engineer depot companies to the ASF depots at Memphis, Tenn., and Ogden, Utah; AGF engineer maintenance companies to ASF equipment repair shops at Kearney, Neb., and Salina, Kan.; and AGF quartermaster depot companies to various ASF depots, including those at Charlotte, N. C., Memphis, Tenn., and New Cumberland, Pa.[80]

AGF control over units in training in ASF installations varied considerably in the different branches. Quartermaster depot companies sent from Camp Shelby

[79] Statement of Lt Col E. J. Gibson, Ord AGF, to AGF Hist Off, 27 Jan 44.

[80] This paragraph is based on interviews with various officers in AGF Special Staff sections in April–May 1945. This source will be cited hereafter as "Interviews with AGF staff officers." The officers interviewed and the dates of interviews are as follows:

Lt Col G. J. Collins	Med Sec	3 Apr 45
Maj L. R. Watson	Engr Sec	3 Apr 45
Col J. B. Hughes	Engr Off	28 Apr 45
Col O. K. Sadtler	Sig Off	1 May 45
Col N. C. Snyder	Ex O, Sig Sec	1 May 45
Maj G. T. Petersen	Ord Sec	2–4 May 45
W/O A. L. Greno	Ord Sec	2–4 May 45
Col H. Edward	QM Off	3 May 45
Maj G. R. Hill	QM Sec	3 May 45

230-171 O - 66 - 35

to Memphis for functional training encamped in a park near the ASF depot. During the day the men went to the depot in such numbers as ASF authorities could conveniently employ in the handling of supplies. At night they returned to their camp. While not working at the depot the men engaged in unit training under their own officers.[81]

While at ASF installations, AGF signal units were placed on a detached service basis. They followed training programs which had been prepared by ASF authorities but submitted to the Army Ground Forces for information and comment. Unit commanders, under supervision of the depot commander, were responsible for basic military training and physical conditioning of their men during the period of detached service.[82] AGF officers, accompanied usually by their opposites in the Army Service Forces, made occasional visits of inspection to personnel in training at ASF installations.[83]

The length of the functional training period varied with circumstances. Engineer units were usually attached to ASF depots for a period of thirty days.[84] In the case of signal units an attempt was made to provide a tour of duty sufficient to permit 75 percent of the specialists to obtain six weeks' training in their duties, but urgency of overseas requirements usually prevented attainment of this goal.[85]

A glimpse of the operation of the collaborative plan, as well as of the reaction of a unit commander to its effectiveness, is given by the following report covering training of the 728th Engineer Depot Company at the ASF depot at Memphis, Tenn.:[86]

This organization is now in its fourth and final week of training in the Engineer Section of this Depot and the following is submitted as statement of training accomplished.

As a result of training in the administrative section it has been possible for our officers and non-commissioned officers to work out a chart for the flow of paper work as we expect it to be done in the field, and each man can see just where his job fits in.

The entire personnel has learned from shipping and receiving sections the two all important questions: How much on hand and where is it? This was done by assigning each enlisted man to a civilian employee doing the same job the enlisted man held under the table

[81] Statement of Col H. Edward, AGF QM, to AGF Hist Off, 3 May 45.

[82] (1) Statement of Col O. K. Sadtler, AGF Sig Off, to AGF Hist Off, 1 May 45. (2) AGF 1st ind, 27 Nov 44, on memo of CSigO for CG ASF, 21 Nov 44, sub: Tng Dir for Sig Dep Cos. 353.01/150.

[83] Interviews with AGF staff officers.

[84] Statement of Col J. B. Hughes, AGF Engr Off, to AGF Hist Off, 28 Apr 45.

[85] Statement of Col N. C. Snyder, AGF Sig Sec, to AGF Hist Off, 10 Jan 45.

[86] 728th Engr Dep Co memo for Engr Sup Off, ASF Dep, Memphis, Tenn, 14 Aug 44, sub: Memo, attached to AGF ltr to CG, XXII Corps, 2 Sep 44, sub: Tng of Engr Dep Cos at ASF Deps. 353/216 (Engr).

of organization. Changes were made from time to time in order to place our men in the job most suited to them. . . .

Not only did the men get training in their own jobs but they were switched around so as to be able to do any assigned work if called upon. . . .

A highlight of the training program has been the talks by officers of the Depot to the officers and non-commissioned officers of this organization. These officers operated depots in all the major Theaters of Operation and brought to us the problems we may encounter and how they should be overcome, giving us the points to stress while we are still training.

The training program was carried on by two methods used for two weeks each. The first method was to divide the company into groups and the groups into teams according to our table of organization. Groups were sent to various sections of the depot and rotated. For the second period of two weeks entire platoons were sent to the same sections and rotated. The second method was preferred, since the officers and non-commissioned officers could instruct their own men and change them to proper T/O positions. Also the men taught each other and learned how much they could depend on each other under pressure. Every opportunity was given to each man to show initiative in his own job and leaders were thereby selected.

Immediately upon arrival here the men were told that the facilities for training were available here, and what they got out of the training depended upon how they applied themselves to their assignments. With few exceptions the interest has been keen and the enthusiasm high.

Critiques were held daily at which time all were given the opportunity to ask questions and express their opinions of the day's operations. A list of questions was given the men and they brought back the answers the next day. . . .

Reactions of Special Staff section chiefs at Headquarters, Army Ground Forces, were also very favorable. The AGF engineer officer stated in May 1945: "Cooperation has been splendid. This is the only way that Ground units can get plenty of materiel on which to work." [87] The AGF signal officer reported: "We had long realized that a person who had had basic and unit training in AGF and specialist training or a service school was not a completely trained person. . . . Advanced on-the-job training at ASF Depots has worked out very satisfactorily." [88]

Service rendered to ASF depots by AGF units in the course of their functional training was a secondary consideration, but in some instances it seems to have been notable. In June 1944 the commanding officer of the ASF depot at Ogden, Utah, from which one AGF engineer unit had just been graduated, requested immediate assignment of another unit to take its place. In explanation of this request he wrote:[89]

[87] Statement of Col J. B. Hughes to AGF Hist Off, 28 Apr 45.

[88] Statement of Col O. K. Sadtler to AGF Hist Off, 1 May 45.

[89] Ltr ASF Dep, Ogden, Utah, to CofEngrs USA, 22 Sep 44, sub: Asgmt of Engr Dep Cos. 353/221 (Engr).

The labor situation in this area is critical. Facilities exist at this depot for quartering a depot company and its value to the Engineer Section of the Depot is unquestioned . . . since this depot is the west coast key and reserve depot for engineer supplies, the approaching peak activities connected with supply for the Japanese campaign place a maximum load upon the depot. It is urgently recommended that a depot company be transferred to this depot for training in the immediate future and that such a company be left at this depot until ordered overseas.

Another instance of closer cooperation between the Army Ground Forces and the Army Service Forces in 1944 was the borrowing of ASF officers to assist in AGF maintenance inspections. Representatives of the Chief of Ordnance and the Quartermaster General were regularly included in the maintenance inspection team which Headquarters, Army Ground Forces, kept in the field a large portion of the time throughout 1944 and the early months of 1945. Requests for loan of the ASF officers arose primarily from the fact that the AGF ordnance and quartermaster officers did not have enough assistants to permit sending their own personnel. The ASF officers in the inspections concerned themselves primarily with technical matters; they did not inspect or evaluate training as such. Copies of their reports were sent both to their chiefs in the Army Service Forces and to Headquarters, Army Ground Forces.[90]

Occasionally ASF officers were borrowed by Special Staff sections of the Army Ground Forces to assist in various other matters that were primarily technical in character. In one case, for example, the AGF engineer officer requested a representative of the Chief of Engineers to assist in the inspection of two engineer camouflage companies, one of which had to be inactivated. The two units were put through their paces before the AGF and ASF representatives, and on the basis of this performance the AGF officer, relying on the advice of his ASF opposite as to technical matters, decided which was to be inactivated.[91]

The trend toward closer cooperation in 1944 was most marked in matters pertaining to training literature and other publications. In May 1945 the AGF quartermaster officer stated:[92]

For the past year all technical and training literature issued by the office of the Quartermaster General has been sent to the AGF Quartermaster for review prior to publication, and vice versa. Material sent to us for criticism and comment included MTP's, courses of instruction at Quartermaster schools, including officer candidate schools, specialist courses, and even

[90] Statements of AGF QM Off, 3 May 45, and Maj G. T. Petersen, AGF Ord Sec, 2 May 45, to AGF Hist Off.

[91] Statement of Maj L. R. Watson, AGF Engr Sec, to AGF Hist Off, 21 May 45.

[92] Statement of AGF QM Off to AGF Hist Off, 3 May 45.

posters on materiel conservation. There is a full and free exchange of opinion on every publication put out by either the Quartermaster General or the AGF Quartermaster. This works to the mutual advantage of both. We benefit particularly from the advice of their specialists. . . .

The Quartermaster General passes on to us reports of all observers sent out by him to the theaters. Moreover, we are invited over to talk with some of the observers personally so that we may share the benefits of their observations.

Beginning in the summer of 1944, the Chief Signal Officer submitted to the AGF signal officer drafts of proposed signal MTP's for comment and suggestion. The AGF signal officer was also consulted about revisions of courses in ASF signal schools attended by AGF personnel.[93]

The trend toward closer cooperation in 1944 was not, indeed, universal and steady; in some instances it was only faint, and in others, partial. One AGF section chief, for example, while reporting closer collaboration in the use of ASF facilities for advanced functional training, complained of increased difficulty in 1944 in gaining the admission of specialists to service schools in the required numbers because of a tendency of the branch chief to give preference to ASF personnel in the allotment of quotas.[94] Moreover, collaborative action sometimes originated on a secondary level—between the AGF section chief and his opposite in the Army Service Forces—and moved from there upward. In one instance the plan to train AGF units at ASF installations, while strongly favored by the AGF section chief and the branch chief in the Army Service Forces, was opposed initially by their superiors. The two section chiefs, by informal collaboration, were able eventually to generate enough pressure to overcome opposition and secure adoption of the plan.[95]

Divergence of opinion among the Special Staff sections as to the extent of collaboration with chiefs of the services in the training of ground personnel is well illustrated by recommendations made prior to V-E Day by the AGF ordnance officer and the AGF signal officer. The former, believing that the Army Service Forces was better equipped than the Army Ground Forces for the training of individual specialists, recommended that after V-E Day the Army Service Forces maintain a pool of 1,800 ordnance specialists, trained by the Army Service Forces, for use as fillers and replacements in Ground Force units.[96] The

[93] Statement of AGF Sig Off to AGF Hist Off, 1 May 45.

[94] (1) Statement of Col J. B. Hughes to AGF Hist Off, 28 Apr 45. (2) AGF M/S, Engr to G-3 Tng Div, 27 May 44, sub: Tng in Parts Sup Dep Procedure. 353/211 (Engr).

[95] Statement of AGF Sig Off to AGF Hist Off, 1 May 45.

[96] Statement of Maj G. T. Petersen, AGF Ord Sec, to AGF Hist Off, 2 May 45.

AGF signal officer, on the other hand, believing that "there is a distinct difference in theoretical training standards between Ground, Air and Service Force signal personnel," advocated that the Army Ground Forces be no longer required to look to the Army Service Forces for training of signal specialists and replacements, but that it establish schools and replacement training centers of its own for training of such personnel.[97]

The weight of sentiment in the Army Ground Forces not only by V-E Day but also throughout the war seemed to favor the position stated by the AGF signal officer. The principal argument for this position was that AGF personnel required a distinct type of training to fit them properly for service in ground units, and that the Army Service Forces tended to think first of its own needs in training and allocating personnel trained in ASF installations. On one point the staff of Headquarters, Army Ground Forces, seems to have been nearly unanimous: namely, that policy should be revised to give the Army Ground Forces control of ground-trained personnel returning from overseas. Complaint was frequent and bitter in AGF headquarters that the Army Service Forces used its control of the processing of individual returnees to screen out the best for its own use and thus leave the dregs for AGF organizations.[98]

[97] AGF M/S, Sig Sec to CofS, 8 Sep 44, sub: Tng Agencies. 314.7 (AGF Hist).

[98] Interviews with AGF staff officers.

III. The Development of the Training Program

Status of the Training Program in 1942

At the creation of Army Ground Forces, nondivisional units engaged in basic training were guided by Mobilization Training Programs (MTP's) prepared during the GHQ period by chiefs of the appropriate arms or services. Those units in advanced stages of training had no detailed charts to follow, since MTP's in most cases did not extend beyond the basic period. During advanced training, units followed weekly schedules drawn up by their own commanders in accordance with directives of a very general nature issued by higher headquarters.[1]

The final weeks of 1942 and the early months of 1943 saw important changes in the training program of nondivisional organizations. The AGF Training Directive effective 1 November 1942 contained general instructions for each major category of spare parts. The sections devoted to artillery indicated what training programs were to be followed, what tests were to be taken, and what subjects were to be stressed. Appropriate directives along the same lines were laid down in the paragraphs covering tank destroyer and cavalry units. Instructions for engineer, medical, ordnance, quartermaster, signal, and chemical units varied somewhat, but in most cases they designated the MTP's to be followed, the subjects to be emphasized, and the objectives to be sought.[2]

Revision of MTP's and Preparation of UTP's

The issuance of the new training directive gave impetus to a movement already under way to revise MTP's and to prepare Unit Training Programs (UTP's). MTP's for service units were in most instances obsolete, lacking in detail, and insufficiently adapted to the needs of units destined to function in close association with combat organizations. Deficiencies observed in combined training and in the theaters in the latter part of 1942 focused attention sharply on the fact that no UTP's had ever been prepared for the guidance of service units.[3]

[1] This statement is based on interviews by the AGF Historical Officer with Special Staff heads and various members of the AGF G–3 Section, January 1944.

[2] AGF ltr to CGs, 19 Oct 42, sub: Tng Dir Effective November 1, 1942. 353/52 (Tng Dir).

[3] Interviews with AGF Special Staff heads, Jan 44. 314.7 (AGF Hist).

Early in 1943 Special Staff sections were directed to revise MTP's covering the individual training period and to prepare UTP's, showing the subjects to be covered, the references to be used, and the hours to be devoted to each subject.[4] The overhauling of MTP's proceeded more rapidly than the drawing up of UTP's. By the autumn of 1943, revision of MTP's for all the services except the Medical Corps had been completed. A UTP for signal units was published on 12 May 1943, but its usefulness was impaired by failure to provide subject schedules. In August 1943 programs for the unit training of engineer and quartermaster organizations were published, and in September a comprehensive UTP was issued by the AGF Ordnance Section. Early in 1944 a UTP was prepared for the guidance of motorized chemical battalions. The Medical Section in January 1944 drafted a directive outlining in general terms a unit training schedule for ground medical organizations.[5]

These modifications of the training schedules of service organizations were paralleled by similar changes in the programs of the combat arms. In January 1943 a thoroughgoing revision of both the basic and the unit phases of the Field Artillery training program was completed. The new program was notable for the detail with which it broke down subjects scheduled for the unit training period.[6] In July 1943 the Antiaircraft Command, using the Field Artillery schedule as a model, worked out a new training program for units under its jurisdiction. All organizations adjusted their programs in 1943 to accommodate provisions in AGF directives calling for greater stress on field exercises, combat firing, and physical and mental conditioning for battle.

The most important purpose served by the new MTP's and UTP's in both service and combat categories was a closer adaptation of training to requirements of modern combat as revealed by battle experience. Revised schedules provided greater emphasis and more specific coverage for such battle-proved subjects as night fighting, patrolling, security, reconnaissance, dispersion, concealment, camouflage, mines, booby traps, first aid, antitank protection, discipline, and physical hardening.[7] The Unit Training Programs filled a vital and long-standing

[4] (1) AGF memo, G–3 for CofS, 23 Jan 43, sub: Tng Program for Serv Units. 461/43 (MTP). (2) AGF M/S, G–4 to CofS, 5 Feb 43, sub: Tng Program for Serv Units. AGF G–3 Sec files, 353/43 (Tng, Gen).

[5] Interviews with AGF Special Staff heads, Jan 44.

[6] (1) AGF M/S, G–3 to Gen McNair, 15 Jan 43, sub: FA UTP. 353/252 (FA). (2) Ltr of Gen McNair to CG R&SC, 16 Jan 43, sub: FA Tng Program. 353/252 (FA).

[7] (1) Interviews of AGF Hist Off with AGF Special Staff heads and members of AGF G–3 Sec, Jan 44. (2) AGF ltr to CGs, 7 Jun 43, sub: Supplement to Tng Dir Effective 1 Nov 42. 353/52 (Tng Dir).

need for detailed and specific guidance of small-unit commanders, many of whom were lacking in military background and experience.

With respect to combined training, the situation in 1943 was less satisfactory than with basic and unit training. During 1943 the demands of theater commanders for nondivisional units, particularly for service units, continued to be so great that many were dispatched overseas without benefit of combined training. Others were deprived of this training by the failure of army, corps, and other subordinate commanders to arrange combined-arms exercises in such a way as to accommodate the maximum number of nondivisional units. On 20 January 1944 Headquarters, Army Ground Forces, sent a letter to subordinate commands urging them to provide a minimum of three weeks' field training for all nondivisional units. Participation in maneuvers was advocated as the most desirable form of field training, but, if circumstances made this impracticable, units were to function with divisions in advanced tactical exercises known as the "D" series or, as a last resort, to operate under field conditions by themselves.[8] The dwindling number of divisions yet to be trained, together with the reduction in the scope of combined training which came with the closing of the California–Arizona Maneuver Area, made the prospects for participation of supporting units in realistic field exercises in 1944 unpromising in the extreme.

Changes in MTP's and UTP's in 1944 and 1945 were of a minor nature, consisting mainly in bringing references up to date and adapting time allotments to the accelerated program of training. When V-E Day came only the Quartermaster Section had within the past fifteen months completely revised applicable MTP's and UTP's, and modifications were mainly of a routine character. The Ordnance, Signal, and Engineer Sections were in the process of bringing their training programs up to date, and the Medical Section was engaged in adapting Army Service Forces MTP's to AGF use. In view of the small number of units being activated in the spring of 1945, revision of MTP's was considered secondary in importance to preparation of redeployment training programs.[9]

Modification of Tests

The summer and fall of 1943 witnessed an attempt to improve the quality of nondivisional training through the adoption of new and improved tests[10] for field

[8] AGF ltr to CGs, 20 Jan 44, sub: Tng of Nondiv Combat and Serv Units. 353.01/102.

[9] Interviews with AGF staff officers.

[10] (1) AGF ltr to CGs, 29 Aug 43, sub: Revision of FA and TD Tests. (2) AGF ltr to CGs, 16 Aug 43, sub: Tng Dir Effective 1 Nov 42. Both in 353/52 (Tng Dir).

artillery battalions, tank destroyer battalions, and tank gunnery crews. Checking of combat intelligence training in all units was facilitated by comprehensive tests prepared in the G–2 Section of Headquarters, Army Ground Forces.[11]

Of considerably greater significance than these changes was the more extensive modification of the testing program in 1944. Early in that year tests, based on those prescribed for field artillery units, were for the first time published for antiaircraft automatic weapons, gun, and searchlight battalions. These tests, prepared by the Antiaircraft Command in close collaboration with Headquarters, Army Ground Forces, and given by the Antiaircraft Command testing teams, did much to improve the quality of antiaircraft training.[12] In August 1944 the Army Ground Forces published tests for checking the proficiency of antiaircraft gun battalions as reinforcing field artillery.[13] Later a similar test was completed for measuring the indirect fire proficiency of tank and tank destroyer battalions.[14]

In March 1944, firing tests for infantry battalions and cavalry squadrons were made more realistic, and in April Tank Destroyer Combat Firing and Tactical Proficiency Tests were revised to standardize firing proficiency for all types of weapons and generally to stiffen requirements for a passing score. In the summer and autumn of 1944 there were minor revisions of Infantry Platoon Combat Firing Tests, Antiaircraft Gun, Weapons, and Searchlight Battalion Tests, Field Artillery Tests, and Cavalry Reconnaissance Squadron Field and Platoon Combat Firing Tests.[15]

POM visits of The Inspector General in the early months of 1944 revealed many instances of service unit personnel being unable to perform their assigned duties in a satisfactory manner. This was found to be especially true of technical specialists. To remedy the situation, General McNair directed chiefs of the Special Staff sections to prepare appropriate tests for the checking of individuals and units in their technical specialties.[16]

Before the end of 1944 Military Occupational Specialty (MOS) Tests for the testing of individuals in their specialist functions had been prepared for all

[11] AGF ltr (R) to CGs, 26 Aug 43, sub: Combat Intel Tng Tests. 250.09/1 (R).

[12] (1) AGF ltr to CG AA Comd, 3 Dec 43, sub: Tests for AAA. With related papers. 353/52. (2) AGF ltr to CGs, 30 Jan 44, sub: Tng Dir Effective 1 Nov 42. With related papers. 353.01/107 (Tng Dir).

[13] AGF ltr to CGs, 1 Aug 44, sub: AGF Test for AA Gun Bns as Reinforcing FA. 353/52 (Tng Dir).

[14] AGF ltr to CGs, 10 Nov 44, sub: Indirect Fire Test for Tanks and TD Units. 353.4/230.

[15] The revised tests (and accompanying papers) are filed in 353.01/52 (Tng Dir).

[16] (1) AGF ltr (R) to CGs, 1 Apr 44, sub: Supervision of Tng of Sub Units. 353.204 (S). (2) AGF ltr to CGs, 27 Jul 44, sub: Tech Inspections of Serv Units. 353/2321.

the services in the Army Ground Forces. In some cases MOS Tests disseminated by the Army Ground Forces were adaptations of tests already in use in subordinate commands; in other instances they were modifications of tests prepared by chiefs of the services.[17]

MOS Tests usually consisted of two principal parts: (1) questions covering the character of the duties required of the individual; and (2) practical application of specialist techniques.[18] For example, the more theoretical portion of the test for MOS 017—Baker, prepared by the AGF Quartermaster Section, contained a question regarding the difference between field and garrison bread. The second and practical portion of the test required the baker, among other things, to operate the Model 1937 fire unit, obtaining the desired oven temperature and load. The Quartermaster and Medical Sections supplemented the MOS Tests with exercises designed to check the qualifications of units to perform their primary missions. For example, the unit test for a quartermaster gasoline supply company required the company to move under tactical conditions from an assembly point to a bivouac area, set up and operate a bulk reduction point and a distributing point, and operate truck convoys between these points. Similarly, the test for a medical collecting company required this unit to collect and transport casualties under tactical conditions. Because both MOS and Unit Tests were already in use in some of the subordinate commands, and in view of variations in local conditions and needs, the tests published by the Army Ground Forces were not made mandatory. The covering letter sent with the tests stated that they were designed "to supplement and not necessarily to replace" tests already in use.[19]

The testing program initiated by General McNair in 1944 produced a wider, more uniform, and more thorough checking of technical proficiency throughout the Army Ground Forces. The ultimate result was a decline in the number of "Not Ready" units reported by The Inspector General.[20]

[17] Interviews with AGF staff officers.

[18] AGF ltr to CGs, 27 Jul 44, sub: Tech Inspections of Serv Units. 353/2321.

[19] (1) Ltr cited in n. 18. (2) AGF ltr to CGs, 26 Oct 44, sub: QM Unit Tng Tests. 353/251 (QM).

[20] AGF units reported "Not Ready" by TIG, Jan 44–Jun 45, inclusive, by quarters, were as follows:

1944								*1945*			
1st Quarter		*2d Quarter*		*3d Quarter*		*4th Quarter*		*1st Quarter*		*2d Quarter*	
Units	*%*	*Units*	*%*	*Units*	*%*	*Units*	*%*	*Units*	*%*	*Units*	*%*
43	13	22	11	21	9	27	11	13	8	7	7

See: (1) AGF ltr (R) to CGs, 21 Jan 45, sub: Readiness of Units for Movement Overseas. 353/1257 (Read) (R). (2) AGF ltr (R) to CGs, 24 Apr 45, sub as in (1). 353/1447 (Read)(R). (3) AGF ltr (R) to CGs, 9 Jul 45, sub as in (1). 353/1541 (Read)(R).

Acceleration of the Training Program

While revision of tests was getting under way, the Army Ground Forces was compelled by urgent overseas demands to curtail the training cycle of non-divisional units. An accelerated schedule of training was published on 14 July 1944. The new arrangement grouped units in three categories according to the source of their fillers. Organizations receiving the bulk of their fillers from reception centers were allowed longer training periods than those which drew their personnel from the replacement training centers or units of other branches. Units made up of personnel from replacement training centers or organizations of the same branch as their own were allowed the shortest training period of all. The principal cut was in unit and combined training. Ordnance units, for example, under the old schedule were authorized to spend 14 weeks in individual training, 16 in unit training, and 8 in combined training; under the accelerated program the allotments for the three periods were, respectively, 14, 7, and 3 weeks for all except maintenance companies, which were permitted 6 additional weeks for unit training. Newly activated units and units that had been stripped were to initiate individual training as soon as they had attained 80 percent of authorized strength and had received 50 percent of their equipment. Units that were following old schedules were to adjust the remainder of their training time to the accelerated program.[21]

The accelerated program did not prescribe combined training for anti-aircraft and several types of service units, but directed them instead to devote three weeks of the unit period to training in the field. Units for which combined training was prescribed, but which for lack of opportunity had to forego this training, were directed to substitute an equivalent period of intensive unit training in the field. Provision was made for subordinate commanders in exceptional cases to request extension of the time allotted under the accelerated program.[22]

The accelerated training program created a serious difficulty in the schooling of specialists. Some types of signal, engineer, and other units were composed largely of personnel whose duties were so technical as to require them to attend service school courses of several weeks' duration. Getting these men to school without disrupting the training program and impairing the integrity of the unit had been a substantial problem under the old schedule. Curtailment of the training period made this problem more acute. Schooling was accomplished in many

[21] AGF ltr to CGs, 14 Jul 44, sub: Accelerated Tng of Nondiv Units. With enclosed chart. 353.01/124.

[22] *Ibid.*

instances only at the cost of having a majority of the personnel absent from the unit after completion of basic training.[23]

Conversion of Units and Adjustments in Training

During the period 1944–45 certain phases of the training of nondivisional units were substantially affected by changes made in the pattern of nondivisional strength to meet shifting requirements of overseas operations. The elements figuring most prominently in these adjustments were heavy field artillery, combat engineer, antiaircraft, tank destroyer, and quartermaster truck units.[24]

Heavy field artillery in particular was affected, experience in the Mediterranean Theater having demonstrated that heavy field artillery had a much more extensive role in modern warfare than was provided for in Troop Basis planning.[25] The number of heavy artillery battalions active in the Troop Basis jumped from 61 on 31 December 1943 to 116 on 30 June 1944 and 137 on 31 December 1944.[26] Similarly, revisions of mobilization planning based on theater experience provided for an increase in both engineer combat and heavy ponton battalions.[27] The trend toward heavier types of equipment and the increased stress on conservation and maintenance resulted in a sharp rise in the activation in 1944 of ordnance heavy maintenance and evacuation units.[28] The increase in quartermaster truck companies was no less marked.[29]

[23] Interviews with AGF staff officers.

[24] For a fuller account of developments outlined in this section see the following studies in *The Organization of Ground Combat Troops:* "Ground Forces in the Army, December 1941–April 1945: A Statistical Study"; "Mobilization of the Ground Army"; and "Organization and Training of New Ground Combat Elements."

[25] This view had long been advocated by Headquarters, Army Ground Forces.

[26] See the table in "Ground Forces in the Army, December 1941–April 1945: A Statistical Study," in *The Organization of Ground Combat Troops.*

[27] On 31 December 1943 active engineer combat and heavy ponton battalions numbered 166; on 30 June 1944 there were 212; and six months later, 240. (See the table cited in n. 26.) Of the 211 engineer combat battalions in existence on V-E Day, 82 were activated in 1944. (Statement of Col J. B. Hughes, AGF Engr Off, to AGF Hist Off, 28 Apr 45.)

[28] Figures on these types of units, as given in WD Troop Bases, 14 Jan 44, 1 Jul 44, and 1 Jan 45, were as follows:

Type of Unit	*Number Active 31 Dec 43*	*Number Active 30 Jun 44*	*Number Active 31 Dec 44*
Auto Maint Med	150	169	168
Hvy Auto Maint	91	136	139
Hvy Maint Field Army	41	59	58
Evacuation	26	51	53

[29] On 31 December 1943 the number of active companies at home and abroad was 611; on 30 June 1944, 814; and on 31 December 1944, 904. (WD Troop Bases, 14 Jan 44, 1 Jul 44, and 1 Jan 45.)

In other types of units the trend in activation during 1944 was sharply downward. The increasing superiority of Allied air power reduced, as Army Ground Forces had predicted, the requirements for antiaircraft to a figure much lower than that set forth in the Troop Bases. Antiaircraft units active in the Troop Basis, numbering 557 on 31 December 1943, fell to 479 on 30 June 1944, to 347 on 31 December 1944, and to 331 on 31 March 1945.[30] All in all, 258 antiaircraft units were inactivated or disbanded by Army Ground Forces between 1 January 1944 and V-E Day.[31] Theater experience showed that the Army Ground Forces itself had greatly overestimated requirements for tank destroyers. Between 1 January 1944 and V-E Day twenty-six tank destroyer battalions were inactivated by Army Ground Forces.[32]

A large portion of the personnel made available by inactivation and disbandment of antiaircraft, coast artillery, tank destroyer, and other types of surplus units were utilized as fillers and replacements in infantry, field artillery, combat engineer, chemical, signal construction, and other types of units for which need increased. Conversion training was given in appropriate replacement training centers or in the new unit.

In many instances units which became surplus in the Troop Basis were converted *en bloc*—except for field-grade officers, who were usually withdrawn prior to conversion—into units for which there was a current requirement. Coast artillery gun battalions were converted into heavy field artillery battalions; antiaircraft barrage balloon battalions into signal construction battalions; antiaircraft weapons and/or gun battalions into field artillery rocket battalions; chemical mortar battalions into engineer combat battalions; chemical decontamination companies into amphibian tractor, field artillery, and tank battalions, or quartermaster gas supply companies; and cavalry squadrons into signal information and monitoring companies.[33] Negro units were converted primarily into service-type units. For example, cadre personnel for amphibian truck and quartermaster truck companies was drawn from air base security battalions, which were then transferred to Army Service Forces for disbandment and reassignment of personnel. Antiaircraft automatic weapons and barrage balloon battalions became signal construction battalions; field artillery battalions became engineer combat and

[30] WD Troop Bases, 14 Jan 44, 1 Jul 44, and 1 Jan 45.

[31] Information compiled for AGF Hist Off by AGF Stat Sec, 15 May 45.

[32] *Ibid.*

[33] These statements are based on a survey of the "321" and "401.1" files in the AGF AG Records, and on interviews with AGF staff officers.

quartermaster truck units; tank destroyer battalions became quartermaster truck, engineer fire fighting, and port units. Other Negro units were stripped to cadre strength and their personnel was transferred to ASF units which urgently needed fillers to meet overseas commitment dates. In August 1943 alone, these included thirteen antiaircraft battalions, ten field artillery battalions, and eight tank destroyer battalions.[34] Some of the stripped units were refilled but eventually most of them, including those refilled, were converted, disbanded, or inactivated to fill service and infantry replacement requirements. Service units in excess of expected needs were also converted; chemical decontamination and smoke generator companies, for example, were converted into engineer dump truck companies, and quartermaster pack troops into infantry.

Conversion of units was not accomplished without considerable difficulty. Personnel had to be given special training for their new duties both in schools and within the organization. Urgency of overseas needs was sometimes so great as not to allow sufficient time for thorough conversion training. Officers and noncommissioned officers were often slow in adapting themselves to their new duties and in consequence lost effectiveness as leaders. A feeling of being pushed about had a deleterious effect on the morale of both officers and men.[35]

A frequent form of reorganization was the change of units from one type to another in the same arm or service. The following cases are typical: the change of ordnance light maintenance companies to evacuation companies; of ordnance medium automotive maintenance companies to heavy automotive maintenance companies; of armored signal battalions, not required after discontinuance of armored corps, to signal operations battalions; of engineer topographic units to maintenance and depot units; and of engineer camouflage battalions to combat battalions.[36]

These reorganizations were, at best, apt to be wasteful because of failure to make full use of specialist training. Speaking particularly of ordnance reorganization, an AGF staff officer stated:[37]

[34] (1) AGF memo for CofS USA, 25 Aug 43, sub: Negro Units in 1943 TB. 322.999/10 (Cld Trs)(S). (2) WD memo (S) WDGCT 291/21 (4 Mar 44) to ASW, 4 Mar 44, sub: Utilization of Manpower.

[35] (1) Interviews with AGF staff officers. (2) Memo of Col Hans W. Holmer for AGF Engr, 16 Aug 44, sub: Inspection of Units at Cp Maxey, Tex, and Cp Howze, Tex, 8–14 Aug 44. 353.02/615 (AGF). (3) Memo of Maj Clovis A. Brown, QM Sec AGF, for G–4 AGF, 27 Nov 44, sub: Rpt of Visit to QM Nondiv Units Located at Cp Polk, La, and Cp Livingston, La, 13–18 Nov 44. 353.02/717 (AGF).

[36] Interviews with AGF staff officers.

[37] Statement of Maj G. T. Petersen, AGF Ord Sec, to AGF Hist Off, 2 May 45.

Usually it would have been better to inactivate the units being reorganized, transfer the personnel to other units of the same type that were understrength or use them as loss replacements and start from scratch with personnel from reception centers. When we made evacuation companies out of maintenance companies we required many men trained to do one type of work to learn to do another type. Their abilities should have been utilized in other maintenance companies, and evacuation companies formed from reception center personnel.

Sometimes sudden changes in requirements made the prior reorganization seem wasteful in the extreme. On one occasion, for example, reorganization of some engineer heavy ponton battalions into light equipment companies was followed in two months by an order to activate more heavy ponton battalions.[38]

Conversion of antiaircraft and tank destroyer units would undoubtedly have been more extensive had not their utility been increased by wider employment in secondary roles. In the theaters tank destroyers were used effectively as artillery in indirect fire missions and for direct fire in support of ground troops, very much after the fashion of self-propelled infantry cannon.[39] Antiaircraft gun battalions employed their weapons to good purpose against ground targets, particularly against pillboxes and other enemy strong points; in the Pacific they turned their high-velocity guns against openings of caves and dugouts to seal the Japanese in their fastnesses. In 1944 training programs were revised to provide for additional training of antiaircraft and tank destroyer units in their secondary missions.[40]

Another significant adjustment was the employment of separate infantry regiments for conversion of certain categories of personnel to infantry, initiated in April 1944 when demand for infantry replacements became urgent. Their enlisted strength having been put in the replacement stream, nine regiments were refilled with men from antiaircraft, tank destroyer, and other types of surplus units, and were launched on a program for intensive training as infantry riflemen. The first four weeks were devoted to individual training, including firing of the rifle for qualification, transition firing, familiarization firing of other infantry weapons, bayonet drill, and grenades. Then came two weeks of tactical training of the individual soldier, followed by as much progressive unit training as time

[38] Statement of Col J. B. Hughes, AGF Engr Off, to AGF Hist Off, 28 Apr 45.

[39] AGF Obsrs MTO Rpt (S) A-323, 5 Mar 45, sub: Comments on Questions Pertaining to TDs. 314.7 (AGF Hist).

[40] (1) AGF Obsrs SWPA Rpt (C) B-236, 28 Mar 45, sub: Employment of AAA Guns as Reinforcing FA. 314.7 (AGF Hist). (2) AGF ltr to CGs, 15 Apr 44, sub: Employment of AAA Guns (Mbl) and (Sem) in Secondary Roles. 353/610 (CA). (3) Memo of Lt Col V. B. Barnes for G-3 AGF, 30 Jun 44, sub: Rpt of Obsns Made on Visit to Memphis, Tenn, Ft Riley, Kans, Cp Campbell, Ky, 13-17 Jun 44. 353.02/570 (AGF).

permitted. Special attention was devoted to the development of infantry noncommissioned officers.[41]

The separate infantry regiments became essentially miniature advanced replacement training centers. They made extensive use of the committee system of instruction common in replacement training installations.[42] Like the centers they suffered greatly from repeated replacement of experienced infantry officers with novices from officer candidate schools and personnel from other branches lacking in infantry experience.[43] On the whole the product of the infantry regiments was not as good as that of the infantry advanced replacement training centers. In the latter, supervision and coordination seem to have been considerably better.[44]

As an expedient for the quick conversion of miscellaneous surplus personnel to infantry, the regiments performed a valuable service. One of these regiments, the 140th, between April and December 1944 trained three increments of replacements. During this period 7,547 enlisted men, more than enough to provide infantry privates for an entire infantry division, were "graduated" from the regiment. Of these, 3,881 went to replacement depots, 2,368 to infantry divisions, and 46 to officer candidate schools. In addition, the regiment sent 153 officers overseas as replacements.[45]

The period 1944–45 witnessed not merely the adjustment of the training program to conversion of units but also its adaptation to the training of experimental units. Several new types of nondivisional units came into existence during this period, mainly in response to needs revealed by theater experience. These included two experimental rocket battalions,[46] and two new types of signal units.[47] Mobilization Training Programs were developed for the new units on an experimental basis.

[41] AGF ltr to CGs, 16 Apr 44, sub: Tng Dir for Sep Inf Regts. 353.01/112.

[42] AGF ltr to CG Second Army, 3 Jun 44, sub: Visit to Cp Chaffee, Ark, 16–17 May 44. 353.02/554 (AGF).

[43] Record of tel conv between Col Mearnes, Fourth Army, and Col V. B. Barnes, AGF, 31 Oct 44. AGF G–3 Sec files, 000/890 (Tel Conv).

[44] (1) AGF M/S, CofS to G–3, 27 Jan 45, sub: WD G–3 Comments on Our Tng at IARTCs. 353/216 (Inf). (2) AGF M/S (C), G–3 to CofS, 17 Jan 45, sub: Regtl Comdrs, Sep Inf Regts. 353.02/115 (AGF)(C).

[45] Regtl History, 140th Inf Regt. AGO Records.

[46] AGF M/S (C), G–3 to CofS, 12 Dec 44, sub: Rocket Bns. 321/108 (FA)(C).

[47] (1) Statement of Col O. K. Sadtler, AGF Sig Off, to AGF Hist Off, 1 May 45. (2) AGF memo for CofS USA, 22 Dec 44, sub: Plan of Opn of Proposed Sig Rad Relay Co, T/O&E 11-137. 321/929 (Sig).

230-171 O - 66 - 36

IV. Obstacles to Effective Training

Personnel Shortage and Turnover

The training of nondivisional units was hampered from first to last by tremendous difficulties of which the most formidable and persistent, unquestionably, was personnel shortage and turnover. This problem was most acute in the early summer of 1942, when adoption of the ROUNDUP plan for invading western Europe the following spring created unanticipated requirements for service units, and again in the summer of 1944, when unusual demands arose in connection with movement into France.

On 30 June 1942 the enlisted strength of spare parts in the Army Ground Forces was more than 120,000 below that authorized by Tables of Organization. Three months later the deficiency had increased to a figure exceeding 150,000. The shortage on each date was about 30 percent of authorized strength. By the end of the year the stepping up of inductions, the curtailment of activations, and the postponement of ROUNDUP had improved the situation somewhat. Nevertheless, deficiencies at that time still approximated 120,000, or 20 percent of authorized strength.[1]

Composite figures do not tell the whole story. Some nondivisional units had full Table of Organization strength, or even surpluses, but a full complement was usually not attained until movement overseas was in immediate prospect. Moreover, the filling of alerted organizations was achieved in most cases by robbing units in intermediate stages of training. Units thus despoiled were compelled either to hobble along at reduced strength or to replenish their rosters from reception centers. The bringing in of green fillers meant, of course, the launching of basic training all over again. It was not unusual for an organization to be forced, through repeated withdrawals of personnel for cadres, officer candidate schools, and transfers, to go through basic training several times. Then when finally alerted it was often so far below authorized strength that it in turn had to rob some unit of lower priority before leaving port.[2] This was a vicious circle, inimical alike to orderly training and to morale.

[1] (1) "Comparative Strength of AGF." 320.2 (Comp Str)(S). Figures for 31 December 1942 are distinctive in that they include authorized overstrength (5 or 15 percent). (2) Comparative Strength compilations in files of AGF Stat Sec.

[2] Interviews with AGF Special Staff heads, Jan 44.

Delay in the provision of fillers and the use of tactical units as replacement training centers were wasteful of time and supervisory personnel at a period when the Army was hard-pressed for both. An AGF study in November 1942 disclosed that the personnel required to operate thirty-one units used for replacement training could, if utilized in replacement centers, train twice as many replacements as were trained in the units.[3]

Personnel deficiencies were greatest among units in early stages of training. It was not uncommon in 1942 for a company, after activation, to remain at skeleton strength for several months while waiting for fillers. When fillers finally began to arrive they frequently came in driblets, requiring either that the launching of the training program be further delayed or that training be conducted on more than one level.[4]

A considerable part of the turnover in personnel experienced by nondivisional units was produced by transfers to the Air Forces and inroads of OCS quotas. These losses had an adverse effect on the general quality of AGF enlisted personnel. General McNair reported to General Marshall in February 1943 that the character of manpower in units under his jurisdiction "declined visibly toward the end of 1942."[5] A specific illustration was afforded by seven tank destroyer battalions which, after heavy losses to Army Air Forces and officer candidate schools, found themselves with over 50 percent of their personnel in Classes IV and V of the Army General Classification Test, whereas normal distribution in these classes was 35 percent.

In early 1942 the problem of those responsible for nondivisional training was complicated also by the fact that existing plans for building nondivisional units contemplated provision of fillers by replacement training centers. But this expectation, never realized to any considerable extent, had to be virtually abandoned during the early stages of ROUNDUP preparations. The training machinery was regeared to accommodate the policy of unloading the raw materials of reception centers directly into tactical units.[6]

Nondivisional training was also handicapped in 1942 by the dearth and inexperience of officers. Ample and efficient commissioned personnel were particu-

[3] AGF memo (C) to CofS USA, 9 Nov 42, sub: Repl Deps. 320.2/222 (C).

[4] (1) Second Army ltr to CG AGF, 30 Jul 42, sub: A Study Showing the Delay in Achieving Combat Proficiency Due to Receiving Filler Repls in Small Increments. 341/8 (Second Army).

[5] Memo (C) of Gen McNair for Gen Marshall, 2 Feb 43, sub: Discipline of Trs in North Africa. 353/1 (MTO)(C).

[6] Statement of Col J. B. Hughes, AGF Engr, to AGF Hist Off, 29 Jan 44.

larly vital to spare parts because of the relative lack of supervision in these units and the technical nature of much of their training.

On 30 June 1942, nondivisional units in Army Ground Forces had only 15,013 officers of an authorized strength of 22,293, and three months later only 19,931 of an authorized 27,141. Shortages were most pronounced in engineer, signal, ordnance, and field artillery units.[7] Typical units of these branches in the lean days prior to December 1942 sometimes had no more than one-third of their authorized commissioned strength present for duty.[8] By the end of the year, owing to a tremendous increase in OCS output in the summer and fall, the overall officer picture had changed from deficiency to surplus: actual strength was 29,369; authorized strength, 28,789. Nevertheless, shortages persisted in some categories, particularly in the signal and engineer branches. The rapid activation of units produced an urgent demand for leaders which resulted all too often in hasty selection and premature promotion of officers.[9] The dire need of technical specialists in some of the service categories led to the direct commissioning of large numbers of civilians. The process known as affiliation was frequently resorted to, particularly by ordnance and signal authorities. Under this scheme a telephone corporation was asked to furnish officer and enlisted personnel for an entire signal construction company, and an automobile manufacturer was called on to produce an ordnance maintenance company. It was contemplated that affiliated personnel would be given a thorough course in military training, but the need for service units was frequently so great as drastically to curtail instructions. Affiliation gave the services vitally needed specialists, and for enlisted personnel technical proficiency was perhaps the primary consideration. But the same was not true of the officers. Company commanders and executives had to be familiar with Army organization, customs of the service, and unit administration in order to discharge their duties effectively.[10]

The placing of men in command of units before they learned their military ABC's produced bad results that were farcical when they were not tragic. Perhaps the worst consequences were those pertaining to discipline. In the automobile

[7] (1) "Comparative Strength of AGF." 320.2 (Comp Str)(S). (2) Comparative Strength compilations in files of AGF Stat Sec.

[8] Eleventh ind (C) by Brig Gen Russell G. Barkalow to notice of Reclassification Proceedings [undated but Feb 44]. 322.98/96 (Comdrs)(S).

[9] Memo (C) of Gen McNair for Gen Marshall, 2 Feb 43, sub: Discipline of Trs in North Africa. 353/1 (MTO)(C).

[10] Interviews of AGF Hist Off with AGF offs: Lt Col L. H. Harrison, Ord Sec, 27 Jan 44, Maj R. E. Peters, Ord Sec, 28 Jan 44, and Col G. C. Black, Sig Off, 28 Jan 44.

plant the assembly-line foreman had been addressed by his underlings in the free and easy spirit of "Hi Joe." When affiliation placed the group in uniform, "Joe," by virtue of his supervisory status as a civilian, became a captain. But the workers, suddenly converted into sergeants, corporals, and privates, found it difficult, notwithstanding the shining bars, the salutes, and the correctly intoned "Sirs," to think of their captain in any other light than "Joe." The situation was not helped by "Joe's" maladroitness in giving commands and his bungling of company administration.[11]

Blanket condemnation of personnel commissioned directly from civilian life would be unfair. Some of the men thrust into positions of command had natural qualities of leadership, learned military ways with remarkable celerity, and in a short time became good officers. Their technical knowledge was of inestimable benefit to the armed forces. Many of the hurriedly selected nonspecialist products of officer candidate schools, promoted rapidly to posts of considerable responsibility, also gave remarkably good account of themselves. But paucity of capable leaders was one of the outstanding hindrances to spare-parts training during the early period of Army Ground Forces. During his tour of the North African Theater early in 1943, General Marshall noted some of the consequences in the form of shabby appearance and slack discipline among organizations,[12] and on his return he urged the importance of corrective action. A War Department staff member, reporting a conference with the Chief of Staff at this time, stated:[13]

> During this discussion the Chief of Staff very pointedly made an issue of the training of battalion and regimental commanders, especially of service units. He commented on the lack of high quality of leadership among otherwise well qualified technical commanders. He stressed the imperative necessity for training these commanders in battlefield leadership. In concluding this particular part of the discussion he stated in substantially these words: "I do not give a —— whether the commander has perfect technical training or not. He does not have to have it if his subordinates have it. What he must have is the leadership and drive necessary to get the right things done at the right time in battle. For example, the commander of a hospital does not have to be a doctor."

Brig. Gen. Floyd L. Parks, Chief of Staff, Army Ground Forces, on receiving

[11] Interviews of AGF Hist Off with Lt Col L. H. Harrison and Maj R. E. Peters, AGF Ord Sec, 27–28 Jan 44.

[12] Memo (C) of Gen Marshall for Gen McNair, 1 Feb 43, sub: Discipline of Trs in North Africa. 353/1 (MTO)(C).

[13] Memo (S) of Col Matchett for Gen White, WD, 29 Apr 43, sub: Informal Conferences with the CofS. WD G–3 Records, "Negro File" (S).

a report of bad disciplinary conditions in an AGF tank destroyer battalion in August 1942, concluded that leadership was "woefully lacking." "I am not worrying about the qualities of the enlisted men," he stated, "but I am extraordinarily alarmed at the dearth of leaders. It will take us quite a while to eliminate the deadwood and bring out the men of ability and character." [14] Future experience showed the accuracy of his prediction.

During the first few months of 1943, in consequence of the abandonment of ROUNDUP and a slowing down of mobilization, personnel resources in general were adequate for nondivisional requirements. But in the fall the situation took an unfavorable turn, and by the end of the year spare parts reported an aggregate enlisted understrength of nearly 20,000.[15]

It might have been expected that the large officer surplus which existed after the summer of 1943 would solve the needs of all units as far as commissioned personnel was concerned. Such did not prove to be the case. Some of the technical services continued to be seriously hampered by an insufficiency of competent officers. In the case of engineers the general surplus of commissioned personnel actually proved a handicap, because it brought a halt to the commissioning of civilian and enlisted specialists and led instead to the transfer to engineer units of officers who lacked technical qualifications for their new assignments.[16]

Medical units experienced the most acute shortages of commissioned personnel. On 30 November 1943, Ground Forces medical units reported a deficiency of 1,505 officers out of an authorized strength of 5,961. Circumstances foreshadowed a situation even more distressing in the future.[17]

In the spring and summer of 1944, nondivisional units experienced a leanness of personnel comparable to that of 1942. In May 1944, when manpower resources were being drained to the limit in preparation for the invasion of western Europe, an AGF staff officer who had just returned from a visit of inspection reported: "Difficulties encountered by units during individual training periods are believed to be 80% personnel and 10% supply problems, and 10% lack of training facilities. . . ." The AGF G-3 scribbled in the margin opposite this comment: "The talk is about personnel, regardless of who goes out." [18]

[14] Personal ltr (C) of Brig Gen Floyd L. Parks, CofS AGF, to Maj Gen R. H. Bull, 8 Aug 42. 333.1/32 (Insps, Fld Forces) (C).

[15] "Comparative Strength of AGF," 31 Dec 43. 320.2/104 (Comp Str) (S).

[16] Statement of Col J. B. Hughes, AGF Engr, to AGF Hist Off, 29 Jan 44.

[17] Data furnished by Lt Col G. J. Collins, AGF Med Sec, 28 Jan 44.

[18] Memo of Lt Col Barksdale Hamlett for G-3 AGF, 23 May 44, sub: Visit to Ft Sill, Okla, Cp Bowie, Tex, Ft Sam Houston, Tex, R&SC, and Ft Bragg, N.C., 14-19 May 44. AGF G-3 Sec Files, 333.1/222 (Inspections by AGF Staff Offs).

One aspect of the personnel problem in 1944 was delay in receiving fillers for newly activated units. Engineer units experienced this difficulty to a greater extent than those of other branches. In May 1944 many engineer combat battalions urgently needed overseas were marking time at cadre strength because of lack of available fillers.[19] An AGF staff officer reported in mid-July that the 286th Engineer Combat Battalion, activated on 17 December 1943, had had to postpone initiation of the individual training program until 10 March 1944, by which date only 50 percent of fillers had been received, and that arrival of the remainder on 5 April 1944 necessitated the beginning of a second echelon of training. He stated further that the 1272d Engineer Combat Battalion activated on 20 April 1944 had by mid-July received only 65 percent of its fillers.[20]

Officer shortages, while considerably less serious on the whole than in 1942–43, remained substantial in medical units, and to some extent in engineer units, throughout 1944. In September 1944 there was a deficiency of about 44 percent in the authorized commissioned strength of AGF medical units.[21] Shortages were still more pronounced in professional specialist categories, such as surgeons and neurologists. A conference held by ASF, AAF, and AGF representatives in the fall of 1944 on redistribution of medical officers resulted in some improvement of conditions in the Army Ground Forces.[22]

One of the major difficulties experienced by nondivisional units in 1944 was turnover of personnel. In November 1944 an AGF staff officer reported that several quartermaster units had had more than 100-percent turnover of enlisted strength in three months' time.[23] Personnel losses of from 50 to 75 percent seem to have been fairly common among all types of nondivisional units except antiaircraft, tank destroyer, and tank battalions.

Several factors were responsible for this enormous turnover. One was the discontinuance early in 1944 of the practice of authorizing units at activation an overstrength to offset losses from normal attrition, thus making it necessary for these units when alerted to replenish their rosters by drafts on organizations of

[19] Statement of Lt Col L. C. Gilbert, AGF Engr Sec, to AGF Hist Off, 21 Jan 46.

[20] Memo of Lt Col G. S. Witters, AGF Engr Sec, for G–3 AGF, 18 Jul 44, sub: Rpt of Inspection Trip, Cp Carson, Colo, Cp McCoy, Wis. AGF G–3 files, 333.1/286 (Inspections by AGF Staff Offs.)

[21] Statement of Maj E. S. Chapman, AGF Med Sec, to AGF Hist Off, 3 Apr 45.

[22] Memo (R) of Maj G. R. Hill, AGF QM Sec, for G–4 AGF, 11 Nov 44, sub: Rpt of Visit to Hq & Hq Det Sp Trs Fourth Army, Cp Swift, Tex, 30 Oct–3 Nov 44. 353.02/49 (AGF)(R).

[23] This statement is based on a study of AGF inspection reports filed in AGF G–3 Sec files, 333.1 (Inspections by AGF Staff Offs) and AGF AG files, 353.02.

lower priority.[24] Another factor was the accumulation in the Army Ground Forces of large numbers of physically handicapped (Class D) men and the War Department's insistence until the latter part of 1944 that these men be tried out in various capacities with a view to finding a place where they could be usefully employed. In many cases personnel not disqualified for overseas service, but physically handicapped to an extent making them extremely hard to place, were passed from one unit to another in an effort to find suitable assignments. In September 1944 G-1 wrote to the Chief of Staff, Army Ground Forces, as follows:[25]

> The War Department has consistently exerted heavy pressure on Army Ground Forces to utilize everyone who could do useful work. They authorized the induction not only of limited service personnel but for several months they authorized the induction of 5% who were *below the minimum standards* of induction for limited service. Prior to the use of the profile system such personnel were habitually assigned to the Army Ground Forces and many trials were required before we could find spots where they might fit in.

In the fall of 1944 War Department policy was changed to permit the Army Ground Forces to get rid of large numbers of Class D personnel, either through discharge or by transfer to the Army Air Forces and the Army Service Forces.[26] This provision greatly accelerated the turnover of personnel.[27] The Fourth Army alone, in the period 1 September–31 December 1944, removed 30,000 physically handicapped men from T/O units.[28] Replacements for those cleared from units in advance stages of training had to be taken from low-priority organizations.

Turnover of personnel was also increased by the practice, common in the summer and fall of 1944, of shipping units before completion of the prescribed training period to meet urgent unexpected overseas requirements. Units whose readiness dates were thus advanced were frequently unable to secure the return of specialists from service schools prior to shipment and were compelled to draft substitutes from other units. In the fall of 1944 the War Department at one stroke ordered shipment in current status of training, that is, before completion of the

[24] AGF memo (C) for CofS USA, 16 May 44, sub: Overstrength of Units to Equalize Losses through Attrition. 320.2/428 (C).

[25] AGF M/S, G-1 to CofS, 13 Sep 44, sub: Pers Turnover. 333.1/1621.

[26] Remarks of Col J. H. Banville, Rpt of Gen Lear's Conference with AGF Units at Ft Ord, 26 Aug 44. 353.02/635 (AGF).

[27] Memo of Maj Clovis A. Brown, AGF QM Sec, for G-4 AGF, 27 Nov 44, sub: Rpt of Visit to QM Nondiv Units Located at Cp Polk, La, and Cp Livingston, La, 13-18 Nov 44. 353.02/717 (AGF).

[28] 1st ind, 9 Jan 45, by Fourth Army on AGF ltr (C) to CG Fourth Army, 31 Dec 44, sub: Adjustment of Unit Str. 320.2/489 (C).

prescribed training period, of 65 engineer combat battalions. Because of this action, 1,800 specialists in attendance at service schools were unable to rejoin their units. Unalerted engineer units were combed for substitutes, but since these sources were too limited to meet the requisition the alerted organizations had to fill many of the specialist positions with ordinary fillers lacking in the required technical training.[29]

The practice of transferring personnel found deficient in POM requirements from an alerted unit to an organization of lower priority was sometimes repeated as many as a half-dozen times. The armies wished to maintain casual detachments in headquarters and headquarters detachments, special troops, for storage and processing of such personnel, but Headquarters, Army Ground Forces, did not favor the plan. Objection seems to have sprung mainly from fear that pooling of the "floaters" would have an adverse effect on morale.[30]

The processing of outgoing and incoming men placed a heavy burden of administration on battalion and company headquarters. Moreover, the breaking in of replacements was disruptive to training. But perhaps the most unfortunate consequence of all was the injury of personnel changes to unit esprit and teamwork.

Turnover of personnel would have been considerably less extensive and disruptive if pools of trained personnel, including qualified specialists, had been maintained in the Army Ground Forces for each of the branches. If such pools had been provided, alerted units might have drawn on them for loss replacements instead of robbing units of lower priority. The need for reserve pools was repeatedly urged by chiefs of special staff sections in the Army Ground Forces, but, mainly because the demands of theaters for units and replacements were so pressing as to prevent escape from a hand-to-mouth basis, pools were not provided prior to V-E Day.[31]

Deficiency in the quality of personnel was a serious obstacle to training in 1944. As the Nation's manpower resources approached exhaustion under existing Selective Service policies, there was a decline in the quality of personnel coming to units through reception centers, and after adoption of the profile system the best of the inductees went to the Infantry. In 1944 nondivisional units received

[29] AGF M/S, Engr Sec to Sig, G–3, and G–4 Secs, 23 Oct 44, sub: Draft No. 2, POM. 370.5/4227.

[30] (1) Memo of Col H. W. Holmer, AGF Engr Sec, for AGF Engr, 16 Mar 44, sub: Rpt of Inspection Trip. 353.02/491 (AGF). (2) Statements of G–3s, Second and Fourth Armies, at Redepl Conferences, Hq AGF, 27–28 Mar 45. (3) Memo of Maj G. H. Murphy, G–1 AGF, for CofS AGF, 10 Nov 44, sub: Inspection of Physical Profile Records and Procedures. 353.02/712 (AGF).

[31] Interviews with AGF staff officers.

their fillers to an increasing extent from organizations declared surplus in the Troop Basis and from the Army's floating population of casuals, which to a considerable degree was made up of discards from alerted units. A vivid picture of the dregs received by some organizations is afforded by the following excerpt from an inspection report, dated 20 June 1944, of an AGF artillery officer:[32]

Physically disqualified men:

415th FA Group: CAC transferred 62 men which are in general hospitals over the United States. Twenty were in station hospitals of converted CAC units. Seventy-two men are blind in one eye; 17 are without an eye; 259 have only one good eye above 20/400.

417th FA Group: CAC transferred 25 men, absent in general hospitals, 110 men unqualified to go overseas; 18 psycho-neurosis and 6 epileptics.

207th FA Group: CAC transferred 50 Class "C" men to each of 3 battalions; two other battalions have 11 per battalion with only one eye; 65 are physically disqualified for drill.

All above men are discards from previously alerted AA and CAC units. They are a serious handicap to training, will never go overseas in a combat unit, and should be discharged. This is only an average example of these problems.

The practice of high-priority units unloading their culls on low-priority organizations resulted, as deployment neared completion, in accumulation in the last units activated of a disproportionate quantity of the physically unfit for which the usual repository, that is, units of the same branch in earlier stages of training, did not exist. In other words, the process of successive unloadings ran out for lack of units on which to unload. Revisions of personnel policy in August 1944 authorized discharge of the physically unfit, but by that time replacement sources had become so impoverished that application of the policy often resulted in the exchange of a man of weak body but good training for one of fair stamina but little training, and possibly with sundry other defects.[33]

Insistence by higher headquarters in the early months of 1944 that every effort be made to utilize Class D men, together with the practice of assigning the best physical specimens to the Infantry, resulted frequently in throwing upon nondivisional units, particularly those of service categories, a heavier load of substandard personnel than they could effectively absorb.[34] In some instances divisions were favored in personnel matters to an extent that was detrimental to

[32] Memo of Lt Col V. B. Barnes for G–3 AGF, 20 Jun 44, sub: Rpt of Obsns Made on Visit to Memphis, Tenn, Ft Riley, Kans, and Cp Campbell, Ky, 13–17 Jun 44. 353.02/570 (AGF).

[33] Interviews with AGF staff officers.

[34] Memo of Maj Robert D. Durst, AGF G–1 Sec. for G–3 AGF, 1 May 44, sub: Rpt of G–1 Representative on Gen McNair's Inspection Trip, 23–29 Apr 44. AGF G–3 Sec files, 333.1/23 (Inspections by AGF Staff Offs).

spare parts. In July 1944 the Fourth Army directed the commanding officer of a headquarters and headquarters detachment, special troops, to screen all physically qualified men from low-priority signal, ordnance, and quartermaster units of his command and report them as available for transfer to divisions as replacements for infantry losses.[35]

Inadequacy of Equipment

Another serious obstacle to nondivisional training was inadequacy of equipment. The difficulties of divisions in this connection, as noted elsewhere, were formidable; the experience of spare parts was even more so because of the failure to set up a minimum equipment list for these units and because of their particular dependence on equipment for adequate training.

The problem of equipment was especially acute in 1942. At Camp Hood, in the spring and summer of 1942, "simulated tank destroyers maneuvered against simulated tanks over terrain almost devoid of roads, firing was conducted on improvised ranges . . . [and] so few radios were available that practically no communications training could be given." [36] As a result of the cutting of ammunition allowances by one-third, artillery officers throughout Army Ground Forces were directed in April "to fire a simulated problem each day . . . using a matchbox, sandtable, some sort of terrain board, or any other expedient," and to put their batteries through simulated service practices.[37]

Signal communications units could not well improvise technical equipment, nor could ordnance and quartermaster maintenance companies service imaginary tanks and trucks. The result of the pervasive shortages of specialist and functional equipment for these and other service organizations was inevitably a loss of training opportunity and the use of poorly prepared units to fill the importunate requests for overseas assignment. Service units, because of their low priority, had shortages of small arms even more pronounced than those in other types of equipment.[38]

The straits to which many nondivisional units were reduced in 1942 is disclosed by the following extracts from inspection reports. On 17 June 1942, after a visit to four camps, Col. John W. Middleton of the AGF G–4 Section reported:[39]

[35] AGF ltr to CG Fourth Army, 8 Jul 44, sub: Visit to Cp Polk, La, and Cp McCain, Miss. 353.02/583 (AGF).

[36] AGF Historical Section, The Tank Destroyer History, Sec VIII.

[37] AGF ltr to CGs, 14 Apr 42, sub: FA Firing. 353.1/92 (FA).

[38] Interviews with AGF Special Staff heads, Jan 44.

[39] Memo of Col John W. Middleton to AGF G–4, 17 Jun 42, sub: Rpt of Inspections: Ft Jackson, Cp Sutton, Ft Bragg, and Cp Pickett. 333.1/1164 (Insps, Fld Forces).

1. 67th QM Troop (Pack). "[Members of] this organization have not been issued their animals. . . . They are over 41 pack horses [short] and short 294 mules."

2. Co. C, 53d QM Regiment (HM). "Short cartridge belts, haversacks, pack carriers, and water containers."

3. Co. D, 53d QM Regiment (HM). "Shortage of tentage, shelter halves, web equipment, field ranges, and motor vehicles."

Following an inspection of signal units at Camp Crowder another AGF staff officer noted on 26 June 1942:[40]

1. 93d Signal Battalion, activiated 18 May 1942. "The arrival of Signal Corps equipment is far behind schedule. In many cases the equipment received is such that little if any training of some types can be accomplished. . . . No telephones of any kind have been received [precluding] not only training in swichboard and switchboard operation, but also wire construction."

2. 96th Signal Battalion, activated 14 June 1942. "Not one solitary item of Signal Corps equipment has been received."

3. 179th Signal Repair Company, activated 15 May 1942. "Signal Corps equipment received consists largely of many items which cannot be used for training purposes without the receipt of key items such as telephones, switchboards, etc."

A special survey made in November 1942 by the Inspector General's Department of service units under AGF control affords a revealing picture of the equipment situation:[41]

1. 63d QM Battalion. "There are only 284 rifles for 1,113 men."

2. 663d Engineer Topo. Co. "Progress in technical training has been delayed by a lack of drafting material and aerial photographs."

3. Company A, 302nd QM Battalion, Sterilization. "Activated 1 May 1942, has had very little opportunity for technical training, there being no clothing and personnel to practice on."

4. 23d Chemical Decontamination Company. "Has completed eight weeks of MTP training, has not been issued either antigas impregnated or impervious clothing."

5. 193d Ordnance Company (Depot) and 60th Chemical Company (Depot). "Had no prospect of stores to handle or warehouses in which to work."

6. 3d Convalescent Hospital. "Has little chance for development . . . because of shortage in T/BA equipment and the lack of useful work to perform."

7. 25th and 33d Chemical Decontamination Companies. "The original allotment of training munitions and agents was exhausted during the initial training period and replacement not obtainable to date."

8. 479th Engineer Maintenance Company. "Lacked mobile repair equipment."

[40] AGF M/S (S), Sig Off to CofS, 26 Jun 42, sub: Inspection of Sig Corps Units at Cp Crowder, Mo. 320.2/283 (S).

[41] Memo of Brig Gen Philip E. Brown, Dep of IG USA, for CG AGF, 11 Dec 42, sub: Sp Survey of AGF Serv Units Other than Divs. 333.1/1415 (Insps, Fld Forces).

Nondivisional combat units were in a somewhat better position with regard to equipment than were service organizations, but the plight of most units in both categories in 1942 was deplorable. An AGF staff member remarked at the end of the year: "Small, separate units have been a weak spot of training in 1942." [42]

The question naturally arises as to how the scantily equipped organizations acquired even a small degree of proficiency in performing the duties required of them. The answer lies, to a large extent, in the capacity of unit and higher commanders for perseverance and their ingenuity in borrowing, pooling, and improvising. Blocks of wood were used for mines, sandbags for ammunition boxes, galvanized iron pipes mounted on ration carts for artillery, sticks for guns, and "jeeps" for tanks, not to mention a long list of mock structures ranging from landing craft to "Nazi villages."[43] To a great extent nondivisional training in 1942 rested upon improvisations, simulations, and expedients.

The equipment situation improved somewhat in the early months of 1943, but many units, particularly those in early stages of training, continued to be hampered by serious shortages. In April 1943 General McNair, convinced that many of the deficiencies revealed by United States troops in combat were due to inadequacies of training equipment, urged the War Department to change existing policies to enable nondivisional units to obtain 50 percent of their equipment, instead of the 20 percent then authorized, at activation, and 100 percent at the end of four months. But no action was taken on this recommendation.[44]

By the summer of 1943 the increasing production of American factories made it possible for some units in early stages of training to obtain a substantial quantity of training equipment in excess of the 20 percent alloted to them at activation. But this favorable situation was upset by adoption, at the suggestion of Army Service Forces, of a policy of preshipping equipment to Great Britain. Hitherto the practice had been followed of shipping units and equipment together. The new policy provided that equipment should be stockpiled in Great Britain ahead of time, and that when units in training departed for ports of embarkation they should leave their guns, tanks, and trucks behind.[45]

[42] AGF ltr to CG Third Army, 31 Dec 42, sub: Visit to Cp Gruber and Cp Barkeley. 353.02/33 (AGF).

[43] See, for example, ltr of CG 3d ABS Tng Gp to CG Second Army, 19 Nov 42. Second Army Files, AG 353-173.

[44] Memo (S) of Gen McNair for Gen Marshall, 3 Jul 43, sub: Policies Governing Issues of Equip. 320.2/22 (TUB 43)(S).

[45] (1) WD memo (S) OPD 400 WMP (3-1-43) to CG AGF, 22 Apr 43, sub: Victory Program TB. (2) ASF memo (S) PAOG 475 to OPD, 19 Jun 43, sub: Policies Governing Issue of Equip. (3) WD memo (S) OPD 400 (19 Jun 43) to CG AGF, 26 Jul 43, sub: Preshipment. All in 320.2/22 (TUB 43)(S).

Army Ground Forces had been apprehensive of the effects of preshipment, and it did cause a temporary decline in the flow of equipment to units in training. In the long run the policy proved a benefit. Production was speeded up by the pressure brought to bear on factories to turn out large quantities of equipment for transoceanic transportation during the summer and autumn months, while British shipping and port facilities were less strained than usual. Moreover, the release of equipment by units ordered to ports of embarkation made it available almost immediately to units in training.[46]

In 1944-45 equipment became available in increasingly large quantities, but shortages in certain items were reported at various times until the end of the war in Europe. In April 1945 the chief of the AGF Engineer Section stated:[47]

> Until recently we had shortages of all types of equipment. The situation improved for a while in the early months of 1944, then it became bad again, as theater demands increased and as the Army Service Forces began to call in equipment for rehabilitation in preparation for overseas shipment. For the past six months we have had only one M-2 Treadway Bridge in the Army Ground Forces, and it had to be used primarily for testing purposes; recently we even lost that. The Ground Forces got its first 2½ ton dump truck for training purposes about February 1945.

Deficiencies were most common and serious in such newly developed items as carrier equipment (for sending messages of various frequencies over the same channel), speech security equipment for signal units, and transporter equipment for ordnance units.[48]

Preferred Status of the Arms

There were some who believed that the basic obstacle to the effective training of nondivisional units was the preferred status enjoyed by the arms. There is no doubt that, in the early period of the war, training of divisions enjoyed definite priority over the training of spare parts, particularly those falling in service categories. Thus, while a detailed plan for the systematic production of divisions was developed at the inception of the Army Ground Forces, a similar plan for the building and training of spare parts was not formulated until March 1943, too late, in view of subsequent personnel shortages, to be of great benefit. The initial focusing of emphasis on divisional training is attributable in part, at least, to the belief that small units could in general be trained more quickly and with less

[46] Statement of Col J. B. Hughes, AGF Engr Off, to AGF Hist Off, 29 Jan 44.

[47] Statement of AGF Engr Off to AGF Hist Off, 28 Apr 45.

[48] Interviews with AGF staff officers.

difficulty than divisions. Experiences of 1942 indicated that this conception was unsound and that the production of dependable and smoothly functioning spare parts required no less careful planning, no less close supervision, and hardly, if any, less time than did the larger units they were to support in combat. But serious and persistent personnel shortages permitted only a partial application of this important lesson. Although the training of spare parts received greater emphasis after 1942, the role of small units seems to have continued to be secondary to that of divisions; after divisional training had been shaken down into good working order in 1943, the spotlight tended to turn to replacements. Reports of The Inspector General leave the impression that personnel and training deficiencies of alerted units throughout the history of the Army Ground Forces were much more common among spare parts than among divisions.

Some of the Special Staff personnel of Headquarters, Army Ground Forces, were strongly of the opinion that the training of service units suffered because of the preferred status of the arms over the services in the planning and administration of the training program. They complained of a reluctance in both Headquarters, Army Ground Forces, and subordinate commands to take Special Staff officers fully into counsel and to clothe them with essential authority.[49] In April 1945 the AGF ordnance officer wrote to G–3 as follows:[50]

> There has been a continued tendency on the part of subordinate commands, as well as this headquarters, to de-emphasize the responsibilities of the ordnance staff officer in these maintenance matters. In fact the Replacement and School Command, for example, does not even have as a part of its headquarters an ordnance section. Another typical example is the Antiaircraft Command . . . in which the ordnance officer of the command must justify to a representative of the office of chief of staff the inspection or visit he plans to make before he can make such an inspection to determine maintenance practices and adequacy of maintenance training in subordinate units. . . . Experience in theaters of operations has proven beyond any possible contention the need for strong Special Staff Sections to supervise, inspect and advise in maintenance matters.

The AGF ordnance officer also objected strongly to what he regarded as a neglect of the services in the training programs prepared by G–3 for the Japanese phase of the war.[51]

[49] *Ibid.*

[50] AGF M/S (S), Ord Sec to G–3, 13 Apr 45, sub: Maint Tng and Procedure. AGF Ord files, "Ord Maint, 1945" (S).

[51] AGF M/S, Ord to G–3, 10 Mar 45, sub: AGF Tng Memorandum No. 1. AGF G–3 Sec files, 300.6 (Tng Memo No. 1).

The view was held by some that relegation of the services to a secondary position in the Army Ground Forces caused an overstressing of military subjects in service units and the allotment of insufficient time and attention to functional training. Thus in April 1945 the AGF engineer officer stated:[52]

> The overwhelming sentiment of the theaters is that we should devote more time to training in engineer duties and less time to marching and shooting. The theater people say that their primary need is road builders but that we send them men who are good at shooting and fighting but who are lacking in ability to organize and execute engineer projects.

It is not unlikely that neglect of service units and of other spare parts was often more imagined than real. In any event, despite many difficulties of personnel, equipment, and supervision, the training of nondivisional units improved during most of the AGF period. Activation procedure had been systematized, training programs had been recast to conform to the actualities of combat, supervision had been intensified by creation of intermediate headquarters, command had been streamlined by the setting up of flexible groups and battalions, checking of training proficiency had been improved by the modernization of tests and testing techniques, and increased productiveness of American factories had reduced to a rare phenomenon the spectacle of spare-parts soldiers using sticks for guns, rocks for grenades, and jeeps for tanks. Accordingly, nondivisional units leaving port in 1945 were considerably better qualified for performing their missions than were those sent overseas in 1942.

[52] Statement of AGF Engr Off to AGF Hist Off, 28 Apr 45.

The Preparation of Units For Overseas Movement

by

Bell I. Wiley

230-171 O - 66 - 37

Contents

I. Initial Procedures and Problems

The culminating function of Army Ground Forces was the delivery of units to ports of embarkation in readiness for theater requirements. Even though in actual practice most units shipped overseas received considerable training after they reached the theaters, Army Ground Forces was held responsible, except in cases of specific exemption by the War Department, for bringing units to a state of complete combat readiness before releasing them to port commanders for staging and shipment.

A casual perusal of training literature might lead to the assumption that normally units were ready for combat when they completed the prescribed cycle of training and that a call for overseas shipment entailed nothing more than a final checking of personnel and equipment and a routine movement to port. But conditions which prevailed during most of the period from 1942 to 1945 made the processing of units a difficult and complicated matter. Chronic shortages of personnel and, especially in 1942–43, of equipment made it impossible to keep units fully manned and equipped. Consequently the earmarking of a unit for movement usually necessitated a hurried draft on other tactical organizations for both men and material. The vicious circle of robbing and replenishing resulted almost without exception in units reaching final stages of training with a heavy admixture of partially trained men. These had to be either replaced or rushed to completion of minimum training requirements.

AGF Responsibilities in Preparation for Overseas Movement

Army Ground Forces had many tasks to perform in the final preparation of units for overseas movement, which came to be known as POM. It was responsible for designating specific units when the War Department gave notice that certain numbers of various types were needed. It informed major subordinate commands of the earmarking of units under their jurisdiction for early overseas shipment. It drafted movement orders for issuance by The Adjutant General to all major commands concerned, specifying units to be moved, shipment code numbers, and the agency charged with execution of the movement, and giving general information as to equipment, clothing, personnel, and mode of travel. It collaborated with other War Department agencies in the preparation and revision of detailed instructions for guidance of all echelons having a part in bringing units to a state of combat readiness and moving them to port. It issued supplementary information on points not covered in movement orders and War Department instructions. It had to coordinate its efforts with those of Army Service Forces to expedite filling of equipment shortages and to assure movement of units within a reasonable time after they were alerted. Periodically, through command channels, it checked pertinent AGF agencies and activities to ensure compliance with current instructions.

Army Ground Forces for a time was also given authority to supervise, in coordination with port commanders, AGF units after they had passed to the temporary control of the Army Service Forces, the agency responsible for the staging and overseas shipment of units. Normally units were transferred to intermediate stations called "staging areas" for last-minute processing before moving to loading docks. Staging areas were regarded as adjuncts to ports of embarkation, and on arrival therein units passed to the control of the port commander.[1]

Only limited instrumentalities for discharge of these functions were provided in the initial organization of Army Ground Forces. The sole headquarters agency specifically charged with such matters was the Task Forces Branch of the Operations Division, which after the reorganization of July 1942 became the Task Force Division of the G–3 Section. The Task Forces Branch consisted originally of six officers and one enlisted man, all of whom came at the inception of Army Ground Forces from the Operations Branch of G–3, War Department.[2] Personnel phases of overseas movement during the early AGF period were handled largely by Col. George R. Stanton, in addition to his other duties as head of the Officers Branch of the Personnel Division.[3] Col. Victor A. St. Onge of the AGF Supply Division performed most of the equipment and supply functions; he too had other duties.[4] Not until December 1942 and March 1943, respectively, were separate task force divisions created in the G–1 and G–4 Sections (sections which in the July 1942 reorganization of Headquarters, Army Ground Forces, absorbed the Personnel and Supply Divisions).[5]

The application of the term "task force" to AGF agencies charged with POM functions requires a word of explanation. The War Department directive of

[1] WD ltr AG 353 (3–24–42) MT–C to CG AGF, 26 Mar 42, sub: Tng of Units at Staging Areas. 320.2/1 (Staging Areas).

[2] Statement of Lt Col S. L. Weld, G–3 Task Force Div AGF, to AGF Hist Off, 24 May 44.

[3] Statement of Maj J. S. Claypool, G–1 Task Force Div AGF, to AGF Hist Off, 26 May 44.

[4] Statement of Col V. A. St. Onge, G–4 Task Force Div AGF, to AGF Hist Off, 23 May 44.

[5] (1) *Ibid.* (2) AGF Daily Bull, 3 Dec 42.

2 March 1942, which created Army Ground Forces, intimated that the preparation of task forces might be a major function of the new headquarters. One paragraph of this directive stated that "the mission of the Army Ground Forces is to provide Ground units properly organized, trained and equipped for combat operations." Another listed among the duties specifically assigned to Army Ground Forces "the organization, equipment and training of such task forces as are directed by The Chief of Staff." [6] During the first few months of its existence Army Ground Forces was charged with organizing and preparing a few task forces. In March, for example, the War Department gave Army Ground Forces the responsibility of setting up a force for Tongatabu, an island in the South Pacific. Duties performed by Army Ground Forces in this connection included selection of the task force commander, activation of a force headquarters, designation of the necessary ground units, coordination with Services of Supply (later called Army Service Forces) for supplies and organization of service units, and movement of elements of the force to the port of embarkation.[7] In July 1942 Army Ground Forces had similar responsibilities for two other shipments.[8] In these cases Headquarters, Army Ground Forces, functioned as General Headquarters, U.S. Army, had functioned. But in each of these instances the size of the force was so small and the objective so limited as hardly to merit the designation "task force" as the term is usually understood.

Late in 1942, the War Department delegated to Army Ground Forces the preparation of a large combat-loaded task force consisting of the 45th Division and attached elements.[9] In July 1943, this force, totaling some 21,000 officers and enlisted men, participated in the Sicily landings.[10] But the three other major

[6] Cir 59, WD, 2 Mar 42.

[7] (1) AGF memo (S) 370.5–OPN for TAG, 14 Mar 42, sub: Orgn and Mvmt Orders, Shipment 0051 (Ground Forces). (See especially M/R atchd). (2) WD ltr (S) AG 370.5 (3–14–42) MC–GN–M to CGs First and Third Armies and V Army Corps, 15 Mar 42, sub: Mvmt Orders, Shipment 0051 (Ground Forces). Both in AGF G–3 files, Shipment 0051 (S).

[8] WD memo (S) OPD 370.5 (7–7–42) to CGs, 7 Jul 42, sub: Task Force for Ostler and Lineout. AGF Movement Orders files (S), Shipment 8408.

[9] (1) OPD D/F (S) 353 Amph Force to AGF, 31 Dec 42, sub: Designation of Units for Amph Tng. 353/53 (Amph Tng Comd–AF)(S). (2) Statement of Lt Col S. L. Weld to AGF Hist Off, 24 May 44. (3) AGF ltr (S) to CG Second Army, 16 Jan 43, sub: Amph Task Force. 320.2/10 (Amph Tng Comd–AF) (S). (4) Ltr (S) of Maj Gen Troy Middleton, CG 45th Div to AGF, 1 Jun 43, sub: Amph Task Force. 320.2/10 (Amph Tng Comd–AF)(S). (5) AGF M/R (S), 12 Apr 43, sub: Equip for 45th Div and Atchd Units. AGF G–4 Task Force files, binder marked "Task Force 45th Div" (S).

[10] Papers filed in AGF G–4 Task Force files, binders marked "North African Books" (S), especially WD ltr (S) OPD 370.5 (4–14–43) to CGs 45th Div, AGF, and ASF, 14 Apr 43, sub: Overseas Mvmt of 45th Inf Div, Re-inf.

combat-loaded task forces organized in this country—those destined for North Africa, Kiska, and Attu—were prepared by other agencies.[11]

In view of the fact that only an insignificant portion of the units prepared for overseas movement by Army Ground Forces were parts of task forces, the task force divisions of Headquarters, Army Ground Forces, were misnamed. These organizations might more appropriately have been called POM divisions.

As far as overseas movements were concerned, the first two months after the establishment of Army Ground Forces were a time of comparative inactivity. In March 1942 only 8 AGF units, with an authorized enlisted strength of 1,187, were shipped to ports of embarkation. In April 16 units, with an enlisted strength of 11,660, were shipped.[12] But in that month steps were instituted by the War Department which promised an immediate and tremendous acceleration of POM activities. These steps had to do with the plan for a cross-Channel invasion of Europe in the spring of 1943.

This plan, known as ROUNDUP, called for the shipment to England of from 750,000 to 1,000,000 men. A variant of the scheme (called the "modified" plan, with code name SLEDGEHAMMER) contemplated invasion by a smaller force whose American contingent would number over 100,000 men, about 1 September 1942.[13]

The Plans Section represented Army Ground Forces headquarters on the War Department committee charged with preparations. In early May the Plans Section, in close collaboration with G–3, completed a tentative movement schedule of Ground Forces units for ROUNDUP. This schedule designated specific units, including 18 divisions, and totaling over 500,000 men, for monthly shipment to the United Kingdom from May 1942 to April 1943.[14] There were many modifications of this schedule to meet changes in estimates of requirements and of shipping facilities. In the late summer, ROUNDUP was laid aside in favor of a plan (code name TORCH) which called for the landing of a large force in North Africa.[15]

[11] Statement of Lt Col S. L. Weld to AGF Hist Off, 24 May 44.

[12] Information compiled from monthly AGF Stat Sec Rpt No. 19 (S), "AGF Units Arriving at PE." AGF Stat Sec files.

[13] (1) Plan for Opn in Western Europe (S). AGF Plans Sec files, Bolero/4 (S). (2) Memo (S) of Lt Col L. L. Lemnitzer, Plans Sec, for CofS AGF, 1 May 42, sub: Meeting of Bolero Committee. AGF Plans Sec files, Bolero/6 (S). (3) *Biennial Report of the Chief of Staff, U.S. Army, July 1, 1943 to June 30, 1945*, pp. 8–9.

[14] "Tentative Movement Schedule, AGF, Bolero Plan, 9 May 42" (S). AGF Plans Sec files, Bolero/19 (S).

[15] (1) *Biennial Report of the Chief of Staff, U.S. Army, July 1, 1943 to June 30, 1945*, p. 9. (2) Memo (S) of Col F. J. Tate, Plans Sec. for CofS AGF, 25 Sep 42, sub: Rpt on OPD Conference on Pers Matters.

The immediate effect of ROUNDUP was to speed up the processing of units earmarked for early shipment. In May 1942, 57 AGF units, with an enlisted strength of 41,218 men and including 2 divisions, were moved to ports of embarkation. In June and July, movements to port fell to about 15,000 men per month, but a definite decision in the late summer to invade Africa in the fall brought a new impetus. In August AGF agencies shipped 49 units and 40,209 enlisted men to ports of embarkation, and in September 1942 the preparation of Task Force A, the force which with elements from England invaded North Africa in November 1942, raised movement to the unprecedented figure of 67 units and 88,636 men—the highest attained during any month prior to January 1944. All told, AGF elements moved to ports of embarkation from 9 March to 31 December 1942 totaled 361 units and 268,107 enlisted men.[16]

Problems of Personnel, Equipment, and Schedules

The processing of so large a number of units and men entailed many difficulties and revealed not a few deficiencies. An initial source of trouble was inexperience. Comparatively few of the officers charged with POM responsibilities, from the War Department on down, had had first-hand contact with problems of overseas movement prior to the reorganization of 9 March 1942, and those who did have experience had acquired it only recently.[17] There was naturally a considerable amount of fumbling until officers of the various echelons learned their jobs. A recurrent handicap, particularly serious in 1942, was the haste with which units had to be prepared. First there was the pressure of ROUNDUP and then of TORCH. Urgency was so great as to preclude the advance planning essential to an orderly and efficient processing. Another general source of difficulty, especially in 1942, was a shortage of virtually everything needed to bring units to a state of combat readiness. The year 1942 was a period of enormous expansion of the armed forces, in which new units vied with old ones for officers, men, and materiel. There was simply not enough to go around.

320.2/114 (S). (3) AGF M/S (S) of Lt Col L. L. Lemnitzer for CofS AGF, 19 Jun 42, sub: Meeting of Bolero Committee, 18 Jun. AGF Plans Sec files, Bolero/35 (S).

[16] Information compiled from monthly AGF Stat Sec Rpt No. 19 (S), "AGF Units Arriving at PE." AGF Stat Sec files. There is a slight discrepancy between the figures in this report and a special composite report, "AGF Units Arriving at PE, March 1942–April 1944," owing to the fact that reports of units arriving at port late in the month sometimes did not arrive at AGF headquarters in time for inclusion in the current issue of Report No. 19. It was deemed preferable in this study for the sake of consistency to use information based on Report No. 19.

[17] Statement of Lt Col S. L. Weld to AGF Hist Off, 24 May 44.

Units earmarked for early shipment overseas were given highest priority, but when movements were ordered at such great speed and volume as in 1942 it was exceedingly difficult to meet the demands of the preferred units and at the same time to leave anything for the swarm of units being activated each month.[18]

Of the many difficulties those having to do with personnel were the most acute. Because of demands for cadres, losses to the Air Forces and officer candidate schools, and other attritional influences, most units were considerably understrength when they were earmarked for overseas movement. The 3d Division had only 65 percent of its authorized strength when alerted, and two other divisions of Task Force A were each short over 2,000 enlisted men on the eve of their call to intensive training.[19] The last-minute filling of depleted units was accomplished at the expense of organizations of lower priority. The units thus robbed were often alerted after only a brief interval, with the result that they in turn had to draw fillers from other organizations; thus an endless sequence of stripping and filling was set in motion.[20]

A similar problem arose in connection with the disposition of personnel disqualified for overseas service. Because of manpower shortages, the difficulty under existing regulations of dispensing with the physically unqualified, repeated additions of untrained filler replacements, and dilatoriness of command in instituting housecleaning measures, units commonly found themselves, on being alerted, burdened with considerable numbers of substandard officers and men. With movement to port imminent, the only feasible course was to direct some units of lower priority to accept the substandard and untrained men in exchange for an equal number of personnel qualified for combat. But unfortunately it sometimes happened that the unit which received the undesirables was itself alerted a short time later. Whereupon it proceeded to unload its recently acquired incompetents, along with substandard personnel of its own, upon some unit further down the line of priority.[21]

The absorption of large numbers of new men and officers on the eve of sailing was apt to be disruptive. An officer of a division shipped overseas in the spring of

[18] (1) *Ibid.* (2) Statement of Col V. A. St. Onge to AGF Hist Off, 30 Mar 44. (3) AGF memo (S) for Col Elliot D. Cooke, IGD, 31 Oct 42, sub: Processing of Task Forces. 320.2/133 (S).

[19] Memo (S) of Gen Marshall for Gen McNair, 28 Nov 42, sub not given. With atchd papers. 353/151 (sep binder) (S).

[20] AGF memo (S) for Col Elliot D. Cooke, IGD, 31 Oct 42, sub: Processing of Task Forces. 320.2/133 (S).

[21] (1) See "The Procurement of Enlisted Personnel: the Problem of Quality" and "The Building and Training of Infantry Divisions," both in this volume. (2) Ltr (S) of CO Boston PE to CofTrans WD, 22 Aug 42, sub: WD Tr Mvmt Orders—Delayed or Not Recd. 370.5/530 (S).

1942 wrote just prior to leaving port: "We drew over 3,000 Inf[antry] at last minute at PE. This is a slug. Men do not know officers and vice versa." [22]

The haste of last-minute transfers sometimes resulted in flagrant cases of misassignment. When Task Force A was on the point of embarkation, "a number of enlisted men who had been trained as machine gunners were assigned as riflemen and consequently did not know how to fire the M-1 rifles which were issued to them practically at the pier." [23]

Equipment gave rise to difficulties no less harassing. Because of the shortage prevalent in 1942, few units when earmarked for overseas shipment had anything like the full allotment of equipment. Service-type units often had considerably less than 50 percent of their authorized allowances. When units were alerted, steps were initiated immediately to supply deficiencies from stock or production. In 1942 the requisitions on these sources frequently could not be met. The only alternative was to take the needed equipment from units in training, thus setting up a vicious circle like that pertaining to personnel.[24]

The completion of equipment, whatever the source, required time. Often shortages were not filled until arrival at port. It was not unusual in 1942 for units in staging areas to rush numbers of men through required firing courses with weapons borrowed from neighboring units or from port commanders.[25]

After requirements had thus been met, it sometimes happened that when allotted weapons finally arrived they were of a model or type different from that which the men had been using. In 1942 units, particularly those in service categories, whose Tables of Basic Allowances called for carbines, were compelled by the prevalent shortage of these weapons to complete training with 1903 or 1917 rifles. But these units always faced the possibility of having their rifles replaced by carbines at staging areas or ports, too late for practice in firing.[26]

Sometimes radical innovations just emerging from production lines were issued to units on the eve of embarkation. In November 1942, "bazookas" were

[22] Personal ltr (S) of Col William Hones, CofS 32d Div, to Col Lloyd D. Brown, AGF, 21 Apr 42. 370.5/4 (32d Div) (S).

[23] Memo (S) of Gen Marshall for Gen McNair, 28 Nov 42, sub not given. With atchd papers. 353/151 (sep binder) (S).

[24] (1) AGF memo (S) for Col Elliot D. Cooke, 31 Oct 42, sub: Processing of Task Forces. 320.2/133 (S). (2) See above, "The Building and Training of Infantry Divisions" and "The Training of Nondivisional Units."

[25] Ltr (S) of Brig Gen Benjamin C. Lockwood to CofS USA, 1 Apr 42, sub: Task Force 0051. AGF G–3 files, Shipment 0051 (S).

[26] II Armd Corps ltr (C) to AGF, 3 Feb 43, sub: Small Arms Tng of Alerted Units. 353/116 (Int Tng) (C).

issued at the last minute to troops in Task Force A "without anybody knowing how to use them or even what they were for." New types of landing nets and radios were also issued to a portion of this force just prior to its sailing.[27]

Sometimes units that had weapons could not obtain shells for them. The commander of an armored corps reported to General McNair early in 1943: "While there are sufficient carbines in the corps to permit rotation on temporary loan to alerted units . . . ammunition . . . is inadequate. . . . Over a thousand Launchers, Rocket AT M-1 are available . . . [but] to date neither M-6 nor M-7 ammunition have been available." [28]

Frequent modification of movement schedules to meet changes of strategic plans, variations of theater requirements, and fluctuations of available shipping were other sources of difficulty. In some instances units that had been directed on one day to prepare for movement in two or three months had to be informed a few days later to expect movement within two or three weeks. In other cases units were alerted and "de-alerted" several times. In still others they were actually called to port and their organizational equipment shipped to the theater, after which they were transferred back to a training status under Army Ground Forces.[29]

Estimates of theater requirements changed so rapidly in 1942 that Army Ground Forces sometimes received conflicting instructions from closely related War Department agencies.[30] On receipt in July of the projected overseas movement schedule for the fourth quarter of 1942, prepared by the War Department G-3, Army Ground Forces commented:[31]

The Ground Forces units listed in the attached memo do not agree with current plans of OPD WDGS, as recently conveyed to this Headquarters. There are differences in the number and types of divisions, and number of Army Corps Headquarters. . . . It is believed

[27] Memo (S) of Gen Marshall for Gen McNair, 28 Nov 42, sub not given. With atchd papers. 353/151 (sep binders) (S).

[28] II Armd Corps ltr (C) to AGF, 3 Feb 43, sub: Small Arms Tng of Alerted Units. 353/116 (Int Tng) (C).

[29] (1) AGF M/S (S), Opns Div G-3 to Sec Gen Staff, 28 Apr 42, sub not given. 370.5/4 (32d Div) (S). (2) Data (S) on overseas movement of 38th Div in AGF G-3 files, Shipment 5264 (S). (3) Data (S) on overseas movement of 29th Div in AGF G-3 files, Shipment 0550 (S). (4) AGF memo (draft) (S) for G-3 WD, 24 Jun 42, sub: Str of Units in Bolero. AGF Plans Sec file, Bolero/47 (S). (5) AGF M/S (S), Opns Div to G-3, 19 Jun 42, sub: Withdrawal of Equip from Divs for Shipment to Bolero. 370.5/407 (S). (6) Statement of Lt Col J. A. Hanson, G-4 Task Force Div AGF, to AGF Hist Off, 10 Mar 45.

[30] Memo (R) of Col F. J. Tate, AGF Plans Sec, for CofS AGF, 2 Sep 42, sub: Confusion at DTC over Conflicting Orders. 370.5/134 (R).

[31] AGF memo (S) for G-3 WD, 31 Jul 42, sub: Tentative Overseas Mvmt Projected Augmentation and Task Forces (Estimate) for Fourth Quarter 42. 370.5/451 (S).

that discrepancies also exist between the list of units on attached memorandum and latest revised plans of OPD.

The effect of changing plans on individual units is illustrated by the experience of the 32d Infantry Division as described by an AGF staff officer:[32]

Late in December 1941, the 32d Division . . . was earmarked for Force Magnet. . . . The Division was placed in a priority for distribution of controlled items of equipment and for assignment of personnel to meet a planned schedule of movement to overseas destination. Shipping facilities retarded the contemplated date of sailing. It was now estimated that this division would sail . . . not earlier than July 1942. At 8:45 A.M. 25 March 1942 telephone information was received from the OPD War Department General Staff to the effect that the 32d Division would sail from the San Francisco P/E not later than April 15. At this time the division was short 4788 enlisted men. In addition its Engineer Regiment had been shipped to North Ireland. It was now necessary to complete the preparation of this unit and place it at the Port in San Francisco all the way across the country from Ft. Devens, Mass. in *three weeks* time, whereas existing schedule of priority provided for completion of its preparation in time to sail in three months. In order to prepare the division within the limited time available, it was necessary to ship fillers and equipment direct to the Port of Embarkation.

Effects of Overlapping Jurisdiction

Another source of difficulty in 1942 was the confusion caused by overlapping authority of the various agencies involved in the processing of units for overseas movement. The situation with reference to staging areas is a case in point. As previously noted, directives in effect when Army Ground Forces was created put units in staging areas under the control of commanders of ports of embarkation and, therefore, of the Services of Supply. This arrangement was based on the assumption that units would not proceed to staging areas until fully trained, manned, and equipped, and that they would remain there only a short time.

But things did not work out as planned. The need for utilizing all available shipping to meet such urgent requirements as ROUNDUP led to the practice of assembling men near ports in numbers that far exceeded normal shipping capacities. Changes in strategic plans, as noted above, sometimes caused postponement or cancellation of shipment after units were moved to staging areas. The result of these and other factors was the overflow of "true staging areas," such as Camp Kilmer, designed and equipped solely for routine steps incident to final processing, into quasi-staging establishments such as Fort Ord, Calif., Indiantown Gap, Pa., and Fort Dix, N. J. Instead of remaining in staging areas for two or three

[32] AGF M/S (S), Opns Div to Sec Gen Staff, 28 Apr 42, sub not given. 370.5/4 (32d Div)(S).

weeks as originally contemplated, units frequently lingered for two or three months. Staging activities, instead of being limited to final processing and maintenance of combat readiness, were extended to include reception of large increments of personnel and equipment, putting considerable numbers of replacements through firing courses and other minimum training requirements, and instructing old and new personnel in the use of recently acquired equipment. In short, staging installations to a large extent became training establishments. But port facilities were not designed for training functions, and port authorities were not familiar with AGF training programs. Consequently the combat fitness of units deteriorated during the long wait for overseas movement.

On 26 March 1942 the War Department took cognizance of these difficulties by giving Lt. Gen. Lesley J. McNair, Commanding General of Army Ground Forces, and Lt. Gen. Henry H. Arnold, Commanding General of Army Air Forces, authority to supervise the training, in coordination with port commanders concerned, of AGF and AAF units awaiting embarkation at Fort Dix, Indiantown Gap, Fort Ord, and other stations used to augment the capacity of true staging areas. But the provision was added that this step was "not to be construed to diminish the control of the unit by the Port Commander." [33]

Army Ground Forces on 10 July 1942 issued a training directive for units in staging areas. But, owing to the adoption concurrently of the policy of preshipping equipment of units destined for England, as well as to uncertainty as to the authority conferred by the War Department letter of 26 March, this directive was couched in terms so general as to be of little practical use.[34]

The plan of having Army Ground Forces supervise the training of units controlled by Services of Supply did not work out satisfactorily. In August 1942 General Marshall indicated to General McNair his desire for a scheme that would give Army Ground Forces greater control over units during the staging period.[35] A staff officer, charged by General McNair with digging out key data on which to base a response to General Marshall's request, reported difficulty in determining precisely what installations were considered as staging areas. "The whole question of staging areas is confused and rather complicated," he wrote.[36] His

[33] WD ltr AG 353 (3–24–42) MT–C to CG AGF, 26 Mar 42, sub: Tng of Units at Staging Areas. 320.2/1 (Staging Areas).

[34] AGF ltr to CGs, 10 Jul 42, sub: Tng Dir for Units During Period from Arrival at Staging Areas to Departure for PEs. 353/1515.

[35] AGF memo (C) for CofS USA, 19 Aug 42, sub: Comd of Units Ordered Overseas. 320.2/1 (Staging Areas) (C).

[36] Memo (C) of Lt Col William J. Eyerly for Gen McNair, 19 Aug 42, sub: Status of Staging Areas. 320.2/1 (Staging Areas) (C).

comment is borne out by a report from the Second Army a short time previously that SOS authorities had attempted to designate Fort Jackson, S. C., as a staging area, and had sent officers there from the Boston Port of Embarkation to supervise POM activities of certain units scheduled for early movement. Backed by Army Ground Forces, Second Army restricted the visitors to liaison functions on the ground that Fort Jackson was a training camp, not a staging area.[37]

General McNair recommended to General Marshall on 19 August 1942 that AGF units sent to Fort Dix, Indiantown Gap, and Fort Ord, the three staging areas where dual responsibility had existed, remain under command of Army Ground Forces, "subject to direct orders by the port commander in connection with administrative measures and other preparations for movement overseas." He observed that most of the difficulty arose from the long sojourns of units in staging areas. "If conditions become such that units could be moved more promptly," he added, "the necessity of the action recommended would be lessened." [38]

General McNair's proposal that Army Ground Forces be given command of units staged at Fort Dix, Indiantown Gap, and Fort Ord was not adopted. On 12 September 1942 a directive issued over General Marshall's signature perpetuated the port commanders' control over units in all staging areas. This control included "continuance of such training as will not interfere with preparation for overseas movement." To provide more effective supervision of nondivisional units the directive required establishment of small permanent command groups in each staging area. Separate command groups of each of the three major forces were authorized in cases where the number of units of each command was large enough to make such action desirable. The Commanding Generals of Army Ground Forces, Services of Supply, and Army Air Forces were required to maintain liaison with these command groups, which were under command of the port commander and therefore of the Commanding General, Services of Supply, and "to cause periodical inspections to be made of their respective units within staging areas, to insure that training is continued and that disciplinary standards are maintained." [39]

On 5 October 1942 Army Ground Forces sent to its principal components a directive which informed them that command groups were soon to be set up in

[37] Second Army 5th ind (S), 30 Oct 42, on ltr of CO Boston PE to CofTrans WD, 22 Aug 42, sub: WD Tr Mvmt Orders—Delayed and Not Rcd. 370.5/530 (S).

[38] AGF memo (C) for CofS USA, 19 Aug 42, sub: Comd of Units Ordered Overseas. 320.2/1 (Staging Areas) (C).

[39] Memo (R) of Gen Marshall for CGs AGF, AAF, SOS, 12 Sep 42, sub: Control of Units in Staging Areas. 320.2/2 (Staging Areas) (R).

the various staging areas and which delegated to appropriate armies and corps the liaison and inspection responsibilities set forth in the Chief of Staff's directive of 12 September.[40]

But while steps were being taken to implement the directive of 12 September, there was much shaking of heads at Headquarters, Army Ground Forces, as to its effectiveness. One staff member commented:[41]

> A duplication of personnel and effort is indicated here. It is not believed that the establishment of these command groups, although directed by the War Department, will accomplish the desires of the Chief of Staff, United States Army. . . . This matter has been tossed about by successive echelons of the War Department, each being farther removed from the original conception, until the final product is a makeshift which, in my opinion, is far from the most effective solution. It merely sets up additional help for the staging area commander and places additional requirements upon Army Ground Forces for personnel.

General McNair felt that Army Ground Forces could exercise its limited training responsibilities in staging areas through existing army and corps inspection systems, and, in view of the prevalent shortage of personnel, he was reluctant to turn officers and men over to the Services of Supply for use in administrative capacities the value of which he could not clearly see.[42] Apparently no one was satisfied with the system instituted by the directive of 12 September. Services of Supply disliked the idea of outsiders coming into staging areas to inspect units that had passed to its command. Army Ground Forces turned a cold shoulder to the suggestion that it provide personnel for command groups which it did not control.[43]

After General Marshall expressed strong dissatisfaction in November 1942 with the circumstances surrounding the final processing of Task Force A, Army Ground Forces again proposed that it be allowed to retain command of AGF units during their staging period. Nothing came of this recommendation.[44]

On 5 January 1943 the War Department, in a general revamping of POM policies, revoked the requirement that Army Ground Forces inspect units in

[40] AGF ltr (R) to CGs, 5 Oct 42, sub and location as in n. 39.

[41] AGF M/S (S), Plans Sec to CofS, 22 Oct 42, sub as in n. 39. 320.2/1 (Staging Areas) (S).

[42] AGF M/S (S), Gen McNair to G-3, 12 Oct 42, sub: Conferences on Control of Units in Staging Areas. 320.2/1 (Staging Areas) (S).

[43] Memo (S) of Lt Col Herbert B. Powell for G-3 AGF, 8 Oct 42, sub as in n. 42. With related papers. 320.2/1 (Staging Areas) (S).

[44] (1) Memo (S) of Gen Marshall for Gen McNair, 28 Nov 42, sub not given. With atchd papers. 353/151 (sep binder) (S). (2) AGF memo (S) of DCofS for CG, 4 Dec 42, sub: Conference. 337/24 (S). (3) AGF memo (C), DCofS for DCofS USA, 17 Dec 42, sub: Preparation of Task Forces. With incl. 322/1 (Task Forces) (C).

staging areas, and at the same time directed port commanders to make every effort to reduce staging periods to a maximum of two weeks.[45] This action did not specifically forbid Army Ground Forces to make inspections of units while they were being staged, but that Army Ground Forces interpreted it in this light is indicated by an incident that occurred in June 1943. On 2 June Brig. Gen. Walter L. Weible, Director of Military Training, Army Service Forces, wrote G–3, Army Ground Forces, that training in staging areas was suffering from lack of proper guidance. "I would appreciate it greatly," he said, "if you would have your training inspectors visit staging areas containing units or individuals of the Army Ground Forces to determine what further steps could or should be taken to improve the training possibilities during their period in the staging area. I would welcome any suggestions on the subject as apparently such training has important effects on morale." This letter was finally sent to the Adjutant General's Records in August 1943, with the pencilled note: "General Lentz desired no further action."[46]

Headquarters, Army Ground Forces, apparently made no effort after the beginning of 1943 to secure control over units in staging areas. Improvement in the shipping situation, repeated protests on the part of Army Ground Forces against the tendency of Army Service Forces to pile up units in staging areas as a cushion against sudden increases of available transports, and the settling down of theater requirements to a somewhat firmer basis reduced instances of prolonged staging periods in 1943 and 1944. This removed to a large extent the basis of objection to Army Service Forces' control. The command groups persisted into 1944, and AGF commands were instructed, through these liaison connections, to "render such assistance as requested by the port commander as may be practicable." Indications are that such assistance was rarely, if ever, requested by port commanders.[47]

Confusion from overlapping authority also arose in connection with the preparation of task forces. This was mainly because of the entrance of another authority, the task force headquarters, into an already complicated picture. The Tongatabu Task Force prepared in the spring of 1942 is a case in point. As previously noted, major responsibility for the organization of this force was dele-

[45] WD ltr (C) AG 320.2 (1–2–43) OB–S–C–M to CGs, 5 Jan 43, sub: Orgn, Tng, and Equip of Units for Overseas Serv. 320.2/2 (Staging Areas) (C).

[46] Memo (R) of Brig Gen Walter L. Weible for G–3 AGF, 2 Jun 43, sub: Continuation of Tng in Staging Areas, PEs. 320.2/4 (Staging Areas) (R).

[47] Statement of Lt Thomas P. Govan, Hist Off, Second Army, to AGF Hist Off, 26 Jul 44.

230-171 O - 66 - 38

gated by War Plans Division to Army Ground Forces. According to plans drafted at Headquarters, Army Ground Forces, the V Corps was directed to organize the bulk of the force from elements of the 37th Division at Indiantown Gap, but one small detachment was to be organized by the First Army at Fort Dix and another by the Third Army at Camp Livingston; shipment was to be from the New York Port of Embarkation, after staging at Fort Dix and Indiantown Gap.[48]

While the army and corps commanders concerned were complying with these arrangements, Brig. Gen. Benjamin C. Lockwood was designated as Task Force Commander, and a force headquarters was set up in the Munitions Building in Washington. The confusion which ensued was depicted in a report made by General Lockwood to General Marshall on 1 April 1942:[49]

The component elements of this force were assembled from numerous stations and many had to be organized just prior to their movement to the staging area.

Numerous new Tables of Organization and Tables of Basic Allowances had to be prepared and issued to the supply services, the units concerned, this headquarters, the two staging areas and to the port of embarkation. Many of these required check and modification to fit requirements.

There was little or no chance for the force commander to assemble this force, get to know the unit commander, and expedite adjustment of numerous problems and difficulties. Actually he had practically no control prior to embarkation. Practically all of the headquarters staff and all organization commanders and units were strangers to the force commander.

. . . .

Many of the difficulties and delays . . . were due to the numerous intermediate commanders and staffs which entered into the picture. For example, upon visiting the Indiantown Gap Staging Area, it was found that the Division Commander of the 37th Infantry Division was requiring the Infantry and Field Artillery components of this force to participate in a review during the last week of their stay in the staging area. The V Army Corps was requiring the Field Artillery battalion to fire a test, using their 75-mm guns which they had already turned in. Last-minute arrangements were made, at my instigation, which resulted in a modification of this test so that the unit could use the 105-mm howitzer and devote the remainder of their short stay to intensive instruction in the new weapon. This was in spite of clear instructions that upon reaching staging areas these units passed to the control of the port commander.

[48] AGF memo (S) 370.5–OPN for TAG, 14 Mar 42, sub: Orgn and Mvmt Orders, Shipment 0051. AGF G–3 files, Shipment 0051 (S).

[49] Ltr (S) of Brig Gen Benjamin C. Lockwood to CofS USA, 1 Apr 42, sub: Task Force 0051. AGF G–3 files, Shipment 0051 (S).

It was little wonder that General Lockwood recommended to General Marshall that in setting up task forces in the future "elements of the task force be assembled in but one staging area as early as practicable so that the task force commander and a portion of his staff can . . . act as intermediary between units and numerous . . . agencies charged with preparing them for the mission." [50]

The Tongatabu expedition was a small affair, consisting of only a few thousand men. In September 1942 Task Force A, numbering more than 60,000 men—the largest combat-loaded task force ever to sail from the United States—was organized for participation in the North African invasion of November. Responsibility for preparation of this force rested with agencies other than Army Ground Forces, but AGF commands, notably the Desert Training Center, were called upon to process a number of nondivisional components.[51]

In August the War Department set up a Force Headquarters in Washington to function directly under the Operations Division in preparing the expedition and designated Maj. Gen. George S. Patton as Task Force Commander. Liaison was established between the Force Headquarters and Army Ground Forces for the selection and processing of AGF units. But the Force Commander complicated proceedings by acting independently of liaison agencies and disregarding established channels of command.[52] A responsible officer of the Desert Training Center, in answer to an inquiry from the Task Force Branch of AGF G-3, stated in September 1942: "Individuals in Washington have called units direct and have given instructions. There have been times when we didn't know whether they were official, personal or what. . . . I think a great many of these calls came from individuals who had been here, had gone to Washington, and had information that we didn't have." [53] This officer cautiously refrained from naming the offending individuals in Washington. But a memorandum of an AGF staff officer drafted the following day established definite identification and threw additional light on the confusion attending preparation of Task Force A:[54]

[50] *Ibid.*

[51] (1) WD ltr (S) OPD 320.2 (ETO)(9-3-42) to CGs AGF, SOS, and Task Force A, 3 Sep 42, sub: Creation of a Task Force. 370.5/6 (binder 1-B)(S). (2) AGF M/S (R), Plans Sec for CofS, 2 Sep 42, sub: Confusion at DTC over Conflicting Orders. 370.5/134 (R). (3) AGF memo (S), Asst G-1 to G-1, 2 Dec 42, sub: Untrained Men in the 9th Inf Div. 353/151 (sep binder)(S).

[52] AGF M/S (R), Plans Sec for CofS, 2 Sep 42, sub: Confusion at DTC over Conflicting Orders. 370.5/134 (R).

[53] Record of conv (R) between Col Schabacker, AGF, and Col Pierce, CofS DTC, 1 Sep 42. 370.5/134 (R).

[54] AGF M/S (R), Plans Sec for CofS, 2 Sep 42, sub: Confusion at DTC over Conflicting Orders. 370.5/134 (R).

Frequent changes of instructions on troop movements have been normal since we entered the war. This condition appears to be getting worse. The preparation of a special task force recently was the most disorderly of any thus far. In this particular case the condition was aggravated by the introduction of . . . General Patton's Headquarters, here in Washington, which dealt directly with the Desert Training Center and issued certain instructions at variance with those issued by this office without notifying this office. . . . In addition to this, the Services of Supply issued directives to its supply agencies to ship equipment direct to the units.

The 45th Division expedition, the only large combat-loaded task force dispatched from the United States after shipment of Task Force A, was prepared under AGF auspices.[55] Conflict of authority was much less pronounced in the preparation of this force than in previous instances. But some difficulty arose over the failure of Operations Division, WDGS, to call Army Ground Forces into early councils on supply problems. In a report covering preparation of this force Maj. Gen. Troy H. Middleton, Task Force Commander, stated that he and his chief of staff had been summoned to Washington in mid-March for consultation on the part which the force was to play in the Sicilian operations. He added:[56]

During the following twenty days numerous conferences were held between staff officers of the division and the OPD, War Department, at which conferences certain policies regarding the procurement of equipment and supplies were set up. The Army Ground Forces, during this period, was not brought into the picture. . . . Some delay and misunderstanding did occur in this operation by reason of the Army Ground Forces not being represented until about April 15.

Processing of units in 1942, whether in task forces or as separate organizations, was complicated by lack of coordination between tactical and supply agencies. Army Ground Forces in September 1942 complained that SOS agencies had contacted units direct "*before* it had *definitely* been determined that the unit was to be alerted either for overseas movement or for equipment and personnel." [57] The effect of dealings out of channel with field organizations, many of which were already jittery with anticipation, was to disrupt final training. The situation was summarized by an AGF staff officer who observed in the early fall:[58]

In general units in the field are on edge and many have been known to alert themselves for overseas movement on rumors of the most meagre information. Inquiries from Washington reference strength of a unit, status of training, or equipment, often have been misinterpreted as being indicative of early overseas movement.

[55] (1) First Annual Rpt (C) of G–4 Task Force Div AGF to G–4 AGF, 10 Apr 44. G–4 Task Force files (C). (2) Statement of Lt Col S. L. Weld to AGF Hist Off, 24 May 44.

[56] 45th Div ltr (S) to CG AGF, 1 Jun 43, sub: Amph Task Force. 320.2/10 (Amph Tng Comd–AF)(S).

[57] AGF memo (R) for SOS, 10 Sep 42, sub: Alert Orders. 370.5/317 (Movement Orders)(R).

[58] AGF M/S (R), Plans Sec for CofS, 2 Sep 42, sub: Confusion at DTC over Conflicting Orders. 370.5/134 (R).

II. Standardization of Preparation for Overseas Movement

Chronic difficulties in preparing AGF units for overseas movement were matched by efforts to correct the conditions which caused them. In September 1942 Army Ground Forces attempted to reduce confusion and duplication within its own administrative organization by consolidating POM instructions issuing from G–1, G–3, and G–4 into a single directive sent out by G–3. At about the same time Army Ground Forces requested the cooperation of OPD in eliminating direct communication with AGF units by task force commanders and other outside authorities. Efforts were made concurrently to prevent premature alerting of AGF units by SOS agencies.[1]

Another remedial step grew out of adverse reports of The Inspector General in September 1942 regarding serviceability of equipment of certain AGF units at staging areas. Army Ground Forces attributed the unfavorable findings of The Inspector General largely to differences in the standards of inspection.[2]

In an effort to provide a single standard for the evaluation of equipment, Army Ground Forces arranged in October for alerted units to be inspected at their home stations by teams from The Inspector General's office, functioning as representatives of Headquarters, Army Ground Forces. Later a follow-up system was devised to assure prompt correction of deficiencies revealed by The Inspector General's reports. When The Inspector General declared a unit unready for combat, Army Ground Forces dispatched to the army, corps, or other agency preparing the unit for movement a letter to the following effect:[3]

> 1. a. Attention is invited to the attached memorandum [of TIG] . . . relative to the overseas readiness status of . . . [unit].
>
> b. Immediate action will be taken to correct the deficiencies set forth in the above cited memorandum.

[1] AGF memo (R) for CofS USA (attn OPD), 15 Sep 42, sub: Confusion at DTC over Conflicting Orders. 370.5/134 (R).

[2] Memo of TIG (S) 333.1 (43d Div) for DCofS USA, 10 Oct 42, sub not given. With related papers. 333.1/29 (S).

[3] This procedure apparently was initiated in the spring of 1943. See AGF form ltrs (R) to subcomds, for example, AGF ltr (R) for CG A/B Comd, 2 Dec 43, sub: Overseas Readiness Status of Hq & Hq Co, 2d A/B Inf Brig. 353 (Int Tng)(S).

2. Necessary action will be taken to prevent the recurrence of similar deficiencies in other units.

3. A report will be submitted to this headquarters when these deficiencies have been corrected.

If The Inspector General's report revealed a flagrant violation of existing instructions, a clause requiring explanation of this circumstance was included in the letter.[4]

To place POM activities on a more efficient and orderly basis Army Ground Forces in October made the following recommendations to the War Department:

1. That a proposal made earlier in the year be implemented at once, namely, creation and maintenance of a pool of trained units so that unexpected requirements of theater commanders might be met without robbing units in training.

2. That the War Department "inform AGF of the numbers and types of units and the conditions under which they will be employed at least four months, and preferably five months, prior to the sailing date of each unit."

3. That specific units earmarked to meet these estimated requirements be automatically authorized full strength in combat personnel and given an A-2 priority for equipment.

4. That units in the reserve pool be kept at full strength and given an A-3 priority for equipment.

5. That "every possible means . . . be directed toward providing complete allowance of equipment in time to permit the unit to conduct three months' realistic training prior to its entry into combat."

6. That Army Ground Forces retain control over personnel assignment to AGF units until they left the continental limits of the United States.

7. That preparation of units for overseas movement be regarded as a continuous process from the time of activation, and that every effort be made to assure completion of this process prior to the staging period.[5]

War Department Directive of 5 January 1943

The War Department, because of the previous suggestions of Army Ground Forces and also in the light of its own experience, particularly with Task Force A, had already developed a favorable attitude toward most of these proposals.[6] The

[4] For example, see AGF ltr (R) to CG AA Comd, 6 Dec 43, sub: Overseas Readiness Status of 129th AAA Gun Bn (Mob). 353/253 (Int Tng)(S).

[5] AGF memo (S) for Col Elliot D. Cooke, 31 Oct 42, sub: Processing of Task Forces. 320.2/133 (S).

[6] See AGF memo (S), DCofS for CG, 4 Dec 42, sub: Conference. 337/24 (S).

improvement of the manpower situation and prospects of more abundant equipment indicated that remedial action was practicable. Further exchange of views among War Department agencies and the three major commands led in late 1942 to tentative revisions which were followed early in 1943 by a general revamping of policies and procedures for overseas movement. Adoption of the revised program was an important episode in that it indicated transition from a period marked by haste, scarcity, and confusion to an era when advance planning and routine administration were predominant.[7]

Fundamentals of the revised procedure were laid down in a War Department letter of 5 January 1943. This document contained the following important provisions:

1. OPD each month was to furnish the three major commands lists of estimated monthly overseas requirements for the succeeding 6-month period, broken down by quantities and types of units. The list would designate unusual operations for which special training was required.

2. Each major command was to designate specific units to meet the War Department requirements. On approval by the War Department of the units selected, a combined list, known as the Six Months List, was to be prepared. This list was to constitute the basis for establishing equipment and personnel priorities and for initiating overseas movement procedures.

3. To meet emergency demands for additional units which had not been previously earmarked for overseas shipment, each major command was to maintain a pool of units completely organized, manned, and equipped.

4. Units designated for overseas shipment were to be placed in priorities for equipment in the following order:[8]

[7] Statement of Lt Col S. L. Weld to AGF Hist Off, 24 May 44.

[8] Priorities for equipment and personnel were designated and broken down as follows:

		Priority	
	Status of Units	*Pers*	*Equip*
a.	Units under orders or earmarked for shipment within 3 months	13	A–2
	1. Units under orders or earmarked for shipment within 1 month	13–a	A–2a
	2. Units under orders or earmarked for shipment within 2 months	13–b	A–2b
	3. Units under orders or earmarked for shipment within 3 months.	13–b	A–2c
b.	Units in emergency pool	....	A–3
c.	Units not under orders but designated for 4th, 5th, and 6th months	14–1 to 999	A–4
	1. Units not under orders but designated for 4th month	14–1 to 299	A–4a
	2. Units not under orders but designated for 5th month	14–300 to 599	A–4b
	3. Units not under orders but designated for 6th month	14–600 to 999	A–4c
d.	Units not definitely earmarked but filled with personnel and authorized to receive replacements from RTC graduates	14–1000 and up	....
e.	Units neither earmarked nor filled and which were to receive personnel from reception centers	3	....

a. Units under orders or earmarked for movement within three months.

b. Units in the emergency pool.

c. Units listed for shipment in the fourth, fifth, and sixth months.

5. To ensure each unit having full equipment in time to complete the final training at its home station, supply agencies were to fill shortages from stock or production forty-five days prior to the estimated date of departure. If such delivery could not be made, supply agencies were to notify the responsible command sixty days prior to the departure date so that equipment could be transferred, if practicable, from neighboring units. Unfamiliar equipment was not, except as a last resort, to be delivered to units at ports or staging areas.

6. Measures were to be taken promptly to clear alerted units of personnel unsuitable for combat and to bring them to full Table of Organization strength. No individual, except certain technical specialists not organically armed, was to be sent to staging areas or ports unless he had completed basic training and fired the prescribed course in marksmanship with his principal weapon.

7. Port commanders were to make every effort to reduce staging periods to two weeks.

8. Instructions to units designated for overseas movement were to be transmitted through normal command channels.[9]

This letter also directed inspection of alerted units by The Inspector General "to determine adequacy and efficiency of personnel, the state of technical training, and the completeness and condition of equipment." Previously The Inspector General had, on his own initiative or on order of the Chief of Staff, U.S. Army, occasionally conducted POM inspections for the War Department. The directive of 5 January 1943 made these inspections standing operating procedure, broadened their scope, and placed at The Inspector General's disposal the personnel needed to carry out the enlarged program. Adoption of the new policy brought to an end the practice, initiated in October 1942, of The Inspector General's inspecting alerted units as the representative of the Commanding General, Army Ground Forces. In evaluating readiness of AGF units for combat, The Inspector General was guided by standards prescribed by the War Department and Army Ground Forces in mobilization training programs, training directives, POM literature, and similar material.[10]

[9] WD ltr (C) AG 320.2 (1-2-43) OB-S-C-M to CGs, 5 Jan 43, sub: Orgn, Tng, and Equip of Units for Overseas Serv. 320.2/2 (Staging Areas) (C).

[10] Statement of Maj Gen Philip E. Brown, The Acting Inspector General, to AGF Historical Officer, 26 July 1945. General Brown cited as factors contributing to adoption of the War Department policy requiring POM inspections by The Inspector General the following: (1) adverse findings of The Inspector General

The 5 January directive approved and carried forward one item previously recognized as standing operating procedure, namely, submission to the Chief of Staff, U.S. Army, by the appropriate major command of a status report covering the organization, training, and equipment of each unit designated for overseas movement.[11]

The new directive included, with variation of details, most of the recommendations made in October by Army Ground Forces. The principal point of disagreement was the control of units in the staging areas. When the War Department G–3 submitted the draft of the directive to Army Ground Forces for comment prior to its publication, the AGF G–1 observed: "We should insist upon complete control and responsibility for everything except movement orders until a unit is actually embarked." [12] The War Department did not concur in this suggestion but compromised by urging restrictions of staging periods to two weeks and requiring transmission of instructions to earmarked units through command channels.[13]

Adoption of the policies and procedures laid down in the letter of 5 January 1943 necessitated a revision of current War Department instructions governing preparation of units for overseas movement. Hitherto the practice had been followed of issuing instructions in several installments, the most important of which was Inclosure No. 1 to the secret movement order sent to the army, corps, or other major command charged with preparing the unit for shipment. Since the movement order often was not published until thirty days (or less) before a unit's departure for the staging area, the unit commander and the local supply agencies frequently did not have adequate time to complete the equipment of the unit

---

in special alert inspections in the fall of 1942 of the 43d and 4th Divisions; (2) dissatisfaction of General Marshall with conditions which came to light in connection with the shipment of units in Task Force A; (3) complaint of theater commanders that units arriving overseas were not ready for combat—that men had not fired their weapons, equipment was in poor condition, and officers were not qualified; (4) a strong desire on the part of the Deputy Chief of Staff, U.S. Army (General McNarney), who since July 1942 had been charged with the responsibilty of certifying combat readiness of all units shipped overseas, to have an impartial agency investigate and underwrite the readiness of alerted units.

[11] (1) WD ltr (C) AG 320.2 (1–2–43) OB–S–C–M to CGs, 5 Jan 43, sub: Orgn, Tng, and Equip of Units for Overseas Serv. 320.2/2 (Staging Areas) (C). (2) Status reports were first required in July 1942, as a result of the policy adopted at that time of having readiness of all units certified by the Deputy Chief of Staff prior to their movement overseas. See OPD memo 370.5 (7–1–42) for CGs AGF, SOS, and AAF, 4 Jul 42, sub: Stat Rpts. 370.5/3402.

[12] AGF M/S (S), G–1 to Plans Sec, 1 Jan 43, sub: Orgn, Equip, and Tng of Units for Overseas Serv. 320.2/145 (S).

[13] WD ltr (C) AG 320.2 (1–2–43) OB–S–C–M to CGs, 5 Jan 43, sub: Orgn, Tng, and Equip of Units for Overseas Serv. 320.2/2 (Staging Areas) (C).

before it left camp. Now that preparation for overseas shipment was set up on a long-range basis, it was deemed imperative that instructions be issued before a unit was alerted for movement; moreover, it was considered desirable that instructions go in the clear, as a single document, to unit commanders as far down as the company level.

To accomplish these ends OPD in January held conferences with representatives of Army Ground Forces, Army Air Forces, and Services of Supply. The result of these consultations was a 34-page War Department document, published 1 February 1943, entitled "Preparation for Overseas Movement," with the short title "POM." This document set forth in detail the duties and responsibilities of each commander and agency involved in the processing of a unit for overseas shipment. It became the bible for all concerned.[14]

"POM" was the result of the accumulated experience of the agencies that shared in its preparation. The contribution of Army Ground Forces was considerable, especially with regard to the definition of general-purpose motor vehicles (paragraph 9*c* (6)) and the tabulation of responsibilities of all commands having a part in movement preparations (paragraph 16). It participated with Services of Supply in the shaping of passages covering original and initial lists of shortages (paragraph 9).[15]

On 19 February 1943 Army Ground Forces dispatched a letter to its subcommands, implementing and elaborating the policies and procedures laid down in the War Department letter of 5 January 1943 and in "POM."[16] A few days later provision was made for placing "POM" and the AGF letter of 19 February in the hands of commanding officers of all units at the time of activation.[17] About the same time the "Alert Instruction" letter, which AGF customarily sent to major subordinate commands approximately three months before units designated therein were scheduled for movement, was revised to conform to the new system.

Other changes in the program of POM made by Army Ground Forces early in 1943 included the addition of the requirement that all individuals go through infiltration courses before proceeding to ports of embarkation, together with issuance of a new directive to guide training in staging areas. The latter simply substituted the general training directive of 1 November 1942 for the one issued in

[14] This document is filed in 370.5/4113 (sep binder).

[15] Statement of Col V. A. St. Onge to AGF Hist Off, 31 May 44.

[16] AGF ltr (R) to CGs, 19 Feb 43, sub: Preparation and Mvmt of Units for Overseas Shipment. 370.5/171 (R).

[17] AGF ltr (R) to CGs, 23 Feb 43, sub and location as in n. 16.

June 1942. Again, as in the original staging directive of 10 July 1942, phrasing was so general as to offer little effective assistance in shaping the training program.[18]

Operation of POM, 1943

As the changes instituted in January and February placed overseas movement procedures on a fairly permanent basis, it is appropriate at this point to summarize the system applied in the spring of 1943.[19]

The first step in the process was transmission to Army Ground Forces by OPD of estimated monthly requirements of various types of AGF units for the next six months. The Task Force Division of G-3, in coordination with the Training Division, and where necessary with subordinate commands as well, designated specific units to fill OPD requirements. Units thus selected became the AGF portion of the War Department's official Six Months List. The list was fundamental to all subsequent POM activities.

From this point activities proceeded along two broad lines—lines which merged or crossed so frequently as to make it difficult at times to distinguish them—one having to do with equipment, and the other with general processing, including phases of equipment. Equipment activities began with publication by the War Department G-3 of an equipment priority list, based on OPD's Six Months List. Units scheduled for movement during the latter half of the 6-month period usually fell in the A-4 group. War Department distribution of the equipment priority list included AGF commands, but it was intended primarily as a guide for supply agencies. It frequently happened that the post commander received the priority list before notice of a change of status reached the responsible tactical commander located at the same station—a situation which sometimes led to confusion. It was normal in 1943 for a nondivisional unit commander to receive the first intimation of the earmarking of his unit through notification by the

[18] AGF ltr (R) to CGs, 12 Mar 43, sub and location as in n. 16.

[19] This summary, unless otherwise indicated, is based on the following sources:

(1) WD ltr (C) AG 320.2 (1-2-43) OB-S-C-M to CGs, 5 Jan 43, sub: Orgn, Tng, and Equip of Units for Overseas Serv. 320.2/2 (Staging Areas) (C). (2) WD document "POM," 2d edition. 370.5/4113 (sep binder). (3) AGF ltr (R) to CGs, 19 Feb 43, sub: Preparation and Mvmt of Units for Overseas Shipment. 370.5/171 (R). (4) Statements of Lt Col S. L. Weld to AGF Hist Off, May 44. (5) Statements of Col V. A. St. Onge and Lt Col J. A. Hanson to AGF Hist Off, May and Aug 44. (6) Various G-3 and G-4 Shipment files in AGF Records. Each alerted unit was given a shipment number. All key papers pertaining to the movement of the unit were henceforth kept in separate files; one, pertaining primarily to personnel and training, was kept by the G-3 Task Force Division, and another, covering equipment matters, was maintained by the G-4 Section — each bearing the unit's shipment number. After arrival of the unit at its destination, these files were transferred to AGF AG Records (Secret). Binders for Shipment 9850 afford an idea of procedures followed in the movement of a unit in 1943.

commanding officer, headquarters and headquarters detachment, special troops, that his organization had been assigned an A-4 equipment priority. This notification had the effect of initiating proceedings laid down in "POM."

The other line of activities springing from the Six Months List began when, two or three months before the date set for a unit's movement, Headquarters, Army Ground Forces, sent an Alert Instruction letter, prepared in the Task Force Division of G-3, to the agency responsible for the unit's movement, that is, an army, separate corps, command, or center. For convenience one may assume that the agency was Second Army and that the unit was "C" Ordnance Company (commanding officer, Captain Smith) assigned to the 11th Headquarters and Headquarters Detachment, Special Troops (commanding officer, Colonel Doe), located at Camp Forrest. The Alert Instruction letter informed the Second Army commander that a list of units, including "C" Company, had been earmarked for early movement, and that training should be completed by a date two months hence. A training paragraph, drafted by the Task Force Division of G-3, directed that a program of intensive training, based insofar as possible on current training programs, be instituted at once. A personnel paragraph, drafted by the Task Force Division of G-1, prohibited further departure of officers or men to schools. It also required the army commander within fifteen days to replace officers and men unqualified for foreign service and to initiate action to bring the unit to full T/O strength, plus known future losses. A supply paragraph, drafted by the Task Force Division of G-4, gave notice of A-2 priority status, and directed compliance with appropriate provisions of "POM" and the AGF letter of 19 February 1943.

Upon receipt of this communication Second Army dispatched an Alert Instruction letter of its own to Colonel Doe, the Detachment Commander at Camp Forrest, informing him that certain units under his command, including "C" Company, had been placed on an intensive training status. This letter, which also contained sections covering training, personnel, and equipment, prepared respectively by the Second Army's G-3, G-1, and G-4, set forth in considerable detail Colonel Doe's responsibilities in accomplishing the objectives laid down in the Alert Instruction letter. Colonel Doe immediately called on Captain Smith, commander of "C" Company, and explained the steps which he was to take in preparing his unit for movement. Colonel Doe also checked with the post commander to see that the latter had been informed of the A-2 equipment priority status. Henceforth there was close collaboration among Colonel Doe, Captain Smith, and the post commander.

About six weeks after dispatch of the Alert Instruction letter, Army Ground

Forces received a secret memorandum from OPD, War Department, directing preparation of certain units, including "C" Company, for movement to North Africa via a port of embarkation to be designated by the Commanding General, Army Service Forces. This memorandum fixed a date three weeks hence by which the unit should be ready to move to the staging area.

Upon receipt of this memorandum the Task Force Division of G–3 notified the Second Army G–3 (Troop Movements Division) that "C" Company was alerted for movement. Second Army immediately transmitted this information to Colonel Doe at Camp Forrest, who in turn alerted "C" Company for movement. About this time Army Ground Forces ascertained from Army Service Forces that the port of embarkation would be Hampton Roads.

During the week following receipt of the OPD memorandum, Army Ground Forces prepared the draft of a movement order for dispatch by the War Department.[20] This draft assigned a shipment number, which for security reasons was henceforth to be used instead of the usual unit designation in all communications and markings. It specified Second Army as the "Agency to Issue Movement Orders" and designated the T/O and T/BA to be followed in completing movement preparations. Hampton Roads was designated as the port of embarkation. The readiness date for personnel was the same as that given in the OPD memorandum; that for equipment was four days earlier.

The draft contained paragraphs on supply and personnel drawn up respectively by the G–4 and G–1 Task Force Divisions. The personnel paragraph elaborated instructions given in the Alert Instruction letter. The supply paragraph directed certain modifications of clothing and equipment prescribed in applicable T/BA's. Other portions of the draft specified modifications of "POM," stated that movement was to be by rail, and required a report of the unit's departure from the home station.

The draft order prepared by Army Ground Forces was combined by OPD with instructions submitted by Army Service Forces, and a single letter was sent to the Adjutant General's Office for publication. Distribution included the Second Army, the Fourth Service Command, the Replacement and School Command, the Hampton Roads Port of Embarkation, the Chief of Transportation, and the chiefs of supply services, as subsequent activities involved coordination among these agencies.

[20] All essential information contained in the movement order had been transmitted to Second Army, by telephone or otherwise, prior to completion of the draft. Statement of Lt Col Weld to AGF Hist Off, 24 Aug 44.

The movement order reached Second Army ten days before the readiness date for equipment, and portions relating to "C" Company were immediately passed on to Colonel Doe. Action indicated in the order had already been initiated by the alert for movement.

During the period ensuing before movement, Army Ground Forces assisted in final preparations by checking to see that the chiefs of supply services were informed of equipment expected of them and by arranging for last-minute transfer from other AGF units of a few scarce items not obtainable from Army Service Forces.

Meanwhile matters had been moving with increasing tempo at Camp Forrest. Immediately following Colonel Doe's visit to tell him that his company was earmarked for early movement, Captain Smith had taken steps to accelerate immunizations, physical checkups, record firing of principal arms, familiarization firing of additional weapons, and other requirements laid down in "POM." He had also made provision for bringing company records up to date. During this period a Second Army inspection team, including representatives of G–1, The Inspector General, and Ordnance, visited the unit and gave advice concerning such matters as removal of undesirable personnel and the completion of training requirements. By informal contact with post supply authorities Captain Smith began the replacement of unserviceable equipment. In all these matters the unit commander consulted freely with Colonel Doe and his staff.

On receipt of alert instructions from Colonel Doe, Captain Smith, assisted by officers of headquarters, special troops, and of the post, conducted a showdown inspection and made an inventory of the company's clothing, supplies, and equipment. From this inspection Captain Smith prepared lists of "original shortages" which were submitted to the station commander. The station commander, through his director of supply, immediately arranged to fill all possible shortages from stocks on hand and from depots which ordinarily served him. He then tabulated the remaining deficiencies in "Initial Lists of Shortages" and forwarded "Action Copies" of these lists by the most expeditious means to the appropriate chiefs of the supply services; information copies were sent by regular mail to the Second Army, Fourth Service Command, G–4 of Army Ground Forces, and the Stock Control Division of Army Service Forces. Deficiencies which developed subsequently, and which could not be filled by the station commander from his own stock or the usual depots, were dispatched as "Supplementary Lists of Shortages." The chiefs of supply services delivered a part of the needed equipment to "C" Company at its home station. Because of factors of time and distance, arrangements had to be made to ship some items to the port of embarkation. The Chief of Ordnance, being unable to procure a few unusually scarce items of ordnance equipment included in the Initial List of Shortages sent to his office, notified the Commanding General, Army Ground Forces, of this fact through the Stock Control Division of Army Service Forces. G–4 of Army Ground Forces immediately arranged for transfer of these items to "C" Company at Hampton Roads from an AGF unit of low priority. The ASF Stock Control Division was then informed of the transfer so that items thus transferred would be replaced as soon as they became available. G–4, Army Ground Forces, kept War Department G–3 informed of critical items transferred.

"C" Company spent a considerable portion of its last three weeks at Camp Forrest greasing and packing the equipment which was to precede it to port. This was a tedious chore as it had to be executed in accordance with detailed rules laid down in "POM" to ensure arrival of equipment overseas in a usable condition.

Equipment was packed by the readiness date designated in the movement order, except, of course, for a few housekeeping and administrative items essential to the unit's welfare at the staging area, and for rifles and individual equipment which the soldiers were to take with them on shipboard. But three days passed without any notice of the expected move. On the fourth day word was received through channels that the port commander had called for delivery of the equipment at Hampton Roads at 1800, two days hence. After the shipping of the equipment there was another wait of five days. Then came the port commander's call—through channels, of course—to the Hampton Roads Staging Area. Upon arrival at the staging area, "C" Company passed from the jurisdiction of Army Ground Forces to that of the Commanding General, Hampton Roads Port of Embarkation.

Amendments of POM, 1943

The foregoing account affords a picture of overseas movement preparations as they might have worked under optimum conditions in accordance with the system prescribed in early 1943. But difficulties often prevented the system from functioning as intended. Shortages of equipment, while considerably less in 1943 than in the previous year, made it impossible to deliver anything like full allowances to units soon after they were earmarked for overseas service. The provision in the War Department letter of 5 January 1943 requiring Services of Supply to notify responsible tactical commanders, sixty days before the estimated movement date, of inability to deliver full equipment to home stations of earmarked units forty-five days prior to their scheduled departure, was a dead letter from the beginning.[21] Preshipment of large stocks of material to Great Britain in the summer of 1943 in order to make maximum use of cargo and dock facilities, was beneficial in the long run, but it had the immediate effect of curbing the flow of equipment to units in advanced stages of training. Because of this and other factors, last-minute transfers of equipment continued to impair the combat readiness of AGF units during the greater part of 1943.

Personnel was also a chronic source of worry. The POM system prescribed early in 1943 was predicated on two assumptions: first, that the 15-percent initial overstrength instituted in the fall of 1942 would enable most units to complete their training with a full complement of personnel; second, that such fillers as were needed by organizations designated for overseas movement could be readily obtained from replacement training centers. But these assumptions were only partially confirmed. Replacement center capacities were diverted very largely to the filling of overseas requirements. By autumn the manpower situation had relapsed into the stark leanness of the previous summer, with the result that once more units of lower priority were stripped to fill those on the verge of overseas shipment. As late as May 1944 Army Ground Forces was attempting to arrest the evil by freezing personnel in units that had been subjected to one or more rounds of robbing and refilling.

The POM system prescribed at the beginning of 1943 also assumed a greater degree of stability in operational and shipping predictions than materialized. Changing estimates by OPD required frequent modification of the Six Months List and adjustments of equipment priorities. In November 1943 and March 1944 Army Service Forces called on Army Ground Forces to deliver at ports on very short notice shipments totaling respectively 22,000 and 15,000 men.[22] More frequently it happened that units which had been alerted for movement and had packed their equipment waited for several weeks beyond the designated readiness date before port commanders issued the call to staging areas. In such cases Army Ground Forces checked with Army Service Forces on the feasibility of permitting units to unpack at least a part of their equipment in order to permit a resumption of training.[23]

[21] Statement of Col V. A. St. Onge to AGF Hist Off, 3 Jun 44.

[22] Statement of Col V. A. St. Onge to AGF Hist Off, 31 May 44.

[23] For example, see AGF memo (S) for WD OPD, 22 Oct 43, sub: Mvmt of Units from Home Stations. 370.5/939 (MO)(S).

In a considerable number of instances units, although their equipment, except for minimum essentials, had been sent to port or perhaps shipped overseas, lingered for several weeks in staging areas while combat proficiency brought to a peak during final training under Army Ground Forces steadily deteriorated.[24] Sometimes units whose shipment was thus delayed were deleted from movement orders because of sudden changes in theater requirements or for other reasons, and were turned back to Army Ground Forces for further training.[25] This necessitated a scurrying about to replace the organizational equipment that had gone overseas.

During 1943, generally speaking, difficulties declined in both number and gravity. Concurrently, there was an upward trend in the movement of AGF units. In April 1943, shipments to ports of embarkation totaled 158 units and 60,992 enlisted men. There was a considerable drop during the next three months, but in August the figures were 193 units and 69,126 men. After another temporary decline shipment climbed in December to 202 units and 81,235 men. From 9 March 1942 through 31 December 1943 Army Ground Forces sent to ports of embarkation 2,067 units, with a strength of 805,848 enlisted men.[26]

The mounting scale of shipments in 1943 was accompanied by continuing modification of movement procedure. In March 1943 the War Department, on AGF recommendation, amended the document "POM" to provide for return to their units of officers who happened to be absent at school when movement orders were issued.[27] The original edition had directed that such officers as could not complete courses prior to their unit's shipment be transferred to other organizations. This provision had made commanders reluctant to recommend their best officers for schooling after a unit reached advanced stages of training. On 1 August 1943 the War Department issued a second edition of "POM." [28] The revision made no significant changes in policy, but it clarified the functions of each of the three major commands and set up instructions in such a way as to facilitate considerably their use. AGF contributions to the revision included amendments to the list of definitions in order to reduce the likelihood of misinter-

[24] For example, see AGF memo (S) to WD OPD, 31 Mar 43, sub: Return of Units to Ground Force Control. 370.5/717 (S).

[25] For example, see AGF memo (S) for CofS USA (Attn OPD), 29 May 43, sub: Amendment to Mvmt Orders, Shipment 9255. AGF Movement Order files, Shipment 9255 (S).

[26] Information compiled from monthly AGF Stat Sec Rpt No. 19 (S), "AGF Units Arriving at PE." AGF Stat Sec files.

[27] AGF memo for G-1 WD and G-3 WD, 24 Mar 43, sub: Amendment to WD Document (short title "POM"). 370.5/4113.

[28] This document is filed in 370.5/4131 (sep binder).

230-171 O - 66 - 39

pretation; sharpening of the differentiation between the roles of Army Ground Forces and of Army Service Forces in the warning process to prevent jittery units from alerting themselves upon notification of changes in equipment priority; and participation with Army Service Forces in preparing reports on status of equipment.[29]

On 10 August 1943 the War Department issued a supplement to "POM" under the title "Identification of Organizational Impedimenta and Preparation of Records Concerning its Shipment" (short title, "IOI").[30] The purpose of this document was to assist unit commanders in the numerous details incident to the segregation, packing, marking, and recording of the organizational equipment which current policies required to be shipped from home stations to ports of embarkation. This document was prepared by the Army Service Forces. The Army Ground Forces contributed to portions covering activities scheduled for the prestaging period.[31]

Army Ground Forces followed up these War Department measures by revising the letter which it had issued on 19 February 1943 to supplement the first edition of "POM." The new letter, dated 28 August 1943, elaborated the purpose and emphasized the importance of status reports. It also attempted to eliminate the all-too-common practice of units prematurely packing their equipment, by making a clear distinction between the date for completion of training specified in Alert Instructions and the readiness date fixed in movement orders. Finally, it required of field agencies a more careful consideration of all factors involved before they reported a unit ready for overseas service.[32]

Despite the practice, instituted in the summer of 1943 as a result of the preshipment program, of having units destined for the United Kingdom leave their organizational equipment behind when they went to port, commanders were still required to hold show-down inspections and submit shortage reports for all items prescribed in current T/BA's and T/E's. On 30 November 1943 Army Ground Forces, in the interest of saving time and effort, recommended that units earmarked for shipment to the United Kingdom be relieved of inspection and shortage reports except for such articles of equipment as they were supposed to take with them. Early in December OPD authorized this procedure

[29] (1) WD AGO Form No. 412. (2) Tab F to AGF ltr 370.5/233 (R) GNGCT (28 Aug 43) to CGs, sub: Preparation and Mvmt of Units for Overseas Serv. AGF G-3 Task Force Div files.

[30] This document is filed in 370.5/4131 (sep binder).

[31] Statement of Col V. A. St. Onge to AGF Hist Off, 31 May 44.

[32] (1) AGF ltr (R) to CGs, 28 Aug 43, sub: Preparation and Mvmt of Units for Overseas Serv. 370.5/233 (R). (2) Tab F to above ltr. AGF G-3 Task Force Div files.

for all units scheduled for movement to the United Kingdom between 1 January and 30 April 1944. The date was subsequently extended to 31 August 1944. Units operating under this modification of "POM"—which comprised the major portion of all those moved during the period indicated—were referred to as being on the "Blue List." [33]

In the summer and fall of 1943 Army Ground Forces held conferences with representatives of its principal components for the purpose of explaining POM functions.[34] In September an AGF officer was sent to Indiantown Gap to attend an ASF conference on procedure in packing, marking, and loading equipment.[35] These and other activities indicated during the final months of 1943 an intensive effort to improve AGF phases of the overseas shipment program.

The corrective program was not wholly efficacious. At the end of 1943 there was still frequent complaint that units were arriving at ports with such flagrant and avoidable deficiencies as "personnel physically unqualified for overseas service, personnel requiring dental treatment, missing or incomplete identification tags, and incomplete immunizations." [36] Headquarters, Army Ground Forces, continued its efforts to secure better results by exercising a closer check over agencies charged with POM responsibilities and by further improving its own part in the program.

The steady trend of improvement in preparing units for overseas movement in spite of difficulties, deficiencies, and increasing theater requirements was strikingly revealed by the quarterly reports of The Inspector General to the Chief of Staff. The first report, covering the first quarter of 1943, showed 18 percent of the ground units inspected "not ready." In the second quarter the figure was 20 percent, in the third quarter 12 percent, and in the fourth quarter 11 percent.[37]

[33] (1) AGF memo (S) to CofS USA, 30 Nov 43, sub: Modification to Current Dir. 370.5–97 (ETO)(S). (2) WD memo (S) OPD 353 (30 Nov 43) for AGF, ASF, TIG, 9 Dec 43, sub and location as in (1). (3) Statement of Col V. A. St. Onge to AGF Hist Off, 31 May 44.

[34] AGF memo (S) for CofS USA, 16 Nov 43, sub: Readiness of Units for Overseas Serv. 353/21 (Readiness Rpts)(S).

[35] 3d SvC ltr to AGF, 7 Sep 43, sub: Conference on Revised POM. 370.5/4131.

[36] AGF ltr (R) to CGs, 10 Jan 44, sub: Preparation of Units for Overseas Serv. 370.5/300 (R).

[37] TIG memo (S) for DCofS USA, 22 Apr 44, sub: Readiness of Units for Movement Overseas. TIG file WDSIG 333.1 Quarterly Rpt (1st) SP (S).

III. The Period of Accelerated Movement, 1944-45

Personnel Turnover and Other Difficulties

Fundamental to many of the difficulties experienced in preparing units for overseas movement in 1944 was the enormous turnover of personnel characteristic of the period. "POM" laid down the principle that processing for shipment should be continuous from activation to embarkation. But, with personnel coming and going as it did throughout most of 1944, continuity for most units was impossible. Unit commanders time and again trained men, gave them their "shots," and fitted them with glasses and dentures, only to lose them to other units of higher priority. This was especially true of specialists, whose replacement in kind was always difficult and frequently impossible, and whose training required considerable time. It was not unusual for a unit to receive a heavy slug of partially trained, incompletely processed fillers only a few weeks prior to shipment. The result was a frenzied effort to have the newcomers "qualified" and "to get them by" the POM inspectors. Under these circumstances there was a tendency to place more emphasis on paper than on proficiency, on crediting a man's record with weapons-firing than on establishing his ability to hit the target, on checking off such requirements as overhead fire, close combat, and "combat in cities" on charts posted in headquarters offices than on actually indoctrinating the trainees for battle and molding them into smoothly working teams.[1]

A common sight in almost any AGF camp in the spring and summer of 1944 was a group of lieutenants herding a batch of recent arrivals from the Army Specialized Training Program, low-priority units, or converted organizations through weapons-firing and combat courses so that they might be put down as "qualified" and taken to port with the unit. Frequently these newcomers were so ignorant of tactics and so unaccustomed to firearms that the lieutenants dared not permit freedom of maneuver, but felt constrained instead to coach them through the exercises, with frequent admonitions to "get back in line" and "don't

[1] (1) Personal observations of AGF Hist Off on visits to divisions in training in Jun, Jul, and Oct 44. (2) Memo of Lt Col Ralph L. Zwicker for G-3 AGF, 26 Feb 44, sub: Visit to Cps Adair, White, and Beale, 18-23 Feb 44. AGF G-3 files, 333.1/75 (Insps by AGF Staff Offs).

fire till I tell you." Circumscribed to this extent, the well-conceived processing became an empty ritual.[2]

Personnel turnover was not a phenomenon limited to a brief period or a few unfortunate units; it was prolonged and extensive, being most acute during the summer of 1944. A study by The Inspector General of 4 divisions and 56 AGF nondivisional units for a 6-month period beginning in March and ending in September revealed that during that time the divisions lost 27,192 men (55.1 percent of their authorized strength) and gained 39,091 (74 percent). The nondivisional units lost 8,852 (38.3 percent) and gained 12,034 (52.2 percent). Some of the men transferred to these units remained only a short time and then were sent on to other units or to replacement depots, thus aggravating disruption and multiplying the burdens of POM.[3]

Many units fared much worse than the average of those included in The Inspector General's survey. The 506th Military Police Battalion, activated in March 1944 with a T/O enlisted strength of 519, between May and October, 1944, gained 870 men and lost 833.[4] The 1282d Engineer Combat Battalion received 470 men from the 2d Coast Artillery Provisional Battalion on 23 June and lost them on 21 July. During the period 7–22 July this unit received 180 men from various military police, quartermaster, ordnance, and paratroop organizations. On 24 July 240 men came in from an antiaircraft battalion. In October, with movement to port imminent, the unit was 41 men understrength, and 30-odd men had yet to be replaced because of physical disqualifications, deficiencies in specialist training, or other reasons. The bad effect of personnel changes on the unit's general proficiency is reflected in the following statement from The Inspector General's POM inspection report:[5]

> The battalion's basic training did not begin until 31 July . . . . Individual technical training has not been satisfactorily completed because of the lack of technicians . . . and because one-third of the squad specialists are insufficiently trained for satisfactory performance of their specialties; also, only limited training has been conducted in construction of roads, laying and removal of mines, booby traps, general construction and combat principles. No unit training has been conducted.

[2] *Ibid.*

[3] TIG memo (C) for DCofS USA, 27 Sep 44, sub: Transfer of Personnel between T/O Units of the Army. TIG file WDSIG 333.9 (Personnel Transfers).

[4] TIG memo (R) for DCofS USA, 9 Oct 44, sub: Overseas Readiness Status of 506th MP Bn. 353/1018 (Readiness) (R).

[5] TIG memo (R) for DCofS USA, 18 Oct 44, sub: Overseas Readiness Status of 1282d Engr Combat Bn. 353/1039 (Readiness) (R).

The 381st Ordnance Medium Auto Maintenance Company, activated in March 1944 with a T/O strength of 112 men, received 71 fillers after it was placed under alert instructions. Sixty-two men obtained late in the training period had to be sent to school immediately to remove deficiencies in technical training. They completed their course a few weeks before the readiness date but not in time to be molded into the team.[6]

In view of the pervasiveness of personnel turnover, there is little surprise in the observation, made by The Inspector General at the end of 1944, that "throughout the year unsatisfactory unit training was the principal reason for declaring units not ready."[7]

A second basic difficulty in the processing of units for overseas movement in 1944 was the practice, common in the summer and fall, of OPD calling for shipment of units considerably in advance of expected dates. In mid-August 1944 seven divisions, the shipment of which had not been anticipated prior to July 1945, were taken from the strategic reserve, earmarked for the European Theater of Operations, and given tentative readiness dates ranging from 9 November 1944 to 27 January 1945.[8] In October, to meet a pressing theater need, the Army Ground Forces was directed to move on very short notice, from one to six months prior to previously fixed dates for completion of training, 66 engineer combat battalions.[9] These battalions were ordered shipped in current status of training, which permitted the waiving of certain "POM" requirements, but in other instances there was no modification of requirements when shipment dates were moved up; in such instances processing had to be intensified to meet the new dates.

POM activities were further complicated by the instability of completion-of-training dates even after they had been advanced by several months. In the fall of 1944 OPD ordered the alerting of the seven divisions the training of which had been planned on the assumption that they would not be moved overseas until after June 1945. Two months later, on 13 October, Lt. Col. Seth L. Weld, head of the G–3 Task Force Division, was called out of bed at 0230 by an OPD officer

[6] TIG memo (R) for DCofS USA, 3 Mar 45, sub: Overseas Readiness Status of 381st Ord M Auto Maint Co. 353/1385 (Readiness) (R).

[7] TIG memo (R) for DCofS USA, 8 Jan 45, sub: Readiness of Units for Mvmt Overseas, 4th Quarter 1944. 353/1378 (Readiness) (R).

[8] (1) AGF M/S (R), G–3 for DCofS, 13 Oct 44, sub: Move-up for Shipment of Inf Divs to ETO. AGF G–3 Task Force file, "Availability, Preparation, and Tng of Units for Overseas" (R). (2) Statement of Lt Col S. L. Weld to AGF Hist Off, 24 Feb 45.

[9] Statement of Maj L. R. Watson, AGF Engr Sec, to AGF Hist Off, 19 Jun 45.

and directed to proceed to his office to receive an urgent message from ETO. The message called for a statement of the earliest possible date on which the infantry regiments of all divisions earmarked for ETO would be ready to move in current status of training. An answer was expected in Paris by 0600.[10]

Colonel Weld immediately placed telephone calls for the headquarters of the Second Army, Fourth Army, and the XXII Corps, but there was considerable delay in getting the necessary information. Between 0600 and 0800 a tentative answer was transmitted to Paris. At a noon conference in the Pentagon it was agreed that 28 October was the earliest date that could be met for the movement of the infantry regiments, except for those of four divisions which were given personnel readiness dates of 13 November, and information to this effect was passed on to ETO.[11]

The divisions were alerted in accordance with the dates agreed on at the conference.[12] Subsequently there were many changes. The following chronology of the alert status of the 65th Division at Camp Shelby, Miss., exemplifies the experience of the divisions affected:[13]

15 Oct 44 — Unit alerted by telegram. Dates for infantry regiments and VQ (provisional headquarters detachment): personnel, 13 November; equipment, 28 October. Dates for other elements later.

17 Oct 44 — Dates for infantry regiments and VQ changes: personnel, 12 November; equipment, no change.

18 Oct 44 — WD movement order received.

19 Oct 44 — Received port call for infantry regiments and provisional headquarters detachment, Camp Shanks, N. Y., 15–17 November.

23 Oct 44 — Readiness dates for division less infantry regiments and provisional headquarters detachments: personnel, 25 November; equipment, 15 November.

25 Oct 44 — Port call for infantry regiments and VQ canceled.

27 Oct 44 — Notice received that new dates would probably be forthcoming by 15 November; spare parts of division directed to stop packing but ordered not to unpack; infantry regiments and VQ 95% complete on packing, none of the balance of division complete; boxes all completed.

3 Nov 44 — Division directed to unpack minimum of equipment necessary to carry on training.

16 Nov 44 — New York announced as port.

[10] AGF M/S (R), G–3 to DCofS, 13 Oct 44, sub: Move-up for Shipment of Inf Divs to ETO. AGF G–3 Task Force file, "Availability, Preparation, and Tng of Units for Overseas" (R).

[11] *Ibid.*

[12] AGF M/S (R), G–3 for CofS, 2 Nov 44, sub: Shipment of Divs to ETO. AGF G–3 Task Force file, "Availability, Preparation, and Tng of Units for Overseas" (R).

[13] Information furnished AGF Hist Off by Lt Col V. P. Mock, G–3 Sec, Second Army, 3 Apr 45.

21 Nov 44—VQ deleted and new readiness given division: personnel, 24 December; equipment, 10 December; advance detachment, 10 December.

25 Nov 44—Port call received for Camp Shanks, N. Y., as follows: advance detachment, 21 December; unit, 26 December–2 January; equipment to arrive no later than 29 December.

The effect of these changes on personnel of the division is not difficult to imagine. Packing and unpacking of military equipment in camp were paralleled by packing and unpacking of household goods by officers' and soldiers' wives in the near-by town of Hattiesburg.[14]

Other difficulties sprang from the enormous volume of overseas movements in 1944. In January 1944 283 AGF units, including 6 divisions, with a T/O enlisted strength of 116,860, arrived at ports of embarkation. During the next seven months shipments were not as heavy, but in September they totaled 385 units (including 9 divisions) and 139,839 men. The all-time high was attained in October with movement to port of 393 units (including 5 divisions) and 149,313 men. Shipments fell off in November and December, but the strength of units moved to ports in each of these months was greater than in any month prior to January 1944. During 1944 movements to port reached a total of 3,418 units (including 49 divisions) and 1,195,046 enlisted men. This exceeded by some 1,350 units and 390,000 men the total of all AGF shipments prior to 1944.[15]

This tremendous volume of movement meant an overloading of installations and an overtaxing of personnel charged with POM functions and responsibilities. In June, the peak month for units on alert status in the Army Ground Forces, there were 474 units in A–2 priority and 604 in A–4 priority. In July 446 units were in A–2 priority and 502 units in A–4.[16] The 12th Headquarters and Headquarters Detachment, Special Troops, at Fort Jackson, S. C., had under its supervision at one time as many as 69 alerted units, a large number of which had been placed on alert status almost simultaneously. The task of supervising this flood of units proved too great for the small headquarters of 18 officers and 51 enlisted men, and some of these units were found "Not Ready" in POM inspections.[17]

[14] Based on personal observations of AGF Hist Off on a visit to Camp Shelby and Hattiesburg, Miss, 30 Oct–3 Nov 44.

[15] Information compiled from monthly AGF Stat Sec Rpt No. 19 (S): "AGF Units Arriving at PE." AGF Stat Sec files.

[16] AGF M/S (C), G–4 Task Force Div to G–4, 6 Apr 45, sub: Second Annual Rpt. AGF G–4 Task Force Div files (C).

[17] AGF M/S, G–4 to CofS, 8 Jan 45, sub: Visit to Ft Jackson, S.C., 12–15 Dec 44. 353.02/730 (AGF).

The work load of staff officers who bore the brunt of POM responsibilities in higher headquarters was also exceedingly heavy. Lights in the Task Force Divisions of the G–3 and G–4 Sections of Headquarters, Army Ground Forces, burned late on many nights during peak periods of summer and fall, as weary personnel labored over preparation of Alert Instruction letters, checked status reports, issued directives for transfer of equipment, and wrote movement orders. The load of office work borne by each individual was made heavier by the necessity of keeping a portion of the staff on the road to assist lower headquarters with their multiplied tasks.[18]

POM activities were also complicated by frequent changes of supervisory headquarters and by rotation of personnel within these headquarters. Corps, group, and battalion headquarters were moved overseas in great numbers in 1944, and, as they usually moved as separate organizations, units attached to them for supervision had to be taken over by other headquarters for completion of training and POM. This made continuity of procedure very difficult. Attachment to headquarters and headquarters detachments, special troops, usually fluctuated less, but changes of personnel within these headquarters in 1944 were frequent. The 716th Engineer Depot Company was supervised by four different headquarters: 1122d Engineer Combat Group, 15 December 1943–8 March 1944; 1152d Engineer Combat Group, 13 March 1944–5 June 1944; 14th Headquarters and Headquarters Detachment, Special Troops, Fourth Army, 8 June 1944–15 July 1944; 1152d Engineer Combat Group, 17 July 1944–21 September 1944; and 1161st Engineer Combat Group, 22 September 1944 until movement to port. The 67th Signal Battalion was at various times supervised by seven different headquarters.[19]

With so many units on alert status at one time, and with supervisory headquarters changing so frequently, it was impossible for units to receive the assistance needed in preparing themselves for overseas movement.

Lack of coordination among the various agencies involved in the POM of units continued to be an impediment in 1944, though to a lesser extent than in 1942 and 1943. On numerous occasions supply agencies, functioning automatically on being informed that a unit had been placed in A–4 priority, began to ship equipment to the post for the unit, in spite of the fact that information received by the unit commander through command channels indicated that the

[18] Statements of various offs of G–3 and G–4 Task Force Divs to AGF Hist Off, Feb 45.

[19] (1) TIG memo (R) for DCofS USA, 2 Oct 44, sub: Overseas Readiness Status of 716th Engr Dep Co. 353/998 (Readiness)(R). (2) TIG memo (R) for DCofS USA, 12 Oct 44, sub: Overseas Readiness Status of 67th Sig Bn. 353/1020 (Readiness)(R).

unit was to move with minimum essential equipment only. When the clouds of confusion had lifted in such cases much equipment had to be repacked and sent back to the supply depots.[20]

Considerable confusion existed also as to the responsibility of the group and of the headquarters and headquarters detachment, special troops, for the POM of battalions and separate companies attached to groups.[21]

Varying standards as to combat serviceability of equipment were another source of misunderstanding and difficulty. Time and again unit commanders whose equipment had been certified as combat-serviceable by army or lower headquarters would a short time later have a portion of that equipment condemned as unserviceable by representatives of The Inspector General in the final POM inspection. The result was a hurried replacement of the equipment rejected and a "black eye" for the unit and its supervisory headquarters for letting such equipment pass.[22] Prior to November 1944 the situation was further complicated by the fact that port commanders passed on the serviceability of small arms and other items of individual equipment, using standards somewhat at variance from those applied by either tactical commands or The Inspector General.[23] Schools on combat serviceability instituted by the Army Service Forces in November 1944, and attended by personnel of the Army Ground Forces, the Army Service Forces, and the Inspector General's Department, developed a closer agreement on applicable standards. Elimination in the fall of port inspection of small arms, except as specifically requested by unit commanders, reduced the number of authorities who had to be satisfied as to certain items being combat-serviceable.[24]

Another obstacle in 1944 was insistence by Army Service Forces on keeping station stock at a very low level, thus necessitating the filling of equipment orders from depots which sometimes were at a considerable distance from units having shortages to fill. This consumed time that often, in view of the accelerated training and movement of units, could ill be spared. Army Ground Forces was con-

[20] Memo of Col Charles H. Bryan for G–4 AGF, 27 May 44, sub: Notes on Trip to Ft Knox, Ky, and Ft Leonard Wood, Mo, 24–26 May 44. AGF G–3 files, 333.1 (Insp by AGF Staff Off) (binder 28).

[21] AGF memo, G–1 representative for G–3, 1 May 44, sub: Rpt of G–1 Representative on Gen McNair's Insp Trip 23–29 Apr 44. 353.02/599 (AGF).

[22] (1) AGF M/S (R), G–3 to CofS, 17 Jan 45, sub: IG Rpt for the Last Quarter. 353/1378 (Readiness) (R). (2) AGF M/S (C), G–4 Task Force Div to G–4, 2 Jul 44, sub: Quarterly Rpt. AGF G–4 Task Force Stat Book (C).

[23] Statement of Lt Col J. A. Hanson, G–4 Task Force Div, to AGF Hist Off, 2 Jun 45.

[24] (1) *Ibid.* (2) AGF M/S (C), G–4 Task Force Div to G–4, 9 Jan 45, sub: Quarterly Rpt. AGF G–4 Task Force Stat Book (C).

cerned also over what appeared to be a tendency of Army Service Forces to regard equipment of low-priority units as a reserve source which might be drawn on in lieu of depot stocks for completing the equipment of alerted units.[25]

Still another source of difficulty was the failure to allow units an overstrength sufficient to absorb losses from attrition, transfers, and other causes. In January 1944, because of dwindling manpower resources, the War Department discontinued the 15 percent initial overstrength that had been authorized since the fall of 1942.[26] In May 1944 Headquarters, Army Ground Forces, made strong representations to the War Department for a 6-percent overstrength for units as soon as they appeared on the Six Months List. Only in this way, the Army Ground Forces insisted, could the necessity of stripping low-priority organizations to fill alerted units be avoided.[27] The War Department responded to this request by authorizing a 2-percent overstrength for units having an A–2 priority.[28] This allotment was both too little and too late.

Of less basic difficulties, those cited most frequently by unit commanders were overabundance of inspections, excess of reports, and multiplicity and redundancy of instructions. The III Corps early in 1944 called on the 91st Division for four status reports; in addition the division was subjected to numerous inspections by officers "with varied ideas as to combat serviceability of equipment." [29] Units at Camp McCoy were inspected periodically by inspection teams of the headquarters and headquarters detachment, special troops, and of the post; moreover, those on alert status were inspected daily by the commanding officer, the executive officer, or the S–3 of the headquarters and headquarters detachment, special troops.[30]

In August 1944 the Army Ground Forces polled lower commands for com-

[25] (1) AGF M/S (C), G–4 Task Force Div to G–4, 2 Jul 44, sub: Quarterly Rpt. (2) AGF M/S (C), G–4 Task Force Div to G–4, 9 Jun 45, sub: Quarterly Rpt. Both in AGF G–4 Task Force Div Stat Book (C). (3) AGF M/S, G–4 to CofS, 30 Apr 45, sub: Equip for Redeployment Tng. AGF G–4 Task Force file, "Chief of Staff."

[26] WD ltr (R) AG 320.2 (15 Jan 44) OB–S–C–M to CGs, 20 Jan 44, sub: Overstrength in Units in the Continental U. S. 320.2/309 (R).

[27] AGF memo (C) for CofS USA, Attn G–3, sub: Overstrength in Units to Neutralize Losses through Attrition. 320.2/428 (C).

[28] WD memo (C) WDGCT 320.2 (16 May 44) for CGs, 19 May 44, sub: Overstrength of Units. 320.2/428 (C).

[29] Memo of Lt Col Ralph W. Zwicker for G–3 AGF, 26 Feb 44, sub: Visit to Cps Adair, White, and Beale, 18–23 Feb 44. AGF G–3 files, 333.1/75 (Insps by AGF Staff Off).

[30] Memo of G–3 representative for G–3 AGF, 12 Jul 44, sub: Visit to Cp Carson, Colo, and Cp McCoy, Wis, 6–8 Jul 44. AGF G–3 files, 333.1 (Insp by AGF Staff Off)(binder 40).

ments on POM procedures, and it received almost universal complaint about the mass and complexity of current instructions. A corps commander observed: "The sources of instruction available to a unit for preparation for overseas movement are so numerous and involved that it is difficult for the unit commander to keep abreast of all requirements." [31] A division commander suggested "that regulations published by each port be coordinated with those of other ports, and that such regulations be thoroughly coordinated with POM and IOI. Instructions in these documents, in some cases, conflict or supplement one another." [32] Fourth Army headquarters stated: "The multiplicity of sources of information on POM requirements is a definite source of delay and lost motion in smaller units. . . . What is desired . . . [is] a consolidated manual of all POM requirements and directives." [33] In another connection a special troops commander, chafing under criticism of a unit under his supervision going to port with some of its equipment combat-unserviceable, remarked: "'. . . combat serviceability,' in the absence of specific information, can only be considered a matter of opinion. Since Circular 296, WD 44, uses such terms as 'approximately 75% of wear expectancy,' 'approximate shade of original color,' and 'degree of light reflection,' this headquarters had endeavored to comply with the last sentence of paragraph 3*c* thereof." [34]

These and other difficulties resulted in numerous deficiencies in the processing of units for overseas movement. A study of various pertinent sources, but mainly of reports of The Inspector General, indicates that the most frequent and persistent shortcomings were as follows:[35]

1. Individual technical training unsatisfactory.
2. Unit training unsatisfactory.
3. Individual and crew-served weapons-firing incomplete.
4. Administration and records unsatisfactory.
5. Discipline and morale unsatisfactory.
6. Maintenance and supply discipline unsatisfactory.
7. Shortage or unserviceability of organizational and individual equipment.

[31] AGF ltr (C) to CGs Second and Fourth Armies, R&SC, and AA Comd, 7 Aug 44, sub: Comments on POM Procedures. With related papers. 370.5/632 (C).

[32] *Ibid.*

[33] *Ibid.*

[34] 2d ind by 7th Hq & Hq Det Sp Trs, Fourth Army, on AGF ltr to CG Fourth Army, 18 Oct 44, sub: Overseas Readiness Status of 65th Sig Bn, Cp Howze, Tex. 353/1024 (Readiness) (R).

[35] For quarterly summaries of deficiencies revealed by TIG reports see AGF letters, sub: Readiness of Units for Movement Overseas, with file numbers and dates as follows:

353/621 (Readiness)(R), 9 May 44
353/822 (Readiness)(R), 5 May 44
353/1046 (Readiness)(R), 29 Oct 44
353/1257 (Readiness)(R), 21 Jan 45
353/1447 (Readiness)(R), 24 Apr 45
353/1541 (Readiness)(R), 9 Jul 45

Changes in Procedures

In the early months of 1944 there was a continuing effort to place the processing of units for overseas movement on a more efficient basis. On 3 April 1944 the AGF letter supplementing POM was revised to require preparation of a personnel status report for each alerted unit. This report, submitted by major subcommands to the Task Force Division of G-1 Section, Headquarters, Army Ground Forces, soon after receipt of alert instructions, indicated what action had been taken to replace unqualified individuals by personnel fit for combat. The revised letter also raised minimum requirements for overseas readiness to include completion of combined training for combat organizations and three weeks of field training for service-type units.[36]

A significant step toward improvement of POM procedure, made by the Army Ground Forces in April 1944, was the initiation of the practice of revealing to armies and other principal agencies all units under their control appearing in the War Department Six Months List immediately after each monthly revision of that list.[37] Hitherto subcommands had been given complete information only as to overseas movements scheduled within the next three months. Now they were told which units were earmarked for the fourth, fifth, and sixth months.

The monthly notification of earmarkings was accompanied by appropriate instructions for initiation of steps prescribed in "POM." Thus for the first time in the war it became possible for responsible agencies to begin a planned program of preparing their units for overseas movement six months prior to the expected date of shipment. It was frankly admitted by AGF staff officers that the new procedure was an experiment and that its effectiveness would depend in large measure on the adequacy of personnel resources and the stability of OPD requirements estimates.[38]

An important change made in the summer of 1944 was the initiation of a modified or "streamlined" system of POM, known as "Red List" procedure for units destined for ETO. The Red List procedure superseded the Blue List system.[39] It will be recalled that the Blue List comprised units shipped to Great Britain prior to the Normandy landings; organizational equipment for these

[36] AGF ltr (R) to CGs, 3 Apr 44, sub: Preparation of Units for Overseas Serv. 370.5/352 (R).

[37] AGF ltr (R) to CGs, 10 Apr 44, sub: Tentative Selection of Units for Overseas Serv. 353/644 (Readiness) (R).

[38] Statement of Lt Col S. L. Weld to AGF Hist Off, 5 Jun 44.

[39] Both designations were suggested by the Task Force Division of the AGF G-4 Section. AGF M/S (C), G-4 Task Force Div to G-4, 6 Apr 45, sub: Second Annual Rpt. AGF G-4 Task Force Stat Book (C).

units was preshipped and picked up by them after their arrival in England. After establishment of the Normandy bridgehead most units shipped to ETO went directly to the Continent or stopped only briefly in England before proceeding to France. In the case of these units it was neither necessary nor desirable to preship equipment.

Units moving under the Red List procedure were, at the suggestion of the AGF G-4 Task Force Division, given a "theater priority" for equipment, which meant in effect that they received complete allowances of combat-serviceable equipment before leaving the United States. As a rule, Red List units took all their equipment with them except general-purpose vehicles; it was found that the latter required 40 percent less space if shipped knocked down in separate cargoes than if loaded with the units. For economy and convenience, certain types of organizational equipment, including special-purpose vehicles, were laid down at the ASF Holding and Reconsignment Point, Elmira, N. Y., and held there until the unit was ready to embark. This prevented the overtaxing of port facilities by advance accumulation of heavy impedimenta at the docks. Supply officers of Red List units were routed through Elmira on their way to port to complete equipment arrangements. The Army Ground Forces assigned a liaison representative to the Holding and Reconsignment Point to assist these officers.[40]

Details of Red List procedure were worked out by a War Department Control Board. The Army Ground Forces was represented on this board by the head of the G-4 Task Force Division.[41]

Red List procedure provided for a certain date, known as the "Date of Delivery" ("DDL"), which was usually about thirty days prior to the personnel readiness date by which supply agencies should aim to complete equipment scheduled for delivery at the home station. Shortages still outstanding on that date were listed on a special report, known as the "DDL Report," which also gave information as to prospective delivery; this report was signed by both the station and the unit commanders. At the suggestion of Headquarters, Army Ground Forces, the report was consolidated with the Nondelivery Information Report usually submitted by the unit commmander forty days after the submission of the show-down shortage list. The DDL Report had the effect of expediting completion of equipment and of keeping all parties fully informed as to the status

[40] (1) AGF M/S (C), G-4 Task Force Div to G-4, 6 Apr 45, sub: Second Annual Rpt. AGF G-4 Task Force Stat Book (C). (2) Statement of Col V. A. St. Onge to AGF Hist Off, 20 Sep 44.

[41] AGF M/S (C), G-4 Task Force Div to G-4, 6 Apr 45, sub: Second Annual Rpt. AGF G-4 Task Force Stat Book (C).

of shortages. Subsequently the date of delivery and the DDL Report were prescribed for all units in POM.[42]

Most units shipped to ETO between September 1944 and February 1945, inclusive, were governed by Red List procedures. All in all, 939 units were moved under Red List provisions; included among these were 32 divisions, 6 corps headquarters, and 1 army headquarters.[43]

Mainly to meet deficiencies in administration and record keeping revealed in POM inspections of The Inspector General, the Army Ground Forces took action as follows:

1. It allotted personnel and classification officers to headquarters and headquarters detachments, special troops, to assist nondivisional units in assignment and other administrative matters.

2. It published instructions on administrative records and procedure in the AGF Weekly Directive.

3. It sent officers to the field at frequent intervals to check up on compliance with AGF directives and to instruct personnel in administrative policies.[44]

Another step for improvement of POM taken by Headquarters, Army Ground Forces, was the strengthening of liaison with various agencies involved in preparing units for shipment. In 1944 and the early months of 1945 Task Force representatives of the Army Ground Forces intensified visits to army headquarters in order to keep them up to date on POM policies, to check up on POM activities, and to secure recommendations for changes in procedure.[45] These visits afforded a means of passing on to one headquarters improvements developed by another, as is indicated in the following excerpt from the report of the head of the G-3 Task Force Division after a trip in November 1944:[46]

> The party obtained from the Second Army their procedure for committing units, POM inspection, and pre-IG inspections in order to carry this information to Fourth Army in an effort to improve Fourth Army's operation in these matters.

Liaison with alerted units, with headquarters and headquarters detachments,

[42] (1) *Ibid.* (2) AGF M/S (C), G-4 Task Force Div to G-4, 2 Oct 44, sub: Quarterly Rpt. AGF G-4 Task Force Stat Book (C). (3) Statements of Lt Col J. A. Hanson to AGF Hist Off, 2 and 21 Jun 45.

[43] M/R (C), 27 Jan 45, sub: Summary of Units under Red List Procedures. AGF G-4 Task Force "Red Unit Book."

[44] AGF M/S (R), AG to CofS, 9 Feb 45, sub: IG Rpt for the Last Quarter. 353/1378 (Readiness)(R).

[45] Statement of Lt Col S. L. Weld to AGF Hist Off, 11 Jun 45.

[46] AGF M/S, G-3 Task Force Div to G-3, 28 Nov 44, sub: POM Inspection Trip to Second and Fourth Armies. AGF G-3 files, 333.1/474 (Insp by AGF Staff Off). This action was desirable in view of the fact that personnel of the Fourth Army Headquarters had undergone a complete turnover.

special troops, and with posts was also strengthened. Prior to the summer of 1944 AGF representatives had visited some of the divisions and other units preparing for movement, but these trips had been occasional, and assistance with POM had been more or less incidental. Beginning about July 1944, POM liaison visits were increased and systematized, and assistance in preparing units for shipment was recognized as a primary responsibility of Headquarters, Army Ground Forces. All the divisions on the Red List, and many of the nondivisional units, were visited at least once between the time of their alert and their departure from port.[47]

Visits were made by teams rather than by individuals. The POM liaison team usually consisted of one or more representatives from the G–1 Task Force Division, the G–3 Task Force Division, the G–4 Task Force Division, and the Distribution Division of Army Service Forces. Whenever practicable the AGF visit was coordinated with that of port of embarkation representatives. Beginning in August 1944 a representative of War Department G-4 accompanied the AGF liaison party on its trips. A conference, arranged by the army or other agency responsible for movement of the units concerned, was held at each station visited by the AGF party. This conference was attended by representatives of all units under POM, by officers from corps, by the commander and key staff members of the headquarters and headquarters detachments, special troops, and by representatives of the post.[48]

At each post where a division was stationed, the division commander or his chief of staff opened the conference by introducing the members of the visiting party. The AGF G–1 Task Force member discussed current POM personnel policies and gave advice on preparation of personnel-status reports and on clearing of officers and men who were not qualified for overseas service.[49] The Task Force Officer from G–4 of the Army Ground Forces talked at length on matters of equipment. For the benefit of units moving under Red List procedures he gave a brief explanation of the purposes and functioning of that system. He then took up such topics as standards of combat serviceability, relations with ASF supply agencies and port authorities, applicable modifications of POM, and various means of expediting equipment deliveries. He laid particular stress on the impor-

[47] (1) Statement of Lt Col J. A. Hanson to AGF Hist Off, 2 Jun 45. (2) AGF M/Ss (C), G–4 Task Force Div to G–4, 2 Jul 44, 2 Oct 44, and 9 Jan 45, sub: Quarterly Rpt. (3) AGF M/S (C), G–4 Task Force Div to G–4, 6 Apr 45, sub: Second Annual Rpt. Both (2) and (3) in AGF G–4 Task Force Stat Book (C).

[48] Statement of Lt Col J. A. Hanson to AGF Hist Off, 2 Jun 45.

[49] *Ibid.*

tance of aggressiveness in pursuing equipment requisitions. "Remember," he said, that "the squeaky wheel gets the grease." [50]

The G–3 Task Force representative discussed the completion of training requirements, but, in view of the fact that in most cases little remained to be done in the way of training, his talk was comparatively brief. G–4 was the principal spokesman for the Army Ground Forces at these conferences.[51]

The port of embarkation representative usually covered the following points:[52]

1. Geography of the port, including approaches, terminals, and lighterage problems.
2. Relations with staging areas.
3. Sequence of dates of calls to port.
4. Reports, including Port Impedimenta Report, Form 413, Shipment Packing List, Initial and Supplemental Shortages.
5. Shipment of baggage.
6. Shipment of organizational equipment.

Conferences were concluded by a question period during which unit and station representatives were able to clear up points of confusion still outstanding. The War Department G–4 representative commented informally on War Department policies and procedures. Following the formal sessions members of the AGF party talked informally with officers of the post, alerted units, headquarters and headquarters detachment, special troops, and corps. These meetings contributed greatly to mutual understanding of problems and to harmonious relations. At some time during the visit representatives of the ASF Distribution Division conferred with the post commander and the post director of supply on matters relating to procurement and distribution of equipment.[53]

Another important liaison step taken in 1944 by Headquarters, Army Ground Forces, was the creation in May of an "IG Reports Branch" in the G–3 Task Force Division. The principal function of this branch was the maintenance of liaison between AGF organizations and the Inspector General's Department. An officer from the branch attended POM inspections, rendering such assistance

[50] Transcript of speech made by Lt Col J. A. Hanson at Cp Chaffee, Ark, 28 Nov 44. AGF G–4 Task Force files (Lt Col Hanson's Book).

[51] Statement of Lt Col J. A. Hanson to AGF Hist Off, 2 Jun 45.

[52] Memo (C) of Lt Col Hanson for AGF G–4, 26 Oct 44, sub: POM Liaison Trip to Ft Benning, Ga; Cp Rucker, Ala; Cp Van Dorn, Miss; and Cp Shelby, Miss. AGF G–4 Task Force files (Lt Col Hanson's Book).

[53] (1) Memo (R) of Lt Col Hanson for G–4 AGF, 4 Dec 44, sub: POM Liaison Visits. AGF G–4 Task Force files (Lt Col Hanson's Book). (2) Statement of Lt Col Hanson to AGF Hist Off, 2 Jun 45.

230-171 O - 66 - 40

as was appropriate to both IGD officers and units under inspection. When deficiencies calling for correction by higher headquarters were found in a unit, the AGF representative could telephone the corps, army, or other responsible agency directly, and quickly secure the necessary actions.[54]

The AGF officer's attendance at these inspections had other consequences which, though not as tangible, were no less salutary. The association of AGF and IGD officers on inspection trips developed personal acquaintance and was conducive to closer cooperation. In former days there had been some inclination on the part of General McNair and his staff to look upon the Inspector General's Department as an arbitrary agency, unduly concerned with impressing its efficiency on the War Department by pointing out a multitude of faults, and interested more in "skinning" than in helping.[55] As AGF and IGD officers came to know each other better through association this feeling subsided. It was common practice in late 1944 and early in 1945 for IGD officers on returning from a trip to telephone the IG Reports Branch of Army Ground Forces and say that a particular unit was in bad shape and needed a visit by AGF officers.[56]

Because of the lack of sufficient personnel AGF representatives did not attend all the POM inspections of The Inspector General, but they did make a generous sampling of them. Between 1 June 1944 and V-E Day the Army Ground Forces was represented at the inspection of some forty units, including eleven divisions.[57]

Still another significant move was made in the period May 1944–May 1945 for better coordination of AGF functions with those of other War Department agencies: the establishment of AGF personnel liaison officers at ports of embarkation. Some of the Task Force staff of the Army Ground Forces had long felt a need of liaison representation at ports, but, apparently because of reluctance of General McNair to enter installations not commanded by him, liaison officers were not authorized until after his incumbency.[58]

The port liaison officers began to function in the spring of 1945. Experience in the period immediately preceding V-E Day indicated the value of the work

[54] (1) Biennial Rpt of AGF, Jun 45 (S), p. 29. 319.1/102 (AGF)(S). (2) Statement of Lt Col H. L. Herberts, IG Rpts Br G–3 Task Force, to AGF Hist Off, 19 Jun 45.

[55] Personal ltr of Gen McNair to Maj Gen A. C. Gillem, Jr., CG XIII Corps, 6 Mar 44. McNair Corrrespondence.

[56] Statement of Lt Col H. L. Herberts to AGF Hist Off, 19 Jun 45.

[57] Biennial Rpt of AGF, Jun 45 (S), p. 29. 319.1/102 (AGF)(S).

[58] For this paragraph and the one following see: (1) Statement of Lt Col J. A. Hanson to AGF Hist Off, 5 Jun 45. (2) AGF M/S (C), G–4 Task Force Div to G–4, 6 Apr 45, sub: Second Annual Rpt. AGF G–4 Task Force Stat Book.

of these officers in helping units through the port and in assuring commanders and their men of the continuing interest of the Army Ground Forces in their welfare after they passed under the control of other agencies. Both officers and men seemed glad to have representatives of the command that trained them present at the dock to bid them Godspeed as the transports cast off for distant shores.

As the Army Ground Forces increased its contacts with alerted units it intensified pressure on subcommands to give these units the assistance and supervision necessary for successful completion of POM requirements. In the fall of 1944, for example, the Army Ground Forces instituted the practice of requiring major subcommands, within twenty-four hours after notification that The Inspector General had rated a unit unsatisfactory, to submit a report covering the following matters:[59]

1. Why the preparation of the unit was such as to result in a "Not Ready" report from The Inspector General.
2. The steps being taken to correct the deficiencies reported by The Inspector General.
3. Whether the deficiencies reported by The Inspector General could be corrected by the readiness date.
4. Any other information pertinent to the readiness of the unit involved.

In part at least because of pressure from above, armies and other subcommands took extraordinary steps to prevent units from being declared unready. For example, in the fall of 1944, when preparations for movement were proceeding at an accelerated pace to meet increased overseas requirements, the Second Army sent a G-3 liaison officer and a G-4 officer to each division alerted. These officers remained with the division, rendering all practicable assistance, until movement from camp was completed. Armies also increased the pressure on corps and headquarters and headquarters detachments, special troops, for more effective supervision of nondivisional units operating under POM.[60] As previously stated, some of the lower headquarters, reacting overzealously to the pressure from above, carried supervision to such extremes as to hinder units in their preparation for overseas movement.

Headquarters, Army Ground Forces, also exercised increased pressure on supply agencies in the interest of more rapid and efficient equipping of units for

[59] AGF ltr (R) to CGs, 11 Nov 44, sub: Preparation for Overseas Mvmt (IG Rpts). 370.5/455 (R).

[60] (1) Statement of Lt Col S. L. Weld to AGF Hist Off, 11 Jun 45. (2) Statement of Lt Col J. A. Hanson to AGF Hist Off, 2 Jun 45.

overseas movement. In the late spring of 1944 the Task Force Division of G–4 persuaded Army Service Forces to raise post stock levels to enable units to receive more of their equipment directly from home stations.[61]

Influenced to some extent, at least, by pressure from Army Ground Forces, chiefs of technical services in the fall of 1944 assigned "expediters" to most camps to assist station and tactical commanders in obtaining equipment for alerted units. These expediters were empowered to bypass intermediate agencies and go directly to their chiefs to meet emergency equipment needs. Their "know-how" and authority were of considerable benefit to AGF agencies.[62]

Prompted by the insistence of the AGF G–4 Task Force Division, representatives of the Army Service Forces, the Inspector General's Department, and the Army Ground Forces held a conference in May 1944 on the clarification of ordnance service standards with a view to reducing confusion over varying interpretations of combat serviceability.[63] Later in the year the Army Service Forces, as stated above, adopted the recommendation of the AGF G–4 Task Force Division to set up schools of instruction in combat serviceability for representatives of The Inspector General, Army Service Forces, and Army Ground Forces.

In August 1944 the Army Service Forces, influenced, no doubt, by continuing AGF insistence on advance information as to equipment deliveries, issued a new manual of supply procedures for organizational equipment. Major changes prescribed in this document were as follows: (1) the fixing of a time limit for depots and stock control points in furnishing equipment-delivery information to the station commander; (2) the taking over by technical service stock control points of all necessary responsibilities in supplying equipment, drawing on depots, and directing shipment to stations; and (3) the designation of a time, known as the "Required Date" (thirty days after receipt by the station commander of a unit's show-down shortage list), by which shortages had to be received at the home station. These changes had practically the same objectives as those sought by the Army Ground Forces in the Nondelivery Information Reports, and they were hailed by G–4 officers as acceptance by the Army Service Forces, after persistent objection, of a view long advocated by Army Ground Forces.[64]

[61] (1) Statement of Lt Col J. A. Hanson to AGF Hist Off, 2 Jun 45. (2) AGF M/S (C), G–4 Task Force Div to G–4, 2 Jul 44, 9 Jan 45, sub: Quarterly Rpt. AGF G–4 Task Force Stat Book.

[62] AGF M/S (C), G–4 Task Force Div to G–4, 6 Apr 45, sub: Second Annual Rpt. AGF G–4 Task Force Stat Book.

[63] *Ibid.*

[64] AGF M/S (C), G–4 Task Force Div to G–4, 2 Oct 44, sub: Quarterly Rpt. AGF G–4 Task Force Div Stat Book.

In the spring of 1945 Army Ground Forces made two other notable gains in its efforts to assure adequate and timely equipment of units in training. First, it succeeded in having the War Department place restrictions on ASF requests for transfer of equipment from low-priority units to fill requisitions of those on alert status. Such transfers had originated in the days when ASF stocks were necessarily low and when production could not keep pace with requirements. But in 1944 and 1945, after the production situation had greatly improved, the Army Service Forces, instead of filling requisitions from stock, continued to make numerous requests for transfers of various items from units in early stages of training. The Army Ground Forces protested that by greater exertion the Army Service Forces could meet most if not all of these needs from production or stock.[65] Influenced by this argument, the Secretary of War in May 1945 directed the Army Service Forces henceforth to report immediately to the War Department each request for transfer of equipment. In so doing it was to state the following: (1) "why each item of equipment reported is not currently available for issue"; (2) "that all other prospective sources of supply of each item reported short have been exhausted, and that there exists no other method of filling the shortage other than by transfer"; (3) the action being taken on procurement of each item; and (4) an estimate of total quantities of each item required in the next ninety days.[66] Following issuance of this directive there was a decline in the number of requests on the Army Ground Forces for transfers of equipment from one unit to another.[67]

The second gain made by the Army Ground Forces with reference to equipment was the issuance by the War Department of a directive requiring that units in redeployment training be given an A-2 priority and be completely furnished with 100-percent combat-serviceable equipment.[68]

These changes in POM equipment provisions were accompanied by revisions of policies governing personnel and training. In November 1944 steps were taken to permit the withdrawal, under certain conditions, of enlisted specialists from schools in cases where units were shipped in advance of expected dates; if students were not withdrawn, and their unit sailed without them, they were not to remain under control of the Army Service Forces on graduation, as had previ-

[65] (1) Statement of Lt Col J. A. Hanson to AGF Hist Off, 2 Jun 45. (2) AGF M/S, G-4 to CofS, 25 May 45, sub: Transfers of Equip. G-4 Task Force Div file, "Chief of Staff."

[66] WD D/F, memo of WD G-4 for CG ASF, 17 May 45, sub as in n. 65. 475/2358 (Equip of Trs).

[67] Statement of Lt Col J. A. Hanson to AGF Hist Off, 23 Jun 45.

[68] AGF M/S, G-4, to CofS, 30 Apr 45 sub: Equip for Redeployment Tng. AGF G-4 Task Force Div file, "Chief of Staff."

ously been the case, but were to revert to AGF jurisdiction.[69] In December 1944, because of the exigencies of conversion, the War Department deleted from "POM" the requirement that each individual must have completed individual training for his arm or service before shipment overseas. Prior to this modification it had been necessary for the Army Ground Forces, before shipping a cook transferred from an engineer to an infantry unit, to give him basic infantry training, despite the fact that there was very little change in his duties. As a safeguard against abuse of the liberalized procedure, the War Department added the provision that agencies preparing units for overseas service should not relax efforts to furnish personnel in the arm or service normally required, together with the stipulation that "in the event that personnel of one arm or service must be used to fill a vacancy in another arm or service, such personnel will be reasonably qualified to perform the job to which they are assigned." [70]

These and various other changes in procedure made after issuance of the second edition of "POM" in August 1943 were embodied in a third edition of that document, dated 15 January 1945 and distributed in March. As in previous revisions, Headquarters, Army Ground Forces, contributed both oral and written suggestions on drafts submitted by the War Department.[71]

Among the changes in the third edition of "POM" which have not been discussed previously, one may note, first, the fact that A–3 and A–4 were not listed as equipment priorities. A–3 was a special priority that had been created late in 1942 for units stored in a pool to meet emergency overseas calls. Reserve pools were maintained for a time in 1943, but increased theater demands in 1944 so depleted these reservoirs that they consisted almost exclusively of units for which there was no overseas requirement and which "floated about" awaiting inactivation or conversion. Hence it was deemed pointless to continue the A–3 priority. The A–4 priority had been provided for units in the fourth, fifth, and sixth months of the War Department's Six Months List. At conferences held late in 1944 for revision of "POM" the Army Service Forces presented these arguments: (1) If units actually received their full allotment of combat-serviceable equipment from three to six months prior to shipment, as contemplated in the A–4 priority, they would wear it out before movement to port. (2) If the units did not receive the equipment the net result of the priority would be a burden of worry and

[69] AGF M/S, G–4 to G–1, 29 Nov 44, sub: Draft No. 2—POM. 370.5/4227.

[70] WD ltr AG 370.5 (23 Dec 44) OB–S–E–SPMOT–M to CGs, 24 Dec 44, sub: Modification to POM. 370.5/4219.

[71] The third edition of "POM," together with a summary of principal changes in procedure made by this revision, is filed in 370.5/506 (sep binder) (R).

paper work. (3) The A-2 priority provided for units receiving the bulk of their combat equipment about ninety days prior to shipment, and this was soon enough. Army Ground Forces, influenced partly by these arguments and partly by the fact that the A-4 priority had never produced any considerable increase in the flow of equipment, agreed to its discontinuance.

A second change was that reports of shortages of uncontrolled equipment to chiefs of supply services after show-down inspections were discontinued, although, under the revised system, an Equipment Delivery Report, made five days prior to the impedimenta readiness date, informed the ASF depot of shortages still outstanding. The Army Service Forces requested this change on the ground that station supply officers could obtain uncontrolled items from depots by routine requisition without troubling chiefs of services.

Third, certain provisions of the Red List procedure and of ASF Manual 414 were included. Among these was the fixing of a "required date" by the time of which supply agencies were to complete delivery of equipment at the home station for the filling of shortages. The required date for units in A-2 priority or under warning on movement orders was thirty days after receipt by the station commander of a unit's show-down shortage report. Station commanders were required to submit Equipment Delivery Reports of all unit shortages not filled at the home station seven days prior to the impedimenta readiness date.

The third edition of "POM" embodied the provisions of "IOI" and certain other instructions that had been issued as separate documents. In bringing these various publications together within the covers of a single booklet, much was accomplished toward removal of one of the principal criticisms of field commanders, namely, the multiplicity and redundancy of POM literature. But there remained considerable room for improvement, including further simplification of terminology.

In November 1944 and again in March 1945 the Army Ground Forces, to bring it into line with changes in "POM," revised the form letter "Preparation and Movement of Units for Overseas Service" addressed to principal subcommands. Moreover, a provision was added requiring that the report to Headquarters, Army Ground Forces, of shortages outstanding forty days after submission of the show-down shortage list should be prepared by the unit commander in coordination with the station commander and that it should be signed by both.[72] This had the effect not only of reducing misunderstanding as to the

[72] (1) AGF ltr (R) to CGs, 26 Nov 44, sub: Preparation and Mvmt of Units for Overseas Service. 370.5/352 (R). (2) AGF ltr (R) to CGs, 17 Mar 45, sub: Preparation and Mvmt of Units for Overseas Serv. 370.5/506 (R).

status of equipment but also of impressing upon the station commander the urgent necessity of completing equipment delivery.[73]

Achievements and Shortcomings

In spite of the tremendous increase in the volume of overseas movement in 1944, the Army Ground Forces was able to maintain a good record in the readiness of units inspected by The Inspector General. Of 1,000 AGF units inspected in 1944 only 113, or 11 percent, were reported as "Not Ready."[74] The following tabulation shows the trend in "Not Ready" percentages from the first quarter of 1943, when TIG readiness reports began, through the second quarter of 1945:[75]

1943				*1944*				*1945*	
1st Q	*2d Q*	*3d Q*	*4th Q*	*1st Q*	*2d Q*	*3d Q*	*4th Q*	*1st Q*	*2d Q*
18%	20%	12%	11%	13%	11%	9%	11%	8%	7%

It will be noted that the percentage of units "Not Ready" during the second quarter of 1945 (7 percent) was the lowest of any quarter covered by The Inspector General's reports. While the number of units shipped during this quarter was relatively small, the period during which they were trained was one in which obstacles to training were unusually formidable.

In the early spring of 1945 it became apparent that the defeat of Germany was imminent and that the movement of AGF units to Europe would soon cease. But the War Department, mindful of von Rundstedt's counterthrust in December and determined to take no chance on being again caught off balance, waited until 30 April, only one week before V-E Day, to suspend the flow of movement to ETO. Shipments to the Mediterranean Theater were not discontinued until 2 May.[76]

On 31 July 1945 the cumulative figure for movement to port of AGF units since the inception of Headquarters, Army Ground Forces, stood at 6,210 units and 2,208,753 enlisted men.[77] This represented an achievement of which the headquarters staff was extremely proud.

[73] Statement of Lt Col J. A. Hanson to AGF Hist Off, 2 Jun 45.

[74] AGF ltr (R) to CGs, 21 Jan 45, sub: Readiness of Units for Mvmt Overseas. 353/1257 (Int Tng)(R).

[75] (1) *Ibid.* (2) TIG memo (S) for DCofS USA, 22 Apr 44, sub: Readiness of Units for Movement Overseas. TIG file WDSIG 333.1 Quarterly Report (1st) SP. (3) AGF ltr (S) to CGs, 24 Apr 45, sub as in (2). 353/1447 (Readiness)(S). (4) AGF ltr to CGs, 9 Jul 45, sub as in (2). 353/1541 (Readiness)(S).

[76] AGF M/S (S), G-3 Sec (Harding) to CofS, 4 May 45, sub: Cessation of Mvmt of Units to ETO and MTO. 370.5/535 (S).

[77] Information compiled from monthly AGF Stat Sec Rpt No. 19 (S), "AGF Units Arriving at PE." AGF Stat Sec files. Since the T/O officer strength of AGF units averaged about 6 percent of the enlisted strength, the over-all T/O strength of AGF units moved to ports of embarkation between 9 March 1942 and 31 July 1945 was approximately 2,350,000.

Behind these figures on units and men sent to port there is a story of progress in procedure, for POM technique was much better by V-E Day than during the pioneer period of the Army Ground Forces. In the early months of 1942 the instructions sent out by the Army Ground Forces for the guidance of subordinate commanders charged with preparing units for overseas movement were lacking in coordination and fullness; in 1945 the directives were comprehensive and well-coordinated. During the first year of the AGF period there was no provision for systematic follow-up of final inspections by The Inspector General to ensure the prompt correction of deficiencies which he found or to prevent their occurrence in other units; in 1945, after each inspection, the Army Ground Forces immediately called deficiencies to the attention of appropriate lower commanders and required of them a prompt report of remedial action. In addition, following each quarterly report of The Inspector General, Army Ground Forces prepared a statistical study of the frequency of POM deficiencies and distributed copies of the study among subordinate commanders for their admonition and guidance. In 1942–43 there was no established liaison with the Inspector General's Department; in 1945, when The Inspector General visited alerted units, an AGF liaison officer was commonly at hand to slash red tape and otherwise expedite such corrective action as was required. In 1942 there was no liaison with ports of embarkation on the level of Headquarters, Army Ground Forces; armies and separate corps were directed to maintain liaison with staging areas, but this provision was ineffective. In 1945 the Army Ground Forces had ample and active liaison staffs in all ports of embarkation. In 1942 visits of the AGF staff to armies and alerted units for advice and assistance in POM functions were occasional and incidental; during the year prior to V-E Day such visits were standing operating procedure.

Gradually during the period 1942–45 Army Ground Forces intensified its supervision of armies, separate corps, and other principal commands charged with implementing POM policies. This evolution was a result in large measure of increasing experience; as the AGF staff acquired experience and a sense of confidence there was naturally a tendency toward stronger control. Intensified supervision was implemented by such devices as the requirement of more detailed status reports, more frequent visits, and specific instruction by telephone and telegraph.

The refinement of the AGF phases of POM was due in part to the initiative of Headquarters, Army Ground Forces, and in part to War Department pressure. The War Department, like the Army Ground Forces, tended to exercise stronger control as its staff became more familiar with POM problems. The last quarter of 1942 represents a turning point in War Department control. Conditions revealed in connection with large-scale shipments in this period, particularly Task Force A, caused the War Department to step in and take a firmer grasp on POM matters. From this development came the important policy changes of January 1943, including comprehensive POM inspections by The Inspector General of alerted units, improved status reports for alerted units, provision of a reserve pool of units trained and equipped for overseas movement, and the War Department document "POM." Undoubtedly these vigorous measures led the Army Ground Forces in turn to intensify surveillance over POM activities of its own domain.

Unfortunately the War Department did not bring about closer collaboration of the Army Ground Forces and the Army Service Forces. Cooperation was better in 1945 than in 1942, but it came slowly and at best left much to be desired. Mutual lack of confidence, exaggerated concern with prerogative, and a tendency of the Army Ground Forces and the Army Service Forces each to regard its activities and functions as separate and distinct from those of the other prevented attainment of that degree of efficiency in POM that might have been realized only by exercise of a stronger control on the War Department level.

Even under the existing system more efficiency could perhaps have been attained had it not been for certain characteristics of the organization and policy of the Army Ground Forces. The organization of the AGF staff contained no section representing the inspectional function. General McNair's strict adherence to the principles of the chain of command and delegation of operating functions to lower headquarters, together with his rigid insistence on a "lean headquarters," tended to delay unduly the establishment of the liaison with ports of embarkation which was found to be necessary. His determination to have his headquarters practice the economy advocated by the War Department also held the staffs of task force divisions in Headquarters, Army Ground Forces, to such meager proportions that during periods of heavy movement it was impossible for them to handle the work passing across their desks without regularly working late at night, much less to visit with needed frequency subordinate commands struggling with the enormous problems of POM.

No improvements in method, however, could have overcome completely the obstacles presented by lack of accuracy in estimates of overseas operational needs, failure to place full allowances of combat-serviceable equipment in the hands of troops well in advance of their movement to port, and turnover of personnel. Over these matters the Army Ground Forces did not have control.

Redeployment Training:
Plans and Problems

by

Bell I. Wiley

Contents

Table

I. The Redeployment Training Program

The program for the redeployment training of ground combat troops had its inception in the early fall of 1944, when G–3 of the Army Ground Forces proposed that the multitude of training tests and directives then in effect, some of which went back to the GHQ period and which altogether made up a mass of paper weighing eight pounds, be brought up to date and compressed into a single document.[1] In October 1944, shortly after the G–3 proposal, instructions were received from the War Department requiring the preparation of a program of training for use during the period that would follow the defeat of Germany.[2] It was decided to combine the proposed streamlining of literature on training with the charting of a redeployment training program.[3]

The War Department directive of 5 October 1944 stipulated that redeployment training be "planned and conducted with the objective of preparing individuals, crews, teams, and organizations specifically for operations against Japan." It also required that the following subjects be stressed:[4]

1. Maintenance of health, including malarial discipline and control.
2. Training of junior officers and noncommissioned officers in leadership.
3. Chemical warfare, including the tactical use of smoke and the offensive employment of toxic gases.
4. Swimming, life-saving, and resuscitation.
5. Japanese tactics, techniques, and weapons.
6. Identification of Japanese planes and equipment.
7. Care and maintenance of arms, vehicles, equipment, and clothing under climatic conditions prevailing in the Pacific.
8. Map and aerial photograph reading.
9. Natural and artificial camouflage.

[1] (1) Statement of Lt Col M. F. Brennan, AGF G–3 Sec, to AGF Hist Off, 10 Oct 45. (2) AGF M/S, G–3 to CG, 30 Mar 45, sub: Tng Memo No. 1. AGF G–3 Sec files, 300.6 (AGF Tng Memo No. 1).

[2] WD memo (R) 353 (5 Oct 44) for CGs AGF, ASF, AAF, 5 Oct 44, sub: Tng after the Defeat of Germany. 353/5 (Redepl)(R).

[3] Statement of Lt Col M. F. Brennan to AGF Hist Off, 10 Oct 45.

[4] WD memo (R) 353 (5 Oct 44) for CGs AGF, ASF, AAF, 5 Oct 44, sub: Tng after the Defeat of Germany. 353/5 (Redepl)(R).

The War Department directed further that special attention be devoted to physical ruggedness, small-unit training, scouting and patrolling, and security against surprise ground attacks. A minimum of two hours a week was required for "orientation," but in no other case did the War Department specify the time to be devoted to a subject. To preserve a high state of morale and discipline during redeployment and to promote efficiency in battle, the War Department ordered that insofar as practicable unit commanders and training instructors be men with combat experience.

AGF Training Memorandum, 1 June 1945

In general, the principles stated by the War Department were in harmony with AGF concepts of redeployment training. They were embodied in Training Memorandum No. 1, the new comprehensive AGF directive, issued tentatively in April 1945 and published in permanent form on 1 June.[5] The chief source on which the Army Ground Forces drew in preparing the new program was its own experience during the years of mobilization and war and the experience of overseas commands as reported by AGF and War Department observers. In short, the redeployment training program was for the most part a simplification and rearrangement of existing training literature to meet the needs of an all-out effort against Japan. No significant change was made in procedure or doctrine, although the redeployment training program did place increased stress on subjects peculiarly applicable to Pacific warfare, such as swimming, small-unit training, security against surprise attacks, Japanese weapons, and Japanese tactics and cave warfare.[6] Its main principles were stated by Col. Syril E. Faine at a conference with representatives of subordinate commands on 28 March 1945: "The attitude of this headquarters is that our first problem is to see that the man is basically trained. We're not worrying too much about the man being sure he knows how to fight the Japs, if he is a basically trained soldier." [7] This was the philosophy that Lt. Gen. Lesley J. McNair, Commanding General, Army Ground Forces, 1942–44, had held from the beginning.

[5] The tentative edition (mimeographed, dated 25 Apr 45) is filed in 353.01/1 (Tng Memos); the final edition (lithographed, dated 1 Jun 45) is in a separate binder of the same file. A typed draft that was circulated among AGF staff sections for comments in March is in AGF G–3 Sec files, 300.6 (AGF Tng Memo No. 1).

[6] Statements in this paragraph are based mainly on comparison of Training Memorandum No. 1 with earlier AGF training literature and on conversations of the AGF Historical Officer with various members of the AGF G–3 Section in October 1945.

[7] Record of Conference on Redepl Policies and Procedures, Hq AGF, 27–28 Mar 45. 337/1 (Redepl) (S).

Training Memorandum No. 1 was divided into thirteen sections, each devoted to a distinct aspect of redeployment training. Section I, "General," set forth certain fundamental principles and provisions deemed applicable to redeployment training. This section was drawn largely from the War Department directive of 5 October 1944 and basic AGF documents of an earlier period, particularly the Training Directive effective 1 November 1942 and the supplement thereto dated 7 June 1943.[8] The portion (paragraph 5) which summarized fundamental combat qualifications, such as strong leadership, rigid discipline, proficiency and ruggedness of the individual soldier, teamwork, security, and ability to fight at night, was taken almost verbatim from the supplement of 7 June 1943. Drawing on this and other AGF directives, the introductory section of the new directive called for emphasis on combat firing, expert use of weapons, small-unit leadership, flame-thrower training, reconnaissance, combat intelligence, air-ground training, chemical warfare training, training in maintenance and supply, and mental and physical conditioning. The keynote sentences of the "Special Battle Courses" letter were repeated: "Soldiers without combat experience must be trained mentally for the shock of battle. They must be subjected in training to every possible sight, sound, and sensation of battle."[9]

Specific adaptations for warfare against Japan were apparent in a number of provisions: (1) Attack of fortified positions was modified to provide for operations against emplacements constructed of earth and logs, with emphasis on the use of flame thrower and bulldozer. (2) The "combat in cities" exercise was redrafted to afford training for attacks in Japanese villages, a sketch being included as a guide for constructing mock-ups of the oriental type of building. (3) Stress was placed on small-unit security, to guard against infiltration, and on camouflage because it was thought that Japanese air strength might be greater than that encountered in Europe after 1943. (4) All personnel, except nurses, of medical detachments and units were to fire the rifle, carbine, and pistol for familiarization and to receive instruction in the unloading of other weapons and the handling of grenades. The ostensible purpose of this provision was to prevent accidental discharge of weapons by medical personnel who cleared armed casualties from the battlefield. Experience in Europe had demonstrated the need of training medical personnel in the safe handling of firearms, but it seems likely that instruction in shooting was included in the redeployment program at least

[8] Both the training directive of 1 November 1942 and the supplement of 7 June 1943 are filed in 353/52 (Tng Dir).

[9] AGF ltr to CGs, 4 Feb 43, sub: Spec Battle Courses. 353.01/61.

230-171 O - 66 - 41

partly because of the reputation of the Japanese for ignoring the Geneva Convention.[10]

Section II of Training Memorandum No. 1 was devoted to the training of undeployed nondivisional units—there were no undeployed divisions—during the redeployment period. The schedule set forth in this section was practically the same as that prescribed by the Army Ground Forces in July 1944 for the accelerated training of nondivisional units.[11] Allotments of training time varied with units of different type and also according to the sources from which they obtained their fillers. Those units whose fillers came from reception centers were allotted considerably more time than those whose fillers came from units or replacement training centers of other branches. Those whose fillers came from units or replacement training centers of the same branch were to have the shortest training periods of all. The content of the training program was to be based on appropriate Mobilization Training Programs and the applicable provisions of Training Memorandum No. 1.

Section III set forth principles for the training of redeployed units during the minimum 8-week period established by the War Department. It included a schedule of subjects designed specifically as a guide for units of the arms. (See the adjoining table.) The training called for in this section was to begin when units had available 80 percent of their Table of Organization strength and 50 percent of essential equipment. It was expected that a "shakedown" period of about a week would be required for the assembly of personnel after their recuperation furloughs.[12]

Headquarters, Army Ground Forces, took steps to facilitate the training of redeployed units in operations peculiar to the Pacific. First, it prepared for War Department publication a comprehensive training circular on Japanese characteristics and tactics. This circular told of the character and training of the Japanese soldier, described his weapons, gave a brief summary of Japanese organization and communications, and outlined the high points of the enemy's offensive and defensive tactics.[13] Second, it supervised the preparation for War Department publication of a training circular on the reduction of Japanese cave fortifications

[10] Record of Conference (S) on Redepl Policies and Procedures, Hq AGF, 27–28 Mar 45 (question and answer session following talk by Col Faine). 337/1 (Redepl) (S).

[11] See above, "The Training of Nondivisional Units."

[12] (1) Training Memorandum No. 1, Sec III, p. 2. (2) See n. 10 above.

[13] (1) Tng Cir 23, WD, 28 May 45. (2) Statement of Col C. N. Hunter (who prepared the draft of this circular), AGF Tng Div, G–3 Sec, to AGF Hist Off, 12 Feb 46.

Redeployment Training Schedule for Units of the Arms, 1 June 1945[a]

Subject	Number of Hours per Week						Total Number Hours
	Individual				Unit		
	1st wk.	2d wk.	3d wk.	4th wk.	5th wk.	6th wk.	
Japanese Tactics and Technique	....	....	2	2	....	....	4
Japanese Materiel	2	2	....	....	....	....	4
First Aid and Sanitation	2	2	....	....	....	....	4
Hygiene and Prevention of Diseases	4	4	....	....	....	....	8
Physical Training (including Swimming)	2	2	2	2	2	2	12
Organized Athletics	4	4	4	4	4	4	24
Chemical Warfare	2	2	....	....	....	....	4
Use of Maps and Air Photos	3	3	....	....	....	....	6
Military Courtesy	1	1	....	....	....	....	2
Inspections	2	2	2	2	2	2	12
Dismounted Drill and Ceremonies	2	2	2	2	2	2	12
Care and Maintenance of Clothing and Equipment	2	2	....	....	....	....	4
Weapons Training	10	10	20	....	....	....	40
Interior Guard and Local Security	2	2	....	....	....	....	4
Tactical Marches and Bivouacs	....	....	....	....	4	4	8
Squad and Crew Training	....	....	6	6	....	....	12
Mines and Booby Traps	....	....	....	2	....	2	4
Unit Training, Tactics, and Techniques (including Scouting and Patrolling)	....	....	....	16	24	20	60
Orientation	2	2	2	2	2	2	12
Open Time	4	4	4	6	4	6	28
TOTAL	44	44	44	44	44	44	264

a The seventh and eighth weeks, consisting of combined training with all available types of supporting arms, are not shown in the table.

(Sphinx Project).[14] This document described in detail the structure of cave fortifications, means of detecting their location, methods of defense, and the planning and execution of attack. Stress was laid on coordination of the various arms in both planning and assault phases. Third, it compiled AGF observer and board reports on Japanese tactics and techniques, for distribution to subordinate training agencies.[15] Finally, AGF headquarters cooperated with the War Department in the organization of fifteen mobile intelligence training units for instruc-

[14] Tng Cir 34, WD, 11 Aug 45.

[15] Statement of Lt Col M. F. Brennan to AGF Hist Off, 10 Oct 45.

tion of unit and replacement training center personnel in Japanese organization, weapons, equipment, and uniforms and in small-unit tactics, maintenance of health, and employment of camouflage. These mobile units were trained at Camp Ritchie, Md., from which six of them were graduated in late June and turned over to the Army Ground Forces for assignment to their instructional duties.[16]

Training Memorandum No. 1 did not include detailed instructions for redeployment training of AGF service-type units or of combat engineer, signal, and chemical units. But provision was made for the drawing up by G–3 and appropriate AGF Special Staff sections of separate redeployment training programs for units in each of the service branches.[17]

Section IV of Training Memorandum No. 1 directed that converted units follow the schedules prescribed in Section II for undeployed units.

Since it was anticipated that many units would have an opportunity to extend their training considerably beyond the minimum 8-week period prescribed by the War Department, Section V, "Supplemental Training," was included to provide systematic guidance during an additional period of indefinite duration. This section, modelled on the program of postmaneuver training outlined in the general AGF directive of 7 June 1943, prescribed four periods of progressive training. These began with squad and platoon exercises in the first period and built up to regimental combat team and division exercises in the fourth. Since no tests were scheduled in the initial eight weeks of redeployment training, the supplementary phase was devoted largely to squad, platoon, battalion, and other testing exercises. The special battle courses were also scheduled for this period, and it was specifically directed that in the village fighting exercise the coordination of infantry with tanks should be stressed. Camouflage exercises, training of tank, tank destroyer, and antiaircraft units in the secondary role of supporting artillery, and the participation of service-type units in technical functions were also emphasized.

Redeployment plans anticipated an accumulation of large numbers of casuals in the Zone of Interior as a consequence of unit inactivations and redeployments.[18] Section VI therefore provided for the organization of AGF casuals into tem-

[16] Record of Conference (S) on Redepl Policies and Procedures, Hq AGF, 27–28 Mar 45, talks by AGF G–2 representative, 28 Mar 45. 337/1 (Redepl) (S).

[17] AGF M/S, G–3 to CofS, 2 Apr 45, sub: Tng Memo No. 1. G–3 Records, 300.6 (AGF Tng Memo No. 1).

[18] Record of Conference (S) on Redepl Policies and Procedures, Hq AGF, 28 Mar 45, talks by Col Faine. 337/1 (Redepl) (S).

porary companies, battalions, groups, and regiments for training under armies and corps. Two training periods were prescribed for casual units: during the first they were to follow the initial 2-week program laid down in Section III for redeployed units; during the second, which was of indeterminate length, they were to receive progressive small-unit and military occupational specialty training.

Section VII provided that schools and replacement training centers should continue training under current Mobilization Training Programs, with adaptation of instruction, whenever practicable, to combat against Japan. Subjects for which emphasis was specifically directed included weapons firing, health, leadership, Japanese equipment and tactics, security, maintenance, and the training of assault teams.

General provisions for training in replacement depots were set forth in Section VIII. These emphasized correction of individual deficiencies, physical and mental conditioning, and final polishing of individual and small-unit training.

Section IX contained detailed instructions on the subjects of information and education. The emphasis which Training Memoradum No. 1 gave to orientation sprang from two principal sources. The first was the concern of the War Department and of Army Ground Forces for the morale of redeployed personnel. The second was the strong personal interest of Lt. Gen. Ben Lear, commander of Army Ground Forces during the latter half of 1944 when planning for redeployment was active, in a broad and forceful indoctrination course. Section IX provided for a comprehensive film-lecture-discussion program of one full hour per week in undeployed units and replacement training centers and of two hours per week for redeployed personnel. This program covered the history of Asiatic countries, American interest in the Pacific, the character of the Japanese, and the scope of the task ahead. It contained little that was new, but its publication as an integral part of the basic training directive of Army Ground Forces gave to orientation an emphasis which was likely to impress its subordinate commanders strongly.

Section X, "Administration and Supply," summarized briefly current AGF doctrines and practices governing supply, maintenance, and ammunition. Commanders of subordinate headquarters were directed "to set up a display of clothing and equipment" in order to demonstrate required maintenance standards.

In Section XI training for infiltration, combat in cities, and close combat was outlined, with appropriate illustrations accompanying the text.

Section XII was devoted to tests. Except for the basic medical and intelligence tests, only those which required firing were included. In some cases established tests were revised for the redeployment program, but modifications, designed to remove deficiencies revealed by experience, were of a minor nature. It was not considered necessary to change testing exercises drastically for adaptation to operations in the Pacific.[19] Section XII comprised about nine-tenths of Training Memorandum No. 1.

Thirty-two tests, some consisting of several distinct exercises, were included in the redeployment program. As stated above, no tests were to be given to a redeployed unit during the first eight weeks of training. The plan to defer all tests to the supplemental training period was based on three considerations. First, the primary needs of redeployed units were orientation in conditions and techniques peculiar to the Pacific and the polishing of small-unit training. Inclusion of tests in initial training periods would interfere with the accomplishment of this basic objective. Second, units remaining in the United States for only eight weeks or less would not have time to grow stale and therefore would have no great need of testing. Finally, units remaining in the Zone of Interior for extended periods would need the refreshing afforded by tests and would have ample time to take them.[20] The prescribed program provided a flexible schedule of progressive testing for an unlimited period.

The final division of Training Memorandum No. 1, Section XIII, summarized the requirements of Preparation for Overseas Movement (POM) for units trained during the redeployment period. Requirements varied with the amount of time available for training. For example, redeployed units which had had the opportunity to complete the second period of supplementary training were required to participate in the combat-in-cities course, while those training for lesser periods were exempted from this requirement. Infantry units which had progressed no further than the first period of supplementary training had to take only squad combat firing tests, while those completing the fourth period were required to take platoon and battalion combat firing tests as well as a series of tests in combat intelligence. In requirements a differentiation was also made between undeployed and redeployed units.

Controversy over the Training Program

G-3's of subordinate commands, called to a redeployment conference in Washington on 27-28 March 1945, viewed the new program favorably. But when

[19] *Ibid.*

[20] *Ibid.*

Training Memorandum No. 1 was circulated in draft form among the staff sections of Headquarters, Army Ground Forces, for comment and concurrence, G-4 and some of the Special Staff heads registered objections to certain of the provisions. The main points at issue were allotment of time for maintenance of clothing and equipment, provision for training in maintenance and supply discipline, relative stress on training of units of the arms as against those of the services, and relative emphasis in service units on tactical as distinguished from technical training.[21]

The principals in the controversy were G-4 and Ordnance on the one hand and G-3 on the other. The position of G-4 and Ordnance may be briefly summarized. First, reports from the European Theater of Operations and findings of The Inspector General indicated that maintenance conditions both overseas and in the Zone of Interior left much to be desired. The only way to correct these conditions was to make specific provision in the training program for the upkeep of equipment and for instruction in maintenance, particularly in preventive maintenance. The four hours earmarked for "care and maintenance of clothing and equipment" in Section III of Training Memorandum No. 1 was considered grossly inadequate; at least twelve hours, it was held, should be set aside for this purpose. Second, the form and provisions of the document were deemed prejudicial to service units. Emphasis throughout was on training in the arms. For example, Section III specified a training program for redeployed units of the arms but confined itself to stating that service units would be guided by separate redeployment training programs to be issued later. This would inevitably tend to give subordinate commands the impression that units of the arms were the primary concern of the Army Ground Forces and that service units were viewed somewhat as stepchildren. It was believed that a more equitable plan would be to divide the training program into two parts, one for units of the arms and the other for units of the services. Third, the program as drafted would result in requiring service units to devote a disproportionate amount of time to tactical training, with consequent neglect of training in their primary technical duties. Finally, Headquarters, Army Ground Forces, should make it mandatory for personnel of service units to take military occupational specialty tests, to assure a check on those units comparable to that provided by the squad, platoon, and battalion tests required of combat units. Mainly because of the predominant role

[21] (1) AGF M/S, G-4 to CofS, 1 Apr 45, sub: Tng Memo No. 1. (2) AGF M/S, G-3 to other staff sections, 3 Mar 45, sub: AGF Tng Memo No. 1 and replies thereto (various dates). Both in AGF G-3 Sec files, 300.6 (Tng Memo No. 1).

of the individual specialist in service units, unit testing of functional proficiency in the services was impracticable and hence was not required. It was therefore all the more important that military occupational specialty tests be made obligatory for individuals. While subordinate commands in some instances required testing of service personnel in their individual specialties, AGF action was necessary to guarantee uniform application of the practice in all ground organizations. Until such action was taken Army Ground Forces could have no assurance that service units sent to port were as well qualified as units of the arms to perform their primary missions.[22]

The position of G–3, on the other hand, stressed in the first place the consideration that care and maintenance of equipment, while important, were secondary to the principal mission of the Army Ground Forces—the preparation of units for combat. There was danger of stressing maintenance to a point where troops would have more concern for keeping their weapons in shiny condition than for expending them in realistic training. Second, G–3 held that maintenance and maintenance training were primarily matters of command and discipline. It was neither necessary nor desirable to set aside considerable periods of time for these activities. A good commander would teach his men to care for their weapons as he trained them in the use of those weapons; he would instruct them in the care of their clothing at inspections and in other phases of training. Third, it was argued that adequate provision for technical training of service units would be made in redeployment training programs subsequently to be issued for units of each service branch. A fourth argument was that tests required by the Army Ground Forces should be kept to a minimum and should not extend to the individual level.[23]

This debate over Training Memorandum No. 1 revealed grievances that had long been smouldering among those who represented the services in Headquarters, Army Ground Forces. These grievances centered in a feeling that the Army Ground Forces was dominated by the arms and that service matters received only secondary consideration. It was believed that G–3 was so overwhelmingly con-

[22] (1) AGF M/S, G–3 to CofS, 1 Apr 45, sub: Tng Memo No. 1. (2) AGF M/S, Ord to G–3, 10 Mar 45, sub: Tng Memo No. 1. (3) AGF memo, G–4 to G–3, 10 Mar 45, sub: Tng Memo No. 1. These three references are in AGF G–3 Sec files, 300.6 (Tng Memo No. 1). (4) Statement of Lt Col G. T. Petersen, AGF Ord Sec, to AGF Hist Off, 4 May and 12 Oct 45. (5) Interview of Col K. M. Matthews and other members of AGF G–4 Sec by AGF Hist Off, 10 Oct 45. (6) Statement of Maj G. R. Hill, AGF QM Sec, to AGF Hist Off, 10 Oct 45. (7) Statement of Col O. K. Sadtler, Office of the CSigO, ASF (formerly AGF Signal Off), to AGF Hist Off, 15 Sep 45.

[23] AGF M/S, G–3 to CofS, 2 Apr 45, sub: Tng Memo No. 1. AGF G–3 Sec files, 300.6 (Tng Memo No. 1).

cerned with the training of combat units that it gave only a minimum of attention to the preparation of service units. Such units, it was held, were put through a routine of training designed primarily for units of the arms, with the result that service personnel were required to spend many hours in marching and shooting that were more vitally needed in perfecting technical specialties.[24]

It is impossible to say that in this conflict of opinion one side was right and the other wrong. The points at issue might have been reduced, if not resolved, had there been more time available for training—time to make both soldiers and finished technicians out of service personnel and more time to care for equipment and provide for maintenance instructions without imperiling other phases of the training program.

The Chief of Staff, Army Ground Forces, upheld G–3's position that no more time than that provided in the draft of Training Memorandum No. 1 could be allotted to maintenance, and that military occupational specialty tests should not be made mandatory.[25] The relative importance of tactical and technical subjects in the training of service units was threshed out between G–3 and the various Special Staff sections in the course of preparing redeployment training programs (RTP's) for each of the services. When work on the RTP's was initiated Special Staff heads were handed a schedule of "must" subjects, including items prescribed in War Department directives, which differed little from the schedule outlined in Training Memorandum No. 1 (Section III, "Redeployed Units") for units of the arms and which left comparatively little time for technical training within the 8-week minimum specified by the War Department. Special Staff heads protested, and in subsequent exchanges of views they secured some adjustment in favor of technical training.[26] In the case of signal units, for example, the time prescribed for dismounted drill and ceremonies was reduced to 4 hours as compared with 12 hours for units of the arms; the time for tactical marches and bivouacs to 6 hours as compared to 12 for the arms. Most of the time saved by these reductions was earmarked for "specialist refresher training" of signal per-

[24] Statements in this paragraph are based mainly on the following sources: (1) Interviews of the AGF Hist Off with officers of AGF Special Staff Secs in 1944 and 1945. (2) Interviews with Col K. M. Matthews and other officers of the AGF G–4 Sec by AGF Hist Off, 10 Oct 45. (3) AGF M/S (S), Ord to G–3, 13 Apr 45, sub: Maint Tng and Procedures. AGF Ord Sec file, "Ord Maint 1945" (S).

[25] Statement of Maj Gen Leo Donovan to AGF Hist Off, 7 Aug 45.

[26] Statements to AGF Hist Off of the following: (1) Col O. K. Sadtler, Office of the CSigO, ASF (formerly AGF Signal Officer), 1 Nov 45, (2) Lt Col G. T. Petersen, AGF Ord Sec, 12 Oct 45, (3) Maj G. R. Hill, 1 Nov 45.

sonnel.[27] Similar adjustments were made for other types of AGF service units, but the redeployment training programs as published in final form on 1 June 1945 fell considerably short of what was regarded by Special Staff heads as a desirable balance between tactical and technical subjects. One concession that was obtained applied to all the services. The following provision was included in the replacement training program of each of the services:[28]

> Unless specifically modified by the Commanding General, AGF, the specifications set forth in TM 12-427, "Military Occupational Classification of Enlisted Personnel," are adopted as the standard of individual training. In order to insure appropriate assignment of personnel, unit commanders will carefully analyze current T/O&E applicable to their units and conduct training to qualify fully each specialist in his MOS.

Innovations of the Training Program

Generally speaking, the redeployment training programs for service units differed in three important respects from previous programs. First, they gave subordinate commanders considerable latitude in arranging the details of training. The engineer program, for example, contained this statement:[29]

> Hours allotted are not sufficient to cover all the above subjects during this phase. Overseas experience and individual unit needs must be considered in allotment of training hours. Additional training needs should be covered by allotment of open time hours or scheduled during the supplemental training phase.

Delegation of broad discretionary prerogatives to lower commanders was prompted by the realization that training needs of returned units would vary greatly because of differences in such matters as prior training, combat experience, and turnover of personnel. In the second place, the redeployment training programs, to a larger extent than earlier programs, were based on lessons learned in combat. This was apparently due to two factors: first, the fact that information on combat experience available to Headquarters, Army Ground Forces, through overseas reports and the testimony of officers returning for reassignment was more complete than ever before; second, the fact that in most cases the spade work of preparing the RTP's had been entrusted to officers who had served overseas.[30] The following are examples of the use of combat lessons in RTP's:

[27] (1) Statement of Col O. K. Sadtler to AGF Hist Off, 1 Nov 45, (2) RTP for Sig Units of AGF (printed), 1 Jun 45. 314.7 (AGF Hist).

[28] Par 5 of printed RTP for each of the services in AGF, 1 Jun 45. 314.7 (AGF Hist).

[29] RTP for Engr Units of AGF (printed), 1 Jun 45. 314.7 (AGF Hist).

[30] (1) Statement of Lt Col R. N. Blancett to AGF Hist Off, 1 Nov 45. (2) Observations of AGF Historical Officer, based on personal acquaintance with officers who prepared the RTPs.

Engineer RTP.[31]

1. Interior Guard and Local Security. . . . Stress should be made on working-party security and day-and-night perimeter defense against snipers, banzai raids and infiltration tactics as used by the Japanese. Against the Japanese there is no so-called "secure" rear area.

2. Specialist Training. . . . All units will conduct technical training of individuals and units concurrent with other training. The training of additional engineer equipment operators will be emphasized. SWP and POA reports indicate a need for additional trained equipment operators in engineer units.

Ordnance RTP.[32]

1. Maintenance companies. . . . In so far as availability of Japanese equipment will permit, all units will be trained in the maintenance and reconditioning of such equipment. Third echelon maintenance companies will stress contact-party procedure . . . [and] provisions must be made for contact-party visits to supported units at least daily. Concurrently the supply section of the maintenance must be so organized and trained that deliveries on requisitions to supported units are on a 24-hour or less basis. Provisions also must be made for an efficient back-order system so that rerequisitioning by supported units will never be required.

Fourth echelon maintenance companies will stress rebuilding of assemblies and major items with sufficient emphasis on fifth echelon rebuild to enable the unit to operate without Base Shop support when necessary. Service personnel will be trained to an especially high degree of proficiency in the manufacture of parts within the capability of machine tools authorized for the unit.

Signal RTP.[33]

1. Training emphasis — communications units. . . .

a. Installation and maintenance of wire facilities under unfavorable conditions of weather, terrain and darkness with particular attention to trouble-shooting procedure.

b. Procedure in event of jamming and fading. Net operation with heavy traffic loads.

c. Intensive practice by cryptographic personnel under heavy traffic loads.

2. Training emphasis—Signal Photographic Company. . . .

a. Training of combat assignment personnel in missions involving photographic reconnaissance from liaison type aircraft and supplementation of other ground-reconnaissance agencies.

b. Pertinent instruction in combat tactics and technique of the individual soldier to assure continued functioning of combat-assigned personnel under battle conditions.

3. Supplemental training—team and section. . . .

a. Training in the technique of organizing day-and-night perimeter defense and the security of wire parties and other signal personnel on isolated missions. Fire discipline to prevent promiscuous firing when in a defensive situation and against aircraft. . . .

b. The development of and training in techniques of active coordination and cooperation with engineer-construction troops by wire-installation personnel whenever possible.

[31] RTP for Engr Units of the AGF, 1 Jun 45.
[32] RTP for Ord Units of AGF, 1 Jun 45.
[33] RTP for Sig Units of AGF, 1 Jun 45.

The third distinctive aspect of redeployment training programs has already been indicated; namely, concentration on a single enemy and a fairly limited geographical area. Former programs had to be general enough to prepare units and individuals for operations against many enemies in widely scattered portions of the world. Now it was possible to point all training activities directly toward Japan.

In general the Army Ground Forces contemplated little change in technique for redeployment training. One innovation, however, should be mentioned—the use of demonstration teams organized and trained on the War Department level to facilitate instruction in complicated equipment and procedures. Reference has already been made to the mobile intelligence training teams trained at Camp Ritchie, Md., for use in acquainting AGF units and replacement centers with Japanese organization, weapons, equipment, and uniforms, and for instructing ground intelligence personnel in foreign maps, Japanese psychology, handling of prisoners, and use of specialist teams.[34] Plans drafted jointly by Headquarters, Army Ground Forces, and the Chemical Warfare Service, Army Service Forces, provided that teams trained by the Chemical Warfare Service should be employed by the Army Ground Forces for the demonstration of chemical-warfare equipment and technique to redeployed divisions. Items scheduled for demonstration included the portable flame thrower, the mechanized flame thrower, the one-shot flame thrower, the mechanized assault-gun flame thrower, the 4.2-inch recoilless chemical mortar, and the 7.2-inch rocket, incendiary, and/or chemical filling. Six mobile intelligence training teams were trained and turned over to the Army Ground Forces in July 1945. V-J Day came while the Chemical Warfare Service demonstration teams were still in the planning stage; none was ever organized.[35]

At the request of the Army Ground Forces, The Quartermaster General in July 1945 conducted a 4-week course in clothing and equipment for seventeen teams (one officer and two enlisted men per team) of armies and other major ground commands. On graduation from this course at Camp Lee, Va., the teams conducted schools for representatives of units and other subordinate installations, who in turn instructed the individuals of their respective commands. The Army Ground Forces planned to give every enlisted man sent to the Pacific at

[34] Record of Conference (S) on Redepl Policies and Procedures. Talks by AGF G–2 representative. 337/1 (Redepl) (S).

[35] (1) ASF ltr (C) SPCVK to CG AGF, 16 Jun 45, sub: Chemical Warfare Materiel Demonstration for Redeployed Divs. With AGF 1st ind, 4 Jul 45. 475/17 (Redepl) (C). (2) Statement of Lt Col T. L. Edwards, AGF Chem Sec, to AGF Hist Off, 5 Nov 45.

least two hours of training in clothing and equipment, and every officer four hours.[36]

Provision of this instruction was suggested mainly by experience in Europe, particularly during the last winter of hostilities. At that time failure of commanders to requisition proper clothing, together with lack of knowledge of officers and men as to its use, caused excessively heavy "cold weather" casualties, particularly from trench foot and frostbite. Subjects emphasized in the new courses included clothing insulation, proper sizing of garments, ventilation in clothing, means of obtaining maximum efficiency from clothing, the relation of food and water to clothing, principles of cleanliness, methods of laundering, and the relation of rest and shelter to clothing. Officers were also instructed in such subjects as the relation of clothing to climate and terrain, the correlation of tactical movement and clothing factors, principles of selecting clothing suitable to the activities of the soldier, clothing inspections, responsibilities of officers in the procurement and proper use of clothing, and accustoming men to unfamiliar garments.[37]

The war came to an end shortly after the first clothing and equipment teams completed their training, but steps were taken in the following months both to increase the scope of special instruction in quartermaster schools and to make specific provisions in Ground Forces training schedules for instruction in the selection and use of clothing.[38]

Training by extraneous and migratory groups might have been construed as a violation of General McNair's fundamental dictum that soldiers should be trained in the unit by the unit commander. But General McNair himself had sanctioned modification of the unit training principle in certain instances where instruction was of a highly specialized nature, as was shown by his approval of training centers for antiaircraft and tank destroyer units. In the case of redeployment training in intelligence, clothing, and chemical subjects, limitation of time was an additional factor calling for the application of mass-production techniques. No radical departure was made, in this or other respects, from the training policies which the Army Ground Forces had developed and applied under the direction of General McNair during the mobilization of the ground forces in 1942–43.

[36] (1) Statement of Col G. H. Chapman, Sp Projects Br, AGF G–3 Sec, to AGF Hist Off, 28 Feb 46. (2) AGF ltr to CGs, 15 Jun 45, sub: Clothing Tng. 352/276 (QM Sch). (3) TM 5, 16 Jul 45, sub: Clothing Instruction. 353.01/5 (Tng Memos). (4) Sundry papers filed in binder marked "Clothing Training—Background." Sp Projects Br, AGF G–3 Sec files.

[37] *Ibid.*

[38] Statement of Col G. H. Chapman, Sp Projects Br, AGF G–3 Sec, to AGF Hist Off, 28 Feb 46.

II. Training Problems, 8 May–14 August 1945

The surrender of Japan on 14 August 1945 brought the war to an end before redeployment training as prescribed in Training Memorandum No. 1 could be put into effect. The first units to return to the United States, including the 86th and 97th Divisions, which arrived on 17 and 24 June respectively, were in the process of reassembly following completion of recuperation furloughs when the end came.[1] In any case, personnel readjustment and other policies after V-E Day had a disruptive effect on units which would have made the implementation of redeployment training plans difficult in the extreme.

Personnel Turnover

Status reports prepared in the European Theater of Operations (ETO) reveal the unhappy effect of personnel turnover on units selected for redeployment. The 28th Division in one week experienced a turnover of 20 percent of its enlisted strength and in 40 days a turnover of 46 percent of its officers. Between V-E Day and V-J Day the 35th Infantry Division lost 285 officers and 3,880 men. During the three months following V-E Day the 804th Tank Destroyer Battalion lost 50 percent of its personnel; the 330th Ordnance Depot Company reported in August 1945 that 73 percent of its personnel had been in the unit less than one month; and the 122d Signal Radio Intelligence Company reported that 95 percent of its strength was above the critical score of credits for early discharge. A large proportion of the men lost under readjustment policies were key specialists and NCO's. To make matters worse, newcomers usually were greatly inferior in training, experience, and leadership to the men whom they replaced.[2]

Personnel problems were increased by unforeseen, last-minute extensions of campaign credits. The 2d Infantry Division, for example, after having replaced all men with scores of 85 or above, shortly before sailing from Europe received credit for two additional campaigns. This made some 2,700 more men eligible

[1] Information furnished AGF Hist Off by Col S. L. Weld, AGF G–3 Sec, 16 Oct 45.

[2] (1) AGF M/S (S), G–3 to CofS, 30 Aug 45, sub: Returning Units Reported Not Fully Qualified. 353/1564 (Readiness)(S). (2) Status Report (R) on 5th Inf Div, 12 Jun 45. 319.1/51 (Redepl)(R). (3) Statement of Brig Gen A. D. Warnock, Asst Div Comdr, 5th Inf Div, to AGF Hist Off, 20 Nov 45.

for discharge.[3] Because of lack of time, the prescribed policy of completing personnel adjustments in Europe, where replacements were available, had to be abandoned and adjustments postponed until return of the organization to the United States. But since the output of replacement training centers was being sent to the Pacific there was no adequate source of replacements in the Zone of Interior; hence provision had to be made for the return from ETO, not only in the case of the 2d Division but for others as well, of a "packet" of about 2,000 low-score replacements to fill the gap left by removal of personnel made eligible for discharge by the addition of battle credits. This arrangement would have been fairly satisfactory if the packets could have been shipped promptly, but lack of shipping space, due partly to concessions to public pressure for the early return of high-point men, caused a delay in the forwarding of these replacements. None had arrived by V-J Day; in fact it was not until October that these packets began to reach American ports. Possibly they would have been given higher priority if the war had continued.[4]

Personnel turnover in the 45th Division, originally scheduled for return to the United States in August 1945, was much greater than in other divisions selected for redeployment. AGF staff officers who visited the 45th Division in July were informed that on the basis of currently applicable discharge scores a turnover of 11,000 enlisted men and 600 officers was anticipated; the division artillery staff was to have only one officer left—the artillery commander himself.[5]

The basis for selecting divisions to be redeployed and for determining the order of their return was not known in Headquarters, Army Ground Forces. But designating for redeployment units such as the 45th Division, which had a preponderance of high-score personnel, while choosing for inactivation many units such as the 63d and 65th Divisions, with comparatively few men eligible for discharge, created formidable difficulties.[6] Certainly the effect of replacing a large percentage of the personnel on the eve of redeployment would have been exceedingly injurious to the team—and the concept of the division as a team had been approved by the War Department and was considered cardinal by the Army Ground Forces. The period of redeployment training was too brief to permit of

[3] AGF memo (S) for CofS USA, 2 Jul 45, sub: Pers for Redeployed Units. 200.3/4 (Redepl)(S).

[4] Statement of Col H. T. Todd, AGF G-3 Sec, to AGF Hist Off, 12 Oct 45.

[5] Statement of Col S. L. Weld to AGF Hist Off, 16 Oct 45. This statement is supported by a memo (draft) of Col Weld to Gen Leo Donovan (undated, but Aug 45), sub: Liaison Trip to USFET. 314.7 (AGF Hist).

[6] (1) Statement of Col H. T. Todd on AGF Hist Off, 12 Oct 45. (2) Statement of Col S. L. Weld to AGF Hist Off, 16 Oct 45.

molding into a team a unit which had lost most of its key specialists and from one-third to three-fourths of its officers and men. The team principle had been disregarded before, particularly in the strippings of 1944 for overseas replacements, and the results, as attested by the performance of rebuilt divisions on the battlefield, were not as bad as had been feared. While it seems not unlikely that the rehabilitated divisions would have given a good account of themselves in the Pacific, the time available in redeployment for remolding the team was by no means as long as in 1944 and the loss of specialists was much heavier.

The Problem of Coordination with ETO

Another difficulty faced by those responsible for redeployment training in the United States was insufficient coordination with the European Theater of Operations. In the early stages of redeployment planning it appeared that coordination would leave little to be desired. On 19 March 1945, key AGF officers conferred at length in Washington with Brig. Gen. G. S. Eyster, G-3 ETO, with reference to redeployment matters. At this conference General Eyster stated:[7]

> There will have to be a closely integrated program between ETO and Ground Forces. For example, when ETO returns a unit they will forward a training status report which may state that the unit has done 120 days of training. Then after returning to the United States and having had furloughs, the unit would start on the 121st day of training.

General Eyster stated further that one of the Army Groups, probably the 6th, would be responsible for supervising redeployment training in ETO, and that the master training program then in preparation should be very closely integrated with programs drawn up by the Army Ground Forces.[8]

Draft copies of AGF Training Memorandum No. 1 were sent to ETO in April 1945 and to the Mediterranean Theater of Operations a few weeks later.[9] Early in May 1945, Colonel Faine and Col. Arthur M. Parsons of the Training Division, G-3 Section, AGF, visited ETO for the purpose of furthering coordination of the Army Ground Forces and ETO on matters of redeployment training. Colonel Faine and Colonel Parsons, after a conference with General Eyster,

[7] AGF M/R (S), 19 Mar 45, sub: Conference with Brig Gen Eyster, G-3 Hq ETO on Matters pertaining to Redepl. AGF G-1 Control Div files, binder marked "Special Planning — Interim Redeployment."

[8] *Ibid.*

[9] (1) AGF M/S (S), G-3 to CofS, 3 May 45, sub: Extract from Final Rpt of Col Hans W. Holmer, Engr member, AGF Bd MTO. (2) AGF ltr (S) for CG MTO, 9 May 45, sub: AGF Tng Memo No. 1, dated 28 Apr 45. Both in 353/6 (Redepl)(S).

met with Brig. Gen. William P. Shepard and other officers of Headquarters, 6th Army Group, to work out details of coordination. Concerning this and subsequent meetings, the AGF representatives wrote in their report to the Ground Chief of Staff:[10]

> The first conference with General Shepard's Group covered the purpose of our visit, and copies of AGF training literature were briefly explained. General Shepard agreed to accept our training memoranda in toto, with minor changes to be made to fit the training facilities to be available to them. We agreed to assist in rewriting these training memoranda. The next several days were spent in the actual rewrite.

The report explained the machinery set up for redeployment training in ETO, by which units were to be readjusted by the 12th Army Group, passed to the control of the 6th Army Group for training, and, after a minimum of eight weeks' training under the supervision of an army headquarters, shipped to an assembly area for POM. The report then stated:

> In addition to the status report which will be furnished OPD by the theater, Sixth Army Group has promised to send a copy of training status report direct to AGF; this report being in more complete detail than the theater report. Their status training report will include a statement as to the operations performed by the unit in combat. . . . At a final conference held on 11 May 1945 with Generals Shepard and Eyster, it was agreed that Hq AGF would recommend to OPD that training officers . . . from each of the special staff sections of AGF would be assigned to the staff of Sixth Army Group; that the Sixth Army Group would in turn select, and return for duty at Hq AGF, an officer of corresponding rank from their special staff sections. It was also recommended by Gen. Eyster that arrangements be made for the establishment of liaison between Hq AGF, Hq ETO, Hq Assembly Area Command, and Port of Le Havre, in order to provide the latest information on AGF units returning to the U. S. General Eyster and General Shepard assured us such a request would be promptly acted upon in the theater.

The report concluded with the statement: "Our visit resulted in Sixth Army Group adopting AGF training programs lock, stock and barrel!"

But the training plans drafted in ETO in May did not work out. Because of various obstacles, including the absorption of units and higher headquarters with occupation duties, inadequacy of training facilities, and acceleration of the shipment schedule, the scheme of training units at home stations in ETO under armies and corps proved impracticable, and, in general, responsibility for training passed to the Assembly Area Commands. But restrictions of space and equipment precluded any but the most limited training by units after they left their

[10] Memo (S) of Col S. E. Faine and Col A. M. Parsons, AGF G–3 Sec, for CofS AGF, 14 May 45, sub: Rpt of Visit to ETO concerning Redepl Tng of Units in that Theater. 353/7 (Redepl) (S).

230-171 O - 66 - 42

home stations in Europe. An AGF officer who visited Europe in July 1945 reported: "Very little, if any, training will be accomplished in USFET by indirectly redeployed units." [11]

The proposals made by General Eyster that the Army Ground Forces send officers periodically to ETO to maintain liaison on redeployment matters also went by the board. An AGF request in May for permission to send a liaison party to Europe elicited a reply from ETO to the effect that such liaison was neither necessary nor desirable. Renewal of the request in June, through General of the Army Dwight D. Eisenhower's Chief of Staff, who was visiting in Washington, met with a favorable response. A party of three officers (Col. Harrison W. Todd, G–3 Mobilization Division, Col. Seth L. Weld, G–3 Task Force Division, and Lt. Col. John A. Hanson, G–4 Task Force Division) left Washington on 7 July 1945 and returned three weeks later. Much valuable information was exchanged, but the trip came too late to yield maximum benefits. The conclusion of the visiting officers was: "The trip should have been made in May as originally recommended." [12]

Liaison was all the more imperative in view of the tardiness and inadequacy of status reports. AGF plans, based on War Department directives, contemplated receipt by air mail of complete and up-to-date reports on organization, status, and training of redeployed units at about the time of their arrival in the United States. But on 11 July 1945 Headquarters, Army Ground Forces, reported to the Chief of Staff, U.S. Army: "To date status reports have been received for only four of the 170 units which are listed to return to the U. S. in June, and no lists of personnel shortages of the units by grade, SSN, and arm or service have been received." [13] The status reports that were received did not give a true picture of either training or personnel because of the practice followed in ETO prior to August 1945. This required that before movement all but the personnel portions of the reports be submitted to the assembly area, where most of the training was conducted, and that twenty days before the readiness date for movement to the staging area personnel paragraphs be filled in. Considerable turnover of personnel occurred after preparation of each phase of the report.[14]

[11] Memo (draft) of Col S. L. Weld, AGF G–3 Sec, for Gen Leo Donovan (undated, but Aug 45), sub: Ln Trip to USFET. 314.7 (AGF Hist).

[12] (1) Memo (draft) of Col S. L. Weld, AGF G–3 Sec, for Gen Leo Donovan (undated, but Aug 45), sub: Ln Trip to USFET. 314.7 (AGF Hist). (2) Statement of Col S. L. Weld to AGF Hist Off, 16 Oct 45.

[13] AGF memo for CofS USA, 11 Jul 45, sub: Status Rpts on Units Scheduled for Redepl. 319.1/6 (Redepl).

[14] Statement of Col S. L. Weld to AGF Hist Off, 16 Oct 45.

The poor coordination between the Army Ground Forces and ETO had other bad effects. First, many authorities in ETO held the erroneous opinion that reinforcements were available in the United States for replacement of high-point personnel. Second, "organization detachments," required by War Department regulations to proceed directly from ports to assembly stations with essential records to prepare the way for the rest of the unit, were not designated and oriented in their duties prior to departure of units from ETO. Third, copies of reports of equipment authorized for return to the United States, intended for dispatch to the Army Ground Forces, were sent to the Army Service Forces.[15]

But what gave most concern to those charged with the receipt and training of redeployed units was that the Army Ground Forces, until the latter part of July, did not receive up-to-date information concerning the shipment of returning ground units. Schedules laid down prior to V-E Day in redeployment forecasts were stepped up considerably by ETO as more shipping became available than had been anticipated, with the result that units expected in August came pouring into the United States in July. AGF officers asked OPD for revised schedules only to find that they were not available in the War Department.[16]

The AGF liaison party that visited ETO in July 1945 obtained up-to-date redeployment schedules and cleared up other major points of misunderstanding mentioned above. But, as previously indicated, this action came too late to be of much benefit.

AGF officers who held key positions in administering the training of redeployed units were of the opinion that many of the difficulties growing out of the return of units from Europe might have been avoided if it had been possible to exercise stronger control of redeployment activities on the War Department level. Lack of coordination seemed due in large measure to the persistence after V-E Day of the previous practice of permitting theater commanders a free hand in overseas activities. This principle, when applied to matters as closely related to responsibilities of interior agencies as redeployment, greatly aggravated the problems of those agencies.[17]

[15] (1) Memo (R) of Lt Col John A. Hanson for G-4 AGF, 22 Aug 45, sub: Ln Trip to ETO. AGF G-4 Task Force Div files. (2) Statement of Lt Col John A. Hanson, Task Force Div, AGF G-4 Sec, to AGF Hist Off, 9 Oct 45. (3) Statement of Col S. L. Weld to AGF Hist Off, 16 Oct 45.

[16] (1) Statement of Col S. L. Weld to AGF Hist Off, 16 Oct 45. (2) Chart (S), Divisional Readiness Dates (undated), prepared by Task Force Division, G-3 AGF. 314.7 (AGF Hist).

[17] Statements of this paragraph are based primarily on conversations of the AGF Hist Off with key members of the AGF G-1, G-3, and G-4 Secs in October 1945.

The Problem of Equipment

The problem of equipment, while apparently not as formidable in redeployment as in most of the prior period, nevertheless gave Headquarters, Army Ground Forces, considerable concern. According to War Department regulations, units, before their departure from Europe, were to turn in to supply agencies all except minimum essential equipment for shipment direct to the Pacific. This meant that equipment required for training in the United States would have to be furnished from ASF stock in the Zone of Interior. In response to AGF insistence, the War Department directed that 100 percent of T/O&E equipment be laid down at the training station in advance of the unit's return and that it be in a condition serviceable for combat.[18] In at least one instance—in connection with provision of 1-ton 2-wheel cargo trailers—the Army Service Forces sought by direct negotiations with the Army Ground Forces to be relieved of the requirement of 100 percent combat-serviceable equipment. But the Army Ground Forces, apprehensive lest this be the first of a series of such requests, gave a firm negative reply.[19]

Two factors, beyond the control of both commands, complicated the equipment problem. One was the acceleration of the rate of return of divisions and other units from ETO. The second was the shifting of division stations to meet unforeseen changes in strategic plans. This shifting is exemplified in the case of the first two armored divisions (the 13th and 20th) scheduled for return to the United States. The Army Ground Forces in mid-April 1945, in reply to an inquiry from the ASF Distribution Division, designated Camp Polk and Fort Benning as the stations to receive the first armored divisions selected for redeployment. The Army Service Forces initiated measures necessary to lay down a complete set of equipment for an armored division at each of these stations. Subsequently, strategic plans were modified to provide for inclusion of the first two redeployed armored divisions in an armored task force attack on the Japanese homeland. Because of this change it became necessary to give the divisions amphibious training; hence Camp Cooke, Calif., was designated as their station instead of the two camps previously selected. The Army Service Forces, notwithstanding the fact that some armored equipment had already been shipped to Fort Benning,

[18] (1) AGF M/S, G–4 to CofS, 30 Apr 45, sub: Equip for Redepl Tng. AGF G–4 Task Force Div files. (2) AGF M/S (S), G–4 to CofS, 30 May 45, sub: Conference on Equip Priorities. AGF G–4 Task Force Div files. (3) Statement of Lt Col John A. Hanson to AGF Hist Off, 9 Oct 45.

[19] ASF memo (C) SPRLR 370.01 for CG AGF, 14 Jun 45, sub: Redepl Tng Demands for Trailer 1-ton 2-Wheel Cargo. With attached papers. 475/11 (Redepl)(C).

was now called on to lay down two complete sets of armored equipment at Camp Cooke.[20]

A type of equipment which was a source of special concern was that required for implementation of the athletic and recreational program directed by the War Department. On 9 March 1945 the Army Ground Forces, to implement this program, requested the Army Service Forces to provide equipment in the following categories for 500,000 men: athletic supplies; dayroom furniture; musical instruments; workshop outfits of various types (artist's, printing, clay modelling, metal craft, carpentry, etc.); soldier show supplies; and photo darkroom outfits. It was estimated that the materials requested would cost about $8,000,000. In submitting the request the Army Ground Forces called attention to the urgent need of laying down supplies at redeployment stations ahead of time to avoid delay in initiating the recreational program.[21]

After waiting more than two months for a reply to its letter of 9 March, the Army Ground Forces on 12 May made written inquiry as to the action contemplated by the Army Service Forces.[22] When the answer to the letter of 9 March finally came, dated 19 May, it reported a decision of the Secretary of War on 18 May 1945 that no additional recreational equipment would be procured, *for use during duty hours,* within the Zone of Interior, and stated that "every reasonable effort is being made to provide equipment and facilities adequate for recreational purposes [in off-duty hours] during the redeployment period." [23]

Taking the view that additional athletic equipment was indispensable to the accomplishment of provisions in the War Department's redeployment training directives, and that procurement of this equipment was not prohibited by the Secretary of War's ruling of 18 May—since it was to be used for after-duty games as well as for on-duty physical conditioning—the Army Ground Forces on 19 June 1945 made a new request for athletic training equipment sufficient for 500,000 men and asked for delivery of 20 percent of the equipment by 15 July.[24] The Army Service Forces replied on 22 June 1945 that G–3 of the War De-

[20] (1) Statement of Col A. L. Harding, AGF G–3 Sec, to AGF Hist Off, 7 Nov 45. (2) AGF 2d ind (draft) 354.1 (R)(11 Apr 45), 21 Apr 45, on WD memo (S) WDGS 11721 for CGs AAF, AGF, ASF, 12 Apr 45, sub: WD Installations. (3) AGF M/S, G–3 to CofS, 29 May 45, sub: Stations for Divs. Both (2) and (3) in files of Col A. L. Harding, AGF G–3 Sec.

[21] (1) AGF ltr (R) to CG ASF, 9 Mar 45, sub: Redepl Tng. (2) AGF M/S (R), G–1 to CofS, 1 Jun 45 sub: Sp Serv Supplies for Redepl Tng. Both in 353/5 (Redepl)(R).

[22] AGF ltr (R) to CG ASF, 12 May 45, sub: Redepl Tng. 353/5 (Redepl)(R).

[23] ASF memo (R) SPOPD 353 for CG AGF, 19 May 45, sub: Redepl Tng. 353/5 (Redepl)(R).

[24] AGF ltr (S) to CG ASF, 19 Jun 45, sub: Athletic Equip for Redepl Tng. 400/3 (Redepl)(S).

partment had interpreted recreational equipment intended for use during duty hours as including athletic equipment and that the AGF request was therefore returned without action.[25]

In the meantime, prospects had become very discouraging for provision of nonathletic equipment intended solely for after-duty recreational purposes. At the end of May, three months after Army Ground Forces put in an itemized requisition for recreational equipment with the Special Services Division of Army Service Forces, the status of the requisition was still unclear. A telephone conversation between the AGF Personal Services Officer and an ASF officer revealed that manufacturing difficulties, lack of appropriations, and uncertainties as to procurement jurisdiction had prevented any of the items from being obtained and that little information could as yet be given as to when or whether they would be available.[26] It appeared that the recreational program was destined to be thwarted by lack of equipment.

Outside of radios, which were eventually obtained through direct negotiations with the Signal Corps, the Army Ground Forces on V-J Day had secured very little of the nonathletic recreational equipment requested in March, and the prospect of getting such equipment remained unpromising.[27] By continuing pressure, it had obtained Enlisted Men's Welfare Funds to the extent of $1.75 per man for purchase of athletic playing equipment for use in both training and nontraining activities. When Japan surrendered, the War Department was considering an AGF request for distribution from ASF stocks in Kansas City of $3.00 worth of athletic clothing (shirts, shoes, and supporters) to each enlisted man in redeployment training.[28] All in all, the efforts of the Army Ground Forces to secure the means of carrying out War Department directives for bolstering the mental and physical health of redeployed soldiers through an intensive program of recreation were disappointing in the extreme.[29]

Acceleration of Operational Schedule

Another difficulty sprang from the acceleration of the operational timetable in the Pacific which took place after the original plans for redeployment had been

[25] ASF 1st ind (S) SPDOD 353 (19 Jun 45), 22 Jun 45, on AGF ltr cited in n. 24. 400/3 (Redepl)(S).

[26] Record of tel conv (R) between Col Waters, AGF, and Maj Murray, Spec Serv Div ASF, 28 May 45. 353/5 (Redepl)(R).

[27] Statement of Col J. F. Waters, AGF G–1 Sec, to AGF Hist Off, 9 Nov 45.

[28] AGF memo (R) for CofS USA, attn: G–3 Div, 1 Aug 45, sub: Athletic Equip for Redepl Tng. 418/1 (R).

[29] Statement of Col J. F. Waters to AGF Hist Off, 9 Nov 45.

put into effect. This threatened to reduce to a fraction the 8-week period of training which had been based on these plans and which was regarded as the minimum for effective training. On 7 August 1945 the War Department gave the 86th and 97th Divisions, the first divisions to be brought back from Europe, new readiness dates which precluded any redeployment training under the Army Ground Forces.[30] If one plan still under consideration on V-J Day had been carried out, the 20th Armored Division would have had only twenty days' training in the United States and the 13th Armored Division only nine days.[31] This situation was particularly disturbing in view of the fact that the scheduled operation was amphibious, and neither division had had amphibious training.[32]

Thus the course of events during the months between V-E Day and V-J Day had been such as to make the prospects of redeployment training most unfavorable. Personnel turnover and other difficulties had been so formidable, indeed, that a key officer in the G–3 Section of Headquarters, Army Ground Forces, was later constrained to remark: [33]

> The capitulation of Hirohito on 14 August saved our necks. With things being as they were it would have been absolutely impossible for us to have sent well-trained teams to the Pacific for participation in the scheduled invasion of Japan.

After V-J Day, units scheduled for occupation service were put through a modified program of redeployment training, but training during that period is part of another story.

[30] AGF memo (S) for CofS USA, 9 Aug 45, sub: Conditions of O'seas Movement of 86th and 97th Inf Divs and Allied Repl Shipment. 353/1559 (Readiness) (S).

[31] Statement of Col S. L. Weld to AGF Hist Off, 16 Oct 45.

[32] Statement of Col S. L. Weld to AGF Hist Off, 5 Mar 46.

[33] Statement of Col S. L. Weld to AGF Hist Off, 16 Oct 45.

Glossary of Abbreviations*

AA	Antiaircraft
AAF	Army Air Forces
AARTC	Antiaircraft replacement training center
A/B	Airborne
AEF	American Expeditionary Forces
AGCT	Army General Classification Test
AGF	Army Ground Forces
AGO	Adjutant General's Office
AR	Army Regulation
Armd	Armored
ASF	Army Service Forces
ASTP	Army Specialized Training Program
ASTRP	Army Specialized Training Reserve Program
AUS	Army of the United States
BIRTC	Branch immaterial replacement training center
Bn	Battalion
CA	Coast Artillery
C–AMA	California–Arizona Maneuver Area
Cav	Cavalry
CE	Corps of Engineers
Ch	Chaplain
CMP	Corps of Military Police
Co	Company
DC	Dental Corps
EM	Enlisted men
ETO	European Theater of Operations
FA	Field Artillery
FM	Field Manual
G–1	Personnel
G–2	Intelligence
G–3	Operations, Organization, and Training
G–4	Supply
GHQ	General Headquarters

*See also War Department, Dictionary of United States Army Terms (TM 20–205).

Gp	Group
GSC	General Staff Corps
HD	Harbor defense
Hq	Headquarters
IARTC	Infantry advanced replacement training center
IGD	Inspector General's Department
Inf	Infantry
IOI	Identification of Organizational Impedimenta
IRTC	Infantry replacement training center
JAGD	Judge Advocate General's Department
MAC	Medical Administrative Corps
MC	Medical Corps
MOS	Military occupational specialty
MTO	Mediterranean Theater of Operations
MTP	Mobilization training program
NATO	North African Theater of Operations
NCO	Noncommissioned officer
NG	National Guard
OCS	Officer candidate school
OPD	Operations Division
OR	Organized Reserves
Ord	Ordnance
PE	Port of embarkation
POA	Pacific Ocean Areas
POM	Preparation for Overseas Movement
POR	Preparation for Oversea Movement of Individual Replacements
Pvt	Private
QM	Quartermaster
QMC	Quartermaster Corps
QMMT	Quartermaster Motor Transport
RA	Regular Army
R&SC	Replacement and School Command
Regt	Regiment
ROTC	Reserve Officers' Training Corps
RTC	Replacement training center
RTP	Redeployment training program
S–1	Personnel

S–2	Intelligence
S–3	Operations
S–4	Supply
SC	Signal Corps
SOS	Services of Supply
SSN	Specification serial number
STU	Special training unit
SWP	Southwest Pacific
TAG	The Adjutant General
T/BA	Table of Basic Allowances
TD	Tank Destroyer
T/E	Table of Equipment
TIG	The Inspector General
TM	Technical Manual
T/O	Table of Organization
T/O&E	Table of Organization and Equipment
USFET	United States Forces European Theater
UTP	Unit training program
VOC	Volunteer officer candidate
Vol	Volunteer
WD	War Department
WDGS	War Department General Staff
WDSS	War Department Special Staff
ZI	Zone of Interior

Guide to Footnotes

No generally accepted practice for citing War Department documents exists. The method adopted in the series on the history of the Army Ground Forces is designed to realize three main objectives: to furnish the reader essential information on the character, the source, the addressee, the date, and the subject matter of the document; to assist the reader who may wish to consult the source; and to make citations as brief as possible.

In general, abbreviations conform to TM 20–205, Dictionary of United States Army Terms, issued by the War Department on 18 January 1944. The file symbols cited are those of the decimal filing system prescribed in *War Department Decimal File System* (revised edition, Washington, 1943), compiled by The Adjutant General.

The following may serve as an example:

> WD ltr (C) AG 320.2 (1–2–43) OB–S–C–M to CGs, 5 Jan 43, sub: Orgn, Tng, and Equip of Units for Overseas Serv. 320.2/2 (Staging Areas) (C).

The meaning of the above citation is as follows:

1. The document was an official War Department directive (WD ltr), classified originally as Confidential (C), and signed by The Adjutant General or one of his assistants (AG).

2. In the Adjutant General's Office it was given the file number 320.2, the prescribed decimal symbol for "Strength of the Army."

3. In the War Department file it can be located under the date of 2 January 1943 (1–2–43), the day on which the basic policy decision authorizing the issue of the directive was made.

4. The final copy of the directive was prepared for signature and distribution by the Operations Branch (OB), Secret and Confidential Section (S) of the Adjutant General's Office, and was based on a G–3 directive (C); the final copy was issued in mimeographed form (M).*

5. The letter was addressed to the commanding generals concerned (CGs) on 5 January 1943.

6. Its subject (sub) was the organization, training, and equipment of units being prepared for overseas service.

*Explanations of this type of symbol may be found in War Department circulars issued periodically whenever major changes in organization occur.

7. The letter was filed in the central records of AGF headquarters in the Strength of the Army file (320.2) with a group of related papers (/2) and in a separate binder under the subheading "Staging Areas." This binder is or was classified Confidential (C).

At all times the classification indicated is that given to the document when issued: (S) for Secret, (C) for Confidential, and (R) for Restricted. Reclassification of documents, a continuous process accelerated since the termination of hostilities, has not been taken into consideration. The classification of information in the text that has been derived from classified documents has been removed by appropriate authority.

The file symbol at the end of the note is given only as an aid to further investigation. It shows where the document, or a copy of it, was located when last consulted. When the symbol is not preceded by the initials of a particular office, as in the example given above, it refers to the records of Army Ground Forces. When the symbol is preceded by "AGO Records," it means that the document was consulted in the files of the Adjutant General's Office of the War Department. In the case of documents originating outside of the Army Ground Forces (as in the example cited above), the original file symbol has generally been incorporated at the beginning, and the location at the time of consultation has been indicated at the end of the citation.

The following list of the types of documents cited in the footnotes is added to assist the reader unfamiliar with War Department and Army usage:

AR. Army Regulations are issued by the War Department and include basic policies and rules for the governing of the Army. They have the force and effect of law to the Army.

FM. Field Manuals are official handbooks containing information and instructions for guidance in training and in the operation and maintenance of materiel and equipment.

Cir. Circulars are temporary directives issued by the War Department or specific headquarters. War Department circulars may later be incorporated in the more permanent form of Army Regulations or Field Service Regulations.

GO. General Orders are announcements of official acts of the Secretary of War or the commanding officer of a headquarters.

Bull. Bulletins are official publications containing matter which is informative or advisory in nature. They are usually employed for notification of legislative or executive actions of importance to the Army.

Memo. The memorandum form of correspondence is normally employed within a headquarters for the transmittal of orders, advice, or information. It is also frequently used among headquarters like the WD, AGF, ASF, and AAF. Sometimes the term "memorandum" is used for published instructions of a more temporary character than those in circulars.

Ltr. The letter form of correspondence is used for the transmittal of orders, advice, or information among different headquarters or field agencies. Whenever personal letters are cited, they are indicated as such.

Ind. An indorsement is used as a reply to a military communication, or as a forwarding note of further transmittal, and is added to the original communication.

M/S. A memorandum slip is used for informal interoffice communication.

WD D/F. A War Department disposition form is the cover sheet for the routing of a staff paper and may contain instructions or comments. For more informal transmittal, disposition or routing slips are used.

Telg, Rad., TWX. These refer respectively to telegrams, radiograms, and teletype messages. Usually no subject matter is indicated. *Radre* is used to indicate replies to radiograms ("reference your radiogram").

Bibliographical Note

The studies in this volume are based almost entirely on documents and recorded interviews. References to the published sources used will be found in the footnotes. Mention of certain other publications bearing on the history of the Army Ground Forces will be found in the bibliographical note in the first volume of the present series, *The Organization of Ground Combat Troops* (Washington, 1947). A list of the studies made or initiated during the war by the Historical Section of the Army Ground Forces will be found at the end of this note.

Documentary research was conducted principally in the central records files of the Army Ground Forces. Supplementary material was secured from the files of staff sections or their divisions and branches in AGF headquarters, from the files of commands and agencies subordinate to that headquarters, and from the AGO Central files and files of the War Department General Staff divisions. The authors have made extensive use of interviews with staff members of AGF headquarters and subordinate commands and agencies, the substance of which has been recorded in notes on file in the Historical Records Section, AGO.

The central records files maintained by Army Ground Forces to furnish the basis for current staff and command action provide the principal record of the operations and decisions of the AGF command, of the steps leading to its decisions, and of the information on which those decisions were based. In general, the central records include the following types of documents:

1. Carbon copies of letters, memoranda, and messages dispatched.

2. Drafts of letters, memoranda, and messages, often annotated by hand, which were not used or which were issued in revised form.

3. Originals of staff memoranda or memorandum slips circulated within the headquarters and usually bearing dated notes or comments of the staff officers concerned, the Chief of Staff, or the Commanding General; these are invaluable for tracing the course of a discussion and the ideas and influences that entered into a decision.

4. Originals of letters, memoranda, or disposition forms addressed to AGF headquarters by agencies of the War Department and by coordinate or subordinate headquarters.

230-171 O - 66 - 43

5. Copies of papers received at the headquarters for information, concurrence, or action.

6. Carbons or typed copies of papers originating elsewhere, received by the headquarters for action, and returned to the sender or indorsed to a new addressee.

7. Mimeographed directives, generally in the form of letters, issued by Headquarters, Army Ground Forces, or by headquarters of subordinate commands, such as those of armies.

The central records files also contain such documents as staff studies, the reports of boards responsible to AGF headquarters, reports of overseas observers, annotated drafts of training circulars, statistical reports and tables, and organizational charts.

The bulk of the central records of Headquarters, Army Ground Forces, is to be found in the General Correspondence files. Files were also kept for the subordinate commands. Within each category papers were filed under the appropriate decimal classification, for example, 353, for papers closely related to training. Within this classification "cut-off" series appear for important subjects, for example, 353 (Training Directives), or 353 (Air-Ground).

The file classifications richest in material for the history of the Army Ground Forces are 320 (Organization and Strength of the Army) and 353 (Training). They contain a large proportion of the records of primary historical or administrative significance. Together these two series constitute the nearest approach to a master or policy file of the command. Other important series dealing with the development and functioning of Army Ground Forces during the war include the following:

210 —Officers
220 —Enlisted Men
319.1—Reports
327.3—Inducted Men
333 —Inspections
337 —Conferences
352 —Schools
354.1—Training Centers
354.2—Maneuvers
370 —Employment and Movement of Troops
381 —War Plans
461 —Publications

Under such numbers in the AGF files papers from other agencies will sometimes be found which were given a different decimal or cut-off symbol by the originating agency.

In the central records the papers relating to a particular course of action are filed together in a group. Each paper in the group is given a group number, which appears after the diagonal following the file classification symbol, for example, 320.2/135 or 335/9 (S). The series of related papers in the group may cover a considerable period of time, and in such cases the chronological sequence of the papers in a given binder of the general series within which it appears is broken. But within each binder the groups are arranged in chronological order in accordance with the dates of the basic papers through which the course of action was initiated. In general, each group contains, if not the documents themselves, clues to the documents needed for a study of the action.

A listing sheet appears on the face of each binder. This lists the individual papers originally contained in each of the groups described above. The date of each paper appears in a separate column; the dates are not in exact chronological order but are of assistance in locating a paper the date of which is known. The listing sheet often provides the only practicable means of finding such a paper.

At the present time (1947), the wartime central records of AGF headquarters are divided between Headquarters, Army Ground Forces, at Fort Monroe, Va., and the Adjutant General's Office in Washington. The former possesses most of the records for 1944 and 1945, while the latter has charge of the records for the earlier years of the war. Headquarters, Army Ground Forces, was not an office of record. Before its central files were transferred to the Adjutant General's Office, mimeographed letters issued by the War Department or its major commands for general distribution were screened out of the records. The cross-index sheets which had originally been inserted to facilitate reference were also removed. A reference to the papers removed can usually be found in the listing sheets on the face of each binder.

Such records of staff sections or their subdivisions at Headquarters, Army Ground Forces, as were not in the central records have been transferred, when believed to be of value for future research, to the Historical Records Section of the Adjutant General's Office. Certain material used in the preparation of these studies is on file in the Historical Division, WDSS. The records of the Replacement and School Command, occasionally referred to in the documentation of the studies in this volume, have been transferred to AGF headquarters at Fort Monroe.

Anyone desiring to trace a special or technical question in the records of Army Ground Forces may find the following procedure helpful:

1. Locate, in the alphabetical subject index to the file manual, the decimal symbol there assigned to the subject.

2. Consult this number in the records.

3. Work by cross reference, or by means of the listing sheet on the face of each binder, to other binders in the records with different decimal classifications.

Studies Prepared during the War by the Historical Section, Army Ground Forces

*Origins of the Army Ground Forces: General Headquarters, United States Army, 1940–42 (R)
A General History of the Army Ground Forces (R)

Mobilization of the Ground Forces

*Ground Forces in the War Army: a Statistical Study (R)
*Mobilization of the Ground Army (R)
**Procurement of Enlisted Personnel for the AGF: the Problem of Quality (R)
**The Procurement and Branch Distribution of Officers (R)
**The Provision of Enlisted Replacements (R)

Organization of the Ground Forces

*Reorganization of Ground Troops for Combat (R)
*Organization and Training of New Ground Combat Elements (R)

Unit Training

**The Building and Training of Infantry Divisions (R)
**Problems of Nondivisional Training in the Army Ground Forces (R)
The Desert Training Center and C–AMA (R)
History of the Second Army (R)
History of the Third Army (R)
History of the Fourth Army (R)
History of the Activation of Headquarters of the Fifteenth Army (R)
**Preparation of Units for Overseas Movement (R)

Special Training of Units

The Amphibious Training Center (R)
Training in Mountain and Winter Warfare (R)
The Mountain Training Center (R)

Training of Specialized Units

The Airborne Command and Center (R)
The Antiaircraft Command and Center (R)
The Armored Force, Command, and Center (R)
History of the Tenth Light Division (Alpine) (R)
The Tank Destroyer History (R)

*Revised and published in the first volume of the AGF series.
**Revised and published in this volume.

Individual Training

**Wartime Training in the Schools of the Army Ground Forces (R)
**Training of Officer Candidates in AGF Special Service Schools (R)
**Major Developments in the Training of Enlisted Replacements (R)
The Replacement and School Command (R)

Equipment

The Role of the Army Ground Forces in the Development of Equipment (R)

Special Problems of Organization and Training

Air-Ground Cooperation (R)
The Training of Negro Troops (C)

Redeployment

*The Role of Army Ground Forces in Redeployment (R)
**Redeployment Training (R)

*Revised and published in the first volume of the AGF series.
**Revised and published in this volume.

UNITED STATES ARMY IN WORLD WAR II

List of Subseries

	Number of volumes
The War Department	8
The Army Ground Forces	2
The Army Service Forces	1
The Western Hemisphere	2
The War in the Pacific	11
Mediterranean Theater of Operations	4
European Theater of Operations	10
The Middle East Theater	1
The China-Burma-India Theater	3
The Technical Services	
Chemical Warfare Service	3
The Corps of Engineers	4
The Medical Department	4
The Ordnance Department	3
The Quartermaster Corps	4
The Signal Corps	3
The Transportation Corps	3
Special Studies	9
The Army Air Forces*	7
Total	82

*Published by the University of Chicago Press.

Index

230-171 O - 66 - 44

U.S. GOVERNMENT PRINTING OFFICE: 1966 O—230-171